AN AUTOBIOGRAPHY

FRANK LLOYD WRIGHT

FRANK LLOYD WRIGHT

AN AUTOBIOGRAPHY

LONDON
FABER & FABER LIMITED
AND THE HYPERION PRESS LIMITED

*First published in Mcmxlv
by Faber and Faber Limited
24 Russell Square London W.C. 1
and the Hyperion Press Limited London
Printed in Great Britain by
R. MacLehose and Company Limited
The University Press Glasgow
All rights reserved*

CONTENTS

BOOK ONE: FAMILY

BOOK TWO: FELLOWSHIP

BOOK THREE: WORK

BOOK FOUR: FREEDOM

BOOK FIVE: FORM

ILLUSTRATIONS

6

FAMILY

PRELUDE

A light blanket of snow fresh-fallen over sloping fields, gleaming in the morning sun. Clusters of pod-topped weeds woven of bronze here and there sprinkling the spotless expanse of white. Dark sprays of slender metallic lines, tipped with quivering dots. Pattern to the eye of the sun, as the sun spread delicate network of more pattern in blue shadows on the white beneath.

'Come, my boy,' said Uncle John to his sister Anna's nine-year-old. 'Come now, and I will show you how to go!'

Taking the boy by the hand he pulled his big hat down over his shock of gray hair and started straight across and up the sloping fields towards a point upon which he had fixed his keen blue eyes.

Neither to right nor to left, intent upon his goal, straight forward he walked—possessed.

But soon the boy caught the play of naked weed against the snow, sharp shadows laced in blue arabesque beneath. Leaving his mitten in the strong grasp, he got free.

He ran first left, to gather beads on stems and then beads and tassels on more stems. Then right, to gather prettier ones. Again—left, to some darker and more brilliant—and beyond to a low-spreading kind. Farther on again to tall golden lines tipped with delicate clusters of dark bronze heads. Eager, trembling, he ran to and fro behind Uncle John, his arms growing full of 'weeds'.

A long way up the slope, arrived at the point on which he had fixed, Uncle John turned to look back.

A smile of satisfaction lit the strong Welsh face. His tracks in the snow were straight as any string could be straight.

The boy came up, arms full, face flushed, glowing.

He looked up at his Uncle—see what he had found!

A stern look came down on him. The lesson was to come. Back there was the long, straight, mindful, heedless line Uncle John's own feet had purposefully made. He pointed to it with pride. And there was the wavering, searching, heedful line embroidering the straight one like some free, engaging vine as it ran back and forth across it. He pointed to that too—with gentle reproof.

Both stood looking back. The small hand with half-frozen fingers was again in its mitten in the older, stronger hand; an indulgent, benevolent smile down now on the shamed young face.

9

And somehow, there was something . . . not clear.

Uncle John's meaning was plain—NEITHER TO RIGHT NOR TO THE LEFT, BUT STRAIGHT, IS THE WAY.

The boy looked at his treasure and then at Uncle John's pride, comprehending more than Uncle John meant he should.

The boy was troubled. Uncle John had left out something that made all the difference.

THE BOY

Back in Wales in the Victorian Era, there lived a hatter, stalwart maker of strange, black, high-pointed cones. The witches wore them when riding on their broom-sticks. The Welsh wore them for hats. The hatter was proud of his work and peddled his hats at fairs. He would throw one down on the ground and, 'Stand on it!' he would say to anyone likely to buy.

On Sundays he preached, a firebrand of a man, questioning how man should be just with God, rejecting the answers most men, and women too, gave him.

He was tall, this Richard Jones, dark-eyed—an impassioned, unpopular Unitarian. The daughter of an old Welsh family, Mary Lloyd, heard him and fell in love with him.

'For there is the just man who perisheth in his righteousness, and there is the wicked man who prolongeth in his wickedness.

'But he that knoweth God and serveth him shall come forth of them all.'

So she believed, and went away with him against her parents' will. If her wealthy family looked askance at her staunch man, what did that matter? She loved him and, so, trusted him.

They had seven children, whose family name became Lloyd-Jones.

Then his outspoken liberality offending conservative popular opinion made America seem a hope and a haven to the Unitarian, and he came with a delicate wife and their seven to The West. He came to find a farm where his stalwart strength might make a home and a place to work in a land where speech was free, because men were.

So the hatter-preacher in his fifty-third year became the Wisconsin Pioneer, with his Thomas, John, Margaret, Mary, Anna, Jenkin and Nannie.

Little Nannie, dying on the way, was left behind in strange ground.

They came by canal-boat and lake-steamer to Milwaukee on their way to Ixonia, Wisconsin. Six years the pioneer couple lived there, where they invoked four more children, Ellen, Jane, James, and Enos, to join their little band before they found the valley by the Wisconsin River.

'The Valley', they all lovingly called it in after life, and lovable it was, lying fertile between two ranges of diversified soft hills, with a third ridge intruding and dividing it in two smaller valleys at the upper end. A small stream coursing down each joined at the homestead and continued as a wider stream on its course toward the River. The lower or open end of the Valley was crossed and closed by the broad and sandbarred Wisconsin, and from the hills you could look out upon the great sandy and treeless plain that had once been the bed of the mighty Wisconsin of ancient times.

When the virgin soil was broken by the grandfather and his sons, friendly Indians still lingered in the neighbourhood.

By the eldest, Thomas, a carpenter, a small house was built on a gently sloping hillside facing south. Balm-of-Gilead trees and Lombardy Poplars were planted by the Mother and her brood around the little house and along the lanes: lanes worm-fenced with oak-rails split in the hillside forests which clung to the northern slopes and hillcrowns.

The southern slopes were all too dry for wood, and were bare except where rock ledges came through. The stables were roofed with straw like the old Welsh thatch. The small simple house, however, was 'modern', clapboarded and shingled by Thomas and his brothers. The kitchen was a lean-to at the rear. An outside stairway led to a cool stone cellar beneath. A root-house was close behind, partially dug into the ground and roofed with a sloping mound of grass-covered earth.

Here in 'The Valley', the family tree of Richard Lloyd-Jones, Welsh pioneer, with its ten branches and one scar, struck root in the America of his hope. It was now his haven.

Up to this time he had preached, even while travelling on the ships or the canal-boats or at the inns where the family stayed. Usually he was listened to with respect. There was fervour, exaltation in him. He read the Bible his own way with strong Welsh accent, but no one could mistake his meaning. It was often new to his lettered betters and would change their thought. He was pioneer, not on the earth alone, but in mighty reaches of the spirit where the earth grows dim.

He had a Church during his years in Ixonia but again, 'where speech was free because men were', the Church proposed to try him. He said, 'You need not. If I am intrusive, I will get out. I cannot quell my spirit.'

He had for family crest, the old Druid symbol: **/|** 'TRUTH AGAINST THE WORLD.'

Grandfather preached as Isaiah preached. 'The flower fadeth, the grass withereth—but the word of the Lord, thy God, endureth forever.' His children had to learn that chapter of Isaiah, the fortieth, by heart so they could recite it.

The boy, his grandson, grew to distrust Isaiah. Was the flower any less desirable because it seemed to have been condemned to die that it might live more abundantly? As they all went to work in the fields, the grass seemed always necessary to life in the Valley, most of all when it withered and was hay to keep the stock alive in winter so the preacher himself might live.

The flowers have closed their eyes beneath the stars, opened to the sun, dropped their seeds into the bosom of friendly earth these thousands of years away from Isaiah and bid fair to be unfaded when the 'word of our Lord', as Isaiah heard it, has been much modified in the mouth. . . .

Might it not be then before all, that this very grass and these flowers, too, are in truth themselves the very word of GOD.

11

There seemed base ingratitude in the boastful thunder of that hateful text.

When storms swept the Valley from bank to bank of its ranges of hills, then black against a livid sky—lashing the trees, drowning the helpless small things, in the destruction that was wrought and the wreck that followed, the boy would see Isaiah's 'Judgment'.

Ah, yes! In this prophet Hell enlarged itself and opened 'her' mouth without measure!

Woe! Woe! that word 'woe' struck on the young heart like a blow—'O Woe unto them that are mighty to drink wine and mingle strong drink!' Nor was there to be pity on 'the fruit of the womb'. Little children were to be trodden under foot.

Isaiah's awful Lord smote the poor multitudes with a mighty continuous smite, never taking away the gory, dreadful hand outstretched to smite more; never satisfied with the smiting already done.

And yet, according to Isaiah, were you willing to argue the matter, to reason with 'Him' (none seemed to know whether Isaiah or His Lord was meant by 'Him'), your sins would be white as snow. Why?

Verily this Holy Warrior was a prophet making GOD in his own image. Turning his own lusts into virtues because they were on the side of pain instead of on the side of pleasure.

What a curse to put upon the mind of any child!

How much too much to thrash him!

How much less than too little to lead him!

His grandson would see the stalwart figure, legs straight in stirrups, of this spiritual brother of Isaiah, his dreaded, beloved Welsh Grandfather, white-bearded and hoary-headed, sitting up straight upon his horse, Timothy, like a Patriarch; stick with shepherd's-crook hung over the left forearm, the Bible of his faith firm against his side. And his grandson would see that he was thus able to whack his horse on the flank without losing his hold on the BOOK.

Week days grandfather believed in the gospel of hard work. Relentlessly he taught his children to add tired to tired and add it again, until the fountain of energy he himself was, working out through his offspring, began to cut away the forests and establish a human decency where the wilderness had been. A human smile, where before had been the Divine Countenance.

The Indians, in passing, sometimes brought venison and laid it on his doorstep and he had tobacco for them. For he smoked a pipe. And this pipe was a great source of shame to his family in after years. Their one shadow of reproach to him. Though he was hard, and, should a child by some slip pour much more sorghum on his plate than intended, Grandfather would righteously make him eat it all ('his eyes should not be bigger than his stomach'), yet this cruelty they respected. The pipe they could neither explain nor forgive.

After all, it was the little Grandmother who loved him and tempered his harshness. She had taught him to smoke as a cure for his asthma.

The asthma he outgrew but his pipe stayed with him while he lived.

Grandmother's gentle spirit had welded together with their father's the strong wills of his ten children in a united affection that was never broken.

Some ten years in the new home and the Grandmother passed painlessly away, carried out into the open air of the arbour which the Grandfather had built with his own hands for her. As if he, too, were transported, Grandfather, the better part of his life gone now, got on his feet and led these children in a prayer which they ever after remembered as the most beautiful they had ever heard.

Eleven years later, eighty-seven years of age, he lay down on his bed to sleep. In the night—painlessly—he, too, slipped away.

But not then was his spirit 'quelled'.

Grandfather's spirit lived on in a typical emigrant establishment on virgin American soil. A little Welsh clan, by himself set in this little corner of that enormous new ground dedicated to Freedom, and parcelled out among all the breeds of the earth, stayed there with the ground.

The ground! What does it not hold impartially in its depths, breadths and beauty for the pioneer like Richard Lloyd-Jones, in league with the stones of the field, himself like the ridges of primeval rock that ribbed the hills in contrast to the verdure rolling over them. He planted a small world within the world that is again within other worlds, without end.

He did not consider the lilies—how they grew.

The little Grandmother was all that to him.

Beauty comes to all strong men, in some guise, sometimes in disguise.

His children, his flesh and blood, were like him but with something of the element added to them of the prayerful consideration for the lilies that was the gentle Grandmother's. Sympathy 'for the flower that fadeth', gratitude for the 'grass that withereth' came a step nearer to them in their mother.

'Mother's Pine' stands on the Hillside lawn, a living child of hers. The little Grandmother planted it there. A small thing. Careless mowing in the yard had injured it. They were going to pull it up and throw it away. 'No, leave it to me,' she said, and, bringing her sewing basket, knelt by the tree on the grass and covered the injury with pitch. She sewed a firm canvas band tight around the damaged trunk.

That white pine is seventy-five feet tall today! Twice, the lightning struck it, but it is still a noble specimen of its fast disappearing tribe.

Occasional Lombardies, of which she was fond, stand isolated in clumps where once their ranks along the lanes up the hillsides were unbroken.

Her Balm-of-Gilead has scattered around the Valley to meet you in unexpected places.

And the Lilacs and Bouncing-Betty of her dooryard have colonized on their own along the roadsides in great masses good to see.

Willing worker in this intensive human-hive of work, song and prayer in rural Wisconsin was the Sister Anna. Her son, the grandson who

13

doubted Isaiah, it was who went in quest of weeds while his Uncle John preached a sermon to the lad with his feet, in the snow.

Sister Anna herself, fourth child of Richard Lloyd-Jones and Mary Lloyd, his wife, was five years old when the immigration from Wales took place. She walked with a free stride like a man, had much dark brown hair above a good, brave brow; a fine nose and dark, dreaming brown eyes. Much fire and energy gave her temper beneath a self-possession calm and gracious.

Education was Sister Anna's passion even while very young. All this family was imbued with the idea of education as salvation. Education it was that made man out of the brute and saved him from the beast. Education it was too (and that was her mistake) that unlocked the stores of Beauty to let it come crowding in on every side at every gate. Although she believed Education the direct manifestation of God to reach it, Sister Anna loved—Beauty. Soon she became a teacher in the countryside, riding a horse over the hills and through the woods to and from her school each day. Old men in the neighbourhood still speak of Sister Anna as their teacher, with admiration and respect.

THE MOTHER

Her school lay sometimes in one direction and sometimes in another, but always miles away. When her horse was needed in the fields she walked, but usually she rode, coming from the still shadows of the wood to the far prospect from the hilltops or overlooking the warm yellow-green sunshine on the meadow-stretches. All blazed with bewildering colour in autumn, and was more beautiful than ever when asleep under wintry coverlets of snow, the shapes of the hills then like huge primeval monsters lying peacefully beneath them. Often she made those journeys after dark alone. Farmsteads were few and miles between.

And often too it rained. She had to go just the same, covered with a blue soldier's cape that had brass buttons and a hood. Bareheaded, otherwise, she went. She knew the ferns, the flowers, by name, the startled animals that ran along the road. There were berries by the roadside too, wild cherries, plums, and grapes. She might reach out and take them on the branches, hanging the branches to the saddle bow, eating from them as she rode.

How it happened that Sister Anna's ideals then are modern now, who can say. Unless first-hand contact with nature in the primitive struggle, and the rugged faith of the father ('at destruction and famine thou shalt laugh, neither shalt thou be afraid of the beasts of the earth for thou shalt be in league with the stones of the field') gave it to her. This 'league with the stones of the field' must have imparted power to her imaginative vision.

The boy of this story was her first child, Frank.

Sister Anna came by him as the law prescribed. She married a man who satisfied her ideal of 'Education'. A man from Hartford, Connecticut. A circuit rider. A musician now going about the countryside near Lone Rock, Wisconsin, teaching folk to sing.

14

She was twenty-nine when she married him. Seventeen years her senior, the music-master was a product of education, one of a family of intellectuals to which James Russell Lowell belonged, and Alice and Phoebe Cary, from which distant branches he got his middle names.

He was William Russell Cary Wright, tirelessly educating himself, first at Amherst, then to practice medicine, soon found by him to be no genuine science. Then the law, but again—disillusion. He was just about to hear the 'call' his preacher ancestors back to the days of the Reformation in England had all been hearing. And Sister Anna was the one to help him hear it. Soon after they were married he too became a preacher. He had his music still, which always consoled him, and music was his friend to the last when all else had failed.

After their son was born something happened between the mother and father. Sister Anna's extraordinary devotion to the child disconcerted the father. He never made much of the child, it seems. No doubt the wife loved him no less but now loved something more, something created out of her own fervour of love and desire. A means to realize her vision.

The boy, she said, was to build beautiful buildings. Faith in prenatal influences was strong in this expectant mother. She kept her thoughts on the high things for which she yearned and looked carefully after her health. There was never a doubt in the expectant mother's mind but that she was to have a boy.

Fascinated by buildings, she took ten full-page wood-engravings of the old English Cathedrals from 'Old England', a pictorial periodical to which the father had subscribed, had them framed simply in flat oak and hung them upon the walls of the room that was to be her son's.

Before he was born, she said she intended him to be an Architect.

In due course of nature, in a little inland town among the hills, Richland Center, Wisconsin, the father preaching and sometimes lawing, still teaching music, her son was born.

That meant invocation ceased and 'Education' took hold.

When the boy was three with a baby sister a year old, the father was called to a Church at Weymouth near Boston.

About this time the father's father died at his home in Hartford, Connecticut, aged ninety and nine. He went upstairs to his room, wrote by candlelight a letter to each of his three sons, addressed each in his own handwriting, went to bed and, like the mother's father, painlessly slept to final sleep.

Leaving the Lloyd-Joneses prospering in their Valley, our little family went west, nearer to Hartford, Connecticut, the father's native place. Went on to activities still religious but to different scenes, a different atmosphere—that of a Boston suburb.

A modest, gray, wooden house near a tall white-brick church in drab old historic Weymouth.

The tall, handsome mother in that house with her boy and the little girl Jane, named after the mother's sister back there in the Valley. A donation party of the previous evening had left twenty-three pumpkin pies on the pantry shelves where there was nothing much else to eat after the party had gone away. No wonder if the mother longed for the Valley for which she seemed always to pine.

BACH

At this time a nervously active intellectual man in clerical dress seated at the organ in the church, playing. Usually he was playing. He was playing Bach now. Behind the organ, a dark chamber. In the dark chamber, huge bellows with projecting wooden lever-handle. A tiny shaded oil lamp shining in the dark on a lead marker that ran up and down to indicate the amount of air pressure necessary to keep the organ playing. A small boy of seven, eyes on the lighted marker, pumping away with all his strength at the lever and crying bitterly as he did so.

Streams of sound went pouring out into the Church against the stained-glass windows *fortissimo*. The boy worked away for dear life to keep air in the bellows, knowing only too well what would happen to him should he give out. Then came a long-drawn-out, softer passage. It was easier to pump—the Vox Humana—faraway beauty, tenderness and promise in it stealing over boy-senses. He stopped, tears and all, entranced. Listening —breathless—he forgot, but suddenly remembered just in time to work away again with all his might to keep air enough for the Bach as it broke into the sound-waves of triumphant, march-like progress. The heroic measures brought him back again to strength and for a while he pumped away with fresh energy, hopefully. But as on and on the wondrous music went, more and more the young back and arms ached until again the tears began to flow. Would father never stop? He felt forgotten, and he was. Could he hold out? Pulling all his energies together now, despair gaining on him, eye on that leaden marker. Should it ever drop? But it will . . . it will . . . for he can't . . . No . . .

Just then the music abruptly ended. The stops knocked back into their sockets. The cover of the keyboard slammed down. His father called him. 'Frank! . . . Frank!' There was no answer.

The figure of the father darkened the small doorway, took in the situation at a glance, took the boy by the hand and led him home without a word.

When they got there his mother, seeing the state the boy was in, looked reproachfully at the father.

It was always so. The differences between husband and wife all seemed to arise over that boy. Mother always on the defensive, father taking the offensive.

So the lad grew, afraid of his father.

His father taught him music. His knuckles were rapped by the lead pencil in the impatient hand that would sometimes force the boy's hand into position at practice time on the Steinway Square piano in the sitting room. And yet he felt proud of his father. Everybody listened and seemed happy when father talked. And Sundays when he preached the small son

16

dressed in his home-made Sunday best looked up at him absorbed in something of his own making that would have surprised the father and the mother more if they could have known.

His pupil always remembered father as he was when 'composing', ink on his fingers and face. For he always held the pen crosswise in his mouth while he would go to and from the desk to the keyboard trying over the passage he had written. His face would soon become fearful with black smudges. To his observant understudy at those times he was weird.

Was music made in such heat and haste as this, the boy wondered? How did Beethoven make his? And how did Bach make his?

He thought Beethoven must have made most of his when it was raining, or just going to, or when the days were gloomy and the sun was soft with clouds. He was sure Bach made his when the sun shone bright and breezes were blowing as little children were happily playing in the street.

Father sometimes played on the piano far into the night, and much of Beethoven and Bach the boy learned by heart as he lay listening. Living seemed a kind of listening to him—then.

Sometimes it was as though a door would open, and he could get the beautiful meaning clear. Then it would close and the meaning would be dim or far away. But always there was some meaning. Father taught him to see a symphony as an edifice—of sound!

At the Centennial in Philadelphia, after a sightseeing day, mother made a discovery. She was eager about it now. Could hardly wait to go to Boston as soon as she got home—to Milton Bradley's.

The Kindergarten!

She had seen the 'Gifts' in the Exposition Building. The strips of coloured paper, glazed and 'matt', remarkably soft brilliant colours. Now came the geometric by-play of those charming checkered colour combinations! The structural figures to be made with peas and small straight sticks: slender constructions, the joinings accented by the little green-pea globes. The smooth shapely maple blocks with which to build, the sense of which never afterwards leaves the fingers: *form* becoming *feeling*. The box had a mast to set up on it, on which to hang the maple cubes and spheres and triangles, revolving them to discover subordinate forms.

And the exciting cardboard shapes with pure scarlet face—such scarlet! Smooth triangular shapes, white-back and edges, cut into rhomboids with which to make designs on the flat table top. What shapes they made naturally if only one would let them!

GIFTS

A small interior world of colour and form now came within grasp of small fingers. Colour and pattern, in the flat, in the round. Shapes that lay hidden behind the appearances all about.

Here was something for invention to seize, and use to create. These 'Gifts' came into the gray house in drab old Weymouth and made something live there that had never lived there before. Mother would go to Boston, take lessons of a teacher of the Froebel method and come home to teach the children. When her housework was done mother and the two children would sit at a low mahogany table with polished top, working with these 'Gifts'.

Fra Angelico's bright-robed angels, some in red, some in blue, others in green; and one—the loveliest of all—in yellow, would come and hover over the table. From their golden harps simple rhythms were gently falling on child minds like flying seeds carried on the wings of the wind to fertile ground. Giotto standing in the shadow at the mother's elbow would have worn a smile beneath his Florentine cap; musing smile prophetic of seedtime and harvest other than his but eternally the same. Again—architecture.

His mother's son has been in Miss Williams' private school for some years, no doubt with the usual Snobbyists and Goodyites. For several years, the minister's son was kept in this fashionable school with the few little Lord Fauntleroys Weymouth afforded.

Let the delicate psychology of biological unfoldings in boys under eleven, important, but so much the same, stand as on record by able artists with a taste for psychological anatomy. In public schools the susceptible little animals encounter and learn things that mothers promptly try to make their boys unlearn and protect them from. So well was this done with him that until marriage in his twenty-first year, personal biological experience was exactly nothing at all, left probably too innocent for his own self-guidance.

But nothing much of this period remains very clear to a boy who dreamed as this lad did. His imagination made a world for himself as he would have it, except where rudely intruded upon by forces that would and could have it otherwise. Music he adored . . . and the Gifts. Meantime he was learning to play the piano. Going to his mother's kindergarten. Learning to paint and draw a little. Learning to sing a little. Reading much all the while.

Boy-like, he discounted his sister. So he played alone usually. There would be an occasional excursion to Nantucket—or a clam-bake at Narragansett. What he was taught in school made not the slightest impression that can be remembered as of any consequence.

For many of the early years of his life when the minister's son was told by his mother that he must not eat a certain thing, 'for it would make him sick', he would always say, 'Well! Let's see if it will then!'

For the first twelve years of life he got a ginger-cookie now and then, gingerbread with a glass of milk, molasses candy, popcorn aplenty, but 'store candies' only when mother didn't know it. No pie. No cake—except at other houses as he grew older. Sometimes, driven to it in the bitterness of thwarted desire, he would hurl this withering sarcasm at his defenceless mother, 'Huh! bringing up your children on graham bread, porridge and religion, are you?'

Probably confirmed by the influence of the father's unhappy essay in

18

medicine, this mother distrusted doses and doctors. Her idea of food was that everything in cooking should be left as simple as possible, natural flavour heightened but never disguised. Her brown bread, stews, baked dishes, roasted meats were delicious without sauces. The frying pan had no place in her sense of things. 'Eat the skins of your baked potatoes.' she would say. If potatoes were boiled, it would be with jackets on, to enhance the potato-flavour. And she would slice the apples for pie or sauce without peeling a certain number of them. She believed the life-giving part of grains or fruit or vegetables was in the colour the sun put in them. That was concentrated in the skins. The apple barrel from the Valley was open between meals or just before bedtime.

If mother picked flowers, she would take the stems long, or the branches, and would arrange them not, as was the mode, in variegated bunches, but freely and separately—never too many together. And she always loved best a glass vase for them showing the stems in water.

In the matter of clothes, she cared little for bright colours. She liked black or white or gray or purple with cream-coloured or black lace at hands and throat. Long, flowing lines. She never believed in corsets. Never wore them. She used to say that a beautiful head of hair was Nature's most precious gift to mortals, and seldom wore more than a scarf on her own head unless she were on duty in her place as Minister's wife.

When she read to her children, as she was fond of doing, it was from Whittier, Lowell or Longfellow, or fairy tales. Usually poetry.

The most lovely thing in the world, she said, was a mother nursing her baby.

Though living in this atmosphere of emphasis on the natural, physically well made and strong, knowing little fear except shyness where his feelings were concerned, her son was too much in the imaginative life of the mind. He preferred reading to playing with other boys—and no wonder! He would rather listen to music than eat his food. He liked to read, listen to music, draw and 'make things', rather than sleep. Above all he liked to dream by himself. And this dreaming he did, with mother's encouragement, regardless of the taunt, 'graham bread, porridge and religion'.

The mother saw which way her man-child was going. She was wise and decided to change it. Change it she did.

TRUTH AGAINST THE WORLD /I\

That Eastern pastorate was wearing out by now. The father had been a Baptist in that land consecrated to Unitarianism. But Unitarianism in the air and the mother's Unitarianism of a more colourful kind at home must have had its effect, for the preacher resigned—a Unitarian.

To the mother, accustomed to the free stride of her life in the country, the meticulous righteousness of the world now her world, the punctilio of her position, the hard-shell 'Godliness' of the provincial Baptist, and the consequent consecration of meanness, probably made every 'donation party' an argument for going back home—'out West'.

19

The minister's pay was a pittance, of course, in keeping with the parsimony and poverty of the ideals of life—intolerance and infallibility—it paid for.

The Unitarianism of the Lloyd-Joneses, a far richer thing, was an attempt to amplify in the confusion of the creeds of their day, the idea of life as a gift from the Divine Source, one GOD omnipotent, all things at one with HIM.

Unity was their watchword, the sign and symbol that thrilled them, the UNITY of all things! This mother sought it continually. Good and evil existed for her people still, however, and for her. The old names still confused their faith and defeated them when they came to apply it. But the salt and savour of faith they had, the essential thing, and there was a warmth in them for truth, cut where truth might! And cut, it did—this '*truth against the world*'. Enough trouble in that for any one family—the beauty of TRUTH! The family did not so well know the truth of BEAUTY. These valley-folk feared beauty, seeing in it a probable snare for unwary feet, and making the straight way their own feet might mark in the snow less admirable in their own sight and as an example for irresponsible youth.

Now came back to the ancestral Valley from the East, by way of Sister Anna and her 'preacher', the 'Unitarianism' worked out in the transcendentalism of the sentimental group at Concord: Whittier, Lowell, Longfellow, yes, and Emerson, too. Thoreau? Well, Thoreau seemed to them too smart. He made them uncomfortable.

This poetic transcendentalism was to unite with their own richer, sterner sentimentality, with results that will be seen.

The luxury of the Lloyd-Joneses was not laughter, but tears.

Until you had water in the eyes of them you really hadn't got them.

Quick in emotional response to human need, sorrow or suffering, good deeds thrilled them always.

The little preacher-family in Weymouth was desperately poor in this scrabby, stony vineyard of the Lord. And but for the children of the mother and the music of the father, body and soul by this time would have been far apart. Maginel, a frail little thing, was born in this lean period. She was, for months, handled carefully on a pillow. Her mother, alone, saving her by giving her own vital energy, manipulating and exercising her for hours.

She came to be added to the responsibilities of the preacher.

Salvage for the Mother? Private schooling for her boy, the Gifts, the household, and the transcendentalism of Concord that was reaching back to the Valley in letters she wrote and books she sent, the books of Channing, Emerson, Theodore Parker, and, yes, Thoreau.

Salvage for the Father? A strange Italian, looking like Paganini came to play. Remenyi, grotesque nose and eyes came, too. Later in the West, to the house at Madison, came the handsome Ole Bull. And, always, there was the church organ in the quiet, deserted church.

So the preacher-father and teacher-mother came back West, forty miles

20

from the Valley, to a modest house on the shore of Lake Mendota, in Madison. Now education of the male child was to begin in earnest.

But this child was to be saved not by, but from, the 'word-of-God' as it was thought to be something written in mighty books or spoken by learned men from platform or pulpit. He was to learn the living, breathing thing it is: 'The flower that fadeth, the grass that withereth.'

ADDING TIRED TO TIRED

A letter to Sister Anna's beloved brother James brought him from the home Valley to the modest Madison town-house by the blue lake.

He drove down the entire forty miles leading a cow tied behind his wagon so that Anna's children might have good fresh milk. There stood Uncle James, tall, strong and brown, with a great shock of waving brown hair on his handsome head, thick brown beard on his face. When he smiled his eyes went nearly shut and witty wrinkles came to their corners. His nephew trusted him at first glance.

The golden curls had been cut off. The mother wept as she cut them. Curls there still were, but shorter and their glory gone. This 'going to work' of her boy costing mother something more than the shedding of the curls. It could be seen now.

Uncle James put his arm around his sister to comfort her. She whispered something to him the boy did not hear. He patted her shoulder and laughed a reassuring laugh. How he always laughed! So clear! Ringing out, it always made you want to laugh too. He promised her something as he took the boy by the hand. 'Ready now, Frank? We're going west. Going to make a farmer of you, my boy.' Mother gathered the child in her arms and wept.

And so the boy went. He went away from Mother, books, music and city boys and father and little Maginel and Jane, idle dreams and city streets to learn to add 'tired' to 'tired' and add it again—and add it yet again. Then beginning all over again at the beginning, he learned to add it all up some more until it seemed to him he would surely break or drop.

A low attic bedroom lit by a single window in one of the white-washed sloping walls, heated by a stovepipe running up through the floor and ceiling above from the room below.

Sharp rapping now on the stovepipe—loud. Again, sharper, louder. The boy rubbed his eyes, shocked by the banging outrage.

A voice below, 'Four o'clock, my boy, time to get up.'

How could it be? He had just gone to bed! But he remembered soon and sleepily called, 'All right, Uncle James—coming!'

He looked down at the things Uncle James had put there by the bed the night before, got up and put them on. It was early spring and he shivered. Two pieces, a 'hickory' shirt, blue-jean overalls with blue cotton suspenders. Coarse blue cotton socks and clumsy cowhide shoes, with leather laces. These last were worst. And there was a hat. That hat!

21

Forthwith, hating hat and shoes he learned to do without both.

Uncle James was waiting for him at the foot of the stairs with that life-giving voice of his and winning smile. After splashing water on his face from the basin on the bench—you got it by dropping into the cistern a bucket tied to a rope—he was ready. His Uncle took him off to the barn. The strange smells sickened him but he dutifully began milking as shown, until his hands ached.

And that very morning he learned to look out for certain cows who, feeling you come in beside them, would lean over and crush the breath out of you against the wall of the stall. Beating them over the back with the milking stool only made them push harder.

Milking done, came breakfast. Potatoes, fried. Fried cornmeal mush, fried pork, green cheese and cornbread. Pancakes and sorghum. Butter-milk, glass of fresh milk. Coffee or tea, but not for the boy.

No cream.

When Gottlieb Munch (for Mensch), red-faced, yellow-haired hired man, would pour sorghum over his big piece of fat pork, he would take the boy's appetite away.

After breakfast, helping Uncle James's wife, Aunt Laura, to feed the calves. Teaching the darned, crowding, pushing, bunting things to suck the milk by holding the fingers in the pail for them to suck. A nasty busi-ness. And often a desperate calf would give the bucket a bunt and send milk flying all over him from head to foot until exasperated by the sense-less bunting and pushing he would lay about him with the pail to keep from being trampled down.

Aunt Laura would laugh then.

After this, carrying sticks of cord-wood to the cross-cut saw, pausing to run errands, maybe, if your Uncle saw you were getting the worst of it, and told you to go. Then dinner. Boiled fresh beef, boiled potatoes, boiled carrots, boiled turnips, home-made bread and butter. Jam, pickles, prunes, sorghum, honey and green cheese, or pie or cake. Tea or coffee, but not for the boy.

No cream.

Afternoon—holding the split oak-rails while Uncle James nailed them to the fence-posts, hands full of slivers, going off to get the cows for the first time, at five. Home to supper at six. Fried potatoes, as regularly as the sun set. Home-made bread and butter. Cornbread, cornmeal mush and milk, honey and home-made preserves. Fried salt-pork or smoked beef, 'creamed', they said. Milk.

No cream!

After supper, milking again.

In bed about half-past seven, too tired to move.

Again outrageous banging on the stovepipe, almost before he had really fallen asleep.

It had begun—this business of adding 'tired' to 'tired', and adding it again—and adding it again.

And so, as it was that day with the eleven-year-old it was next day and

22

the day after and the day after that until the clothes he drew on in the morning to the violence of that rapping on the stovepipe were sweat-stiffened. They went on stiff and stayed stiff until he limbered them up by working in them.

On Saturday night he got a bath by carrying soft water from the cistern, heating some of it on the stove. He threw the stark things aside for his city clothes on Sunday morning. And already in April, for the first years, he would begin to look forward to September seventeenth when school would begin for him. Longing for the time to come. How sore! If mother only knew.

She came before long. Seeing him, she clasped him to her bosom and burst into tears. The boy wondered why she was so sad to see him?

And then after she went away work went on some four or five weeks and he began to wear down. His back ached so. His fingers were stiff and sore. Knees and elbows; feet, too. He was ashamed to let it be known—but one afternoon, he decided to change it himself. Having a difficulty with Aunt Laura over the free use of a hammer he seldom put back in its place, he got it, threw it in the creek for good and all, and departed. He took a kitchen-knife with him, intending to get home somehow, anyhow.

He started across the hill toward the river to find the ferryboat that would take him to Spring Green. He was footsore. Crestfallen; his legs stiff. Guilty, his back lame. Ashamed of running away; his hands bleeding in places.

Uncle James knowing what was good for the boy had given it to him until, well—here he was, running away: home or somewhere—what did he care where, if he couldn't go where he could find comfort?

Yet, his nephew adored Uncle James. Uncle James could do everything, and so well that the others liked to stop and watch him do it. Break colts to harness for the neighbours. Handle a kicking cow that Gottlieb, the hired man, would be afraid to touch. Swing an axe with such ringing accuracy that the clean-cut chips whizzed furiously around your head as you tried to dodge them. Could run all the machines. Always knew how to fix what was the matter with them—and there was always something the matter with them. Was always laughing at the same time and never afraid of anything. As the boy thought of him now he wanted to turn back and 'stick'. But he was too sore in body and mind. So he limped along. The home by the blue lake and mother seemed very dear and all he wanted, but—how far away!

As the road ran over the hilltop above Uncle Enos's, soft, white sand-rock cropped out in long, thin ledges beside it. Fascinated by whatever there is in sand that bewitches boys, he scraped away at it with his knife and took the soft piles of pure white in both his hands. To the right were pink ledges. He scraped those. To the left, yellow, and he scraped those. Put a layer of yellow over a layer of white, then pink and then white, and, even in his misery, it occurred to him to cut through the pile with his knife and take one half away and look at the colour streaks in the section he thus made.

23

This diversion ruined his enterprise though he did not know it. His anguish grew less and he thought about going back before Uncle James came home and found him gone. But he had started something now, on his own. So he went on to the ferry.

He was sitting on the barge-board of the old ferryboat, legs over the side in the flowing water, waiting for a start. He sat there for some time, watching the eddies marking the sand along the shore. Then, feeling something, he looked up and saw Uncle Enos!

He liked Uncle Enos, mother's youngest brother.

Uncle Enos was fond of him. They had wrestled and played together often.

Word had gone out from Uncle James to look for the boy. It would soon be getting dark. Uncle Enos's instinct had been the right one. In a kindly tone he asked, 'Where are you going, Frank?'

No answer.

Tears . . .

Uncle Enos took the boy by the hand and led him to the grass on the bank overlooking the river. The boy cried it out, telling his woes and his resentment.

'Yes, yes. I know, my boy. Work the soreness out by keeping right on working! You will grow stronger by keeping at it, no matter how it hurts. Soon you'll be so strong you'll like it and can do things like Uncle James. The only way to do. Just keep on when you are sore and tired and stiff and think you're discouraged. But you never *are* discouraged. No . . . And by keeping on, still more, and again more, you'll see you can do most anything and never feel it too much.' He gripped the biceps in the soft arm. 'As much muscle as a blackbird's got in his legs,' he said. Then stretching out his own arm, 'Feel this,'—and the boy felt his Uncle's iron upper-arm with admiration. 'Your muscles will be like that, Frank, if you keep on at it. Then you can laugh too, like Uncle James, and never be afraid of anything. Work is an adventure that makes strong men and finishes weak ones.'

'Aunt Laura? . . . Well, Aunt Laura is a bit hasty. Not very well just now. Something is going to happen. You needn't mind her too much. Think of your mother and Uncle James. How disappointed they both would be if you went on with this. Shall we go back now?'

'Yes!'

Under cover of darkness, hand in hand, they made their way back. The boy went ruefully up to his bed in the attic.

Next morning—as though nothing at all had happened—the rapping on the stovepipe, perhaps not so loud, but relentless just the same.

And it began all over again.

Something Uncle Enos had said stuck in his mind. 'Adventures make strong men and finish weak ones.'

But Uncle Enos had said 'work' was that adventure. The connection of adventure with 'work' got lost in the impressionable mind for the time being. But later he was to find it.

24

The rebel ran away again before long. Got farther this time. Brought back by Uncle James himself. Unregenerate, he slipped to hiding in the strawstack as soon as they got inside the farmyard gate. All night, not answering by any sign, he lay there hidden in the straw; listening to the anxiety and confusion in the dark, as one or the other of the household would call him from different directions, near or far away.

Thus, the truant boy took his revenge for the hurts that were his—by hurting them. A reprobate element of character, of course, this 'eye for an eye, and tooth for a tooth'. Worthy of Isaiah. This ulcerous Mosaic-root of human misery had shown itself in him before.

He fell asleep.

Fearing some evil had befallen him, so glad were they to find him in the morning that his punishment was in Uncle James's hand, and light. Aunt Laura stood aside for the time being.

That was the last of running away.

What Uncle Enos had said, and Uncle James had said too, began to come true. Work *was* adventure, when you were fit for it. And there was a small boy's mind fixed upon that spring-water stream flowing over the soft mud-bottom as it passed below the house. And whenever he could get into that stream, his was 'recreation' in building dams of sticks and stones across it, sailing his shoes along the banks, wading and playing in it tirelessly whether he might or might not. Fascination for a child . . . running water!

Whenever it rained, running out into the rain for a shower bath, naked, was irresistible. Mother had started it when he was several years old by taking off his clothes and setting him running out of doors in thunderstorms.

'Uncle James!'

How many million times his earnest young disciple's voice had called that name first to last. The young novice's questions were so incessant, Uncle James finally hesitated to take him to town as he usually did, the small legs dangling from the spring seat of the lumber wagon, just because he wanted a little peace!

The restless, inquisitive one, further, was a simpleton looking for a little, white bird which no one could make him believe he would not see. He had seen blue ones, and blue-birds, they said, were for happiness. And he had seen many red ones: scarlet tanagers, yellow thistle-birds and orioles. He had seen black and black-and-red ones and many colours mixed. Brown ones. But none all white. No, never one. Why was there no white bird? Uncle James would assure him there were none in that region except doves and hens. But they wouldn't do. Much to his Uncle's annoyance he believed a white one existed. He continued to look for it just the same. But he never saw one and has never seen one yet.

The boy dreamed now, again. Sitting a long time, never moving, a look on his face that Uncle James came to recognize and he would call him. 'Frank! Frank! Come back! Come back, Frank!' But the open sky was overhead, the woods surrounded the fields in which work was forever going on in a routine that was endless. Endless, the care of the animals, horses, cows, pigs, sheep.

His early lot was cast with the cows.

TO HER!

Cow! What a word! And, cow-bell! The cows! My boy. The cows! Always—'the cows!'

The Valley cows were red—Durhams—until Uncle James later got a black-and-white Holstein bull, envy of all the township. And so the herd, from year to year, grew to black and white. In three years the cattle in the Valley all changed from red to black and white.

Why is any cow, red, black or white, always in just the right place for a picture in any landscape? Like a cypress tree in Italy, she is never wrongly placed. Her outlines quiet down so well into whatever contours surround her. A group of her in the landscape is enchantment.

Has anyone sung the song of the patient, calf-bearing, milk-flowing, cud-chewing, tail-switching cow? Slow-moving, with the fragrant breath and beautiful eyes, the well-behaved, necessary cow, who always seems to occupy the choicest ground anywhere around?

She is the dairy farm, the wealth of states, the health of nations.

How many trusties and lusties besides her lawful calf have pulled away at her teats these thousands of years until the stream flowing from them would float fleets of battleships, drown all the armies the world has ever seen.

How the cow has multiplied the man!

And yet, so battened upon, she is calm, faithful, fruitful.

As companion, she endures all—contented, even indifferent.

But the Minnesingers down the ages have given small place to the cow in poetry or song.

She is just a Cow.

Yet, to go through the herd lying on the grass, as the dew falls all quietly chewing their cud in peace together, is to find a sweetness of the breath as it rises, a freshness of Earth itself that revives something essential to life lying deep in the instincts of the human race.

Is the cow now mother to the man to such an extent that his 'instinct' begins to be aware of her in this exhalation from her nostrils?

And the dung that goes from her to the fields by way of sweating youths and men saturated, struggling in the heavy odour and texture of her leavings! This indispensable wealth that goes to bring back the jaded soil to a greenness of the hills, bring fertility to life itself—for man!

Yes, where her tribe flourishes there the earth is green, the fields fertile. Man in well-being and abundance.

She is Hosanna to the Lord! For where she is, 'at destruction and famine man laughs', as he salts her, fodders her, beds her, breeds her and milks her. Thus tended she contentedly eats her way from calfhood clear through to the digestive tract of humanity—her destiny. Her humble last farewell to man—the shoes upon his feet!

'Come, my boy, the cows,' or that dread cry like an alarm of fire: 'The cows are in the corn!'

His special duty was getting the cows back home and taking them out to grass again. There were no fences about the woods in those days. Few roads, even, and no cow-paths except near the farmsteads, so that each time he went out to find them and bring them in was an adventure. The plaintive tinkle of that far-away cow-bell!

How many small boys in the homes of the brave on these grounds-of-the-free were, or for that matter at any moment since are, listening to the measured tinkle of that far-away bell—anxiously hearkening, stopping to listen, hearing it again. This time—yes—nearer! By losing it altogether and starting to listen all over again.

The tinkle of the cow-bell has steadily called the boys of Usonia. And, in some form, will call them always.

Usonia—Samuel Butler's appropriate name for the United States of America, roots in the word 'union'. If the United States is 'America', then Georgia is South America and New York is North America, the Canadians are Americans, the Mexicans too. South America is jealous of the term 'America'.

Now he went through the moist woods that in their shade were treasuring the rainfall for the sloping fields below or to feed the clear springs in the ravines, wending his way along the ridges of the hills gay with Indian-pinks or shooting-stars, across wide meadows carpeted thick with tall grass on which the flowers seemed to float. The field-lilies stood there above the grass like stars of flame. Wading the creeks, sometimes lost in the deep shade and deeper shadows of white-oak woods, he would go to find and bring home the cows.

He had to start early in order to get them home before dark, but sometimes it would be after dark before he brought them back. Sometimes he found them not at all and Uncle James would have to get on a horse and go after them.

It was his duty to help milk while the herd was standing in the yard if very warm, or at the stanchions in the cow-stable roofed with straw, if cooler. At this milking, each milker would sit balanced on a one-legged stool, bare head against the warm flank of the cow, drawing away at the teats with a slow rhythmical squeezing pull of the hands to the music that was the sound of the milk-streams striking into the foaming milk in the pail. Occasionally a gushing stream of warm milk caught in the mouth, a trick learned from Gottlieb.

Everyone had to milk, even Aunt Laura, who wasn't very well.

The cows all had names—like Spot, who broke into the granary, ate her fill of ground feed, drank all the water she could, and died—a glorious heroine's death in her tribe, no doubt.

The death of Spot was a blow for she was a kindly old cow with a long tail. It was a help. There were other tails to hang to and they served but none so willing for the purpose as Spot's.

In these adventures alone—abroad in the wooded hills to fetch the cows, he, barefoot, bareheaded urchin, was insatiable, curious and venturesome. So he learned to know the woods, from the trees above to the shrubs below and the grass beneath. And the millions of curious lives living hidden in the surface of the ground, among roots, stems, and mould. He was soon happy in such knowledge. As a listening ear, a seeing eye and a sensitive touch had been given naturally to him, his spirit was now becoming familiar with this marvellous book-of-books, Experience, the only true reading, the book of Creation.

One eleven-year-old was learning to *experience* what he heard, touched or saw.

From sunrise to sunset there can be nothing so surpassingly beautiful in any cultivated garden as in the wild Wisconsin pastures.

Night shadows so wonderfully blue, like blue shadows on snow.

Chokecherry pendent blooms to become black clusters of berries that puckered your throat.

Solid depths of shade, springs—a glittering transparency in the cool shadows.

Sunlight, aslant through the leaves on the tree trunks, plashing the leaf-covered ground beneath.

White birches gleaming.

Wild grape festooning fences and trees.

The Sumach, braided foliage and dark red berry-cones.

Herbs, and dripping leaves in soft rain.

In the fields, milkweed blossoming to scatter its snowy fleece on every breeze.

Sorrel reddening on the hills, far and wide.

The world of daylight gold would go through violet passing to the deep blue of the night.

He would dawn now as the day, and studious experiences began in the swarming insect life, in the warm living breath of fern beds. In the marvel of mosses. In leaf-mould.

In the damp grasses under bare feet.

In the strange life going on in them.

There was the feel of mud between the toes and burning sand under the feet, the cool, fresh grass on the open slopes.

He knew where the lady-slippers grew and why, where to find yellow ones and where those rare ones, white and purple, were hidden.

He could lead you surely to where Jack-in-the-Pulpit stood in the deep shade of the wood; to wild strawberries in the sunny clearings of the hills, to watercress in the cool streams flowing from hillside springs.

Always he was the one who knew where the tall, red lilies could be found afloat on tall meadow-grass. Where nuts and berries abounded, there he would be.

The spot of red made by a lily on the green always gave him an emotion.

Later, the red square as spot of flame-red, became the crest with which he signed his drawings and marked his buildings.

Soon the young ear could tell what flew overhead. What sang and where and why. He studied, by the hour, the tumblebugs, black-beetles: scarabs, rolling their marbles of cow manure in the hot sun of the dusty road. Mysterious folk!

The ant-hills were busy cities. Catkins cutting circles making patterns on still water. He would go catching sleek frogs, or poking stupid toads, chasing crazy grasshoppers. Listening at night to the high treble of the frog-song as it rose from the marshes. He delighted in devil's darning needles, turtles, too: their fascinating structure, colour pattern, strange movements—ever curious about them all. He was studying unconsciously what later he would have called 'style'.

And there were enemies: skunks, snakes, and hornets.

There were always too many toes to stub. Mosquitoes. Flies. Cut-grass, nettles. Poison ivy. What that poison ivy could do to young blood and tender skin! Quicksand in the streams. And hornets' nests in the barn-rafters, their wonderful house-nests sometimes hanging from the bushes. The lightning: always the lightning.

Cruel winds that seemed to be the enemy of every growing thing swept the valley sometimes. But he learned their value later.

'Wild Rose!' A legendary woman, gone wild, living in a hut in the hills and wandering about. He had not seen her. All seemed afraid of her, and liked to frighten him.

Such, teeming in the sun, quiet under clouds, drenched with rain, were the then-time pastures of the cow.

And the trees stood in it all like various, beautiful buildings, of more different kinds than all the architectures of the world. Some day this boy was to learn that the secret of all styles in architecture was the same secret that gave *character* to the trees.

Work was hard, sometimes interfering with dreaming studies or studious dreams. At other times, dreams went undisturbed beneath or above the routine. These dreaming moments must have had characteristic expression in him for he would again and again, as before, hear Uncle James calling, 'Come back, Frank! Come back!'

SUNDAY

Sundays were salvation for the 'tired to tired' added during the week.

Uncles and aunts, some of them graying, some white-haired now, would sit at chapel in the old-fashioned rocking chairs provided for them round the platform on which the pulpit stood. The pulpit on which the family Bible lay was covered with a purple cloth and, Sundays, was usually smothered in wild flowers, brought by the children.

Of course, the 'help' were included, too.

Sometimes the neighbours came.

When Uncle Jenkin preached there was the genuine luxury of tears. Going gently to and fro in the rocking chairs below the pulpit as tears were shed and, unheeded, trickled down. His sermons always brought the family to emotional state—but then—so did readings from the transcendental classics or the singing of the children. Tears, too, when all rose in strength and in the dignity of their faith straightened themselves to sing—'step by step since time began we see the steady gain of man'. The faltering, the falsetto and the flat would raise that favourite hymn to the boarded ceiling of the little chapel and go swelling out through the open windows and doors and—to the young mind looking out toward them—seemed to reach far away and fade beyond the hills. This surrender to religious emotion was fervent and sincere! There was true heart in the favourite hymns for them all, and for all . . . water in the eyes of them.

Uncle Thomas, who was poet of the group, had planted the fir grove beside the chapel so that future Sunday picnics might have shade.

On the east side of the shingle-sided chapel, with its quaint belfry opposite the fir grove, was the churchyard where the simple white marble obelisk did reverence to the memory of 'EinTad' and 'EinMam'—their Welsh for father and mother.

Grouped around that tall central slender obelisk were the family graves.

Every Sunday, spring and summer of these youthful years, up to September fifth, the boy would put on his city clothes and go to sit on a chair at these chapel gatherings.

It was his work to decorate the pulpit.

Early in the morning—while still cool—his cousins would go with him to get what flowers and branches he wanted. Tremendous riches were within easy reach along the roads as the team jogged along and stopped, jogged and stopped, until the wagon box was piled high.

The result, broad masses of bloom and verdure freely arranged, mingled pretty much as they grew . . . only more so. Rostrum and pulpit, Sundays, were a gracious sight.

The little wooden chapel stands in fair repair in the Valley. It is almost hidden by the sober, towering, green mass of Uncle Thomas' fir trees under which pine-board tables used to be bountifully spread for young and old of a united family. Uncles and aunts, ten. With husbands and wives, eighteen. Girls and boys all told, forty. An audience, with the neighbours and help of about seventy-five. That is, unless something special was going on like Uncle Jenkin's preaching, a wedding, a funeral or a camp meeting. Then the whole countryside would be there.

This family chapel was the simple, shingled wooden temple in which the valley-clan worshipped images it had lovingly created. In turn the images reacted upon the family in their own image. Those sunny religious meetings were, in reality, gatherings of the clan.

But in midsummer the meetings became an orgy of visiting divines and divinity. William C. Gannett, Henry M. Simmons, J. T. Sunderland and Dr. Thomas of Chicago were family favourites. From time to time there were many others. The visitors would come at preacher's vacation-time and camp meetings, reunions, picnics and birthday celebrations would greet them.

Uncle Thomas with his gentle, rather downcast mien was always for picnics. 'Come now, girls,' he would say to his sisters, 'let us go for a picnic. Do not bother at all, a little graham bread, a little cheese, a drink of milk—let us all be together.'

Preparations would begin. All the children, they had begun to swarm by now, would be called in to help. Soon the 'graham bread, bit of cheese, a drink of milk', would swell into roast pig, roast turkey. Maybe fresh corn-on-the-ear to be roasted. Roast chicken, delectably stuffed. Chicken, fried. Boiled ham, hard-boiled eggs. Sugared doughnuts. Turnovers. Cinnamon-covered Dutch rolls. Corn bread. White biscuits, brown bread and butter. Ripe tomatoes. And maybe fresh cucumbers, whole, to be peeled, eaten in the hand, like a banana with salt. All kinds of sandwiches and pickles. Fat and sugary green-apple pies and pumpkin pie. Green cheese and cream cheese. Sorghum and honey. Of course, home-made preserves that ran the gamut from strawberry to watermelon rind. Interesting inventions in the way of pickles. All kinds of dark and light cookies, slabs of ginger-bread. Each household's favourite frosted or layer or plain cake. Plums or berries might be thereabouts for the picking. Coffee would be made on the fire. Milk, buttermilk and clabbered milk to drink would be set in the spring water. All in abundance until there was hardly anything left out that could or ever had gone into a Jones at one time or another and pleased or profited him.

Pharaoh, no doubt, fared worse.

All this would go into baskets and each family go with its basket and its children into the family wagon. The first wagon ready would draw up and wait for the others. Dressed for the occasion they would, soon after waiting for all to get together, go off in a procession large enough to have been the funeral of some prophet—even Moses himself.

But it was just a Lloyd-Jones picnic.

Bright-coloured cloths would be spread on green grass in some cool selected spot, probably in the shade of beautiful trees. If possible always near a spring or stream. All the preparations would be gorgeously spread out. Swings would be hung from the trees for the children. After the feast the children would sing and speak 'pieces'. Father would play the violin and sing, leading the uncles and aunts in favourite hymns. Some of the older ones knew songs in Welsh. They used to sing them in Wales. There would be *Esteddvod* then and there. His son, the 'modern' note, would give 'Darius Green and his Flying Machine' or the 'Wonderful One Hoss Shay'. All—grownups and children too—would have something or other to speak or sing. But the hymn-singing—in unison, of course—was the most satisfying feature of the day, unless it was Uncle Jenkin's preaching. All would join in, tears—under the circumstances—reaching their best.

At a distance you would hear the harmonicas and jew's-harps of the hired men, walking about by the banks of the stream with the hired girls.

31

Preaching and psalm-singing hadn't the same delight in it for them as for the Lloyd-Joneses.

These sons and daughters of Richard Lloyd-Jones, Welsh Pioneer, in his Valley, had already gone far toward making the kind of life for themselves he would have approved. The united family had its own chapel, its gristmill (Uncle John's), and owned, cultivated or pastured pretty much all the land in sight in the Valley and its branches.

Lloyd-Jones family life was growing in human welfare and consequence.

This spring and summer life of the Valley in spring and summer and of the city in fall and winter, was now established. It was to last five years more for the boy until he was coming sixteen. But the twelve-year-old now comes home in September to the modest brown-wood house by the blue lake in Madison where were Mother, Father, Jennie and Maginel.

Madison is a beautiful city. From near or far away the white dome of the State Capitol on a low spreading hill shone white in the sun between two blue lakes, Mendota and Monona. Two more, smaller, not so blue, Wingra and Waubesa, were flung one side for good measure.

The State University stood on its own hill beside Madison; a collection of noncommittal, respectably nondescript buildings.

Its hill, too, was crowned by a dome—a brown and gold one.

Both domes were in debt for life to Michelangelo. But it was no discredit. As anyone might see, they were doing the best they could. The young student saw both domes destroyed within a few years. The mortgage of time (not Michelangelo's) on human fallibility foreclosed.

The city was laid out as a sort of wheel with eight spokes radiating from the Capitol dome, one of the spokes hitting the campus below the University dome.

Madison was a self-conscious town. A city, but provincial beyond most villages. And the University gave it a high-brow air—the air, that is, of having been educated far beyond its capacity.

There were a few good residences—good for their day. The Vilas home, the best of them. These better places bordered on the lakes. As to the rest, it was Sun Prairie, or Stoughton or any Wisconsin village of one to five thousand on a somewhat larger scale.

The intelligentsia, as was proper, ruled in Madison. The University, their badge of brief authority.

There was influx and exodus of ambitious legislators from the various provinces of the State once a year, coming to immortalize their services by making laws and more 'laws'.

The Capitol then wrested the honours from the University.

At all times, there was a feeble 'Town and Gown' rivalry. But it never became exciting enough to attract much notice.

The lakes saved the city and its population from utter weariness by self-imposed importance in this provincial matter of intellectual-respectability.

ROBIE

One 'William C. Wright', teacher and music master, started a Conservatory of Music above some kind of store in Pinckney Street. The Madison ward schools were, at that time, good. And at the Second Ward School—his ward—on the bank of the lake, near the music-master's home —his son found Robie Lamp. Red-headed Robie Lamp—'the cripple'. Boyish enterprises grew out of the circumstance. More than ever shy, the boy had need of few friends but somehow always needed one intimate companion. He couldn't live, move and have his being, so it seemed, without a heart-to-heart comrade. No, not even at that early day.

Robie Lamp fourteen years old became that inseparable companion.

Robie's legs were shrivelled, and dangled dead as he moved along on crutches. He had a good large head well covered with coarse, bright-red hair. His face had the florid complexion and blue eyes of a Teuton. His arms and chest did the work of the legs that 'went out on him'—to use Robie's Pa's phrase. So arms and chest were fine and strong although his hips were withered and twisted. The arms were much stronger because the legs were helpless.

All there was of Robie was the splendid head, brawny shoulders, chest, arms and hands and—the Robie spirit.

'Lamp' was a good name for him, he was so effulgent. His well-earned nickname was 'Ruby' but his eyes were turquoise ringed with white, clear and wide open.

The schoolboys teased the cripple—unmercifully.

Savagely, squat-on-the-ground, he would strike out at them, those powerful arms of his swinging the brass-shod crutches. His tormentors were careful to keep out of reach but enough of them together could get him and in this autumn, at the moment when he comes in here, they were burying him in the fallen leaves until he was all but smothered, wherefrom he would emerge raging, sputtering and crying.

Plucked up by his farm training of a season, the boy rescued him. Drove off the boys so cruelly picking on him; got the crutches they had wisely thrown far out of his reach; dusted him off; got him up on them and on his smile again. This was the first meeting with 'Robie'.

The boys were fast friends thereafter till Robie, forty-four, died in a little cream-white brick house with a roof-garden filled with flowers, designed for him by this rescuer of his.

At the boy's home in Madison was the irascible, intellectual father, with his piano and violin, now—and more frequently—writing and reading in his study. The household was peaceful at such times. Father was trying to make his Conservatory go and preaching occasionally. The modern refinement of the home grew under the yearning, ambitious mother's hands: the new-laid white, waxed maple floors; the cream-coloured net curtains hanging straight beside the windows and partly over them; pictures (good engravings) hanging on the walls—framed in narrow maple-bands. The centres of the room floors were covered with

India rugs—cream-coloured ground with bright-coloured patterns and border. Maple and rattan furniture. And everywhere, books. Simple vases were gracefully filled with dried leaves.

The 'son-of-his-mother', as might be expected, had ideas about fixing things up. He was coming along by way of architecture, whether he knew it or not. Sometimes he did know it.

The flat, wooden door to his attic bedroom was marked in large loose letters, 'SANCTUM'. It opened with a latch and a string. This attic room with its sloping sides was decorated with dried leaves and the pod-topped weeds we have seen in the snow. In spite of Uncle John's 'lesson', there they were. The woodcuts of the English cathedrals, which the boy saw soon as he opened his eyes to see anything, were on the walls and as many 'things' as were not needed below. 'Things' at this stage were just so many objects to compose—with which to 'fix up effects', the childlike desire to make 'pictures' of everything, yes, including himself.

There were his own drawings and some 'oil paintings' he had made during that pastorale in Weymouth as disciple of Miss Landers, a friend of mother's who vainly imagined oil painting a useful accomplishment maybe for any architect and certainly a social asset.

'Oil paintings?' One of them he carefully made invited your consideration of a card-board cock-robin on a leadpipe branch looking nowhere, on guard beside his wife's four speckled eggs. She had thoughtfully laid them in a cast-iron nest tipped toward you under a baby-blue sky. Another was a 'landscape' with one hairy tree and oilcloth water deep-sunk in a really fine plain-gold frame chosen by Miss Landers herself. This 'painting' was committed in the bushy brush work of the 'buckeye' of that period. The 'buckeye', as you may remember, was profitably distributed about the villages for a dollar to two dollars each, or painted while you waited. A virtuosity. Sometimes because it was so slight, curiously effective. He always liked that frame.

But the paintings were Miss Landers' own innocent crimes to which the innocent mother had allowed her innocent son to become an innocent party. Innocent yet indubitably 'crime'. In due course suitably punished.

A certain earthenware churn—he stippled it with colour and decorated it with plumblossoms scratched through the paint while it was fresh— was better. It was a later work and untaught. Really a kind of *sgraffito*, he afterward came to know.

But the son had given up this precocious 'painting' by way of Miss Landers. He was learning now to play the viola in the orchestra his father was getting together from Madison pupils—boys and girls. Jennie played the piano.

Robie, too, was taking violin lessons of the father. 'Ma' and 'Pa' would always sit and listen while their Robie practised. They saw in it a career for him perhaps.

A small printing-press with seven founts of De Vinne type, second-hand, was set up in the old barn at first, and later a quite complete printing-office fixed up in the basement of the house.

Books read together: 'Hans Brinker', Ruskin's 'Seven Lamps of Architecture', a gift from the Aunts Nell and Jane. Jules Verne's 'Michael Strogoff', 'Hector Servadac'. Goethe's 'Wilhelm Meister'. The 'Arabian Nights' as always—Aladdin and his Lamp—and many tales. Not much poetry. Whittier, Longfellow, Bryant. If they were not poets, they were at least, poetic.

A seductive touch upon dreaming life were the enchanted and enchanting pages of the 'Arabian Nights'!

Enchantment, no less, the tattered illiterature of thrills—the Nickel Library—secretly read. Hidden at the reading for hours. The culprit appearing at mealtime—still elsewhere—would fail to answer in time. Mother would perhaps be anxious.

'What has happened to you, Frank? Are you feeling well?'

'Oh, Mother, I'm all right. I was just thinking.'

'Thinking of what?'

'Oh, just how wonderful the lives of some people are—and what wonderful things happen to them. And we live along just the same every day. Nothing ever happens.'

'Frank, what have you been reading?' Mother would ask, fixing him with her searching eyes.

He would come out with it then and he would lose that one too and never know if they got the Scarlet Rover in the ambuscade at the river-crossing or not.

IN MEMORIAM

Was the Nickel Library really bad? Why would mother or father or teacher take the blood-and-thunder tales away and burn them if they caught us with them? Greasy, worn and torn like old bank-notes they would secretly circulate in exchange for a glassie or an aggie or two. One would go from pocket to pocket until it would have to be patched together to be read, fragments maddeningly missing at critical moments. Stark, they were, with the horror of masks and corpses—dripping with gang-gore—but cool with bravery in the constant crash of catastrophe. The *bravery* thrilled. The daring hero, usually some lad like ourselves, triumphant all the time. Going down, only to come right-side up through scrambled Indians and half-caste cut-throats, carcasses, bowie knives, and cutlasses.

The movie requires no imagination. The Nickel Library did. And (just like 'the movies') all was utterly arranged in every detail to the perfect satisfaction of the girlish heroine, whose virtue, meantime, was tested and retested from every possible angle, and ambush—she too, at the critical moment emerging manhandled but unspotted—with style all the while!

This ill-assorted pair—Frank, good legs and Robie, bad legs—lived many lives.

One with the lake.

35

One, typesetting, printing, and composing. Inventing, designing.

Another with music in the evenings and reading.

The girl-friends of the boy's sisters came in often to sing and play.

Gay evenings! Young, eager, happy voices and clear-shining eyes. Gilbert and Sullivan lyrics were then not only popular—they were the rage. Born of true lyrical genius that never failed to charm the singers who sang them and those who heard them no less. Nor did they ever fail to yield new effects in the experiments made with them. How could *they* have come out of the hideous artificiality of the Victorian Era? Gilbert and Sullivan must have been Victorian 'relief'. A *genuine* gaiety.

These evenings were no concerts. They were happy riots. No one could tell where laughter left off and singing began. Nor where singing left off and laughter began.

Musical education, however, stopped short for the youth when he entered the University and his father had gone. Somehow, the undergraduate got the unpardonable idea that being musical was unmanly, and started in to harden up with the boys.

Naive perspectives were already opening outward into the world in many directions, but in one direction all the others were steadily converging: this direction encouraged in skilful ways by the mother. Her son was to be an architect. He was to get beautiful buildings built. Bridges and dams were fascinating him now. Any construction whatsoever would do to pore over. And he would make what he called 'designs'.

Both Frank and Robie had real passion for invention, and were banged, pinched, stained or marred or were 'had' somewhere by perpetual experiment going on.

A water-velocipede was started—to be called the 'Frankenrob'. Drawings made for a 'Catamaran' that cost too much to happen. The boys made a cross-gun, bows and arrows, and long bob-sled on double runners. They painted them—the joy of striping them in colours! They had them 'ironed' by the blacksmith according to design. A new style newspaper—a scroll. Another kind of ice-boat. Fantastic new kinds of kites of coloured paper. Kites with fantastic tails. A water-wheel. Who could remember how many schemes were hatched, patched up and scrapped during these winter-schooling periods of adolescence. And there was the excellent scroll-saw and the inevitable turning lathe. The boys were perpetually making designs. Drawing always. Always making drawings for fun. Especially by lamplight, evenings.

But—of the schooling itself? Not a thing he can remember!

A blank! Except colourful experiences that had nothing academic about them. Like dipping the gold braid hanging down the back of the pretty girl sitting in front, into the ink-well of his school desk and drawing with it. Getting sent home in consequence.

There was the cruel torture of speaking once a month.

The mortification of the nickname 'Shaggy' pursued him, earned by the still abundant curls that made any hat he put on his head deciduous.

Distant worship of several pretty girls. Goodie Storer, Carrie Jacobs,

Floy Stearns. And Robie at this time began to contract his secret hopeless passion for little blue-eyed Etta Doyon, next door. Golden curls and brown eyes, the boy then preferred. Ella Gernon had both to perfection!

Etta's younger brother, Charlie, more innocent of heart, if possible, than the pair, wanted to come into the printing office with them.

Mr. Doyon was rich for that town and time. Charlie was told that if his father would lend 'the firm' two hundred dollars to buy a larger Model Press and more type, they would let him in. Charlie got the money easily. And the 'papers' were offered by Mr. Doyon and signed by the boys.

Such was the origin of the firm of 'Wright, Doyon and Lamp, Publishers and Printers'. Charlie's share in the enterprise was 'capitalist'. All he had to do was to sit around and look as though he owned the whole thing, and owned the boys too, just because they owed his father money. And he would 'pie' the type when things went altogether wrong for him.

Is anything more pleasurable to the mind than unsullied paper? The studious comparisons and selection of 'stock' in textures and colours of cards and paper?

Letters are works of art, or should be.

The choice of type—a range of choice to tease the most ample taste.

The absorbing mechanics of actual press work.

What room for space invention—'composing'!

A real toy—the press—for growing boys as well as for grown-up rich men.

And what *is* the fascination to the average man or boy of seeing his name in type, even on a business or visiting card? It is phenomenal! A secret is there of intense human interest.

But the schooling! Trying to find traces of it in that growing experience ends in finding *none*. What became of it? Why did it contribute so little to this consciousness-of-existence that is 'the boy'? It seems purely negative and for that reason it may not have been positively harmful. Difficult for one to say. You can't let boys run wild while they are growing. They have to be roped and tied to something so their parents can go about their business. Why not a snubbing post or—school, then? A youth must be slowed-up, held in hand. Caged—yes—mortified too. Broken to harness as colts are broken, or there would be nothing left but to make an 'artist' of him. Send him to an Art Institute.

But certain episodes were harmful and remain so to this day. 'Speaking pieces', for instance. The accomplishments after all seem most devastating as one looks about either before or after.

At this period features in the spring and summer life at the Valley were the country cousins of the city boy—Dick, Tom, and Ed. The city boy practised on them too. They looked upon their cousin with faith and confiding interest. Fully conscious of their admiration. He beguiled them, showed off for them, used them, fooled them and loved them sincerely. But this life-of-the-imagination in him wrought havoc with them.

One time, the four all day together in the fields. The young Aladdin (that's me) suddenly got the idea of a 'party'. The party grew so real in his imagination, as he rubbed his lamp, that it became due for that very evening given by mother at grandfather's where she was then on a visit. It grew so real he began to talk about it to the boys, and as he talked about it the party grew in his imagination. As the day wore on he built it up, touched it up here and there to his satisfaction. There were to be presents for Tom, Dick, and Ed. Things he knew they longed for. There were to be goodies of all sorts. And surprises were cleverly hinted at, to work up excitement. The possibilities grew as he talked until expectations were boundless. Three mouths were watering. His own no less.

When they all turned toward home, they could hardly wait for the party to come with the evening.

Tom, Dick and Ed's parents had heard nothing of all this, but told by the boys, believed them, scrubbed them clean and dressed them up in their Sunday best. By this time the enthusiasm of invention had cooled in the hatching architect and a certain uneasiness came uppermost in him as he half-remembered what he had done. But he said nothing. The invited guests arrived early. Mother in the middle of her work received them, wondering—with 'Hello, boys! Why! Why are you so beautifully dressed? Where are you going?'

'We've come to Frank's party.'

'Party?' said his mother, and looked at her son! One look was enough. And she soon found from the guests they were expecting presents and goodies.

She rose to the occasion to her son's delight and gratitude. Perhaps he knew she would, who knows! Anyhow, she found something in the way of presents so there was only partial disappointment. She made molasses candy, gave them popcorn and ginger cookies, got father to play 'Pop Goes the Weasel' on his violin and sing for them too. And sent them home in an hour or so—her precious son's reputation saved, she hoped.

Now he was facing mother as to his idea of this party. 'Why did you want to fool your cousins, Frank?'

Indignantly, he denied wanting to *fool* them.

'Why did you promise them all those things when you knew they were not going to get them?'

'Well, why did they have to spoil it all by *believing* they were going to get them? It was fun already to think about getting them, wasn't it? Then why did they have to come to the party? Couldn't they just let it alone?'

And mother understood. Nobody else. Clearly they were not up to the game.

A MAN

Time came a year or two later when the boy drove Pont (short for Pontius) and Pilate afield alone, on his own for the first time. That was a day for him! The day before he had been only a boy on the farm. Today he was a man among men. To be a man is to do a man's work. The job in

38

hand now was driving the 'plankers' to finally smooth the harrowed fields for the marking of the rows before corn-planting. The whiffle-trees of Pont and Pilate were hitched to a clevis fastened to the planks at the middle of the side, dragging them crosswise along over the fields. You stood upright on the planks at the centre or to one side as you wanted them to drag, and drove with short hold on the lines, close up to the horses.

All went well. Home at noon as good as the best. In the afternoon, toward four o'clock, coming down the sloping field the planker caught on a rotten stump half-hidden in the ploughed ground. The jerk broke the top off the stump. The 'planker', thus suddenly released jumped forward on to the horses' heels throwing the boy on to Pont's rump. Instinctively the lad grasped the breeching of each horse with his hands as they jumped, kicked, and started to run. The clinging boy was so close to Pont he was lifted each time the horse kicked. And Pont was kicking continually as he ran. Pilate running close but, fortunately, not kicking.

If he let go his hold on Pont's breeching, or the straps broke, the plankers would go over him. To hold on and hope nothing would break was the only hope.

There were no cries, no words, as the team came tearing down the side hill, the boy rising and falling with the running kicks of the horse. Adolph Sprecher, the good-hearted hired man, at work elsewhere marking the field, saw the dangerous flight and with all his brawny might ran over the ploughed ground to head off disaster. Grabbed at the horses' heads, missed and fell. Got up and fortunately as the breeching was pulling Pont's check-rein on one side, causing him to run in a wide circle, he could cut across and he got him just in time.

The lad promoted to man's work dropped on the planks and lay there to get the breath back into the body that crazy horse had kicked the breath out of. All that Pont-horse ever needed to indulge in similar performances was a horsefly on the job in earnest. Many a tussle the amateur had under this professional protestant from first to last.

Adolph Sprecher, for some time, could not believe the boy was not seriously hurt. Begged not to tell Uncle James, he agreed, but broke his promise. The fact was—the boy stuck for another hour's work, went home and did his chores. Next morning, his body was so stiff and black and blue and sore that he simply could not make it go. Then the story came out.

His Uncle James had sent him with hired man number two, with confidence in Adolph. And for some time after this he was sent out in company. But he always liked best to be sent off alone—to be treated like a man. He was soon trusted and sent alone.

That summer he 'bound' his station after the reaper.

In those days the reaper, pride of the farm, was a 'rake-off McCormick'.

A bright-red affair with a varnished wood grain-platform on to which bright-blue, green, yellow and red reels knocked the yellow grain as it was cut by the busy to and fro of the gleaming sickle. This machine, gaily painted, like a toy, no doubt for the same reason, would leave the bundles raked off neatly on the stubble behind, to be bound by four or five men spaced around the field as the crop of grain was light or heavy, and the bundles would be tossed aside out of the way of the horses as they made the next round.

Taking a wisp of the grain-straw in the left hand for a band, dividing it in two parts, deftly twisting it together at the head and in the right hand—stopping and reaching under the bundle with the hand—lifting the bundle in the arms, bringing the ends of the band together over it, dropping it to the ground under the knee as the band would be pulling the band up sharply—then twisting and tucking the ends of the 'band' tight under with a thrust of the fingers, tossing the bundle away—bound!

The young harvester's fingernails would be worn to the quick and bleeding before the last band on the bundles of the season's grain was 'tucked in'.

There was the hauling of the grain in the ample grain racks that also served for hay racks. The pitching of the bundles with a long-handled three-tined fork. And the stacking. The stacking was expert, entrusted to few. The whole thing might come down. Sometimes it did 'slide'. There had already been hauling of the hay and the pitching of hay to the stack.

Aching muscles in the morning always had to be limbered up again by the first few hours of the next day's work.

Soon he learned to endure the routine of continuous labour by finding in it a sort of sing-song. 'Hum-drum'—but for one's imagination.

He would actually sing to the ever-recurring monotonies of rhythm. Hum variations or whistle them when he was at it or in it or of it. Here was the secret of endurance for the imaginative.

Any monotonous task involving repetition of movement has its rhythm. If you can find it the task can soon be made interesting in that sense. The 'job' may be syncopated by changing the accent or making an accent. Binding grain and shocking it, or pitching bundles to the wagon and racks. Pitching hay, hoeing, dropping corn with a 'checker'. Cultivating corn as the green hills passed regularly four feet apart between the shovels— planted four feet apart each way.

All machinery makes some recurrent noise, some clack or beat above the hum that can be made into the rhythm of song-movement—a rhythm that is the obvious poetry in the mathematics of this universe. Maybe.

The body in performing heavy labours for hour after hour can get into a swinging rhythm with music to accompany it, rhythm to be whistled or sung aloud or kept in the mind.

Folk dances originate in this way, no doubt. Sacred dances no less.

Walking there after the plough, bare feet in furrow, was ideal opportunity to indulge this inner rhythm and adjust it to outward movement.

This sense of rhythm, entering into monotonous repetition, naturally led to arrangement of sound to go with it—sometimes a song with words.

The idea—no, it could have been no idea. It was instinct, or whatever it was, for him to suit this naive release of the within to inspirit the work in hand. Work would be better done. Without fatigue.

Milking was the perfect opportunity to turn monotony into music. The sound of the streams at first, soon to be modified by the foaming of the milk in the pail—a kind of music! And usually, the boy sang to this rhythm while he milked. Gottlieb—his red face turned down and sideways, yellow hair against the cow's flank—would sometimes sing with him. You see here, *within himself*, he had found release. He had found a way to beat 'tired to tired'. And Uncle James would not have to call, 'Come back, Frank! Come back!' For he would be satisfactorily active while he dreamed.

More significant than all else at this time was this sense-of-rhythm in him.

Life impelling itself to live?

Notwithstanding this release coming up in him, and out from him continuously, he was doing a man's work on the farm and at the age of fourteen (Uncle James was generous) getting a man's pay—nineteen dollars a month and his board and clothes.

Yes, Uncle James was doing pretty well by him—because . . .

THE HORSE

Now the amateur 'hired man' had come by experience to intimate knowledge of The Horse: to the ways of bits and bridling . . . saddling, haltering, harnessing. Eternal buckling and unbuckling. He knew whiffle-trees, neck-yokes and whips; tugs, breechings, and collars; straps, hooks, bits; hoofs and fetlocks; withers and hocks . . . all man's part in the horse! He saw—procreation. The rearing gorgeous pride of the Clydesdale stallion with his noble head and quivering nostrils. Sleek, meek mares. Young colts, if unluckily male, forthwith sex-degraded to geldings struggling against the inevitable with no sound.

The work horses: he was forever getting them up. Currying them. Brushing them. Getting them over while getting the stables clean under them and behind them. Always this cleaning up to do, behind them. Braiding their tails. Hitching them. Unhitching them. Sometimes ditching them. Switching them. Feeding them. Leading and coaxing. Driving them. Riding them bareback or saddled before and after they were broken. Seeing Uncle James break them, sometimes himself all but broken by them. Getting thrown off them. Getting run-away-with by them. Getting run over, kicked or stepped on. Angry and jerking a horse shamefully, feeling ashamed. Getting the horses shod. Putting the horses with alternate patience and exasperation to the plough, to harrows, seeders, markers, plankers, cultivators and lumber-wagons—sulkies, buggies and logging-trucks—milk-wagons, reapers, and turntables. To threshing-machines. Saws. Hayracks. Hayrakes. And there he would work the horses, and take them away to again feed, water, curry them and bed them.

And these gaily-painted accessories to the horse had to be greased, to get them to go. Getting the life-sized man-toys to stop was sometimes desperation.

41

Learning to swear in the style proper to the hired man and the horse's taste. So, this amateur young master of the HORSE.

Noble excitement comes to a growing boy in this fellowship with the horse. Most respectable of all man's animal associates it is, romantic, too. . . . But, there was . . .

THE SOW

Daily fodder to haul and the boiling pumpkins or something or other—for the hogs. This grunting boar with foaming mouth and ugly tusks, heavy brood sows, bellies almost dragging the ground, always grunting. The clean, pink little pigs. Ringing all snouts at four months so they could never root and spoil the sod. Catching and holding unlucky young boars—screaming infernos of despair as they were degraded into 'barrows'. Loading all—eventually—into the hogracks and hauling them to market.

Perpetually someone was running to get the pigs out of the corn. Get them out of the garden. Get them out of the neighbour's fields. Getting them—well, always 'getting' them out or 'getting' them into—something, himself breathless and perspiring and oftentimes despairing. And then, this business of getting the heavy sows off their own little pigs. He knew they were lying on them by the infernal heart-rending squeals. Sometimes they would eat their newly born. The call of 'P-o-o-i-g! P-o-o-i-g! P-o-o-i-g'. The tenor of that call would do credit to Grand Opera.

Sickened at butchering by seeing the knife stuck deep in the fat throat, hot blood gushing and streaming from the pig marked for family 'pork'. Smell of their yard—devastating! Utter degradation in smells. Procreation, too, of the pig. This unreconciled assistant to the hog now knew these devastations full well. Fortunately less of it went into his experience than . . .

THE COW

His first farm familiars.

He was always afraid of the heavy-necked, bellowing Holstein Bull. Sex slave with ring in his nose but pride and terror of every farm just the same. First farm familiars—the Cows. Calling them—'So Boss! So-o Boss! So-o-o Boss!' A baritone call. For years and years—and years—would they never end?—getting the cows in from early pasture. Getting the cows into their proper places in the barn. Feeding them. Milking them early in the morning. Milking them later in the evening, eaten up by flies. Cruelly twisting their tails to make them stamp their hind legs and stand over to be milked. Getting the vile manure off their bags before milking them, to keep the milk clean. Getting the lazy creatures up. Milking them week days. Milking them just the same on Sundays. Milking them—always milking them. Getting bare feet soiled—'cut' the farm-boys used to say—in the warm, fresh cow-flops, in the stable or in the lane. Always cleaning away at the stables. Always cleaning up to be done—never quite done till next time and next time was always soon. Getting the slow-moving bovines out to pasture again. Adventuresome ones to get out of the corn. The whole tribe would get into the grain. Hooked. Beating a cantankerous old cow goring a young sister, the gored one bellowing agony, head stretched out, big eyes bulging in terror rolled back until the whites were all you could see. Fixing a wooden poke on the neck of the 'leader'—the one first to jump the fence and lead the others to glory while it lasted. He would see the torture of the poor adventurer punished for her innocent initiative as that adventurer in all skins is always punished in some form . . . secretly he would take the cruel 'poke' off without permission. Getting reprimanded when next the cows were in the corn, but taking the cruel poke off again—just the same.

Feeding the calves. '*Sukem* suke suke-suke, *suke*-suke-suke-suke.' Tenor again. Soprano preferred. Catching and tying the luckless bull calves while, bawling in fear, they were degraded into steers—or hauled to market for veal after six weeks of here-on-earth. Seeing a fine steer knocked in the head with a maul—dropped with a thud like lead, throat cut in a flash. Helping to strip off the heavy skin for leather and dress the steaming carcass for beef. Getting the cows in, getting them out, day in and day out—summer after summer. Occasionally helping Uncle James to haul one out, when she got stuck in the mud of the creek. Haul the cow out with a team of horses hitched to a rope tied around her neck. No harm to her whatever.

Always procreation—in season. And always in season, some.

Chased by the bull but never tossed, this go-getter of the Cow knew cow-business now, habitually, as the cattle chewed their cud. Meantime, scattered about in all this was

THE HEN

O Cock, with the scarlet comb! Squire of the Hens. Hundreds were all over the place. Crowing. Scratching. Clucking. Cheeping. Squawking. He would have to get up at night to look into the hen-house when a terrific squawking commotion indicated some prowling enemy in their midst. It was given to him sometimes to catch and strike off the heads of superfluous young roosters when their turn came to be eaten. It invariably came. Throwing the flapping convulsive fowl aside in headless tumble over wood-pile and door-yard in frantic letting go of life. Eggs. Always hunting eggs. Setting eggs. Sucking eggs as taught by Gottlieb. Chucking or ducking cross old hens who should have known better, into the water-trough to cool maternal ardour. Dropping them into the bottom of a barrel with water in it to let them 'set' on that. Getting pecked by the lousy things. Getting actually covered with lice. This young fowler, admiring the cock and his brood but never liking them and detesting their procreation—perpetual. But he did like guinea fowl with the raucous cry and speckled gray plumage, formed like a quail.—The peacock fascinated him—a spiritual element in all this because peacocks seemed introduced for love of beauty—ornament? That element hovers over everything . . . this

43

sentiment for beauty. Man cannot drive it entirely away! No—even when he domesticates the animals it will linger there and it will cling even to . . .

THE HOE

Whosoever would sow must hoe.

And if he who hoes would reap—he must weed.

The Garden! A comparatively peaceful place that Garden—when not raided by unnatural domesticated enemies from over the none-too-good-fence—chickens, little pigs, and some few non-conformist sows. To say nothing of natural enemies underground—grubs, worms and the marching armies of insects. Insects! Will they eventually win the battle and exterminate man?

Weeding is an art, though the back breaks. The boy learned to twist his fingers around the weed-stems close to the ground and with a sidewise twist—thumb as a lever—bringing the narrow side of the hand to the ground—prying, while pulling, he would get them out with roots unbroken while the skin on his fingers lasted.

Thus the process would go on for hours a day, all the days the garden was young, until back and arms were stiff and fingers sore in the continued effort to clean the weeds out from between the plants known to be useful as the garden grew older.

And this amateur hired-man hoed. Hoed lettuce. Hoed radishes, beets, carrots, parsnips and turnips. Cabbages. Tomato plants. Onions. Always he seemed to be hoeing in the season of early summer. Hoeing and weeding, weeding and hoeing until the palms of his hands were thick and hard —as shiny as the hoe handle—both like glass. And finally they would have to come and cut down the triumphant weeds with a sickle or scythe and burn them up!

The wielder of the hoe would wonder why weeds couldn't be studied, possibilities found and then maybe cultivated. The 'crop' eliminated. Perhaps the 'crop' was weeds once upon a time just because the farmer didn't know what they were for. Tobacco was a weed once. And corn? Seems there never was wild corn. And potatoes. And tomatoes were once thought by Europeans to be poison. Love apples they called them. Cancerous? Nearly everything was a weed once upon a time. Maybe, sometime, there would be no 'weeds' and then? But meanwhile weeds seemed fittest to survive in this unequal strife—in this contending, never-ending competition between Good and Evil or whatever the competition should be named.

What vitality these 'weeds' had! Pusley, for instance. Chess (velvet weed). Pigweed. Dock and Ragweed. Quack grass—king of all. Canada thistle—queen! Would the weeds become feeble, if they were cultivated, and 'crops' become as vigorous as 'weeds' if left alone to flourish on their own?

What of such science and art? Ask the professors?

And yet, afield in June, he saw as reward of toil, forethought and some art and science, the sweeping acres of clover-bloom floating in perfume, heard the hum of busy bees as the tall, round spires of the timothy stood above, slender spires bending to the sweeping of the breeze. Soon there would be the large round cones of the yellow grain-stacks standing in the transparent stubble-fields in August, gathered together from the orderly ranks of yellow grain-shocks dotting the tawny stubble—in the midst of July green. The silvering rows on rows of haycocks in June to end in purple haystacks tomorrow. In September would come the wigwam rows of Indian corn-shocks; solid-gold pumpkins lying thick in the reddening sun over the fields between the 'wigwams'.

And at the red barns there he would be—handling the dangerous hay-fork, choking in the dust of the great hot haymows, 'tailing' on the straw-stacks, struggling to keep from being choked and buried alive in the chaff that fell from the end of the straw-carrier of the threshing machine, his features obliterated by grime, sweat and dust. And later, body dripping with sweat, in the silos he would be putting away the alcoholic silage. Turning tedious grindstones under sickles, scythes and axes. Turning the crank of the fanning-mill to the limit of endurance. Working the wood handle of the old green pump, until his arms were numb.

Did wet weather bring a rest from all these labours? Except for digging post-holes and fencing—yes.

Someone should do the barbed-wire fence in song and story. It would be the story of the march of our later civilization. Together with the tin can, has it made man's conquest too easy? Enough.

On the farm there was always the glib Axe. The honest Bucksaw. And the persuasive Hammer. The pliers! The vice! No farm could have a farmer without these. And, yes, almost forgotten, the tragic Monkey wrench! Whose song is that? What disorganization could be wrought with a monkey wrench? and what about the precious Jack Knife? Has anyone sung the song of the Jack Knife?

MAIN STRENGTH AND AWKWARDNESS

So it is that farm-boy life is continually at the mercy of hoofs, horns and blades. Gleaming plowshares, flashing scythes, poisonous stings and bites and briars. Boy-life there is one continuous round of fatal ups and downs and disastrous ins and outs. Too dry! Too high! Too low! Too wet! Too hot! Too cold! Too soon! Too late! Drought and Frost—major enemies, the farmer must learn to defeat or he will go down like his crops with his animals.

Warfare? Comparatively fancy business. The farmer must make constant demands upon refractory or dull tools. His world is a desperate merry-go-round of ill or happy contrivances painted bright-red, poison green or red, white, blue and gilt, fascinating to him as toys are fascinating to children. Contrivances that will or will not work; main-strength and awkwardness the never-failing final resource in every end.

And—continually there is this perpetual restless movement of perverse or willing perspiring, labouring animal-bodies strapped tied to, and

45

straining at those machines. Machines that would kill them if not managed. Machines that ploughed and dug, cut, piled and tore, ground and bound if you mastered them—or killed you if you didn't—but gaily painted just the same. Machines all in some way dangerous, all rusting in vital spots and, oil and oiling notwithstanding, at some time or other all—damned! Scrap!

Such is the amazing, endless category of parts, every one necessary to the stupendous complex whole into which a boy on the farm is thrown—to survive if he can.

Thus the encounter with the Cow, the Sow, the HEN! served by the humbled HORSE—and himself. Meantime, yes already all imposed upon by fascinating machines. The matter helped by them—perhaps. Who really knows? But the time is coming when man must know or perish.

PEACE! BEAUTY! SATISFACTION! REST!

The divine discontent of the Creative Spirit made havoc with all that, then and there—as things were. And as they are now. Anyone might have seen this and have avoided it if he could. But the boy didn't know. No one warned him.

He was unsuspecting.

So fearlessly did this human item live the life of the imagination in all he did.

Sometimes when the day had been too hard, too tired to sleep he would get out of bed, sweaty jeans pulled on, rolled above his knees, and barefoot and bareheaded slowly climb the path up the hill behind the house. Climb to the long, quiet ridge that ran to the north high in the moonlight, ornamented here and there with scattered hazel-brush and trees. Climbing to wander and look forward and imagine, enjoy waking dreams in a high place.

Going over that ridge later in life, many times, he would wonder how a barefoot boy could safely take that stony way in daylight not to speak of moonlight.

On either side of the ridge lay fertile valleys luminously bathed and gentled by the moon. The different trees all made their special kinds of pattern when the moon shone on them and their favourite deep-dark silhouettes when it shone against them. The flowers had no colour, but their cups and corollas glistening with dew were like pallid gems. The barefoot's feet and legs were wet with the cool freshness of the dews fallen in the long grasses. Broad, shallow mists, distilled from the heavy dews, floating in cool, broad sheets below were lying free over the tree-tops in long, thin, flat ribands. All would be quiet except for the drowsy singing undertone of summer insects. The ancient element of moisture seemed to prevail there as a kind of light flooding all. The deep shadows held mysteries alluring and friendly.

There was no haste now.

He could listen to music religiously as though it were the last strain he might ever hear, and make more in the heart of his mind. Or he would hear the strains of Beethoven that had come to him from his father's playing as, early in life, in his bed he lay listening. Entranced, he would now be uplifted.

The intimate fairy princess drew near, she who was growing up somewhere preparing herself and looking forward, as dreamily, to him. Listening too. Sometimes fair and sometimes dark she was always beautiful as only adolescent boys can picture girlish beauty. Great deeds would rise in him then. Unquenchable triumphs until the evanescent scene faded into many-coloured achievements and boy-sized glory. There was no feeling that the dreams could ever be desecrated by failure. Out of the character they arose into the mind as waking dreams, in magical, mystic, pale-amber and amethyst nights, and settled quietly on the spirit to refresh a mortal weariness as the dew came upon the flowers that stood beside his naked legs.

Looking back now, the dreams seem not great. But then how he thrilled with them and walked in the tall dew-laden grass among moon-struck flowers as on air. Feeling no stones beneath his naked feet. Half-consciously he would wander back, come down and climb into bed again to sleep—deep sleep with no dreams at all.

After one thousand two hundred and sixty todays and tomorrows like those yesterdays the boy was coming sixteen. Farm-days for him were over. He was about to enter the University of Wisconsin.

These farm-days had left their mark on him in a self-confidence in his own strength called courage. Muscles hard. Step—springing. Sure-footed, and fingers quick as thought and quick *with* thought. Mind buoyant with optimism. Optimism that came through seeing sunshine follow clouds and rain—working out success succeeding failure. It had come to him self-consciously, out of his daily endeavours, as an underlying sense of the essential balance of forces in nature. Something in the nature of an inner experience had come to him that was to make a sense of this supremacy of interior order like a religion to him. He was to take refuge in it and grow in it. Besides, coming sixteen, for several years the youth had been doing a man's work. He had learned how to do much and do much well, do most of it happily, feeling himself master where he would. That gave him a whip-hand.

He was afraid only of people. The fearful unknown to him—people. Not to mention girls. The sight of a girl would send him like a scared young stag, scampering back into his wood.

THE FATHER

By now, family life was not so well at the small town house by the blue lake. There was no longer much agreement between father and mother.

The father on this eve of the entrance of his son into the university was himself deep in learning to write Sanskrit. Mother for some years had been ailing. Poverty pinched.

47

The youth would see her self-denial at table. See her eating only what the others did not want. Drinking her tea without sugar and not because she preferred it so: when, rarely, a chicken from the small coop in the back yard would be killed and come to the table—pretending to prefer the neck of the roast chicken so well you almost believed she did.

Provisions often arrived from the farm—potatoes, vegetables, barrels of apples. The father's earnings were small and shrinking. Music wasn't much of a livelihood in Madison. Irregular preaching there and in surrounding towns less so. And the father grew irascible over this and crosscurrents of family feeling. The Joneses didn't much approve of Anna's privations. And he, being a proud man, resented their provisions. His helplessness irritated him.

The lad was his mother's adoration. She lived much in him. Probably that didn't help either.

For some disobedience about this time, the father undertook to thrash the young man. It had happened in the stable and the young rebel got his father down on the floor, held him there until his father promised to let him alone. He had grown too big for that sort of thing. 'Father ought to realize it,' said the boy, as he went into the home, white, shamed, and shaken to tell his mother.

The youth hardly had known himself as his father's son. All had gone well enough on the surface that was now broken. The son had sympathy for his talented father as well as admiration. Something of that vain struggle of superior talents with untoward circumstance that was his father's got to him, and he was touched by it—never knowing how to show father. Something—you see—had never been established that was needed to make them father and son. Perhaps the father never loved the son at any time. Memories would haunt the youth as they haunt the man. . . .

His father's son listening at the closed study door, hearing father walking—walking to and fro studying; reciting as he walked: practising for readings he sometimes gave at churches. Experimenting with changes of intonation and accent, evidently reading the poem, book in hand and occasionally trying over certain passages again and again. This time listening to 'The Raven'. Measured footsteps, father's voice reciting . . .

> . . . *As of someone gently rapping—*
> *Rapping at my chamber door.*
> *"Tis some visitor,' I muttered,*
> *'Tapping at my chamber door;*
> *Only this and nothing more.'*

Interval:

Slowly walking *And the silken, sad, uncertain*
> *Rustling of each purple curtain*
> *Thrilled me—filled me with fantastic*
> *Terrors never felt before . . .*

Silence . . .

48

Now	*Darkness there and nothing more. . . .*
	Darkness there and nothing more. . . .
	Merely this, and nothing more.
Pause . . .	
Footsteps,	*Let me see, then what thereat is,*
measured	*and this mystery explore. . . .*
as before	*and this mystery explore;*
	'Tis the wind, and nothing more. . . .
	'Tis the wind, and nothing more.
Silence.	
Walking	*'Prophet still, if bird or devil! . . .*
faster . . .	*Prophet still, if bird or devil! . . .*
All quiet for a	*'Is there—is there balm in Gilead?*
time and . . .	*Tell me, tell me, I implore.*
	Quoth the Raven, "Nevermore!" . . .
	Quoth the Raven, "Nevermore!" '

the youth would tiptoe away to hear no more.

Sometimes, after all had gone to bed he would hear that nocturnal rehearsal and the walking—was it evermore?—would fill a tender boyish heart with sadness until a head would bury itself in the pillow to shut it out.

One day when difficulties between father and mother had grown unbearable the mother, having borne all she could—probably the father had borne all he could bear too—said quietly, 'Well, Mr. Wright'—always she spoke of him and to him so—'leave us. I will manage with the children. Go your way. We will never ask you for anything except this home. The savings of my earnings as a teacher have gone into this, and I have put into it so many years of my life.

'No—we will never ask you for help.

'If ever you can send us anything, send it. If you cannot we will do the best we can.'

Who can know what, in the eighteen years preceding, gradually and inevitably led to the heartbreak under simple words—spoken so quietly?

Like some traveller taking the long road to some point where another road branches to the left or to the right, the turn is taken with nothing to mark it as an event, yet direction, destination, perhaps all of life—are changed. Destruction too may wait on that turn. All real crises in Life, are they not finally so simple? And who may judge the silent changes gradually taking place in the human heart like organic changes taking place in trees or plants, and like them, when manifest as complete, to be accepted?

What presumptuous folly to rise against them with a 'No!' Senseless hazard to encourage them! What mischief to advise; idiocy to 'judge'!

The father disappeared and never was seen again by his wife or his children. Judge Carpenter quietly dissolved the marriage contract.

The mother's people deeply grieved, shamed because of her 'disgrace'.

She herself bowed down in grief. Although believing in the rightness of separation for her children's sake, she had not believed in her heart—it seems—their father would take advantage of her offer to release him.

And, until he died fifteen years later, she never ceased to believe he would come back. There was never a thought of another man in her life, nor thought of another woman in his. Perhaps it was that their life together had worn its soul away in the strife of failure after failure added to failure: the inveterate and desperate withdrawal on his part into the arid life of his studies, his books and his music, where he was oblivious to all else.

So the boy himself, supersensitive, soon became aware of 'disgrace'. His mother was a 'divorced woman'. His faith in her goodness and rightness did not waver. Therefore there was injustice to her. Did this injustice to her serve some social purpose?

The wondering resentment grew in him. It became a subconscious sense of false judgment entered against himself, his sisters, Jennie and Maginel, innocent of all wrong-doing. His mother's unhappiness—was it a social crime? Why must she, as well as they, be punished? Just what had they all done?

He never got the heavy thing straight, and just accepted it as one more handicap—grew more sensitive and shy than ever. And he began to be distrustful—of what he could not have told you then.

The mother was alone with her son and his two sisters. She found a place for the budding architect with blue-eyed Allen D. Conover, Dean of Engineering at the University of Wisconsin, himself a competent civil engineer. He had an office of his own and a private practice in Madison and probably really needed some boy to work for him. How can one be sure? Professor Conover was a cultivated and kindly man. He allowed the youth to work for him afternoons so that he might have the mornings for classes. He gave him thirty-five dollars a month. This arrangement left the freshman free to study evenings. Architecture, at first his mother's inspiration, then naturally enough his own desire, was the study he wanted. But there was no money to go away to an architectural school. There were classes in engineering at the home university. That was the nearest to architecture within his reach.

So the youth was enrolled at the University of Wisconsin as a prospective civil engineer.

Fortunately, too, by the limitation, he was spared the curse of the 'architectural' education of that day as sentimentalized in the United States with its false direction in culture and wrong emphasis on sentiment.

Every morning he walked to the University—a couple of miles away. After recitations there he walked back down to the Conover office at noon to eat the lunch he carried. And, an afternoon's work done at the drawing-board, he walked home again to eat his supper and to study. Robie Lamp and he were still 'chums' though other associations now drew the youth away from Robie, for Robert Lamp had not entered the university! It made such a difference in those days!

The retrospect of university years is mostly dull pain. Thought of poverty and struggle, pathos of a broken home, unsatisfied longings, humiliations —frustration. Mathematics excepted, there seemed little meaning in the studies. At least mathematics 'worked'. But mathematics was taught by Professor Van Velzer, an academic little man with side-whiskers who had no feeling for romance in his subject. A subject when rightly apprehended most romantic. Music itself but sublimated mathematics.

Consequently the punctilio of the conscientious little professor opened for his pupil the stupendous fact that two plus two equal four. Is it unreasonable to suppose that a professor of mathematics should be a poet? Or a civil engineer be a creative composer of symphonies?

French? Miss Lucy Gay, a charming honest person whom everyone loved and respected, taught him that. He read the 'Romance of the Poor Young Man,' 'Le Cid,' etc.

English Composition was taught him by Professor Freeman. A handsome gentleman, deeply afflicted, so it seemed, by a too strong expression of professional dignity.

The youth yearned to read and write his own language—yearned to speak it—supremely well. He had no chance, under the pompous professor. His compositions were all marked 'good', 'thought excellent', when he already knew both to be dishwater. And barring the correction of gross grammatical errors, which he seldom made anyway, what did he get from that 'marking' business? Merely nothing with less subtracted for pleasure or good-measure. English to this day remains more or less a mystery. He was never taught just why English is English—just what it is that makes it English as distinguished from all other languages and what its peculiar and individual resources are. What its limitations are, and how they may be turned to advantages. He was left to find out for himself if he could, and without material.

The hungry student read at this time, at home, Carlyle's *Sartor Resartus, Heroes and Hero Worship, Past and Present*, the father's calf-bound copy of Plutarch's *Lives*, Ruskin's *Fors Clavigera, Modern Painters, Stones of Venice* (gift of Aunt Nell and Jane), Morris's *Sigurd the Volsung*, and Shelley, Goethe's *Wilhelm Meister*, a little of William Blake, *Les Misérables*, Viollet-le-Duc's *Raisonné de l'architecture*. But he doesn't know in the least what he read in the school course.

Professors Conover and Storm Bull were the engineers to whom he reported; they looked over his work in Stereotomy, Graphic Statics, Analytical and Descriptive Geometry. All as painfully spread by him upon his drawing-board in the drafting room in the old dormitory on the hillside campus. But it was with Professor Conover, in that practice of his, that the youth really learned most.

51

THE FRESHMAN PARTY

Charlie Ware saw May White, his cousin, explained the matter, diffidences, etc., made the engagement after the formality of a call with the fool who was about to go fearfully in where the angels happily tread.

The morning of the party, a beautiful day, the freshman, chesty as a young cockerel, went for a walk. He ran into Charlie.

'Say, Charlie, I ought to know what I do at this party anyhow, and how do I, or ought I, to do it.'

Said Charles, 'Nothing much to know, man. Get May. Take her in. Dance a few dances with her. Keep off her toes. Then get some of the fellows to dance with her. There you are! Dance with some of the other girls yourself. After the last dance—and you dance that with May—mind you—take May back to "Ladies' Hall".'

But the freshman, somehow, thought it good form to kiss the girl when you left her at the door after the party. It was more of this he had been thinking than anything else. Charlie laughed. 'Oh', he said, 'that's optional.' And left the freshman still up in the air.

The class-party was to occur in Assembly Hall, next door to Ladies' Hall. But a carriage was 'good form', so carriage it was.

Dressed. White tie. Black suit. Patent-leather pumps. White gloves in hand. Bouquet for lady. Boutonnière for black coat. So far so good—far too good. He had an uneasy feeling himself that it was too good.

Got to Ladies' Hall, found May ready. May found her escort too embarrassed to say anything at all. But May had been informed. She got him safely back to the carriage. No sooner started, May White and Frank Wright sitting a respectful distance apart, than the carriage stopped at the Hall. Nothing whatever said. The young couple got out and the amateur led the way to the entrance.

They got in only to find a crowd of the 'fellows' chaffing each other. No ladies in sight.

Blushing painfully, he realized he had brought May to the men's entrance. Helplessly he looked around. Where was the women's dressing room, anyway? May evidently didn't know either.

He went sick with shame.

Charlie Ware, from the other side of the room, took in the situation at a glance and rushed over, 'Come with me, May!'

She straightway left the freshman stranded; standing out from the crowd, he felt, like the bull's-eye of a big target. Some boy took pity on him and showed him where to stow his coat and hat. Then he went back to look for his unfortunate lady. He couldn't find her.

Came the promenade. No lady!

Came the first waltz! No lady!

The waltz nearly over and he about to cut it all, when May's voice: 'Why here you are! I waited a long time at the dressing-room door. Then I thought you didn't recognize me. You see, you don't know me very well so I came to find you'

He felt he should indignantly deny not knowing her among a thousand like her. But could only murmur—neither ever knew what!

They danced together. Charlie came when the dance was over and got May's programme filled. Got May's partner himself a dance or two for good measure—Charlie was what 'Charlies' usually are. All of which went off without resistance or remarks from the green partner. Now he hung around and waited for that last dance with May, wondering if it was going to be expected of him to kiss her when he said 'Good night'.

He couldn't picture it. But although an amateur, he wanted not to be a duffer and disgrace Charlie. So he made up his mind he would go through with it.

He felt he ought to tell May her dress was pretty and that she danced well. He really admired her dress and white shoes and the way she wore her hair. All he could say was 'We're having a good time, aren't we?'

'Are we?' said May—a bit miffed by now.

The pair got into the carriage after anxious moments when the escort would have given his college education to be well out of the affair forever.

But no more absurdities until—'We had a good time, didn't we?'

'Did we?'

That kiss seemed far away from me! Standing on the steps, time to say good-bye. . . . 'Well,' he stammered—he felt miserably foolish—he felt . . . 'Thank you,' said he, and ran to the waiting carriage leaving his lady to open the door for herself. He had faith that she got in. But he didn't know.

When home, he lit his lamp, took off the infernal togs he had so miserably betrayed. Threw them aside. Took *Sartor Resartus* to bed for consolation; but was inconsolable. He went over the whole affair and made himself brilliant—irresistible. He staged himself and played the part to perfection—too late! It was next term before he had courage to try again. A nice town girl named Blanche Ryder took pity on him and asked him herself. Tactfully she saw him through.

TRAGEDY

About this time a vivid tragedy had its life-long effect upon the incipient architect. Passing by the new north-wing of the old State Capitol, he was just in time to hear the indescribable roar of building collapse and see the cloud of white lime dust blown from the windows of the outside walls, the dust cloud rising high into the summer air carrying agonized human-cries with it. The white dust cloud came down to settle white over the trees and grass of the park. Whitened by lime dust as sculpture is white, men with bloody faces came plunging wildly out of the basement entrance blindly striking out about their heads with their arms, still fighting off masonry and falling beams. Some fell dead on the grass under the clear sky. Others fell insensible. One workman, lime-whitened, too, hung head-downward from a fifth-story window, pinned to the sill by an iron-beam on a crushed foot, moaning the whole time.

A ghastly red stream ran from him down the stone wall.

53

Firemen soon came. Crowds appeared as though out of the ground and men frantically tugged and pulled away at the senseless mass of brick and beams to reach the moans for help of the workmen dying beneath them. Soon white-faced women, silently crying, went about looking for husbands, brothers or sons.

A sudden movement of alarm and scattering of the crowd startled him, as someone pointed to a hand sticking out between chunks of brick-work on which the crowd itself was standing. After pulling away bricks, finally scarlet plaster, a mangled human being was drawn out—too late. One of the sobbing women knelt over it on the grass. And so it went all day long and far into the night.

The youth stayed for hours clinging to the iron fence that surrounded the park, too heartsick to go away. Then he went home—ill. Dreamed of it all that night and the next and the next. The horror of the scene has never entirely left his consciousness and remains to prompt him to this day.

Only outside walls were left standing. The interior columns had fallen and the whole interior construction was a gigantic rubbish heap in the basement.

The huge concrete piers in that basement, on which rested the interior cast-iron columns supporting the floors and roof, had collapsed and let the columns down. Of course that meant all the floors and interior walls as well.

Architect Jones, good and conscientious architect, had made those piers so excessively large that the contractor thought it no sin to wheel barrows full of broken brick and stone into the hearts of them. They were found rotten at the core where the columns stood. Poor Architect Jones! He was now guilty of manslaughter—tried by a jury of his peers and condemned. He never built another building. He was no kinsman, fortunately.

The University of Wisconsin had its beautiful situation on the hill by Lake Mendota, but the life of the University then was not as it is now. The herd of hungry students less by many thousands and more hungry. The buildings were few and badly furnished. Nor were the professors particularly able or distinguished. It was more like a high school to-day, only less sophisticated than the modern high school. It had the airs, dignitaries and dignities assumed by a university. But all values being relative, it served then as it serves now.

In love with the grand gesture and in common with the others—he got himself a black mortar-board with a beautiful red-silk tassel hanging overboard: a pair of light-grey, skin-tight pants—in vogue then: toothpick shoes. And he dressed and acted the part with his hair still rather too long for it all. An incorrigible sentimentalist.

But his heart was never in this education. It never seemed to be for him. Where was architecture in all this?

This 'education' meant nothing so much to him as a vague sort of emotional distress, a sickening sense of fear—of what he could not say.

54

The inner meaning of nothing came clear. Besides there was something embarrassing in the competitive atmosphere. Something oppressive and threatening in the life of rules and regulations. Both hampered him.

So the university training of one Frank Lloyd Wright, Freshman, Sophomore, Junior, and part-time Senior was lost like some race run under a severe handicap, a race which you know in your heart you are foredoomed to lose: a kind of competition in which you can see nobody winning anywhere. Nor quite knowing why anyone should want to win. Just for the degree? Emulation? Just to be one of the countless many who had that certificate?

Things would start but nothing would seem to happen.

It wasn't like the farm. Doctrine, it was. Perfunctory opinion administered the doctrine. He was being doctored in a big crowd and the doses never seemed to produce any visible effect at any vital spot whatever; and anyway, he didn't feel sick. Science Hall was in course of construction. So was the machine shop and chemical laboratory. He didn't get into those new buildings.

His course didn't lead him into any shop at all, although he did get a beautiful red and white field rod and a fine transit into his hands and went surveying with his classmates. And there was the testing of materials. But finally he did get to work on the buildings themselves by the way of his generous employer, Professor Conover.

At the time Science Hall was being built by a Milwaukee architect out of Professor Conover's office, the professor being superintendent of buildings for the University. So the young sophomore got a little actual contact with this construction. He was entrusted with the working out of some steel clips to join the apex of the trusses of the main tower roof. . . . They wouldn't go together and the workmen, disgusted, left them hanging up there against the sky by the few bolts that would go in.

It was dead of winter—only the iron beams of the floors were in place in the floor levels below. All was slippery with ice, but he went up there, climbing the lattice on the chords of the trusses to the very top, with nothing between him and the ground but that forest of open steel beams. Got the clips loose. Dropped them down.

That was educational?

And the office work with Professor Conover was a great good for him. As he realized then and since. That work was truly educational. But in the university, notwithstanding certain appearances, he was and remained outsider, yearning all the while for the active contact with the soil or for the tests of a free life of action—waiting for something to happen that never happened. Now he realizes that it never could have happened, for 'they' were all there to see that it did not and should not happen.

Reading Goethe only made matters worse, for action, again action and more action was his urge.

The boy already wondered why 'Culture'—that was what the University stood for wasn't it?—shouldn't consist in getting rid of the inappropriate in everything. Whereas 'Education' as he encountered it was as

55

inappropriate as the rubbish wheeled by the contractor into the foundation piers of the Capitol. This he couldn't have told you then, but he felt it somehow—as resentment.

But his 'Classical' course whenever he compared it with the life on the farm seemed to him to be the very *practice* of the inappropriate; so any human edifice reared up on it was likely to fall down like the Capitol.

Gestures were here, fine enough, but—how about *work*? Reality?

The feeling about this best period of youth, lasting three and one-half years, is not so much that it was wasted.

How foolish to say anything is wasted in the living of any life!

Were one thing different, all were different.

So what weakness to regret any incident or turning.

'Might-have-beens' are for the 'Never-weres'. Uncle James said that.

Nature is organic in Man's character-making as in other forms. His instinct was not to criticize her work unless he could know her method and discern her ends: thanks, for this, to the farm.

But Man's puny mind so affronts 'Nature' continually! He never knows what happens to him because of his philosophy, his 'wisdom' usually something *on* life and seldom *of* life.

Motoring to and from Taliesin—seeing masses of the ten or more thousand students increasingly thronging grounds and buildings of the University, overflowing University Avenue, comes the same feeling of unhappiness. Something tragic in it all: a seeming futility or betrayal? The feeling is indefinable, but deep. A resentment against the mass product? Deeper than that. A conviction of betrayal.

Small wonder that we grow 'old'. Educated so soon.

Now in his eighteenth year, dreaming architecture, seeing it more and more in everything, the feeling of depression regarding his one-two-thousand-five-hundredth share in the education afforded by the University of Wisconsin was growing unbearable. Added to dissatisfaction with it and himself, there was a sense of shame in accepting the mother's sacrifices for so little in return. True, he turned over his Conover stipend to her, but the demands of college-education forever pressed in one mean form or another.

He had sold some of his father's books to meet them. The father had taken with him nothing but his clothes and violin—his mother's beautiful gold Swiss watch had now gone to Perry, the pawn-broker, by way of her son. Evenings he had made things, or during holiday vacations, with his scroll-saw, and sold them to be used as 'Christmas presents'. Making these things was recreation, too, in a sense. But his situation in 'college' was all hopelessly inappropriate so far as he could see.

In spite of everything he was the heavy item of expense in that household. But for this miserable college education mother and sisters could get along well enough for a while. Mother would never consent to his giving up so near the time for graduation. Only another winter and spring term?

A sacred sacrifice she was making. But the spring term of his senior year was just ended. Why go on with it?

For mother's sake? Look at her. She was ailing and unhappy. Why not go to Chicago where Uncle Jenkin Lloyd-Jones was building a new church, get work in some architect's office, really help her and be getting nearer architecture himself?

He would plead—'There are great architects in Chicago, mother, so there must be great buildings too. I am going to be an architect. You want me to be one. I am nowhere near it here. Professor Conover is fine but he isn't an architect. Here in the university I am doing nothing but draw and draw and see professional generalities glitter, spending money we haven't got or you have to slave to get.

'Do you believe in it yourself, mother? In your heart I mean? It isn't real you know, like the farm. Why won't you ask Uncle "Jenk" why I can't begin to be an architect right now? Soon it will be too late. I was eighteen last June, remember.'

And then threatening: 'I'll go anyway. It's time I put a stop to this foolish waste motion myself. You are willing to starve for it because all the Joneses, every one of them, is cracked about education. "Education?" You sent me to the farm yourself for *experience*, didn't you? Well, it's experience I want now. You spoiled me, yourself, for this marking time. It's vicious, I tell you! I was sick of it long ago. It's no good for me. Can't you see, mother? It's no good.'

Finally the mother, continually thus beset, did write to Uncle Jenkin who was making a great name for himself as teacher and prophet in his work in Chicago for a larger religion. Came back from the great preacher the answer, 'On no account let the young man come to Chicago. He should stay in Madison and finish his education. That will do more for him than anything else. If he came here he would only waste himself on fine clothes and girls.'

Mother was shocked, and relieved too. Her son now would graduate. But for the son, that insulting misjudgment settled it. It really didn't apply to him. He intended to go. If there was no more sympathy or understanding of him and the pathetic situation there than that letter showed, well—he would show the writer of the letter something . . . some day.

A few days later he left. He had managed to get seven dollars in his pocket, after buying the ticket to Chicago, most of the money got from old man Perry at the pawn-shop for his father's—and his—favourite calf-bound copy of Plutarch's 'Lives', thumbed edges—by the son—at the life of Alcibiades: A finely bound set of Gibbon's 'Decline and Fall', which by the way he detested. Several other books from the father's library, and a mink collar that had been his mother's, but fitted by her to his overcoat!

Well . . . mother wouldn't know he had gone until he didn't come home tomorrow night. He had arranged all to deceive her that far ahead; but he would surely write her from Chicago as soon as he had a job, and that couldn't be long . . .

He put 'University' behind him; a boundless faith grown strong in him. A faith in what? He could not have told you. He got on the Northwestern for Chicago—the Eternal City of the West.

Here is the bravery of all life, in this tragic break with background, in this stand against clear sky—whatever fear, superfluous: This is my own earth now! A song in the heart.

Say good-bye to 'the boy'.

Henceforward, on my own, I am 'I'.

The sentimental son of a sentimental mother grown up in the midst of a sentimental family planted on free soil by a grandly sentimental grandfather . . . the Welsh pioneer.

BOOK TWO

FELLOWSHIP

INTERLUDE

It is seed time.

The field is brown with the unctuous purple-brown of freshly turned earth.

The sowing has been harrowed home.

Life stirs at the root.

Sap rises to flow again into accustomed channels and course'to new growth.

A faint tinge of green comes over the brown field. The wood is flecked with green and touched with delicate pink. The bobwhite has been calling the spring for two weeks past. The boy, as he rakes the leaves and rubbish from the fresh green grass of the door-yard, wonders as he notices that plum trees, apple trees, berry bushes, flower beds show no sign of Spring. He goes over to the beds to rake off the clean cane-stalks holding down the dead leaves when . . .

'Frank! Let them alone! Not safe to let them up yet.'

The beautiful, warm, clear day.

A clear, high night. Stars. A slender moon in the sky when the boy went to bed.

Next morning Winter returned unexpectedly while he slept and spread a rime of thick, white frost afield.

The warm sun came out in the still morning. The tiny flecks of green and the pink tinge over the wood—went black.

Nipped in the bud!

'I thought so,' said Uncle James. 'I was afraid of it!' Let the bobwhite whistle another week. Keep the frost in the roots of the flowers and the fruit.

And the boy knew for the first time why 'cover' was carefully spread over the flower beds after the ground had been frozen deep, and was spread around over the roots of the fruit trees.

To keep the frost in the roots until safe for them to wake!

The young sentimentalist has recourse to the oracle. 'Uncle James! why don't the trees and flowers know when to come out?'

'Well, that's something I can't tell,' said his uncle.

A vague fear settled over the spirit of the seeker after Truth. Had the spring been singing about something it knew so little as to be set back like this?

Did Uncle James know more about 'spring' then, than Nature knew herself? No, of course not.

He just knew how to play some trick on the ground that would make the trees and flowers wait—make them feel it was still winter when it wasn't winter, so he could be sure to have lots of fruit. Well, it was just like making the cows have calves to get the milk, wasn't it? Like making the pigs have little pigs so you could eat them?

That didn't explain anything.

And that wasn't nature at all.

Not the real thing. That was just how men got their living out of nature. Just craft. Perhaps art?

This boy wanted to know something deeper.

This young sentimentalist already in love with truth!

Is there a more tragic figure on earth—in any generation?

THE APPRENTICE

Chicago. Wells Street Station: Six o'clock in late spring, 1887. Drizzling. Sputtering white arc-light in the station and in the streets, dazzling and ugly. I had never seen electric lights before.

Crowds. Impersonal. Intent on seeing nothing.

Somehow I didn't like to ask anyone anything. Followed the crowd. Drifted south to the Wells Street Bridge over the Chicago River. The mysterious dark of the river with dim masts, hulks and funnels hung with lights half-smothered in gloom—reflected in black beneath. I stopped to see, holding myself close against the iron rail to avoid the blind, hurrying by.

I wondered where Chicago was—if it was near. Suddenly the clanging of a bell. The crowd began to run. I wondered why: found myself alone and realized why in time to get off, but stayed on as the bridge swung out with me into the channel and a tug, puffing clouds of steam, came pushing along below pulling an enormous iron grain boat, towing it slowly through the gap. Stood there studying the river-sights in the drizzling rain until the bridge followed after and closed to open the street again. Later, I never crossed the river without being charmed by sombre beauty.

Wondered where to go for the night. But again if I thought to ask anyone, there was only the brutal, hurrying crowd trying hard not to see.

Drifted south. This must be Chicago now. So cold, black, blue-white and wet. The horrid blue-white glare of arc-lights was over everything. Shivering. Hungry. Went into an eating place near Randolph Street and parted with seventy cents, ten per cent of my entire capital. As I ate, I was sure of one thing, never would I go near Uncle Jenkin Lloyd-Jones nor ask his help nor use his name.

Got into the street again to find it colder, raining harder. Drifted south and turned left, shivering now in front of the Chicago Opera House on Washington Street, the flood of hard lights made the unseeing faces of the crowd in the drizzle, livid—ghastly. Under a great canopy that made a shelter from the rain were enormous posters—'Sieba'—Extravaganza by David Henderson, Grand Corps de Ballet. And there the dancers were,

60

life-size almost, out on the sidewalk, holding their colour in spite of the glare.

The doors were just open and a dollar let me go in to wait nearly an hour for the show to begin, where it was dry and warm. During that waiting . . . went back to the home by the lake—to see mother, Jennie and Maginel . . . wondered what they would feel when they knew I had gone for good . . . never to come back? But they were all coming to me in Chicago. There must be clean, quiet 'home' places in Chicago. Near the lake, maybe. I wondered if they were anxious about me, hardly realizing I wouldn't be missed until tomorrow night. Saw mother's sad eyes and pale face as she sat quietly—waiting. She seemed always waiting now. A pang of homesickness already, but the orchestra filed out from under the stage.

Tuning up began, always exciting. Then the florid overture. I knew it wasn't good music—good music was not so sentimental (my father's term of contempt)—but I was glad to hear it. The Henderson Extravaganzas in those days were not unduly extravagant. This one took the roof off an unsophisticated mind.

Went out after all was over, drifting with the crowd to Wabash Avenue. Cottage Grove Avenue cable cars were running there. My first sight of the cable car. So, curious, I got on the grip-car beside the gripman and tried to figure it all out, going south in the process until the car stopped, and 'All out!' That car was going to the barn.

Got one coming out headed north now. Not sleepy nor tired. Half-resentful because compelled to read the signs pressing on the eyes everywhere. They claimed your eyes for this, that, and everything beside. They lined the car above the windows. They lined the way, pushing, crowding and playing all manner of tricks on the victim's eye. Tried to stop looking at them. Unfairly compelled to look again. In self-defence kept on reading until reading got to be torture.

There were glaring signs on the glass-fronts against the lights inside, sharp signs in the glare of the spluttering arc-lamps outside. Hurrah signs. Stop signs. Come-on-in signs. Hello signs set out before the blazing windows on the sidewalks. Flat fences lettered both sides, man-high, were hanging out across above the sidewalks and lit by electric lamps. Coming from extravaganza, here was the beginning of phantasmagoria.

Supersensitive eyes were fixed by harsh dissonance and recovered themselves: reasoned and fought for freedom. Compelled again—until the procession of saloons, food shops, barber shops, eating houses, saloons, restaurants, groceries, laundries—and saloons, saloons, tailors, dry goods, candy shops, bakeries and saloons became chaos in a wilderness of Italian, German, Irish, Polack, Greek, English, Swedish, French, Chinese and Spanish names in letters that began to come off and get about, interlace and stick and climb and swing again.

Demoralization of the eye began: *names* obliterating everything. Names and what they would do for you or with you or to you for your money. Shutting your eyes didn't end it, for then you heard them louder than you saw them. They would begin to mix with absurd effect and you need take

61

nothing to get the effect of another extravaganza. Letters this time. Another ballet, of A. B. C. D. E. F. G., L. M. N. O. P., X. Y. and Z., the première-danseuse intervening in fantastic dances.

It would have been a mercy not to have known the alphabet. One pays a heavy toll for the joys of being eye-minded. Ear-minded, too.

Got to bed at the Brigg's House north on Randolph Street, wrapped a sheet around myself—it seemed awfully like a winding sheet as I caught sight of it in the mirror—and slept. A human item—insignificant but big with interior faith and a great hope. In what? I could not have told you. Asleep in Chicago. And Chicago murderously actual.

CHICAGO

Next day I began on Chicago.

My hand in my pocket after breakfast, I could feel sure of three silver dollars and a dime. Took the city directory and made a list of architects, choosing names I had heard in Conover's office or names that sounded interesting. All only names to me and missed the names of all names important to me. The name of the architect of my uncle's new church, 'All Souls', I knew by heart—J. L. Silsbee, Lakeside Building, Clark Street, Chicago. But I wasn't going there. Tramped through street after street now seeing Chicago above the sign-belt.

And where was the architecture of the great city—the 'Eternal City of the West'? Where was it? Hiding behind these shameless signs? A vacant block would come by. Then the enormous billboards planted there stood up grandly, had it all their own way, obliterating everything in nothing. That was better. Chicago! Immense gridiron of noisy streets. Dirty . . . Heavy traffic crossing both ways at once, managing somehow: torrential noise.

A stupid thing, that gridiron: cross-currents of horses, trucks, street cars grinding on hard rails mingling with streams of human beings in seeming confusion and clamour. But habit was in the movement making it expert, and so safe enough. Dreary—dim—smoked. Smoked dim and smoking. A wide, desolate, vacant strip ran along the waterfront over which the Illinois Central trains puffed, shrieked and ground incessantly, cutting the city off from the lake.

Terrible, this grinding and piling up of blind forces. If there was logic here who could grasp it?

To stop and think in the midst of this would be to give way to terror. The grey, soiled river with its mist of steam and smoke, was the only beauty. And that smelled to heaven.

Young engineer looking for work? 'Sam Treat' looked me over. 'University man, eh?' The kindly intellectual face under a mass of grey hair smiled. 'Sorry.' Caught a glimpse of a busy draughting room full of men as I came out.

Well!—there was 'Beers, Clay and Dutton'. More tramping through brutal crowds that never seemed to see anything. Mr. Clay came out and looked me over—a twinkle of kindly humour in his black eyes. I have remembered that HE seemed to see ME and was amused. Why? Was it the longish hair again, or what? Took pity on me maybe, for he asked me to call again in a few weeks if I found nothing. In a few weeks! And I had just three dollars and ten cents!

Over now to 'S. S. Beman' in the Pullman Building way south on Michigan Avenue.

College 'tooth-picks' made in vain if made for walking. Souvenir of sophomore vanity on right little toe 'raising Cain' now. Perspiring freely. Found Mr. Beman not in! Foreman look me over. I. K. Pond?

'University man? What college, Ann Arbor?'

'No, University of Wisconsin.'

'No, nobody wanted at present, later perhaps—in a few months.' In a few months! I felt the small change in my pocket.

The famous Pullman Building had come into view. It looked funny— as if made to excite curiosity. Passed the Palmer House, on the way down, that famous Chicago Palazzo. It seemed curious to me: like an ugly old, old man whose wrinkles were all in the wrong place owing to a misspent life. As I went on my way to 'W. W. Boyington's' office I passed the Chicago Board of Trade at the foot of La Salle Street. Boyington had done it, had he? This?—thin-chested, hard-faced, chamfered monstrosity? I turned aside from Boyington's office then and there.

Chicago architecture! Where was it? Not the Exposition Building, a rank, much-domed yellow shed on the lake front. No, nor the rank and file along the streets. The rank and file all pretty much alike, industriously varied without variety. All the same thought, or lack of it. Were all American cities like this one, so casual, so monotonous in their savage, outrageous attempts at variety? All competing for the same thing, atten- tion, in the same way? Another senseless competition never to be won?

So thinking I got on toward Major Jenney's office. Mundie came out. He was president of the Chicago Architectural Club as I knew. 'Ah, Uni- versity man. Engineer?' Yes.' Had I any drawings? No? First time I had been asked for any drawings. 'Why don't you come around to the Club meeting Saturday night? You might hear of something there. Bring some of your drawings along with you,' he added.

Strange! I had not thought to bring any drawings with me. But some were in the bag, still checked at the Station. Mundie with his sunken eyes in an impassive frozen face was a little kindly warmth in the official atmo- sphere of a Chicago architect's office.

Too late to go to any more offices now. Got my bag to the Brigg's House not knowing where else to go, hungry. Asked for a cheaper room. Clerk sympathetic—one for seventy-five cents, almost as good. For supper, what twenty cents would buy at the bakery. I had found Kohlsatt's bakery- lunch. Tempting pastry piled high in plain sight, all that I had been denied or allowed to eat only occasionally. And things beside, I had never

63

even dreamed of. A hungry orphan turned loose in a bake-shop? Lucky for me I had little money.

To bed, dog-tired, not at all discouraged. On the whole everyone had i een rather kind. Must be someone who needed me. Tomorrow, maybe!

Two days gone from home. Mother knew now. The thought of her was anguish. I turned away from it to action and repeated the performance of the day before in other offices, this time taking my drawings. Mundie was out. At five other offices, no success.

No lunch. No supper. During the day ten cents invested in bananas.

That night, a weird dream. Up in a balloon. Mother frantically holding to the rope, dragged along the ground, calling Jennie and Maginel to help . . . all dragged along. I shouted down to hitch the end of the rope to something, anything, and make it fast. But it tore out of the helpless hands and I shot up and up and up—until I awoke with a sense of having been lifted miles to the strange ground of another world.

Awakened rudely to the fourth day. Got started again, pavement-sore, gaunt. Something had to happen today. Tired again, three more offices. Same result.

There was still Silsbee's office. He was building my uncle's 'All Souls' church, but he needn't know who I was. After noon I went there. Liked the atmosphere of the office best. Liked Silsbee's sketches on the wall. Liked instantly the fine-looking, cultured fellow with a pompadour and beard, who came forward with a quiet friendly smile—Cecil Corwin.

'Hello!' he said as though he knew me. He looked the artist-musician. Through the gate in the outer office railing he had come humming from the 'Messiah'. I smiled and said, 'So you sing?' He smiled, looking at my hair-cut, or lack of it. 'Yes . . . try to . . . Do you play?' 'Yes . . . try to.' I had found a kindred spirit.

He sat down by me in the outer office. His sleeves were rolled above the elbow. His arms were thickly covered with coarse hair, but I noticed how he daintily crooked his little finger as he lifted his pencil. He had an air of gentleness and refinement. I told him my trials.

'You are a minister's son.'

'Yes, how did you know?'

'Didn't know, something about you. I am one myself. The "Old Man" (moving his head in the direction of Silsbee's private office) is one too. And there are two more here already, Wilcox and Kennard. If you come in here, there would be five of us.'

We laughed.

'Well . . . could I by any chance come in?' I said anxiously. He looked me over. 'I believe we could get along,' he said. 'Let me see your drawings.'

He looked carefully at the sketches. 'You made these just to please yourself?'

'Yes.'

'You've got a good touch. Wait a minute.' He took them and went in

64

through a door marked 'Private'. Presently he appeared at the door with a tall, dark-faced, aristocratic-looking man, gold eye-glasses with long gold chain hanging from his nose. He stood in the door looking carelessly at me with a frown. It was Silsbee. 'All right,' he said, 'take him on. Tracer's wages—$8.00.'

And he turned and shut the door after him.

'Not much, but better than nothing,' said Cecil. I agreed.

How far from my expectations! '$8.00.' With my 'experience' I should be able to earn three times as much. But no one thought much of my experience. Cecil saw the disappointment following elation. 'Had your lunch?' No. 'Come with me.' We went downstairs a block away to Kinsley's. Cecil insisted on a good portion of browned corned-beef hash for me, and coffee.

'Thank you, no coffee. I don't drink it.'

'Well then'—amused—'milk?' And ever since, when feeling really hungry, nothing has tasted so good to me as browned corned-beef hash.

'Got any money left?' he said abruptly.

'Oh, yes!'

'How much?'

'Twenty cents.'

'Had anything to eat yesterday?' This was getting rather too personal so I didn't answer.

'Come home with me tonight and we'll concertize with my new grand piano.' It was Saturday. I was not to report for work until Monday morning.

So I got my bag from the Brigg's House and went home with Cecil. A nice home. Met his benevolent preacher-father, a Congregational missionary. His mother had died some years ago, but his sister Marquita looked after the father and her bachelor brother. She was 'musical' too.

After a 'musical' evening together, we went up to the room that was for me. Cecil found how anxious I was about things back home, gave me paper, pen and ink to write. I did.

And then: 'Would you lend me ten dollars to send my mother? I'll pay you back two dollars a week.' Here started a characteristic process continuing to this day.

He said nothing, took a ten-dollar bill from his pocket and laid it on the table. I put it in the envelope and we took it to the nearest box to post. A load went off my heart. I had a job. But better still, I had a friend. No mean one in any sense, as anyone might see. I could go now and see my uncle's new church, 'All Souls'. Cecil himself had been looking after the building of it so I asked him about it.

He said, Would you like to see 'The Church', with curious emphasis on 'Church'. 'We'll go down to Oakwood Boulevard and Langley Avenue after dinner and have a look at it.' We went. Why the curious emphasis? I knew now. It was in no way like a Church, more like a 'Queen Anne' dwelling. We used to say Queen Anne front and Mary Ann behind. And this was. But interesting to me. Again, not beautiful—but . . . curious.

Taking advantage of the unexpected visit, Cecil went about looking after details in the nearly completed building. I went along Oakwood Boulevard to look it over in perspective. Was standing back, looking over from across the street when a hand from behind took me firmly by the collar and a hearty voice like a blow, 'Well, young man! So here you are.' I recognized the voice instantly, Uncle Jenkin Lloyd-Jones! I was in for it.

'I've been expecting you, young fellow. Your mother wrote—distracted. I'll telegraph you're found.'

No!—Please. I said, I wrote last night telling her I had a job and I sent her some money . . .

A job? 'Where have you found a job?'

'Silsbee's office.'

'Silsbee's? Of course. That was mighty good of him. Told him who you were I suppose? said Uncle Jenkin.

No! I said, I didn't! He looked suspicious. But got the point quickly. All right, he said. Then Cecil came up and greeted him. Where did you get hold of my young nephew? said Uncle Jenkin.

He's your nephew? I didn't know it, Cecil said in astonishment. That proved my case.

Well,—where are you going to stay now? asked the maternal uncle. I didn't know. You're coming to stay near here where I can keep an eye on you. Tonight you must come and stay with us.

No! said Cecil, he's going to stay with me tonight.

All right then, Monday night.

Isn't the opening to 'the way' usually as simple? Here came the chance end of a sequence that like the end of twine in a skein of indefinite length, would unwind in characteristic events as time went on. Not at all as I had expected! It seldom is as much or perhaps at all as we expect. But Cecil was already more in himself than I could ever have imagined. His culture similar to mine, yet he was different. And so much more developed than I. So I began to go to school to Cecil. Soon we were together everywhere.

SILSBEE

Silsbee was doing Edgewater at the time, the latest attempt at high-class subdivision, and doing it entirely for J. L. Cochran, a real-estate 'genius' in his line. A genius being, naturally, a man who can make much money easily. Silsbee could draw with amazing ease. He drew with soft, deep black lead-pencil strokes and he would make remarkable free-hand sketches of that type of dwelling peculiarly his own at the time. His superior talent in design had made him respected in Chicago. His work was a picturesque combination of gable, turret and hip, with broad porches quietly domestic and gracefully picturesque. A contrast to the awkward stupidities and brutalities of the period elsewhere. He would come out to the draughting room as though we, the draughtsmen, did not exist, stand talking a moment with Cecil, one lank leg turning one long foot over sidewise, the picture of indifference or scorn as he stood on the other, grudging of words and shy of patience. All awed by him. Not so Cecil.

The office system was a bad one. Silsbee got a ground-plan and made his pretty sketch, getting some charming picturesque effect he had in his mind. Then the sketch would come out into the draughting room to be fixed up into a building, keeping the floor-plan near the sketch if possible. But the sketches fascinated us. 'My God, Cecil, how that man can draw!'

'He can. He's a kind of genius, but something is the matter with him. He doesn't seem to take any of it or take himself half seriously. The picture interests him. The rest bores him. You'll see. He's an architectural genius spoiled by way of the aristocrat. A fine education and family in Syracuse, but too contemptuous of everything.'

And I did see. I saw Silsbee was just making pictures. And not very close to what was real in the building—that I could see, myself. But I adored Silsbee just the same. He had style. His work had it too, in spite of slipshod methods. There was something finely tragic in his sombre mien; authority in the boom of his enormous voice pitched low in his long throat with its big Adam's apple. I learned a good deal about a house from Silsbee by way of Cecil.

Monday night I had gone to Uncle Jenkin to spend a few days in the parsonage. Interesting people came there to dine. Dr. Thomas, Rabbi Hirsh, Jane Addams, Mangasarian and others. I enjoyed listening.

A letter had come from mother. She wrote regularly every week. She seemed glad after all that I was at work. Told me to stay close to Uncle Jenkin. He was a good man beset by the countless trials of his position but he'd help me all he could. And I was not to worry about her.

She had sold father's library and a few hundred dollars had come to her from her brothers, her small share in grandfather's farm. If I got along and needed her she would sell the Madison place and come down and make a home for me. There were the usual anxieties about diet, warm underwear, companions.

'I would have you', she wrote, 'a man of sense as well as sensibility. You will find Goodness and Truth everywhere you go. If you have to choose, choose Truth. For that is closest to Earth. Keep close to the Earth, my boy: in that lies strength. Simplicity of heart is just as necessary for an architect as for a farmer or a minister if the architect is going to build great buildings.' And she would put this faith of hers in many different forms as she wrote on different subjects, until I knew just what to expect from her.

Always very brave, she was, but I knew what she wanted—she wanted to come down to live with me. And as soon as I could earn eighteen or twenty dollars a week I intended to have her come. Little Maginel was not yet very strong and Jennie had gone to teach school in the country.

I have always been fond of Uncle Jenkin's son, my cousin Richard. He was good-looking, fair-haired, brilliant 'city guy', initiated and unabashed, his views of what went on around him keen and amusing.

Richard had ambition, a certain affection but small reverence. He was a good specimen of minister's son, too. His mother was older than his father and more intellectual, I believe. She adored her son and never tired of quoting him. He was quotable; I will say that for him, although Aunt Susan continually did overdo Richard. Mothers are apt to have the habit of overdoing their sons.

His father found a boarding place for me at the Watermans', a block away on Vincennes Avenue. I got my clothes into a wheelbarrow one night late with Dick's help and we started down the deserted boulevard. It was so smooth I proposed to beat him the two blocks to the corner, I wheeling the barrow. We lit out. And I did beat him but in trying to turn to Vincennes, over went wheelbarrow, clothes, helter-skelter into the dirty street, myself following head first in a cruel slide as though I'd been shot out of a cannon, Dick tumbling after doing a cart-wheel into the wreck. Both of us were scratched and scraped, not hurt. Laughing—we were always laughing—we gathered dusty underwear, ties, Sunday clothes, shirts far and wide as the wind entered into the spirit of the thing and carried on . . . that boulevard dust in my things as near permanent as any dye.

The Watermans' was a quiet, decent place. I saw Harry, a lad nearly my own age, once in a while. But they were all rather pessimistic folk, saddened, it seemed to me, by something of a family nature. Did it follow me everywhere, or did I see it because of my own experience?

Richard and I went about together. Dick knew the ropes as Dick knew how to laugh. We would get to laughing and keep at it, the bait going to and fro between us until both were tired out.

And there was quite a social life going on at the church. Evening events, lectures and meetings of one sort or another. Sociables. Browning classes. I got 'Rabbi Ben Ezra' into my system about that time and 'The Ring and the Book'. Study classes of all kinds. All Souls had a circulating library, was a neighbourhood centre in which were many activities intellectual, social and literary. A kindergarten there too. The church was never closed.

My uncle's soul seemed a sort of spiritual dynamo that never rested. His preaching, like grandfather's, had force and fervour. And brains, but I began to suspect him of sentimentality. But he was evidently becoming an active spiritual force in Chicago, his influence rapidly on the increase.

Cecil was often taking me home and we went to the Apollo Club Concerts or any good concert wherever we could find one. And to theatres sometimes. I had then, as now, a passion for the theatre as for music.

The work in the office was easy for me and I soon made myself useful. We took on a new man about that time, a few months after I had entered —George Maher. He had asked Silsbee for eighteen dollars a week and got it as he had much experience. After three months I had been only raised to twelve.

I soon found George no better draughtsman than I was, if as good. So I made up my mind to try for a raise. If Silsbee could pay George eighteen, he could pay me twenty.

'The old man's here now—go in and talk to him,' said Cecil. I went in.

Silsbee looked at me and frowned. Evidently he knew what my being there meant.

'Well!'

'Mr. Silsbee, I can't get along on twelve dollars a week. Don't you think I can earn fifteen dollars at least—now?'

'You've just had a raise, Wright. No! Perhaps—the first of the year.'

I was sure injustice was being done me. So then and there, I 'quit'.

Mr. W. W. Clay, of Beers, Clay and Dutton, had interested me when I was job-hunting, and I went straight over to see him.

'One of Silsbee's men?' he asked. A man in Silsbee's office could usually draw and design in his style and was in demand by architects less capable in design—

'Yes, sir.'

'How much do you expect to earn?'

'Eighteen dollars.'

He got up and went out with me to the foreman of the draughting room.

'Lockwood,' said he, 'take this young man on. We will pay him eighteen dollars a week. His name is Wright.'

Cecil and I were still together noons and evenings. Mr. Clay, more than kind, seemed interested in me. But I soon found myself entrusted with work beyond me. Designing what I should be learning how to design.

I realized I had made a mistake in the long run. In a few weeks I went in to tell Mr. Clay so. He was astonished.

'Aren't we good to you here, Wright? Isn't the work interesting?'

'Oh, yes,' I could truthfully say.

'Don't you like me?'

'Yes.' And I really did.

'Well, out with it. What's the matter?'

I told him I didn't feel ready to give out designs. Wanted to learn how to make them. There was no one there skilled as a designer. I could learn very little.

'I see,' he said dryly. He was hurt. I think he thought me a young coxcomb.

'What are you going to do?'

'I'm going back to Silsbee.'

'Will he take you?'

'I don't know.'

'Hadn't you better find out before you quit?'

'No.'

'Why not?'

I had no answer.

69

'All right! Go out to Lockwood and tell him to give you your wages.' But he thought that rather rough and went with me himself. 'Lockwood,' he said gently, 'give Wright his wages and let him out. Either he's got the big head or he's right. I don't know which.' And he shook hands with me, the characteristic half-humorous look coming again into his eyes.

I went as straight back to Silsbee as I had left him. Told him the story. He smoked away without a word.

'You've quit already, have you?'

'Yes, sir.'

'What for?'

'Well, I didn't want it to look as though you were taking me away from Mr. Clay, if you let me come back.'

He smiled that bitter smile of his, went to the door and called, 'Corwin!' Cecil came. 'Wright is coming back. His wages will be eighteen dollars.' The Silsbee private office door closed behind me as I came out.

Cecil and I went dancing around the big table in the centre of the room in a friendly tilt.

During these later months at Silsbee's Cecil and I were inseparable. Discussed everything in the heavens above, the earth beneath and the waters thereof. We would go to Madame Galle's Italian table d'hôte and various other cosy restaurants. Or, if we had a little money, to the Tip Top Inn in the Pullman Building.

Theodore Thomas was giving his famous concerts in the old Exposition Building. We went there. In the rear of the audience there were tables and refreshments in comfortable German style. Loving concerts, I've never enjoyed any concerts more.

They were just beginning to build the Chicago Auditorium. The papers were full of its wonders. Adler and Sullivan, the architects, were frequently mentioned. I wondered how I had come to miss that firm in my search for work.

Usually I went to All Souls, Sunday mornings. Perhaps to dinner at the parsonage above. I had noticed interesting people in the congregation but made no acquaintances, although a number of the people who knew me as the pastor's nephew asked me to come and see them or invited me without that formality to dine. But I didn't go. I preferred Cecil's company. If I couldn't have that, I would find something to do.

From the library of All Souls I got two books you would never expect could be found there. Owen Jones' *Grammar of Ornament* and Viollet-le-Duc's *Habitations of Man in All Ages*. I had read his *Dictionnaire*, the *Raisonné* at home, got from the Madison city library.

I believed the *Raisonné* was the only really sensible book on architecture in the world. I got copies of it for my sons, later. That book was enough to keep, in spite of architects, one's faith alive in architecture.

The Owen Jones was a reprint but good enough. I read the 'propositions' and felt the first five were dead right. I didn't know about the others. It seemed these five were equally sound applied to human behaviour. And they were. I got a packet of onion skin, a delicate, strong, smooth tracing paper and traced the multifold designs. I traced evenings and Sunday mornings until the packet of one hundred sheets was gone and I needed exercise to straighten up from this application.

I had been eager to learn to box while at the University and had practised a little with Jimmie Kerr who had a similar ambition. One of the items that rolled over the dusty boulevard when, moving, I upset the barrow and Dick and myself, was a set of boxing gloves. I used to put on the gloves with Harry Waterman. And I used to walk sometimes nearly forty blocks downtown to work. A number of times, out of carfare, I had walked the whole distance.

A PRETTY GIRL IN PINK

Study classes at All Souls were busy with Victor Hugo's *Les Misérables* under the guidance of the Pastor. Students were to complete this study with a costume party, characters of the tale appearing as Victor Hugo designed them. The affair was to be a sweeping one, music, dancing and a supper. Therefore a large hall was hired somewhere near. I wasn't a regular member of the classes, but 'Enjolras,' young French officer, fell to my lot. My rôle was simple, so they said. All I needed was a pair of high-heeled shiny black boots coming above the knee, clanking spurs, not to mention white, tight trousers, scarlet military jacket with stiff collar, gold braid and epaulettes. And I would need a small red cap on my head. And should have hanging alongside on a leather harness, a sword! I don't know where I got all the things—some costumer's, I suppose. They were probably as correct as Victor Hugo himself sometimes wasn't. Cecil helped the great work on. When I was dressed and ready he said, 'Maybe not anything like "Enjolras", Frank, but certainly something to look at.'

I pulled out the sword, stuck it point down on the floor and made a leg. 'You'll do,' he said. 'I almost wish I had agreed to come when your uncle invited me.'

'Come on anyway!' I begged. But he wouldn't. So putting on my overcoat capewise, I buttoned it, sleeves hanging, to put the glory out. Holding the sword by my side I walked down the boulevard to the hall, late, not to be conspicuous.

The scene, after I had stowed my coat and opened the door to the hall, was really brilliant. There they were—happy *misérables* all of them.

But my plan had worked out wrong, for coming late I *was* conspicuous. The first dance over, the characters were standing around the sides of the large room regarding that large central area as I came upon it—an empty dancing floor! Many groups of prettily dressed French peasant girls and young yokels were standing about. Marat I saw, terrible as he needed to be, and perhaps wasn't. The best character there, seen at a glance, was my Aunt Susan, the preacher's wife as the Abbé. Suddenly a group of lasses in

71

bright bodices, short skirts and pretty caps came rushing over the floor. In the lead Miss Emery. 'Here you are at last,' she said.

And she turned to introduce me to the others.

She was older somewhat than I. 'Finished' in a fashionable eastern school she spoke with pretty accent the broad 'a'. Too pretty to be natural and yet, somehow, it probably was hers, after all. . . .

Glad to be taken in hand I danced with the church girls I knew but slightly. The infernal slab-sided sword was slung so low that if I took my hands off, it got between my legs. If I took my mind off, it got between my partner's legs with disastrous effects—some laughable.

No longer shy, I danced pretty well. But that sword sank me. I tried schemes to control it. I wouldn't spoil the fine figure I was making by taking it off. I was going to hang on to that swinging, dangling, clanking sword if I mowed the legs off the whole 'Misérables' tribe. Some of the girls entered into the spirit of the thing and were helpful holding on to it themselves while dancing or at psychological moments otherwise.

Miss Emery sat out a few dances with me or rather we went out into a half-dark auditorium opening into the hall. I felt quite at home in her company. Glad I came. But when I wasn't in trouble with that sword, she was.

Felt I was having a bully time. Outside the gathering, I could take off the superfluous weapon. She seemed to like to hold it—probably felt safer when *she* had it.

At ten o'clock came a lull in the evening. Refreshments to be served. There was a general rushing about to restore the various units to their several places with their parties. Rushing across the dancing floor to join Miss Emery's group, halfway over, a tall, pretty peasant girl in pink, blonde curls dancing my way while looking the other, was upon me before I could avoid her. Striking her forehead square against mine she was knocked to her hands and knees. I myself seeing stars managed to pick her up. Laughing it off bravely enough, she was still blinking. I saw the bump already on her forehead as I led her over to her parents to apologize, but she wouldn't have it. 'All my fault,' she insisted. The parents were Mr. and Mrs. Tobin, and this was their Catherine. Her father called her 'Kitty'. I had noticed her in church, a gay-spirited, sunny-haired young girl of probably sixteen, with a frank, handsome countenance. Her parents I remembered had once asked me to dinner. They asked me again now for Sunday—tomorrow. I said I would come. I hoped the bump, beginning to swell, would not be too painful.

Soon after I noticed they had left.

Next day, a bump on my own forehead.

The course of the party changed for me. At eleven o'clock, the hour for church parties to end, I saw Miss Emery into her carriage and walked home alone along the boulevard.

An ancient oracle might have stretched a prophetic hand over that crash.

Next morning, turned by the party toward Victor Hugo, I remembered

72

a chapter in *Notre Dame*, 'The Book Will Kill the Edifice,' wherein the amazing Frenchman had disposed of the European Renaissance as 'that setting sun all Europe mistook for dawn'. When I got up I went to the Church library.

Found a different translation. This chapter-heading, instead of using as in the original French, *Ceci Tuera Cela* (This will kill that), was 'The book will kill the edifice'. I took it home and read it again instead of going to church.

Victor Hugo loved diffuse discussion in abstruse style. But this essay was one of the truly great things ever written on architecture. Again I felt its force. My own gathering distrust was confirmed. Splendid writing. How 'modern' the great romanticist must have seemed in his time! Yet this chapter was omitted from some editions.

Excited by the great poet into thinking about the difference between romanticism and sentimentality, I got started late, walking down Drexel Boulevard to the Tobin home. Late to dinner. Catherine opened the door, 'Les Misérables' bump 'most gone. Easy to like hearty Father Tobin. He carried everything before him in a bluff, easy way; Mother Tobin was different—fine-looking, auburn-haired woman; both beloved by their children—but the mother ruled, evidently mistress of her nice new home.

Catherine, eldest, was sixteen. Charlie and Robert were twins. They were twelve. Arthur, youngest, a pretty, affectionate boy of seven, came and sat on my knee. All devoted to Jenkin Lloyd-Jones were disposed to lionize his nephew.

Diffidence disappeared in this warm home: a warmth I had lost since coming to the city. Girlish and lovely, Kitty vivaciously adopted me at once. She was in the Hyde Park High School. Also one of Professor Tomlin's pupils in music. Evidently Catherine had pretty much her own way in that household. Yet she seemed a sensible girl. Everything revolved around her. Not only was she accustomed to having her own way but having it without any trouble whatever. At table I noticed she ate on her own particular plate with her own particular knife and fork and spoon. A hangover from childhood. The idiosyncrasy seemed natural. The dinner went off gaily. After dinner Kitty came in dressed to go out, tall laced boots, gloves and short plaid walking jacket. A tam-o'-shanter topped her mass of ruddy curls.

She took me by the hand, simply, and said she was going to take me to see the new Kenwood houses. That meant to see some curious effects, because Kenwood was in process of becoming the most fashionable of Chicago's residence districts. So we went down the front steps hand in hand like children. She *was* one, although so tall and seeming to have such good sense. I was grown up pretty well in architecture, the sphere in which I lived in earnest. But where people were concerned, I had nearly everything yet to learn.

More months went by until, after a year with Silsbee, and coming twenty soon, earning the necessary $18.00 per week I felt mother should sell the Madison home by the lake and come to Chicago. Soon she did come.

The North Shore then attracted me, but mother was afraid of the raw winds of the lake for me and for Maginel too. She didn't seem to want to be too near All Souls either, for some reason. So we went to see Miss Augusta Chapin, a friend of mother's in Oak Park. Again a preacher and this time a woman. She was Oak Park's Universalist pastor. Miss Chapin was thick-set, a woman's woman of about forty, usually dressed in rustling black silk, a gold chain around her neck to hang a gold cross upon her breast. She wore, alternately, a very kind and very severe expression.

Miss Chapin and mother worked out some temporary arrangement whereby we were to come in to the red-brick on Forest Avenue with her for some time to see if Oak Park was really the place to choose for our permanent home.

OAK PARK

Oak Park's other name was 'Saint's Rest'. So many churches for so many good people to go to, I suppose. The village looked like a pretty respectable place. The people were good people most of whom had taken asylum there to bring up their children in comparative peace, safe from the poisons of the great city. The village streets were generously shaded. It had a village government of its own, too, accounting to some extent for its subsequent growth.

I remember Superintendent Hatch, a kindly dark-faced man, driving about in an open buggy from school to school. My sister Jennie, now, owing to Miss Chapin's kind offices, one of his teachers at the Chicago Avenue School.

I remember the old Scovill place, occupying a whole square of the town, standing up there shamelessly tall, to say the last word for the depravity characterizing the residence architecture of that period; this lean wooden house.

The quiet village looked much like Madison to mother. That settled it.

Opposite the red-brick on Forest Avenue and well within the centre of the village was the Austin lot, another whole square competing with the Scovill square. This one untouched natural wildwood. A newly built all-shingle home in the entering mode, Queen Anne, took the middle of a cleared space at the Lake Street front. To one side and to the rear of the house next to Forest Avenue stood an old-fashioned barn vertically boarded and battened. It had good proportion and was an interesting rusty colour where the festoons of vines let colour through. Built in a much earlier period, being only a barn, it had been allowed to live. I liked the barn better than the Austin house. The old barn was honestly picturesque whereas the house only elaborately tried to be so. But Forest Avenue residents thought it outrageous that Mr. Austin, Oak Park's leading citizen, should leave this barn there on the best street in town.

Mr. Austin, short, slow-moving solid Scot, carried his head well down

74

in his shoulders on a short neck and wore a quizzical look on his short, bearded face.

This Austin wood-lot was especially inviting to me in that aggregation of uninspired carpenter work: endless rows of drab or white painted wood houses set regularly apart, each on its little painted cardboard lawn. High front-steps went straight up to jigger-porches wriggling with turned balusters, squirming with wanton scroll-work. And this prevalent porch-luxury was seldom of use, but still the roofs continued to shut out the sun from the parlours and sitting rooms. These enemies of Mr. Austin's barn all had the murderous corner-tower serving as bay-window in the principal corner room. Where did that soul-destroying motif come from? Never from earth. This popular fetish—for it was more than a 'feature'—was either rectangular across the corner, round or octagonal, eventuating above into candle-snuffer roofs, to turnip domes, or corkscrew spires. I walked along the miles of this expensive mummery, trying to get into the thinking processes of the builders, but failed to get hold of any thinking they had done at all. The forms were utterly meaningless, though apparently much scheming and copying had gone into them.

The houses were senseless; most of them looked equally comfortless. No more so in Oak Park than anywhere else; rather better, because here in Oak Park there were more trees and vines and wider shaven lots to cloak their ugliness. Those who lived in this ambitious Eastlake mimicry—called Queen Anne—were blissfully unaware of any serious losses or self-inflicted insults. And yet the monotonous iteration of the suburban-house parade like the sign-parade in Chicago streets compelled my attention willing or not.

The sign-parade—phantasmagoria—had at least some basis, some meaning. This procession—monogoria—had none whatever. My father's complaints and criticisms of music came to mind. 'Sentimentality' spoiled music for him in the making or the playing. Did it apply here?

As I walked and walked about, a helpless spectator, again a rank outsider, it would seem a senseless reiteration. A monologue reciting in monotone. . . .

Nobody home! Nobody home! 'They' stay here but they don't live here. We never knew life. But we are just as good as anybody's houses, just as good: just as good as 'they' are—better, maybe.

Fooled? Maybe they are fooled. What do we care? Everybody is—everybody is! 'They' are. We are. Everybody is. We suit them all. They suit us. Why should we mean anything if they don't mean anything?

We're as good as 'they' are? We couldn't think if we would. They wouldn't think if they could. They buy what thought there is in us ready-made, and what's in them, too. It's easier—maybe better because cheaper. How do you know:

Houses are just like clothes, aren't they? We're just clothes too, so we have to be in fashion, don't we? Or we'll be laughed at! Won't we? Don't you see—boy? They'll be laughed at too—What then?

Fools are we? Maybe—but fools on the laughing side.

75

CULTURE

What was the matter? More painful all this than Chicago sign-parade. More pitiful because this was 'Culture' while that was only mongering. Here was a mess. Were these meaningless monstrosities like the people whose houses they were—like the men and women who lived in them? Was all this waste what they deserved? Or had education been playing tricks with them—too? If 'they' were so far wrong in this expression of themselves, so lacking in feeling and perception of the natural—what were their other institutions like if you looked them square in the face? Were 'they' really right about anything at all above the alimentary canal and reproductive tract? Weren't even those being corrupted and spoiled in a confusion of spurious ideals that ignored needs? Why were they all satisfied with pretentious attitudes and stupid gestures? Were they all merely falsely sentimental instead of really sensible?

I used to take these doubts to Cecil. For wasn't Silsbee doing the same thing in the pictures he made, only that he did it as an artist? Silsbee's houses were merely 'arty' then? What thought there was in them was just the same as this?

I began to be more than ever dissatisfied with Silsbee. He seemed to me to be making matters worse. Making a lie or a vain boast more pretty by his skill, therefore making this shameful swindle easier.

Going by, I would sometimes lean on the Austin fence, an affair of dead oak-tree branches with the bark on—therefore 'rustic'. As I was leaning there looking at the wood one Sunday morning, Mr. Austin came up and spoke to me. 'Won't you come in?' he said. 'You live next door? Young architect? Miss Chapin has spoken of you.'

'I had wanted to get about a little in that oasis,' I said, pointing to the wood. I asked him how he came to let it alone in the midst of all those harsh houses. He looked at me from under bushy eyebrows: 'Don't you like their houses? Eh?

'They want me to move my old barn there, but'—looking toward it, eyes twinkling—'I like the looks of my barn better than I do their houses.' He winked!

'I would rather live in it myself,' I said.

'Come, let's look in it.' And he led the way.

Above, the old barn was fixed up inside as a playroom or ballroom, being decorated now for a party to be given for his daughter, Sophie, who was returning from finishing school. There was a son, Harry, too—away somewhere at college.

Mr. Austin had turned his back on his new house to go to the old barn and never asked me what I thought of the house. The next Sunday he asked me in to meet Mrs. Austin. The interior of the house was livable and homelike and I could say nice things about it. The exterior was never mentioned between us. It seems it was an old home with a new outside and so it looked. Mrs. Austin, a placid invalid, sat in a wheel-chair by the window.

76

Mr. Austin and I went back out to the barn.

'Now what would you do with this room for an *occasion?*' he said.

I made a few spontaneous suggestions which happened to appeal to him. —a decorative scheme of some sort; I have forgotten. 'Will you come over and help carry it out?'

Then he took me several blocks away to a lot at the corner of Forest and Chicago Avenues, tanglewood of all sorts of trees, shrubs and vines belonging, he said, to a Mr. Blair, Scottish landscape gardener. He laid out Humboldt Park in Chicago. Mr. Austin had the greatest affection and respect for him. He never tired talking of the old gardener. I never met the gardener, but kept this lot of his in mind.

Mr. Austin got into the way of calling for me regularly Sunday mornings to go for a little walk. I had found a quiet and, as circumstances proved, a staunch friend in Oak Park. A friend he remained while he lived.

CECIL

Some months later Cecil and I were, as usual, talking over doubts gaining on me and making me less useful in the office.

'Frank, look out!' he would say. 'Heresy in religion is bad enough, but nothing compared to heresy in fashion and culture. Read your Bible. Remember Jesus' instructions to His disciples?'

We happened to be at the Oak Park red-brick on a Sunday. I went after Miss Chapin's Bible. Cecil turned to Matthew and read: 'Go ye not into the way of the Gentiles! And into any city of the Samaritans, enter ye not. And into whatsoever city or town ye enter inquire who in it is worthy. And there abide till ye go home. Behold, I send you forth as sheep in the midst of wolves. Be ye, therefore, wise as serpents and harmless as doves. But beware of men, for they will deliver you up to the councils and they will scourge you in synagogues. And ye shall be brought before governors and kings for my sake for a testimony against them and the Gentiles.' He put the book down.

'The Gentiles and Samaritans today, Frank, and the Pharisees, too, for that matter, are the people proud of those homes: satisfied with them. The architects who work for them are, literally, the "scribes". The "professional men" today are in much the same social relation to the people as the "scribes" were to the Pharisees then.'

He took up the book again. ' "Give not that which is holy unto the dogs, neither cast ye your pearls before swine" . . . "swine" meaning those whose appetites for gain or fame or pleasure rule their judgment . . . "lest they trample them under their feet and turn again and rend you. Beware of the leaven of the Pharisees and of the leaven of Herod".' He shut the book. Sat silent a moment. Then he said quietly, 'Silsbee is right. Silsbee doesn't interfere with their beliefs or upset their ideas of themselves. He does the thing they have already accepted but does it better than the others do it. That's all. And in consequence he is considered radical enough by them and—God knows—has had enough trouble with them on that account.'

Now I had waited, to be sure of what I wanted to say.

'But, Cecil, is Silsbee doing the best he can? I mean, could he do better if he would?'

'What does that matter if he's doing the right thing?'

'But he's not doing the "right thing" if he is not doing as well as he knows and *all* he knows how to do.'

'Why not?'

'Because if there is God He can be trusted to use the best He has made or He wouldn't have made it. If He *is*, He can be trusted to make the modifications—not Silsbee. This God of my grandfather—the first thing *He* would put upon every member of creation, conscious or unconscious, would be just that thing—*to do the best he knew how to do*. Not as he was *told* to do it, but as he *saw* it for himself. Else what meaning has "He"?'

Cecil laughed. 'That mother of yours is going to have occasion to weep for you, Frank.'

'Maybe, Cecil, but not on that account if she is grandfather's daughter. And she is.'

'Have you ever talked these things over with her?'

'No, because it's only now just coming clear to me. I am not afraid of what she'll say, though.'

'But *whom* are you going to build homes for? If you go against their wishes and try to give them what *you* think right and not what they think they want?'

'That's just where a wise Creator must come in, Cecil. I won't need but one man in ten thousand to work for—even one man in a hundred thousand would keep me more than busy all my life, because that man will need me as much as I need him. He will be looking for me. I've been thinking about old Mr. Austin.'

'Yes,' said Cecil. 'Look at his house!'

'Well, I am looking at it. He got the best architect he knew. It happened to be Fred Shock, of Austin, and the old man did all he could with him and got disappointed. What he got isn't his own house and he knows it. He's one man in Oak Park I could work for on the basis of the best I've got in me. He's getting the *"modified* Gospel", when he ought to have got it straight. If God is on the job and not loafing in heaven—there in Mr. Austin would be one client for me.'

'Yes,' laughed Cecil, 'and all you'd need do would be to find him and for him to find you.' Sarcastically, 'A simple matter as things are?'

'Well, I did find him and I could make others like him find me if I had anything to show them. I know what Mr. Austin needs and what he missed. And I believe he missed it because the "Gospel is modified", as you suggest. And yet you defend it and say it is the right thing. Man alive! Isn't making these modifications, taking God away and sitting in his place? We are all given *choice* and left free to choose. We live or die as we are fit to do, to the extent of our natures, only when *free to choose*. Not

78

when somebody is allowing us to choose only what *they* think we want; cheating us out of what we might have but for their interference. And only by such choice, can we fulfil the Law.'

'What Law?' said Cecil. 'That irreligious, inhuman "survival of the fittest"?'

I said 'No', feeling my way to the proper answer. 'No. The process of nature-selection.' I knew I had slipped . . . I tried again—'Well—no—keeping the truest and best of which man is capable where man can use it.'

'If they can find it,' said Cecil. 'How are you going to put it in the show-window?'

'How do I know? That isn't *my* business either.'

'Going to put that up to God?'

'And why not?' I said. 'And look here, Cecil, what's more—I see it now —that's just what's the matter, too, with the Gospel as preached today in churches: Jesus was doing the best He knew how. The truth was in Him. He preached it. But *He*, the Nazarene Carpenter (I wonder if the carpenter wasn't the architect in those days), was modified by His disciples in the next place.

'The disciples were sincere enough and did the best they could but they "modified" Him. Again the preaching was modified by the disciples of those disciples. Again "modified" to suit the "needs of mankind". And not as Jesus or His Father saw those needs. No. Only as your father and my father saw them. Hasn't the sentiment of Jesus become sentimental-ized sentimentality in the mouths of His disciples? Where is there 'clear wine to drink' on any such basis?'

'Who wants clear wine?' said Cecil. 'The water bottle stands beside the chianti on the table. We use it unless we want the linings of our stomachs corroded beyond repair.'

'That won't do! I'm not talking about chianti. That, you said, was made from the skins of grapes anyway. I am talking about Champagne or Moselle or Burgundy or Port—who wants water in real wine?'

'All watered at some time to some extent,' said Cecil. And the discussion had fizzled out.

I began to wonder if, after all, my father's life had not been such a sacrifice to sentimentality, and tried to get it clear. What had the Lloyd-Jones sentimentality done to him? What had it done to me—to them all? To Mother? What was rank sentimentality doing to the life of the world?

Next Sunday, it had begun with Catherine. Sometimes evenings I had taken her home from church. One chill evening, I tried to put my coat on her to keep her warm but she indignantly refused to let me. We compro-mised by walking with an arm around each other to keep *both* warm. Sometimes her mother would let us go together to Theodore Thomas' concerts in town. The daughter began to wait for me to sit by her in church, and if I was late, to wait with a vacant place by her side. I would take her home to the Sunday dinner after services.

I told mother about Catherine. She had already heard—Uncle Jenkin probably. And, as now appeared, she had been anxious. The affair *was* conspicuous by now. Kitty had begun to fall off in her school studies. She was being unmercifully teased by her school-fellows. Young people at the church already took us for granted.

Cecil met her occasionally when she came to pick me up at the office. He thought her a gay, charming youngster. She's awfully fond of me, Cecil, I said.

'Well,' he said, 'so am I. So is your mother. So are your sisters. Maybe others would be too, if you gave them a chance. I don't see that *that* gives her any special claim on you, does it? You don't know other girls at all, Frank. What do you know about women by merely knowing Kitty?'

He himself knew few girls. They were much older than I. Uninteresting, I thought. He was such an attractive person I often wondered why he didn't know more interesting ones.

'Why,' I said, 'does anyone have to know *many* if he finds himself at home with one?'

'Did you ever kiss one—except her?'

'How do you know I've kissed her?'

'I'm clairvoyant,' he said. 'Didn't you know?'

'No, but . . .'

Cecil interrupted me: 'Exactly, "*but*". You are going into this thing heels over head. "At home with her." " *At home*",' he repeated excitedly. 'Yes, that's what I was afraid of. Don't you know she's a child? *You're* a child? Before you can construct any family life worth having you must know what women are?'

'So you mean I have to kiss and *take* women, to study women before I know what I want? Is that what you are driving at? I can understand how a man might kiss a girl in a kind of game. But—how can a man *take* a girl he doesn't love and doesn't want to live with?'

He looked out of the office window, his gentle face drooped—didn't answer.

'Cecil, what is it? What's the matter, old man? I want to know.'

'No use. Why talk? No one ever listened in this world—in these matters.' Bitterly: 'No, not since time began. I see where you are going. And your best friend can't stop you, nor can anyone.'

He was so earnest and really sad, I tried to understand the 'danger'. I sat trying to imagine and couldn't. It all seemed beautifully right to me not to have experimented, lucky to have found the one I wanted, who wanted me, without all that wiseacre evil-thinking.

I felt sorry for Cecil. He didn't know; of course he didn't. Poor fellow. Look at the women he knew compared to the glowing Catherine. She was more of a woman than he thought, too. No child at all. Really a very sensible girl. She wanted me to save money and had offered to take care of it for me and was doing it to some extent. And she was sensible and careful about things, whereas—well—in that way I wasn't there at all, as anybody could see.

1. WINSLOW HOUSE. 1893

2. JOSEPH W. HUSSER HOUSE. 1895-6

3. ARTHUR HEURTLEY HOUSE. 1902

4. The first sealed air-conditioned building in the U.S.A. Red brick and Karsota red sandstone

LARKIN COMPANY ADMINISTRATION BUILDING. 1906

5. Office interior. The building is fire-proof. Steel filing system beneath windows. Steel furniture—chairs attached

Then it flashed over me, 'Look here. Have you been talking to mother about this thing?'

'No. She talked to me about it.'

'What did she say?'

'You might ask *her*.'

I was hurt. My own mother talking over my private affairs with my best friend, saying nothing to me. I was angrily ashamed of the situation and began to feel both Catherine and I were betrayed. She now seemed to need my care and protection. A feeling that had been merely warm and affectionate began to deepen.

'Well,' said Cecil, 'let's not quarrel. You couldn't manage an acquaintance with more than one anyway. You are a born "soloist". I know you. You'll have to go it alone in everything all through life. Only why go so desperately fast? You'll go far enough soon enough. Why try to put into a month what would last any reasonable fellow a year at least? I wish I had more of your sensibility and steam, Frank, and you had more of my sense and laziness.

'Don't feel I'm unsympathetic or that I am saying anything against Catherine. For all anybody knows she may be just the girl for you.'

On the way home to Oak Park that evening I was going over the scene I knew coming with mother.

I got home and sat silent at supper with mother, the girls, and Miss Chapin. Mother's looks inquiring silently. Upstairs in my room after supper she came in to see what had gone wrong with the day.

'What is it, my son?'

'Mother! Why go around to Cecil about Kitty and me?'

She didn't even look surprised. 'Why, indeed?' she said and smiled.

It didn't seem a smiling matter to me, so I burst out with—'Why all this anxiety and fuss over a perfectly natural thing? What's it all about anyway? You are making nature monstrous. Where *is* the sense in it?'

'Frank, have you thought of the consequences to this young girl of your singling her out to the exclusion of all others?'

She had begun on a vulnerable spot. Her first shot went home. 'No, of course I haven't. But isn't she the best judge of what that means to her? I don't see how I can judge for her. And if she can't, how about her father and mother?'

'Her mother's in trouble with her over this already. It seems beyond her mother's control.'

'So you went to see her mother too?'

'Yes. Catherine, accustomed to having her own way, has been giving her mother trouble. She seems to be unreasonable, as you are.'

'Well, that proves, doesn't it, that it's all all right for her? So why this worry, anxiety, anguish, curiosity and prying, praying and gossip, to make a perfectly natural thing scandalous? I don't get it at all. I've never seen *you* like this, mother. It doesn't seem like you. You have always said, "If you have to choose between the good and the true, choose truth." And, God! Mother—what in this matter *is* Truth?'

'Don't swear, my son.'

This was too much! 'Swearing? What is the name of the almighty God for if not to be called upon in extremity? I *mean* it. I think I see a conspiracy to force Catherine and me to give up everything fine and happy in our relationship and think of getting married. What a state of mind! Is only one thing possible to boys and girls in this world? Only one thing that everyone sees, thinks about, watches and believes? Who made things so damned fearsome and artificial anyway?'

'Frank, you are swearing again before your mother.'

' "Damned" is swearing, too? Then how get along on the farm? "Damned", a wonderful, necessary word! Can you dispose of your feelings about contrary things without that word? What other word have we got in English? Is "damned" swearing just because all extremes are profane?'

'In your present frame of mind,' said mother, 'I see no use in talking to you, my boy.'

'Just what old man Cecil said. Why, all of you are ready to weep, wring your hands and wail!' Mother quietly got up and left.

But, just the same, she had done what she had set out to do. 'Have you thought of the consequences to this young girl of singling her out to the exclusion of all others?' It would seem something had been left out of my education. The social instinct.

After this turmoil I saw the object of all the contention but once. Something had been spoiled. I felt a sort of pity for Catherine and shame for myself. I said, 'Catherine, everybody is anxious and unhappy about us. Maybe I *am* doing you harm by being with you so much. "They" say so anyway.'

'How perfectly ridiculous,' said she. 'I've had pretty nearly everything myself but an out-and-out spanking. If I can stand it don't you think you can?'

'Of course, I can. But you don't see. They are right in one thing. You don't know any boys but me and . . .'

'I do, too; know dozens!' And she started to name them.

'No. You know what I mean.'

'Anyhow, I'm not coming down here so often and I am going to keep away in church.'

This from her: 'Well, let them have their way for awhile—I will write to you.'

'Yes,' I said, 'there can't be harm in that.'

A week later I learned by a note from her she had been sent to visit relatives in Mackinac. For three months!

I began to see that in spite of all the talk about Nature, 'natural' was the last thing in this world they would let you be if they could prevent it. What did they mean when 'they' used the word nature? Just some sentimental feeling about animals, grass and trees, the out-of-doors? But how

82

about the nature of wood, glass and iron—internal nature? The nature of boys and girls. The nature of law? Wasn't that Nature? Wasn't nature in this sense the very nature of God?

Somehow I had always thought when I read the word 'nature' in a book or used it in my own mind that it was meant that interior way. Not the other measly, external way.

'Fools!' They have no sentiment for nature. What they really mean by 'nature' is just a sentimentalizing of the rudimentary animal. That's why they suffer all this confusion of ideas and make all these senseless rules— foolish regulations and unwise laws.

'What do "*they*" work them out for? Do they really *know* anything at all?'

Now thrown more in on myself by Catherine's being away, I brought the work in Silsbee's office to bar only to find it more than ever wanting in any true meaning to the life of the folk who owned and lived in them. It was all pose, that's what it was. Aimed to be uncommon—unusual— pictorial. Yes, it *was* sheer ordinary sentimentality.

ADLER AND SULLIVAN

Wilcox, preacher's son number four, came excitedly in one day and leaned on my table. 'Wright,' he said, looking around to see that no one heard, 'I know where you can get a good job if you want it.'

'Where?'

'Adler and Sullivan.'

My heart jumped. I had already formed a high idea of Adler and Sullivan. They were foremost in Chicago. Radical—going strong on independent lines. Burnham and Root their only rivals. 'How do you know, Wilcox?'

'Well, I've just been there myself. Sullivan turned me down. He's looking for someone to make the finish drawings for the interior of the Auditorium. I can't make them, but you can. I told him about you and he asked me to send you over to see him.'

'You did, Wilcox? I . . .' Then I thought of Cecil. I called him. Silsbee was away. We sat in his private office to talk.

'Go on, Frank,' he said, 'you've got pretty much all there is here to get. Sullivan is the coming man in the West. He may be just what you need. Anyway, no harm to try and we won't get lost.'

I swept some of my work together and went over to the Borden Block, top floor.

'Would Mr. Adler do?' Mr. Sullivan was about to leave for St. Louis, Architects' Convention.

'No. Mr. Sullivan wanted to see me—it will only be for a moment.'

'Name?'

'Wright.'

The easy-natured old clerk came back, held the gate open, and I came in.

Mr. Sullivan was a small man immaculately dressed in brown. His out-

standing feature his amazing big brown eyes. Took me in at a glance.
Everything I felt, even to my most secret thoughts.

'Ah yes! The young man Wilcox mentioned. What have you there?' he
said.

I unrolled the drawings on the table. He looked them over.

'You know what I want you for, do you?'

I said, 'Yes.'

'These aren't the kind of drawings I would like to see, but . . . no time
now. I'll be back Friday morning. Make some drawings of ornament or
ornamental details and bring them back then. I want to look at them.'

He looked at me kindly and *saw* me. I was sure of that much.

'Of course I will,' I said eagerly, and left.

The door to the big draughting room was open. At work there must
have been twenty men or more as near as I could see. Whatever the
number was I was going to make one more. A large, tall, rather ungainly
young man with a pointed head, black, bristling pompadour and thin,
black beard looked at me as I stood a moment in the door, his eyes a good
deal like Mr. Sullivan's, I thought. He looked too big for his age and the
black beard seemed out of place on his face. Evidently he was foreman.

'Looking for Mr. Adler?' he said.

'No,' I said. 'Just looking at you.' And I walked away before his astonished expression could change. It was Paul Mueller, the office foreman,
growing a beard to look the part.

I went back to Cecil, elated.

'The job's mine.'

'How do you know?'

'How does one know anything? He *saw*, I tell you, that I can do what
he wants done. Making the drawings for him is just a formality.'

'Just the same,' said Cecil, 'I'd make them as well as I could.'

'Of course I will, but it will be all the easier and I'll do it better now because I know I have the job.'

Cecil gave up. It was hopeless.

'What will Sullivan pay you?'

'Forgot to mention it, but I'll ask for $25.00. And it will be all right.'

When I got to Oak Park that evening after telling mother the good
news I went to work on a drawing board in the room where I had T-square
and triangle; but I used them only for guide lines. I was going to show
Louis H. Sullivan what my free hand could do.

I took some of Silsbee's own drawings of mantels and ornament and
drew them my own way, directly and simply with clear definition. Not
sentimental or 'sketchy'. Silsbee's way was magnificent, his strokes were
like standing corn in the field waving in the breeze. So in some few drawings I imitated his style, just to show I could do that. Then I improvised
ornaments such as I had seen on the Adler and Sullivan buildings. I had
studied them a little since I learned of their work. Three o'clock when I
got to bed. Next evening the same thing. Another evening I took the

84

onion-skin tracings of ornamental details I had made from Owen Jones, mostly Gothic, and made them over into 'Sullivanesque'.

When Friday morning came I had a lot of things to show. I got to Mr. Sullivan.

I took the work out in order:

'First: imitations of Silsbee,' I said.

'I see. You've traced Silsbee's drawings to show me?'

'They are not traced. I drew them. You see? They are not on tracing paper.'

'But you might have transferred them.'

I laughed. 'Too much trouble.'

He looked me over with that glance of his that went clear through.

'Second: imitations of Sullivan.'

'Well! You couldn't have traced those. Not half bad,' he said to himself, scratching his scalp with the sharp point of his lead pencil. Some white dandruff fell on the drawings. He blew it off.

'Third: improvised Gothic from Owen Jones.'

'Owen Jones? Who is he?'

I thought him joking. I said, 'You know, *The Grammar of Ornament*?'

He looked puzzled. 'Anything like Raguenet?'

'I don't know Raguenet.'

'Oh, yes, of course,' he said. 'I do remember the book. So you are trying to turn Gothic ornaments into my style just to please me, are you?'

I said, 'You see how easy it is to do it.' And I saw I had displeased him. Unconsciously I had reduced his ornament to a mere 'sentimentality'.

'Fourth: here are some things, perhaps original—I don't know.'

He was immediately interested. Said nothing. He was sitting on a high stool at his draughting board where he had been drawing. After looking over the drawings he made no comment but drew aside the cover sheet from his own board. I gasped with delight. 'Oh!' I said, 'and you asked me to show you mine?' He seemed to have forgotten me now and went on drawing. I was standing there thinking—'If Silsbee's touch was like standing corn waving in the fields, Sullivan's was like the passion vine in full bloom.' I wondered what mine might be like if I developed one some day. I wanted to ask but, suddenly, 'You've got the right kind of touch, you'll do,' he said. 'How much money have you been getting?'

'Not enough,' I said.

'Well, how much is enough?'

'Twenty-five dollars.'

He smiled, for I might have asked forty dollars and got it.

'All right, but understand you've got to stick until the drawings for the Auditorium are finished. But I don't mean you are to work for that salary during all that time. We'll come to an arrangement after you take hold. Can you come Monday morning?'

'I can come,' I said, 'for there is not much work at Silsbee's. He'll be glad to let me go.'

That was how I got into the Adler and Sullivan office and how I first met the master for whose influence, affection and comradeship I have never ceased to feel gratitude.

Elated, I went back to Silsbee's and to Cecil. Cecil was glad and sad, too, as I could see.

'Go in and tell the old man,' was what he said.

I went in.

'Mr. Silsbee.'

'Well?' wheeling around from his desk.

'I haven't been doing very well for you or myself for some weeks.'

'I've noticed it.'

'I've asked Mr. Sullivan for a job.'

'Did he give you one?'

'Yes, he gave me one that will last a long time, I believe.'

'When are you going?'

'Next Monday, if you don't need me?'

He thought a moment. 'This doesn't seem quite up to your usual standard, does it, Wright?'

'You were away when the chance came. I was going to wait to come to you first, but I dreaded to wait for many reasons. The chance came unexpectedly. But if you need me I would stay.'

'No! I don't need you. I wanted to know your reason for falling down on your principles—that's all.'

'Mr. Silsbee—I was so sure my usefulness here was ended and you would be relieved.'

'But is that the point?'

'Not the point at all. No! I am wrong. Dead wrong. I should never have gone to Mr. Sullivan without first talking with you. It's clear enough.'

'Never mind, Wright. You may like it with Sullivan. Not my style but maybe a genius, who knows?'

I hated to leave that way. No matter what I felt about Silsbee's shortcomings I adored him just the same. And I knew I left him like any tramp draughtsman when he had been really handsome to me. What could I say? I sat helpless. Nothing at all to say. If he saw my face, and I guess he did, he must have forgiven me. If he can see into my heart now, he will see what he saw in my face then. I got out.

I never saw Silsbee again.

LET THE DEAD BURY THEIR DEAD

Has every forward movement in human lives as it is realized, its own peculiar pang, I wonder.

The cause of this 'pang' was definitely a fault of mine. I might have waited to talk with Silsbee at the proper moment and have quit with none.

As usual, I had taken too much for granted.

And yet, do the trees know pain when top branches float leaves on the breeze? Shut the sun from the branches below so those branches must die?

Do perennial plants suffer too, when they rise up in spring through the dead growth of last year, rise to greater glory and abundance this year?

Does the snake slough off its skin with regret, do you think?

Does each stage of our own interior growth cost enough vital energy in suffering so that our span is measured—the allotment of our lives' duration made by the number of pangs we can sustain at each successive forward step or upward movement?

Must human beings eventually die of the pangs of growth?

When we see a delphinium taller, more resplendent than the rest, a tree more superb than the others, a human being in character and achievement outstanding from his fellows—are we to think: what magnificent resistance to suffering was there!

'*Let the dead bury their dead*' was said by the gentlest, wisest and most awful of men.

Is this merely a human weakness or a human fault that growth, then, should have its pang? Or is it all merely the natural evil consequence of the so-called virtues which man in self-love is earnestly making for himself?

I see that I left Silsbee as I left college, and as later, with anguish, I left home—for the same reason, with the same suffering, the same hope, obedient to a principle at work in me taking its toll to this hour as I write. Old as man's moral life is this urge to *grow*. Listen to the Apostle Paul: 'Brethren, I count not myself to have apprehended: but this one thing I do, forgetting those things which are behind and reaching forth to those things which are before.'

And I, too, whether I would or not, like Lieber Meister was going to ask of my generation in my own way, 'Do ye reject the commandment of God, that ye may keep your traditions?' and this in order that my generation should realize that traditions may be kept in the letter after the spirit had fled, only by such rejection.

Louis Sullivan, Lieber Meister, had come to this understanding. He was already at grips with the joys and sorrows of this affirmation—in action.

Monday morning. Some little time before nine o'clock in the draughting room of Adler and Sullivan. The 'firm' then occupied most of the top floor of the old Borden Block, corner of Randolph and Dearborn Streets, now torn down. Paul Mueller was there. No one else. 'Where can I get you?' He looked about. Fixed upon one place—changed his mind several times—finally landed me against the south wall between two large windows. Good place but too closely surrounded by other tables. One of a crowd. Not like the studio-atmosphere of Silsbee's. Might have been in the rank and file of any large business office where many clerks were working.

'I'll have Anton "stretch" some boards for you,' he said, calling the office cub. Said the cub, Anton, 'How many?'

'Ach! I didn't tell you. What you can find loose. What you can find

87

loose, loose, LOOSE,' he shouted. Mueller was awkward, energetic, emotional and under something of a strain? Too young, I was sure, to have any business with that beard.

'What did Mr. Sullivan tell you to do?' he said.

'He didn't tell me.'

'Wait, then—wait till he comes. I've got enough to do without what he wants. He wants you for the designs anyway. My work is construction. I used to work for Tsilsbee myself. Yes, Tsilsbee, he is a great designer.' I loved the way he said 'Tsilsbee' and wanted to hear him say it again. 'Three years ago, Tsilsbee—he wanted an engineer. He took me. Then I came to Mr. Adler over here.'

'How long have you been foreman?'

'More than a year.'

'Like it?' I said.

'Ach!' he said, 'too much to do. What is it? Mr. Adler wants me. . . . Yes, I like it.'

I saw my question was stupid. The men were filing in by now and he went to his table by the entrance door where I had first seen him. Mueller almost never sat down.

Tony, the office cub, had found several boards 'loose, loose, LOOSE' with the manila-paper stretch in general use there. I laid one good one on my table, delighting in the paper surface. A smooth untouched sheet of fine paper is one of the fairest of sights. My back was to the room so I did not see the fellows as they filed in.

Evidently they were a noisy crowd. They chaffed each other a lot as they settled down. A few remarks evidently intended for me. But there was some discipline in the office apparently, for they were soon quietly at work. Tired of looking at the paper I looked to the left. Got their names afterwards. Next table to mine Jean Agnas, a clean-faced Norseman. To the right Eisendrath—apparently stupid. Jewish. Behind me to the left Ottenheimer—alert, apparently bright. Jew too. Turned around to survey the group. Isbell, Jew? Gaylord, no—not. Weydert, Jew undoubtedly. Directly behind, Weatherwax. Couldn't make him out. In the corner Andresen—Swedish. Several more Jewish faces. Of course—I thought, because Mr. Adler himself must be a Jew. I had not seen him yet. I marked time, feeling alone in all that strange crowd, drawing on the margin of my 'stretch'. Had a notion to call up Cecil to say hello and hear his voice.

About 10.30 the door opened. Mr. Sullivan walked slowly in with a haughty air, handkerchief to his nose. Paid no attention to anyone. No good mornings? No. No words of greeting as he went from desk to desk. Saw me waiting for him. Came forward at once with a pleasant 'Ah! Wright, there you are,' and the office had my name. And evidently, in Sullivan's unusually pleasant address, also 'my number'.

'Here, Wright,' lifting a board on to my table, 'take this drawing of mine. A duffer I fired Saturday spoiled it. Re-draw it and ink it in.' And they all knew what I was there for. He wandered about some more in a

88

haughty sort of way seeming to have no respect at all for anybody there except perhaps Paul Mueller. My eyes had been following him when he was observable. Finally he stopped just behind me at Weatherwax's table.

'What the hell do you call that?' he said in a loud voice, without even bending to look. I had turned my head in time to see the man flush angrily and straighten up.

'What the hell do you call that?' Mr. Sullivan said, louder than before. The whole room was now waiting for Weatherwax.

'What do *I* call it?' he said, evidently hot, as though struck by a lash. 'Hell! It's a church, can't you see? *Christ!* What do you want?'

With trembling hands he was undoing the strings of his little black apron as he spoke. With violence he threw his pencil down on the board, grabbed the leather case of drawing instruments and deliberately walked out.

Mr. Sullivan, as though he had heard nothing, changed not a hair, looked a moment at the unhappy drawing while he blew his nose into a fresh handkerchief, then turned on his heel to the next table or two—I could see the cringing fear of him wherever he went—and walked slowly out of the room as he had come in, without another word. There had been no sound in the draughting room during the episode. Evidently all were used to something of the kind. When he had gone out there was a rustle, whispering and low talking which Mueller put down with warning looks.

My reaction to this one was, 'I'm afraid I won't last long here after all!' Evidently no one did where he was concerned. And then, I thought, 'This is not the real Sullivan. I've seen a different one.'

What was Dankmar Adler like? Just before noon he opened the same door through which Mr. Sullivan had entered. A personality, short-built and heavy, like an old Byzantine church. He was not gutty, just broadly and solidly built, one to inspire others with confidence in his power at once. I felt comforted.

He walked with deliberate, heavy-legged, flat-footed steps over to Mueller's desk and stood talking to him. The while his deep bass voice rumbled, he went about with his hands stuck under his coat-tails, looking with a frown at drawings. A word of greeting occasionally. He would sit down at the board and make suggestions in a fatherly sort of way. Finally he got to me. Looked at me pleasantly from his deep-set eyes under the bushy brows.

'Hello!'—kindly. 'Sullivan's new man?'

'Yes, sir!'

He sat down on the stool I had vacated to stand up to him. As he put one leg over the other, I noticed his enormous mannish feet. They spread flat like the foundations for some heavy building.

'Sullivan needs help, Wright. It's difficult to find anyone to "catch on" to what he wants. I hope you will succeed!'

He got up abruptly almost as soon as he had sat down and, as though suddenly remembering something, went heavily out among the draughting tables like a barge making its way between river craft. Dankmar was the name for him.

Thus began an association lasting nearly seven years. Mr. Sullivan had been interested and interesting. His drawings a delight to work upon and out. His manner toward me was markedly different from his manner toward the others. Mark me it might, and mark me it did. I soon found my place in that office had to be fought for.

The work was going well. I could do it. The master was pleased. And I had got his permission to get George Elmslie over from Silsbee's to help me and incidentally make it a little less lonesome for me there. George wasn't a minister's son but ought to have been. He was coming over in a few days. This evident favouritism of the master together with my own natural tendency to mind my own business, coupled with a distaste for most of the Adler and Sullivan men, had, in the course of a few weeks, set them against me. I was unpopular from that first day. And I was baited in various ways. My hair of course. My dress, a bit too individual, I suppose. There would be casual conversation behind me with unmistakable reference to me. Studied interference with my work. The gang had evidently combined to 'get' me. Their phrase. Mueller didn't see much of it all. He was an innocent soul. It was kept pretty well out of his way. I couldn't say anything about it if I would. And I wouldn't if I could.

There was a back room devoted to blue-printing, where Isbell, Gaylord and a few others would go at noon to eat their lunch and box a few rounds. Isbell was supposed to be pretty good, if talk meant anything. And Gaylord was candidate for pugilistic honours in the First Regiment Armoury.

They wanted me to 'box'. Evidently the longish-hair, flowing tie, and fastidious clothes gave them the idea I would be easy, a good spectacle.

I saw I would have to do something to square myself with that crowd.

I had boxed some and had no doubt about my wind or ability to stand punishment. But not much science. So, one noon, I went to see old Colonel Monsterry who had a fencing and boxing academy in the old Athenaeum next door, and engaged for a course of twelve lessons, all twelve to be given in the course of two weeks. I told the old Frenchman I wanted to learn how to hit hard and stop body-blows. I could already take pretty good care of my head.

But why not the foils? 'It is so much more a gentleman's game,' he said.

'I'm not involved with gentlemen. I've got a battle on hand with a pretty tough bunch. I want some rough training.'

'All right,' he said as he handed me the gloves. I put them on and put up my guard. 'No,' he said, 'college boy! This way,' and he put one hand down, the other out in front like a feeler and provocative. 'Now, look out.' He struck at me a number of times to see where I was. 'Not so bad. Now, I'm going to hit you,' he said. 'Go ahead.' He did, and the jolt jarred me to the heels. I thought if it was that easy to reach me I was far from that back room. Took the bout for an hour. Felt wonderful as I got out from under the shower into my clothes and back to the office.

Meanwhile the nagging went on. I had almost the two weeks of training. It wasn't a case of getting into condition, I knew. I was in better condition than either of the office stars.

COMBAT

And the daily practice with the old Colonel had, by now, taught me all he knew. I don't think it was much because he was a swordsman, not a boxer. But it might be enough. I could now take care of myself fairly well. I liked it and began to look forward with some pleasure to the event.

I looked at Isbell's heavy, prominent nose sometimes and thought—what a mark! He was a loud-voiced, blond-haired, well-built, conceited fellow, always keeping up a running fire of jibes and jokes when Mueller was out. Jaunty. And undoubtedly strong. Gaylord was awkward and slow, but stronger.

About two months had gone by since I had entered the office and had steadily minded my own business. But the taunting had grown, and was quite open now. As the noon rustle began just before the men went out, I turned to Isbell. 'Boxing this noon?' He looked puzzled. 'Sure. Coming in to look on?' 'Yes, I might as well,' I said.

'All right. Why look on? Put on the gloves! We won't hurt you.'

I hesitated. 'You fellows must be pretty close to professionals, practising in there all the time. But—well, all right. I might as well.'

I saw the look of triumph, winks passing between the office strong men. The other members of the gang were smiling, but incredulous. I went in alone. But they had their gang, six or seven of them. Coats, vests and collars were off. I drew on the gloves—dirty ones. Isbell wanted the first 'crack' at me and put on another pair, also dirty.

I knew nothing about his style, but struck him—on the nose—just as he fairly got up his guard. The blood came into his face and his blue eyes went hard and cold. He came after me heavily. I saw he was a slugger.

So I let him slug.

Stopped him, when I could, took it when I had to. Standing up to him and backing away, continuously drawing him on. He was breathing hard, rather white. I had taken it easily, good wind anyhow.

The crowd so fresh at first, was a little flat now. Not just what they expected.

'Time!' called Gaylord. 'Time? Not yet,' I said. 'This is a one-round contest,' and I banged Isbell on the nose, hard this time, with my left.

The blood came. First blood for me!

But no applause.

And now Isbell was out for blood. We rushed back and forth, crashing around the room; the fellows raced out of the way knocking over everything that could come loose. Raging Isbell!

Again I got him on the nose. Soon he was a sight. My lip was cut and bleeding, but I sucked in the blood and swallowed it. I felt a wonderful lift. Still had the steam I started with.

'Izzy' was getting the worst of it and the gang saw it.

'Time!' yelled Gaylord. 'Time, Hell,' I said, 'this is a one-round contest,' and I banged Izzy on the nose again. The abnormally large nose that had begun to swell. This was too much for Billy Gaylord. 'Here, Izzy! Give me those gloves. It's my turn now.'

'Yes? Your turn now?' I said. I was waked up and felt nothing could ever stop me. I stood eagerly striking one fist into the open palm of the other while Gaylord put on the dirty gloves. 'Billy' leaned way back, rocking to and fro, crouching low, weaving his arms in and out continually. Crafty. I couldn't wait for him for my blood was up by now and while Billy Gaylord had been comparatively decent, and I half liked him, this cutting in was a dirty trick. I was going to beat all the hell there ever was in him out of him, or die trying.

So I stepped up to him like a flash and slapped him down on the top of the head three times with all my might with my open glove. My foot was behind his and as he pulled back to recover he went over backward into the gang. He got up red and angry. 'That's a hell of a way to box. Two fouls,' he said.

'Fouls, nothing,' I retorted. 'Who said this was a boxing match? What are you doing in here before I finished with Isbell? Come on, damn you, foul *me*. And damn you all, anyway. You wanted to get me in here to do me up and have a laugh. Now come and get it, take your gloves off, you coward.' I threw mine away.

This wasn't quite what they looked for. The crowd interfered.

'Aw, pass him up, Billy. He's crazy-mad and wants to fight. It won't do in here. Let's fix it up for some other time.'

'All right,' I said. 'You fix it! A fine sporting gang you are. If one of you can't win, you put another in on top of that one,' and I went out, too excited to want anything to eat.

The afternoon was quiet. Ominously quiet.

I knew I had lost my case by getting mad. If I had coolly taken Gaylord on, unfair as it was for him to cut in on Isbell, and had good-naturedly made a good showing with him, it would have probably been all over in my favour. By getting angry and sailing into them I made enemies of them all.

Then and there I made up my mind to stay in that office till I could fire every one of the gang, and said so. Ottenheimer, the ringleader, an active, intelligent little Jew was not present. He got the report from the gang next day and I heard him say, 'Ooi, the god-damn son of a bitch! Leave him to me.'

I might as well finish the story. Now I was subjected to the refined cruelty of Ottenheimer's open taunts and skilful innuendoes. Ottenheimer evidently thought he had a drag with 'the old man', that is to say, Mr. Adler. But it was easier to stand the isolation even though it had become downright enmity, now. I had George Elmslie at my side to talk to, a sort of understudy to help in my work. George was a tall, slim, slow-thinking, but refined Scottish lad who had never been young. Faithful, very quiet and diffident. I liked him. I couldn't get along without somebody—ever.

We were both staying in to finish some work for the blue-printer one noon, some weeks after the boxing-bout failure. Ottenheimer, at the table behind me and over one to the left, staying to study for Beaux Arts exams he was soon to take. He was whistling and jibing as was his habit. He had thrown my hat down the stair-well just the day before. He was insolent always. 'You're just a Sullivan toady anyway, Wright. We all know it.' I had stood, without flinching, far worse than that.

But it was 'time'. I laid down my pencil, swung around on the stool and looked at him. He sat at his table, a heavy-bodied, short-legged, pompadoured, conceited, red-faced Jew, wearing gold glasses. His face, now red as a turkey-cock's wattles. 'I think I've had enough from you,' I said. I got up and walked slowly over to him and without realizing he was wearing glasses, or hesitating, struck him square, full in the face with my right hand, knocking him from his stool to the floor, smashing his glasses. I might have blinded him.

With a peculiar animal scream—I've heard something like it since from a Japanese mad with *sake*, but never anything else—he jumped for the knife, a scratcher-blade with a long handle, lying by his board. Half-blinded, he came at me with it.

I caught his head under my arm as he came, and was trying hard to put him out, while with his free arm behind me, he was stabbing away at the back of my neck and shoulders. But his head was too close—tight against my side. Upsetting stools and overturning tables, George, white-faced and scared, looked on. I could feel the blood running down my back and legs into my shoes. They 'cheeped' as though I'd been walking in puddles.

Finally, I wound my right hand in the back of his collar and with all the strength of despair, hurled him away from me. He went staggering, toppling backward across the draughting room to the opposite wall, struck with a heavy bang against the door leading to the next room and went down—but not out. He had dropped the knife near by where he fell. He got up on his feet again and with that same curious animal scream grabbed the knife and came on—a blood-thirsty little beast. Quick as a flash, as he came toward me, I grabbed the long, broad-bladed T-square on my board by the end of the long blade, swung it with all my might, catching Ottie with the edge of the blade beside his neck just above the collar. The cross-head snapped off and flew clear down the length of the room.

The knife dropped from his hand as he wavered a moment. Then he wilted, slowly, into a senseless heap on the floor like a sail coming down.

My heart sank. 'Good God! George! Get some water quick.' George seemed paralysed. It had all happened in a minute. 'Wake up. Quick, man! Come on, George! Don't you see?'

Slow-moving George got back with some water in a dipper and I threw it in Ottie's face. No sign. 'More, George.' I threw more in his face.—He sighed, opened his eyes. I stood there, waiting and trembling. 'Are you badly hurt, Ottie?' No answer. Blinked—seemed to be 'going out' again.

'Water!'

'No! Quit . . . I'm all right,' from Ottie.

He got up by degrees. Stood white and shaking. 'I'll pay you for this, Wright,' he choked. 'You'll get yours for this. You'll see.'

He went back to his desk, shakily gathered up his instruments as I sat smiling, watching him. It was good to see him move, for I thought I had killed him in that wild moment. I never saw Ottenheimer again. He had intended to go to the Beaux Arts in Paris before long. He went without ever coming back to the office.

The affair had taken place at noon, when everyone was out for lunch but George, Ottie and me.

My shoes were full of blood. 'George! Call Cecil. I want to see how badly that little cuss has cut me.'

George called him. He happened to be in and came the five blocks in no time. He pulled off my coat and pushed my shirt down to the waist. 'Man!' he said, counting, 'you're stabbed on the shoulder blades in eleven places, to the bone, all of them. Lucky for you none on the spine. But near it on each side. I don't think any one of them is serious. Let's go over to Arthur's and get them dressed.' Arthur was a physician, his brother.

Today I wear the welts of Ottie's fancy work on my shoulder blades. But not because I turned my back on him.

The disappearance of Ottenheimer broke the persecution for a time. Isbell had been laid off. Gaylord was rather friendly now.

Billy Gaylord was a decent chap on the whole. But occasionally I would surprise sullen looks from Eisendrath and Weydert. I had them to deal with, later. Nor did Mueller or Mr. Sullivan know about the feud until several years after I had finally cleaned up the Adler and Sullivan gang.

THE MASTER

The Master's very walk at this time bore dangerous resemblance to a strut. He had no respect whatever for a draughtsman, as he more than once confided to me in later years. Nor, as far as I could see, respect for anyone else except the big chief—Dankmar Adler, whom he trusted and loved—and Paul Mueller.

None of his contemporaries ever won from Louis Sullivan much but contempt—except H. H. Richardson. Richardson he condescended to criticize, and he was not so hard on John Wellborn Root—as on all the others. Evidently he liked him.

But Richardson at this time had a decided effect upon Sullivan's work, as may be seen in the outside of the Auditorium Building, the Walker Wholesale and other buildings. The effect is unmistakable, although he seemed to hold Richardson in no very high esteem.

I believe Sullivan, the Master, used to talk to me to express his own feelings and thoughts, regardless, forgetting me often. But I could follow him. And the radical sense of things I had already formed intuitively got

94

great encouragement from him. In fact the very sense of things I had been feeling as rebellion was at work in him.

He was absorbed in what seemed extravagant worship of Wagner at the time. I could not share this but I could understand. He would often try to sing the leitmotifs for me and describe the scenes to which they belonged, as he sat at my drawing board. He adored Whitman, as I did. And, explain it however you can, was deep in Herbert Spencer. He gave Spencer's *Synthetic Philosophy* to me to take home and read. He himself had just written *Inspiration*. He read it to me. I thought it had a kind of baying at the moon. Again too sentimental.

I never liked his writing in those early days. Here again was this insidious sentimentality showing even in him. What had been suspicion now began to ripen into rebellion against sentimentality in general.

Soon, the Auditorium finished, other work came on—Pueblo Opera House (since burned down), Salt Lake City Hotel, foundations laid, but never built—one of the office tragedies. I worked hard on the plans with him.

From the very beginning my T-square and triangle were easy media of expression for my geometrical sense of things. But, at the time, Sullivanian ornament was efflorescence pure and simple. Mr. Sullivan would still talk of John Edelman. He had known him in Paris and had visited him in New York. John Edelman was his most respected critic, not to say teacher. I conceived a respect for Edelman, knowing no more than this about him. I have a number of drawings made by Louis Sullivan in Paris and dedicated to John Edelman.

Whenever the Master would rely upon me for a detail I would mingle his sensuous efflorescence with some geometric design, because, I suppose, I could do nothing else so well. And, too, that way of working to me seemed to hold the surface, give needed contrast, be more architectural. Again—less sentimental. But I couldn't say this to him and I wasn't sure.

Often he would pick me up on this point—and try to 'bring me alive', as he said, until I could make designs in his manner so well that toward the end of his life he would sometimes mistake my drawings for his own.

I became a good pencil in the Master's hand, and at a time when he sorely needed one. And because I could be this to him he had more freedom now than he had enjoyed before.

At this time Healy and Millet were his comrades. The three men had known one another in Paris. Sullivan spent much of his time in their company and in the company of Larry Donovan of the 'Yale and Towne'.

CATHERINE

About this time (I was now twenty) I wanted to marry. I told him so.
'Who is the girl?'
'A young girl—still in Hyde Park High School—Catherine. She's seventeen years old. I met her at All Souls Church.'
'Ah-ha! So soon.'

'They all think it too soon, and object!'

'They would,' he said.

'I have no visible means of support for one thing.'

'No? Well . . . we can fix that up. How about a contract? Adler!' he called.

Adler came.

'Wright wants to get married,—no visible means of support. What do you say to a five-year contract?'

'All right,' said Adler. 'You fix it, Sullivan!' And he went out—his usual exit—as though suddenly remembering something that demanded instant attending to.

Meanwhile, as fellowship was taking its course in apprenticeship in the offices of Adler and Sullivan in the Auditorium Tower, let us go back to another fellowship—go back to the girl in the Hyde Park High School.

You have already had a glimpse of our first meetings, the struggle with the circumstance of family that had now led to this announcement to Lieber Meister.

This other phase of fellowship—the sunny-haired, tall, slenderly handsome high-school girl, now seventeen, was the engaging Catherine herself.

She walked with a kind of light-hearted gaiety: mass of red curls, rather short, bobbing in the breeze. White skin. Cheeks rosy. Blue-eyed, frank and impulsive. Generous to see and to me.

'Kitty,' idol of the Tobin household still had pretty much her own way about everything. And everyone except White Grandma.

After the stabbing I received as my share in that row at the office I had gone directly to her at Kenwood. There had been no mention of love—or marriage, no proposal. Why talk about it? It was all a matter of course, so far as that went—sometime . . .

But Catherine, recently back from the North where she had been sent, was quite changed. She was thinner and pale. Her blue eyes were not so happy now, her manner was less gay than usual. She would fall silent. Listless.

And for some time past, I myself had felt that we were in a false position. Catherine was doing nothing much in school. I knew 'Kitty' was running the gauntlet there with the school girls who knew of her attachment to me. I knew because I saw the drawing of a large-eyed kitty— with the legend 'Perfectly Frank' beneath. They had sent it to her from school.

And at home, too, though holding her own with all but 'White Grandma', she was under her discipline. With no knowledge at all we had come to the boy and girl intimacy, no longer satisfied with sheepish looks and perfunctory visiting or playing or talk or music.

Freedom is necessary to any beauty in any fellowship. Otherwise it becomes something mean and shameful by implication. It was shameful even to suspect we were being watched. So I decided to clear it all up.

The consequence of this announcement to Lieber Meister now enabled

96

6. General view

DARWIN
D. MARTIN
HOUSE.
1906

7. Passage con-
necting the con-
servatory with
the house

8. Concrete monolith throughout; exterior treated to expose gravel aggregate. First expression of interior space as the reality of the building

UNITY CHURCH. 1906

9. Organ and choir screen of the auditorium. Sand-finished walls. Wooden light fixtures with exposed, silk-covered wiring

a boy and girl courtship lasting a year to end in marriage. Protests—sensible as well as sentimental ones, still. They were there. But, withstanding all, marriage!

Young husband-to-be just twenty-one, the young wife-to-be not yet eighteen.

Wedding on a rainy day. More resembled a funeral. The sentimentality I was learning to dread came into full flower. The heavens weeping out of doors—all weeping indoors. Mother of the groom fainting. Father of the bride in tears. Pastor performing—the now ceremonious uncle—affected likewise himself.

I turned to Mr. Sullivan with a new idea. 'Mr. Sullivan, if you want me to work for you as long as five years, couldn't you lend me enough money to build a little house, and let me pay you back so much each month—taken out of my pay envelope?'

Mr. Sullivan—it seemed—had a good deal of money of his own at the time. He took me to his lawyer, Felsenthal. The contract was duly signed, and then the Master went with me—'the pencil in his hand'—to Oak Park to see the lot I knew I wanted. It was Mr. Austin's gardener's, the plain lot, the lovely old tanglewood. The lot was on Forest and Chicago Avenues. The Master approved the lot and bought it. There was $3,500 left over to build a small home on that ground planted by the old Scottish landscape-gardener.

'Now look out, Wright!' said Mr. Sullivan, 'I know your tastes . . . no "extras".'

I agreed. 'No, none.'

But there was $1,200 more to be paid toward the end. I kept this dark, paid it in due course as best I could out of what remained of my salary.

The contract at that time made me the best-paid draughtsman in the city of Chicago, so Mr. Adler said. But all the same, the children that followed during those years made creditors a familiar sight—or was it the 'tastes'? To have both gratified was what made the sleeves pull and the coat split across the back.

And the children grew up with similar 'tastes' in an environment that invited their tastes to develop—and continually invited more creditors of course.

TRUTH IS LIFE

I had carved in the oak slab above the fireplace in the living room, 'Truth is Life!' A challenge to sentimentality, I thought. Soon after it occurred to me that Life is Truth. And I could not make it say what I really meant. It was done.

I could not alter it. It was built. Anyway it seemed to me some improvement over the challenge of Grandfather's 'Truth Against the World'. But it wasn't.

THE MASTER AND I

Now went along these matchless early years of master and apprentice. Louis Sullivan, the Master and I, the open-eyed, radical and critical, but always willing apprentice. We had already moved to the top floor of the Auditorium tower, where I had a small room next to him, and a squad of thirty draughtsmen or more to supervise in the planning and detailing that was now my share. Mueller had the engineers and the superintendents reporting to him, at the opposite end of the long room with its row of windows to the north. Adler and Sullivan now stood well to the forefront of their profession. Commercial work, chiefly office buildings, theatres, and clubs, all came steadily in unbroken procession through the office. It was the most progressive and one of the most successful offices in the country.

Dankmar Adler had been an Army engineer. He commanded the confidence of contractor and client alike. His handling of both was masterful. He would pick up a contractor as a mastiff might pick up a cat—shake him and drop him. Some would habitually fortify themselves with a drink or two before they came up to see him. All worshipped him. He was a good planner, a good critic but all for Sullivan. He always called him Sullivan, never Louis. Adler had implicit confidence in Sullivan's genius.

It seems he had taken Sullivan in as a draughtsman when as a young man Sullivan returned from the Beaux Arts. Later he took him into partnership to be what was known, even then, as a designing partner. Architects all put the architecture on the outside—in those days. So there was one man to make it—another man to 'handle' it. But Adler and Sullivan were not quite like that.

Dankmar Adler was a Jew. Louis Sullivan an Irishman. The clients all being Adler's clients, many objected to Sullivan. It did not matter. They had to take Sullivan or lose Adler. In those days Sullivan's attitude and ego may be seen in the fate of Weatherwax, the unfortunate draughtsman who went out of the office the day I came into it. But I had, from the first, seen a different side of Sullivan. He loved to talk to me and I would often stay listening, after dark in the offices in the upper stories of the great tower of the Auditorium building looking out over Lake Michigan, or over the lighted city. Sometimes he would keep on talking seeming to have forgotten me—keep on talking until late at night. Probably liking the exercise. And I would catch the last suburban car for Oak Park and go to bed without supper.

As I have since reflected, he seemed unaware of the machine as a direct element in architecture, abstract or concrete. He never mentioned it. And he was interested in 'the rule so broad as to admit of no exception'. For the life of me I could not help, then or now, being most interested in the exception proving the rule useful or useless.

But this outpouring to a worshipful and sympathetic though critical listener soon enabled me to understand him. Like all geniuses he was an absorbed egocentric—exaggerated sensibility, vitality boundless. This

98

egotism, though, is more armour than character, more shell than substance. It is the usual defence for exaggerated sensibility—a defence become a habit. And with all his synthesis and logical inclination, his uncompromising search for principle, he was an incorrigible romanticist. I have learned to see this as not inconsistent, except as the romanticist degenerates to the sentimentalist. Louis Sullivan himself did sometimes sentimentalize. What rich nature does not at times, and when least suspecting the truth indignantly deny the 'soft impeachment'?

But during all this period when General Grant Gothic was the prevailing mode, Chicago itself the centre of the united fundamentalist ugliness of the United States, the synthesis of his common sense cut clean.

The buildings of the romantic Richardson and the susceptible Root were beginning to appear, but buildings like the Potter Palmer house on the Lake Shore Drive were still supreme. The Palmer home, Palmer House and the Board of Trade were then popular architecture. Adler and Sullivan buildings stood clean and sharp by comparison. See the Borden Block, Gage Building and others in the Chicago wholesale district of this early period. John Edelman's influence may be seen in the ornament of those early buildings.

THE AUDITORIUM BUILDING

The Auditorium interior was the first *great* room for audience that really departed from the curious prevailing traditions. The magic word *plastic* was used by the Master in reference to his ornament, and the room itself began to show the effects of this ideal. The ideal began to enter into the Auditorium interior. Not consciously, I believe. Subconsciously.

Mr. Adler himself had invented the sounding-board as an architectural principle in earlier theatres he had built. That is to say, the sloping surface, extending above the proscenium, opening into the audience room, was the sounding-board. Owing to this simple invention no public hall ever built by Adler and Sullivan was acoustically bad. The Master developed this sounding-board into the concentric, elliptical arches as you may still see them in that great room. And while no advantage was taken of the arched elliptical form to carry the loads above, the inner shell itself being carried—suspended from the level trusses above it—still the form was appropriate, suitable to its purpose and prophetic.

The opening night of the great Chicago Auditorium was a gorgeous civic and social event to be remembered. Adelina Patti was among the score of opera stars that sang upon that occasion. The great room for opera was found to be perfect for its purpose. It was acknowledged to be the greatest building achievement of the period and to this day is probably the best room for grand opera yet built in the world, all things considered.

Off to the beloved Valley for the honeymoon.

A few weeks later, the young bride and groom came back to Oak **Park,** where the new house, made possible by the contract with Adler and Sullivan, was being built. On the way across town from the St. Paul R. R. station to Northwestern R.R. station, came the first *meum* and *tuum*.

I wanted to carve mottoes on the panels of the doors of the rooms of the new house. The decided Kitty, with better sense, accustomed to having her own way, too, said, 'No, no mottoes.' But the reason she gave was not good. 'Didn't like mottoes.'

I—new husband, lugging a heavy suitcase, tired and tried by the useless effort to keep the damn thing off my legs—was surprised to find my superior taste in matters pertaining to my own work disputed. And I was caught red-handed in my own 'sentimentality'. It was forever claiming me and every time it did I would not only lose face, but my patience: and someone or something to blame.

I put the suitcase down, wiped the sweat from my face, more indignant to be caught sentimentalizing than anything else. Picked it up again and refused the offer of help. Not in those circumstances. Thank you. We walked wide apart.

SIX CHILDREN

The little home was ready to move into and we moved into it.

Young husband more interested in the house than in his bride, so the young wife said to him.

No—no children were provided for, but of course they came. The first one came within the year. A son—Lloyd. Then, two years later, another son—John. The several grandmothers came in often to help and advise and keep domesticity working right side up. In two years another. A girl—Catherine II. Two years later, another! Boy, David. Those grandmothers were kept pretty busy around there for years to come. And the several grandmothers agreed none too often. This was something not at all in my reckoning. But just the same, two years later, another. A girl— Frances. Five years went by and Llewelyn came.

The young husband found that he had his work cut out for him. The young wife found hers cut out for her. Architecture was my profession. Motherhood became hers. Fair enough, but it was division.

With Silsbee, I had gained considerable light on the practical needs of the American dwelling. Adler and Sullivan refused to build residences during all the time I was with them. The few that were imperative, owing to social obligations to important clients, fell to my lot out of office hours. They would, of course, check up on them in good time. Sullivan's own home on Lake Avenue was one of these, as were his southern house at Ocean Springs and the house next door for the Charnleys.

The city house on Astor Street for the Charnleys, like the others, I did at home evenings and Sundays in the nice studio draughting room upstairs at the front of the little Forest Avenue home. But this draughting room soon became two bedrooms for the children—the children that had been left out of the reckoning in the building of that house. In this Charnley city-house on Astor Street I first sensed the definitely decorative value of the plain surface, that is to say, of the flat plane as such. The drawings for the Charnley house were all traced and printed in the Adler and Sullivan offices, but by preparing them for this purpose at home I helped pay my pressing building debts with 'overtime.'

Other debts pressing toward the end of the five-year term, I accepted several houses on my own account, one for Dr. Harlan, one for Warren McArthur and one for George Blossom. I did not try anything radical because I could not follow them up. I could not follow up because I did these houses out of office hours, not secretly. And Mr. Sullivan soon became aware of them. He was offended and refused to issue the deed to the Oak Park house; the deed was due because the little house was now paid for. But, although I had not realized this, I had broken my contract by doing this outside work. So I protested. I asked the Master if I had been any less serviceable in the office lately.

'No,' he said, 'but your sole interest is here, while your contract lasts. I won't tolerate division under any circumstances.'

This seemed unjust to me. If I could work over-hours at home for Adler and Sullivan and keep up my work in the office what harm in doing likewise for myself to relieve my own necessities? All the same I was wrong— I saw it, but angered now by what seemed the injustice of the Master—it was the first time he had said harsh words to me—I appealed to Dankmar Adler.

Mr. Adler interceded, which more deeply offended the Master than ever and —more offensively still—he refused to issue the deed.

When I learned this from the Master in none too kindly terms and with the haughty air now turned toward me, it was too much. I threw my pencil down and walked out of the Adler and Sullivan office never to return. Within a few months my five-year contract would have expired. This five-year term added to the previous time would make more than six years with Adler and Sullivan.

Again I was in the wrong. More so than my Master. But again out on my own, this time to stay.

Nor for more than twelve years did I see Louis Sullivan again or communicate with him in any way. The deed to the home duly followed, by Mr. Adler's hand.

From now on the young architect's studio workshop was on Chicago Avenue. The young mother's home and kindergarten had continued and still kept on growing on Forest Avenue. The corridor through which the great sprawling willow tree grew and covered the house with the shade of its spreading green—connected the two establishments.

I knew only a few of the neighbours' names. The young wife knew only a few of her husband's clients' names or what buildings he was building.

The children were well born and handsome. Each and all, they were fine specimens of healthy childhood, curly-headed, blue-eyed, sunny-

101

haired, fair-skinned like their beautiful mother. They all resembled her. Every one of them was born, so it seemed, directly in his or her own right. You might think they had all willed it and decided it all for themselves.

They were seemingly endowed with the resistance and will of the father, inheriting his perverse qualities. They inherited their mother's good looks.

That little home-department on Forest Avenue soon became a lively place. Things began to smash. Cries to resound. Shrieks. Quarrels and laughter. Someone or another or several or something in a pickle, and in a pickle all of the time. Destruction of something or other happened every minute.

Works of art and craft, crockery, toys—all went together. Then followed destruction of Mother's peace and patience! I, their legitimate father, would hear all about it when I came in to be fed, or if I came in early to go to bed—which I seldom did.

The children were their mother's children and up to her except when the two young parents themselves made eight children all together at playtime. And early in the morning. Warren McArthur, friend and early client of mine, something of a wag, dining with us one Sunday, caught one of the children and called to me, 'Quick now, Frank, . . . what's the name of this one?' It worked. Surprised by the peremptory request I gave the wrong name.

Sometimes pursuing a kind interest in my state someone would ask: 'And are there children?'

The answer 'Yes, six' would leave the kindly one interested, wide-eyed, wondering. I am afraid I never looked the part. Nor ever acted it. I didn't feel it. And I didn't know how.

FATHERHOOD

We two had a joint bank-account. Drew cheques until they began to come back N.S.F.—in red. Then we knew the money was gone. Never mind! The first of the month was only two weeks off. There would be some more. Why worry? The father in the architect took the children's future to heart in that I wanted them to grow up in beautiful surroundings. I intended them all to be infected by a love for the beautiful. I then called it so in spite of growing prejudice against the sentimental. So I built a beautiful large playroom for them all on the upper floor at the rear of the little house. Before I could get it all paid for a benevolent sheriff came and sat in it all of one night. It was next morning before I could get the eighty-five dollars somewhere to send him on his way. I remember, to this day, that it was eighty-five dollars, but I can't remember where I got it. Probably Wheaton, the old business clerk at Adler and Sullivan's, advanced it on my pay. He did such things for me. Sometimes.

But the children didn't know about such things then. Never mind, they learned all about such things later on.

But the playroom was a beautiful playroom and did its work well. The allegory at the end—the Fisherman and the Genii from the Arabian Nights: the Genii, first design, done in straight-line pattern. A lesson was to be drawn from the subject matter by the children. I forget what it was. Perhaps never to be too sentimental, or curious, or meddlesome, or there would be consequences.

The neighbours' children, too, came to kindergarten there. The home overflowed with children until one fell out of the window. Youngest son —Llewelyn. He was not hurt very much because his dress caught on the playroom windowsill and held him a moment.

There was little sickness, but when there was, gloom settled over everything. A sick child and the place ceased to live until improvement came and the child got well again. Fortunately little redheaded Doctor Luff lived only several doors away. And fortunately such sickness as came never lasted long. The six children were six happy, healthy, going, independent institutions not to say constitutions. And they all had their own way in the end. Yes. Always. They had about as much respect for their father as they had each for the others. And at times, later on in years, it was hard to tell which was father and son when together, whether by language, attitude or appearance of age.

That household was pretty much the children all the time—all together. But it was a double-barrelled establishment. A three-ring circus on the one side. A stimulating excursion into the future here and now on the other side. Both were regardless. A good time was had by all until something or other would happen. And something or other always did happen. The establishments began to compete. The architect absorbed the father in me—perhaps—because I never got used to the word nor the idea of being one as I saw them all around the block and met them among my friends. I hated the sound of the word *papa*.

Is it a quality? Fatherhood? If so, I seemed born without it. And yet a building was a child. I have had the father-feeling, I am sure, when coming back after a long time to one of my buildings. That must be the true feeling of fatherhood. But I never had it for my children. I had affection for them. I regarded them as *with* me—and play-fellows, comrades to be responsible for. But their wills were set alongside mine, never across or against mine unless I was trying to protect myself from them. Though I did have to take in hand the upbringing of six-year-old Frances. I took her into the bathroom and punished her until her cries (Frances could open her mouth wide and cry enormously) were heard by all the next-door neighbours. I had closed the door but had forgotten to close the window. Finished with it, she rushed out of the house, slammed the door and went down the street to stay 'forever' with 'Blue' Grandma. The unusual indignity that outraged her had shocked and shamed me no less. And she was always bringing in some dirty stray cat, or strange mangy dog she had found at large in the streets and no one wanted. She adopted them with a passionate clinging—pathetic or ridiculous according to the point of view. When her animals were turned out, Frances would stand

103

stockstill, outraged, open her mouth wide and pour out the wailing only Frances or 'de la Parma' knew how to wail.

And if there is any meaner feeling man makes for himself than when he strikes a child, what may it be, I wonder? The coward, ninety-nine times out of a hundred, is only releasing personal vexation or some cheap peevish resentment for upset '*authority*'.

Spare the rod and spoil the child? Yes, another Mosaic root of human misery: the special invention—in self-defence—of that imposition called Fatherhood. 'Fatherhood?' An *institution* I suppose in the interest of bigger and better domesticity.

These youngsters that grew up alongside my coming of age now call me Dad. I shouldn't be surprised if they were to call me Frank, nor ever would be.

They often started to do it, too, when they were little, but their mother would treat it as a form of disrespect, and insist upon 'Papa', accent long on the first 'a' making a more offensive word '*paa*-pa' than even when accented on the last and it became 'pa-*paa*'. There is a stuffy domesticity about the sound applied to the male that was always intolerable to me, as I have said.

'Father' is tolerable after fifty. '*Paa*pa' never!

THE HOSE

I remember sitting on the terrace in front of the little Forest Avenue home waiting for Lloyd's mother to come home from Church. Two-and-a-half-year-old Lloyd had been left with me. It was spring. I had turned on the revolving sprinkler to water the lawn. The two-year-old spied the revolving water thing and wanted it. 'No, Lloyd,' I said, 'you can't have it —keep away! You'll get your new clothes all wet.'

Unable to conquer desire himself I assisted by gently leading him back to the steps. And I sat him down there by me in full view of the whirligig, out of the way of the water but where he could see and enjoy the swish and whirl. A moment and he got up to go after it again, regardless of warnings. Again I seated him. Again up and going. Threats now as to dire consequences. He seemed not to hear any of them. He was fascinated. Though roughly seated again—he was up and going. 'Come back, young fellow!'

But he was helpless to return. Again I got up and brought him back, angry, by now, myself. Should I punish him? Sunday, people coming home from church. So far as that went, yes, but what good?

By the time this thought got through my mind, there he was in the zone of the sprinkler. The lusty little redhead gasped and stopped a moment.

'Come back, Lloyd, or you'll be drowned,' I called in a tone that might have blasted him where he stood. No sound from him. He went in further. Drenched thoroughly, he gasped again, turned his face aside and stood his ground.

'All right,' I thought, 'maybe this *is* the best way.' I sat down on the steps to watch the struggle.

His mother had dressed him freshly clean. He had looked nice. All that was already a total loss.

He now shut his eyes, held his breath and, his hand stretched out in the act, staggered in closer to grab the coveted thing.

Too much! Drenched, he fell in the mud. Bawling lustily now but not giving an inch he got up and turning his face aside stood there bawling loudly, angry.

He was a sight but there he was, only a few feet away from his desire, the water taking his breath every time he turned to go forward.

'Come back, lusty boy,' I said. 'Can't you see you can't get it? Come back here!' Myself angry to see him so. He didn't know I called, apparently, because another totter brought him so close I thought he had the whirling thing, but no—he fell. Gurgling, bawling and gasping he lay there for a moment, but rolled over again on to his hands and knees, head down toward the whirling spray.

'All right,' I thought cruelly. 'Let's see what stuff he's made of!' And I let him lie there half drowned, literally, to see what he would do. Features already obliterated with water, mud and anger, still howling desire, he got up on his feet, fell inarticulate with the water but he had what he wanted. In both hands. I ran now and picked him up, mud from head to heels, gasping but hanging on to the whirligig, just in time to hear a piercing scream as his mother rushed to snatch him from me, publicly reproaching me as she sobbed over the half-drowned infant. 'My child,' she sobbed. 'My child!' And her own beautiful spring costume was a sight—too.

All right. He was good stuff.

And that hose was the cause of many a divertissement. Myself coming home one Sunday, but not from Church, I found Lloyd and John playing the hose on the lawn, already too wet. None too pleased I called, 'Boys, put up that hose!' No inclination to put it up. 'Lloyd! John! Put up that hose or I'll put you all up a tree and leave you there.' A challenge. John had the hose and, at this, swung it around toward me. Just a little warning to me, that's all. By now angry, I called—'Boys, put down that hose!'

Nothing of the sort.

Both boys took the hose and turned it on me. I had to jump back a few strides. 'Look here, you . . .' but the neighbours were coming from church and some of them had stopped to see what would happen next. This gallery excited the boys but restrained me.

I walked around to flank them from the shrubbery.

They were waiting for me and wet me down.

'Boys, come on, be good sports—put down that hose.' I coaxed now.

Not their idea of sport.

'Let's see you get it!' said John, ringleader in the mischief by this time. They danced around and came toward me with it. I got back out of the swishing water. The neighbours, a group on both sides of the street, were laughing, enjoying this show at paternal expense. Authority was getting a bad break. I was already wet so I charged the pair. They turned the hose full on me and ran.

And so it went.

EDUCATION

I took cold baths myself in the morning those days and I would fling the boys into a tub of cold water, failing to drown their yells which would lift the roof. Then after they were rubbed dry—putting one hand in my pocket and a boxing glove on the other, I would take them on, gloves on both their hands and both boys working together until they grew too big even to be handled with both my hands gloved and free or later more than one at a time.

To each child, early in his life, I gave a musical instrument. To learn to play it was all I asked of their education.

Lloyd—Cello.

John—Violin.

Catherine—Voice.

Frances—Piano.

David—Flute.

Llewelyn—Guitar and Mandolin.

Their mother played the piano, reading. I played the piano a little myself, trying to improvise, letting the piano play itself.

Later this incipient orchestra was presided over by Lloyd, conducting with the bow of his cello. He would reach out so skilfully with it to rap the skull of the player of a wrong note that he would not even interrupt the rhythm of his playing. The howls and wails that mingled with the music gave a distinctly modern effect to every performance.

The connecting door to the Studio would open cautiously, when some rather important client would be in to go over the plans. And I would see curly heads and mischievous eyes challenging mine, knowing I could do nothing about it in the circumstances. There was a balcony around the draughting room reached from the connecting corridor with the willow tree in it. The children always loved to get up in that balcony and peer down at the goings-on. They would break out into a roar and scamper back before unkind words could overtake them.

One day a fashionable fastidious client from the North Side. Mrs. Aline Devin. Her first visit to the studio. Sitting together at the big central office table, facing the corridor—I was just about to show her plans to her for the first time, always a strained situation—when I saw the door open and saw Catherine's dirty little face. A dirty little hand was on the door jamb.

I looked tons of 'go away'. But no fear. The door opened wider. In came the Catherine, one stocking down over one shoe—broadly chewing gum. Where did she get that gum? Gum was forbidden. The dirt was familiar enough.

106

She marched sidelong to the opposite side of the table, perfectly conscious of the effect she was having upon me. Her little jaws worked carelessly and freely while she deliberately regarded Mrs. Devin curiously—apparently unfavourably.

Then suddenly, stretching out her dirty little hand: '*Paa*pa! Mama wants a dime!'

I didn't have one. So I made merry over the break, escorted Catherine II to the corridor door and turned the key.

Fatal error.

There she was now up in the balcony above, looking down—freely chewing, as ever....

'*Paa*pa! Mama wants a dime!'

Her mother finally came to get the persistent creditor dunning me for the dime I didn't have. I will say Catherine made herself charming, if dirty—all the while.

Mrs. Devin was highly amused. And so must I have been, or worse, for I've never forgotten the moment.

Those children!

They are worthy a monograph, each.

NINETEEN YEARS

Life and work went on in Oak Park for nineteen years.

Food, clothing, shelter, education and amusement for my six meanwhile accomplished somehow. The older boys went from The Hillside Home School to college. The other boys from the Oak Park High School to universities. The girls went to private schools, Frances to Penn Hall and to Sophie Newcomb. Catherine was sent to New York to study music. All had musical educations of a sort. All seemed talented individuals, yes, pretty much in their own right. They were happy only when they were on their own. They knew how to be, even at that very early age and I guess they knew how before they ever got here at all.

So long as we had the luxuries, the necessities could pretty well take care of themselves so far as we were concerned. Season tickets to the Symphony; the children always tastefully dressed, in expensive things, the best that could be had. Their good looks made this agreeable extravagance. Catherine herself wore so well the clothes I designed for her that it was always a temptation to get new dresses. Designing them was fun.

This love for beautiful things—rugs, books, prints or anything made by art or craft or building—especially building—kept the butcher, the baker, and the landlord always waiting. Sometimes waiting an incredibly long time.

GROCERIES, RENT

Our kind grocer, down at the corner, Mr. Gotsch, came around once, I remember, with a grocery bill for eight hundred and fifty dollars. How many months old, I do not remember. But I do remember the kindly way in which he sat down to plead his side of the case with me. He showed me how much cheaper he could serve me if I would pay his bill regularly.

'Then,' I said, 'you are charging me for giving me credit, are you?'

'Of course,' he said, 'I must. I have children of my own.' And I knew them—nice children. He went on to say: 'If I didn't protect myself I would soon be unable to give them even a small part of what you are pretty freely giving yours.'

He didn't press the matter. He just showed me the folly of such neglect as mine. And I felt remorse, even though I *had* paid in cash for my own neglect. I somehow got the money and paid him. I would resist the next adventure into art and craft, perhaps resist for several months. But this self-denial would not last. So, always, the necessities were going by default to save the luxuries until I hardly knew which were necessities and which luxuries.

It was my misfortune, too, that everybody was willing to trust me. I don't know why they were willing, either, because I don't imagine my appearance or my way of life would appeal to a businessman any more than my buildings appealed to the local bankers a little later on. But I always found in those early days the merchants kind, indulgent to unbelievable extremes. And this, too, tended to make me dreadfully careless. Only the banks would 'N.S.F.' us. So we came to distrust and despise banks. But they were really doing us the only favour they knew how to do. The mistrust grew cordially mutual in the course of time.

But the group of children big and little in the little gabled house on the corner with the queer studio alongside had unusual luxuries. Unusual advantages in education. Eventually, though I never knew *how* nor quite *how much* they all came to, I managed to pay for the necessary luxuries plus delinquency tax of course, which was considerable.

I remember 'rent' in the Schiller Building when offices were later opened there. Rent would sometimes be seven or eight months behind. And I hear Mr. Dose, the manager of the building say, when I would realize the enormity of the circumstances by being brought to book and would apologize and promise, 'Never mind, Mr. Wright: you are an artist. I have never yet lost any rent owed me by any artist. You will pay me,' said the heavy, severe-faced agent of my landlord.

And, of course, I did pay him. After that, as regularly as I could.

I don't believe anyone ever lost a penny either in rent or on credit in all those haphazard years—except myself. It cost me handsomely in the end to allow the necessities to drift. How much? Say twenty-five per cent. Perhaps it was worth it. Who knows?

I remember walking into a little, thrifty, French investment broker's office one day and seeing on the wall the framed motto, 'Spend what you earn.' I told him he was corrupting the youth of this country. No such motto would ever get anybody anywhere. 'Make the motto read: "Earn what you spend," and you will have everybody working hard for you and to better purpose.' I might have said that he would also have everybody

108

to whom the youth owed money working on the youth, to make him work.

Nevertheless, during those years always there was a very real undertone of worry, owing to this heavy drag of debt that fell to my share. I believe no one ever really forgets a money-obligation. It goes along with him wherever he goes. Pricking him sharply, from underneath at times, coming to mind wakeful nights. And I believe, too, while debt is stimulating to some, it is stultifying to others. I suppose it is just a question as to how much punishment one can stand. The buying and selling of money has introduced a shopkeeping code into the bookkeeping ethics of modern life and made preachers and teachers as well as profligate spenders all money-raisers.

The secret information of the credit-detective systems, instalment buying finance companies, their back-stair ruses and fine-print extortions, their refinancings. All this commercialite machinery takes terrible toll from any man who gets in too deep. Or he who lets his bills go by. We partly owe all these unpicturesque institutions to this tendency of youthful human nature to put off paying until tomorrow. It gives jobs to a good many, and rich opportunities to the sharks.

This 'weakness' has bred a whole school and new type of money-shark. And this 'system'—a meretricious, preposterous 'absolute'—has its teeth in the lives of nearly everyone today. The victim of the shark and the teeth will wake up some day to realize how costly these 'mañana' money-men are, and, by avoiding them make them, too, go to work.

BOOK THREE

WORK

THE FIELD

Midsummer sun floods the field of smoothly rippling grain. The swath of yellow stubble left by the rounds of the gay reaper shows faint undertone of living green. The gaily painted reaper, pulled by three white horses, cuts its way around round after round.

The stubble is interlined by the big wheel of the reaper as it is also patterned by grain-shocks. Adolph in a bright blue shirt is setting up the shocks. The bundles—six of them—he stands butt-end down firmly on the stubble and caps them by putting two bundles crosswise on the top.

The entire field is becoming a linear pattern of Work.

Coming along after the noisy red, blue, green, yellow and white man-toy—jerkily sweeping the grain into regular piles on the stubble—are four more men, each binding the bundles raked off on his side of the square of still standing grain. Each must finish binding his side of the square, his station, before the reaper comes around again or he falls hopelessly behind.

Rhythm is regular and patterned order is everywhere established in this work of the harvest.

After the stooping and rising men comes a bareheaded boy running barefoot to and fro in the stubble picking up the bundles. He gathers eight together in a pile. The shocker, coming along behind, grasps the bundles two at a time, standing all eight up together.

The twelve-year-old, brown as a walnut, sits down on a bundle in the hot blaze of sun.

Nearby in the shadow of a shock is a brown stone jug filled with spring water. He goes to the jug, uncorks the nozzle, slips two fingers through the stone handle. He manages to lift the jug, letting it drop over on to his forearm as he has seen the men do. Head thrown back he takes a thirsty pull, water gurgling from the jug down his young throat, wipes the sweat from his tanned face and water from his chin with the blue gingham sleeve on his forearm. Head up, he listens a moment.

The Meadow Lark!

Looks down at his bleeding fingers, nails worn to the quick by the too many straw bands already to his credit. Then, to carry on, he gets up and picks up the bundle on which he had been sitting. From the butt-end of the bundle a rattler unwittingly bound into the sheaf a few moments before by one of the binders and tossed aside, slips to the ground.

Smoothly, the snake swiftly coils in the stubble and—tail upended—rattles, darting a forked tongue—narrow hostile eyes gleaming.

The barefoot starts back his own eyes narrowing at sight of the splendid enemy.

Instantly, clear consciousness of the whole scene comes full upon the boy: the golden blaze; the giddy whirl of the gay reaper; voices of the men—one singing; the distant rattle of the sickle mingling with the ominous rattle of the snake. The beautiful brown embroidery of its golden body makes the reptile belong. Some fascination holds the lad. A sense of something predestined—lived before. To be lived again? Something in the far distant past comes near—as repetition?

Held by this, he stands still, eyeing the snake as narrowly as the snake eyes him. Yes—as hostile.

A three-tined pitchfork stands against the shock sheltering the stone jug. He leaps for the fork, turns and with a thrust swift as the darting tongue pins the rattler to the ground. The piercing tines of the fork hold fast in the ground as the seething coils of the enraged serpent vainly struggle to get free.

Now what?

With the bottom of the stone jug he flattens the evil-spitting head and picks up the gorgeous thing by the rattles. Nine!

The reaper, come opposite, stops. His uncle drops off the driver's seat and comes toward him.

'See, Uncle James! I've got him—nine rattles!'

'Why didn't you get away from him and let Adolph kill him?'

'Why?' the boy answers, missing the approval he felt earned.

'Why? You are barefoot. You might get worse than hurt.'

But the boy holds the limp snake as much higher as he can, looking at its length.

The rhythm and routine of the harvest field go on again all as before. But with no warning at all something dreadful had suddenly happened to challenge the order of the peaceful harvest field.

Work—the plan—was, for a moment, interrupted by something not in the plan, or the reckoning: something over a part of Life but ever a threat to 'the plan'. Something that bothered the men who made the Bible. Is the Devil the only answer?

WORK

Come with me to the offices of Frank Lloyd Wright, Architect, offices at 1501 Schiller Building where the arches loop beneath the top-storey motif—the square mass of the top glooming against the sky. An Adler and Sullivan building now called 'the Garrick'.

It is late in the year Eighteen Hundred and Ninety-three. A fateful year in the culture of these United States. 'They' are about to go Pseudo-Classic!

The Columbian Fair opened and closed its turnstiles to the crowd. Upon leaving Adler and Sullivan, Cecil Corwin joined me (not as a partner) and

111

we opened offices on this tower-floor in the Schiller Building, Chicago—a building that, owing to Sullivan's love for his new home in the South, had been more largely left to me than any other. Accustomed to the view from a high place and feeling a little nearer Adler and Sullivan by being there, I suppose, I wanted that space.

Cecil and I had a draughting room, each, either side of the common central room for business. Defending this room was an anteroom or vestibule with the ceiling dropped down to the top of the doors. A straight line glass-pattern formed this ceiling—glass diffusing artificial light. The effect of this indirect lighting in the small anteroom was like sunlight, no light-fixtures visible. There was a large flat oak chest of drawers each side of the door with some of Hermon MacNeil's Indian statuettes standing on them. The walls were entirely plain. At either end were two plain square chairs. We liked to stand there and talk about the future—Cecil and I. And we would greet a coming client or linger there to talk with one leaving, enjoying the atmosphere.

The outside entrance door to this anteroom, like the inner door to the business space itself, was a single clear plate of glass bordered by the usual wood stiles and rails of the usual width. A single clear glass plate from side to side ran top to bottom with our names lettered in gold on one side of the outside door at the top of the plate-glass. On the inner door, 'Private'. Also in gold.

These single-panel clear plate-glass doors had style. They were new. Anyone could see directly not only into the anteroom from the elevator hall, but into the business space as well, so we had a shade on each door to pull up from top to bottom. But the shades were seldom used, the effect was so pleasant.

At the centre of the inner business-space was a huge, flat-topped table with four square chests of drawers for legs, leaving leg-space at the middle on four sides. Four comfortable chairs were placed one at the centre of each side. We could thus sit on both sides with clients or contractors on the other sides. This table was seven feet square and in the centre was a glass globe usually filled with flowers from our small garden. Sitting there I could see directly out as anyone could see directly in. This had various consequences.

I see one of the consequences as I write, in the yellow face and evil eyes of Shimoda, a Japanese draughtsman fired for cause and warned never to come back. The cause was speaking obliquely of a lady who got into the habit of leaving flowers in the glass globe on the big office table.

And yet, one noon, as I glanced up, there stood Shimoda.

A scared look came over the yellow face as I jumped to my feet. My time to be out so he was taken as much by surprise as I was. Probably he had come back with no worse intent than to see the boys, but I had warned him never to come back.

He turned to run but I could open those two doors quickly by now, owing to much practice. Before he could get away I reached him. A well-directed intimate kick landed him well down the half-flight on the main public stair running from directly in front of the entrance door down the half-landing below. He lay there in a whimpering heap and I turned back into the office and sat down—waiting.

But not satisfied with his salutary welcome he carried the tale to my reverend uncle of All Souls Church. Described the event with enlarged details—my big riding boots—insinuating I had them on that morning for no other business and no other intention than to kill him.

'Very rough business for me,' said Yerrow Socks as his familiars always called him because 'l' was not in his vocabulary.

For this characteristic carrying of the tale I did the work more thoroughly next time he came—which strange to say he did some weeks later, again thinking I was out of town—by continuing the work, this time, on down from the landing to the floor below.

This finally settled it and Shimoda disappeared from the American scene, not very much worse for wear.

No, Shimoda was not a good Japanese.

To this clear plate with the small gold letters—

FRANK LLOYD WRIGHT, ARCHITECT
CECIL CORWIN, ARCHITECT
—came my first client.

You notice the order? By seniority Cecil should have been first but he wouldn't have it so.

And, you see, opening an office was all that simple. It usually is in Chicago. Rent an office to your liking. Take out the door panels, all of them. Substitute a single beautiful clear plate of glass. Sit down and letter your own name in the size and style preferred. Hesitate a moment becomingly—then add 'Architect'. Get a thrill out of this, as you regard it for a moment with none too adequate realization of the implication. Get a sign writer to put in all in gold leaf on the glass, and—there you are. Another architect come to town. How many of the boys who have listened to the far-away tinkle of the cowbells, have had that same thrill—'professing' something or other? Opening an office?

Truth Against the World is a heavy standard. A flagrant banner. I had left it off the door. But it was sitting there inside. But individual preferences are a compelling circumstance. Babies are too.

Combine the several circumstances with the preferences and what have you? Or what is it that has you?

W. H. Winslow of the Winslow Ornamental Iron Works had often been to Adler and Sullivan's to consult with me about the work of that office. W. H. turned up now to give me my first job. I was to be the architect of his new home at River Forest. I could hardly believe I really had a job. Difficult to believe the initiative I had taken was now a reality. But I soon enough found out that it was.

The Winslow house was to stand across the drive from Mr. Waller's own house in the Waller park in River Forest. Mr. Waller was the handsomest and most aristocratic individual I had ever seen. He had become my friend. He much admired the Winslow house. The building of that house should have a story, but it has none yet. Edward C. Waller and Daniel H. Burnham, the partner of John Root, were old friends. John Root had just died.

Mr. Waller brought about a meeting with 'Uncle Dan', as they all called Daniel H. Burnham—inviting Catherine and me to meet Mr. and Mrs. Burnham at his home. 'Uncle Dan' had seen the Winslow house and straightway pronounced it 'a gentleman's house from grade to coping'.

After dinner Mr. Waller led the way to his cosy library. He wanted to show his friend some work in it I had done for him. I saw him turn to lock the door after we were in. I wondered why. Then and there began an argument which I have never forgotten.

Sitting there, handsome, jovial, splendidly convincing, was 'Uncle Dan'. To be brief, he would take care of my wife and children if I would go to Paris—four years of the Beaux Arts. Then Rome—two years. Expenses all paid. A job with him when I came back. It was more than merely generous. It was splendid. But I was frightened. I sat embarrassed, not knowing what to say.

Mr. Waller got up, walked to and fro telling me what a great opportunity it all was for me. I sat there trying to find the right words to say.

'Another year and it will be too late, Frank,' said Uncle Dan.

That was my cue. 'Yes, too late, Uncle Dan—It's too late now I'm afraid. I am spoiled already. I've been too close to Mr. Sullivan. He has helped spoil the Beaux Arts for me, or spoiled me for the Beaux Arts, I guess I mean. He told me things too, and I think he regrets the time he spent there himself.'

Uncle Dan: 'You are loyal to Sullivan I see, Frank, and that is right. I admire Sullivan when it comes to decoration. Essentially he is a great decorator. His ornament charms me. But his architecture? I can't see that. The Fair, Frank, is going to have a great influence in our country. The American people have seen the Classics on a grand scale for the first time. You've seen the success of the Fair and it should mean something to you too. We should take advantage of the Fair.'

He went on: 'Atwood's Fine Arts Building, Beman's Merchant Tailor's Building, McKim's Building—all beautiful! Beautiful! I can see all America constructed along the lines of the Fair, in noble dignified classic style. The great men of the day all feel that way about it—all of them.'

'No,' I said, 'there is Louis Sullivan. He doesn't. And if John Root were alive I don't believe he would feel that way about it. Richardson I am sure never would.'

'Frank,' he said, 'the Fair should have shown you that Sullivan and Richardson are well enough in their way, but their way won't prevail—architecture is going the other way.'

'But, it is essentially the uncreative way . . . isn't it?'

'Uncreative?—What do you mean uncreative? What can be more beau-

114

tiful than the classic lines and proportions of Greek architecture. That architecture will never be surpassed. We should be taught by it and accept its rules. Without a good education in the Classics how can you hope to . . . succeed?'

'I know. Yes—I know, Uncle Dan, you may be quite right but somehow it just strikes on my heart like—jail. Like something awful. I couldn't bear it, I believe. All that discipline and time wasted, again waiting for something to happen that could never happen. I just can't see it as living. Somehow—it scares me.' I actually began to look for some avenue of escape; the window was partly open. I knew the door was locked.

Mr. Waller now interfered, manifestly provoked at my obstinacy, if not my stupidity, indeed.

'Frank, don't you realize what this offer means to you? As you choose now, remember, so you will go on all the rest of your life.'

'Yes, Mr. Waller—that's just it,' I said. 'I know. They all do. I have seen the men come home from there all one type, no matter how much they were individuals when they went.'

'Individuals? Great architecture *is* severe discipline,' said Uncle Dan.

'Think of your future, think of your family,' said Mr. Waller.

I felt the weight of the occasion.

I saw myself influential, prosperous, safe; saw myself a competent leader of the majority rule. That much faith I had in it all. There would be no doubt about that, with Daniel H. Burnham's power behind me, if I qualified—and there was no doubt in my mind but that I could qualify. It was all so definitely set, too easy and unexciting as I saw it. And it was all untrue. At the very best a makeshift.

This was success as I had dreamed of it then? Was it? Right here, within my grasp? I, too, had already seen the effect of the Fair. But I could not respect it, though I believed Uncle Dan spoke the truth. I did fear and believe it was going to *prevail* as he said. I would have given a good deal to know my Master Sullivan's reaction to all this. But that was all over. I could not go to him now.

The two friends mistook my depression for a weakening in favour of the Beaux Arts.

'Well?' said both, smiling kindly—affectionately.

I felt like an ingrate. Never was the ego within me more hateful to me than at that moment. But it stood straight up against the very roof of my mind.

'No, Mr. Burnham, no, Mr. Waller—I can't run away.'

'Run away, what do you mean?' said Mr. Waller.

'Well, you see, run away from what I see as mine, I mean what I see as *ours* in our country, to what can't belong to me, no, I mean *us*, just because it means success. You see—I can't go, even if I wanted to go because I should never care for myself, after that.'

I don't believe either of the two great friends believed me. They thought I must be showing off—I saw that by their expressions, I thought. 'It may be foolish. I suppose it is, somehow, but I'd rather be free and a failure and "foolish" than be tied up to any routine success. I don't see freedom in it . . . that's all. Oh yes, I mean it. I really do. I'm grateful to you both though; but I won't go.' I got up on my feet. Suddenly the whole thing cleared up before my eyes as only keeping faith with what we then called 'America' and I now call Usonia.

'Thank you both,' I said again. 'I know how obstinate and egotistic you think me, but I'm going on as I've started. I'm spoiled, first by birth, then by training, and'—this had now come clear under pressure—'by conviction, for anything like that.'

Mr. Waller unlocked the study door, opened it and stood aside—hurt, I could see—to let me pass. I helped Catherine on with her things, and we went home. I didn't mention to her what had happened until long afterward.

The Winslow house had burst on the view of that provincial suburb like the Prima Vera in full bloom. It was a new world to Oak Park and River Forest. That house became an attraction, far and near. Incessantly it was courted and admired. Ridiculed, too, of course. Ridicule is always modelled on the opposite side of that shield. This first house soon began to sift the sheep from the goats in this fashion:

Mr. Moore, a lawyer on Forest Avenue near my own house, was going to build. I had learned of this, and I had given up hope that he might ask me to build for him, when, one day, sure enough—could I believe my eyes? I saw Mr. and Mrs. Moore standing outside the full length clear-plate in the outer door of the Schiller Building office. I opened it—excited. The Moores came in and sat down.

'How is it, Mr. Wright,' said Mr. Moore, 'that every architect I know or have ever heard of and some I never heard of have come in one way or another to ask to build my house and you live across the street from me but I haven't had a word from you?'

'Did Mr. Patton come?' I asked. He was the head of the American Institute of Architects, the A.I.A., at the time and lived in Oak Park.

'Yes, he was the first one to come. Why didn't you come?'

'I knew if you wanted me, you knew where to find me. And how did I know you wanted me? . . . You are a lawyer,' I said. 'Would you offer yourself to someone you knew needed a good lawyer?'

'I thought that was it,' he said.

'Now we want you to build our house . . . but—I don't want you to give us anything like that house you did for Winslow. I don't want to go down backstreets to my morning train to avoid being laughed at. I would like something like this,' and he laid some pictures of English half-timber work on my table.

Three children were now running around the streets without proper shoes. How money was needed in that little gabled house! (I had been insulted several times by guesses as to whether the house was 'sea-side' or 'colonial'.) None knew so little as I where money was coming from. Could I take Mr. Moore on? Could I give him a home in the name of English

116

half-timber good enough so that I would not 'sell out'? It was worth trying anyway. I tried it . . .

They were delighted with the house, and so was everyone but me. Did I always resent the praise bestowed upon it because a mention of it made me think of my brave stand before Mr. Waller and Uncle Dan? But it was better to stand back and make way with a single house—wasn't it, than with a whole lifetime of them? Or was it?

So I consoled myself. At any rate it was the one time in the course of a long career that I gave in to the fact that I had a family and they had a right to live—and their living was up to me. The tragedy of the binomial theorem!

Yes, I often had occasion to remember and regret 'giving in' in the years immediately following. I can look back now and see that young professional architect—I soon left off the affix as beside the mark—sitting at that big platform table—let's say the flowers were lilacs—listening to you expectantly. I suspect the ego in him invited or repelled you as you happened to be made yourself.

'You wish to build a house? . . . Oh? Like the one I built for Mr. Moore?'

There is a feeling of disappointment that gets to you. I hear myself saying, 'But why like that house for Mr. Moore?' And the argument is on.

Anyone could get a rise out of me by admiring that essay in English half-timber. 'They' all liked it and I could have gone on unnaturally building them for the rest of my natural life. It was the first time, however, an English half-timbered house ever saw a porch. The porch was becoming to the house.

But, by the time an hour or so had passed, I was quite likely to have made that client see why and how it was the wrong thing, especially now wrong, to build anything more like that in our country, wrong in Usonia where men were free, and old enough to know that licence even in taste is not freedom.

The offices in the Schiller (now the Garrick) saw the making of the Winslow plans; the plans for the Moore house. Mr. Baldwin, another Oak Park lawyer, had come in and laid a cheque for three hundred and fifty dollars on the table as a retainer. He had evidently heard from Mr. Moore. The Francis Apartments I built for an estate. The Husser and Heller home, the Lexington Terraces, the Wolff Lake Resort. A number of other buildings all characterized to a certain extent by the Sullivanian idiom, at least in detail. I couldn't invent the terms of my own overnight. At that time there was nothing in sight that might be helpful. I had no Sullivanian models, even, for any of these things.

A remark of the Master had come back to me by way of my client Winslow: 'Sullivan says, Frank, it looks as though you were going to work out your own individuality.'

So he was interested in me still, was he?

Cecil had been working on some jobs of his own, Rush Medical College in particular. We were not partners. I did not see much of him now for I was intensely busy, and meantime he had found some new intimates. We sat talking in the business office we used in common. He looked discouraged, I noticed.

'What's the matter, old man Cecil?'

'Not much, in general, Frank. In particular, I don't believe I'm an architect, that's all.'

'What's the matter with Rush? Don't you like it?'

He looked at me as he tilted gently back and forth in a creaking office chair—sadness and some whimsey in his look.

'You know. Why ask me?'

'Because it's a fine piece of work.'

'Is it architecture?' he said quietly.

'Well, it's better than ninety-nine out of a hundred architects are doing —better than their barbering and make-up. And, Cecil, you are only beginning. You have such fine feeling for proportion—you know it—and good taste, and . . . Why are you looking at me, that way? You are worth more to any client than any architect I know.' Again I asked, 'What is the matter with you?'

'All right, I'll tell you, young fellow. I've found out there's no joy in architecture for me except as I see you do it. It bores me when I try to do it myself. There's the truth for you. You *are* the thing you do. I'm not and I never will be. And worse than all, I'm not sure any longer, lately, that I want to be. There's joy in it for you—but there's obsession too. You live in your work. You will wake up some day to find that you can't do that, altogether, and then there'll be trouble, I foresee.'

All this seemed to open a chasm where I thought all fair enough. I had lost sight of him. He had been lagging behind. Dear old Cecil. After all, was architecture everything? But worse was coming.

'I'm going East, Frank. I'm interested with Dr. Buchanan—we're going into something together. You can take over my room and, as I see, you'll need it.'

This was unbelievable. I reproached Cecil because I had an uneasy sense of having betrayed him and so—inclined to blame *him*. Never would I have believed this *of* him. I was finding it hard to believe it even *from* him.

I argued, pleaded. All of no use.

'I might as well make a clean breast of it, Frank. I don't want to go on seeing you do the things I can't do. Already I'm where I can do less than I could when we came in here together, and I really care less. Caring less, this isn't so difficult as you imagine it to be.'

It flashed through my mind that I was right. This abnegation on his part was genuine discouragement due to my own neglect—and I felt ashamed of myself. Why not take him in with me? But that was not what this meant. And I knew he wouldn't come.

But I said, 'Why not join me, Cecil—I need you to help me and maybe I could help you out of this. How do you know?'

'No, I'm not the man you need for a partner, Frank. I'm no business man at all. I despise business—it's too gabby and grabby and selly for me

118

—and I'm no architect. I know it now. You do need me for a friend, and I'll always be one. You are going to go far. You'll have a kind of success; I believe the kind you want. Not everybody would pay the price in concentrated hard work and human sacrifice you'll make for it though, my boy.' He added, 'I'm afraid—for what will be coming to you.'

There was no bitterness in this; I could see that a load seemed to have slipped off his mind. He got up. His expression changed. He looked happy again. I was miserable.

Cecil was something of a prophet.

Cecil went East and—God knows why—never have I seen him since.

That place in the Schiller Building soon seemed nothing at all without him. I had met Robert Spencer, Myron Hunt, and Dwight Perkins. Dwight had a loft in his new Steinway Hall building—too large for him. So we formed a group—outer office in common—workrooms screened apart in the loft of Steinway Hall. These young men, new-comers in architectural practice like myself, were my first associates in the so-called profession of architecture. George Dean was another and Hugh Garden. Birch Long was a young and talented 'renderer' at this time and we took him into the Steinway loft with us.

Now and then I went with them to talk at women's clubs until they could all speak the language as well as I. But when they undertook to build, what a difference to me! So I decided to let them do the speaking. I would do the building.

About this time came the incipient Arts and Crafts Society at Hull House. And there I read the paper, protestant and yet affirmative—'The Art and Craft of the Machine'. Next day there was an editorial in the *Chicago Tribune* commenting upon the fact that an artist had said the first word for the use of the machine as an artist's tool. Jane Addams herself must have written it, I suspect. She sympathized with me, as did Julia Lathrop.

But my novel thesis was overwhelmed by Professors Zueblin and Triggs and the architects and handicraftsmen present that evening. The Society went 'handicraft' and was soon defunct. Never have I found support for radical or organic ideas from architects or professors. But there was nevertheless by now a certain cautious emulation on all sides. Soon it was like seeing one's own features distorted in an imperfect mirror. The emulation disturbed, when it did not anger me.

Never having known Sullivan much themselves, at this time these young architects were all getting the gospel modified through me. And I should have liked to be allowed to work out the thing I felt in me as architecture with no reflections or refractions from them or libellous compliments until I had it all where I felt it really ought to be. But that was not possible. I was out in the open to stay. Premature though it might be.

To this new Steinway loft came Ward Willets, client number one. And I did the streamlined prairie house for him on Sheridan drive in Highland Park. Others soon followed in this vein which was now really my own.

119

About this time 'Romeo and Juliet', amateur engineering architecture
—an idea of structure working out into architectural form—the future in
embryo—got itself built. These creations of ours. I see as we look back
upon them, or as we look at them and try to re-create them, how we ourselves belong to them. And because it *was* the engineering architecture of
the future in the amateur embryo, here is the tale.

ROMEO AND JULIET

At this time in the Valley were two matriarchal maiden sisters of
Mother's. They were my Aunts Nell and Jane.

The buildings for the Lloyd-Jones Sisters' Hillside Home School for
boys and girls were designed by amateur me. The first one in which to
mother their forty or fifty boys and girls was built in 1887. This school,
too, had for its crest, 'Truth against the World'. 'The Aunts' built the
school on the site of Grandfather's old homestead, adding several new
buildings. And—the better to guard the development of this beloved
school with a high aim, therefore with trouble ahead—its founders made
a compact with each other never to marry.

Around about the Hillside Home School farm were the farms of their
five patriarchal brothers, my uncles. They always referred to my aunts as
'the girls' and with true clan-faithfulness watched over their sisters' educational venture and over them too. Anything 'the girls' needed they got,
if all the surrounding farms went to rack and ruin. That, at least, was the
complaint the wives of some of my uncles used to make. Meantime their
brothers were proud of their sisters' school. Boys and girls from a dozen or
more states freely called them all 'Uncle' and called the Lloyd-Jones sisters
Aunt Nell and Aunt Jennie no less than the legitimate nephews and nieces
—some thirty or more of whom foregathered there to be educated. Eventually the native nephews and nieces were all 'educated' out of the
beloved Valley—by way of learning—educated into white-collarites in
the big cities.

The school prospered.

When working with architect Silsbee in Chicago I had made the
amateurish plans for the very first school buildings; Cramer the local contractor had built them. But inventing new construction to make itself
beautiful as architecture was not a Cramer habit.

Now, a big reservoir for a new water system has been scooped out in
the white sand-rock of the hilltop above the school. This reservoir finished
the Aunts intended to erect a windmill over it. This was decided upon by a
family gathering which the clan usually held to make such decisions concerning the school or important affairs of their own.

Said Aunt Nell, managerial mind of the school: 'Why not a pretty
windmill tower in keeping with our school building instead of an ugly
steel tower or, for that matter, the timber ones I have seen? I am going
to ask Frank for a design.'

'Nonsense, Nell,' said preacher-brother Jenkin (he happened to be there on one of his frequent visits). 'A steel tower like all the others is good enough. I never ride my horse in this countryside that I don't welcome the sight of one. They are practical and cheap.' The other brothers thought so too.

Aunt Jane, emotional, warmly humane mind of the school, disagreed with the brothers. She said, 'The hill is visible from all over our several valleys. Something should be there to go with the school buildings. I agree with Nell. Let's ask Frank to send us a design.'

The meeting grumbled. But when Nell put her foot down, all usually gave up quietly. She put her foot down now.

So, Uncle James said, 'Well, let's see what the boy will do then.'

The design came. A perspective sketch of the tower in the trees on the hilltop was included with the structural details. The sisters liked it and thought it becoming to the dignity of the beloved school. To the Uncles it looked expensive and foolish.

Cramer, builder 'and good enough architect, too, for around there', was called in to take the drawings away with him to make an estimate. The family waited in vain for Cramer to come back. So brother James went several towns away to look for Cramer. James came back alone. The brothers got together to consider carefully the facts Uncle James had from Cramer.

'Cramer says wasting time and money to build that tower. Blow down sure as Death and Taxes. Sixty feet high! Fourteen-foot wheel top of that. He says the thing is just a sort of big octagonal wood pipe, 4×4 posts at each corner, boards nailed around to the posts, inside and outside. Then all shingled all over on the outside. The whole thing is just like a barrel, only the staves run around across instead of running up and down. There's a diamond-shaped part cutting into the octagon part, or barrel, to the very centre. And the outside half of the diamond makes a "storm prow". Frank named it "storm prow" on the plan. The "storm prow" . . . looks like a big blade running up to the very top on the sou'west side of the barrel. Up the centre of this diamond-shaped part runs a big wood post six inches by six inches—runs up and out of the diamond to carry the big mill-wheel at the top. The boy wants a big heavy stone foundation under the whole thing, eight big strap-bolts built into it, the straps to stick up out of the stone six feet alongside the posts and be bolted to them.

'Cramer laughed. It looked crazy to him. He said we could tell the girls about it ourselves. Frank wants to try some experiment or other.'

Anxious family gathering.

AUNT NELL: 'Did Cramer positively say he knew Frank's tower would fall down?'

UNCLE JAMES: 'Positively.'

UNCLE JENKIN: 'To suppose such a thing could stand up there sixty feet high to carry a fourteen-foot wheel in the storms we have in this region! Why, Nell, it's nonsense. Trust Cramer. Why build something none of us ever saw the like of in our lives? Nor Frank, either, if I know him.'

AUNT JANE: 'Poor boy, what a pity his tower won't stand up. How can he know it will? I do not for the life of me see. Dear me! How he will be disappointed.'

Aunt Nell said nothing, just walked over to the window with her hands behind her back as usual, and looked up at the hilltop. She may have seen the tower there among the trees, the wheel spinning; who knows? All she said was, 'I'll telegraph Frank.'

To all present this seemed like temporizing with the devil. But there was nothing to do but wait for an answer. The telegram—'CRAMER SAYS WINDMILL TOWER SURE TO FALL. ARE YOU SURE IT WILL STAND?' Signed AUNT NELL—reached the young architect, by now on his own in Chicago.

Came back the answer: 'BUILD IT.'

Consternation! Into peaceful family relations came war. Aunt Nell's work was cut out for her. It was clear to them all; she was going to build that foolish tower!

'That boy will be the ruination of his aunts.' That conviction settled firmly around there and became a slogan. Cramer came down to argue and expostulate.

But with her back to the wall Aunt Nell said, 'Does the boy want to build anything that will fall down any more than we do? He has even more at stake. He says, "*Build it*." Maybe he knows better than all of us? He would not be so confident unless he had his feet on something in this design.'

Said Aunt Jane, 'He is never willing to explain fully, but somehow I do believe he knows what he is about, after all.'

'Cramer,' said Aunt Nell, as she turned around to face the practical builder, 'how much will it cost to build this tower just as Frank planned it?'

'Nine hundred and fifty dollars,' he said.

'How much would a steel mill cost?'

'Two hundred seventy-five dollars,' he said.

'Only six hundred seventy-five dollars for all that difference,' was her unexpected reaction. (This was in the country about 1896.) 'Of course we are going to build it.'

The anxious committee ruefully disbanded.

DEAR AUNTS NELL AND JANE:

Of course you had a hard time with Romeo and Juliet. But you know how troublesome they were centuries ago. The principle they represent still causes mischief in the world because it is so vital. Each is indispensable to the other . . . neither could stand without the other. Romeo, as you will see, will do all the work and Juliet cuddle alongside to support and exalt him. Romeo takes the side of the blast and Juliet will entertain the school children. Let's let it go at that. No symbol should be taken too far. As for the principle involved, it *is* a principle but I've never seen it in this form. No. But I've never seen anything to go against it, either.

Yes, I could explain the way the storm-strains on the harmonious pair

122

will be resolved into one another and be tuned into a pull on the iron straps built deep into the stone foundation. But, after all, for the life of this harmoniously contrasting pair I am chiefly betting on the nails driven into the boards by the hammers of Cramer's *men* to fasten them to the upright corner-posts. We'll see that there are enough nails and long enough. Nails are not engineering but they are 'practice'. Of course you will build it. I will come out.

Lovingly,
FRANK.

N.B. Romeo and Juliet will stand twenty-five years which is longer than the iron towers stand around there. I am afraid all of my uncles themselves may be gone before 'Romeo and Juliet.' Let's go.

Cramer, the local builder, 'good enough architect too, for around there', was sincere in his belief that the thing would fall down. 'Sixty-foot post to the spring of the wheel,' said he, shaking his head. 'And a fourteen-foot wheel,' he added,—really dejected.

'It beats heck,' said he, 'the way those two old maids dance around after that boy. He comes up here with his swell duds on, runs around the hills with the school girls and goes home. You wouldn't think he had a care in the world nor anything but something to laugh at.'

'Well . . .' He finally stopped grumbling and went to work.

Five grey-bearded uncles religiously kept away from the scene of impending disaster. Two grey-headed, distinguished-looking maiden aunts, between whiles mothering their boys and girls, daily climbed to the hilltop, anxious to see what was going on. Timothy, family friend and excellent old Welsh stone-mason, incorrigible in his quaint misuse of the word 'whateverr', had by now got up the stone foundation. Timothy, alone, gave them comfort. He knew well the aunts liked a good word for their nephew.

'The boys [meaning my uncles] don't know what's in the young man's head, whateverr. They'll be looking to him one of these days. . . . Yes, whateverrr. Could any wooden tower pull that stone foundation over?' And he built the rods in solider and deeper than they were called for . . . a staunch mason, and man too, that Welshman. Whateverr.

As the frame went up into the air, the workmen were skittish at first. If the wind came up they came down.

But the big windmill wheel was finally shipped way up there in the blue. . The tower swayed in the wind several inches as it should have done but this sway made the men nervous. Some quit for one specious reason or another. It did look very far down to the ground when you were up in the little belvedere—named for Juliet. The tower lifted from the apex of the hill and from up there you looked all the way down the sides of the hill. Vertigo was the consequence of this combined verticality. I came out, once, to make sure all was going all right and the boards were properly nailed to the corner uprights outside and inside. I knew I could count on Timothy for the anchorage.

123

It was all simple enough. You see, the wooden tower was rooted as the trees are. Unless *uprooted* it could not fall for it would not break, notwithstanding the barrel simile. Try, sometime, yourself to break a barrel!

Romeo and Juliet stood in full view from five farmhouses on five brotherly farms and Aunt Jane could see it from her sitting-room window. Several months after it was finished the first real sou'wester struck—in the night. As promptly as Aunt Jane's and Aunt Nell's, at sun up the anxious faces of five grey-bearded farmer brothers all came to as many farm-house doors shading their eyes to peer over at the new tower. It was still there. The Aunts promptly took their tower for granted. But the brothers kept on peering. For 'what was one storm, after all'. A few years later Uncle Thomas, arch-conservative, died.

But year after year this little drama of unfaith—typical of scepticism directed toward the Idea everywhere on earth—went on in the beloved valley. Storm after storm swept over. But each storm only left all nearer the conviction that the next must be the last. The uncles would shake their heads doggedly after coming to the door to look at the tower, each storm the tower weathered. Cramer, the builder, died ten years later. The staunch Timothy, stone-mason, followed the builder to the mysterious 'whatever' to which during his long and simple lifetime he had made allusion.

Then Uncle James died. Uncle John, the miller, died some years later. Some twenty-five years after the tower came to stand on the hill both the Lloyd-Jones sisters passed away to rest, their tower still standing. Uncle Philip, arch-sceptic, soon after moved away to the city, an old, old man. Uncle Jenkin died. But Uncle Enos, Sister Anna's younger brother, aged and alone now, never failed true to the habit of that long vigil, to come to the door after a storm and shading his eyes with his hand peer over at the tower to see the damage it had suffered at last. Now he too has moved away to the city where he can no longer see the tower.

Had the tower fallen at any time during that period, unfaith would have found and uttered judgment.

Now nearly forty-four years have gone by since the amateur windmill tower—'Romeo and Juliet'—took its place on the hill in the sun overlooking the beloved valley. I, the author of its being, hair getting white now as Aunt Nell's was when, before the tower was built, she first walked to the window to see its wheel spinning there among the trees, look over from Taliesin. Seemingly good as ever the wooden tower that was an experiment still stands in full view. Shall I take it down, faithful servant serving so well, so long? Or shall I let it go until it falls just as I myself must do—though neither tower nor I show any signs of doing so.

The tower is weatherbeaten. My hair is grey. One never knows. But when we fall, there will surely still be those to say, 'Well, there it is— down at last! We thought so!'

No. Romeo and Juliet shall live to crash down together.

About the time Romeo and Juliet came to stand on the hill known as 'Hillside', I had begun work on the Middle Western prairies: the buildings that came later to be known as 'New School of the Middle West'.

A contract with the Luxfer Prism Co. of Chicago, I to be consulting engineer for making prism-glass installations in office buildings throughout the country, had enabled me to build the workroom—then I called it a 'studio'—next to our little Oak Park dwelling-place.

An old willow tree still stood in the corridor connecting the house with the big work-room. I had succeeded in making the roofs around the tree trunks watertight in a manner that would permit the tree to grow, and the great, sprawling old tree gave us a grateful coolness in the studio in summer. I liked the golden green drooping above the amateurish buildings. If I could have covered the buildings all over with greenery, I would have done so. They were so badly overdone.

Here, in this studio, I worked away with various boys and girls as helpers and apprentices, to get the houses built that now stand around the prairie and have influenced many of those built in North, Northwest, Southwest, and West. And soon, owing to this proximity to the draughting board, my own children were all running around with thumbtacks in the soles of their shoes.

At last, my work was alongside my home, where it has been ever since. I could work late and tumble into bed. Unable to sleep because of some idea, I could get up, go downstairs to the 'studio' by way of the connecting corridor, and work.

As I had regularly gone to and fro between Oak Park and my work with Adler and Sullivan in Chicago, here at hand was the typical American dwelling, the 'monogoria' of earlier days, standing about on the Chicago prairie. That dwelling got there somehow and became typical. But by any faith in nature, implicit or explicit, it did not belong there. I had seen that far in the light of the conception of architecture as natural. And ideas had naturally begun to come to me as to a more natural house. Each house I built I longed for the chance to build another. And I soon got the chance. I was not the only one sick of hypocrisy and hungry for reality around there, I found.

What was the matter with the kind of house I found on the prairie? —let me tell you in more detail.

Just for a beginning, let's say that house *lied* about everything. It had no sense of Unity at all nor any such sense of space as should belong to a free man among a free people in a free country. It was stuck up and stuck on, however it might be done. Wherever it happened to be. To take any one of those so-called 'homes' away would have improved the landscape, and cleared the atmosphere. It was a box, too, cut full of holes to let in light and air, an especially ugly one to get in and out of. Or else it was a clumsy gabled chunk of roofed masonry similarly treated. Otherwise joinery reigned supreme; you know—'Carpenter and Joiner', it used to read on the signs. Floors were the only part of the house left plain and the housewife covered those with a tangled rug-collection, because otherwise the floors were 'bare'—bare, I suppose, only because one could not very well walk on jigsawing or turned spindles or plaster-ornament.

It is not too much to say that as an architect my lot in Oak Park was

125

cast with an inebriate lot of sinners hardened by habit against every human significance except one—and why mention 'the one touch of nature that makes the whole world kin'? I will venture to say that the aggregation was the worst the world ever saw—at the lowest esthetic level in all history. Steam heat, plumbing and electric light were coming in as its only redeeming features.

My first feeling therefore had been a yearning for simplicity. A new sense of simplicity as 'organic'. This had barely begun to take shape in my mind when the Winslow house was planned. But now it began in practice. Organic simplicity might be seen producing significant character in the harmonious order we call nature. Beauty in growing things. None were insignificant.

I loved the prairie by instinct as a great simplicity—the trees, flowers, sky itself, thrilling by contrast.

I saw that a little height on the prairie was enough to look like much more —every detail as to height becoming intensely significant, breadths all falling short. Here was tremendous spaciousness but all sacrificed needlessly. All space was cut up crosswise and cut up lengthwise into the fifty-foot lot—or would you have twenty-five feet less or twenty-five feet more? Salesmanship cut and parcelled it out, sold it with no restrictions. In a great, new, free country there was, then, everywhere a characteristic tendency to huddle and in consequence a mean tendency to tip everything in the way of human habitation up edgewise instead of letting it lie comfortably and naturally flat with the ground. Nor has this changed much since automobilization made it stupid as an economic measure and criminal as a social habit. I had an idea that the horizontal planes in buildings, those planes parallel to earth, identify themselves with the ground—make the building belong to the ground. I began putting this idea to work.

The buildings standing around there on the Chicago prairies were all tall and all tight. Chimneys were lean and taller still—sooty fingers threatening the sky. And beside them, sticking up almost as high, were the dormers. Dormers were elaborate devices—cunning little buildings complete in themselves—stuck on to the main roof-slopes to let the help poke their heads out of the attic for air. Invariably the damp, sticky clay of the prairie was dug out for a basement under the whole house and the rubble stone-walls of this dank basement always stuck above the ground a foot or so—and blinked through half-windows.

So the universal 'cellar' showed itself above ground as a bank of some kind of masonry running around the whole, for the house to sit up on—like a chair. The lean upper house walls of the usual two floors above this stone or brick basement were wood and were set up on top of this masonry chair. Preferably house walls were both sided and shingled, mixed up and down or crosswise, together or with mouldings. These overdressed wood house walls had cut in them, or cut out of them to be precise, big holes for the big cat, and little holes for the little cat, to get in or get out for ulterior purposes of light and air. These house walls were be-corniced or fancy-

126

bracketed up at the top into the tall, purposely, profusely complicated roof. Dormers plus. The whole roof was ridged and tipped, swanked and gabled to madness before they would allow it to be either watershed or shelter. The whole exterior was bedevilled, that is to say, mixed to puzzle-pieces with corner-boards, panel-boards, window-frames, corner-blocks, plinth-blocks, rosettes, fantails, and jiggerwork in general. This was the only way 'they' seemed to have then of putting on style. The wood butchery of scroll-saw and turning lathe were at that moment the honest means to this fashionable and unholy but entirely moral end as things were.

Unless the householder of the period were poor indeed, usually the ingenious corner tower as seen in monogaria, eventuated into a candle-snuffer dome, a spire, an inverted rutabaga, radish or onion. Always elaborate bay-windows and fancy porches rallied around this imaginatively unimaginative corner fetish—ring around a rosie. And all this the builders of the period could do nearly as well in brick as in stone. It was an impartial society. All materials looked pretty much alike to it in that day and do today.

Simplicity was as far from this scrap-pile as the pandemonium of the barnyard is far from music. But easy enough for the architect. Oh yes. All he had to do was call, 'Boy, take down No. 37, and put a bay-window on it for the lady.'

BUILDING THE NEW HOUSE

First thing in building the new house, get rid of the attic, therefore the dormer. Get rid of the useless false heights below it. Next, get rid of the unwholesome basement, yes absolutely—in any house built on the prairie. Instead of lean, brick chimneys bristling up everywhere to hint at Judgment, I could see necessity for one chimney only. A broad generous one, or at most two. These kept low-down on gently sloping roofs or perhaps flat roofs. The big fireplace in the house below became now a place for a real fire. A real fireplace at that time was extraordinary. There were mantels instead. A mantel was a marble frame for a few coals in a grate. Or it was a piece of wooden furniture with tile stuck in it around the grate, the whole set slam up against the plastered, papered wall. Insult to comfort. So the *integral* fireplace became an important part of the building itself in the houses I was allowed to build out there on the prairie.

It comforted me to see the fire burning deep in the solid masonry of the house itself. A feeling that came to stay.

Taking a human being for my scale, I brought the whole house down in height to fit a normal one—ergo, 5' 8½" tall, say. This is my own height. Believing in no other scale than the human being I broadened the mass out all I possibly could to bring it down into spaciousness. It has been said that were I three inches taller than 5' 8½" all my houses would have been quite different in proportion. Probably.

127

House walls were now started at the ground on a cement or stone water table that looked like a low platform under the building, and usually was. But the house walls were stopped at the second-storey windowsill level to let the bedrooms come through above in a continuous window series below the broad eaves of a gently sloping, overhanging roof. In this new house the wall was beginning to go as an impediment to outside light and air and beauty. Walls had been the great fact about the box in which holes had to be punched. It was still this conception of a wall-building which was with me when I designed the Winslow house. But after that my conception began to change.

My sense of 'wall' was no longer the side of a box. It was enclosure of space affording protection against storm or heat only when needed. But it was also to bring the outside world into the house and let the inside of the house go outside. In this sense I was working away at the wall as a wall and bringing it towards the function of a screen, a means of opening up space which, as control of building-materials improved, would finally permit the free use of the whole space without affecting the soundness of the structure.

The climate being what it was, violent in extremes of heat and cold, damp and dry, dark and bright, I gave broad protecting roof-shelter to the whole, getting back to the purpose for which the cornice was originally designed. The underside of roof-projections was flat and usually light in colour to create a glow of reflected light that softly brightened the upper rooms. Overhangs had double value: shelter and preservation for the walls of the house, as well as this diffusion of reflected light for the upper storey through the 'light screens' that took the place of the walls and were now often the windows in long series.

And at this time I saw a house, primarily, as livable interior space under ample shelter. I liked the *sense of shelter* in the look of the building. I still like it.

The house began to associate with the ground and become natural to its prairie site.

And would the young man in Architecture believe that this was all 'new' then? Yes—not only new, but destructive heresy—ridiculous eccentricity. All somewhat so today. Stranger still, but then it was *all* so *new* that what prospect I had of ever earning a livelihood by making houses was nearly wrecked. At first, 'they' called the houses 'dress reform' houses because Society was just then excited about that particular reform. This simplification looked like some kind of reform to the provincials.

What I have just described was on the *outside* of the house. But it was all there, chiefly because of what had happened *inside*.

Dwellings of that period were cut up, advisedly and completely, with the grim determination that should go with any cutting process. The interiors consisted of boxes beside boxes or inside boxes, called *rooms*. All boxes were inside a complicated outside boxing. Each domestic function was properly box to box.

I could see little sense in this inhibition, this cellular sequestration that implied ancestors familiar with penal institutions, except for the privacy of bedrooms on the upper floor. They were perhaps all right as sleeping boxes. So I declared the whole lower floor as one room, cutting off the kitchen as a laboratory, putting the servants' sleeping and living quarters next to the kitchen but semi-detached, on the ground floor. Then I screened various portions of the big room for certain purposes like dining, reading, receiving callers.

There were no plans in existence like these at the time. But my clients were all pushed toward these ideas as helpful to a solution of the vexed servant problem. Scores of unnecessary doors disappeared and no end of partition. Both clients and servants liked the new freedom. The house became more free as space and more livable too. Interior spaciousness began to dawn.

Thus came an end to the cluttered house. Fewer doors; fewer window holes though much greater window area; windows and doors lowered to convenient human heights. These changes once made, the ceilings of the rooms could be brought down over on to the walls by way of the horizontal broad bands of plaster on the walls themselves above the windows and coloured the same as the room-ceilings. This would bring ceiling-surface and colour down to the very window tops. Ceilings thus expanded by way of the wall band above the windows gave generous overhead even to small rooms. The sense of the whole broadened, made plastic by this means.

Here entered the important new element of plasticity—as I saw it. And I saw it as indispensable element to the successful use of the machine. The windows would sometimes be wrapped around the building corners as inside emphasis of plasticity and to increase the sense of interior space. I fought for outswinging windows because the casement window associated house with the out-of-doors gave free openings outward. In other words, the so-called casement was not only simple but more human in use and effect. So more natural. If it had not existed I should have invented it. But it was not used at that time in the United States so I lost many clients because I insisted upon it. The client usually wanted the double-hung (the guillotine window) in use then, although it was neither simple nor human. It was only expedient. I used it once, in the Winslow house, and rejected it forever thereafter. Nor at that time did I entirely eliminate the wooden trim. I did make the 'trim' plastic, that is to say, light and continuously flowing instead of the prevailing heavy 'cut and butt' carpenter work. No longer did trim, so-called, look like carpenter work. The machine could do it all perfectly well as I laid it out, in this search for quiet. This plastic trim enabled poor workmanship to be concealed. There was need of that much trim then to conceal much in the way of craftsmanship because the battle between the machines and the Union had already begun to demoralize workmen.

Machine-resources of this period were so little understood that extensive drawings had to be made merely to show the mill-man what to leave off. Not alone in the trim but in numerous ways too tedious to describe in words, this revolutionary sense of the *plastic* whole began to work more and more intelligently and have fascinating unforeseen consequences. Nearly everyone had endured the house of the period as long as possible, judging by the appreciation of the change. Here was an ideal of organic simplicity put to work, with historical consequences not only in this country but especially in the thought of the civilized world.

SIMPLICITY

Organic Simplicity—in this early constructive effort—I soon found depended upon the sympathy with which such co-ordination as I have described might be effected. Plainness was not necessarily simplicity. That was evident. Crude furniture of the Roycroft-Stickley-Mission style, which came along later, was offensively plain, plain as a barn-door—but was never simple in any true sense. Nor, I found, were merely machine-made things in themselves necessarily simple. 'To think', as the Master used to say, 'is to deal in simples.' And that means with an eye single to the altogether.

This is, I believe, the single secret of simplicity: that we may truly regard nothing at all as simple in itself. I believe that no one thing in itself is ever so, but must achieve simplicity—as an artist should use the term—as a perfectly realized part of some organic whole. Only as a feature or any part becomes harmonious element in the harmonious whole does it arrive at the state of simplicity. Any wild flower is truly simple but double the same wild flower by cultivation and it ceases to be so. The scheme of the original is no longer clear. Clarity of design and perfect significance both are first essentials of the spontaneous born simplicity of the lilies of the field. 'They toil not, neither do they spin.' Jesus wrote the supreme essay on simplicity in this, 'Consider the lilies of the field.'

Five lines where three are enough is always stupidity. Nine pounds where three are sufficient is obesity. But to eliminate expressive words in speaking or writing—words that intensify or vivify meaning is not simplicity. Nor is similar elimination in architecture simplicity. It may be, and usually is, stupidity.

In architecture, expressive changes of surface, emphasis of line and especially textures of material or imaginative pattern, may go to make facts more eloquent—forms more significant. Elimination, therefore, may be just as meaningless as elaboration, perhaps more often is so. To know what to leave out and what to put in; just where and just how, ah, *that* is to have been educated in knowledge of simplicity—toward ultimate freedom of expression.

As for objects of art in the house, even in that early day they were *bêtes noires* of the new simplicity. If well chosen, all right. But only if each

130

were properly digested by the whole. Antique or modern sculpture, paintings, pottery, might well enough become objectives in the architectural scheme. And I accepted them, aimed at them often but assimilated them. Such precious things may often take their places as elements in the design of any house, be gracious and good to live with. But such assimilation is extraordinarily difficult. Better in general to design all as integral features.

I tried to make my clients see that furniture and furnishings that were not built in as integral features of the building should be designed as attributes of whatever furniture *was* built in and should be seen as a minor part of the building itself even if detached or kept aside to be employed only on occasion.

But when the building itself was finished the old furniture they already possessed usually went in with the clients to await the time when the interior might be completed in this sense. Very few of the houses, therefore, were anything but painful to me after the clients brought in their belongings.

Soon I found it difficult, anyway, to make some of the furniture in the abstract. That is, to design it as architecture and make it human at the same time—fit for human use. I have been black and blue in some spot, somewhere, almost all my life from too intimate contact with my own early furniture.

Human beings must group, sit or recline, confound them, and they must dine—but dining is much easier to manage and always a great artistic opportunity. Arrangements for the informality of sitting in comfort singly or in groups still belonging in disarray to the scheme as a whole: *that* is a matter difficult to accomplish. But it can be done now and should be done, because only those attributes of human comfort and convenience should be in order which belong to the whole in this modern integrated sense.

Human use and comfort should not be taxed to pay dividends on any designer's idiosyncrasy. Human use and comfort should have intimate possession of every interior—should be felt in every exterior. Decoration is intended to make use more charming and comfort more appropriate, or else privilege has been abused.

As these ideals worked away from house to house, finally freedom of floor space and elimination of useless heights worked a miracle in the new dwelling place. A sense of appropriate freedom had changed its whole aspect. The whole became different but more fit for human habitation and more natural on its site. It was impossible to imagine a house once built on these principles somewhere else. An entirely new sense of space-values in architecture came home. It now appears these new values came into the architecture of the world. New sense of repose in quiet streamline effects had arrived. The streamline and the plain surface seen as the flat plane had then and there, some thirty-seven years ago, found their

131

way into buildings as we see them in steamships, aeroplanes and motor-cars, although they were intimately related to building materials, environment and the human being.

But, more important than all beside, still rising to greater dignity as an idea as it goes on working, was the ideal of plasticity. That ideal now began to emerge as a means to achieve an organic architecture.

PLASTICITY

Plasticity may be seen in the expressive flesh-covering of the skeleton as contrasted with the articulation of the skeleton itself. If form really 'followed function'—as the Master declared—here was the direct means of expression of the more spiritual idea that form and function are one: the only true means I could see then or can see now to eliminate the separation and complication of cut-and-butt joinery in favour of the expressive flow of continuous surface. Here, by instinct at first—all ideas germinate—a principle entered into building that has since gone on developing. In my work the idea of plasticity may now be seen as the element of continuity.

In architecture, plasticity is only the modern expression of an ancient thought. But the thought taken into structure and throughout human affairs will re-create in a badly 'disjointed', distracted world the entire fabric of human society. This magic word 'plastic' was a word Louis Sullivan himself was fond of using in reference to his idea of ornamentation as distinguished from all other or applied ornament. But now, why not the larger application in the structure of the building itself in this sense?

Why a principle working in the part if not living in the whole?

If form really followed function—it did in a material sense by means of this ideal of plasticity, the spiritual concept of *form and function as one* —why not throw away the implications of post or upright and beam or horizontal entirely? Have no beams or columns piling up as 'joinery'. Nor any 'features' as *fixtures*. No. Have no appliances of any kind at all, such as pilasters, entablatures and cornices. Nor put into the building any fixtures whatsoever as 'fixtures'. Eliminate the separations and separate joints. Classic architecture was all fixation-of-the-fixture. Yes, entirely so. Now why not let walls, ceilings, floors become *seen* as component parts of each other, their surfaces flowing into each other. To get continuity in the whole, eliminating all constructed features just as Louis Sullivan had eliminated background in his ornament in favour of an integral sense of the whole. Here the promotion of an idea from the material to the spiritual plane began to have consequences. Conceive now that an entire building might grow up out of conditions as a plant grows up out of soil and yet be free to be itself, to 'live its own life according to Man's Nature'. Dignified as a tree in the midst of nature but a child of the spirit of man.

132

I now propose an ideal for the architecture of the machine age, for the ideal American building. Let it grow up in that image. The tree.

But I do not mean to suggest the imitation of the tree.

Proceeding, then, step by step from generals to particulars, plasticity as a large means in architecture began to grip me and to work its own will. Fascinated I would watch its sequences, seeing other sequences in those consequences already in evidence: as in the Heurtley, Martin, Heath, Thomas, Tomek, Coonley and dozens of other houses.

The old architecture, so far as its grammar went, for me began, literally, to disappear. As if by magic new architectural effects came to life—effects genuinely new in the whole cycle of architecture owing simply to the working of this spiritual principle. Vistas of inevitable simplicity and ineffable harmonies would open, so beautiful to me that I was not only delighted, but often startled. Yes, sometimes amazed.

I have since concentrated on plasticity as physical continuity, using it as a practical working principle within the very nature of the building itself in the effort to accomplish this great thing called architecture. Every true aesthetic is an implication of nature, so it was inevitable that this aesthetic ideal should be found to enter into the actual building of the building itself as a principle of construction.

But later on I found that in the effort to actually eliminate the post and beam in favour of structural continuity, that is to say, making the two things one thing instead of two separate things, I could get no help at all from regular engineers. By habit, the engineer reduced everything in the field of calculation to the post and the beam resting upon it before he could calculate and tell you where and just how much for either. He had no other data. Walls made one with floors and ceilings, merging together yet reacting upon each other, the engineer had never met. And the engineer has not yet enough scientific formulae to enable him to calculate for continuity. Floor slabs stiffened and extended as cantilevers over centred supports, as a waiter's tray rests upon his upturned fingers, such as I now began to use in order to get planes parallel to the earth to emphasize the third dimension, were new, as I used them, especially in the Imperial Hotel. But the engineer soon mastered the element of continuity in floor slabs, with such formulae as he had. The cantilever thus became a new feature of design in architecture. As used in the Imperial Hotel at Tokio it was the most important of the features of construction that insured the life of that building in the terrific temblor of 1922. So, not only a new aesthetic but proving the aesthetic as scientifically sound, a great new economic 'stability' derived from steel in tension was able now to enter into building construction.

THE NATURE OF MATERIALS

From this early ideal of plasticity another concept came. To be consistent in practice, or indeed if as a principle it was to work out in the

133

field at all, I found that plasticity must have a new sense, as well as a science of materials. The greatest of the materials, steel, glass, ferro- or armoured concrete were new. Had they existed in the ancient order we never would have had anything at all like 'classic architecture'.

And it may interest you, as it astonished me, to learn that there was nothing in the literature of the civilized world on the nature of materials in this sense. So I began to study the nature of materials, learning to *see* them. I now learned to see brick as brick, to see wood as wood, and to see concrete or glass or metal. See each for itself and all as themselves. Strange to say, this required greater concentration of imagination. Each material demanded different handling and had possibilities of use peculiar to its own nature. Appropriate designs for one material would not be appropriate at all for another material. At least, not in the light of this spiritual ideal of simplicity as *organic plasticity*. Of course, as I could now see, there could be no organic architecture where the nature of materials was ignored or misunderstood. How could there be? Perfect correlation is the first principle of growth. Integration, or even the very word 'organic' means that nothing is of value except as it is naturally related to the whole in the direction of some living purpose, a true part of entity. My old master had designed for the old materials all alike; brick, stone, wood, iron wrought or iron cast, or plaster—all were grist for his rich imagination and his sentient ornament.

To him all materials were only one material in which to weave the stuff of his dreams. I still remember being ashamed of the delight I took at first in thus seeing—thanks to him too—so plainly around the beloved Master's own practice. But *acting* upon this new train of ideals brought work sharply up against the tool I could find to get the ideas in practical form: the Machine. What were the tools in use everywhere? Machines—automatic, most of them. Stone- or wood-planers, moulding shapers, various lathes and power saws, all in commercialized organized mills. Sheet-metal breakers, gigantic presses, shears, moulding and stamping machines in the sheet-metal industry, commercialized in 'shops'. Foundries and rolling-mills turned out cast-iron and steel in any imaginable shape. The machine as such had not seemed to interest Louis Sullivan. Perhaps he took it for granted. But what a resource, that rolling or drawing or extruding of metal! And more confusion to the old order, concrete-mixers, form-makers, clay-bakers, casters, glass-makers, all in organized trade unions.

And the unions themselves were all units in a more or less highly commercialized union in which craftsmanship had no place except as survival-for-burial. Standardization had already become an inflexible necessity. Standardization was either the enemy or a friend to the architect. He might choose. But I felt that as he chose he became master and useful or else he became a luxury and eventually a parasite. Although not realized then at all nor yet completely realized by the architect, machine standardization had already taken the life of handicraft in all its expressions. If I was to realize new buildings I should have to have new technique. I should have to so design buildings that they would not only be appropriate to

134

materials but design them so the machine that would *have* to make them could make them surpassingly well. By now, you see, I had really come under the discipline of a great ideal. There is no discipline so severe as the perfect integration of true correlation in any human endeavour. But there is no discipline that yields such rich rewards in work, nor is there any discipline so safe and sure of results. (Why should human relations be excepted?) The straight line, the flat plane were limitations until proved benefits by the Machine. But steel-in-tension was clearly liberation.

After the Winslow house was built in 1893 and Mr. Moore did not want a house so 'different' that he would have to go down the back way to his morning train to avoid being laughed at, our bulkheads of caution blindly serving Yesterday—our bankers—at first refused to loan money on the 'new' houses. Friends had to be found to finance the early buildings. When the plans were presented for estimates, soon, mill-men would look for the name on them, read the name, roll the drawings up again and hand them back to the contractor with the remark that 'they were not hunting for trouble'. Contractors, of course, more often failed to read the plans correctly than not. The plans were necessarily radically different simply because so much nonsense had to be left off the building. Numbers of small men went broke trying to carry out their contracts. This made trouble. Fools would come walking in where angels were afraid to tread. We seemed to have the worst of the contracting element in Oak Park to deal with. Clients usually stood by, excited, often interested beyond their means. So when they moved into the house they had to take their old furniture in with them whether they wanted to or not. This was tragedy because the ideal of an organic simplicity seen as the countenance of perfect integration, abolished all fixtures, rejected all superficial decoration, made all lighting and heating apparatus architectural features of the house and, so far as possible, all furniture was to be designed by the architect as a natural part of the whole building. Hangings, rugs, carpet —all came into the same category. So this particular feature gone wrong often crippled results. Nor was there any planting to be done about the house without co-operation with the architect. This made trouble. No sculpture, no painting unless co-operating with the architect. This made trouble. Decorators hunting a job would visit the owners, learn the name of the architect, lift their hats with exaggerated courtesy and turning on their heels leave with a curt, sarcastic 'Good day',—meaning really what the slang 'Good night!' meant some time ago. And the owners of the houses were all subjected to vulgar curiosity. Often to sincere admiration. But more often they submitted to the ridicule of that middle-of-the-road egoist, the one hundred per cent American provincial.

Each new building was a new experience. A different choice of materials and a different client would mean a different scheme altogether. Concrete was just then coming into use and Unity Temple at Oak Park became the first concrete monolith in the world. That is, the first total building designed for and completed in the wooden forms into which it

135

was poured as concrete. Even plastered houses were then new. Casement windows were nowhere to be seen except in my houses. So many things were new. Nearly everything, in fact, but the law of gravitation and the personal idiosyncrasy of the client.

THE FIRST PROTESTANT

The Larkin Building was the first emphatic protestant in architecture. Yes—it was the first emphatic outstanding protest against the tide of meaningless elaboration sweeping the United States as Uncle Dan Burnham, calling it by a different name, had prophesied it would do. The United States were being swept into one grand rubbish heap of the acknowledged styles, instead of intelligently and patiently creating a new architecture.

The Larkin Administration Building was a simple cliff of brick hermetically sealed (one of the first 'air-conditioned' buildings in the country) to keep the interior space clear of the poisonous gases in the smoke from the New York Central trains that puffed along beside it.

It was built of masonry material—brick and stone; and in terms of the straight line and flat plane the Larkin Administration Building was a genuine expression of power directly applied to purpose, in the same sense that the ocean liner, the plane or the car is so. And it's only fair to say that it has had a profound influence upon European architecture for this reason.

The character and brutal power as well as the opportunity for beauty of our own age were coming clear to me. In fact I saw then as now that they are all one. I saw our own great chance in this sense still going to waste on every side. Rebellious and protestant as I was myself when the Larkin Building came from me, I was conscious also that the only way to succeed, either as rebel or as protestant, was to make architecture genuine and constructive affirmation of the new Order of this Machine Age.

And I worked to get that something into the Larkin Building, interested now also in the principle of *articulation* as related to that order. But not until the contract had been let to Paul Mueller and the plaster-model of the building stood completed on the big detail board at the centre of the Oak Park draughting room did I get the articulation I finally wanted. The solution that had hung fire came in a flash. I took the next train to Buffalo to try and get the Larkin Company to see that it was worth thirty thousand dollars more to build the stair towers free of the central block, not only as independent stair towers for communication and escape but also as air intakes for the ventilating system. It would require this sum to individualize and properly articulate these features as I saw them.

Mr. Larkin, a kind and generous man, granted the appropriation and the building as architecture, I felt, was saved.

This entire building was a great fireproof vault, probably the first completely fireproof furnished building. The furniture was all made in steel and magnesite built into place—even the desks and chairs we made with the building. The wastepaper baskets were omitted. I never had a chance to incorporate them later—or design the telephone I had in mind as the office had already arranged for both these items. All else was of or with the building.

Magnesite was a new material to us then, but it was probably the cement used by the Romans and good in Rome until today. We experimented with it—finally used it—throughout the interior. And I made many new inventions. The hanging water-closet partition, the long automatic multiple chair-desk, the wall-water-closet, were only several among them. All were intended to simplify cleaning and make operation easy. The dignified top-lighted interior created the effect of one great official family at work in day-light, clean and airy quarters, day-lit and officered from a central court. The top-storey was a restaurant and conservatory, the ferns and flowers seen from the court below. The roof was a recreation ground paved with brick. The new architecture was in every detail practical or it was only another sentimentality, to further demoralize the country.

The officers, D. D. Martin, William R. Heath and the employees all appreciated the building in practice. But it was all too severe for the fundamentalist English tastes of the Larkin family. They were distracted, too, I imagine, by so many *experiments,* some of which, like the magnesite, delayed the completion of the building. A few minor failures annoyed them—and made them think the whole might be—merely queer? They did not really know. They never realized the place their building took in the thought of the world—for they never hesitated to make senseless changes in it in after years. To them it was just one of their factory buildings—to be treated like any other. And I suppose from any stand-point available to them, that was all it was. In architecture they were still pallbearers for the remains of Thomas Jefferson and subsequently all built colonial houses for themselves in Buffalo.

Now Unity Temple and the Buffalo dwellings of D. D. Martin and W. R. Heath came into work at Oak Park.

Several invitations to submit work in competition came along also. But no matter how promising the programme nor how many promises were made I steadily refused to enter a competition. I have refused ever since.

The world has gained no building worth having by competition because: (1) The jury itself is necessarily a hand-picked average. Some constituency must agree upon the jury. (2) Therefore the first thing this average does as a jury, when picked, is to go through all the designs and throw out the best ones and the worst ones. This is necessary in order that the average may average upon something average. (3) Therefore any architectural competition will be an average upon an average by averages in behalf of the average. (4) The net result is a building well behind the times before it is begun.

This might seem democratic if mediocrity is democratic ideal in architecture. No. Competitions are only opportunity for inexperienced youth to air precocious propensity.

137

Moreover, to further vitiate the competitive objective every architect entering any competition does so to win the prize. So he sensibly aims his efforts at what he conceives to be the common prejudices and predilections of the jury. Invariably the man who does this most accurately wins the competition.

A competition was first thought of for Unity Temple, but the idea was abandoned and the commission was given to me after much hesitation and debate among the committee.

Committee decisions are seldom above mediocre unless the committee is dominated by some strong individual. In this case the committee was so run by Charles E. Roberts—inventor. He was the strong man in this instance or Unity Temple would never have been built.

Let us take Unity Temple to pieces in the thought of its architect and see how it came to be the Unity Temple you now see.

DESIGNING UNITY TEMPLE

Had Doctor Johonnot, the Universalist pastor of Unity Church, been Fra Junipero the style of the Unity Temple would have been predetermined—'Mission'. Had he been Father Latour it would have been Midi-Romanesque. Yes, and perhaps being what he was, he was entitled to the only tradition he knew—that of the little white New England church, lean spire pointing to heaven—'back East'. If sentimentality were sense this might be so.

But the pastor was out of luck. Circumstances brought him to yield himself up in the cause of architecture. And to that cause everyone who undertakes to read what follows is called upon to yield a little.

Our building committee were all good men and true. One of them, Charles E. Roberts, the mechanical engineer and inventor I have mentioned, was himself enlightened in creation. One, enlightened, is leaven enough in any Usonian committee lump. The struggle began. It is always a struggle in architecture for the architect where good men and true are concerned.

First came the philosophy of the building in my own mind.

I said, let us abolish, in the art and craft of architecture, literature in any symbolic form whatsoever. The sense of inner rhythm deep planted in human sensibility lives far above all other considerations in art. Then why the steeple of the little white church? Why *point* to heaven?

I told the committee a story. Did they not know the tale of the holy man who, yearning to see God, climbed up and up the highest mountain —climbed to the highest relic of a tree there was on the mountain? There, ragged and worn, he lifted up his eager perspiring face to heaven and called upon God. He heard a voice bidding him get down . . . go back!

Would he really see God's face? Then he should go back, go down there in the valley below where his own people were—there only could *he* look upon God's countenance. . . .

138

Why not, then, build a temple, not to God in that way—more sentimental than sense—but build a temple to man, appropriate to his uses as a meeting place, in which to study man himself for his God's sake? A modern meeting-house and a good-time place.

The pastor was a liberal. His liberality was thus challenged, his reason was piqued and the curiosity of all was aroused. What would such a building look like? They said they could imagine no such thing.

'That's what you came to me for,' I ventured. 'I can imagine it and I will help you create it.' Promising the building committee something tangible to look at soon—I sent them away.

The first idea was to keep a noble room for worship in mind, and let that sense of the great room shape the whole edifice. Let the room inside be the architecture outside.

What shape? Well, the answer lay in the material. There was only one material to choose—as the church funds were $45,000—to 'church' 400 people in 1906. Concrete was cheap.

Why not make the wooden boxes or forms so the concrete could be cast in them as separate blocks and masses, these grouped about an interior space in some such way as to preserve this sense of the interior space, the great room, in the appearance of the whole building? And the block-masses might be left as themselves with no facing at all? That would be cheap and permanent and not ugly either.

What roof? What had concrete to offer as a cover shelter? The concrete slab—of course. The reinforced slab. Nothing else if the building was to be thoroughbred, meaning built in character out of one material.

Too monumental, all this? Too forthright for my committee I feared. Would a statement so positive as that final slab over the whole seem irreligious to them? Profane in their eyes? Why? But the flat slab was cheap and direct. It would be nobly simple. The wooden forms or moulds in which concrete buildings must at that time be cast were always the chief item of expense, so to repeat the use of a single form as often as possible was necessary. Therefore a building, all four sides alike, looked like the thing. This, reduced to simplest terms, meant a building square in plan. That would make their temple a cube—a noble form in masonry.

The slab, too, belonged to the cube by nature. '*Credo simplicitatem.*' That form is most imaginative and happy that is most radiant with the aura or overtone of super-form. Integrity.

Then the Temple itself—still in my mind—began to take shape. The site was noisy, by the Lake Street car-tracks. Therefore it seemed best to keep the building closed on the three front sides and enter it from a court to the rear at the centre of the lot. Unity Temple itself with the thoughts in mind I have just expressed, arrived easily enough, but there was a secular side to Universalist church activities—entertainment often, Sunday school, feasts, and so on.

To embody these with the temple would spoil the simplicity of the room—the noble Room in the service of man for the worship of God. So I finally put the secular space designated as 'Unity House', a long free

139

space to the rear of the lot, as a separate building to be subdivided by movable screens for Sunday school or on occasion. It thus became a separate building but harmonious with the Temple—the entrance to both to be the connecting link between them. That was that.

And why not put the pulpit at the entrance side at the rear of the square Temple, and bring the congregation into the room at the sides on a lower level so those entering would be imperceptible to the audience? This would preserve the quiet and the dignity of the room itself. Out of that thought came the depressed foyer or cloister corridor on either side, leading from the main lobby at the centre to the stairs in the near and far corners of the room. Those entering the room in this way could see into the big room but not be seen by those already seated within it.

And, important to the pastor, when the congregation rose to disperse, here was opportunity to move forward toward their pastor and by swinging wide doors open beside the pulpit allow the entire flock to pass out by him and find themselves directly in the entrance loggia from which they had first come in. They had gone into the depressed entrances at the sides from this same entrance to the big room. But it seemed more respectful to let them go out thus toward the pulpit than turn their backs upon their minister as is usual in most churches.

So this was done.

The room itself—size determined by comfortable seats with leg-room for four hundred people—was built with four interior free standing posts to carry the overhead structure. These concrete posts were hollow and became free-standing ducts to insure economic and uniform distribution of heat. The large supporting posts were so set in plan as to form a double tier of alcoves on four sides of the room. I flooded these side-alcoves with light from above to get a sense of a happy cloudless day into the room. And with this feeling for light the centre ceiling between the four great posts became skylight, daylight sifting through between the intersecting concrete beams, filtering through amber glass ceiling lights. Thus managed the light would, rain or shine, have the warmth of sunlight. Artificial lighting took place there at night as well. This scheme of lighting was integral, gave diffusion and kept the room-space clear.

Now for proportion—for the concrete expression of concrete in this natural arrangement—the ideal of an organic whole well in mind. And we have arrived at the question of *style*. For observe, so far, what has actually taken place is only reasoned *arrangement*. The 'plan' with an eye to an exterior in the realm of ideas but meantime 'felt' in imagination as a whole.

First came the general philosophy of the thing as repeated in the little story to the trustees. All artistic creation has its own philosophy. It is the first condition of creation. However, some would smile and say, 'the result of it'.

Second there was the general purpose of the whole to consider in each part: a matter of reasoned arrangement. This arrangement must be made with a sense of the yet-unborn-whole in the mind, to be blocked out as

140

appropriate to concrete masses cast in wooden boxes. Holding all this diversity together in a preconceived direction is really no light matter but is the condition of creation. Imagination conceives here the PLAN suitable to the material and the purpose of the whole, seeing the probable possible form clearer all the time.

Imagination reigns supreme, until now the form the whole will naturally take must be seen.

But if all this preliminary planning has been well conceived that question in the main is settled. This matter of style is organic now.

We do not choose the style. No. Style is what is coming now and it will be what we *are* in all this. A thrilling moment in any architect's experience. He is about to see the countenance of something he is invoking with intense concentration. Out of this inner sense of order and love of the beauty of life something is to be born—maybe to live long as a message of hope and be a joy or a curse to his kind. *His* message he feels. None the less will it be 'theirs', and rather more. And it is out of love and understanding that any building is born to bless or curse those it is built to serve. Bless them if they will see, understand and aid. Curse them as it will be cursed by them if either they or the architect fail to understand each other. This is the faith and the fear in the architect as he makes ready—to draw his design.

In all artists it is somewhat the same fear and the same faith.

Now regard this pure white sheet of paper! It is ready for recording the logic of the plan.

T-square, triangle, scale—seductive invitation lying upon the spotless surface. Temptation!

'Boy! Go tell Black Kelly to make a blaze there in the work-room fireplace! Ask Brown Sadie if it's too late to have Baked Bermudas for supper! Then go ask your Mother—I shall hear her in here—to play something—Bach preferred, or Beethoven if she prefers.'

Now comes to brood—to suffer doubt, hesitate yet burn with eagerness. To test bearings—and prove ground already assumed by putting all together in definite scale on paper. Preferably small scale study at first. Then larger. Finally still larger scale detail studies of parts.

An aid to creative effort, the open fire. What a friend to the labouring artist the poetic baked-onion! Real encouragement to him is great music. Yes, and what a poor creature, after all, creation comes singing through. About like catgut and horsehair in the hands of a Sarasate.

Night labour at the draughting board is best for intense creation. It may continue uninterrupted.

Meantime glancing side reflections are passing in the mind—'design is abstraction of nature-elements in purely geometric terms'—that is what we ought to call pure design? . . . This cube—this square—proportion. But—nature-pattern and nature-texture in materials themselves often approach conventionalization, or the abstract, to such a degree as to be

141

superlative means ready to the designer's hand to qualify, stimulate, and enrich his own efforts . . . What texture this concrete mass? Why not its own gravel? How to bring the gravel clean on the surface? . . . I knew. Here was reality. Yes, the 'fine thing' is always reality. Always reality? . . . Realism, the subgeometric, is the abuse of this fine feeling. . . . Keep the straight lines clean and keep all significant of the idea—the flat plane expressive and always clean cut. But let texture come unto them to qualify them in sunlight.

Reality is spirit—the essence brooding just behind all aspect. Seize it! And—after all you will see that the pattern of reality *is* supergeometric, casting a spell or a charm over any geometry, and is such a spell in itself.

Yes, so it seems to me as I draw with T-square, triangle and scale. That is what it means to be an artist—to seize this essence brooding everywhere in everything, just behind aspect. These questionings arising each with its own train of thought by the way, as the architect sits at his work.

Suddenly it is morning. To bed for a while.

But returning to the drawing board, here we see pencilled upon a sheet of paper, the plan, section, and elevation in the main—all except the exterior of Unity House, as the room for secular recreation is to be called. To establish harmony between these buildings of separate function proved difficult, utterly exasperating.

Another series of concentrations—lasting hours at a time for several days. How to keep the noble scale of the temple in the design of the subordinate mass of the secular hall and not falsify the function of that secular mass? The ideal of an organic architecture is often terribly severe discipline for the imagination. I came to know that full well. And, always, some minor concordance takes more time, taxes concentration more than all besides. Any minor element may become a major problem to vex the architect. How many schemes I have thrown away because some one minor feature would not come true to form!

Thirty-four studies were necessary to arrive at this concordance as it is now seen. Unfortunately the studies are lost with thousands of others of many other buildings: the fruit of similar struggles to co-ordinate and perfect them as organic entities—I wish I had kept them. Unity House looks easy enough now, for it is right enough. But it was not.

Finally, see the sense of the room not only preserved—*it may be seen as the soul of the design*. Instead of being built into the heart of a block of sculptured building material, out of sight, the sacrosanct space for worship is merely screened in . . . does it come through as the living 'motif' of the architecture?

Many studies in detail as a matter of course yet remain to be made, in order to determine what further may be left out to protect the design. These studies never seem to end and in this sense no organic building may ever be 'finished'. The complete goal of the ideal of organic architecture is never reached. Nor need be. What worth-while ideal is ever reached?

Unity Temple is a complete building on paper, already. There is no

142

'sketch' and there never has been one. There seldom is in a thought-built building.

The hardest of an architect's trials is to show his work for the first time to anyone not entirely competent or perhaps unsympathetic.

Already the architect begins to fear for the fate of his design. If it is to be changed much he prefers to throw it all away and begin all over again. Not much hope in the committee except Mr. Roberts. Why not ask him to see the design and explain it to him first? This is done. He is delighted. He *understands!* He is himself an inventor. And every project in architecture needs this one intimate friend in order to proceed. Mr. Roberts suggests a model. Without it nothing can be done. So the model is soon made.

All right; let the committee come now. They do come—all curious. Soon confounded—taking the 'show me' attitude. At this moment the creative architect is distinctly at a disadvantage as compared with his obsequious brother of the 'styles', he who can show his pattern-book, speak glibly of St. Mark's at Venice or Capella Palatine, impress the no less craven clients by brave show of erudite authorities.

But the architect with the ideal of an organic architecture at stake can talk only principle and sense. His only appeal is fresh and must be made to the independent thought and judgment of his client such as it is. The client, too, must know how to think a little or follow from generals to particulars. How rare it is for an architect to go into any court where that quality of mind is on the bench! This architect has learned to dread the personal idiosyncrasy—offered him three times out of five—as a substitute for the needed, hoped-for intelligence.

But hoping, we try. And we use all our resources, we two—the inventor and I—and we win a third member of the committee at the first meeting. Including the pastor, there are now four only left in doubt. One of the four openly hostile—Mr. Skillin. Dr. Johonnot, the pastor, is himself impressed but cautious—oh very—but tactful. He really has a glimpse of a new world. There is hope, distinctly hope, when he makes four as he soon does and the balance of power is with us. We need three more but the architect's work is done now. The four will get the others. The pastor is convinced. He will work! Doubts and fears are finally put to sleep—all but Mr. Skillin's. Mr. Skillin is sure the room will be dark—sure the acoustics will be bad. Finally the commission to go ahead is formally given over his dissent and warnings. Usually there is a Mr. Skillin on every modern building project in Usonia.

Now, who will build the Temple? After weeks of prospecting, no one can be found who wants to try it. Simple enough—yes—that's the trouble. So simple there is nothing at all to gauge it by. Requires too much imagination and initiative to be safe. The only bids available came in double, or more, our utmost limit. No one really wanted to touch it. Contractors are naturally gamblers but they usually bet on a sure thing—as they see the thing.

Now Paul Mueller comes to the rescue, reads the scheme like easy print. Will build it for only a little over their appropriation—and does it. He takes it easily along for nearly a year but he does it. Doesn't lose much on it in the end. It is exciting to him to rescue ideas, to participate in creation. And together we overcame difficulty after difficulty in the field, where an architect's education is never finished.

This building, however, is finished and the Sunday for dedication arrives. I do not want to go. Stay at home.

When the church was opened the phone began to ring. Happy contented voices are heard in congratulation. Finally weary, I take little Francie by the hand to go out into the air to get away from it all. Enough.

But just as my hat goes on my head, another ring, a prosaic voice, Mr. Skillin's: 'Take back all I said. . . . Light everywhere—all pleased.'

'Hear well?'

'Yes, see and hear fine—see it all now.'

'I'm glad.'

'Goodbye.' At last the doubting member, sincere in praise, a good sport besides.

Francie got tossed in the air. She came down with a squeal of delight.

And that is how it was and is and will be as often as a building is born.

Now, even though you are interested in architecture this story is more or less tedious and partly meaningless to you, as you were fairly warned at the beginning it would be. Without close study of the plans and photographs as it is read it must bore you. I have undertaken here, for once, to indicate the process of building on principle to insure character and achieve style, as near as I can indicate it by taking Unity Temple to pieces. Perhaps I am not the one to try it. It really would be a literary feat and feast were it well done.

A CODE

Concerning the traditional church as a modern building! Religion and art are forms of inner-experience—growing richer and deeper as the race grows older. We will never lose either. But I believe religious experience is outgrowing the church—not outgrowing religion but outgrowing the church as an institution, just as architecture has outgrown the Renaissance and for reasons human, scientific and similar. I cannot see the ancient institutional form of any church building as anything but sentimental survival for burial. The Temple as a forum and good-time place—beautiful and inspiring as such—yes. As a religious edifice raised in the sense of the old ritual? No. I cannot see it at all as living. It is no longer free.

Of course what is most vitally important in all that I have tried to say and explain cannot be explained at all. It need not be, I think. But here in this searching process may be seen the architect's mind at work, as boys in the studio would crowd around and participate in it. And you too, perhaps, may see certain wheels go around.

Certain hints coming through between the lines that may help someone who needs help in comprehending what planning a building really means.

144

10. AVERY COONLEY HOUSE. 1909. Rough-wood trim, plastered walls with in-laid tile-mosaic frieze; copper-barred window-glass; pink tile roofs

11. AVERY COONLEY KINDERGARTEN. 1911. Kinder-symphony in the glass of the windows

12. Interior court. Concrete and brick. Garden for music, dining and dancing. The tall poles are electric light fixtures, the lights protruding from the sides of the steel shafts

MIDWAY GARDENS. 1913

13. Street front

But this brief indication of the problem of building out of the man will not clear up the question as to what is style, either. But a little by way of suggestion, maybe.

Man's struggle to illuminate creation, especially his own, is another tragedy, that's all.

About this time Mr. and Mrs. Avery Coonley came to the Oak Park workshop to ask me to build a home for them at Riverside, Illinois.

They had gone to see nearly everything they could learn that I had done before they came.

The day they finally came into the Oak Park workshop Mrs. Coonley said they had come because it seemed to them they saw in my houses 'the countenance of principle'. This was to me a great and sincere compliment. So I put my best into the Coonley house. Looking back upon it, I feel now that that building was the best I could then do in the way of a house.

The story of this dwelling, most successful of my houses from my standpoint, is not included, as descriptions of ideals and the nature of my creative effort in house building already given apply particularly to this characteristic dwelling.

KUNO FRANCKE

Kuno Francke was Roosevelt exchange-professor in aesthetics at Harvard. He came out to the Oak Park workshop from Chicago. He had seen the new type house standing about on the prairies, asking the name of the architect each time, and again getting the same name for an answer. Mine.

A German friend, finally, at the professor's request, brought Francke and his charming wife to Oak Park for a short visit. Kuno Francke stayed all day and came back the next day. He, too, as had Mr. Waller and Uncle Dan, wanted me to go to Europe; but he wanted me to go to Germany, stay there and go to work.

'I see that you are doing organically', he said, 'what my people are feeling for only superficially. They would reward you. It will be long before your own people will be ready for what you are trying to give them.'

I had always loved old Germany—Goethe, Schiller, Nietzsche, Bach—the great architect who happened to choose music for his form—Beethoven and Strauss. And Munich! This beloved company—were they not Germany? And Vienna. Vienna had always appealed to my imagination. Paris? Never!

It would be wonderful to go!

But I had resisted up to this time, only dreaming of Europe.

Earlier, C. R. Ashbee of the London Arts and Crafts movement, while lecturing in America as the representative of the Natural Trust for Planes of Historic Interest and Natural Beauty, had come at Jane Addams' instigation to see me. He had stayed to urge a not dissimilar mission upon me He had been made to see the future I saw in the United States. Now how to make Kuno Francke see it. . . . I tried the same argument, not so dissimilar to the one I used with Uncle Dan.

'But, where will you be when America gets around to all this?' said the Herr Professor of Aesthetics. 'Do you expect to live one hundred years longer, at least?'

'Oh, no, but I hope to live long enough to see it coming,' I said. 'America is growing up fast. This is a free country!' I boasted. And I told him the story of the Chicagoan at the Ashbee banquet who stood Ashbee as long as he could, and then got up on his indignant feet to say that Chicago wasn't much on Culture now, maybe, but when Chicago *did* get after Culture, she'd make Culture hum! We laughed the usual laugh and that was that.

Soon after this inspiring visit came a proposal from Germany—from the very able publisher Wasmuth in Berlin—to publish a complete monograph of my work if I would send over the material. This proposal of the German publisher, was, I think, one net result of Kuno Francke's visit to the Oak Park workshop—though I never really knew.

(I had written the above when word by way of a news-clipping falling on my desk this morning told me that Kuno Francke was dead.)

THE CLOSED ROAD

This absorbing, consuming phase of my experience as an architect ended about 1909. I had almost reached my fortieth year. Weary, I was losing grip on my work and even my interest in it. Every day of every week and far into the night of nearly every day, Sunday included, I had 'added tired to tired' and added it again and yet again as I had been trained to do by Uncle James on the farm as a boy. Continuously thrilled by the effort but now it seemed to leave me up against a dead wall. I could see no way out. Because I did not know what I wanted I wanted to go away. Why not go to Germany and prepare the material for the Wasmuth Monograph? . . . I looked longingly in that direction.

Afternoons after four o'clock I had been in the habit of riding Kano, my young black horse (named after the Japanese Master), over the prairies north of Oak Park, sometimes letting him run wild as he loved to do, sometimes reining him in and reading from a book usually carried in my pocket, for I've always loved to read out-of-doors—especially Whitman.

Ever since boyhood, horseback riding, swimming, dancing, skating and omnivorous reading. Always music-hungry. Motoring (just that much added or was it deducted?) had come along to interfere with these recreations, a little. The motor car brought a disturbance of all values, subtle or obvious, and it brought disturbance to me.

Nevertheless, changing work to recreation and recreation to work as I might; the intensity of effort; unrelenting concentration; giving up the best in me to an ideal loved better than myself; all this had done something to me that reacted now upon every effort.

Everything, personal or otherwise, bore heavily down upon me. Domesticity most of all. What I wanted I did not know. I loved my children. I loved my home. A true home is the finest ideal of man, and yet—well, to gain freedom I asked for a divorce. It was, advisedly, refused. But these conditions were made: Were I to wait a year, divorce would be granted. The year went by. Legal freedom still refused by Catherine and all concerned in the promise. There remained to me in the circumstances only one choice—to take the situation in hand and work out the best life possible for all concerned. I could not keep my home because, to keep the ideal high, well . . . these three necessities have emerged from struggles precipitated at this time. I will set the three down here, as a means to honest life, instead of intruding the personal details of my own experience:

First: Marriage not mutual is no better, but is worse than any other form of slavery.

Second: Only to the degree that marriage is mutual is it decent. Love is not property. To take it so is barbarous. To protect it as such is barbarism.

Third: The child is the pledge of good faith its parents give to the future of the race. There are no illegitimate children. There may be illegitimate parents—legal or illegal. Legal interference has no function whatever in any true Democracy where these three fundamentals are concerned except:

Concerning the three foregoing conclusions:

First: Legal marriage is but a civil contract between a man and woman to share property and together provide for children that may spring from that marriage. So, in this respect legal marriage is subject to the legal interpretations and enforcements of any other contract. But legal marriage should be regarded as no mere licence for sexual relation. That relation should not as the law now makes it be the shameless essence of legal marriage in any such respect.

Second: Love, so far as laws can go to protect it, is entitled to the benefit of hands-off and the benefit of the doubt—unless degraded to a matter of commerce. So degraded, it should be subject to the laws that govern any other degraded traffic.

Love should be its own protection or its own defeat—if it is to grow strong.

Third: The child being the pledge given to society by love, it is the duty of the State to make and enforce laws that protect the substance of that pledge. The substance of the pledge is that, provided by its parents, every child born shall have good shelter, good food, good treatment and an open door to growth of body and mind. Added to this the child should have whatever in addition the circumstances of its birth may present to it—the most desirable thing of all being love. . . . *But this latter can be no concern of the laws.*

What I have tried to set down here was working in great detail in my mind during that miserable year of misunderstanding, overstatement, probation and demoralization. It was working more or less clearly as any man's right to live. The denial of that right not only worked against

147

reconstruction more than anything else but invited, if indeed the deliberate denial did not insist upon, the destruction of my home.

So, turning my clients' plans and draughtsmen over to a man whom I had but just met, a young Chicago architect, Von Holst, and making the best provision I could make for my family for one year, I broke with all family connections, though never with such responsibilities as I felt to be mine in that connection, or that I felt I could discharge.

Resolutely, with the same faith I'd had when leaving home and college, I took the train for Chicago. I went into the unknown to test faith in freedom. Test my faith in life as I had already proved faith in my work. I faced the hazards of change and objective ruin inevitably involved with our society in every inner struggle for freedom. I have since learned that objective struggle for inner freedom is a far deeper and more serious matter never finished on this earth. Notwithstanding or withstanding, all rebellion went its way in exile. A volunteer.

IN EXILE

In ancient Fiesole, far above the romantic city of cities Firenze, in a little cream-white villa on the Via Verdi, the rebel. How many souls seeking release from real or fancied domestic woes have sheltered on the slopes below Fiesole!

I, too, now sought shelter there in companionship with her who, by force of rebellion as by way of love, was then implicated with me.

Walking hand in hand together up the hill road from Firenze to the older town, all along the way in the sight and scent of roses, by day. Walking arm in arm up the same old road at night, listening to the nightingale in the deep shadows of the moonlit wood—trying hard to hear the song in the deeps of life. So many Pilgrimages we made to reach the small solid door framed in the solid white blank wall with the massive green door opening toward the narrow Via Verdi itself. Entering, closing the medieval door on the world outside to find a wood fire burning in the small grate. Estero in her white apron, smiling, waiting to surprise Signora and Signore with the incomparable little dinner: the perfect roast fowl, mellow wine, the caramel custard—beyond all roasts or wine or caramels ever made, I remember.

Or out walking in the high-walled garden that lay alongside the cottage in the Florentine sun or in the little garden by the pool arboured under climbing masses of yellow roses. I see the white cloth on the small stone table near the little fountain and beneath the clusters of yellow roses, set for two. There were long walks along the waysides of those undulating hills above, through the poppies, all over the hill fields, toward Vallombrosa.

The waterfall there, finding and losing its own sound in the deep silences of that famous pine wood. Breathing deep the odour of great pines—tired out, to sleep at the cloistered little mountain-inn.

Back again walking hand in hand miles through the hot sun and deep dust of the ancient winding road: an old Italian road, along the stream. How old! How thoroughly a Roman road!

Together again tired out, sitting on benches in the galleries of Europe, saturated with plastic beauty, beauty in buildings, beauty in sculpture, beauty in paintings, until no Chiesa however rare and no further beckoning work of human hands could waylay us any more.

Faithful comrade!

A dream? In realization ended? No. Woven, a golden thread in the human pattern of the precious fabric that is life: her life built into the house of houses. So far as may be known—forever!

AFTERMATH

Characteristic newspaper publicity pursued me now wherever I happened to go. Concerning that relentless persecution all I have to say at the moment I will try to set down clearly as three simple corollaries drawn from my own experience at this time of my life. I was pursued and exploited by publicity, together with all those I loved and was trying to respect, while I was making a desperate effort to re-establish a better life for us all upon a fairer, firmer basis for all.

Corollary One: Since all publicity in the United States is privately owned, any exploitation damaging or insulting to any individual in respect to the three fundamentals before stated should be seen as demoralizing.

Corollary Two: No publicity exploiting these profoundly personal matters should be marketed for profit, but such publicity should be limited to the purview of the laws unless crime or perversion harmful to all three interests be proved to exist. The burden of proof should be put upon the exploiter and not upon the exploited.

Corollary Three: These three human interests are more sacred than any property interests whatsoever.

How can any social structure deliberately intefering with the three conclusions or neglecting these three corollaries, hope to endure free?

The passions have all contributed to the progress of life. Sacrifice began as selfishness and even love began as lust. And still so begins. Legislation can be no friend to moral growth except by the 'Hands off!' or the 'Stand back, please', that allows the individual in the purely private and deeply personal concerns of his own life, to do or die *on his own.* I, too, believe that for any man to have found no lasting relationship in love in this brief life is to suffer great waste. Flogging, ridicule nor censure are needed to make such waste socially exemplar and effective.

Anyone not blinded by fear or eager to play the part of a wrathful Jehovah may see this. But how the laws of our own government are continually used as weapons of blackmail or revenge because the government stays in the sex-business as the government went into the liquor business —by way of prohibition and punishment—all this is obvious enough. Naturally, laws will be abused where they interfere with life and try to

149

assume responsibility which they have no business to assume in any decent society. Only where culture is based upon the building of character by freedom-of-choice will we ever have the culture of true Democracy.

Such exaggeration of government must continually resist continual exploitation of itself either as a weapon or a tool in the hands of unscrupulous or passionately vindictive individuals seeking public redress for private and personal wrongs.

Thomas Jefferson, most intelligent founder of our Republic, honestly declared, 'That Government is best Government that is least Government.'

The sense of all this I am trying to say in this way was fundamentally right. It was the same faith that characterized my forefathers from generation to generation. I suppose that faith carried them as it now carried me through the vortex of reaction, the anguish and waste of breaking up home and the loss of prestige and my work at Oak Park. Work, life and love I transferred to the beloved ancestral Valley where my mother foreseeing the plight I would be in had bought the low hill on which Taliesin now stands and she offered it to me now as a refuge. Yes, a retreat when I returned from Europe in 1911. I began to build Taliesin to get my back against the wall and fight for what I saw I had to fight.

TALIESIN

Taliesin was the name of a Welsh poet, a druid-bard who sang to Wales the glories of fine art. Many legends cling to that beloved reverend name in Wales.

Richard Hovey's charming masque, 'Taliesin', had just made me acquainted with his image of the historic bard. Since all my relatives had Welsh names for their places, why not Taliesin for mine? . . . Literally the Welsh word means 'shining brow'.

This hill on which Taliesin now stands as 'brow' was one of my favourite places when as a boy looking for pasque flowers I went there in March sun while snow still streaked the hillsides. When you are on the low hill-crown you are out in mid-air as though swinging in a plane, the Valley and two others dropping away from you leaving the tree-tops standing below all about you. And 'Romeo and Juliet' still stood in plain view over to the southeast. The Hillside Home School was just over the ridge.

As a boy I had learned to know the ground-plan of the region in every line and feature. For me now its elevation is the modelling of the hills, the weaving and the fabric that clings to them, the look of it all in tender green or covered with snow or in full glow of summer that bursts into the glorious blaze of autumn. I still feel myself as much a part of it as the trees and birds and bees are, and the red barns. Or as the animals are, for that matter.

When family-life in Oak Park that spring of 1909 conspired against the freedom to which I had come to feel every soul was entitled, I had no choice, would I keep my self-respect, but go out a voluntary exile into the uncharted and unknown. Deprived of legal protection, I got my back against the wall in this way. I meant to live if I could an unconventional life. I turned to this hill in the Valley as my grandfather before me had turned to America—as a hope and haven. But I was forgetful, for the time being, of grandfather's Isaiah. His smiting and punishment.

And architecture by now was quite mine. It had come to me by actual experience and meant something out of this ground we call America. Architecture was something in league with the stones of the field, in sympathy with 'the flower that fadeth and the grass that withereth'. It had something of the prayerful consideration for the lilies of the field that was my gentle grandmother's: something natural to the great change that was America herself.

It was unthinkable to me, at least unbearable, that any house should be put *on* that beloved hill.

I knew well that no house should ever be *on* a hill or *on* anything. It should be *of* the hill. Belonging to it. Hill and house should live together each the happier for the other. That was the way everything found round about was naturally managed except when man did something. When he added his mite he became imitative and ugly. Why? Was there no natural house? I felt I had proved there was. Now I wanted a *natural* house to live in myself. I scanned the hills of the region where the rock came cropping out in strata to suggest buildings. How quiet and strong the rock-ledge masses looked with the dark red cedars and white birches, there, above the green slopes. They were all part of the countenance of southern Wisconsin.

I wished to be part of my beloved southern Wisconsin, too. I did not want to put my small part of it out of countenance. Architecture, after all, I have learned—or before all, I should say—is no less a weaving and a fabric than the trees are. And as anyone might see, a beech tree is a beech tree. It isn't trying to be an oak. Nor is a pine trying to be a birch, although each makes the other more beautiful when seen together.

The world had had appropriate buildings before—why not appropriate buildings now, more so than ever before? There must be some kind of house that would belong to that hill, as trees and the ledges of rock did; as grandfather and mother had belonged to it in their sense of it all.

There must be a natural house, not natural as caves and log-cabins were natural, but native in spirit and the making, having itself all that architecture had meant whenever it was alive in times past. Nothing at all I had ever seen would do. This country had changed all that old building into something inappropriate. Grandfather and grandmother were something splendid in themselves that I couldn't imagine living in any period-houses I had ever seen or the ugly ones around there. Yes, there was a house that hill might marry and live happily with ever after. I fully intended to find it. I even saw for myself what it might be like. And I began to build it as the brow of that hill.

It was still a very young faith that undertook to build that house. It was the same faith, though, that plants twigs for orchards, vineslips for vine-yards, and small whips to become beneficent shade trees. And it planted them all about!

I saw the hill-crown back of the house as one mass of apple trees in bloom, perfume drifting down the Valley, later the boughs bending to the ground with red and white and yellow spheres that make the apple tree no less beautiful than the orange tree. I saw plum trees, fragrant drifts of snow-white in the spring, loaded in August with blue and red and yellow plums, scattering them over the ground at a shake of the hand. I saw the rows on rows of berry bushes, necklaces of pink and green gooseberries hanging to the under side of the green branches. I saw thickly pendent clusters of rubies like tassels in the dark leaves of the currant bushes. I remembered the rich odour of black currants and looked forward to them in quantity.

Black cherries? White cherries? Those too.

There were to be strawberry beds, white, scarlet and green over the covering of clean wheat-straw.

And I saw abundant asparagus in rows and a stretch of great sumptuous rhubarb that would always be enough. I saw the vineyard now on the south slope of the hill, opulent vines loaded with purple, green and yellow grapes. Boys and girls coming in with baskets filled to overflowing to set about the rooms, like flowers. Melons lying thick in the trailing green on the hill slope. Bees humming over all, storing up honey in the white rows of hives beside the chicken yard.

And the herd that I would have! The gentle Holsteins and a monarch of a bull—a sleek glittering decoration of the fields and meadows as they moved about, grazing. The sheep grazing too on the upland slopes and hills, the plaintive bleat of little white lambs in spring.

Those grunting sows to turn all waste into solid gold.

I saw the spirited, well-schooled horses, black horses and chestnut mares with glossy coats and splendid strides, being saddled and led to the mounting-block for rides about the place and along the country lanes I loved—the best of companionship alongside. I saw sturdy teams ploughing in the fields. There would be the changing colours of the slopes, from seed-ing time to harvest. I saw the scarlet comb of the rooster and his hundreds of hens—their white eggs and the ducks upon the pond. Geese, too, and swans floating upon the water in the shadow of the trees.

I looked forward to peacocks Javanese and white on the low roofs of the buildings or calling from the walls of the courts. And from the vegetable gardens I walked into a deep cavern in the hill—modern equivalent of the rootcellar of my grandfather. I saw its wide sand floor planted with celery, piled high with squash and turnips, potatoes, carrots, onions, parsnips. Cabbages wrapped in paper and hanging from the roof. Apples, pears and grapes stored in wooden crates walled the cellar from floor to roof. And cream! All the cream the boy had been denied. Thick—so lifting it in a spoon it would float like an egg on the fragrant morning cup of coffee or ride on the scarlet strawberries.

Yes, Taliesin should be a garden and a farm behind a real workshop and a good home.

I saw it all, and planted it all and laid the foundation of the herd, flocks, stable and fowl as I laid the foundation of the house.

All these items of livelihood came back—improved from boyhood.

And so began a 'shining brow' for the hill, the hill rising unbroken above it to crown the exuberance of life in all these rural riches.

There was a stone quarry on another hill a mile away, where the yellow sand-limestone uncovered lay in strata like outcropping ledges in the façades of the hills. The look of it was what I wanted for such masses as would rise from these native slopes. The teams of neighbouring farmers soon began hauling the stone over to the hill, doubling the teams to get it to the top. Long cords of this native stone, five hundred or more from first to last, got up there ready to hand, as Father Larson, the old Norse stone mason working in the quarry beyond, blasted and quarried it out in great flakes. The slabs of stone went down for pavements of terraces and courts. Stone was sent along the slopes into great walls. Stone stepped up like ledges on to the hill and flung long arms in any direction that brought the house to the ground. The ground! My grandfather's ground. It was lovingly felt as intimate in all this.

Finally it was not so easy to tell where pavements and walls left off and ground began. Especially on the hill-crown, which became a low-walled garden above the surrounding courts, reached by stone steps walled into the slopes. A clump of fine oaks that grew on the hilltop stood untouched on one side above the court. A great curved stone-walled seat enclosed the space just beneath them, and stone pavement stepped down to a spring or fountain that welled up into a pool at the centre of the circle. Each court had its fountain and the winding stream below had a great dam. A thick stone wall was thrown across it, to make a pond at the very foot of the hill and raise the water in the valley to within sight from Taliesin. The water below the falls thus made was sent by hydraulic ram up to a big stone reservoir built into the higher hill, just behind and above the hilltop garden, to come down again into the fountains and go on down to the vegetable gardens on the slopes below the house.

Taliesin, of course, was to be an architect's workshop, a dwelling as well, for young workers who would come to assist. And it was a farm cottage for the farm help. Around a rear court were to be farm buildings, for Taliesin was to be a complete living unit genuine in point of comfort and beauty, yes, from pig to proprietor. The place was to be self-sustaining if not self-sufficient, and with its domain of two hundred acres was to be shelter, food, clothes and even entertainment within itself. It had to be its own light-plant, fuelyard, transportation and water system.

Taliesin was to be recreation ground for my children and their children perhaps for many generations more. This modest human programme in terms of rural Wisconsin arranged itself around the hilltop in a series of four varied courts leading one into the other, the courts all together forming a sort of drive along the hillside flanked by low buildings on one side

153

and by flower gardens against the stone walls that retained the hill-crown on the other.

The hill-crown was thus saved and the buildings became a brow for the hill itself. The strata of fundamental stone-work kept reaching around and on into the four courts, and made them. Then stone, stratified, went into the lower house walls and up from the ground itself into the broad chimneys. This native stone prepared the way for the lighter plastered construction of the upper wood-walls. Taliesin was to be an abstract combination of stone and wood as they naturally met in the aspect of the hills around about. And the lines of the hills were the lines of the roofs, the slopes of the hills their slopes, the plastered surfaces of the light wood-walls, set back into shade beneath broad eaves, were like the flat stretches of sand in the river below and the same in colour, for that is where the material that covered them came from.

The finished wood outside was the colour of grey tree-trunks in violet light.

The shingles of the roof surfaces were left to weather silver-grey like the tree branches spreading below them.

The chimneys of the great stone fireplaces rose heavily through all, wherever there was a gathering place within, and there were many such places. They showed great rock-faces over deep openings inside.

Outside they were strong, quiet, rectangular rock-masses bespeaking strength and comfort within.

Country masons laid all the stone with the stone-quarry for a pattern and the architect for a teacher. The masons learned to lay the walls in the long, thin, flat ledges natural to the quarry, natural edges out. As often as they laid a stone they would stand back to judge the effect. They were soon as interested as sculptors fashioning a statue; one might imagine they were as they stepped back, head cocked one side, to get the general effect. Having arrived at some conclusion they would step forward and shove the stone more to their liking, seeming never to tire of this discrimination. Many of them were artistic for the first time, and liked it. There were many masons from first to last, all good. Perhaps old Dad Signola, in his youth a Czech, was the best of them until Philip Volk came. Philip worked away five years at the place as it grew from year to year—for it will never be finished. And with not much inharmonious discrepancy, one may see each mason's individuality in his work at Taliesin to this day. I frequently recall the man as I see his work.

At that time, to get this mass of material to the hilltop meant organizing man and horse-power. Trucks came along years later. Main strength and awkwardness, directed by commanding intelligence, got the better of the law of gravitation by the ton as sand, stone, gravel and timber went up into appointed places. Ben Davis was commander of these forces at this time. Ben was a creative cusser. He had to be. To listen to Ben back of all this movement was to take off your hat to a virtuoso. Men have cussed between every word, but Ben split the words and artistically worked in an oath between every syllable. One day Ben with five of his men was moving

154

a big rock that suddenly got away from its edge and fell over flat, catching Ben's big toe. I shuddered for that rock as, hobbling slowly back and forth around it, Ben hissed and glared at it, threatening, eyeing and cussing it. He rose to such heights, plunged to such depths of vengeance as I had never suspected, even in Ben. No Marseillaise nor any damnation in the mouth of a Mosaic prophet ever exceeded Ben at this high spot in his career as a cusser. William Blake says exuberance is beauty. It would be profane perhaps to say that Ben at this moment was sublime. But he was.

And in Spring Green (the names in the region are mostly simple like Black Earth, Blue Mounds, Cross Plains, Lone Rock, Silver Creek) I found a carpenter. William Weston was a natural carpenter. He was a carpenter such as architects like to stand and watch work. I never saw him make a false or unnecessary movement. His hammer, extra light with a handle fashioned by himself, flashed to the right spot every time like the rapier of an expert swordsman. He with his nimble intelligence and swift sure hand was a gift to any architect. That William stayed with and by Taliesin through trials and tribulations the better part of fourteen years. America turns up a good mechanic around in country places every so often. Billy was one of them.

Winter came. A bitter one. The roof was on, plastering done, windows in, men working now inside. Evenings the men grouped around the open fire-places, throwing cord-wood into them to keep warm as the cold wind came up through the floor boards. All came to work from surrounding towns and had to be fed and bedded down on the place somewhere during the week. Saturday nights they went home with money for the week's work in pocket, or its equivalent in groceries and fixings from the village. Their reactions were picturesque. There was Johnnie Vaughan who was, I guess, a genius. I got him because he had gone into some kind of concrete business with another Irishman for a partner, and failed. Johnnie said, 'We didn't fail sooner because we didn't have more business.' I overheard this lank genius, he was looking after the carpenters, nagging Billy Little, who had been foreman of several jobs in the city for me. Said Johnnie, 'I built this place off a shingle.' 'Huh,' said Billy, 'that ain't nothin'. I built them places in Oak Park right off'd the air.' No one ever got even a little over the rat-like perspicacity of that little Billy Little.

Workmen never have enough drawings or explanations no matter how many they get—but this is the sort of slander an architect needs to hear occasionally.

The workmen took the work as a sort of adventure. It was adventure. In every realm. Especially in the financial realm. I kept working all the while to make the money come. It did. And we kept on inside with plenty of clean soft wood that could be left alone pretty much in plain surfaces. The stone, too, strong and protective inside, spoke for itself in certain piers and walls.

Inside floors, like the outside floors, were stone-paved or if not were laid with wide, dark-streaked cypress boards. The plaster in the walls was mixed with raw siénna in the box, went onto the walls natural, drying out

155

tawny gold. Outside, the plastered walls were the same but greyer with cement. But in the *constitution* of the whole, in the way the walls rose from the plan and spaces were roofed over, was the chief interest of the whole house. The whole was supremely natural. The rooms went up into the roof, tent-like, and were ribanded overhead with marking-strips of waxed, soft wood. The house was set so sun came through the openings into every room sometime during the day. Walls opened everywhere to views as the windows swung out above the tree-tops, the tops of red, white and black oaks and wild cherry trees festooned with wild grape-vines. In spring, the perfume of the blossoms came full through the windows, the birds singing there the while, from sunrise to sunset—all but the several white months of winter.

I wanted a home where icicles by invitation might beautify the eaves. So there were no gutters. And when the snow piled deep on the roofs and lay drifted in the courts, icicles came to hang staccato from the eaves. Prismatic crystal pendants sometimes six feet long, glittered between the landscape and the eyes inside. Taliesin in winter was a frosted palace roofed and walled with snow, hung with iridescent fringes, the plate-glass of the windows shone bright and warm through it all as the light of the huge fire-places lit them from the firesides within, and streams of wood-smoke from a dozen such places went straight up toward the stars.

The furnishings inside were simple and temperate. Thin tan-coloured flax rugs covered the floors, later abandoned for the severer simplicity of the stone pavements and wide boards. Doors and windows were hung with modest, brown checkered fabrics. The furniture was home-made of the same wood as the trim, and mostly fitted into the trim. I got a compliment on this from old Dan Davis, a rich and 'savin' ' Welsh neighbour who saw we had made it ourselves. 'Gosh-dang it, Frank,' he said. 'Ye're savin' too, ain't ye?' Although Mother Williams, another neighbour, who came to work for me, said 'Savin'? He's nothin' of the sort. He could 'ave got it most as cheap ready-made from that Sears and Roebuck . . . I know.'

A house of the North. The whole was low, wide and snug, a broad shelter seeking fellowship with its surroundings. A house that could open to the breezes of summer and become like an open camp if need be. With spring came music on the roofs, for there were few dead roof-spaces over-head, and the broad eaves so sheltered the windows that they were safely left open to the sweeping, soft air of the rain. Taliesin was grateful for care. Took what grooming it got with gratitude and repaid it all with interest.

Taliesin's order was such that when all was clean and in place its coun-tenance beamed, wore a happy smile of well-being and welcome for all.

It was intensely human, I believe.

Although, thanks to 'bigger and better publicity', among those who be-sieged it Saturdays and Sundays from near and far, came several charac-teristic ladies whose unusual enterprise got them as far as the upper half of the Dutch door, standing open to the living room. They couldn't see me. I was lying on a long walled-seat just inside. They poked in their heads and looked about with Oh's and Ah's. A pause. In the nasal twang of the more aggressive one, 'I wonder . . . I wonder, now, if I'd like living in a regular home?'

The studio, lit by a bank of tall windows to the north, really was a group of four studies, one large, three small. And in their midst stood a stone fireproof vault for treasures. The plans, private papers, and such money as there was, took chances anywhere outside it. But the Taliesin library of Genroku embroidery and antique coloured wood-block prints all stayed safely inside. As work and sojourn overseas continued, Chinese pottery and sculpture and Momoama screens overflowed into the rooms where, in a few years, every single object used for decorative accent became an 'antique' of rare quality.

If the eye rested on some ornament it could be sure of worthy entertainment. Hovering over these messengers to Taliesin from other civilizations and thousands of years ago, must have been spirits of peace and good-will? Their figures seemed to shed fraternal sense of kinship from their places in the stone or from the broad ledges where they rested.

Yes. It all actually happened as I have described it. It is all there now.

But the story of Taliesin, after all, is old: old as the human spirit. These ancient figures were traces of that spirit, left behind in the human procession as Time went on its way. They now came forward to rest and feel at home, that's all. So it seemed as you looked at them. But they were only the story within the story: ancient comment on the New.

The New lived for itself for their sake, as long ago they had lived, for its sake.

The storms of the north broke over the low-sweeping roofs that now sheltered a life in which hope purposefully lived at earnest work. The lightning in this region, always so crushing and severe, crashed (Isaiah) and Taliesin smiled. Taliesin was minding its own business, living up to its own obligations and to the past it could well understand. But the New, failing to recognize it as its own, still pursued and besieged, traduced and insulted it. Taliesin raged, wanted to talk back—and smiled. Taliesin was a 'story' and therefore it and all in it had to run the gauntlet. But steadily it made its way through storm and stress, enduring all threats and slanderous curiosity for more than three years, and smiled—always. No one entering and feeling the repose of its spirit could ever believe in the storm of publicity that kept breaking outside because a kindred spirit—a woman—had taken refuge there for life.

Gradually creative desire and faith came creeping back to me again. Taliesin was there to come alive and I to settle down to work.

Chicago business offices were now in the Orchestra Hall Building, though the studio-workshop was still at Taliesin. A number of buildings went out from that studio. The neighbourhood playhouse of Mrs. Coonley was among them, and the Midway Gardens on the Plaisance near Chicago University. As the Gardens were a product of the first re-establishment and are associated in my mind with the tragedy at Taliesin and because they were so new in so many ways, here is the story of that adventure. A tale of the Architectural 'Arabian Nights'.

THE TALE OF THE MIDWAY GARDENS

Some time ago, it was in the fall of 1913, young Ed Waller's head got outside the idea of the Chicago Midway Gardens and he set to work. First on me. One day when I had come into Chicago from the Taliesin studio-workshop, he began on me.

Said Ed: 'Frank, in all this black old town there's no place to go but out, nor any place to come but back, that isn't bare and ugly unless it's cheap and nasty. I want to put a garden in this wilderness of smoky dens, car-tracks, and saloons.'

This sounded like his father whom you have seen in the experience with Uncle Dan in the library of the house at River Forest.

'I believe Chicago would appreciate a beautiful garden resort. Our people would go there, listen to good music, eat and drink. You know, an outdoor garden something like those little parks round Munich where German families go. You have seen them.

'The dance craze is on now, too, and we could have a dancing floor inside somewhere for the young folks. Yes, and a place within the big place out-side near the orchestra where highbrows could come and sit to hear a fine concert even if they did want to dine at home.

'The trouble of course is the short season. But we could fix that up by putting a winter-garden on one side for diners, with a big dancing floor in the middle. And to make it all surefire as to money we would put in a bar [the 'affliction' had not yet befallen] that would go the year around. We would run the whole thing as a high-class entertainment on a grand scale —Pavlowa dancing—Max Bendix's full orchestra playing—you know Max. Music outdoors starting at seven o'clock. Between orchestral num-bers there would be a dance-orchestra striking up, back there in the winter-garden, so the girls could get the boys to dance. Special matinees several days a week. Features every night. I see people up on balconies and all around over the tops of the buildings. Light, colour, music, movement— a gay place!

'Frank, you could make it unique,' he went on.

'I know I could,' I said, 'where I can get the ground. Down on the South Side just off the Midway. The old Sans Souci place. Been on the rocks for years. Stupid old ballyhoo. It's just big enough, I think. About three acres. You'll get paid for your drawings anyway.'

All Ed didn't know was where he could get the money. He said 'but that is the easiest part of it'. He would fix that.

'What do you think of the idea?'

Well, Aladdin and his wonderful lamp had fascinated me as a boy. But by now I knew the enchanting young Arabian was really just a symbol for creative desire, his lamp intended for another symbol—imagination. As I sat listening I was Aladdin. Young Ed? The genie. He knew apparently where all 'the slaves of the lamp' could be found. Well, this might all be necromancy but I believed in magic. Had I not rubbed my lamp with what seemed wonderful effect, before this? I didn't hesitate.

'When you get back to the office, Ed, send me a survey of the old Sans Souci grounds. Then come back Monday,' I said. 'You'll see what ... you'll see.'

He came back Monday. The thing had simply shaken itself out of my sleeve. In a remarkably short time there it was on paper—in colour. Young Ed gloated over it.

'I knew it,' he said. 'You could do it and *this is it*.'

Paul Mueller it was whom we both desired as 'slave of the lamp'. We got Paul-the-builder interested in the scheme. With accustomed energy he started in to make the dream reality. His 'organization', as he called it, of partners, foremen, workmen skilled and workmen unskilled, all belonged to various departments of the great big Chicago building contractor known as 'The Union'. Mueller rented slaves from the Union by making the usual terms. But he himself, as usual, was really the organization, so far as that went, in getting the Midway Gardens built.

Nor could Young Ed wait for any process very long. He was very young. The genie started all this on the fly and he kept it flying.

In another several days old Sans Souci's several acres had begun to boil. The Union was on the job as usual with watchful, jealous eye. Soon all of old Sans Souci there was left in plain sight was a rusty old steel-tower standing up in one corner of the lot. Labourers started to wreck it but the Union simply raised its warning hand. The rickety old tower was iron, therefore consecrate to the steel-workers. Skilled steel-workers only should dare demolish it. This meant a thousand or so wasted, but no time to argue —the Union knew that too. Skilled steel-workers took the thing down.

Mueller, now slave-driver, stood up six feet two inches tall in all this commotion madly shouting through a megaphone to five points of the compass all at the same time, giving directions to seemingly insane activity.

Excavators, steam shovels, wagons, dumping materials and trucks hauling dirt away, barrows, mules, more trucks, concrete mixers, derricks, gin poles, mud, water and men. Cement-bags, sand, brick, beams and timber came piling up into great heaps. Masons, hod-carriers, bricklayers, plasterers, carpenters, steel-workers all over the place found the proper thing to do at the proper time because capable foremen were correctly reading the architect's blue-prints in the little board-shanty that had now taken the place of the consecrated iron tower. 'Paul F. P. Mueller & Co., Builders' was the legend painted in big black letters across the small edifice.

You know without being told where the blue-prints came from. And Young Ed, genius of all this hubbub—and expected to pay for it—hovered over it all, excited. To date, this was the time of his life.

In Ed's office was Charlie Matthews, a cultivated chap. Artistic, music-mad Charlie. He too went off his head over the scheme for the Midway Gardens. Got others into a state of mind to buy stock in the enterprise. And while this frenzied army of workmen were busy—Ed, Charlie and their friends were busy too. Trying to raise money. But, as subsequently appeared, there was only about sixty-five thousand dollars in hand to meet the three hundred and fifty thousand to be paid. No one knew that at the time unless it was Ed. And I doubt if even he did. Anyhow, that is about all the real money there ever was with which to build the Midway Gardens.

But all unaware of that fact, the Gardens were well above ground, rapidly moving up toward the blue overhead. Even Chicago weather permitted, entering into the conspiracy, if there really was any conspiracy outside the Union. I knew of none except the conspiracy to get the Midway Gardens done in ninety days, the diners seated, dinner on the tables and the music playing. The date of the opening was fixed for May 1, 1914.

The Midway Gardens were planned as a summer garden: a system of low masonry terraces enclosed by promenades, loggias and galleries at the sides, these flanked by the Winter Garden. The Winter Garden also was terraced and balconied in permanent masonry without and within. This Winter Garden stood on the main street, opposite the great orchestra shell. The Bar, 'supporting economic feature', was put on the principal corner. Ed argued that a bar should be right across a man's path, a manifest temptation. That boy knew a lot about human weaknesses—among other things. This bar, as manifest temptation, was going strong when the nation-wide affliction befell.

At the extreme outer corners of the lot toward the main street were set the two tall welcoming features, flat towers topped by trellises intended to be covered with vines and flowers and ablaze with light to advertise the entrances to both summer and winter gardens. The kitchen, of course, as stomach is to man, was located beneath and at the very centre of the building scheme, short tunnels leading direct to the Gardens for quick service, service stairs leading straight up into the winter-garden terraces above it. A waiter could with reasonable ease get direct to all the various terrace levels, balconies and roofs. And the waiters were legion.

'Quick service and hot food,' said John Vogelsang. John was to regale the inner man, interior-decorate him, while Max Bendix charmed his ears, the Gardens charmed his eyes, and all together charmed the dollars out of popular pockets into the eager Midway Gardens coffers. 'Quick service and hot food are the secret of contented diners.' John knew. He was a Chicago restaurateur and a success at the time he was talking. So, after getting the kitchen located and appurtenances properly connected up, we made all the kitchen arrangements 'according to John'.

But the orchestra shell became a bone of contention.

Out of a good deal of experience in such matters with Adler and Sullivan

14. Garden front

FRANCIS W. LITTLE HOUSE. 1907-8

15. Living room

16. Plaster model. The model was lost in transit to the U.S.A. Earthquake-proof construction; flexibility and tenuity the principle of construction, instead of rigidity. Foundations of concrete pins inserted in layer of top soil over sixty feet of mud. Building floats on mud as a battleship floats on salt water

IMPERIAL HOTEL, TOKIO. (1916)-1922

17. Emperors' entrance. Brick wall sheets reinforced with steel, formed with concrete and cut lava members. Blue copper roof. Perforated cornices

—they designed the Chicago Auditorium and twenty-six other successful opera houses—I had designed the shell, sure it would work out.

Here is where Charlie Matthews' knowledge of music came in, because Charlie having been a director himself was appointed committee of one to see this important feature a success. As anyone knows, acoustics are tricky unless you know them to be simple and scientific. This was little known then. So the first thing Charlie did was to run around the United States interviewing musicians. Each musician wanted it different from the way I had it. I wouldn't change it. Then Charlie got mad and called in experts. The experts were all agreed that the open sides that I wanted in order to distribute the sound well to the sides of the Gardens were a mistake. Charlie said, 'Change it.'

I said, 'No, Charlie, not just for that. Give me a better reason.'

Said Charlie, now unbecomingly heated, 'Hell, Frank, do you think you are the only one in the world who knows anything about orchestra shells?'

'No, Charlie,' I said, trying to keep my case in court, 'but about this particular orchestra shell, utterly yes. I am sure I do.'

A little later Ed's voice on the phone—'Say, Mr. Architect, are you sure that shell will be all right?'

'Perfectly sure, Ed.'

'Then go ahead and build it. Don't change it for anybody.' And I knew 'anybody' meant Charlie.

In regard to this shell, you see, I was in the position the Union was in toward the Gardens. Success to the dictator lay in this matter of *time*, for the thing had to be done without delays. All this conflict did make me a little anxious. But had I shown it, all would have been down with the shell, just because it is impossible to build anything more than one way at one time. Had I lost my nerve I should have had to build it six different ways at least at the same time and then, after all, probably tear it down. So I proposed something that made friends with Charlie. The shell was cupped well out above over the orchestra, rising with no complex curves from a wall behind the musicians, a wall about nine feet high. The sides were only partially closed and those open sides being the chief contention, I proposed to make the sides at this point doors that could be swung outward if that proved necessary. If not necessary then they were there as features to carry the programme-numbers and signs in electric lights.

This expedient restored harmony.

The Midway Gardens, meantime, were fast growing up out of chaos. Long, low, level lines and new rectangular masonry forms were taking definite shape. They could be seen now, far enough along to make one wonder what in the world was coming.

At the time the Midway Gardens were designed, 1913, *l'Art Nouveau* was dying in France, where it originated, and gasping wherever else it happened to have caught on, and various experiments in the 'abstract' in painting and sculpture were being made in Europe, exciting the aesthetic vanguard and insulting the rank and file.

But the straight line, itself an abstraction, and the flat plane for its own sake, had characterized my buildings from the first hour on my own account I had become building-conscious.

Never much interested in 'realism', I was already dissatisfied with the realistic element in any building. Like 'Breaking Home Ties' in painting, the Rogers Groups in sculpture, or *Liberty* covers today, the work of the period was flat on its stomach to the 'realistic'. Or else the buildings were the usual dull and vulgar imitations of the old styles, false and imitative. I admired nothing going on in architecture at the time this design for the Midway Gardens became due to happen.

I clearly saw my trusty T-square and aspiring triangle as means to the Midway Garden end I had in view.

I meant to get back to first principles—pure form in everything; weave a masonry-fabric in beautiful pattern in genuine materials and good construction, bring painting and sculpture in to heighten and carry all still further into the realm of the Lamp in the same Spirit. A synthesis of all the Arts.

Yes, why not have the whole Gardens as consistently a unit for once in a century as anything in noble music Max Bendix could find to play in them. Why then not go back to the source, bring form alive again in my own way, making a true chime to the tune of imagination in Chicago. Forms could be made into a festival for the eye no less than music made a festival for the ear. I knew. And this could all be genuine building, not mere scene painting.

Well, yes, but how about the Chicago audience? Would Chicago be able to see that if it did happen? Chicago was far behind in judging qualities in either form, sound or colour. But I believed that was because she never had a chance to choose the real thing. Notwithstanding 'The Fair', the Arts were yet to come to Chicago. A painting still had to be a picture; and the more the picture could be mistaken for the real object, the better Chicago liked the work. Sculpture the same way. That too had to look 'real' and if it could seem so to the touch, why, that was greatest sculpture. Would Chicago respond to adventure into the realm of the abstract in the sense that I wanted to go into it? Did Chicago know what 'abstraction' meant anyway? Perhaps not. Certainly not. Why be silly.

But I didn't argue these points with anyone but myself. I kept still about them. After all, what did these subjective matters signify to others? Fortunately, human beings are really childlike in the best sense when directly appealed to by simple, strong forms and pure, bright colour. Chicago was not sophisticated. Chicago was still unspoiled. So probably all this could go straight to the Chicago heart if it would.

Meantime the straight line, square, triangle and circle I had learned to play with in Kindergarten were set to work in this developing sense of abstraction, by now my habit, to characterize the architecture, painting and sculpture of the Midway Gardens. Most places of the kind I had seen at home or abroad were phantasy developed as a cheap, erotic foolishness. A kind of papier-mâché scene painting. In the Midway Gardens there was

162

to be no eroticism. No damned sentimentality either. There was to be permanent structure. The lovely human figure might come into the scheme but come in only to respect the architecture, dominated by a proper sense of the whole. The human figure should be there but humbly, to heighten the whole effect.

The human figure? Well, the sprites of these geometrical forms themselves: they might come in to play and share in the general geometric gaiety. How far these ideas would go in flat colour I determined when I handed the general schemes for colour-decoration to William Henderson and Jack Norton of the Art Institute, and Jerry Blum of the Orient. The schemes for sculpture to young Ianelli whom I brought east for the purpose.

Here in the Midway Gardens painting and sculpture were to be bidden back again to their original places and to their original offices in architecture, where they belonged. The architect, himself, was here again master to them all together. (Making no secret of it, whatever.) But artists are very sensitive beings in their own right. In modern times they have not become accustomed to sitting in the orchestra to play a mere part in an architect's score, so to speak. The incumbent *altogether* means less to them than it did to their ancient progenitors. As an obligation it grinds on them. They lose face when they regard it. But I am glad I got them in anyway. About their own feelings later I am not so sure. I've taken you into confidence in this explanation while these thoughts were taking visible and novel effect in brick and concrete there in the Gardens. The work was going on night and day. My son John helped superintend. I myself sometimes slept at night on a pile of shavings in a corner of the Winter Garden when worn out. John would keep going.

'Look here, Wright,' said the exasperated Mueller to me one day. 'What's this you got here—this young bull-dog that he is. He follows me around and around. Every little while he sticks his teeth in the seat of my pants and I can't get away from him. Can I pull over everything that goes wrong in this work? Can I? Not if I get these Gardens finished up, already to open on time some day, I can't. Take him off me!''

But that sounded good to me and I didn't take him off. John was in it all up to his ears, and his teeth were serviceable.

We had built a couple of wooden shanties for the modelling of the sculpture. Dicky Bock and Ianelli were working away in them with helpers and a female model. This model was the mysterious object of continuous and extensive male curiosity. Although unable to read, she carried a volume of Ibsen's plays coming and going. Scientifically she had reduced her garments to one piece plus shoes, stockings, gloves in hand and hat so she could 'slip on' and 'slip off' easily. Her Mona Lisa smile is evident in the figure pieces of the Gardens (thanks to Ianelli).

While sculpture was going on in the shanty painters were working on wooden scaffolds within the buildings of the Gardens. The painter boys had got some of their Art Institute pupils to help them, among them an accomplished girl, Catherine Dudley.

One day a plug-ugly stuck his head in the door of the modelling shanty. The Union! Again for about the seventh time on various pretexts.

He said, 'Say, what about it? What about that skirt y' got up there doin' paintin'? She ain't no artist, 's she?'

'Sh' is,' I said, 'and damned clever.'

'Aw, come in. Sh' is just one o' them too good lookin' society dames. Say,' he went on, lowering his head and sticking out his jaw, 'you get that skirt off'n there or these Gardens, may be . . . they'll *never* open. See? And them three other guys yu' got out there a-paintin' with smockkies on a-smokin'. Don't look like no artists to me neither. Get cards for them, too. See!'

'Artists? Man,' I said, 'they are. And so good, they're teachers at the Art Institute.' (I thought that should impress him.) 'Go and ask.'

'Naw, I ain't askin' nobody. Cards f'r 'em, see? Get 'em.'

He glanced at sculptors Bock and Ianelli. The curtains had hastily been drawn across the model.

'What yu got in there behind that curtain?'

'Now look here. You are going pretty strong, aren't you? What business have you got in here, anyway?'

'Business?' he said. 'I'll show you what business I got 'n here. Ye're hid'n men out on me that ought to be 'n the Union, scabs, see?'

He gave the sculptors a dirty look. 'Where's their cards?'

'Don't need cards. They're Artists, too—sculptors. Can't you see they look that way?' (I couldn't resist this.)

'Naw, n' more'n the carvers and modellers we got in the Union. Not's much,' he said. 'They got to get their cards or this show don' go on.'

I called Dicky down from the scaffold where just before this ugly break he had been working away on the model for four big capitals for the great piers of the Winter Garden. I took him aside.

'Dicky, this looks funny to me. The Union is bad enough, God knows, but this fellow's drunk. Got any money in the bank, Dicky?'

'About seven dollars, I guess.'

'Fine! Got your checkbook, Dicky?'

'Yes.'

I got over to the plug-ugly.

'Look here, rough-boy. How much for these two great Artists?'

'Thirty-five apiece.'

'Seventy dollars?'

'Seventy.'

'All right. Dick, give the Union a cheque for seventy dollars.'

'Name?'

He got the cheque, turned, gave another dirty look at the curtains which and when just then parted. Hatted, gloved, volume of Ibsen under arm, the Mona Lisa, eyes properly downcast, stepped forward into view.

The ugly grinned. 'Yeah! So I see,' said he, and laughed himself out of the door.

'My God,' said Dicky. 'When that thug finds out there's no money back of that cheque, he'll come back here and murder me—hands up.'

'Let's see if he will,' I said.

The Union had held up the work a half dozen times on one pretext or another but no issue was ever made of this matter for some reason. The artists *per se*, as such, carried on with no more help from 'the Union'. I suppose that cheque cashed by the 'delegate' had bounced and inasmuch as he had taken too great a personal interest in it—it was best on the whole to say nothing.

The Gardens, owing to high pressure and night-shifts, were nearly done. The electric needles that I made out of wrought-iron pipe punctured to let the lamps through thickly at the sides, now stood delicately up into the sky and irradiated the whole place for night work.

Seen from afar, they were good advertisements for the Gardens—but not good enough for John Vogelsang. No, no, not for John. He had secretly started a campaign for a great big electric sign above it all with 'MIDWAY GARDENS' blazing in coloured lights. I discovered this and fought him. I won for a little while but eventually—sometime after the opening—he did get it up there. The first severe blow to the scheme.

We didn't have any money to colour the walls as intended, by inlaying scarlet and green flash-glass in the relief patterns made of concrete. We had no money to finish the sky-frames on the four towers of the Winter Garden intended to be garlanded with vines and flowers like the tops of the welcoming features. Nor any to plant the big trees at the corners of the Gardens. I mean that we had nothing at all that even promised money. Even the stage money was all gone now. Gay coloured balloons of various sizes in great numbers were to have flown high above the scene, anchored to the electric needles and tower features. They couldn't get these. They wouldn't have cost much, but that little was too much at that time.

Money troubles now. Anxiety. Anger. But still hopes and active promises aplenty.

Mueller stood in the breach with his young partner Seipp, and carried on else the Midway Gardens would never have opened at all. We all had faith that when opened, the Gardens themselves would settle the financial question the first season. They did.

And then, one noon while I was eating a late luncheon in the Winter. Gardens came the terrible news of tragedy at Taliesin that took me away from the Gardens and from all else for a time.

When the Midway Gardens were nearly finished—my son John and I were sleeping there nightly in a corner on a pile of shavings to keep track of the night work now necessary to finish the Gardens on time—at noon as we were sitting quietly eating our lunch in the newly finished bar, came a long distance call from Spring Green. 'Taliesin destroyed by fire.' But no word came of the ghastly tragedy itself. I learned of that little by little on my way home on the train that evening. The newspaper headlines glared with it.

165

Thirty-six hours earlier I had left Taliesin leaving all living, friendly and happy. Now the blow had fallen like a lightning stroke. In less time than it takes to write it, a thin-lipped Barbados Negro, who had been recommended to me by John Vogelsang as an ideal servant, had turned madman, taken the lives of seven and set the house in flames. In thirty minutes the house and all in it had burned to the stone work or to the ground. The living half of Taliesin was violently swept down and away in a madman's nightmare of flame and murder.

The working half only remained.

Will Weston saved that.

He had come to grips with the madman, whose strength was superhuman, but slipped away from his grasp and blows. Bleeding from the encounter he ran down the hill to the nearest neighbour, Reider, to give the alarm, made his way back immediately through the cornfields only to find the deadly work finished and the home ablaze. Hardly able to stand, he ran to where the fire hose was kept in a niche of the garden wall, past his young son lying there in the fountain basin—one of the seven dead—got the hose loose, staggered with it to the fire and with the playing hose stood against destruction until they led him away.

The great stone chimneys stood black and tall on the hillside, their fireplaces now gaping holes. They stood there above the Valley against the sky, themselves tragic.

She for whom Taliesin had first taken form and her two children—gone. A talented apprentice, Emil Brodelle; the young son of William Weston the gardener; David Lindblom; a faithful workman, Thomas Brunker—this was the human toll taken by a few moments of madness. The madman was finally discovered after a day or two hidden in the firepot of the steam boiler, down in the smoking ruins of the house. Still alive though nearly dead, he was taken to the Dodgeville jail. Refusing meantime to utter a word, he died there.

A primitive burial in the ground of the family chapel. Men from Taliesin dug the grave, deep, near grandfather's and grandmother's grave. Uncle Enos had come to say it would be all right. But I felt that a funeral service could only be mockery. The undertaker's offices—too, his vulgar casket—seemed to me profane. So I cut her garden down and with the flowers filled a strong, plain box of fresh, white pine to overflowing. I had my own carpenters make it.

My boy, John, coming to my side now, helped me to lift the body and we let it down to rest among the flowers that had grown and bloomed for her. The plain box lid was pressed down and fastened home. Then the plain, strong box was lifted on the shoulders of my workmen and they placed it on our little spring-wagon, filled, too, with flowers—waiting, hitched behind the faithful Darby and Joan . . . We made the whole a mass of flowers. It helped a little.

Since Taliesin was first built Darby and Joan were the faithful little sorrel team that had drawn us along the Valley roads and over the hills, in spring, summer, autumn and winter, almost daily.

Walking alongside the wheels now I drove them along the road to the churchyard where no bell tolled. No people were waiting. John followed. Ralp and Orrin, two of my young Hillside cousins, were waiting at the chapel gate. Together we lowered the flower-filled and flower-covered pine-box to the bottom of the new-made grave. Then I asked them to leave me there alone.

I wanted to fill the grave myself . . .

The August sun was setting I remember on the familiar range of hills. Dimly, I felt coming in far-off shadows of the ages struggling to escape from sub-consciousness and utter themselves . . . Then slowly came darkness . . . I filled the grave, staying there in the dark. It was friendly.

And no monument yet marks the spot where she was buried.

All I had left to show for the struggle for freedom of the five years past that had swept most of my former life away, had now been swept away.

Why mark the spot where desolation ended and began?

AGAIN

In the little bedroom back of the undestroyed studio workshop I remained in what was left of Taliesin I.

No one seemed near to me. Not even she who had been struck down.

The gaping black hole left by fire in the beautiful hillside was empty, a charred and ugly scar upon my own life.

This tragedy resulting in the destruction of Taliesin the first left me in a strange plight.

From the moment of my return to that scene of devastating horror I had wanted to see no one. And I would see no one but the workmen. Work only was bearable.

For the week following there was no one on the hill at night but me and the watchman who sat on the steps with a gun across his knees. The whole countryside was terrified by the tragedy—not knowing what more to expect. Before the murderer was discovered groups of the neighbours had searched cornfields and woods for the black-man.

Those nights in the little back room were black, filled with strange unreasoning terrors. No moon seemed to shine. No stars in the sky. No familiar frog-song coming from the pond below. There was a strange, unnatural silence, while drifts of smoke still rose from the ruin.

Unable to sleep, numb, I would get up, take a cold bath to bring myself alive and go out on the hills in the night, not really knowing where. But I would come safely back again with only a sense of black night and the strange fear, no beauty visible any more. Grope how I might—no help from that source. And I would find my way back to bed.

Something strange had happened to me. Instead of feeling that she, whose life had joined mine there at Taliesin, was a spirit near, she was utterly gone.

167

After the first terrible anguish, a kind of black despair seemed to paralyse my imagination in her direction and numbed my sensibilities. The blow was too severe.

I got no relief in any faith nor yet any in hope. Except repulsion, I could feel now only in terms of rebuilding. I could get relief only by looking toward rebuilding—get relief from a kind of continuous nausea, by work.

That relief by habitual action was all I really had—the only colour life kept for my work and music. They had thrown my piano out of the window to save it and, legs broken, it was now blocked up by the studio fireplace. I could sit there and try to play.

But everything else had been swept away or lurked in the strange oppression of some darkened forbidding room in which strange shadows moved.

As I looked back at that time, I saw the black hole in the hillside, the black night over all. And I moved about in sinister shadows. Days strangely without light would follow the black nights. Totally—she was gone.

No, this is not fanciful word painting. I am trying to tell what happened. Gone into this equivocal blackness near oblivion for several years to come was all sense of her whom I had loved as one having really lived at all.

This was merciful? I believe the equivalent of years passed within my consciousness in the course of weeks. Time, never very present to me, ceased to exist. As days passed into nights I was numb to all but the automatic steps toward rebuilding the home that was destroyed by hateful forces.

The routine of the day's work, eating the three meals a day that were brought to me: this went on by sheer force of habit. But I began to go down. Physically I sagged. Boils (I had never had any in my life before) now broke over my back and neck. I lost weight. Finally I got back to my little home at 25 East Cedar Street and lived there alone except for an Irish caretaker, Nellie Breen.

I had never needed glasses, but now I had to have them.

These came between me and my work for the first time.

Nature is merciful as she is cruel. I believe any spiritual faculty as well as physical faculty, overtaxed, becomes numb. The real pain in that realm, too, comes when healing begins. It is thus the spirit seems subject to the same laws as the body.

A horrible loneliness now began to clutch at me, but strange to say I longed for no one I ever loved or that I had ever known. My mother was deeply hurt by my refusal to have her with me. My children—I had welcomed them eagerly always—but I did not want them now. They had been so faithfully kind in my extremity. I shall never forget.

But strange faces were best and I walked among them.

I do not understand this any better now than I did then. Months went by, but they might have been and I believe they were for me an actual lifetime.

168

Perhaps a new consciousness had to grow as a green shoot will grow from a charred and blackened stump?

Whatever the truth may be, the fact remains—until many years afterward, to turn my thoughts backward to what had transpired in the life Mamah and I had lived together at Taliesin was like trying to see into a dark room in which terror lurked, strange shadows moved—and I would do well to turn away in time.

I could see forward only. I could not see backward. The pain was too great.

And it looked for some time as though I might not be able to see at all.

It was this that, like a lash, made me get to work upon myself none too soon. Have I been describing despair? A feeling unknown to me.

Waves of unkind, stupid publicity had broken over Taliesin again. The human sacrifices at Taliesin seemed in vain. Its heroism was ridiculed, its love mocked. Its very heart, struck from it at a blow, was profaned by a public sympathy harder to bear even than public curiosity had been.

'Tried and condemned,' some said. Well . . . was this trial for heresy too? Was this trial, like grandfather's, at some judgment seat, to quell a spirit that would not be quelled?

And was this unconventional believer in the good, the true and beautiful seeing it as work, life and love, actually in the midst of all three, thus similarly struck down?

Some months before, sitting on the stone terrace overlooking the valley below, I saw one of the finest cows of the countryside, Taliesin's Holstein Maplecroft, a thoroughbred worth several hundred ordinary cows, standing beneath an oak tree. Two other cows were standing there beside her, comparatively worthless. A lightning flash of flame there below simultaneous with a stunning crash. Two cows walked away beneath the tree unharmed. It was Maplecroft that lay there dead by stroke of lightning. Why peerless Maplecroft?

Why Taliesin?

So many too willing answers to 'Why Taliesin?' were publicly made by good men and true. They now had a text upon which to preach. But no preaching was more reasonable than that the 'unconventional' gathers the enmity of the conventional until, charged beyond the containing point, explosion in some form, obvious or occult, follows. Did this apply to Maplecroft's unconventionality? Hers consisted in being thoroughbred among the 'grades'. Did the envy or displeasure of ordinary numbers attract destruction to her?

Utter nonsense!

So the rage that grew in me when I felt the inimical weight of human censure concentrated upon me began to fade away until I finally found refuge in the idea that Taliesin should live to show something more for its mortal sacrifices than a charred and terrible ruin on a lonely hillside in the beloved ancestral Valley where great happiness had been.

In action there is release from anguish of mind. Anguish could not

169

leave me until action for *renewal*, so far as might be, began. Again, and at once, all that had been in motion before at the will of the architect, if not the man, was set in motion. Steadily, stone by stone, board by board, Taliesin II began to rise from the ashes of Taliesin I.

Where scenes of horror had identified the structure with ugly memories, I changed it all. Where tragedy had been most obvious, an open stone-floored loggia looked up the Valley toward the Lloyd-Jones family Chapel.

A guest unit was added to the west, and a great fireplace. It was for my mother and aged aunts. I intended to bring them home to Taliesin now.

There was to be no turning back nor any stopping to mourn. What had been beautiful at Taliesin should live as a grateful memory creating the new, and, come who and whatever might to share Taliesin, they would be sure to help in that spirit.

So I believed and resolved.

As one consequence of the ugly publicity given the terrible tragedy hundreds of letters had come to me from all over the country. I tied them up together into a bundle now and burned them. Unread. I went to work. The salt and savour of life had not been lost. That salt and savour will always be the work one does best.

TALIESIN II

More stone, more wood, more work—a more harmonious use of them all. More workmen, more money—sacrifices, not only more creative work on my part but desperate efforts to find and eventually earn the necessary money.

Another fall, another winter, another spring, another summer and late in 1915, Taliesin II took the place of the first Taliesin. A more reposeful and a finer one. Not a chastened Taliesin. No, up in arms now, declining to take the popular Mosaic-Isaian idea of punishment as worthy the sacrifice demanded and taken at Taliesin. Demanded? By whom? Taken? For what? And the sentimental or superstitious or profane answers from all sides, and from top to bottom, answered nothing.

But something was coming clear, now, through all the brutalizing Taliesin had received. Something—no, not rebellion. Conviction. Purpose now lifted the crown of the head higher. Made the eye see clearer. The tread that faltered for a moment in weakness and confusion became elastic and more sure as Work came alive again.

Meantime the Gardens, though still unfinished, had opened in as brilliant a social event as Chicago ever knew. Not finished yet, no, nor were they ever finished. The decoration in the entrance-features remained to be done. The towers of the Winter Garden had no decoration. Certain other things all about. But the atmosphere aimed at, that was there. In a scene unforgettable to all who attended, the architectural scheme and colour, form, light and sound had come alive. Thousands of beautifully

170

dressed women and tuxedoed men thronged the scene. And this scene came upon the beholders as a magic spell. All there moved and spoke as if in a dream. They believed it must be one. Yes, Chicago marvelled, acclaimed, approved. And Chicago came back and did the same, marvelling again and again and again. To many it was all Egyptian, Maya to some, very Japanese to others. But strange to all. It awakened a sense of mystery and romance in the beholder. Each responded with what he had in him to give. And for the remainder of the season, Chicago, the unregenerate, came to rendezvous with a new beauty. The coffers of Ed's company began to fill. It looked as though such a success could not be a failure for anyone concerned.

I returned from Taliesin and tragedy to Chicago when this popularity was at its height. Still dazed by tragedy I was trying to realize this myself. The acoustics proved to be all anyone could hope for, thanks to a perfect orchestra shell. Charlie Matthews was silent. But the unfinished final touches so significant and telling in any work of art were lacking. This hurt and marred my sense of the thing as a success. It is usually so.

These were also days of world tragedy. War soon broke out. Chicago as all the United States was unnaturally excited. The course of normal human life everywhere was soon upset. The Gardens opened the following season in financial difficulties, but promising enough if the second season equalled the first. Pavlowa danced. The orchestra was superb.

But the official safe was robbed while the creditors were not yet half paid. Dissension came in the management now. Ugly suspicions and threats were rife.

Finally the Edelweiss Brewing Company took advantage of this stupid confusion, virtually chaos, to buy the Gardens for a song. They brought their beer to the Gardens—the beer was good—but they brought no imagination and only beer-garden management. The Gardens never were 'beer gardens' in any sense. The Edelweiss did not know that. So the proud Midway Gardens fell into hands beneath their level and languished in consequence. The Edelweiss tried to 'hit them up'—hired someone to come in, paint the concrete, stencil the plain surfaces, and add obnoxious features out of balance and nasty. The whole effect was cheapened to suit a hearty bourgeois taste. The scheme that had once been integral was now 'decorated' in the meanest and worst of the popular sense of the word. Where there had been form integral with materials and purpose here was raw red, dead white, and bad blue *paint*. Another 'World's Fair' effect.

And then the affliction befell. The nation went 'dry'. And that was the final blow to the misdirection and insult already befallen the Gardens. Because the country went dry, all the more reason for the sort of thing the Midway Gardens originally represented; the greater the need of gaiety in beauty, beauty in gaiety; the greater the need of some artistic rendezvous for the people of the great city where some stimulating beauty to drink, managed with imagination, could be found.

171

But the Gardens had sunk to the level of the beer-garden—now without beer. No imagination on that level could bring it back into its own. The once distinguished Garden languished now dreaming of past glory—of possibilities untouched, of a life different from this one of the Chicago gridiron—as sometimes a beautiful woman dreams who has once known honour, position, homage, but—dragged down by inexorable circumstance—knows only shame.

So it went on from this bad to much worse. The place changed hands again, as they say of saloons. These new hands carved it up and over into a dance hall. The Gardens themselves were flooded for a skating rink. The new 'They' carried it all to the mob. For this the interiors were bedizened still more. They rouged its cheeks, put carmine on its lips and decked it out in gaudy artificial flowers.

'They' painted the chaste white concrete sculpture in more irrelevant gaudy colours, stencilled more cheap ornament on top of the integral ornment, wrecked the noble line and perfect balance of the whole. All semblance of the original harmony vanished. Yes, a distinguished beautiful woman dragged to the level of the prostitute is now its true parallel. I often thought, 'Why will someone in mercy not give them the final blow and tear them down?'

Now, at last, they have been mercifully destroyed to make room for an auto-laundry. I am thankful. The contractor who removed the buildings found them so solidly constructed that he lost more on the contract than it was worth.

The German Monograph published by Wasmuth had duly appeared in beautiful format. The work was a success in Germany and Darwin D. Martin helped me to control the sale of the book in America. But the 500 copies reserved for that purpose went up in smoke when Taliesin burned. Some thirty copies only were saved. The pile in the basement smouldered and smoked for three days after the house had burned to the ground.

Now came relief, a change of scene as—promptly—I was called to build the Imperial Hotel in Tokio, Japan. A commission including the Japanese architect, Yoshitaki, and the intelligent manager of the Imperial Hotel, Aisaku Hayashi. Both had gone around the world to find a model building. Reaching the Middle West they saw the new houses. They were immediately interested in them. Such buildings though not at all Japanese, they thought would look well in Japan. So they came to the reconstructed Taliesin, Taliesin II, to see me. Taliesin itself impressed them. Said Hayashi San, 'I am taken back to Jimmu Tenno's time.' He fell in love with the place as did his gentle wife, Takako-San.

Hayashi's young Takako-San was a beautiful presence at Taliesin at this time, with her exquisite Japanese wardrobe. I regret so few pictures have been preserved for others. Very quiet and reserved in manner, she was very frankly curious about everything, especially our foreign ways. One evening at dinner she said, 'Wrieto-San, what means "goddam"?'

172

'Goddam?' I wondered where she got that.

'Oh, Takako-San, goddam is a polite word for "very". You might say it is a goddam fine evening, or it is goddam fresh butter. Or after dinner you say to your hostess, "Thank you for your goddam good dinner." '

'O, O!' she said. ('O' was her invariable English exclamation.) 'O, I see. Please, Wrieto-San, pass me the goddam fresh butter.' And she goddam'd her way through the dinner to a running accompaniment of laughter. Afterward she turned to her host and with perfect naïveté thanked him for the 'goddam good dinner'.

Was she wiser than she seemed? I was naïve enough to wonder if she hadn't known all the time what the laughter meant. Hayashi, whose laughter had joined in, wouldn't enlighten me. I didn't deserve it.

Then and there in the workroom that had escaped destruction I made a preliminary plan according to Hayashi San's general requirements. The little commission after a week at Taliesin went back to Tokio. Some months later an official invitation came back to come on at once to Tokio. I went as soon as I could. Yes, I was eager to go, for again I wanted to get away from the United States. I still imagined one might get away from himself that way—a little. In spite of all my reasoning power and returning balance I was continually expecting some terrible blow to strike. The sense of impending disaster would hang over me, waking or dreaming. This fitted in well enough with the sense of earthquake, from the actuality of which I should have to defend the new building. But at this time I looked forward to Japan as refuge and rescue. The lands of my dreams—old Japan and old Germany.

JAPANESE PRINTS

During my later years at the Oak Park workshop, Japanese prints had intrigued me and taught me much. The elimination of the insignificant, a process of simplification in art in which I was myself already engaged, beginning with my twenty-third year, found much collateral evidence in the print. And ever since I discovered the print Japan had appealed to me as the most romantic, artistic, nature-inspired country on earth. Later I found that Japanese art and architecture really did have organic character. Their art was nearer to the earth and a more indigenous product of native conditions of life and work, therefore more nearly modern as I saw it, than any European civilization alive or dead.

I had realized this during a first visit in pursuit of the Japanese print in 1906. I had gone there to rest after building the Larkin building and the Martin residence, all but tired out.

A SONG TO HEAVEN

Now again, as the ship's anchor dropped in Yokohama Bay, I was to have earlier feelings deepened, intensified. Imagine, if you have not seen

173

it, a mountainous, abrupt land, the sea everywhere apparently risen too high upon it, so that all gentle slopes to the water's edge are lost. All shore lines abrupt. It is morning. Pure golden skies are seen over far stretches of blue sea dotted in the distance by flocks of white sampan sails—white birds at rest on the blue water.

Imagine, if you can, sloping foothills and mountain sides all antique sculpture, carved, century after century, with curving terraces. The cultivated fields rising tier on tier to still higher terraced vegetable fields, green-dotted. And extending far above the topmost dotted fields, see the very mountain tops themselves corrugated with regular rows of young pine trees pushing diagonally over them. Reforestation, the Imperial Government's share in the pattern, everywhere visible.

Look at the clusters of straw-thatched villages nesting in the nooks of the mountainous land naturally as birds nesting in trees. Or clinging there like the vegetation itself to steep slopes. Turn about, and look at the ruddy-bronze naked bodies of fishermen gleaming red in the sun as they go sculling by. Turn again and see the toilers in the fields, animated spots of true indigo-blue, spots that live in the landscape like the flowers and birds. The birds strangely without song: few of the flowers with any perfume at all but so boldly made, so brilliant and profuse as to seem artificial. I often touched many in flower arrangements to see whether they were real or artificial.

Glance as you go ashore for the first time into the village streets at the swarms of brightly clad, happy children, babies thrust into the bright kimonos on their backs, for the child is the Japanese treasure of treasures. Observe the silhouette of the clothed female figures—young or old—a simple swelling curve from nape of neck to white cotton-covered heels as all go clogging about with short scraping steps, white feet thrust into tall wooden clogs. These white feet will tell the story of the dwelling ancient Shinto religion built there in that land of the living as a matter of every-day life, and everywhere! The cotton-clad white feet are more significant in the telling of the tale of the Japanese house than anything else could be. Men and women so care for their very young, and their very old, it is said their country is the paradise of old age and of childhood. Old age is a qualification, not a disqualification, in Japan. A proof of civilization, sadly lacking in our own?

And all these patient human beings from the very young to the very old seem gladly and humbly resigned to loving one another, respecting one another as they clog along bowing and smiling to one another politely, scraping over damp bare-earth streets the feet made white with *tabi*, kept white. These significant 'tabi' are merely a soft-fitted white-cotton low sock-shoe. When going out, the *tabi* are thrust into the wooden geta or clogs waiting at the door. The 'geta' are a sort of detachable stilted wooden hoof to be left outside on the dirt or stone pavement of the entry as the 'white-feet' leave and step up inside onto spotless *tatami* of the dwelling. The removable sections of firm, padded straw-matting of their house floors are called *tatami*.

So clean are these straw mats of their floors that I have seen women, men too, kneeling on the long side-benches of the railway trains going to and from Tokio—facing the car windows: therefore sitting on their feet in a posture which left the bottoms of their feet nicely put together underneath them but toward you. And, as anyone might see, the very bottoms of their feet were spotless white.

Be clean! Yes—'Be clean' was the soul of Shinto, this ancient religion of Japan the Buddhists found when they came from China. Shinto spoke not of a good or a moral man but of a *clean* man. Spoke of clean hands—of a clean heart. And the Shinto religion finally made the Japanese dwelling the cleanest of all clean human things because it is no less *clean* a thing of the spirit. The Japanese have the sense that abhors waste as matter out of place: therefore dirt. Therefore ugliness is dirt. Dirt is ugly. As the centuries went by, every Japanese home whether of the coolie or of the aristocrat has been gradually worked out in this 'be clean' spirit. It is as a temple.

Becoming more closely acquainted with things Japanese, I saw the native home in Japan as a supreme study in elimination—not only of dirt but the elimination of the insignificant. So the Japanese house naturally fascinated me and I would spend hours taking it all to pieces and putting it together again. I saw nothing meaningless in the Japanese home and could find very little added in the way of ornament because all *ornament* as we call it, they get out of the way the necessary things are done or by bringing out and polishing the beauty of the simple materials they used in making the building. Again, you see, a kind of cleanliness.

At last I had found one country on earth where simplicity, as natural, is supreme. The floors of these Japanese homes are all made to live on—to sleep on, to kneel and eat from, to kneel upon soft silken mats and meditate upon. On which to play the flute, or to make love.

Nothing is allowed to stand long as a fixture upon the sacred floors of any Japanese home. Everything the family uses is designed to be removed when not in use and be carefully put in its proper place. It is so designed and made. Beautiful to use only when appropriate and use only at the right moment. Even the partitions dividing the floor spaces are made removable for cleaning.

And strangely enough, I found this ancient Japanese dwelling to be a perfect example of the modern standardizing I had myself been working out. The floor mats, removable for cleaning, are all three feet by six feet. The size and shape of all the houses are both determined by these mats. The sliding partitions all occur at the unit lines of the mats. And they all speak of a nine, sixteen or thirty-six mat house, as the case may be.

The simple square, polished wooden posts that support the ceilings and roof all stand at the intersections of the mats. The sliding paper *shoji*, or outside screens that serve in place of windows and enclose the interior room spaces (they are actually the outside walls), all slide back into a recess in the walls. They too are removable. The wind blows clean beneath the floors. The sloping tiled roofs are padded with clay under the heavy curved roof tiles and above the beautiful, low, flat, broad-boarded ceilings to make a cool overhead. The *benjo* or earth-closet is usually made on one side of the garden and set well away from the 'devil's corner'. And as if to prove that nearly every superstition has a basis of sense, I found that corner to be the one from which the prevailing breezes blow. Semi-detached from the house, the *benjo* is reached under shelter on polished plank floors. Beside it stands always a soft-water cistern, perhaps made of some hollowed-out natural stone or a picturesque garden-feature made or set up out of various natural stones. Or it may be a great bronze bowl brimming with water. A delicate little bamboo dipper lies across the pool of water to be lifted by the little housemaid who will pour clean water over the hands of the master or of his guests as either leaves the *benjo*. Another libation to the Shinto God of Cleanliness. A little confusing at first perhaps to the foreign guest, and no little embarrassment.

And the kitchen? Go down several steps to find that, for it is tiled flat with the ground and also goes high up into the rafters for ventilation. It is like a cool, clean, well-ventilated studio. Its simple appointments are of hand-polished concrete or fine hard stone. The kitchen is hung with a collection of copper kettles and lacquer-ware that would drive a Western collector quite off his head, and often has.

But the bathroom! This holy of holies is a good-sized detached pavilion, too, again flush with the ground and floored over with stone or tiles so pitched that water thrown from a bucket will drain away. Over the stone floor is a slat-floor of wood on which to stand in bare feet, the water going through freely. The built-in tub is square and deep and wood, made to stand up in. It is always heated from beneath.

As with every native so I have often been soaped and scrubbed before I was allowed to be tubbed. After that only might I step in and cook the germs off me. To any extent I was able to stand up to. Yes, that Shinto bath is a fine and religious thing, but so is everything else about the establishment. And bathing is perpetual. It has been made easy. The Japanese man or woman may loosen only the girdle and the garments all slip off together in one gesture. They put them all on again the same simple easy way. In their costume too, see simplicity, convenience, repose—their bodies as easily kept clean as their houses. Shinto made it and will have it so, the Buddhist notwithstanding. I found it wholly convenient and I wore the native costume whenever in the Japanese inn or dwelling. And much impressed the native inns.

For pleasure in all this human affair you couldn't tell where the garden leaves off and the garden begins. I soon ceased to try, too delighted with the problem to attempt to solve it. There are some things so perfect that nothing justifies such curiosity.

By heaven, here was a house used by those who made it with just that naturalness with which a turtle uses his shell. It is as like the natives as the polished bronze of their skin, the texture of their polished hair or the sly look in their slant and sloe eyes.

176

Belonging to this domestic establishment, this 'domestication of the infinite', everywhere there is to be seen a peculiar concentration on the part of *Ochsan*, the kindly-faced housewife. And even as yet, on the part of her coy daughters *O Kani-san* and *O Hisa-san*. As they all go about their domestic tasks, there must be some religious consecration in their minds to what they do. Or, in their hearts maybe.

'The simplest way with no waste.' That is daily Shinto ceremonial in Japan, I found after trying to work it all out that way for my people. You may see this in the most dignified and valued of all Japanese ceremonials —their tea ceremony. All cultured Japanese women, rich or poor, must learn to properly perform the tea ceremony according to cultural rules laid down by the celebrated master-esthete, Rikkyu. He was master too of flower arrangement. I tried to learn it. But this high tea ceremony came simply out of the science or art of most gracefully and economically getting a cup of tea made and reverently serving it to beloved or respected guests. Such reverent concentration as this tea ceremonial carries the ideal of 'be clean' to such heights—and lengths too—as weary us of the more direct West. We have not the spirit of it nor could we stand it—very long. But in this ceremony the very sense of 'be clean' becomes the spiritual attitude that not only abhors waste as matter out of place—therefore dirt—but places disorder of any sort in the same category.

That attitude prolonged, the West finds unbearable. This practical direct application of their ancient Shinto religion would see most of our domestic arrangements tumbled out of the windows into the street, a rich harvest for some junk man. Nevertheless, if Christian houses were ever treated by 'Christians' to proper spiritual interpretation such as Japanese interpretation of 'Shinto' the resulting integrity of spirit would immediately bankrupt our cherished 'pictorial homes'. Even if, yes especially *if* such interpretation did not enrich the soul of the West.

How our 'good taste' reacts upon and poisons them! By contact with us they have suddenly seen how difficult and unnecessary such painstaking aesthetic integrity is. They are seeing now how such discipline as theirs is no longer necessary feature or even part of the temporal authority or power and affluence we exercise. They discover it to be otherwise in the great West they emulate.

Spiritual significance is alive and singing in everything concerning the Japanese house. A veritable song. And it is in perfect unison with their Heaven.

It interested and refreshed me to see the Japanese gratify their desire for fine things—as something naturally added to them. The desire for beauty is no more natural to them than it is to us? But they always have a little recess in even the most humble houses devoted only to appropriate Fine Art entertainment. They call this little treasure-alcove the *Tokonoma*. A single rare painting will be hung for a day in proper season against the quiet-toned plaster walls of the *Tokonoma*. A single cultured flower arrangement in a beautiful vase will be set beside the painting, or

Kakemono, in this *Tokonoma.* One fine piece of sculpture too, or some abstract form in fine material on a polished lacquer surface, is allowed below that. The three arts are thus brought together by agreeable contrast so that we may see and admire the individual taste of the owner of the house. Never is the trinity without true cultural reference to some poetic significance of the day, occasion or season. Literature, too, would be near by, represented by some poet's profound saying in fine writing framed and hung—usually on the *ranma*—above the interior *shoji,* or sliding paper screens. All these things, however fine, mind you, must be appropriate. And they must be in season or they are not appropriate. They must take the rank of the masterpiece, though, in whatever art.

Truly cultivated people, the Japanese lavish loving care on their beautiful things. To them beautiful things are religious things and their care is a great privilege.

All is in their houses designed for kneeling on soft mats? Of course it is. But the same significant integrity or integrity made significant would work out just as well on one's feet—for us—as it worked for them on their knees. I am trying to work it out for us as I would like to help them do for themselves.

We of the West couldn't live in Japanese houses and we shouldn't. But we *could* live in houses disciplined by an ideal at least as high and fine as this one of theirs—if we went about it for a half century or so. I am sure the West needs this source of inspiration. For once, it can't very well copy. The ethnic eccentricity is too great. The West can copy nearly everything easier than it can copy the Japanese house or Japanese things for domestic uses.

Isn't real barbarism mostly ignorance of principle? Isn't barbarism merely trusting to instinct? Which is just what all our taste does or is with us. Instincts such as ours of the West, demoralized by opulence, are none the less barbaric because they have intellect they don't use, or a past culture they sentimentally abuse. Such demoralization is more dangerous and offensive to life, I should say.

On tortured knees I have tried to learn some of these lessons fro m t h Japanese. I have painfully participated in this 'idealized' making of a cup of tea following a Japanese formal dinner, trying to get at some of these secrets if secrets they are. I confess that I have been eventually bored to extinction by the repetition of it all and soon I would avoid the ordeal when I could see an invitation coming. And I freely admit, such discipline is not for us. It is far too severe. Yes, far too severe! We are not yet civilized enough to go that far in idealizing anything in life, not to mention our environment. Or be capable of making our living into ceremonial of any kind except occasionally: for the moment. Our joys and sorrows come and go otherwise. Our recreations mainly—different. And I always become painfully aware of our crudity in the more cultured Japanese environment. Their thumbs fold inward naturally as ours stick up and out. Their legs quietly fold beneath them where ours must stick out and

178

sprawl. It could be said that the culture of our civilization is founded upon the silken leg, the shapely thigh, balanced on the high heel. Theirs is founded upon the graceful arm, the beautifully modelled breast and the expressive hand. The finely moulded leg rising from the shapely shoe indicates our heaven. The finely modulated breast and arm and expressive hand indicates theirs. There is a difference.

But the truth is the Japanese dwelling is in every bone and fibre of its structure honest and our dwellings are not honest. In its every aspect the Japanese dwelling sincerely means something fine and straightway does it. So it seemed to me as I studied the 'song' that we of the West cut ourselves off from the practical way of beautiful life by so many old, sentimental unchristian expedients? Why are we so busy elaborately trying to get earth to heaven instead of seeing this simple Shinto wisdom of sensibly getting heaven decently to earth?

In the morning land I found this simple everyday singing of the human spirit—a 'song to heaven' I am calling it—to be the everyday, Shinto-made dwelling place of the Japanese people. I see that song as just as truly a blossom of interior-nature as trees and flowers and bees are blossoms. And I have learned as much for us in our lives from this singing as I could hear or bear. I have seen it on reverent knees beside poor old Baron Kuki—lonely aged diplomat still celebrated for his cuisine and his 'collections'. Or when some other Japanese gentlemen would send for me to come and dine, as so frequently happened, and the solemn tea ceremony as laid down by Rikkyu would inevitably follow the twenty-four or more artistic courses of the formal Japanese dinner.

All this had settled as past experience in my thought of Japan. And the question of modern architecture seemed more involved with Japanese architecture in native-principle than with any other architecture. So in the circumstances—frustration and destruction behind me—I turned hopefully and gratefully toward Japan, once more to live. But as nature and character—both are fate—would have it, I had not come alone as I might have done. And should have done?

Several months after the terrible catastrophe at Taliesin had come a short note expressing sympathy in kindly terms that understood suffering. It came evidently from a developed artist-intelligence. I somehow thought it from some fine-spirited, gray-haired lady-mother who had suffered deeply herself. I spoke of the note to my mother. And, for some reason lonely and spent now, I acknowledged it with a few grateful words. A reply came back asking if the writer might come to see me. She was a sculptress. She said life had crashed for her with much the same sorrow for her as mine. A luckless love affair. And she gave me some helpful suggestions as to thought. The philosophy was not so new to me but I had neglected it and needed it now. I wrote, appointing a time at the Orchestra Hall office. She intimated that she preferred to come after office hours.

179

That was how Miriam Noel appeared in my life. It was she I had taken to Japan.

I was—frankly—astonished. She was the reverse of everything I had expected. I could not connect her letters with her appearance. But as she sat opposite me at the office desk, when she spoke I understood how she could have written them.

She looked the Parisian by adoption and preference. Brilliant. Sophisticated, as might be seen at a glance. She had evidently been very beautiful and was so distinguished by beauty still. A violet pallor. Mass of dark red-brown hair. Clear-seeing eyes with a green light in them. Carriage erect and conscious—figure still youthful. She was richly dressed in the mode, a sealskin cape and cap. On her small hands were several rings. Around her neck she wore a gold chain with a jewelled cross—a monocle, too, was suspended from her neck on a white silken cord. She played with this as she talked. She laid a dainty cigarette case upon the office table. I lit for her the cigarette she took from it—not caring to smoke myself because I did not know how. In her left hand had been a small, black, limp book. She laid this on the desk. It was a copy of *Science and Health* by Mary Baker Eddy. Her latest study in psychology, I thought.

'How do you like me?' she said. A trace of some illness seemed to cling to her in the continuous, slight but perceptible shaking of her head. She looked at me, waiting for some answer to her simple question.

'I've never seen anyone like you,' I said honestly.

I learned that her two daughters were married. Her own son a travelling man. She had no one, she said—'nowhere to go and no desires'. Her health 'had been broken by the tragedy of the luckless love affair which was parallel to mine'.

And finally she had been driven from Paris along with the other Americans by the recent declaration of war. So she was staying for a time in Chicago with one of her married daughters, Norma. She had heard of me in Paris from the Horace Holleys—had read there of the terrible tragedy. The reading had touched her, and she apologized for being so bold as to write and offer her help. There she was.

Outside the routine of my work I had scarcely spoken to anyone but my mother since the tragedy.

Drowning men—they say so—clutch at straws. Here was no straw but enlightened comradeship, help, more light than I had to see by. Salvation maybe from blackness—blindness. I did not know. And here began the leading of the blind by the blind.

How do sentimental people ever manage to live on good terms with themselves, at all? By hypocrisy? I have often asked that question of the most sentimental person I ever knew. Myself. And I am sure the answer is yes—hypocrisy. Hypocrisy with oneself—which is the foundation of all hypocrisy towards others.

Now on the way to Tokio the truly brilliant Miriam was alongside.

When I arrived in Yokohama Bay for the third time, there stood Fujiyama the venerable, white-hooded and inviolate God of Nippon, against a golden sky. After the usual half sea-sickness that always made every hour that would go slowly by on board ship be counted wearily as one hour nearer this landing, the *Empress of China* now rides at anchor in the harbour at dawn. The engines stilled at last—the soft tread of Chinese boys, keeping step with the silence. Remembered beauty of earlier experiences comes rushing to refresh the jaded senses. The jinrikshas roll off the dock to familiar sights.

We two have come here two years after the second crossing to build the Hotel Imperial. High work to be done. Foundation tests already completed, the building is to begin and continue in earnest the better part of four years to come.

Contrary to popular superstition concerning a voluntary, open intimacy between grown-up independent men and women, there is usually a high ideal of life and great self-respect on both sides. There must be. Any sincere attempt to be true to one's self and to each other meets life's demands upon a higher plane of excellence than is ordinary and so a more exacting code of ethics continuously makes demands upon the personal quality and integrity of both the man and the woman. Comradeship makes constant demands that legal marriage may and does dispense with. Especially upon the woman does a voluntary relationship make these increasingly difficult demands. The woman brave enough or foolish enough to go honestly into one has that relationship alone to live by and to live for. Because—it is inevitable—she will owing to environment and circumstances be cut off from society in ways hard enough to bear at first and harder if not impossible to bear as time goes on.

A developed interior life of no mean character is the condition of any success whatever, even temporarily, in any unconventional life a man and a woman may undertake to live openly together.

I was still 'illegitimate'—that is to say I was still unable to get any legitimate freedom from the marriage contract with Catherine. No arguments availing. Therefore any woman foolish enough to be interested in me in the circumstances, if she cared enough for me to live openly with me, would be compelled to take that step into unconventional life or go under cover. Any tragedy after in these circumstances is double the similar tragedy in legal marriage, because the relationship is not only utterly defenceless, but is mercilessly assailed, and its failure quite generally welcomed by 'good' Society.

Well, I had never in my life learned to hide. And if I had learned I should have declined any partnership on those terms with anyone, because unconscious hypocrisy is bad enough. Conscious hypocrisy is a sure and swift corrosion of the soul of any creative artist. No coward ever did creative work, I believed then. And I believe it now.

Equivocal conduct hurts those who practise it ten times more than it hurts those it is practised upon. Secrecy and hypocrisy both do something to the character never to be repaired. And while the hypocrisy of others is

181

hard enough to bear, it is better to *bear* it than to *be* it. It is not the honest living of any life that endangers society, is it? Aren't the *pretended* lives the rotten threads in the social fabric?

I am sure that, while marriage in true sense is only for those who do not need it, yet it is so difficult to live long above marriage without the protection it affords and gives that only a coarse character or a very rare virtue can ever hope to survive without the formality of legal marriage.

The management of the Imperial allowed me to build a modest little nook for myself in the new temporary annex. The hotel had built this annex from my plans to take care of increase in guests while the New Imperial was building. The annex was just finished.

The windows of this little apartment looked out to the south over the Japanese garden and the apartment itself was connected to the hotel for complete service. I had a Japanese boy for my own uses. The fascinating mystery of Tokio was all around us. Tokio is very much like London in many respects. There is so much room in it for surprises. A dingy street outside and palaces immediately within the humble street doors, casual gates and quiet entrance ways.

In this particular nook in Tokio was a small living room with a fireplace —fire always burning—a balcony filled with dwarf-trees and flowers, a bedroom with balcony and bath, a small dining room where meals were served from the hotel. All were on the main floor of the apartment. But a narrow stair led up from the entrance way to a commodious studio-bed-room built as a penthouse above the roof. I slept there and had set up my drawing board there where I could work disturbing no one and could tumble into bed when tired out. Into these charming quarters we now went. And for a time a peaceful, mutually helpful relationship. There was a small grand piano—there were few in Tokio, and our friends were all capable of making good music. There was much good reading, study, rambles through Tokio by night, motor trips sometimes, usually on Sunday, by day. These recreations together with the few friends always faithful in such cases because they understand the situation and respect the characters involved, made up the world we lived in. We knew a good many interesting people and some charming Russians in Tokio, among them the talented Polish Count and Countess Lubiensky, Princess Tscheremissinoff, Count and Countess Ablomov, the Ivanoffs, Olga Krynska, a talented pianist and linguist, and the Japanese Hanis of the wonderful little 'School of the Free Spirit'. I built a school building suitable to their purpose—one of the rare experiences of my life.

But the clairvoyant Miriam, herself—as I had soon discovered—had for many years been the victim of strange disturbances. Sometimes unnatural exaggerations, mental and emotional. They would spoil life entirely for both of us for days at a time. I had hunted causes. Yes—I had looked into myself, too, as a possible cause.

It was true that nervously she had suffered wreck. Strange disabilities still appeared to cling to her. All would go happily for some days. Then strange perversion of all that. No visible cause. An unnatural exaggeration of emotional nature that grew more and more morbid. The mystifying reactions became more violent until something like a terrible struggle between two natures in her would seem to be going on within her all the time and be tearing her to pieces. Then peace again for some time and a charming life.

This undertow of strange—often weird—disturbance with happy intervals lasted four years during the construction of the Imperial Hotel. But the outbreaks grew more destructive as years went by. Domestic drama increased at the expense of good sense and domestic peace. Misery and disquiet not only ran alongside the gruelling effort I had to make on the building of the Imperial, but everywhere life itself now went, various galling disturbances would take place.

But for me there was always the quest for Japanese prints. And the mysterious, wonderful Yedo to explore. The print is more autobiographical than you may imagine. If Japanese prints were to be deducted from my education, I don't know what direction the whole might have taken. The gospel of elimination of the insignificant preached by the print came home to me in architecture as it had come home to the French painters who developed *Cubism* and *Futurism*. Intrinsically the print lies at the bottom of all this so-called *modernism*. Strangely unnoticed, uncredited. I have often wondered why.

CAME YEDO

Like Ancient Rome, Ancient Yedo was a capital of seven hills, every hill crowned by gay temples and the highways leading over the hills or to them were hung with red paper lanterns. Yes, the illuminated sign is ancient! But here, the glowing 'advertising' did not repel the eye. The characters, so beautiful in themselves, were ideographs as appropriate to the eye as the lantern.

This teeming, enormous area is fascinating Yedo. A vast city channelled but with wide bare-earth streets swarming with humanity their interminable length, beaten down hard by traffic, lined both sides with blue-grey tile-roofed two-story wooden buildings. A great city that is a gigantic village. One of the largest cities in the world. Several millions of people are already there. Here come natives in crowds pulling or pushing at loaded carts, others peddling, or they go strolling or bargaining along the shopfronts; queer little horses drawing loads so balanced just behind on two great cart wheels that they help push the cart along; strange hump-backed horses being led along through the throngs by their masters. No drivers. Big black bullocks, turquoise headdress wound about their big black horns, come labouring slowly along, head down, sullenly drawing enormous loads of logs or merchandise. And sprinkled all through the moving masses of sober-robed people, hand carts, back-boxes and horses, picturesque strollers and heaving bullocks, innumerable gaily clad children are happily playing. Japanese children seem to always have the right of way; they are gaily dressed as flowers in the sun.

Scarlet and gold shuttered sedan-chairs, the *kagos*, blinds drawn, occasionally go by, slung to long black beams carried on the thick shoulders of stout naked-legged coolies, two coolies in front, two in the rear. Mystery is everywhere. Maintained—as privacy? Weird figures wander by us as from no earthly world. But notwithstanding this tremendous activity, there is brooding quiet over all as though some enchantment wrought an unnatural scene. Yet everywhere a pleasant gaiety gives assurance of intimate human contentment.

Dusk is falling. The softly brilliant globes or cylinders, red-paper lanterns patterned with strange characters in white or black, begin to glow in the street vistas of this twilight. And there are rows of soft red lanterns countering on rows along the streets, and always there are more clusters of the beautiful things and occasionally a simple large one. On every building they hang and move to and fro as the breezes blow. Some hang above the street on bamboo poles. Light, here, is something soft to beguile the eyes. Evidently here too is the ancient advertising medium of a limitless city. The illuminated sign is ancient.

Along all the highways and byways are the shops; all the second stories lining the upper sides of the swarming streets are dwelling-places. The sliding paper closure of the openings is usually protected by vertical wooden slats in so many clever geometrial patterns. As evening falls these screens become luminous from within as in daylight they were luminous from without. Charming silhouettes are all the time flickering on them, the play to and fro made as human figures pass. The plaintive twang of samisen strings plucked by a broad ivory blade of the hands of the shop-keeper's daughter—Hirani-san or Nobu-san—maybe, is heard coming into the glowing unnaturally quiet scene. Yes, it all looks—*just like the prints!* It does.

The lower stories of buildings lining the labyrinth of earthen highways and byways are all shops and wide open to the street from side to side. All are ingeniously crammed to overflowing with an orderly array of curious or brilliant merchandise: on all seven hills are famous temples and gardens, famous places celebrated by the prints and at this moment—the year is 1800.

Therefore the quiet but gay life of this ancient-modern capital is aware of Toyonobu, Harunobu, Shunsho, and Shigemasa. Utamaro Hokusai and Hiroshige are soon to come to work. Commodore Perry has not yet insisted upon international co-operation. No Hollanders have arrived. Will Adams, hardy Englishman stranded there, is the only Westerner to have seen this land of mist, snow, flower—and woman—until we reconstruct it from the prints. This hardy, shipwrecked sailor is there now as much because he wants to be as because the shoguns will not allow him to leave. Through him, only, does this singular culture, developing in complete isolation, learn anything at all of Western ways. And by way of the print alone does the West know anything of Japanese ways in ancient Yedo.

All life in Yedo is familiar to the teeming streets. All the charming children seem to be playing there. Exuberance is beauty.

And there is laughter in Yedo—always laughter. Always too the sound of the scraping clogs. Always these weird calls and cries of street vendors. Always snatches of weird song and strange animal cries. Japanese music seems to us an animal cry. At night—the mysteries of Silence deepen. Song-like sounds that might be—but are not—made by the wind are everywhere. The nasal twang of samisen-strings punctures it all at intervals. And the sweet wail of flutes comes to us like lovely coloured ribbons of sound from the private family gardens behind the shops. Heard over all this staccato as running accompaniment to this festival for the eyes is the ceaseless crescendo and diminuendo of the measured, scraping sound made by innumerable geta in the gravelled street of the thronging city—a continuous diapason to an obbligato of far-off cries—like strange animals calling to each other. The ripple of soprano laughter and the glad voices nearby are reassuring.

But see everywhere warm family affection. True contentment. The night life of Yedo meantime is industry even until midnight, wherever there is light to see by. This strange night-scene is always pervaded by ceaseless quiet movement. Wherever the fascinating red and white paper lanterns glow, deep shadows quiver and hover around, for Yedo is not bright at night. All is subdued like some modern society-woman's red-shaded drawing-room, and the streets are as orderly, mannerly and clean as her carpets.

All the human figures of this scene are so simply robed. They may be, as simply, unrobed.

And the life of Yedo swarms with a perpetual swarming.

But, within, behind the shopfronts, all is repose. Kindly, glowing, humane and homely repose. And yet, at night, behind all the softly glowing lights of the gently swinging lanterns with their mysterious messages and the lambent flambeaux of open shops there is always this undergrowth of dark and of mystery. A group of sinister, black-robed, double-sworded figures come with black hoods on their heads, swords alongside that make all other swords seem innocuous, as they pass by us again: gallant strides, reckless swagger. Such side and *style* would make Fifth Avenue gasp. Adventurous *Samurai* are abroad! Here come now enormous, bulky, brutal figures but with such kindly faces. Their long black hair is brushed back high from the forehead. They are the giant strong-men and are followed by several attendants and shuffling of adoring crowds. The bulk of several Japanese is in any one of these: they are the Sumo or professional wrestlers bred in Tokio for that purpose alone and for many centuries. When famous, the Sumo, too, are celebrated by the prints. To inbreed human beings for a special purpose as we breed horses! Yes, they did it.

See those elegant figures? They are the *Komuso*, aristocratic street adventurers. Faces concealed by huge bell-shaped head-cover of woven straw, going about with short-swords stuck in their belts.

185

Tea houses are everywhere. This one by Tokyo-bay is inviting because it is so thickly hung with gay red-paper lanterns. The entrances are curtained with indigo blue hangings patterned with the huge white 'mon' of the keeper's household. Push through the hangings with us and enter to find, looking down at us from the matted floors just beyond the entrance, smiling pretty Japanese girls down on their knees bowing low and bowing lower—rising eagerly to take us by the hand and lead us in. Our shoes? Well, we take the things off, step up in stocking feet on to clean, fresh-smelling straw mats.

Look about you now and see for the first time what severe simplicity of form and beautiful materials left clean for their own sake can do for a scene of shifting colour and quick movement. All clean and silent for soft white-shod feet. How can anything human be so polished and clean?

So we pass by the rooms and glimpse charming sights. Guests robed in silks, fan in hand, heads gleaming with polished black. Ah! you see—in everything inimitable, imperishable style! Black, in itself a property, is revelation here.

Little cages of fireflies hang to the posts, as post by post we pass along the open corridors against the outside dark. Finally all will open along one entire roomside to an enchanted scene: the Japanese garden! Samisen notes come from all directions like pervasive insect-notes in a summer field. We hear the tender wail of flutes more distinctly here as though a door had opened; we see moon-lanterns glowing under spreading pine trees as high moonlight streams down over all; soft light of the new moon gleams on the still water, softly glances from the cool plashing of gently falling water from on high over great black stones. Thin silver streams cascade down piles of fantastic rugged rock half hidden in dark masses of dark green sonari; bright flowers and blooming shrubs are massed about the rocks and rugged tree trunks down to the water's very edge.

This seems an ancient countryside, this garden. Or an opal empire. But it may be, yes, *it must be*, very small. How small would be unbelievable! Twenty-five feet square!

We had come here from another, noisier, more vulgar world and we gratefully knelt on sombre silken cushions, subdued, entranced—looking humbly upon this environment of simple perfect art.

A work of art as marvellous now enters the scene. She is fashioned upon the head, hand and breast instead of upon the leg and thigh as she would have been fashioned in the West. With modest mien she enters, smiles sweetly and bows gracefully to the floor again and again. She softly asks what the most honourable gentlemen will be pleased to have her unworthy self bring to them, this most tender of evenings, for their good pleasure? Black heads meantime are everywhere moving within the adjoining rooms. Black gleams over smooth oval powder-whitened faces punctuated by lips of living scarlet, the scarlet to match the saki cups?

Black! the science and the art of 'black' is in everything. Decorous black eyes slyly slant upon you from every direction as the little artful beings

186

move noiselessly about, grace and refinement in every movement. For what, might we ask? Crudely, but with a smile we say simply, 'Gohan'. Leaving all to them. What else to do?

Now take the clean pine twin-sticks in your fingers, break them apart. The *hashi* are fresh, for use but once, and do your best by the steaming rice as the cover is lifted from the big black lacquered bowls. Rice like that is cooked only in Japan. The pretty maid fills and refills our smaller red lacquer bowls from the large black one. The perfectly done fish on the Nabeshima china on the trays may please you. Savoury fish-soups under cover in the delicately lacquered patterns of the covered golden bowls may not. You are unaccustomed to fish-soup? Curiously designed sweets are laid out on the painted, gaily decorated stands. They are disappointing to us, not sweet enough as we know sweets. Meantime distant drums have been beating beneath the other sounds—beating, as we now become aware, in strange, secretly frustrating rhythms. The ear strives and fails to catch the rhythm—syncopated like nothing so much as raindrops falling from the eaves on hollow metal. Then, tired of eating or the attempt to eat, the little *musme* bring in pretty woven baskets, in each a steaming wet towel wrung dry, and they offer it to us in a separate basket. We refresh our hands and faces. They are gently regarding us the while with shy amusement. The little *musme* break into gales of laughter as we groan and awkwardly stretch our legs to take the strange kinks out of them, or as we fall back to our knees in the attempt to rise after sitting so long on our heels. *Saki* had nothing to do with it but it might have had.

All the while, to and fro in the corridors, Geisha parties undulate noiselessly to and fro, samisen in hand, faces crimsoned slightly at the temples, foreheads and cheeks whitened all over to the brilliant-scarlet lips. All just as Harunobu, Kiyonaga and Utamaro, Shunsho and Shigemasa faithfully recorded it so the world might never lose it. A fine lady plays the koto, the koto's graceful length laid upon the expanse of matting. She kneels over it and caresses minor chords from it. Then say—as you will—'such gentleness!' ' Such good sense in elegant simplicity!' With what disciplined beauty Japan has mingled the uses and purposes of everyday life! Mingled? No. *Made* the necessities of life beautiful. This *is* civilization, you say. Feeling it all too good to be true. There must be some sinister side to the picture, lurking out there in the dark! Maybe! This is the East you know— And the scepticism from the West looks warily about. Now we have seen nothing, yet, immoral.

But of course it is. It must be.

Ugliness being a kind of virtue in the West, beauty must be immoral in the East. But it all *seems* so innocent, naïve and charming.

Come now and we shall see the Oriental Courtesan, favourite subject of the prints and the basis of much reproof.

Immoral in this land of the rising sun? No. Only unmoral.

But can what is naturally sordid be made beautiful?

Well, we climb into a sitting posture, knees up to our chins, crammed into the romantic Kago, glancing as we pass by into miles of open shop-fronts, many of them 'news' shops, that is to say, shops full of prints. We pass pedlars, pilgrims with jangling-staffs, carrying slender cabinets on their backs filled with trays. The trays were sometimes filled with exquisite prints of every sort by popular artists of the day, making the portraits of popular favourites on the stage, all the prints to be sold in public places. These are the animated news-stands of that period. These pedlars were then all the newsboys there were.

We see posted in the shops coloured pictures, prints, of gorgeous Oiran or Courtesans and their Komuso, or little pupils.

'Advertising' was active then as now, but the artist's individuality never suffered on account of it then. Why?

Ahead of us now looms a great black gate and directly in front of the gateway a great cherry tree is in bloom, like drifted pink snow in the light of innumerable red and white lanterns. Just inside the gate we come upon the Oiran or Yoshiwara procession. The prints have prepared us for that. The procession is now prepared for us.

In the centre of each group of the elaborate pageant is a gorgeous feminine creature exaggerated by resplendent robes and extravagant head-dress. She is slowly moving with feminine traits deliberately exaggerated, undulating with stately artificiality on white-clad feet thrust into high black-lacquered clogs. Her face is plastered dead-white, her lips painted the limit of scarlet. The only animate human thing in the ensemble of gorgeous robes, impassive face and black and gold head-dress is the pair of sly black eyes. They move in the white mask and regard you for one brief, seeing moment—with mischief in their depths. With measured tread and artificial grace she moves on in slow, stately pomp, surrounded by other creatures as feminine but far less gorgeous. And following just behind the gorgeous 'Oiran' come two Komuso, plaintive little creatures, wonderfully dressed, made likewise in little. And being as stately as small editions can be. Such splendours as you can only call barbaric are there before you. The procession centring about the barbaric queen, too queenly for any but barbarism, moves slowly to the gate, herself now softly flecked by the falling petals of the great cherry tree. Other gorgeous 'Oiran' are coming, all of them surrounded by similar groups lit by dancing coloured lanterns as was the queen of the Yoshiwara.

As the gorgeous procession turns to go back again, sober-robed men like grey moths hovering about some glittering flame, follow, fascinated. Such splendour dazzles duller lives. An apparition of heaven to them.

Individuality marks each Oiran and her group, in spite of the severely conventional style that seems to be imposed upon them all.

Here, as the high black-lacquered clogs scrape slowly over the roadway now pink with fallen cherry-flower petals, is the ceremonial glorification of something we of the West have never been allowed to understand, if indeed we are able to understand it.

Here, it appears, a woman is raised to nth power as symbol among men.

You will try to understand that these creatures are not 'women' but Woman. Woman aggrandized, Institutionalized. Demoralized? No. Only *Professionalized* on a plane that here seems to carry a premium in place, grace, and preferment. Here is compelling power made artistic and deliberately cultured. Not yet awakened to 'moral' discrimination, so not sinful. Was there pride, think you, in doing surpassingly well this pleasuring of men? Was there conscientious sense of the value of the office—and a real ambition to deserve well of the luxury and opportunity to shine resplendent as the object of man's desire?

Well, judging from the poetic inscriptions on the prints of that period that advertise and celebrate the Oiran—Yes.

The social power or some natural power at this stage of Japan's culture had placed this premium of '*woman*' upon these professional women. In all extravagance. If exuberance is beauty, here it was again. Artists like Utamaro lived and designed that popular series of prints wherein woman was made symbol of almost everything. And it was here in the Yoshiwara that the next artist enjoyed and criticized and was enjoyed and criticized. Here in the Yoshiwara of Yedo the literati of the times came to remember to forget. Here the Samurai in black masks came seeking release. And romance in the intoxication of a freedom they could never otherwise know made them lay their swords aside.

The social graces and such fine arts of music, poetry, dancing as Japan knew were the running accompaniment to the conviviality, here on no bestial plane. The 'moral' element that could make it bestial was lacking. As it was with the Philosopher and the Hetaira in Rome and in Athens itself, so probably it was here in Yedo except that here it was an aesthetic rite.

Then all this knew nothing of its own degradation?

If we look at it similarly we may see the beauty it had. If we bring to it eyes confirmed in assumption of the 'unclean', then will we see only that.

But in the artist's celebration of this life as we find it illustrated in the now antique Yedo daily journal, the prints of the ukiyoye, we see proof not of vice but of innocence.

As the prints show it to us we see that love of life and beauty was a poetic theme running like a thread of fine silk through all that Yoshiwara life of the Yedo courtesan. There was raw but elemental romance in it. It could not be so now in the degradation that remains of the institution as it exists in Japan and as it has always been in the West, and it is not. It would be money now and therefore no romance at all except the fortuitous romance of luck.

We find it all so recorded in the most exquisite piece of illustrated magazine making in this world—a graphic journalistic report by Shunsho Shigemasa called 'Beauties of the Little Green Houses', showing, as it does, the elegance of these lives of *filles de joie* of old Japan a century or more ago.

So, while the conception of the great hotel grew, and when later the building itself began to rise, Yedo was a presence always in which to

189

search for the invaluable record of that time, in prints. A window through which I looked upon my own work. A byroad by which I saw it. Yet I must not linger more with the great heart of Japanese life, antique Yedo, but pass on to the telling of the building of the New Imperial Hotel of Tokio. Yedo of 1915.

BUILDING AGAINST DOOMSDAY (WHY THE GREAT EARTHQUAKE DID NOT DESTROY THE IMPERIAL HOTEL)

From infancy, a sort of subjective contemplation, the minds and hearts of the Japanese are fixed upon the great calm mountain God of their nation—the sacred Fujiyama brooding in majesty and eternal calm over all. They deeply worship as the mountain continually changes moods, combining with sun and moon, clouds and mist in a vast expression of elemental beauty the like of which in dignity and repose exists nowhere else on earth.

It is not too much to say that the sacred mountain is the God of old Japan; Japan the Modern Ancient.

And yet the dreaded force that made the great mountain, continually takes its toll of life from this devoted people, as the enormous weight of the deep sea beside the tenuous island, the deepest sea in the world, strains the earth-crust, opening fissures in the bottom of the great valley in which it rests and the sea rushes down to internal fires to become gas and steam expanding or exploding internally, causing earth convulsions that betray the life on the green surface. Great wave movements go shuddering through the body of their land, spasmodically changing all overnight in immense areas. Whole villages disappear. New islands appear as others are lost and all on them. Shores are reversed as mountains are laid low and valleys lifted up. And always flames! The terror of it all invariably faces conflagration at the end.

Trained by these disasters of the centuries to build lightly on the ground —the wood and paper houses natural to them may be kindled by any spark. When fire starts it seldom stops short of several hundred homes and usually thousands, or complete destruction. So, when the earthquake is violent, fire finishes the terrible work.

The dead not swallowed up, are buried, and once more *Shikata-gai-nai* (it cannot be helped) goes patiently on as before. Naturally the earthwaves seem fate and unconquerable. A force useless to combat in strength alone, for it is mightier than any force at man's command. *Shikata-gainai!* This stoicism I have seen and lived with four years or more while preparing to meet this awful force by building on ground which the seismograph shows is never for a moment still—prepare to meet it by other means than rigid force.

The foreigner with the advent of Commodore Perry came to share Japanese joys and sorrows, and soon a building was needed to shelter the foreign element of Tokio, the capital of Japan. A social clearing house became necessary to official Japan as a consequence of the new foreign interest in them, because, for one reason, no foreigner could live on the floor. The need steadily increased. At that time the Mikado took it upon himself to meet the need, and asked the Germans to build one of their characteristic national wood and plaster extravaganzas for the purpose.

That wretched marvel grew obsolete and the need of another, a great one, imperative. The Imperial household, this time, proposed to share the task of providing the new accommodation with the capitalists of the Empire, shipowners, cement manufacturers, bankers, tobacco interests, etc., and I, an American, was chosen to do the work.

No foreigner yet invited to Japan had taken off his hat to Japanese traditions. When foreigners came, what they had back home came too, suitable or not, and the politely humble Japanese, duly impressed, took the offering and marvelled. They tried to do likewise in their turn. And yet Japanese fine-art traditions are among the noblest and purest in this world, giving Chinese origins due credit. It was my instinct not to insult them. The West has much to learn from the East—and Japan was the gateway to that great East of which I had been dreaming since I had seen my first Japanese prints—and read my first Laotze.

But this terrible natural enemy to all building whatsoever—the temblor!

The terror of the temblor never left me while I planned the building nor while, for more than four years, I worked upon it. Nor is anyone allowed to forget it—sometimes awakened at night by strange sensations as at sea, strangely unearthly and yet rumbling earth-noises. Sudden shocks, subsidence—and swinging. Again shock after shock and upheaval, jolting back and swinging. A sense of the bottom falling from beneath the building, terror of the coming moments as cracking plaster and groaning timbers indicate the whole structure may come crashing and tumbling down. There may be more awful threat to human happiness than earthquake. I do not know what it can be.

The Japanese turn livid, perspiration starts on them, but no other sign unless the violence becomes extreme, then—panic. I studied the temblor. Found it a wave-movement, not of sea but of earth—accompanied by terrific shocks no rigidity could withstand.

Because of the wave movements, deep foundations like long piles would oscillate and rock the structure. Therefore the foundation should be short or shallow. There was sixty to seventy feet of soft mud below the upper depth of eight feet of surface soil on the site. That mud seemed a merciful provision—a good cushion to relieve the terrible shocks. Why not float the building upon it? A battleship floats on salt water. And why not extreme lightness combined with tenuity and flexibility instead of the great weight necessary to the greatest possible rigidity? Why not, then, a building made as the two hands thrust together palms inward, fingers interlocking and yielding to movement—but resilient to return to original position when distortion ceased? A flexure—flexing and reflexing in any direction. Why fight the quake? Why not sympathize with it and out-wit it?

That was how the building began to be planned.

The most serious problem was how to get the most carrying power out of that eight feet of cheese-like soil that overlay the liquid mud. During the first year of plan-making, I made borings nine inches in diameter eight feet deep and filled them with concrete. Arranged to test the concrete pins thus made. Got carloads of pig iron and loaded the pins until they would drive into the ground. Kept the test figures of loads and reactions. Took borings all over the site to find soft pockets. Water stood in the holes two feet below the surface, so the concrete had to go in quickly as the borings were completed. Later, tapered piles were driven in to *punch* the holes and pulled out—the concrete thrown directly in as soon as the pile was out of the way.

These data in hand, the foundation plan was made to push these concrete pins two feet on centres each way over the entire areas on which the wall footings were to spread. The strength of the whole depth of eight feet of top soil was thus brought to bear at the surface. That was simple. But here was a compressible soil that might take a squeeze under the broad footings to add to the friction of the pins. Experiments showed the squeeze could safely be added to the friction. This meant a settlement of the building of five inches, the building itself driving the piles that much deeper. This was economy, but dangerous and more complicated.

But finally the building was computed pound by pound and distributed according to test data to 'float' below the grade of the ground surface— and it did. With some few slight variations it stayed there.

This foundation saved hundreds of thousands of dollars over the foundations then in use in Tokio. But had the owners of the Imperial superficially known what was contemplated something might have happened to prevent it. Rumour nearly did prevent it. Here, however, was the desired shock-absorber, a cushion, pins and all, to be uniformly loaded and put to work against the day of reckoning.

Now how to make the flexible structure instead of the foolish rigid one? Divide the building into parts. Where the parts were necessarily more than sixty feet long, joint these parts clear through floors, walls, footings and all, and manage the joints in the design. Wherever part met part, through joints also. So far, good sense, and careful calculation.

But a construction was needed where floors would not be carried between walls, because subterranean disturbances might move the walls and drop the floors. Why not then carry the floors as a waiter carries his tray on upraised arm and fingers at the centre—*balancing* the load? All supports centred under the floor slabs like that instead of resting the slabs on the walls at their edges as is usually the case?

This meant the cantilever, as I had found by now. The cantilever is most romantic, most free, of all principles of construction, and in this case it seemed the most sensible. The waiter's tray supported by his hand at the centre is a cantilever slab in principle. And so concrete cantilever slabs continuous across the building from side to side, supported in that way, became the structure of the Imperial Hotel at Tokio.

192

Roof tiles of Japanese buildings have murdered countless thousands of Japanese in upheavals, so a light hand-worked green copper roof was planned. Why kill more?

The outer walls were spread wide, thick and heavy at the base, growing thinner and lighter toward the top. Whereas Tokio buildings were all top-heavy. The centre of gravity was kept low against the swinging movements and the slopes were made an aesthetic feature of the design. The outside cover-hangs of the cantilever slabs where they came through the walls were all lightened by ornamental perforations enriching the light and shade of the structure. The stone everywhere under foot in Tokio was a workable light lava weighing as much as green oak. It was considered sacrilege to use this common material for the aristocratic edifice. But finally it was used for the feature material and readily yielded to any sense of form the architect might choose to indicate. And the whole structure was to be set up as a double shell—two shells, an exterior of slim cunning bricks, and an interior one of fluted hollow bricks raised together to a convenient height of four feet or more. These shells were to be poured solid with concrete to bind them together.

The great building thus became a jointed monolith with a mosaic surface of lava and brick. Earthquakes had always torn piping and wiring apart where laid in the structure and had flooded or charged the building. So all piping and wiring was to be laid free of construction in covered concrete trenches in the ground of the basements, independent even of foundations. Mains and all pipes were of lead with wiped joints, the lead bends sweeping from the trenches to be hung free in vertical pipe shafts, from which the curved lead branches were again taken off, curved, to the stacks of bathrooms. Thus any disturbance might flex and rattle but not break the pipes or wiring.

Last but not least there was to be an immense reservoir or pool as an architectural feature of the entrance court—connected to the water system of the hotel and conserving the roof water.

Thus the plans were made so that all architectural features were practical necessities, and the straight line and flat plane were respectfully modified in point of style to a building bowing to the traditions of the people to whom the building would belong. The *nature* of the design too, I wanted to make something their intensive hand methods could do well, because we didn't know what machinery could be used. It was impossible to say how far we could go with that. Probably not very far.

Finally the plans were ready.

No estimates could be had. It was all so unfamiliar, no commercial concern would touch it. Nothing left but to abandon the whole or organize to build it ourselves. The Imperial Hotel and its architect and builder. The language was a barrier. The men and methods strange.

But the foreign architect—with eighteen or twenty architectural students from the Japanese universities, several of whom were taken to Wisconsin during the plan-making period—and one expert foreign builder, Paul Muellor of Chicago, two foreigners, all else native, we organized with the hotel manager, Hayashi-San, as general manager. We had already bought pottery kilns in Shizuoka and made the long slim cunning bricks, of a style and size never made before for the outside shell. They were now ready for use. We had also made the fluted hollow bricks for the inside shell, the first in the Empire. We bought a fine lava-quarry at Oya near Nikko for the feature-material and started a flood of dimension stone moving down to the site in Tokio—a stream that kept piling into the building for four years. The size of the hole left in the ground at Oya was about like the excavations for the Grand Central Terminal.

We had a hundred or more clever stone choppers beating out patterns of the building on the greenish, leopard-spotted lava, for that period. On an average we employed about 600 men continually for four years. As a large proportion of them came from the surrounding country they lived round about in the building as we built it. With their numerous families, there they were—cooking, washing, sleeping. And we tried faithfully—sometimes frantically and often profanely—to teach them how to build it, halfway between our way and their way.

We tried the stone-planer with the stone-cutters. It was soon buried beneath the chips that flew from their busy stone-axes. Tried derricks and gin-poles and hoists. They preferred to carry heavy loads and enormous stones up inclined planes on their shoulders. We tried to abolish scaffolding and teach them to lay brick from the inside. Not to be done. They lashed tapering poles together in cunning ways as for centuries and clung with prehensile toes to the framework.

How skilful they were! What craftsmen! How patient and clever. So instead of wasting them by vainly trying to make them come our way—we went with them their way. I modified many original intentions to make the most of what I now saw was naturally theirs. The language grew less an obstruction. But curious mistakes were perpetual. It is true that the Japanese approach to any matter is a spiral. Their instinct for attack in any direction is oblique and volute. But they make up for it in gentleness and cleverness and loyalty. Yes, the loyalty of the retainer to his *Samurai*. They soon educated us and all went pretty well.

The countenance of the building began to emerge from the seemingly hopeless confusion of the enormous area now covered by the building materials of its terraces and courts and hundreds of families. And the workmen grew more and more interested in it. It was no uncommon thing to see groups of them admiring and criticizing too as some finished portion would emerge—criticizing intelligently.

There was a warmth of appreciation and loyalty unknown in the building circles of our country. A fine thing to have experienced.

The curse of the work was the holiday. There were no Sundays, but a couple of holidays every fortnight instead, and it took a day or two to recover from most of them. So the work dragged. And the rainy season! The Japanese say it rains up from the ground as well as down from the sky —in Tokio. We did succeed in abolishing the expensive cover-shed of tight roof and hanging matting sides under which most buildings are built

194

in Japan. We congratulated ourselves until we found they knew their climate better than we did. Had we protected them from the rain and the burning sun the buildings would have been finished about seven months sooner—besides making all more comfortable and so more efficient.

A few more such 'successes' would have been enough.

The directors met regularly for a couple of years and began to complain.

Rumours reached them from the English (the English love the Americans in Tokio) and Americans (why are Americans invariably so unpleasant to one another abroad?) to the effect that the architect of their building was mad. In any earthquake the whole thing would tumble apart—and the whole building would sink out of sight in the mud beneath. There was room enough for it in that cushion of mud. Where all had been pleasant enthusiasm, things began to drag. The loyalty of my own office force never for a moment wavered, but manager Hayashi was daily hectored and censured. At this critical time it became apparent that three and a half million yen more would be necessary to complete and furnish the work. Things looked dark.

By now a small army was working away in the lower stories of the building as it was completed. As soon as one portion was built it became a hive of frantic industry. The copper features and fixtures and roof tiles were all made there; the interior woodwork and furniture—the upholstery and many other things went on in the vast interior spaces as soon as the floor slabs covered them over.

I had brought examples of good furniture from home and took them apart to teach the Japanese workmen how to make them according to the new designs which made them all part of the structure. They were fine craftsmen at this. Rug designs had gone to Pekin. The rugs were being woven there to harmonize with the interior features of the great rooms and the guest rooms. We were about two-thirds of the way over with the building itself. The foreigners had no way of keeping track of costs or finding out much about them in detail. So things had gone on for several years.

The crash came.

The directors were called together.

Baron Okura was chairman of the board—representing besides his own interests, the interest of the Imperial Royal Household, sixty per cent, besides ownership of the ground. There was also Asano-san—a white-haired Samson of the shipping interests—a powerful man with shaggy white brows and piercing eyes. Murai of the tobacco interests—a peace-maker, with pleasant ways always. Wakai, the banker, as broad as he was long, with a beard that reached below the table when he stood up. Kanaka, a half dozen others.

Baron Okura had rather sponsored me from the beginning. He was in trouble now. The meetings had been held in the old hotel building and were pleasant social affairs with refreshments. This one was not. It looked black. A long time, it had been threatening. The Baron, a black-haired youth of eighty—a remarkable man regarded as one of the astute financial powers of the Empire—sat at the head of the table. I sat on his left. On

195

his right sat his cultivated secretary, a Harvard graduate, who was interpreter. It doesn't matter where the others were. They were there and all talking at once. I answered the leading questions without end. The foundations. Always the foundations—and the money. The money!

The Baron was patient and polite—for some time. His lower lip had a trick of sticking out and quivering when he became intense. This personal idiosyncrasy of his was evident now. Suddenly he rose—leaned forward, head thrust forward, angry, hissing, pounding the table with both fists—extraordinary conduct for him.

The crowd went back and down as though blown down by the wind.

There was silence—the Baron still standing looking over toward me. Not knowing what it was all about I instinctively rose. The interpreter rose too, and said, 'The Baron says that if the "young man" (all things are relative) will himself remain in Japan until the building is finished, he the Baron will himself find the necessary money and they could all go to ——' whatever the Japanese word is for the place they could go to.

Although homesick by now and sick besides I reached out my hand to the Baron. The compact was made. The meeting was over. The directors filed out, red and angry to a man, instead of happy to have the responsibility lifted from them.

Was it Pericles who enacted some such role as the Baron's when the Parthenon was building? Anyway, the building of the new Imperial went on. Now every director became a spy. The walls had ears. Propaganda increased. My freedom was gone. I worked under greater difficulties than ever. But my little band of Japanese apprentices was loyal and we got ahead until another storm broke.

'Why not,' said the directors to the Baron, 'eliminate the pool and save 40,000 yen?' The Baron saw sense in this and sent for me. His mind was made up. No arguments took effect. I told him via interpreters that it was the last resource against the quake. In disaster, the city water would be cut off, and the window frames being wood in the 500-foot building front along the side street where wooden buildings stood, fire could gut the structure even though it withstood the quake. I had witnessed five terrible fires in Tokio already—walls of flame nothing in any degree inflammable could withstand.

No matter. The pool must come out. No, I said, it is wrong to take it out, and by such interference he would release me from my agreement and I could and would go home with no further delay. And I left his office. But I did not leave Tokio and the pool went in to play its final part in the great drama of destruction that followed two years later.

Another year and I could go home. The Tokio climate, so moist and humid summer and winter, depressing except in fall and early spring, together with the work and anxiety were wearing me down.

But now came a terrible test that calmed troublesome fears and made the architect's position easier.

The building construction was about finished. The architect's workroom had been moved to the top of the left wing above the promenade

196

entrance. It was nearly noon. The boys in the office, reduced to ten, were there, and workmen were about. Suddenly with no warning a gigantic jolt lifted the whole building, threw the boys down sprawling with their drawing boards. A moment's panic and hell broke loose as the wave motions began. The structure was literally in convulsions. I was knocked down by the rush of workmen and my own boys to save their own lives. It is a mercy there were not more workmen in the roof space beyond, or I should have been trampled out. As I lay there I could clearly see the ground swell pass through the construction above as it heaved and groaned to hideous crushing and grinding noises. Several thunderous crashes sickened me, but later these proved to be the falling of five tall chimneys of the old Imperial, left standing alone by the recent burning of that building.

At the time it seemed as though the banquet hall section, invisible just behind the work-room, had crashed down.

Only one faithful assistant stayed through this terrible ordeal. Endo-San, loyal right-bower—white to the teeth—perspiring. Otherwise the building was utterly deserted. We got up shaking to the knees and went together out onto the roofs. There across the street were crowds of frightened workmen. They had thrown down their tools and run for their lives, even those working in the courts. There they all stood strangely silent, pasty-faced, shaking. A strange silence too was everywhere over the city. Soon fires broke out in a dozen places. Bells rang and pandemonium broke. Women dragging frightened children ran weeping and wailing along the streets below.

We had just passed through the worst quake in fifty-two years. The building was undamaged. A transit put on the foundation levels showed no deviation whatever.

The work had been proved.

Hayashi-San, when reports of the damage to the city and none to the building came in, burst into tears of gratitude. His life had barely been worth living for more than a year, so cruel were the suspicions, so harassing the doubts. The year passed. The building was now so nearly complete there was no longer pressing need for the presence of the architect.

Another wing remained to be finished but it was a duplication of the one already done and furnished. So I could go home with a good conscience. My clients, headed by the Baron, were generous, added substantial proof of appreciation to my fee, and I was 'farewelled' first at a champagne luncheon by the Baron and his directors; then at a tea house entertainment by the building organization itself, all with unique expressions of esteem; finally by the workmen after their no less generous fashion. Witness:

The day of sailing came. To get to my car I had to pass from the rear through the new building to the front. All was deserted and I wondered. Arrived at the entrance courts, there all the workmen were, crowding the spaces, watching and waiting. Already there had been gratifying evidence of appreciation—I thought—but here was the real thing. This could have happened nowhere but in Japan. Here was the spirit I had tried to compliment and respect in my work.

197

As their architect came out they crowded round, workmen of every rank from sweepers to foremen of 'the trades', laughing, weeping, wanting awkwardly to shake hands—foreign fashion. They had learned 'aw-right', and mingled it now with 'arigato' and '*sayonara* Wrieto-San'.

Too much, and 'Wrieto-San' broke. They followed the car down along Hibiya way to the station, running, shouting 'Banzai, Wrieto-San, banzai!'

The dock at Yokohama, eighteen miles away, was reached by train, to find that sixty of the foremen had paid their way down from Tokio to shout again and wave good-bye, while they faded from sight as the ship went down the bay. Such people! Where else in all the world would such touching warmth of kindness in faithfulness be probable or even possible?

Two years later—1923—in Los Angeles. News of terrible disaster shouted in the streets. Tokio and Yokohama wiped out! The most terrible temblor of all history!

Appalling details came day after day. Nothing human, it seemed, could have withstood the cataclysm. Too anxious to get any sleep I tried to get news of the fate of the New Imperial, of Shugio, Endo, San Hayashi, the Baron, and the host of friends I had left over there. Finally, the third night and about two in the morning the telephone bell rang. The *Examiner* wished to inform me that the Imperial Hotel was completely destroyed. My heart sank but I laughed, 'How did they *know*?' The night editor read the dispatch, a list of Imperial University, Imperial Theatre, Imperial Hospital, Imperial this and Imperial that.

'You see,' I said, 'how easy it is to get the Imperial Hotel mixed with the other Imperials? I am sure if anything is above ground in Tokio it is that building. If you print its destruction as "news" you will have to retract.'

Their turn to laugh and hang up the receiver. Ten days of uncertainty and conflicting reports, for during most of that time direct communication was cut off. Then a cablegram . . .

CLASS OF SERVICE | SYMBOL
Telegram |
Day Letter | Blue
Night Message | Nite
Night Letter | N L

WESTERN UNION
WESTERN UNION
TELEGRAM
NEWCOMB CARLTON, PRESIDENT   GEORGE W. E. ATKINS, FIRST VICE-PRESIDENT

CLASS OF SERVICE | SYMBOL
Telegram |
Day Letter | Blue
Night Message | Nite
Night Letter | N L

RECEIVED AT MAIN OFFICE 608-610 SOUTH SPRING ST., LOS ANGELES, CAL.
1923 SEP 13 PM 6 00
AA656 27 COLLECT NITE
SPRINGGREEN' WIS 13
FRANK LLOYD WRIGHT C454 99-10 HW
OLIVE HILL STUDIO RESIDENCE B 1645 VERMONT AVE HOLLYWOOD CALIF
FOLLOWING WIRELESS RECEIVED FROM TOKIO TODAY HOTEL STANDS UNDAMAGED
AS MONUMENT OF YOUR GENIUS HUNDREDS OF HOMELESS PROVIDED BY PERFECTLY
MAINTAINED SERVICE CONGRATULATIONS SIGNED' OKURA: IMPEHO "

For once good news was news and the Baron's cablegram flashed around the world to herald the triumph of good sense. Both the great Tokio homes of the Baron were gone. The splendid museum he gave to Tokio and all its contents were destroyed. The building by the American architect, whose hand he took and whose cause he sponsored, was all he had left in Tokio—nor could love or money buy it now or buy a share of stock in it.

When the letters began to come in and nearly all the friends were found to be safe the news most gratifying to the architect was the fact that after the first great quake was over, the dead rotting there in unburied heaps, the Japanese in subsequent shocks coming in droves dragging their children into the courts and onto the terraces of the building, praying for protection by the God that has protected that building; then as the wall of fire, driving a great wail of human misery before it, came sweeping across the city toward the long front of the building, the hotel boys formed a bucket line to the big pool, the water there the only water available anywhere. And then kept the window sashes and frames on that side wet to meet the flames that came leaping across the narrow street.

The last thought for the safety of the New Imperial had taken effect.

Following the construction of the Imperial Hotel, I lingered in Los Angeles aided by my son Lloyd working on the new unit-block system I had conceived.

But experience with the Imperial had made all probable experience for some time to come quite tame. When I first came back, I took really little interest in such prospects as would present themselves for solution from time to time. No appetite for less than another 'Imperial', I suppose. Or, perhaps, satiated, exhausted by such incessant demands upon my resources as that intimate experience with building represented, I had enough for a while.

For the better part of four years I had been standing in the thick of creative effort, badgered by increasing domestic infelicity, perplexities and finally the characteristic serious illness that attacks men of the North in that humid Pacific lowland. My aged mother, now eighty years old, hearing that my condition was desperate, in spite of all dissuasion had crossed the Pacific to be near. The fact that she came blew the remnant of my relationship with Miriam Noel back across the Pacific in insane fury.

Luckily the Japanese made much of Mother—old age is a qualification in Japan. So, toward the end of her life, she enjoyed many happy and remarkable experiences, one of them a gratifying appearance at the Emperor's Garden Party where she looked a queen, though looking happier than a queen usually looks.

Shugio, the remarkable connoisseur Emperor Mutsushito had placed in charge of all Japan's foreign art exhibitions was immensely kind to her, taking her about. All my friends in Tokio came often to the little Imperial place to see her and take her to various 'occasions'. I think she had no lonely hours in Tokio. Some four months later though, having met with a painful accident while driving to Miyanoshita in my motor car, she got back to America, much the better for her heroism. Tscheremissinoff was devoted to her.

A world in itself—a transition world—began to take shape in that transition-building. It was created spontaneously as any ever fashioned by the will of a creator in the Middle Ages. Most all of the plans I had prepared at Taliesin were thrown away and my presence on the work enabled me to make such changes in the work itself as were required or I desired. This comprehensive work had been completed by the hand of one architect. In ancient times such was seldom the case, the work on any great building continuing from the architect of one generation to an architect of the next generation. I could take off my hat to the culture I had learned to revere. Something no foreign architect had ever done before. In a measure I accomplished what I had meant to do.

Again in Hollywood, I was still dreaming of the great edifice not long since completed. I lived over again this romance of one thousand and nine days and nights in Tokio—once Yedo.

Meantime, during the building of the Imperial the building of a home for Aline Barnsdall was going forward. She called the house Hollyhock House before it was born. I called it a 'California Romanza', this time being frankly on holiday. I met Miss Barnsdall shortly after the tragedy at Taliesin, while I was still in Chicago at the Cedar Street house. Henry Sell brought her to see me in connection with a project for a theatre in which she was interested in Los Angeles. Her very large, wide-open eyes gave her a disingenuous expression not connected with the theatre and her extremely small hands and feet somehow seemed not connected with such ambition as hers.

Later I made the preliminary studies for the theatre she intended to build in Los Angeles. And now coming home from the land of Laotze, Tao, Zen and Bushido, I went to work as I might for the Christians in Hollywood, for a time.

At last there stood Hollyhock House, a silhouette up there on Olive Hill. It had been finally completed with great difficulty, partly owing to my absence in Japan, partly because I had to leave it in amateur hands. Here is the minor strain of Aline Barnsdall's. . . .

HOLLYHOCK HOUSE IN HOLLYWOOD

Architecture, the mother art, is a greater art than music, if one art can be fairly said to be greater than another. I believe one can say it only for the sake of argument. Nevertheless I have secretly envied Beethoven, Bach, and the other great music-masters. After concentration upon creation, they lifted an ivory baton or perhaps merely gracefully significant hands and soared into execution of their designs with the alert obedience of two score or more kindred, willing hands and minds: the orchestra.

200

And that means a thousand of fingers trained and quick to perform every nuance of the general effect the master precisely wanted, on instruments whose effects were definitely understood.

That remarkable resource is comparatively modern.

Bach and Beethoven are invariably inspiration, even information, to me.

What facility great masters of music were afforded by various forms moving according to their mood, from fugue to sonata, from romanza to concerto, or proceeding from them all to the melodic grandeur and completeness of the symphony. I suppose it is well no architect has such facility nor can ever get it. Consequences to the country are bad enough, facility such as it is.

As a small boy long after I had been put to bed I used to lie and listen to my father playing Beethoven—for whose music he had a passion—playing far into the night. To my young mind music spoke a language that stirred me strangely and, as I have since learned, music is the language—beyond all words—of the human heart. The symphony, as my father first taught me, *is* an edifice of sound. I now felt Architecture not only might be but ought to be symphonic in character.

So, when called upon by Aline Barnsdall—her metier the theatre—to build a home for her in Hollywood, why not make architecture stand up and show itself on her new ground, Olive Hill, as California Romance? A bit sentimental withal, Miss Barnsdall had pre-named the house for the Hollyhock she loved for many reasons, all of them good ones, and called upon me to render her favourite flower as a feature of Architecture, how I might.

Unlike many 'patronesses of the arts' Miss Barnsdall wanted no ordinary home, for she was no ordinary woman. If she could have denied she was one at all, she might have done so. But the fact claimed and got her continually, much to her distress and the confusion of her large aims. If any woman ever hitched her wagon to a star, Aline Barnsdall hitched hers thereto. And so far as Hollyhock House and the building of the New Theatre, that was to carry her 'Art of the Theatre' a generation to two ahead of itself, were concerned—at the moment—she chose her architect as that bright and particular star.

Now, these words, 'poetry', 'romance', are red rags or flags or reproachful tags to those hopelessly confused house-owners who drift and drift and continue to happen to 'period' architects as clients. Romance is—no wonder!—something clients would rather not hear about. Because nearly all good people who spoke the language and sought the romantic in good faith, when they became clients drew baleful booby prizes in this lot-lottery of Los Angeles and fell ill of the plague—sentimentality—all infected by the systematically 'tasteful' architects who stick to that region. An exception found his way there, long ago, in Irving Gill. But his antiseptic simplicity did not please the fashionable at all.

So, this hectic quest for sentimental bosh in architecture in our beloved country has wasted billions of perfectly honest dollars, done spiritual harm, more or less violent, to millions of otherwise pretty good people. For that reason perhaps it would be better to say, as I have said of Taliesin, that Hollyhock House was to be a natural house in the changed circumstances and naturally built; native to the region of California as the house in the Middle West had been native to the Middle West.

Suited to Miss Barnsdall and her purpose, such a house would be sure to be all that 'poetry of form' could imply, because any house should be beautiful in California in the way that California herself is beautiful. She wanted no ordinary house.

Yes, our nice word romance is now disreputable, implying rather escape from life than any realization or faithful ideal of our own life. Either by inheritance or as evil consequence, it is a loose attempt at illusion and that is now what is the matter with the word, for that is what it usually is. Such 'Romance' lies loose in the heart, askew in the mind, something fanciful, unlike life. Unlifelike. Results, at best, are exotic. At worst, idiotic. So Romance in the United States has become a sickly simpering mask for a changed new life. 'Romance' attempts to escape from the deadly pressure of the facts of life in this machine age, and go into a beyond each poor earthworm fashions as he may for himself and—if he happens to be an architect—for others.

But, in music, *romanza* is only free form or freedom to make one's own form. A musician's sense of proportion is all that governs him in the musical romanza: the mysterious remaining just haunting enough in a whole so organic as to lose all evidence of how it was made. Now translate 'sounds and the ear' to 'form and the eye', romanza seems reasonable enough in Architecture? In California.

No master of the orchestra, however, I have to conquer a hard-boiled industrial world stewed in terms of money, and persuade or please idiosyncratic, sometimes aristocratic clients, in order to render any romanza whatever or achieve even a modicum of integrity in any building. My lot was cast with a hod of mortar and some bricks or a concrete-mixer and a gang of workmen, the Union, and the Machine. And last, but not least, the client. All these as one '*medium of expression*'.

Out here in Hollywood in Hollyhock House were met Circumstance and Opportunity. The situation didn't look equivocal to me. Not at all. Nevertheless, these oblique remarks are prompted by trying to remember the circumstances now—many of which I have purposefully tried to forget—of this holiday adventure in Romanza.

Miss Barnsdall turned this beautiful site, Olive Hill, over to me as a basis on which we were to go to work *together* to build under the serene canopy of California blue.

We went to work—or I did. My client, I soon found, had ideas and wanted yours but never worked much nor for long at a time, being possessed by incorrigible wanderlust that made me wonder sometimes, what she wanted a beautiful home for—anyhow, anywhere. Later, I came

202

to see that *that* was just *why* she wanted one. A restless spirit—disinclined to stay long at any time in any one place as she travelled over the face of the globe, she would drop suggestions as a war-plane drops bombs and sails away into the blue. One never knew where or from where the bombs would drop—but they dropped.

Now, to add to this discomfort, the fates picked me up and were dragging me to and fro over the Pacific for four or five years, to build the Imperial Hotel at Tokio. I would hear from her when I was wandering about in the maze of the Imperial Hotel in Japan while she was in Hollywood. She would get my telegrams or letters in Spain when I eventually got to Hollywood. And I would hear from her in New York while I was in Chicago or San Francisco. Or, hear from her from some remote piney mountain retreat in the Rockies when I was sea-sick out on the Pacific Ocean. During the building of Hollyhock House there was no radio, only the telegraph. So Hollyhock House had mostly to be built by telegraph so far as client and architect had anything to do with it or each other. Yes, until it was all too late.

Now, with a radical client like Aline Barnsdall, a site like Olive Hill, a climate like California, an architect head on for freedom, something had to happen even by proxy. This Romanza of California had to come out on Olive Hill.

Sublimated mathematics is Music?

Well—mathematics in co-ordinated Form is architecture. I would still use the straight line and the flat plane. I had now become accustomed to using them. But would use them here together with a third mathematical element clearly defined—*integral ornament* modifying or emphasizing both elements to allow suggestion, proper scope, and appropriate rhythms to enter: these, I offer as component parts not only of the California Romanza but of Romanza.

Would Aline Barnsdall be happy with the outcome of all this for a house? Probably not, but happier. Why not? She was neither neo, quasi nor pseudo. She was as near American as any Indian, as developed and travelled in appreciation of the beautiful as any European. As domestic as a shooting star. Conscience troubled me a little. That 'voice within' said, 'What about the machine crying for recognition as the normal tool of your age?'

Well, my critics, one does weary of duty. Even of privilege—while young, I again told the voice to 'go to' for a time. Hollyhock House was to be another holiday for me.

The architect's plans joyfully travelled this fascinating upward road of poetic form and delighted Miss Barnsdall. I could scarcely have keyed the romanza too high for her, I found, had I made it a symphony.

But my client was in a hurry and I was urgently needed in Tokio. If we accomplished more than the preliminary plans themselves in the way of actual building, we would have to amplify the sketches into plans as best we could, making such added notes and details as we went along as would suffice to get the building properly built and turn it over to the help. The manner of work being what it is, this was not unreasonable at the time.

My own son Lloyd introduced the Union in the person of a contractor —Robertson. By all evidence obtainable Robertson should have been competent *Konzertmeister* with the sympathetic aid of my untried amateur superintendent Schindler. But, while Robertson could read the average score, he couldn't read this one, as it turned out. And the superintendent didn't if he could. Rudy Schindler was too smooth a party ever to learn how to be serious, which was one reason why I liked him. But that was bad for the house. Soon I would hear of trouble clear away across the Pacific.

Robertson said it was all because the plans were so hastily prepared. Only partially true. Every contractor will say that and *always—in any circumstances*—it will be partly true. But he knows the allegation plausible alibi for him because every contractor has seen it, times without number, take effect. The truly unreliable contractor never fails to use it with excellent results, so far as he is concerned, which is mostly all he cares about.

And this is all in his day's work. The contractor is seldom contractor for anyone's health but his own and never precisely for that. The drawings were sufficiently complete. But details were being constantly added to educate the contractor as and when his feeble grasp fell short.

Now, *the* penalty (one of the many, probably) for being feminine, with extremely small hands and feet, rich, alone and mundane, is to have an entourage of 'friends'. And employees who yearn to justify themselves as *friends*, by undertaking to guard the feminine employer's financial interest in such manner that they will look faithful until the employer rudely awakens. As employers do. As this one did.

Collectively this insurance-brigade of Miss B's knew about as much about this building as Sodom knew of Sanctity. Unless checked they could only insure defeat. Here enters at the psychological moment the eternal triangle, Architect, Owner, Contractor. All too often the Owner at first sign of trouble with the Architect takes refuge in the Contractor. And this is what now happened. She did.

My client had by now been angered by certain failings of her architect. They got tangled up with his virtues, among them one difficult to untangle and that one, most offensive at this time, was a distinct failure to regard the mere owner of a work of art in hand like the romanza, as of ultimate importance in the *execution* of the design. There were forthright refusals to allow her to take the life of the work itself by thoughtless changes suggested by these cerebratious guardians of hers without due reference to the architect's opinion. The consequence was a challenge to combat.

So, the building about half done—a fortuitous decision. 'They' should build the house. Now this is where I should have left Hollyhock House forever. But do you know the feeling of a sentimental architect for his

204

creation? You love your child, don't you? Well, so does he. I couldn't go and leave the upbringing entirely to them.

So, on the eve of sailing for the ninth time on the Pacific as far as Tokio, I consented to hang on by way of my affable superintendent Schindler and my son Lloyd, plainly seeing nevertheless that my client as well as I would finally have to take the consequences of her insurance brigade and eventually of the usual conspiracy. Now this on my part was due to utter weariness, or else was utter cowardice.

And it might have some moral effect upon the prospects of other paternal architects and self-willed clients to tell of consequent griefs of the owner's administration when driven to unseemliness and hasty acts by their employer's fiats from long-distance. And to speak in detail of the makeshifts the insurance brigade employed, in her behalf of course, 'to save money'. Makeshifts usually cost more than the real thing. And to dramatize, as warning to other architects, some of the architect's own serious mistakes; among these his unjust treatment of a naturally resourceful, forceful and now roused and suspicious client.

But enough. Ownership on Olive Hill in Los Angeles took whip hand of art by way of her own insurance brigade, and with the best intentions, with all the justification there was. And that justification was myself.

Shades of Beethoven and Bach—Romanza did I say? Rude awakening.

And yet—all too aware of the stubborn facts—a poetic idea was to be born. It had to conquer this stubborn, suspicious, mean, possessive old world—all of its refractory materials in between—in order to appear at all on that hill. Yes—and now this treacherous pack of detractors clambering over the whole, besides.

My client's own momentum—it was Irish and considerable—had wantonly cut the ground from beneath herself, and her architect, by making him alien, angered, dazed and puzzled by all this to and fro for nothing.

I am foolishly telling all this in detail to try to show that once started building along any unusual characteristic scheme, no timid owner has any other salvation, never had nor ever will have, in the agonizing triangle— infernal A.I.A. invention—of client, architect and contractor. However fearful any owner, it will inevitably appear that the real interests of owner and architect are one and indivisible all the time and were so at all essential points. But the contractor, by no fault of his, sits there as actually the born enemy of both architect and owner: except as his moral worth may rise superior to the very nature of his office. Usually it is necessary from the start to defeat the contractor's experienced and subtle advices to the client. He, the contractor, is by the very nature of the *characteristic* 'unusual' building, himself the novice. But he will never openly admit that fact of his novitiate. He would lose his case before he began.

Nevertheless from out this confusion, from this welter of misunderstanding and misapplied heat and fury—enough to have consumed the work out of hand and finally resulting in brutal violence—a shape appeared, inviolate. A strangely beautiful 'form' crept inexorably into view. Even the quarrelling pack began to see and be impressed by it.

205

Something had held all this shifty diversity of administration together enough to enable a new significance to come out and adorn that hill crown. Was it the marks on paper that this quarrelling was all about, these traces of a design that, no matter how abused, *would* show itself in spite of friction, waste and slip? Of course.

But rather, and *somehow*, by way of the downright brutality, insolence and persistence of the architect and the client's desire, too, though both architect and client were torn to tatters—'Form' got into the building in spite of all the folly.

This it is that seems to me the miracle as I saw Hollyhock House on its hill now on returning from Tokio. And it is a miracle to this day.

But, even at this distance, I am sure I exaggerated all this warfare just as any parent, fearful for the well-being of an infant, would exaggerate the storm after the danger is over. I am underestimating the fine quality of Miss Barnsdall herself, who really desired a beautiful thing in her heart and, capable of loving it, kept coming back to it again and again, fending off her own organization and really seeing beyond the barrage of petty strife in which, partly owing to her own timidity, she continually involved herself. Or, well, but what does it all matter now? As you read between the lines and see me taking an outfit for a ride, I was chiefly to blame myself. Because I flouted my client—unable to understand her as I now see I was not.

Like it or leave it. There stands Hollyhock House in Hollywood—conceived and desired as a California Romanza. No, not so domestic as the popular neo-Spanish of the region. But comfortable to live in well, with true pride in itself. Yes, Hollyhock House is a very proud house.

And Aline Barnsdall came back, finally. She stayed in her house longer at a time than she had ever stayed anywhere before. With son Lloyd to help she planted greenery and colour around it some more, and she cared for it and tried to correct some of the mistakes that grew out of the initial mistakes made in the struggle of client and architect to build it all mainly by proxy.

Some of the mistakes neither she nor I could correct. But she took it all now in good part as the sunshine began to build up the green around it. Loving pines because of the mountain carpets they made, she planted pine-groves behind on the hill and great masses of the eucalyptus to enclose the pines. She planted great carpets of brilliant flowers for ground cover beside and in front of the house like the carpets woven in Austria for the inside floors. She brought home a few choice *objets d'art* from Europe to add to others from the Orient builded into the walls of the rooms themselves, and to go with the furniture that was made part of the house-design itself.

It looked for a time as though she would become a valuable Hollywood institution and do more beautiful things there. Next, perhaps make the dream of her life come true, the New Theatre, by now already planned and already to be seen in a new white plaster model.

206

Up there on Olive Hill above hillsides furrowed with rows of grey-green olive trees, the daughter of one of America's pioneers had con-structed a little principality her very own, free to live in it as a queen. There was nothing like it anywhere in the world. She—the second generation—came and went, within her consciousness a new sense of home to be handed on to the third generation. To her 'Sugar-top'. Above all friction, waste and slip, Aline Barnsdall had so far succeeded.

And then, as the little queendom grew in beauty and importance, yes, even as the ideas that built it—on holiday—grew in significance around the world she began to feel alone in the possession of it—became more lonely because of it than she had ever felt without it.

Artists came and admired it. Hollyhock House became known as a work of fine art in the various ateliers of the continent where she would go every summer. Europeans came and saw in it something of the higher harmony of the spirit of man. The newer protestant felt—perhaps justly, who knows?—that the architect had indulged himself again regardless of the task with the machine to which he had set himself. But this Romanza in California was just another phase of the greatest of arts—Architecture. Call that phase what you will. Call it poetry. Call it what you like if you do not want to call it architecture, as I shall call it still.

They said in Hollywood, Aline Barnsdall was a Bolshevik—a 'parlour Bolshevik', said some. They rather sneered did some of these little people living in names—those to whom names were ideas and ideas names—at one whose ideas were 'proletariat' and hard while living soft herself like a princess in aristocratic seclusion unrivalled by other princesses who lived merely in the traditional and therefore in a more or less hackneyed style. She now lived above commonplace elegance like any princess but better, because in a matchless style all her own. So far as that went, she lived in an atmosphere rare as poetic. Herself a pioneer this daughter of the pioneer lived up to integral romance when all about her was ill with pseudo-romantic in terms of neo-Spanish, lingering along as quasi-Italian, stale with Renaissance, dying or dead of English half-timber and Colonial.

Well, no one may say what moved her finally. The motives of human deeds lie so deep-buried beneath seemingly irrelevant debris or are so mixed in the tangled threads of feeling in the depths of the human heart. She made up her mind to give it all away; the precious hill-top by now sought for by every realtor of the realm as a prize. She determined to give it away. Together with its ideal buildings, to Los Angeles the city.

And she did give it away, as it stood. Even the faithful Japanese cook, George—he went along, too.

And she gave it, most wisely, to be used by the class most needy in these United States, the class most abjectly mendicant at this time owing to the triumphant march of the Machine. But not, be it said, to the most grate-ful. She gave it to the artists of California, to be their California Art Club home. She restricted the gift so that the house should not be touched or altered for fifteen years. By that time, she said, what she felt to be its real riches, its imaginative Californian Form, would have had its way with them. So far as she herself was concerned, it might then go on its way to destruction.

Out there where almost everything is speculation and soon or late for sale, and where—perhaps just because of that—so few of the many having riches have ever given anybody anything culturally worth while, the wandering daughter of the oil pioneer bequeathed her enjoyment in her home, her faith in its beauty regardless of its faults, gave it wearing the Los Angeles realtor's tag of a 'million dollars'. This she did to help up to the level of life again, if possible, struggling artists, stranded in an era they may never survive. How can they?

Hollyhock House now disintegrates, listens to these artists as they chide, complain and admonish. As they admonish it so it admonishes them. And perhaps—as its donor meant it should do—Hollyhock House goes along with their personal issues into fresh life in a new key, looking gratefully toward her whose home it once was. Yes, and whose home it still truly is to a greater extent than ever; because, since without her it never could have been, her spirit is manifest in it, to all.

Why should all Usonian houses, so-called, when they are anything but Usonian, be of so-called domestic mould when all Usonian people are not so? Why should Aline Barnsdall live in a house like Mrs. Alderman Schmutzkopf or even like Mrs. Reggie Plasterbilt's pseudo-Hacienda on the Boulevard-Wilshire. Individuality is the most precious thing in life, after all—isn't it? An honest democracy must believe that it is. And the thing Usonia is going to fight, tooth and nail, to preserve as things are going, if the superficial fashionable standardizing we have seen every-where on the Los Angeles surface has any meaning beneath the eclectic's latest mode—the passing calling itself the 'international style'.

Again and again within my limited experience the 'fashionable' thing is ever the outworn carcass of the early tomorrow. If you would have your house 'fashionable' be sure it is on its way out of luck even as it is being built.

In any expression of the human spirit it is principle manifest as char-acter that alone endures. Individuality is the true property of character. No . . . not one house that possessed genuine character in this sense but stands safe outside the performance of the passing show. Hollyhock House is such a house.

THE ANGELS

Meantime, Hollyhock House as near finished as it would ever be, here I was looking around me in Los Angeles—trying to hope but disgusted. There the Anglicans were busy as could be with steam-shovels tearing down the hills to get to the top in order to blot out the top with a house in some queasy fashionable 'style', some aesthetic inanity or other. The eclectic procession of to and fro in the rag-tag and cast-off of all the ages was never going to stop—so it seemed to me. It was Mexico-Spanish just

208

18. Great Banqueting Hall. Seating one thousand at table. Lava-brick, copper, and polychrome decorations

IMPERIAL HOTEL, TOKIO
(1916)-1922

19. View showing the lift shaft, the perforated copper cornice and a lava figure 'The Orient'

20. Entrance lobby. Perforated bricks of the piers shed light

21. A detail of the banquet hall. Carved lava peacock, twelve feet square,
over doorway

IMPERIAL HOTEL, TOKIO. (1916)-1922

now. Another fair, in San Diego this time, had set up Mexico-Spanish for another run for another cycle of thirty years. The mode was busy making pretty pictures thus—and anywhere at all. Making pretty pictures cheap, getting 'art and decoration' in to prettify the little plastered caverns. They made them 'comfortable' by piling pillows up and stuffing the interiors with 'overstuffed' furniture.

During all the several years I had been trying to get substantial work out there in Anglicor no reality could be seen in any building where the house owners or the builders were themselves 'art-conscious' or where they were socially amenable for that matter. Every time I thought I had a client, I found the client had nothing except that he really had me.

That desert of shallow effects! All curiously alike in their quite serious attempts to be original or 'different'. But more plain surface was gradually coming in sight—always a relief. But the same old lack of thought was to be seen everywhere. Taste—taste, taste, the usual matter of ignorance—had moved toward simplicity a little, but thought or feeling for integrity had not entered into any of this architecture. All was flatulent or fraudulent with a cheap opulence. Tawdry Spanish medievalism was now rampant. What would such taste for effects be tomorrow? Some other inane reaction with the same dreadfully significant insignificance. Oh, yes. Undoubtedly.

WHAT FORM?

Soon began the gnawing of the old hunger for reality. I saw no escape from reality. I had not yet descended to make believe. Could I go deeper now? I could.

Always the desire to get some system of building construction as a basis for architecture was my objective—my hope. There never was, there *is* no architecture otherwise, I believe.

What form? Well, let the form come. Form would come in time if a sensible, feasible system of building-construction would only come first. What about the concrete block? It was the cheapest (and ugliest) thing in the building world. It lived mostly in the architectural gutter as an imitation of 'rock face' stone. Why not see what could be done with that gutter-rat? Steel welded to it by casting rods inside the joints of the blocks themselves and the whole brought into some broad, practical scheme of general treatment, why would it not be fit for a new phase of our modern architecture? It might be permanent, noble, beautiful. It would be cheap.

There should be many phases of architecture equally modern.

All that imagination needed to make such a scheme feasible architecture was a plastic medium where steel would enter into inert mass as tensile strength. Concrete was the inert mass and would take compression. Concrete is a plastic material—susceptible to the impress of imagination. I saw a kind of weaving coming out of it. Why not weave a kind of building? Then I saw the shell. Shells with steel inlaid in them. Or steel for warp and masonry units for woof in the weaving. For block-size—say man-handled units weighing 40 to 50 pounds—all such units or blocks for either weaving or shells to be set steel-wound and steel-bound. Floors, ceilings, walls all the same—all to be hollow.

I had used the block in some such textured way in the Midway Gardens upper walls. If I could eliminate the mortar joint I could make the whole fabric mechanical. I could do away with skilled labour. I believed I could and began the experiment on La Miniatura. A home and bookshop for Mrs. Alice Millard.

Lightness and strength! Steel the spider spinning a web within the cheap plastic material wedded to it by pouring an inner core of cement after the blocks were set up.

The 'shell' as human habitation. Why not? Another phase of architecture organic. The straight line, the flat plane, now textured. The sense of interior space coming through, the openings all woven together as integral features of the shell. The rich encrustation of the shells should be visible as mass, the true mass of the architecture. Here ornament would become a legitimate feature of construction.

Decoration asserts the whole to be greater than any part and succeeds to the degree that it helps make this good. Genuine mass in this sense will always be modern. A pity were the United States to have only one arrow to its bow, or neglect indigenous riches at any point.

I drew my son Lloyd into this fresh effort.

I was getting interested again.

THE ALTER EGO

Meantime some of the young men who had begun their architectural careers with me were at work out here—in the midst of the popular falsification as I have described it in this land of the *realtoresque* taken as substitute for the picturesque. What were they all doing to modify popular meanness and qualify imitative Usonia? There were many such— fifty or sixty—young men working in the United States or Europe or Japan as architects by now. They had come to me from all parts of the world to enter into my work. Not so much as students; I am no teacher. They came more as apprentices, beginning with no pay—except their living at Taliesin—or with small pay if more competent to help. As they grew helpful they received a small salary in keeping with the work done, or to be done in the office or in the garden, over and above their living.

In the workshop at Oak Park, inasmuch as they had to shift for themselves, all received a nominal wage—the equivalent of board and lodging at the beginning. With the exception of some six or seven I have never had reason to complain of their enthusiasm for their work nor of their loyalty to me. But, of their loyalty to the cause—yes. And after all, were they not taken on, in that cause?

This process of natural selection on their part had its advantages. Some disadvantages. Never going out of my way after the material I really need but always taking those who want to come to me—I do make some sacrifices for sympathetic co-operation, oftentimes not so efficient as it should be. I am fond of the flattery of young people. They indulge me and I indulge them. It is easy for them and for me to do this. But they get the idea that when the master's back is turned, to draw his ideas in his own way, or in theirs, does make those ideas and his way their own. Later on, they must do something to justify them in this 'reflection'. Soon, consciously or unconsciously, this type of *alter ego* becomes a detractor. I am in his way unless good-naturedly I will let him trade on me. Or in me.

But the individuality of my work has never swerved from first to last. It grows steadily on its own centre line. The system, or lack of it—I have never had an 'office' in the conventional manner—has become fixed habit and works well enough—but only because I stay directly with it in every detail, myself. When I go away there is usually trouble and sometimes unpremeditated treachery. No. There was never organization in the sense that the usual architect's office knows organization. Nor any great need of it so long as I stood actually at the centre of the effort. Where I am, there my office is. My office is me. And therein is one great difference between my own and current practice. A severe and exacting limitation instead of the freedom I intended.

THE NOVICE

It was always hard to turn a boy down. An instance:

Sunday morning at the Oak Park studio. Had worked late the night before but I was called. A boy in the studio to see me. I got up and went down. There, standing by the big detail table in the centre of the draughting room, a small boy, face covered with adolescent pimples, blushing furiously. Wanted to be an architect—liked my buildings, believed he would like to build that kind.

Name?

Frank Byrne—young Irish lad.

Where working?

Montgomery Ward's.

What doing?

Wrapping packages.

Getting how much?

Ten dollars a week.

A good preparation for architecture, I observed. Common school only? Studied at home?

A little.

Rather sudden, isn't it—getting into architecture right off the reel like this?

Yes—he thought so, too.

What did he think he could do for me to earn ten dollars a week—knowing nothing about draughting?

Well, he could be office-boy—sweep the floors, wash the windows—anything. But, I said we have already several boys doing that. His face fell.

211

There was something touching, and fine too, in this straightforward break in the direction of his ambition, that appealed to me. Such breaks always do. It looked as though there might be something in this boy. He stood there, pale now. I didn't need him. I didn't want him, but there he was. He was—young, unspoiled—how know what might be in him?

All right, lad, I said—come in.

This boy stayed four years and turned out better than many who had many years the start of him in every way. He was my first Catholic. 'Catholic' helped him when he got out on his own.

This episode might stand as typical, although many apprentices were nominal architects and many were college graduates. And a number of cultivated European architects joined the work at Taliesin. But all on the same basis, whatever their qualifications. Apprentices—when they qualified—would stay from two to ten years.

The same formula was impressed upon all: not to imagine they were coming to school. They were coming in to make themselves as useful to me as they could. I was an architect at work. They would see work going on under their eyes and would be taken into the work as far as they could go. Their living was assured meantime but they would get much or little else from their experience, as they were able. It was all up to them. The discussions in the studio—pro and con—schemes and sketches for buildings in general and more often in detail were made by myself in the midst of the studio-group, each man or boy taking over finally, as he could, whatever I assigned to him to do. Some would soon drop out—unable to stand the great freedom—abusing it. Some would take it and go away with what they could pick up to sell it as their own. Others would thrive on freedom. A fine loyalty characterized all but very few as they were with me in full freedom of their own choice—entirely on their own.

Well, how about them? What have they accomplished?

The architectural world into which they emerged was wholly commercialized and fashionably if not fatuously inclined now toward the 'great' styles. The profession of architecture itself—because it had no basis of principle—is further commercialized by the functioneer architect professing the practical, nevertheless exploiting 'taste'. I have had occasion to reproach some of my young men for what seemed to me selling out—going too easily with the current of commercial degeneration. The usual answer was 'Mr. Wright, we have to live.'

'Why?' I have said.

And I don't see why anyone 'has' to live, at any rate not live as a parasite at expense of the thing he loves. Why not try something else where a living might be had honestly, had fairly to all concerned?

Some identified themselves with other movements: 'It is so hard to stand alone.' Others became competitors, the 'also-ran' and no less. There had been nothing much in my work they didn't have themselves anyway.

I know all too well the weight of opposition all encountered and I am inclined to sympathize with them. It should be much easier for them now and it is so, though many of us must still be ground up, and buried perhaps, before it will be easy enough. Many of my boys are giving a good account of themselves, Middle-West, North-West, South-West and West, and across the Seas. But current life mocks most of our effort forward, breaks it to fragments if it can. To save only a few pieces for future reference as life goes on its way is all we have a right to expect.

Nevertheless, principle alone is defence and refuge from chaos. Otherwise utter defeat.

This digression is here because several young men were at this time doing good work in California on their own—while the work on La Miniatura was going forward. The block experiments had been made and I was ready to start the first one. Its owner named it La Miniatura—the first block house. Since we are in work now here is the story of

LA MINIATURA, FIRST-BORN OF CALIFORNIA

La Miniatura happened as the cactus grows, in that region still showing what folk from the Middle-Western prairies did when, inclined to quit, the prosperous came loose and rolled down there into that far corner to bask in eternal sunshine.

Near by, that arid, sunlit strand is still unspoiled desert. You may see what a poetic thing this land was before this homely mid-west invasion. Curious tan-gold foothills rise from tattooed sand-stretches to join slopes spotted as the leopard-skin with grease-bush. This foreground spreads to distances so vast—human scale is utterly lost as all features recede, turn blue, recede and become bluer still to merge their blue mountain shapes, snow-capped, with the azure of the skies. The one harmonious note man has introduced into these vast perspectives, aside from the long, low plastered wall, is the eucalyptus tree. Tall, tattered ladies, these trees stand with careless feminine grace in the charming abandon appropriate to perpetual sunshine, adding beauty to the olive-green and ivory-white of an exotic symphony in silvered gold and rose-purple. Water comes, but it comes as a deluge once a year to surprise the roofs, sweep the sands into ripples and roll boulders along in the gashes combed by sudden streams in the sands of the desert. Then—all dry as before.

No, not all, for man has caught and held the fugitive flood behind great concrete walls in the hills while he allows it to trickle down by meter to vineyards, orchards and groves. And—yes—to neat, shaven lawns two by twice. Little 'lots' just like those back home in the Middle West. Those funny and fixed little features—the homes—stare above the lawns wearing as many different but curiously unvaried expressions of the same fixed face as there are different people looking out of the windows at each other. They too are as much the same.

This newcomer from the fertile midwestern prairies came here to make sunshine his home. But at first the home did not know how to bask any more than he himself did. Shirt sleeves were his limit and his home had no shirt sleeves nor anything at all easy-going about it. No indeed, that home of his was still as hard and self-assertive as the flat sticks he made it out of: as defiant as ever it was in the mud and snows back there at home at zero. This Yankeefied house, for that is what it was, looked even more hard in perpetual sunshine where all need of its practical offences had disappeared.

Nor when the sunshiners turned to the planting of their places out there was the result very much better. They could easily grow in that sunshine all kinds of strange plants and trees. They did so, as a neat, curious little collection all nicely set out together on the neatly shaved lawns of their little town-lots. And the porch and the parlour had come along with the pie and the ice-water, the rocking chair, and the chewing-gum with the appropriate name.

But long before, Fra Junipero and Father La Tour had been there and they began to have incidental influence now; for it gradually appeared that the Italo-Spanish buildings of the early missionaries' own 'back home' had just happened to be more in keeping with California.

This Southern type of building had already given shelter from a sun that could blister the indiscreet in Spain or Mexico just as it was able to do now in Southern California. So it came to pass that the old Catholic Missions as buildings lived long enough to transform a little and somewhat characterize the details of the Middle-Westerner's home in California— although the *actual* mission was at first rejected as being far from Mid-Western spiritual conviction.

Finally the mid-western sunshiners fell to copying Fra Junipero's buildings, copying his furniture, copying his gardens and style. Fell to buying his antiques. But though the invading Middle West had fallen for all that, it still clung *in toto* to its hard straw hat, English coat, trousers and boots and other customs in general. As a concession to climate, however, the Middle-Westerner himself occasionally did put on a shirt with a soft collar and forget his hat. But when 'dressed' he was not one iota budged. And he looked in his Fra surroundings as the Fra himself or a silken Spaniard would have looked in little Mid-Western parlours. Only for the Fra it would be plus—for the sunshiner it was forever minus.

Spain, by way of despised Mexico, gradually moved up into the midst of this homely invasion. The plain, white-plastered walls—so far so good —of little pictorial caverns gleam or stare at you through the foliage in oases kept green by great mountain reservoirs. A new glint of freshness, a plainness that is a refreshing foil for exotic foliage. There are cool *patios* there too, patios for the Joneses and Smiths. Luxurious haciendas, even, for the richer Robinsons. Arched loggias and vine-covered pergolas run about loose. Rude Spanish-tiled roofs drink in the sunshine, staining it dull pink. Adzed beams or rude beam-construction real or imitated is there, covered by gay stretched awnings. They even put awnings over the windows in the plastered walls.

Thus California has retraced the first steps of an earlier invasion by priests who came there from a climate more like California climate than that of the Middle West. But the Californians of today—née Iowan, Wisconsiner, Ohioan—have yet nothing to say for themselves in all this except superficially acquired taste for Spanish antiques to go with the missionaries' houses. Nevertheless, the town-lot on the gridiron; the modern bathroom; the incorporation of the porch and the kitchenette with the cosy breakfast-nook; all these prize possessions of his own 'back-home' are now features of the 'mission style'. Such is progress. To have and to hold all you can hold, while merely seeming to *be*. But California, if given to drink, smothers the whole in eucalyptus and mimosa arms as she gently kisses all with roses. Thus are buried the mistakes of the decorative picturizing architect whose art and decoration have entirely taken the place of architecture out there.

Here, then, at some length is the pictorial background against which La Miniatura, the little studio-house, is to stand: the flourishing sentimental taste into which it was born.

All true building in this our land of the brave and home of the free, is a soul-trying crusade. I assure you it is, just as Fra Junipero Serra's mission that failed was that kind of crusade. But his building that thus succeeded was not high adventure because he only brought it with him from 'back home' because and solely—he had none other to bring.

Not so La Miniatura. This little building scientifically and afresh began to search for what was missing in all this background. And what was missing? Nothing less than a distinctly genuine expression of California in terms of modern industry and American life—that was all.

Few out there seem to miss anything of the sort. But La Miniatura desired to justly call itself *architecture* and be able to look itself in the face. Mrs. George Madison Millard from those same Mid-Western prairies near Chicago was the heroine of its story: Mrs. Alice Millard, slender, energetic —fighting for the best of everything for everyone. Be it said she knew it, too, when he saw it. Got it if she could.

The Millards had lived in a little wooden dwelling I had built for them fifteen years ago at Highland Park near Chicago. I was proud now to have a client survive the first house and ask me to build a second. Out of one hundred and seventy-two buildings this made only the eleventh time it had happened to me.

So, gratefully, I determined she should have the best I had in my portfolio. That meant, to begin with, something that belonged to the ground on which it stood. Her house should be a sensible matter entirely—an interpretation of her needs in book-collecting for book-collectors. Alice Millard, artistic herself, with her frank blue-eyed smile beneath her unruly hair, didn't fully know that she was to be lightly but inexorably grasped by the architectural fates and used for high exemplar. She probably suspected it though. Now I don't yet know why houses have so much grief concealed in them if they try to *be* anything at all and try to live as themselves. But they do. Like people in this I suppose. Gradually I unfolded to her the scheme of the textile block-slab house gradually forming in my mind since I got home from Japan. She wasn't frightened by the idea. Not at all.

215

We would take that despised outcast of the building industry—the concrete block—out from underfoot in the gutter—find a hitherto unsuspected soul in it—make it live as a thing of beauty—textured like the trees. Yes, the building would be made of concrete blocks, but as a kind of tree itself standing there at home among the other trees in its own native land.

All we would have to do would be to educate the concrete blocks, refine them and knit all together with steel in the joints and so construct the joints that they could be poured full of concrete by any boy after they were set up by common labour and a steel-strand laid in the interior joints. The walls would thus become thin but solid reinforced slabs, impressionable to any desire for pattern imaginable. Yes, common labour could do it all.

We would make the walls double, of course, one wall facing inside and the other wall facing outside, thus getting continuous hollow spaces between, so the house would be cool in summer, warm in winter and dry always. Inside, the textured blocks—or the plain ones—would make a fine background for old pictures, fine books, and tapestries. Outside—well, in that clear sunshine, even the eucalyptus tree would respect the house and love it for what it was. Instead of a fire-trap for her precious book-collections and antiques she would have a house fireproof. I talked this idea over with her, and the more she listened to it the more she liked it. I made some tentative plans. Provided the whole has an old-world atmosphere, said Alice Millard, I will like it. I said it would have.

I forgot to mention that Alice Millard had just ten thousand dollars to put into the house—might get two thousand more, probably not. Bankers were Yesterday, out there too, and hostile to ideas as everywhere. The greater the idea the greater this banker-phobia. So the whole scheme must be excessively modest. For instance, Alice Millard wanted only an unusually large living-room with a great fireplace, a beautiful balcony over it from which her own sleeping room might open. That bedroom should be roomy too, with dressing room, a balcony in that too and a bath, of course. One for the balcony would be nice to have.

Then there must be a good-sized guest-room that might be an office when not in use otherwise, and a bath. Two baths of course. And a dining-room, not so small either—little parties—with pantry, kitchen, servants' bedroom, store-rooms and baths. Making three baths. My client's tastes were good. She did not want cheap woods. She did not want, of all things, cheap hardware. She abominated poor workmanship and knew it when she saw it. She never failed to see it. There was to be nothing shoddy about that house. And a garage was to be thrown in as integral feature of the whole just for good measure. She would be glad to have all this permanent, have it fireproof, and have it as beautiful as it was going to be for $10,000.00 (the first sum mentioned).

So one day after the plans were ready she came enthusiastically to say: 'I've found just the man to build our "thoroughbred" house. I've been talking with him and went with him to see a house he's just finished for a friend of mine. It cost her less than he said it would. He gave her lots of

216

little extras and never charged for them at all. He was so good and efficient they scarcely needed an architect at all. Let's go and see the house.'

Here the other leg of the triangle showed its foot once more—its toes at least in the door with an ingratiating smile. But I could not refuse to go to see his house—yet. And so we went.

That house was not badly done, a lot for the money, almost as much as Alice Millard wanted. I talked with the contractor, and she even went so far as to say, by now, she wouldn't have anyone else build her house anyway.

'I feel', said she, 'we can trust him "utterly".'

Now, she had been just as uncompromising as that about her architect. So I understood her regard for her new-found friend the contractor. But here was already familiar and pretty slippery ground to go on.

'How do you like him?' said she, brightly, but as I could see, anxiously.

'Well,' I said, 'a woman's intuition is valuable even in these matters. He does seem intelligent. He has had a good deal of independent experience. He likes this block-slab idea and volunteers to take the contract without any profit—for the sake of experience. So he says. Therefore he *is* a volunteer. Since you won't have anyone else build for you anyway, why . . . I am inclined to take him at face-value.'

She sighed with relief.

She felt now quite safe. I had no good reason to oppose her ultimatum. But—I wish I had felt as safe as she. In honesty I should add to this that I knew of no one else, not in that region at the time, anyway. Who could, or would, make such sacrifices for her? Some material supply-men recommended the man highly. I called them up. That was how we got the godfather to the new idea.

Here the familiar A.I.A. villain the contractor enters the piece in disguise. Alice Millard's ultimatum was my flimsy excuse. But I knew just how staunch her faith could be and I dreaded any attempt to change it. Had she not disregarded the warnings of all her friends, a lone woman has hundreds, and consented to the loss of some life-long friendships in order to embark with me in this innocent challenge to their ways and what they approved?

And, he began well. They all do.

You see I explain this in detail to show how every idea, even as with the Romanza, enters and encounters life as does a new-born child, pretty much as things happen to be—to take all when and where it may come. The idea then begins to grow up, to work like yeast in these haphazard conditions and it may survive, become important, or dwindle and die as the child may. It is at every moment squarely up to the author of its being to defend it. He has to save its life—continually. And he has a chance if all the cards are on the table!

But, here's for confession—let's see how good for the soul it is in this affair.

Let's call this builder-fellow the god-father of our idea. I could add appropriate adjectives to the word god and to the word father. But after a while, you do it. Alice Millard trusted this gift of the gods for she felt she needed him. I am ashamed to say this, because she should have trusted me instead. Out there where, as I learned, no one ever thinks of trusting anyone or anything she trusted *him*. And because everything and everyone is too much on the surface, or too recent, or too something-or-other, she was rash.

I didn't know this characteristic of the place at the time.

But I've hardly ever trusted anyone since, myself, nor has Alice Millard—scarcely even me, although she wouldn't admit it.

As you may see by now, architect and client were by nature incorrigibly young. Firmly believing in Santa Claus, both were encouraged by Mrs. Millard's builder to believe they could accomplish their mission for around eleven thousand some odd dollars. That was the contractor's estimate. Unhesitating, he signed a contract.

Why should he not sign a contract? Or sign anything at all?

Meantime we had rejected the treeless lot originally purchased by Mrs Millard, as my eyes had fallen upon a ravishing ravine near by, in which stood two beautiful eucalyptus trees. The ravine was reached from the rear by Circle Drive. Aristocratic Lester Avenue passed across the front.

No one would ever want to build in a ravine out there, I believed. They all got out onto the top of everything or anything to build and preferably in the middle of the top. It was a habit. I considered it a bad habit but because of this idiot-syncrasy of the region we could get this lot very cheap. We got it at half price—and it was better than the best at full price.

We would head the ravine at the rear on Circle Drive with the house, thus retaining the ravine as a sunken garden, at the front toward Lester Avenue. The house would rise tall out of the ravine gardens between the two eucalyptus trees. Balconies and a terrace or two would lead down into the ravine from the front of the house. The neighbours on either side liked this idea, as we left the entire front of the lot next their home for an open garden.

We began to build. The builder grew in Mrs. Millard's estimation until well over life-size. He settled down full in the saddle. I could not fail to see this with some alarm and chagrin. It is not pleasant for an architect to see his client clinging to a contractor as safe insurance against what might prove to be too single-minded devotion to an idea on the part of her architect. Her friends had got that far with her? Or perhaps it was her nature. I don't know. But she would not have admitted this for unfaith, I do know, so I admit it for her here with wrinkles at the corners of my eyes. The architect has not infrequently in this region—for some peculiar reason, perhaps it is the climate—to endure this rivalry for the confidence and esteem of his client. I had learned this before from others. But what is this 'something' about a contractor or builder that inspires confidence in the client—especially if the client be a woman? Of course, it is easy for her to believe that he is, before all, practical. It is easy for her to believe that *he* is the man who really builds the building, in spite of the too ambitious, troublesome architect. He knows clapboards and shingles and so he must

218

know concrete blocks, etc., etc. Always, to the woman client, the appeal of the practical man is irresistible. Woman is far more objective than man anyway. She is more susceptible to the obvious every time. Nature made her that way.

So, still smiling, though I will say I resented this rivalry, I cheerfully did nothing about it. Let me admit, if less cheerfully, that I *could* have done nothing about it anyway, had I wanted to. So I helped along, every day on the ground myself, as best I might. I made more studies and details until finally we finished the flasks and boxes in which to make the blocks; got the right mixture of sand, gravel and cement, which we carefully chose; and so varied it that the blocks would not all be the same colour. The builder had picked up some relations of his in Los Angeles to make them. We needed no skilled labour yet and so more of the builder's relatives set the blocks, carrying them up ladders on their shoulders to their scheduled places in the walls. You see, this model house had to be clumsily home-made as it might be, for the price was very low. A good deal would have to be put up with on that account. Otherwise everything went along according to design—smoothly enough. And, by now, that house represented about as much studious labour over a drawing board and attention to getting construction started, as was required by the Cathedral of St. John the Divine in New York City, for instance. Certainly more trouble to me than the architect had with the Woolworth Building.

Inventive effort was all thrown in, of course. It always is where the architect is employed.

But never mind, the house was to me, by now, far more than a mere house. Yes—Mrs. Millard's friends were quite right. Her architect had gone so deep into his idea that concentration upon it was now amounting to a passion. The blocks began to take the sun and creep up between the eucalypti. I, the Weaver, dreaming of their effect. Came visions of a new architecture for a new life—the true life of this romantic, beautiful California—the coming reaction upon this hitherto unawakened people. Other buildings sprang full-born into my mind from this humble beginning. They arose in bewildering variety and peerless beauty. Gradually all complications, all needless expense of the treacherous and wasteful building system of a whole country, all went by the board. Any humble cottage might now live as architecture with the integrity known only to former ages. The machine should be no longer the bar to beauty in our own. At last, here I was grasping the near-end of a great means to a finer order. Standardization *was* the soul of the machine, and here I was the Weaver taking it as a principle and knitting a great future with it. Yes, crocheting with it a free masonry fabric capable of stunning variety, great in architectural beauty. And, well, I might as well admit it—I quite forgot this little building belonged to Alice Millard at all. Palladio? Bramante? Sansovino? Sculptors—all! Now here was I, Frank Lloyd Wright, the Weaver. What might not now grow out of this little commonplace circumstance?

'The Weaver' concentrated on other studies and drawings to carry the idea further. Yes, argued the Weaver—is anyone smiling?—have not all great ideas in art had an origin as humble as this or more so? At last: a real building-method was beginning in this little house; here at last was a weaving in building that could go on forever and not go wrong for anyone: by nature, a prohibition of affectation, sham or senseless extravagance: integrity in architecture in the realm prostitute to the expedient! Mechanical means to infinite variety no longer an impractical dream! Thus I—already too far beyond poor little La Miniatura!

But to come back again rudely to my story, how lucky to have found the intelligence in a client to go through initial steps with me—go along with comprehension and faith complete in her contractor—some in me yet, and no matter what anybody said. For that is what she did, although I seem to take it lightly in this tale.

Thus the home got well above the second storey level and Alice Millard to Europe for the summer. She paid her builder herself before she left, without a word to me. No vouchers asked. She wrote me she had done this. Under the circumstances, by this time, existing between us all, to ask for vouchers from him would have been to look a regal gift-horse in the teeth. . . . This was the final blow to my self-esteem. But I was above hurt —or beneath it—by now!

I drove over daily to carry on, but found no builder day after day. I chafed, complained and drove to and fro elsewhere to find him. Finding him I got promises. Finally Mrs. Millard's builder came to me for more money, explaining that if he got it he could forge ahead. I gave him some more money myself. He didn't forge ahead. Mrs. Millard did, when she came back with renewed enthusiasm for the whole thing, and found so little done. The idea had grown on her, too. Doubt crept into our triangle. I investigated her builder—well, *our* builder by now and . . .

Let's have the matter over with even if no one ever trusts me to build a house again:

I finally found him building a new house for himself way off somewhere. Tile floors throughout. New furniture. Grand piano. Strange. But we investigated some more. Found everything absolutely all right because everything was in his wife's name.

Here we were about half way through: money two-thirds gone. Some of it, maybe, gone into tile floors? New furniture? Grand piano? Why harrow the details. The builder now quit, angered by my own angry ungrateful attitude toward him in this whole matter. Mrs. Millard left in deep water with her inventive architect! And I must say her architect made me especially tired myself at this juncture just as he is making you tired right now, and very much for the same reasons. I now believed her friends were justified in their opposition to her architect. They could now all enjoy their 'I told you so' with me.

Perfect justice.

Now here in this tragi-comic situation is where my client rose and made herself the heroine of this piece.

She said, 'We are going to finish that building if it takes every cent I've got in the world or can get to do it. I see that it's going to be beautiful—and while it's not going to be so well-built as I hoped—I know something worthwile is coming out of that block-pile there in the yard.' That was that. And better than I deserved.

Somewhere, sometime a prospective client asked me how much I could build a ten-thousand-dollar house for. I said I didn't know exactly but I supposed it could be built for about what it would be worth, with something fine thrown in for good measure that money couldn't pay for. That home cost $18,000.00. The owner admitted it was worth it. It looked as though Alice Millard's $11,500.00 studio-house would beat this now. And I knew she couldn't stand it. So I wrote home to see if my credit could be strained to go into it with her to that extent. By submitting to a collection of financial humiliations it could be. I felt that I deserved to be fined enough money to finish that house, and so I fined myself with the six thousand available. Saying nothing about that at the moment, we will go ahead.

We were adrift among the Monyana men who were all in demand in this busy place so well over-sold and so badly under-built. I knew no one but the Hollyhock House crowd and they wouldn't do. They had already done. There were heart-rending trials of faith and friendship as one slippery human agency after another was seized from among the flotsam and jetsam of Monyana-land and put to work. I knew my client was avoiding her best friends. It is the least one can do when in trouble.

And I knew Alice Millard's heart was breaking. But she stood up to everything with a brave smile. With never-failing energy she again kept bringing in new builders with assumed cheerfulness. She could find them when no one else could find them. But they kept fading away until I found one who promised well. This man of mine put the final work into place and was no better than the rest. All told, I should say he was even worse.

And here we were now, facing deficits and duns, ridicule, threats, liens, insults. More liens. Finally lawsuits, or anything else they had around there. Let me tell you that region is particularly rich in all such active ingredients. Lucky I had that six thousand ready.

A lawsuit was brought by our trusty builder himself. I never knew just what the lusty fellow wanted or expected to get until the judge fined him $500 and costs. For his effrontery—I believe. And fired him. That cleared the matter up a little for us, although I still believe he brought the suit because he couldn't refrain from trading a little further upon the beautiful credulity he had found in us both. It really was very beautiful!

Well, anyhow the little studio-house was there, battered up a little, patched somewhat, but believe it or not—not so awfully badly built after all. Alice Millard had some grief over it—her standards were high and Monyana men not so good because really, they don't get much pay. But she had joy in the building now. She had fought a good fight.

Both having taken so much trouble with it from first to last, we had a fool's pride in it. Of course. And how with the added terrace walls, balconies and other things it could ever have been built even for the sum it had now cost, we couldn't see—though we knew some of the money had been—well, perhaps not wasted, but . . . who knows?

We rested. We enjoyed installing the old books and the other old things especially appropriate, which its tasteful owner with her usual discrimination had picked up in Italy. We sat at the tea-table in the afternoon, a blazing fire in the now charming fireplace. The interior was all either of us had dreamed of, it had an old-world atmosphere. And if you didn't go looking too hard for nicked edges or something like that where the Monyana men had run into one another with the blocks or fallen down with one, it wasn't so badly built. Its owner with her taste for fine materials and workmanship, though, would stop in the midst of enjoying the general result—to point to a manifest mechanical defect as though shot through the heart. Nevertheless, she enjoyed a triumph—a satisfaction that goes far, this seeing of one's desires established on earth by means of what had been, less than ten months before, only an idea.

The ravine had become a lively little garden, a pool reflecting the block mass and the trees.

The whole mass and texture of the home made the eucalyptus trees more beautiful, they in turn made the house walls more so.

And the appropriate but expensive garden terraces, balconies and roof gardens that had come to join the original inexpensive programme of interior rooms made the whole so naturally a part of that ravine that no one could even think of that building anywhere else or regret what the additional features cost. A miracle had come to pass. The old ravine got for half price—was one that was used to take away the street water. It had been converted before our very eyes through all confusion and treachery into a complete living home with infinite charm. Oh, yes—it had charm! There was a quality living and holding it all together through friction, waste and slip that so blessed the result. For such *is* an Idea.

La Miniatura. New-born entity where before was emptiness . . . a sunken ravine.

But the Gods will allow no creative effort of man's to go untested. The Japanese themselves believe them jealous, purposely leaving some glaring fault in a conspicuous place to placate them. The Monyana men had done this in many places but we had not done so. And just for that came an unusual cloudburst concentrating on that ravine, it seemed. In every fair-weather region like this it is always the unexpected that happens. No one in fifty years ever saw the culvert that now took the street water away below the basement of the house, overflow. But the heavens opened wide, poured water down until it got to the level of the pretty concrete dining-room floor, determined to float the house if the thing could be done. The flood must have mistaken the house for another Ark, but this time, failing utterly to move it, it left a contemptuous trace of mud on the lower terraces, put out the fires in the sub-basement, burying the gas heaters beneath solid mud. And went away. Mrs. George Madison Millard's spirit, faith, and pride went out with the fires. She wept.

But soon we got this little matter fixed up by aid of the city of Pasadena. Even this was not to be enough to add to what had already been. Depths of misery were yet to be plumbed.

Cyrano de Bergerac, high-adventurer, after a lifetime of triumphs as idealist was inadvertently knocked on the head by a flower-pot. The pot fell from a window ledge above him as, rapier in scabbard, he passed below. And I've always believed there was only a common red-geranium in that pot.

Well, La Miniatura's hard-fought and all-but-won idealism was now to share a like fate. Yes—let no one imagine that because this region is perpetual sunshine the roof is any more negligible a feature of house-happiness than back there in rain and snow and ice. The sun bakes the roof for eleven months, two weeks and five days, shrinking it to a shrivel. Then giving the roof no warning whatever to get back to normal if it could, the clouds burst. Unsuspecting roof surfaces are deluged by a three-inch downpour.

I knew this. And I know there are more leaking roofs in Southern California than in all the rest of the world put together. I knew that the citizens come to look upon water thus in singularly ungrateful mood. I knew that water is all that enables them to have their being there, but let any of it through on them from above, unexpectedly, in their houses and they go mad. It is a kind of phobia. I knew all this and I had seriously taken precautions in the details of this little house to avoid such scenes as result from negligible roofs. This is the truth.

The details were perfect, and were proved so to everyone's dissatisfaction. But what of it? What defence when any roof chooses to leak? It subsequently was found that our builder had lied to me about the flashing under and within the coping walls—that's all. I had cautioned him concerning this before leaving, when called away to Lake Tahoe. But not until I had safely escaped to Taliesin did the La Miniatura roofs decide to leak. I knew nothing of it. Saying nothing to me, not wishing to hurt my feelings, I imagine, Mrs. Millard deliberately invited somebody if not anybody and everybody in to talk it all over and try to fix up that roof. The roof was easy to fix, for there would be no rain for another year. You may feel that by confessing this shameful incompetence in this manner I am making light of a bad matter. But really I am doing penance here. Maybe, I am only making a bad matter worse. However that may be, Mrs. George Madison Millard's spirit, though dampened, was not one made to be broken even by this last trial. Enough of left-handed confession. I finally fixed the house when I found out about it.

Yes, the strength of Alice Millard's determination, the real courage of her faith in La Miniatura, lived to laugh at that trial too. Yes, we two laugh about it all now. But we couldn't then.

Now, sometimes, when I think what La Miniatura would have gained for the future of our Architecture and my own petty fortunes had the gods not been jealous of it and given the local A.I.A., Mrs. Millard's private secretaries, her too many vigilant and confidential advisers, the local realtors, aspiring inferior desecrators, convincing contractors, roofers, loafers, lawyers, plumbers, tourists, butchers, grocers, rooters and servants —all working for the 'I told you so' brigade—this last fatal chance to assassinate it. It leaked! This fatal last chance for all, I curse still. These eager publicists had all the while been roosting à la flower pot—to get the satisfaction of this final knockout blow. We ourselves survived the untoward circumstances—yes, because the house was mainly all right all the time. But not so for them, because La Miniatura had insulted them all by what it aspired to be. 'They' had no wish for it to *survive* anything at all. Not if they could help it.

Well—Cyrano is dead, but La Miniatura is not dead. It is still too young to die. La Miniatura, first-born Californian in architecture, takes place in the esteem and affectionate admiration of our continental judges in architecture across the sea, at least. The process that built it is now in use 'over there', as here. And the humble concrete-block building gives to architects another simple means to establish an indigenous tradition instead of aping styles, buying apples from abroad. Thus, it appears in this shameful and perhaps too light recital of far too serious woes, that no creative impulse as a genuine idea ever does or ever can choose its hour or choose its means or control its ends, once started. The Idea starts and if really one soon shows itself so much bigger than the puppets it plays with fast and loose, that they take, miserably or thankfully as may in them be, whatever they happen to get. And go their way. If meantime they get ungratefully troublesome they may get into court, be fined $500 and costs by the judge, and 'fired'. But inevitably as the sun shall also rise, after some reactions and a few bad days, there will come to the seeker for integrity something beyond fashion, beyond price, beyond all neighbourly cavil.

I believe that reward is the only atonement that can be made for the privilege of being able to build a house at all.

La Miniatura stands in Pasadena against blue sky between the loving eucalyptus companions, and in spite of all friction, waste and slip is triumphant as Idea. Friction, waste and slip did not destroy it—and cannot now. Alice Millard lives in it. She says she would have no other house she has ever seen. She fought for it and finally won—whoever may think she lost. It is her home in more than ordinary sense. It is the reward anyone has a right to enjoy in any sincere high adventure in building.

Seeking simplicity in the spirit in which it was sought in La Miniatura, you will never fail to find beauty—though contractors do betray, workmen botch, all your friends backslide, bankers balk, and the dread jaws of

224

22. The house upon its hill

23. The court

HOLLYHOCK HOUSE, 1920

24. Fireplace on left under top-light pools on either side. Stone mural—bas relief, 'King of the Desert'

25. CHARLES ENNIS
HOUSE 1921-2
A detail of one of the
Hollywood block houses.
A system of reinforced
concrete precast block
construction, of which
there are five in Cali-
fornia

26. THE MILLARD
HOUSE (1923) is a
typical example of the
block house

heaven open wide to hitherto unsuspected deluge—even if all the gods but one be jealous.

As for me—probably living too long as a hermit—and reading mostly in the book of creation—I may have got these things sadly out of drawing —because I would rather have built this little house than St. Peter's at Rome.

Months before La Miniatura was finished, many improvements and changes were made in block technique. Other block houses began to grow up in that equivocal region, even as the first was being completed. The Storer House was one. The Freeman House was another. And then the Little Dipper, kindergarten for Aline Barnsdall, which she destroyed half-way through. And she employed my superintendent of Hollyhock House, himself—by the way, he was all ready—to turn it into a garden terrace.

The little palace, the Ennis house, was fifth of the block-shell group. I had drawn my son Lloyd into this effort and after completing the plans and details for this latter house I entrusted it all to Lloyd to build—and I, too soon, went back to Taliesin.

Some one hundred and seventy-nine buildings, as this is written—both large and small—had been built from my own hand by now and are known as this work of mine. About seventy more, the best ones, had life only on paper. The most interesting and vital stories might belong to these children of imagination were they ever to encounter the field. Say, the Lake Tahoe Project, the Doheny Ranch Project, San Marcos in the Desert, St. Mark's Tower and others.

Such stories of actual buildings as are included here are intended to be typical in some way of the characteristic ills that mean success or failure and of certain phases of the whole group of buildings, although the building of many was untroubled and a delight to all concerned—about three out of five were so I should say.

Many another building, as I see, might have served here the better purpose: say the Winslow House at River Forest; the Hillside Home School buildings; the first 'Dampfer House'—that is to say the Robie House down by Chicago University, now belonging to the Congregational Church. Especially the Coonley House at Riverside. The Martin House at Buffalo. The little 'School of the Free Spirit' in Tokio. The interesting Fukuhara Country House at Hakone—it parted in two during the great earthquake —the great living-room at the front following the rock-cliff on which it had stood, down the mountainside some thousands of feet into the valley below—all being in the bedrooms behind it, no one harmed. The establishment of the Bitter Root Community in Montana—and many others. Success might be thus emphasized. Instead I have spoken of failure, of a kind.

It would be worthwhile to tell the story of the house for Henry Allen at Wichita, Kansas. Henry was as colourful a client as all out-doors. And of the new home I did not build for William Allen White because Will had an animal fear of being turned out of the old one.

I would like to tell of the home at Peoria for Francis Little, himself an intelligent builder and manager of civic gas plants for John R. Walsh. Mr. Little retired and sold the Peoria house to Bob Clarke. And—amusing to me—tell of the second and especially of the third beautiful home I built for him on the shore of Lake Minnetonka, Minnesota. I liked the house much and the Littles more, but it has never been published. I could tell the amusing story of how I got the Hotel and Bank block to build at Mason City, Iowa. And tell of the Aeroplane House, Submarine, the Coach-and-Four, the Polar-star and of Perihelion. The Dana House at Springfield—dear old Mother Lawrence, salt-risen bread, blackberry preserves and the way we kept faith with the old homestead. Tell, especially of the lifelong interest and loyalty of Darwin D. Martin and the building of several houses for him—under fire from Mrs. Martin—who finally joined us. Of the help of the inventive Charles E. Roberts at Oak Park.

So many come trooping to mind, as children troop into school at the ringing of the bell after recess. And I can say truthfully enough if not modestly, that not one building great or small but was the working out of some single-minded far-reaching idea, the practical demonstration of many principles at work and for that reason as of record, not one has yet been lost to the record. Although many have been torn down to make way for changes in the city they have not been lost. A number of dwellings have 'Changed hands'—as the advertisement used to read—because of the rapidly shifting changes in the lives of the people for whom they were built—inevitable in a young and rapidly changing country. Two were bought back again by the same people who had built them and sold them, because they said they could not feel at home in any other. Especially I should like to tell the story of 'the house that was never built'. It was, of course, the best house I ever built.

Kaleidoscopic! These gratifications of social-shifts demanded and taken by the restless to and fro of our artificial, hectic, economic life in the United States. What European would understand it? The people of these United States live under it, familiar with it but do not understand it themselves.

But there have been stories enough. In choosing the tales of Hollyhock House and La Miniatura I have wilfully taken those experiences in which I was most at disadvantage owing to the vicious triangle, or by way of Time, Place and Circumstance, or by way of my own fault—intending as I have said, to show how all creative effort in the direction of any ideal is continually at the mercy of human nature—the trivial idiosyncrasy characteristic in the circumstances, and the vicious building system of our country. But I should retract. Where creative effort is involved there are no trivial circumstances. The most trivial of them may ruin the whole issue. Yes, eternal vigilance is the only condition of creation as well as Freedom in our architecture in Usonia.

Certainly it is only fair to include one's mistakes and errors of judgment—any characteristic failings that at any time had relation to results as a whole, in this presentation of architecture as essentially human stuff.

During the two years passed in the beautiful Southwest, building conditions there had seemed to me a shallow sea of cheap expedients. Nearly every effort I made out there was afloat on the surface and in some way for sale. I felt that were I to stay longer I too would be knocked down cheap to the highest bidder—if any. Desire for depth, for the quality that is genuine, seemed to be all far away in the future. Everybody and everything was getting by with something to sell, selling themselves. Always selling, eventually sold.

So coming back to Taliesin once more I continued work on the preliminary plans for a cantilever glass office building. I had begun it in Los Angeles—plan-making now to go forward for Mr. A. M. Johnson, President of the National Life Insurance Company of Chicago. He had offered to grubstake me with $20,000.00 to prospect in his behalf with this structural idea for a skyscraper as I had already laid it before him the year before.

Cantilever construction was one of the principal features that brought the Imperial safely through the great quake, and Mr. Johnson was interested to see how this cantilever principle, so successful there, could be adapted to modern skyscraper requirements. How would it all work out in a great office building for the site he owned on Water-Tower Square, Chicago?

Ideas attracted this insurance man. He kept saying, 'Now, Mr. Wright, remember!'—with his characteristic chuckle—'I want a virgin. I want a virgin.'

The studies were finally in presentable order. I took them in to him and he took them to his house and put them in his own bedroom. The glass of one of the drawings, the colour perspective, one day being broken by the houseman, he put the drawing in his car, took it over to the framer, waited until it was fixed and brought it back home himself. He wanted no one to see the design but himself. Intensely interested in ideas, I believe, though not himself the kind of man inclined to build much, he seemed rather of the type called conservative who, tempted, will sneak up behind an idea, pinch it in the behind and turn and run. There is this type of man bred by our capitalist system, not the captain, nor the broker or the banker but a better sort not quite contented with the commonplace, not quite courageous enough to take risks. I have met many such men.

THE BUSINESS MYSTIC

I believe that a good part of this is due to the fact that so soon as an idea attracts a man of that kind—all the agencies he is connected with or definitely knows react for him. The engineers shake their heads, rental experts will shake theirs, banks will hang out the 'busy' sign on him. The architects will stand together and ridicule the idea—until the business man who had a moment of illumination and some desire for initiative is by sheer weight of the circumstances in which he has himself taken root, pushed back—where he belongs, I suppose. But he is quite lost. He may be our chief asset in time. He is far ahead of the conservatism that battens and fattens on the capitalist enterprise of the true captains—and turns the vision of real men into the perquisites of the parasite. To this latter type of conservative nothing much happens, either way. He is the middle-of-the-road egotist. The middle of the road is the place for him, so it is the place for everybody. He will have plenty of company there. And he feeds upon company such as it is.

At any rate, here was Mr. Johnson paying a round sum to see how an idea would work out. In his behalf? Why not.

A. M. Johnson was a strange mixture of the fanatic and the mystic, Shylock and the humanist. Withal he was extraordinarily intelligent. His back had been broken in a railway accident but by sheer strength of intelligent will, he had survived. A slight stoop stayed in the way of his walk. We took a trip together into Death Valley, where he and Death Valley Scotty had made a place in which to live. He drove his own car, a Dodge, and as I rode beside him Nature staged a show for us all the way.

He was a convert to Billy Sunday, a revivalist famous for his religious activities, or rather his activities in religious matters. So he was fundamentalist, a controversialist of no mean order. Religiously we were at the poles apart, but he grub-staked me in search of an idea just the same.

There are no pigeonholes in nature, human or otherwise, in which to put anyone. A singular man, a singular trait of Mr. Johnson's was this singular friendship for Scotty. Scotty who was suspected of having murderous connection with gold mines on some location known only to him. But I suspect A. M. Johnson was Scotty's gold mine.

THE GLASS SKYSCRAPER

A lot of approximately 300 × 100 facing 300 feet long to the south.

Sheet-copper and glass were the mediums I chose for the thin pendent wall-screens to be carried by the outer edges of cantilever floor slabs, and to avoid the prejudice I saw in my client's hard mind against excessive glass surface I decided to make the exterior area of this project about $\frac{1}{4}$ of copper and $\frac{3}{4}$ of glass. Sheet metal—copper—would therefore characterize this building as much as the glass.

At work upon this scheme—the metal and glass house—the metal and glass service station, brother to the car and the plane, seemed near at hand. For the Machine-age should have a great many types. It should have at least as many types as there are materials and methods of construction: all genuine. Why not? All might become characteristic as architecture. But now, what form? I had not gone very far into steel-construction before.

So these plans for the insurance building were opportunity to devise a more practical solution of the skyscraper problem than current, because the advantages offered by modern materials and methods add up most heavily in their own favour where they can go farthest—either up and down or crosswise. So standardization here might come completely into its own because standardization is in the nature of both the sheet-metal process and of reinforced concrete. Here, again the life of the Imagination must awaken life within the very limitations of the architect's problem.

Now, exterior walls as such disappear—instead see suspended, standardized sheet-copper screens only slightly engaged with the edges of the floors. The walls themselves cease to exist as either weight or thickness. Windows in this fabrication are a matter of units in the screen fabric, opening singly or in groups at the will of the occupant. All outside glass of the building may be cleaned from the inside with neither bother nor risk. The vertical mullions (copper shells filled with non-conducting mastic) are large and strong enough only to carry from floor to floor. The mullions themselves project much or little as more or less light is wanted. If much projection, the shadows are enriched. Less projection dispels the shadows and brightens the interior. These projected mullions which are really vertical blades of copper, act in the sun like the blades of a blind.

The unit of two feet both ways is small because of Mr. Johnson's fear of too much glass. In this instance the unit is emphasized on every alternate vertical with additional emphasis laid on every fifth unit to enlarge the metal areas and create a larger rhythm. There is no emphasis needed on the horizontal units. They would catch water or dust. The edges of the various floors are bevelled to the same section as is used between the windows where engaged with the wall screen, so these appear in the screen as one of the horizontal divisions occurring naturally on the two-foot unit lines. The floors themselves however do appear at intervals in the recessions of the screen. This in order to bring the concrete structure itself into relief seen in relation to the screen as well as in connection with it, thus weaving the two elements of structure together.

The outer building surfaces become opalescent, iridescent copper-bound glass. To avoid all interference with the fabrication of the light-giving exterior-screen, the supporting pylons were set back from the lot line, the floors carried by them thus becoming cantilever-slabs. The extent of the cantilever is determined by the use for which the building is designed— in this case twelve feet. These pylons are continuous through all floors and in this instance are exposed at the top. The pylons are enlarged to carry electrical, plumbing, and heating conduits which branch from the shafts, not in the floor slabs at all but all in piping designed into visible fixtures extending beneath each ceiling to where the outlets are needed in the office arrangement. All electrical or plumbing appliances may thus be disconnected and re-located at short notice with no waste at all in time or material, and are free of the building in vertical shafts.

Being fabricated upon a perfect unit system, the interior-partitions may all be made up in sections, complete with doors ready to set in place. Designed to match the general style of the outer wall-screen. These interior partition units thus fabricated may be stored ready to use and any changes to suit tenants made overnight with no waste of time and material. Mr. Johnson was an experienced landlord and these simples appealed to him.

Again it was the kind of standardization in building that gave us the motor car.

The increase of glass area over the usual modern skyscraper fenestration was only about ten per cent (the margin could be increased or diminished by expanding or contracting the copper members in which the glass is set), so the expense of heating was not materially increased. Inasmuch as the copper mullions were to be filled with insulating material and the window-openings all tight (mechanical units in a mechanical screen), this excess of glass was compensated. The radiators cast as a railing set in front of the lower glass unit of this outer screen-wall were free enough to make cleaning easy. The walls of the first two storeys, or more, were of unobstructed glass suspended from the floor above. The dreams of the shopkeeper in this connection fully realized.

The connecting stairways necessary between floors are here arranged as a practical fire-escape forming the central feature, as may be seen at the front and rear of each section of the whole mass, and though cut off by fire-proof doors at each floor the continuous stairway thus made discharges upon the sidewalk below without obstruction.

The construction of such a building as this would be at least one-third lighter than anything in the way of a tall building yet built—and three times stronger in any disturbance. The construction balanced as the body on the legs, the walls hanging as the arms from the shoulders, the whole heavy only where weight insures stability.

Of chief value as I see it is the fact that the scheme as a whole legitimately eliminates the matter of masonry architecture that now vexes all such buildings. And this scheme takes away from field construction all such elements of masonry from the architectural exterior or interior either. Architecture in this scheme now is become a complete shop-fabrication. Only the most complicated part of the building prefabricated need be assembled in the field.

The mere physical concrete construction of pylons and floors is noninvolved with any interior or exterior. Indestructible, the fabric is made entirely independent of anything hitherto complicating it and mixed up with it in our country as 'architecture'. As practised at present the skyscraper's so-called architecture is expensively involved but entirely irrelevant. In this design 'architecture' is entirely relevant but uninvolved.

Also the piping and conduits of all appurtenance systems may be cut in the shop, the labour in the field reduced to assembling only. No fitting. Screwing up the joints all that is necessary in either heating, lighting or plumbing.

Thus, literally, we have a shop-made building in all but the interior supporting posts and floors, which may be reinforced concrete or concrete-masked steel cast in place in the field. In this design, architecture was frankly, profitably and artistically—why not?—taken from the field to the factory. A building is here standardized as any mechanical thing whatsoever might be from penny-whistle to a piano, and it is dignified, imaginative, practical. The economic advantages are enormous and obvious.

There is no unsaleable floor space in this building—nothing at all created for effect, as may be observed.

There are no 'features' inside or outside manufactured merely 'for architectural effect'.

To gratify the landlord, his lot area was now saleable to the very lot-line itself and on every floor, where ordinances do not interfere and demand that they be reduced in area as the building soars.

Architecture in evidence here is a light, trim, practical commercial fabric—every inch and pound of which is in service. There is every reason why it should be beautiful. But it was best to say nothing about that to Mr. Johnson. And I said very little about it.

The aim in this fabrication employing the cantilever system of construction was to achieve absolute scientific utility by means of the Machine. To accomplish—first of all—a true standardization which would not only serve as the basis for keeping the life of the building true as architecture but enable me to project the whole, as an expression of a valuable principle involved, into a genuine living architecture of the present.

I began work on this study the winter of 1920, the main features of it having been in mind ever since the building of the Imperial in 1917. I had the good fortune to explain the scheme in detail and show the developed preliminary drawings to liebermeister Louis H. Sullivan shortly before he died. Gratefully I remember—and proudly too—he said: 'I had faith that it would come. It is a work of great art. I knew what I was talking about all these years—you see? I could never have done this building myself, but I believe that, but for me, you could never have done it.'

I know I should never have reached it, but for what he was and what he himself did. This design is dedicated to him.

During this period while building the Imperial Hotel and the block buildings in Los Angeles, life of legal necessity—legal divorce was still denied me—remained unconventional. Voluntarily still in exile. Taliesin meantime had become refuge to the misfortune of the unfortunate Miriam Noel. She who had gone with me to Japan.

But life when resumed at Taliesin II had changed much. There were no longer carefree walks over friendly hills, nor swimming in the river below. No horseback riding along the country lanes, no coasting and skating or happy sleighing in winter. There was no freedom, no singing. Involuntarily, all intention otherwise, life seemed paralysed by subtle poison. Taliesin—so it seemed—had encountered subtle disintegration from within. Fortunately, this life that entered Taliesin II as new, soon left it and went to Japan.

Only caretakers and one faithful apprentice, William Smith, stayed there. Restlessly during these years following, Taliesin had languished, called in vain. But the calling was rewarded each year by a visit of several months from the land on the other side of the globe.

Dust settled on the heads of the ancient gods at rest upon the broad ledges. But Taliesin had been calling me all these years and I was looking forward to the time when it should come alive again for me and all those I loved. Now I had come back. Miriam and I had been married several months before. Marriage resulted in ruin for both. Instead of improving with marriage, as I had hoped, our relationship became worse.

With marriage she seemed to lose what interest she had in life at Taliesin and become more than ever restless and vindictive. Finally under circumstances altogether baffling—she left 'to live a life of her own'. To oppose her now in the slightest degree meant violence. I did not really wish to oppose her.

She went first to Chicago. But even now I would not give up hope or effort to make good a human relationship gone so far wrong. Suffering and sacrifice had already entered in on both sides. Shame to me too—an unfamiliar moral cowardice had kept me from acknowledging defeat, although by nature and equipment I was unfitted for the task I had now undertaken. But the circumstances becoming more than ever violent, even dangerous, I consulted Dr. William Hixon, a famous psychiatrist of Chicago now at Geneva. A tardy consultation because long dreaded it had been deferred.

Convinced by his observation that the struggle of the past six years had been hopeless from the beginning and that Miriam had all along been a danger not only to herself but especially to anyone with whom she might live in close association, I agreed to arrangements to end the relationship, modifying only somewhat the terms dictated by herself. She had returned to Los Angeles. Dr. Hixon said that the only hope for a longer freedom for her lay in letting her have her head. To oppose her would only be to burn her up more quickly in the circumstances.

So the final arrangements for a divorce were made by Judge James Hill while I stayed on at Taliesin.

Young people had come from all over the world attracted by Taliesin's fame abroad to share its spirit; to learn I suppose what message the indigenous United States had for Europe. And, evenings, after good work done, the piano, violin and cello spoke there the religion of Bach, Beethoven and Handel. William Blake, Samuel Butler, Walt Whitman and Shelley often presided. Carl Sandburg, Edna Millay and Ring Lardner, too, had something to say or sing. And life in the hills revived for the little cosmopolitan group eager to know this 'America', for Taliesin was at work quietly Americanizing Europe while American architects Europeanized America.

But peace even for these gentle seekers from afar was not to last. There were but eleven months of growing good-will. The living things of art and beauty belonging now to the place as the eye to the face, become like Taliesin's own flesh, each and all became a loneliness and a sorrow. Occasionally a living thought would go over them as they stood dignified but neglected. Taliesin dreamed, meditated, worked and slept.

Primeval fire-places sent streams of light and warmth into the house itself, but it no longer seemed to know how to live. Dissension and discord had shamed the peace, outraged its lifting walls and friendly ceilings.

A hope only lived there, wishing as always to bring back happiness.

232

ISAIAH

When about a year after I had finally separated from Miriam, one evening at twilight as the lightning of an approaching storm was playing and the wind rising, I came down from the evening meal in the little detached dining room on the hill-top to the dwelling on the court below to find smoke pouring from my bedroom. Again—there it was—Fire!

Fire fanned by that rising storm meant a desperate fight. My heart was sad as I realized all had gone from the place for the evening but two besides myself. Mell, the driver, and Kameki, a Japanese apprentice.

I called for water. And water came to the constant cry of 'Water!' for two hours. I thought I had put the fire out when an ominous crackling above the bedroom ceiling indicated fire had got into the dead spaces beneath the roof. I sent alarm out again, and again the people of the countryside came in and turned to fight flames at Taliesin.

The rising wind blew the flames—raging now beneath the roof surfaces—out above the roof in a dozen places. 'Let us save what we can of the things inside,' they cried.

'No, fight the fire. Fight. Fight I tell you. Save Taliesin or let all go!' I shouted, like some dogged, foolish captain on the bridge of a sinking vessel doomed to all eyes but his.

Water! More water was the cry as more men came over the hills to fight the now roaring sea of devastation. Whipped by the big wind, great clouds of smoke and sparks drove straight down the lengths of Taliesin courts. The place seemed doomed—even to me. That merciless wind! How cruel the wind may be, cruel as fire itself.

But I was on the smoking roofs, feet burned, lungs seered, hair and eyebrows gone, thunder rolling as the lightning flashed over the lurid scene, the hill-top long since profaned by crowds of spectators standing silent there—but I stood there—and fought. Isaiah?

I could not give up the fight. Now it had become a fight to save the workrooms. But everyone else had given it up. Taliesin as a whole, they said, was gone.

The destruction had reached to the workrooms—had begun to take hold of them too—water gone, human energy gone. Men were lying about the roofs to recover strength and breath to keep on fighting the flames.

Suddenly a tremendous pealing roll of thunder and the storm broke with a violent change of wind that rolled the great mass of flame up the valley. It recoiled upon itself once as the rain fell hissing into the roaring furnace. But the clouds of smoke and sparks were swept the opposite way. It was as though some gigantic unseen hand had done it and that awed the spectators. Super-human Providence perhaps—the thought in their minds.

In that terrible twenty minutes, the living half of Taliesin was gone—again!

The heat had been so intense that plate glass windows lay, crystal pools in ashes on hot stone pavements.

Smouldering or crumbled in ashes were priceless blossoms-of-the-soul in all ages—we call them works of art. They lay there broken, or had vanished utterly.

Another savage blow struck at Taliesin.

Now left to me out of most of my earnings since Taliesin I was destroyed, all I could show for my work and wanderings in the Orient for years past were the leather trousers, burned socks and shirt in which I now stood defeated. But what the workshop contained was still intact.

But Taliesin lived wherever I stood! A figure crept forward to me from out the shadows to say this. And I believed what Olgivanna said.

Lightning had struck again. Is human carelessness and fallibility all the wrath of God there is?—The fire seemingly had originated in a house-telephone that had given trouble as it stood by the head of my bed. Again searching causes I wondered. Everything of a personal nature I had in the world, beside my work, was gone. But . . . this time reason to be thankful —no lives were lost except those images whose souls belonged and could now return to the souls that made them—the precious works of art that were destroyed.

I had not protected them. Yes . . . a poor trustee for posterity, I. But they should live on in me, was the thought with which I consoled myself. I would prove their life by mine in what I did. I said so to the suppliant figure standing on the hill-top in the intense dark that now followed the brilliant blaze.

That lurid crowd! During the terrible destruction the crowd had stood there on the hill-top, faces lit up by the flames. Some few were sympathetic. Others half sympathizing were convinced of inevitable doom. Some were already sneering at the fool who imagined Taliesin could come back after all that had happened there before. Others stood there stolidly chewing tobacco—entertained?

Were they the 'force' that had struck again? Were they really 'Isaiah'?

Well—counselled by the living—there I was, alive in their midst, at least. Was I the key to a Taliesin nobler than the first if I could make it? I had faith that I could build another Taliesin! Taliesin III.

A few days later clearing away still smoking ruin to reconstruct, I picked from the debris partly calcined marble heads of the Tang Dynasty, fragments of the black basalt of a splendid Wei-stone, soft-clay Sung sculpture and gorgeous Ming pottery that had turned to the colour of bronze by the intensity of the fire. All sacrificial offerings to—whatever gods may be, I put the fragments aside to weave them into the masonry fabric of Taliesin III. Already in mind it was to stand in place of Taliesin II. And I went to work again to build better than before because I had learned from building the other two.

So, again after confusion, destruction, desolation, I was at work again in the workshop at Taliesin, out in the fields—walking, swimming in the river, driving over the hills, skating in winter. Appetite for creation was still lagging—a little. But coming rapidly alive once more. Hunger for the creative life was not far away.

REUNION

Meantime just before the destruction of the Taliesin I, liebermeister and I had come together again.

Things had not been going well with him since the separation from Dankmar Adler shortly after that triumphant disaster the Columbian 'Fair'. The Guarantee Building, Buffalo, had just come into the office when I left. It was the last building built under the Adler and Sullivan partnership.

To go back many years into Adler and Sullivan history: owing to the nature of such creative work as theirs Adler and Sullivan, Architects, had made no money. Their work cost them as much, often more, than they received for it, although they were paid as well as any first-class architects —probably better paid than most. The depression following the Columbian Fair therefore hit Adler and Sullivan hard. At this psychological moment Crane of the Crane Company came along as tempter. He offered Dankmar Adler $25,000 a year to sell Crane Elevators. In a fit of despondency he accepted. Some money had to be earned by someone. Sullivan left alone was resentful.

The clientele had been mostly Adler's, as Sullivan now found out. And Louis Sullivan soon faced the fact that he was where he must take what was left to him from the Adler connection and start to build up a practice anew for himself. Only one Adler and Sullivan client stayed with the now lonely Sullivan: Meyer, of Schlesinger and Meyer, who employed him to design his new retail store building on State Street.

Meantime, as I got the story, a curious mishap had befallen Crane's new lion. He went to New York to sell Crane Elevators for the new Siegel Cooper Building. The opposing bidder, Sprague Electric, simply pulled out a report Adler the architect had made concerning their elevator for use in the Auditorium Building some years previous. It gave the Electric everything—yes, including the Siegel Cooper work. Mr. Adler came home. Some words from Crane. The lion was unused to being talked to in that tone of voice, especially from one who had hitherto come to him for justice or for favours. The result of the interview was a cheque from Crane to Adler for a year's salary and a contract cancelled.

All now hoped to see the two partners together again. But no, the Master was resentful still and the Big Chief had had enough.

About this time Mr. Adler at the Union League Club called me. I went to talk things over with him. As yet I had not communicated with Mr. Sullivan since leaving. The old chief seemed morose. He had been greatly worried by the risks he had taken to please his clients in certain features of the Auditorium Building; the addition to the height of the tower to please Sullivan; the addition of the banquet hall over the trusses spanning the Auditorium to please Ferdinand Peck *et al.* Movement had not yet stopped. The tower was settling down and taking down the adjoining portions of the building.

I noticed a great change in him. He spoke bitterly of Sullivan, who had published the Guarantee Building with Adler's name deleted from the plans.

'But for me, Wright, there would have been no Guarantee Building!'

'Yes,' I said. 'But I am sure the omission was not Mr. Sullivan's fault. Probably the publisher's. Why don't you make sure?'

'I'm sure enough,' he said.

I tried him out concerning Sullivan. I told him there was such general disappointment over the separation—believed they needed each other—and if ever two men did, they did—had done such great work together—the depression couldn't last. And many other private arguments for resuming the old relationship.

'No, Wright,' thrusting out his bearded chin in characteristic fashion, 'I am going to keep my office in my hat so far as I can—there's nothing in the big office with big rent and a big salary list. I'll do the few buildings I can do, and instead of earning $50,000, keeping $1000—I'll earn, by myself, $5000 and keep $2000.'

Looking at me sharply under his honest, shaggy eyebrows: 'Take this from me, do you do the same, Wright.'

'No architect on that individual basis ever needs a partner,' he added.

I saw something that had lived between the two men who so needed each other, burning up or already burned out.

We walked over to the several small rooms he had taken on the Wabush Avenue side of the Auditorium—while Sullivan was still carrying on up in the tower. It seemed a heart-breaking situation. But I still believed they would come together. I said so when I left. Worry and disappointment had already done something to the grand old chief. This was no way of life for him.

In a short time he was dead.

Some seven years later the Master and I met again. I saw instantly that he too had gone from bad to worse. The Auditorium management finally had refused to carry him further in the splendid tower offices, and offered him two rooms below, near by those Adler had occupied on the Wabash Avenue front. He accepted them, but later even these were closed to the Master. On that occasion he had called me over long-distance. Luckily I was able to reinstate him. But habits engendered by his early life in Paris had made havoc with him. He had 'gone off', as they say, frightfully.

He was much softened though, and deepened too, I thought. He gently called me 'Frank'. I loved the way the word came from him. Before that it had always been 'Wright'.

His courage was not gone. No, that would never go. His eyes burned as brightly as ever. The old gleam of humour would come into them and go. But his carriage was not the same. The body was disintegrating.

I remember sitting on his desk noticing that it was uselessly littered with his papers. There were photographs of the small bank-building he had been doing. These showed only remnants of the great genius that flashed upon him in the Wainwright Building in St. Louis as in the old days in the tower. He was leaning heavily now on George Elmslie who was still with him at the time these buildings were done.

But at least liebermeister was safe in an armchair by a fireside. He had been made a life-member of the Cliff Dwellers. It is one of the great virtues of that organization that it did this for him. I had corresponded with him while in Japan, and from Los Angeles. Whenever I got to Chicago I took a room at the Congress for him, next mine. He was now staying at the old Hotel Warner way down on Cottage Grove Avenue, an old haunt of his with little else to recommend it. He had taken great pride in the performance of the Imperial Hotel, wrote two articles concerning it for the *Architectural Record*. 'At last, Frank,' he said, 'something they can't take away from you.' (I wonder why he thought 'they' couldn't take it away from me? 'They' could take anything away from anybody, if not by hook, then by crook.)

Several architects in Chicago befriended him, had been kind to him. Gates of the American, and Lucas, Hottinger, and others of the North-western Terra Cotta Company especially so. But he was no more tolerant of his contemporaries in architecture now than ever before. Rather less so.

For many years he had been compelled to see great opportunities for work he could do so much better as to make comparison absurd—going to inferior men, going just because his personal habits had given provincial prejudice a chance to 'view with alarm' or dislike, though the matters involved were no concern of theirs nor directly connected with his efficiency as an architect. Ignorant prejudice, provincial, quotidian, was his implacable enemy. A genius? Well, that term damned him as it was intended to do. It will write any man off the commercial scene we live in.

Finance beware! Tiptoe to safety when that word comes through!

But now his efficiency was actually impaired by himself. He had in-creasingly sought refuge from loneliness—frustration—yes, and betrayal too, where and as so many of his gifted brothers have been driven to do since time was.

But had opportunity really opened even at this late in his life, he might have been saved for years of remarkable usefulness. But popular timidity and prejudice encouraged by jealousy had built a wall of ignorance around him so high that the wall blinded his countrymen and wasted him. At times his despondency would overcome his native pride and natural buoyancy. Even his high courage would give way to fear for his livelihood. Then all would come clear again. For a while.

He was caustic when he chose, was the old Master. When he was in a bitter mood, a dozen or so of his hard-boiled contemporaries would come tumbling from their perches on high, top side down, inside out. His blade could cut and flash as it cut.

He was writing the *Autobiography of an Idea* at this time. Occasion-ally he would read chapters to me. He had always loved to write. Now

237

completely shut off from his natural medium of expression, he turned more and more to writing. Soon he was again the Master there. The book meant much to him now, I saw.

He had visited Taliesin some years before. But it proved rather a strenuous experience for him—a bad cold, the result. At this time, two years later, his breath was shorter still and after several cups of the strong coffee he loved much too much, his breath was so short he would take my arm to walk—even slowly.

He was sinking. I continued to see him oftener than every week if I could.

Some weeks passed and a telephone call came to Taliesin from the Warner. I went to Chicago and found the Warner place up in arms against him. He had fallen very sick. Violent spells came over him now more and more often. I made peace with the manager—after raising Cain over the condition I had found his room in. The manager was really devoted to Sullivan as he said he was, but now at his wit's end. We finally got a nurse who would stay. His devoted comrade, the little henna-haired milliner who understood him and could do almost anything with him, was herself in the hospital at the time.

'Don't leave me, Frank,' he begged. 'Stay.'

I stayed. He seemed to be himself again toward evening. We talked about the forthcoming book, *The Autobiography of an Idea*. He hoped there might be some income in it—for him.

He had everything to make him comfortable, so late that evening after he had fallen asleep, I went back to Taliesin again with a promise from the nurse to call me if I was needed.

In town a few days later, I went to see him again.

He seemed better. There—at last—the first bound copy of the *Autobiography*! It had just come in and was lying on the table by his bed. He wanted to get up. I helped him, put my overcoat round his shoulders as he sat on the bed with his feet covered up on the floor. He looked over at the book.

'There it is, Frank.'

I was sitting by him, my arm around him to keep him warm and steady him. I could feel every vertebra in his backbone as I rubbed my hand up and down his spine to comfort him. And I could feel his heart pounding. This heart, his physician said, twice its natural size owing to coffee and bromide.

'Give me the book! The first copy to you. A pencil!' He tried to raise his arm to take the pencil; he couldn't lift it. Gave it up with an attempt at a smile.

And I have never read the book. All I know of it are the chapters he read to me himself. I could not read it. My copy was lost in the fire at Taliesin.

But yes, his courage was still there. He cursed a little—gently enough. The eyes were deeper in their sockets, but burning bright. He joked about the end he saw now, and cursed—under his breath. For the first time he would admit to himself that the end was near. But to me he looked as though he were better, notwithstanding that helpless arm. But he seemed indifferent. He didn't want to talk about it at all, either way. Life had been pretty hard on him. Such friends as he had could do little to make up for the deep tragedy of his frustration as an architect. In solitude only a year or so before he had made the beautiful drawings for the *System of Architectural Ornament*, his hand shaking as with palsy until he began to draw, then firm as could be. And these drawings that he made then show little falling off either in style or execution from his best at any time. His ornament was his inextinguishable gift and to the last. I had passed through many situations with him that had looked worse than this one. So I put him back to bed again—covered him up—and sat there by him on the edge of the bed. He fell asleep. Another crisis had apparently passed. He seemed to sleep well, to breathe deeply enough and easily once more. The nurse had stepped out for a moment. An imperative call came in from Taliesin. I left a note for the nurse to call me immediately if there was any change in him for the worse.

At Taliesin I listened anxiously for the telephone. No call coming I felt reassured.

But the day after the next I learned of his death from the newspapers and a long-distance call from Max Dunning. He had died the day after I left.

Several architects, warm-hearted little Max Dunning one of them, happened to come just at the end to see him and had taken charge. I was not sent for.

The Master had nothing in the world he could call his own but the new clothes it had been a pleasure of my life to see him in—these and a beautiful old daguerreotype of his lovely mother, himself and his brother, aged about nine, seen standing on either side of her.

Knowing he was dying he had given this prized possession to the nurse to give to 'Frank'.

I should have liked to keep the warm muffler he had worn about his neck. But—what use? He was gone!

Nor did anyone think to advise me concerning any of the funeral arrangements. His other friends picked his body up, planned an ordinary funeral at Graceland, at which Wallace Rice, his crony at the Cliff Dwellers, spoke. I attended. Later they designed a monument for him . . . a slab of ornament designed for his grave. In his own vein! 'They' caused this to be designed by George Elmslie, the young understudy I had brought over to Sullivan from Silsbee's because the Master wanted me to train someone to take my place in case anything should happen to me. George had taken my place when I left, and he stayed with the Master ten years or more. But to me, who had understood and loved him, this idea of a monument to the great Master was simply ironic. There was nothing to be done about it worth doing. It was their own best thought for the man now, and no monument was ever more than a monument to those who erect it, is it?

By the Eternal. These monuments! Will we never make an end of such banality, such profanity?

What great man ever lived whose memory has not been traduced, made ridiculous or insulted by the monument 'they' erected to themselves in his name when he was dead! Abraham Lincoln to mind. Monuments are made by those who, voluntarily or not, never did anything but betray the thing the great man they would honour loved most, those who were 'charitable' when he was in need; officious when he died. May hell hold them all!

I wrote something in the fullness of my heart, at the time published somewhere. I forget where. This is it:

THE MASTER'S WORK

The New in the Old and the Old in the New is ever, Principle.

Principle is all and single the reality my master Louis Sullivan ever loved. It gave to the man stature and gave to his work great significance.

His loyalty to principle was the more remarkable as vision when all around him poisonous cultural mists hung low to obscure or blight any bright hope of finer beauty in the matter of this world.

The buildings he has left with us for a brief time are the least of him. In the heart of him he was of infinite value to his country, the country that wasted him, the countrymen who wasted him not because they would: but because they could not know him.

Any work, great as human expression, must be studied in relation to the time in which it insisted upon its virtues and got itself into human view.

So it should be with the work he has left to us.

Remember, you who can, the contemporaries of his first great building, the Chicago Auditorium.

They were the hectic Pullman Building, W. W. Boyington's 'Board of Trade', the hideous Union Station and many other survivors in the idiom of that insensate period.

Outside the initial impetus of John Edelman in his early days, H. H. Richardson, the great emotional revivalist of Romanesque, was one whose influence the Master felt. And John Root, another fertile rival of that time who knew less than the Master but felt almost as much, sometimes shot very straight indeed. But they were his only peers. And they were feeling their way. But he was thinking *and* feeling his way, to the New.

Dankmar Adler, master of the plan and master of men, was his faithful partner.

The Auditorium Building is largely what it is, physically, owing to Dankmar Adler's good judgement and restraining influence. But it was Louis Sullivan who made it sing.

The Getty Tomb in Graceland Cemetery was entirely his own, a piece of sculpture, a statue, a great poem, addressed to human sensibilities as such.

But—when he brought the drawing board with the motive for the Wainwright Building outlined in profile and in scheme upon it and threw it down on my table, I was perfectly aware of what had happened.

This was the great Louis Sullivan moment. His greatest effort. The sky-scraper as a new thing beneath the sun, an entity imperfect, but with virtue, individuality, beauty all its own as the tall building was born. Until Louis Sullivan showed the way, tall buildings never had unity. They were built up in layers. All were fighting tallness instead of grace-fully and honestly accepting it. What unity those false masses had that now pile up toward the New York and Chicago sky is due to the master mind that first perceived the tall building as a harmonious unit—its height triumphant.

The Wainwright Building prophesied and opened the way for these tall office building effects we now point to with so much pride. And to this day, the Wainwright remains the master key to the skyscraper so far as a skyscraper is a matter of architecture.

Only the interior of the Chicago Auditorium, the pictorial Transporta-tion Building for what it was worth, the Getty Tomb, the Wainwright Building are necessary to show the great reach of creative activity that was Louis Sullivan's. Other buildings he did, but all more or less on these stems. Some were grafted from them. Some were grown from them. But all were relatively inferior in point of the quality which we must finally associate with the primitive strength of the thing that got itself done or born regardless and stark to the idea.

The capacity for love—ardent, true, poetic—was great in him. His system of ornament in itself, alone, would prove this. His work in this was esoteric. Is it the less precious for that?

Do you realize that here in his system of ornament is no body of culture evolving through centuries of time but here is a scheme and 'style' of plastic expression which an individual working away in the poetry-crush-ing environment of a more cruel materialism than any seen since the days of the brutal Romans made out of himself. He in this was an individual who evoked the goddess that whole civilizations strove in vain for cen-turies to win, wooed her with this charming interior smile—all on his own in one lifetime all too brief.

Regarding this achievement we may see that the time will come when every man may have that precious quality called style for his very own.

Then where on earth I ask you are the others?

Ah, that supreme erotic adventure of the mind that was his fascinating ornament!

Genius the Master had, or rather, genius had him. Genius possessed him. It revelled in him. And he squandered it.

The effect of any genius is seldom seen in its own time. Nor can the full effects of genius ever be traced or seen. Human affairs are flowing. What we call life is plastic in everything; it is a becoming and is so in spite of all efforts to fix it with names, all endeavours to make it static to man's will. As a pebble cast into the ocean sets up reactions lost in distance and time, so does a man's genius go on infinitely, forever. For genius *is* an expression of principle. Therefore in no way does genius ever run counter to genius nor ever could.

We may be sure that the intuitions and expressions of such a nature as his in the work to which he put his hand no less than the suggestion he was himself to kindred or aspiring natures, is more conservative of the future, the Architecture of our country than all the work of all the schools of all the time combined with all the salesmanship of all the functioneers everywhere.

Not long ago weary, in a despondent moment, he said to me—'It would be harder now to do radical work and more difficult to get radical work accepted now than it ever was.

'The people have stopped thinking!

'The inevitable drift toward mediocrity, taking the name of Democracy in vain, has set in. I see it so.'

No, my Master, believe me it is not so. There is never an inevitable, contrary to love of life. The torch flung to your master-hand from the depths of antiquity, from the heart of this human world—kept alight and held aloft for twenty years at least by you—shall not go out. Ever it has been flung from hand to hand and never yet—since time began for man—has it gone out.

TALIESIN III

My mother is gone now. She was only eighty-three years of age.

The Master, gone before his time.

Three beloved homes gone. The first—the cottage and studio at Oak Park—stood for nineteen years. The second, Taliesin, withstood five years. The third, Taliesin II, stood eleven years. And Taliesin III?

Now the fourth home built by my own hands. A new home built out of a battered and punished but still sentimental self in the same quest—life!

Help came as ever from the deeps of life. Understanding and ready for any sacrifice. Sympathy makes the real friend. Came Olgivanna. A woman is, for man, the best of true friends, if man will let her be one. The idea as to personal life that had come with Taliesin II was conviction, still.

That idea? Simply said, that any man had a right to three things if he is honest with all three. Had I been, could I be, honest with them all?

Honest with the man's life?

The man's work?

The man's love?

There is no answer in the prospect, the only answer lies in the retrospect. But I set to work again. Another spring of co-ordinate effort even more in love with life than ever before. Another summer came and another autumn. Another winter and, early in 1925, came one more chance to live and work in peace in another and yet the same Taliesin.

Talieson III, none the less proudly, if ruefully, took its place where the ashes of Taliesin I and Taliesin II, together with the life lived in each, had fallen in ruins.

The limestone piers, walls and fireplaces of Taliesin II had turned red and crumbled in the fire, but I saved many stones not so destroyed, dyed by fire, and built them together with the fragments of great sculpture I had raked from the ashes into the new walls adding a storied richness to them unknown before. Whereas the previous buildings had all grown by addition, all could now be spontaneously born.

So, taught by the building of Taliesin I and II, I made forty sheets of pencil studies for the building of Taliesin III. I was still in debt for the second, but no discretion whatever could detain me now from beginning work on the third. 'Life is like that!'

Waves of publicity, this time neither ribald nor unkind, had broken over the ruins. After all, even newspaper folk are kind when they really understand. The frustration of the life of the seven years past had ended in the destruction of everything the frustrated life had touched. I sought comfort in that thought as one fine thing after another I had loved and learned from would rise out of its ashes and reproach me with a shameful sense of loss.

And now, again, more and better building materials. More and, by this time, better trained workmen. More intelligent planning and execution on my part, more difficulties in ways and means. I myself had more patience, a deeper anxiety. More humility. Yet in the same faith, moving forward.

Taliesin's radiant brow was marked now by both shame and sorrow but it should come forth and shine again with a serenity unknown before. In this third trial, granted by Life itself, new life itself helped build the walls and make them more noble than before. A real comrade.

And after many years of sorrow, trial and defeat, Taliesin III was re-freshed by the gift of a little new soul, long desired to bring back to Taliesin something it had not found, or, finding, had lost.

Taliesin III was built by and for Olgivanna, Iovanna and Svetlana.

No doubt Isaiah still stood there in the storms that muttered, rolled and broke again over low-spreading shelter. The lightning often played and crashed above us. But the happy friendliness sheltered there was ready for any sacrifice if only Taliesin might come to Life and give one more proof of quality.

The Mosaic Isaiah with eyes aslant where the beautiful would show its face or the lovely dare to lift its head with curly locks or black abundant tresses—was waiting there behind the hills to strike, should life at Taliesin rise from its ashes a third time?

If the angry prophet had struck twice he could strike again.

Human obliquity still going on hand in hand with bigger and better publicity conspired with the ruthless prophet, this self-appointed agent of an angry Jehovah, to do 'righteous' work. This time do it not by death and fire but by madness. Taliesin the gentler prophet of the Celts and of a more merciful God was tempted to lift an arm to strike back in self-defence but suffered in silence and waited.

Again a hue and cry of 'punishment' reached the doors of public officials. Some were moved by it. Knowing only the hue and cry they added blows to give richness to the hue, adding injury to the insult of the cry until the sovereign insult in the gift of its own people—those who should have protected it and many of those who would have protected it had 'Isaiah' not blinded them too—was put upon Taliesin. Taliesin raged, wanted to strike back. Again he held his arm. Strike at what?

Like Isaiah—at little children and women, torn in the streets and bleeding?

No. Taliesin instead turned to work, for work is defence even against Isaiah. At least life was no longer to be betrayed *within* sheltering walls, however it might be beset from *without* by any wrathful jealous prophet whatsoever.

And this stand stood there firm while newspapermen, editors, reporters, cameramen, publishers, lawyers, petty officials, federal, state, county, local officials, lawyers in Washington, lawyers in Minneapolis, lawyers in Chicago, lawyers in Milwaukee, lawyers in Madison, lawyers in Baraboo and in Dodgeville and in Spring Green; newspapermen everywhere, judges, commissioners, prosecuting attorneys, process-servers, sheriffs, jailers, justices of the peace, federal immigration officers, police officers, Washington officials, senators and congressmen, governors—has 'Authority' anything else?—did their worst. And that is, their best. All this rolled over Taliesin once more.

Finally it all ended by the interference of my friends and clients to save Taliesin from wreck and myself too for more work there. Work again a saving clause.

Isaiah is the vengeful prophet of an antique wrath. I say Taliesin is a nobler prophet, not afraid of him. The ancient Druid Bard sang and forever sings of merciful beauty. Wherever beauty is, there Taliesin is singing in praise of the flower that fadeth, the grass that withereth. Taliesin still loves and trusts—man. But men not so much too much, now.

And now standing where and how Isaiah, the Jew, may stand in this third and nobler construction in the name of Taliesin—Taliesin the Celt humbly declares not only an architecture on this soil for a conscious United States of America but declares and for the same reason—the right of every aspiring man, so long as the man shall be as honest as he knows how to be with all three, to his own life, his own work, and his own love.

But, to leave the abstract figure I have employed, to be homeless and without work when life and work have become synonymous terms, and be powerless to protect either; to see home and work and loved-ones at the mercy of the exploitation of irresponsible insane fury by bigger and better publicity, is to go to the bottom of the vulgar pit any man may dig for himself by his own acts. Not the least of my trials now was to see the weakness and helpless exaggeration of a hostile woman incited to destroy herself and destroy all that had ever touched her or been touched by her

244

to make holiday copy for those who neither cared for her nor really for anything she cared for—except news.

And 'news' is bad tidings. If the tidings are not bad . . . they must be made bad, or no news.

The trials by heartless, vulgar imposition that followed in the wake of self-inflicted failure are always harder to bear, I believe, than those failures we cannot trace to our own fault. For three years I had self-inflicted failure to bear as open secrets became open sores by way of scandal that finally reached the depths of outrage, humiliation and falsification. But never have I been allowed to bear any failure alone. So I remember and record and leave the rest to life. At least sensational distortion and exaggeration will here meet quiet fact for the first time. And that perhaps is the purpose of this premature autobiography, every word of which is at least true.

With this extraordinary public excitement, a poor sense of the dignity and human-value of our institutions got to Olgivanna, the figure that crept forward out of the shadows cast by the lurid flames that were destroying Taliesin II.

I was ashamed, sorry that she should be compelled to see this obnoxious phase of American life first. I tried to explain all these gratuitous performances of a public character making up this charivari. I said we had been betrayed into seeming disrespect of the established order, and tried to take the blame upon myself as I should. Olgivanna took it all with suffering—but without resentment. And we stood our ground.

Born in Montenegro of people not unlike my own Welsh forebears, her upbringing had much in common with my own. At the age of nine she had gone to her married sister at Batoum in the Caucasus in order to have the advantages of an education in Russia. Her father was Chief Justice of Montenegro for nearly thirty years. During the latter years of his life he was blind. He never saw the little daughter who used to lead him by the hand through the streets of Cettinje. He was still Chief Justice for many years while blind. Her mother was the daughter of 'Vojevoda' Marco— Balkan general to whom popular credit went for preserving Montenegro's independence. For Montenegro, like Wales and the country of the Basques, was a mountainous little country whose people were never conquered.

Olgivanna herself had grown up in a patriarchal family in an official society with a mind and will of her own.

When we first met I considered myself free in the circumstances, as did she. Though she never had met Miriam Noel, she knew as much about the circumstances of my life as I did. We both knew that only the final signature remained to be fixed to the divorce that settled my separation from Miriam Noel, a separation in effect for more than one year before I met Olgivanna. That signature *was* added soon. But these facts were not in the news. The term 'Montenegrin dancer' was invented by the fancy of the more imaginative reporters. They wrote their stories on that, and

245

implied character according to their usual devices with whatever slant seemed to suit the sheet that paid them for their work.

I play the piano, but that doesn't make me a pianist? Olgivanna dances, but only as a feature of the training at the Gurdjeef Institute at Fontainebleau. This institution, too, came in for a measure of low implication in order to complete the picture desired or not as the case might be.

Unexpectedly, thus, came another public charivari to add to two since past.

I managed to get Olgivanna to Hollis, safe with her brother, Vladimir. I like Vladimir, and his wife. Love and protection around her. A great change from the humiliation and misery of the last fortnight. Her people insisted on my coming to stay at Hollis too. I would go back to town with Vladimir in the morning, to roam the streets of New York alone. I didn't care to see anyone at the time for fear of revealing our whereabouts to the newspapers' pursuit of news.

It was then I began to write. I tried to write some inpressions of the big city. 'In Bondage' was one. 'The Usonian City' another; later to begin this work.

But Olgivanna did not improve as rapidly as she should. The weather was cold and disagreeable, the situation too severe. After Christmas at Vlada's I began to wonder where we could go, and hit on Puerto Rico. A long shot. But it would be warm at least. And it was. Puerto Rico was now a possession of the United States of America. We would need no difficult passports. As a matter of fact, anywhere we went in the United States we were likely to splash more muddy water over the public dam represented by the press.

So, incognito, we took the boat for what remained of Atlantis. We put up at a pleasant inn—the Coamo—far down the island. The Coamo had natural hot-sulphur springs piped into enormous old Spanish stone baths in which we could go for a swim. At night we went under mosquito nets, but had to make constant war on the pests. The days and nights were sultry and oppressive until we would drive up into the mountains. The air there was delightful. These old mountain roads of Spanish Puerto Rico are remarkable.

The primavera was in bloom, enormous white tree trunks, white limbs loaded with brilliant scarlet blooms lying in great high drifts, in the beautiful landscape. Roads covered with falling scarlet splendour.

We hung our young daughter, Iovanna, in a basket in front of the tonneau from the cross ribs of the top of the open car. She was comfortable swinging there and explored the island.

We would have our lunch put up at the Coamo and go over the island every day. Slight showers would fall frequently but would soon clear away.

Puerto Rico is beautiful but Puerto Ricans are pitiful. They seem small, fine-featured remains of a highly civilized race. Gentle, apathetic. Poor beyond belief. The 'Americans' had already bought up the sugar-plantations. Most of them were in the hands of capital from the States. Wages

246

were seventy cents a day and no raise in sight. It would affect the price of sugar.

Evidence of poverty spoiled the beautiful place for Olgivanna. She was touched by the sight of so many ill-fed, mournful-eyed children, and frail-looking women with sorrowful faces. And the men were no better.

So poor the Puerto Ricans were! We remember a man coming down, from miles away, to Coamo on a peaked little horse carrying a small chicken covered with a red handkerchief, to sell this one chicken to the hotel. To get a little money. Such sights were everywhere.

So, after two months we said goodbye to the beautiful islands with the romantic history—why not a fragment of Atlantis?—and returned to Washington where the first signs of spring were beginning to appear.

Iovanna had her airing every morning in the sunshine at the foot of the native Capitol. The faithful Alma never left the baby out of her sight, nor did the mother leave either out of her sight.

By this time Olgivanna was a shadow. The kind proprietor of the hotel, solicitous, asked if there was not something especial he might prepare for her. She ate so little.

These peregrinations had to cease. The anxieties were too great. We needed a home.

And so, braving the persecution, we returned to Taliesin to take the consequences. Anything was better and safer than this equivocal, danger-ous migration from place to place.

In this connection, I remember the time when and the circumstances by which I was soon thereafter forced to leave Taliesin because I had legally lost it. The bank, by formal process, asked me to get out. The drain of the two fires and lost collections at Taliesin, the consequent years of forced inaction, wasteful legality, so many lawyers—had left me finally at the mercy of rented money and its machine process. That process is interesting to me because it shows how, when legal machinery goes wrong, it is like other machinery no better or worse than the intelligence that drives it. It is like any other cherished man-toy—strapped to the animals on the farm.

Some time before that finality came, I had against my will taken my lawyer's advice to take Olgivanna and Iovanna and Svetlana from Taliesin and go away again—this time to entirely lose ourselves for three months at least, and leave him, the lawyer, to work out the situation now so complicated through the advantages taken, on every side—of my own indiscretion.

'Go away,' said Levi Bancroft, 'and I'll have your situation straightened out in three months. Publicity will then quiet down. There will be no further excuse for such performances as are being staged by Miriam Noel and the sensational press.

'So long as there is any chance she will perform for them and you will be good for headlines and "stories". They may get the authorities stirred up,' said Levi. 'The minor official of our country is owned by the newspapers

247

because he gets or loses his office pretty much as they are with him or against him; more often he gets it that way than any other. Newspapers, to get a story, will put officials in some position or other where they will have to act to arrest you. And Olgivanna, too.

'Think it over,' said Levi.

He went on: 'They are working on the cupidity and weakness of an irresponsible woman with nothing to lose except her insane appetite for publicity and fancied revenge. They will stop at nothing. She can't. There is nothing there to stop with.

'She overturned her arrangements with you after she had agreed to them and signed them because they made her see she had a good chance to put you where you would have to give her everything you had left in the world.

'And now if you don't give it to her she thinks, and probably is so advised by her lawyers, that she can take it away. It isn't and won't be their fault if you have a cent to your name or any place to lay your head.'

I listened, knowing it all to be too true. I had seen something of publicity years ago. Taliesin, 1911. I had seen the shameless manner in which Miriam Noel had been exploited by her lawyers and the press and I had every reason to believe such exploitation would continue.

When I walked out of the Dane County Court rather than blacken the character of two women—I had found there that I would have to do this in order to get a divorce—I left this woman who was posing as the 'outraged wife' free to attach and confiscate by way of contingent-fee lawyers everything I owned. I now owed the Bank of Wisconsin a round sum of forty-three thousand dollars—owing to the building of Taliesin III, the loss a second time of the collections I had made in China and Japan, and the plans upset in work by previous and present storms of publicity which prevented me from earning anything.

In the circumstances Judge Hill and Levi Bancroft, both were my lawyers now, said, 'Go to the bank. The president—Hopkins—is your friend. He will be glad to help you in order to protect himself.

'For a loan give the bank a blanket mortgage on everything you have. Don't leave out anything. Cover your plans, collections, drawing instruments, your tools in the studio and on the farm. Write it all in. Do this until we can get time to turn around against this enterprise.'

'A man who has a lawyer but takes his own advice has a fool for a client.' Judge Evan Evans handed that to me.

Jim, and they don't make them any better than Judge Jim Hill, took me to the bank and explained the situation.

'All right,' said the bank, 'we'll help.'

Jim had to catch his train and left me alone in the president's office at the Bank of Wisconsin.

I waited an hour at the bank for elaborate papers to be drawn up by the bank's attorney. 'Here,' said the bank, 'sign here.' I did. A check for fifteen hundred dollars was handed to me, and I had nothing else in the world except by sufferance, or on honour of this bank.

This was now the situation at Taliesin.

Levi touched upon that too. 'The bank will look after things for you while you are gone.

'Everything is in their hands and they'll do that to protect themselves.'

'But I have a feeling, Levi, that if I turn my back on this fight and hide or run away as you suggest, I'll lose what I have been fighting for. It isn't my conviction nor my style. I don't know how to carry on along those lines. I already regret what I did with the bank.'

I pleaded: 'Why not let me stand up to this business and fight it out? Use me. I am all right—ethically if not morally—much as it may look the other way. You know it. Now why not allow me the courage of my convictions—and to stand by?'

Said Levi, 'You forget, Frank. There is your child. There is where they have you. And Olgivanna can't stand any more of this. She is under a terrible strain.'

'I know,' I said, 'But so long as we are all together, that can't matter so much as it would if we were separated.'

'Well,' impatiently, 'you'll all be together—the way I suggest. Think it over.'

I did. And I refused.

But Levi wouldn't give up. Olgivanna herself thought it wise to go. And by appeals on behalf of Olgivanna and the child—Levi won his point. One had to respect his forceful sincerity. As a lawyer, he was right enough. And his uprightness has never been questioned.

My little family and I were to set out in the Cadillac for somewhere. Why not go to Minneapolis? Minnetonka was beautiful. The Thayers were there. It was September. That was not what Levi wanted. He was thinking of Canada, I guess. But I knew if Olgivanna left the country in the circumstances I would have a hard time ever getting her back again.

I wasn't going that far. Together we might stand—divided we would surely fall.

So we drove up the Mississippi along the river and over it at La Crosse into Minneapolis.

We didn't know at the time that we had by doing so given the Federals a chance to declare a federal crime. Had we known enough to get out and walk across the line we should have committed no crime. That is the way laws work.

We found a charming cottage at Minnetonka owned by a Mrs. Simpson. I persuaded her that she needed a vacation and she let us take the house as it stood and for three months—the time Levi had specified. She let her accounts stand as they were in her name. We to be her guests in her absence.

We were to be the Richardsons or something. We kept forgetting to remember who we were.

We stowed the Cadillac with the Victoria top away in the Simpson garage and took to Cleaver's sailboat on the lake and went walking in the

249

countryside. We were now in hiding. It was for the first time in my life. The Thayers were in on the secret. And soon their friends, the Devines.

I had already begun this book at Olgivanna's earnest solicitation and was working away on the first two portions in Mrs. Simpson's cottage with Maude Devine coming in afternoons to do the typing.

Well, we learned from the newspapers before long that we were 'fugitives from justice'. A nice legal phrase for reporters, with possible sensational consequences.

The father of Svetlana, it seems, from whom Olgivanna had been divorced, now making common cause with the lawyer of the persecution —was taken to Taliesin a few days after we had left. Finding us gone and Svetlana, too, he was taken by the mutual lawyer to the county seat of Baraboo to swear out a warrant of arrest for the 'abduction' of his nine-year-old daughter. The devices of the law are devious resources but they are more useful to the unscrupulous than they are to the conscientious. Not for nothing are lawyers inventive. But we knew no better than to keep on hiding. So we were cautious, and really believed we were incognito. It was hard to take any of the business as more than hocus-pocus, knowing what was at the bottom of it all and back of it all, too. So we went on living and I kept on working at this book. My son John came down to get instructions about clearing up certain details of work at Taliesin. And we settled down. To what? We didn't know.

You see.
I had made a fatal error.
Flight had given colour to the low accusations.
And had given courage, too, to the insane persecution.
The implications that were fed to the public by the press gained life-like colour by this disappearance.

Six weeks went by. The lawyer son of Mrs. Simpson came down from Minneapolis on some pretext or other. To look for his fishing tackle? In his mother's attic he said it was. I saw him sizing us up intently—but dismissed him from my mind. Olgivanna saw him too and worried. 'Never mind,' I said, 'He is his mother's son. She is a lady.'

We had just dined. The baby had been put to bed. Svetlana was asleep in her bed on the porch. Maude Devine was typing away at the book. Fire burned in the grate. All was warm and cosy on a late September evening. About half-past nine o'clock came a rude knock on the door of the living room toward the street. I went to the door and opened it. A dozen or more rough-looking characters—led by Miriam Noel's lawyer—now mutual with Svetlana's father—and accompanied by members of the press, several of whom I had seen somewhere before. They shouldered their way into the room and surrounded us.

'You are all under arrest,' said the heavy-handed one, the bigger sheriff. There were three of them, each of a different size and type.

Olgivanna shows her quality in any emergency.

250

She got up and asked them to kindly step out into the next room. I opened the glass door and they all did exactly as they were bid—a little ashamed. They could still watch through the glass door, however, and so were content to stay.

They recovered after finding themselves there, and the heavy-faced lawyer employed by Miriam Noel said loudly with a swagger, 'Well, here they are . . . at last. Now, where's the kid?'

He opened the door to the bedroom and went in. I went in after him and saw him jerk the blanket from the sleeping infant. He laughed 'Yeah! here it is!'

The sheriffs each took an arm, all I had, and said, 'No violence. Take it easy. Take it easy.'

To the sheriffs' credit be it said, they moved that plug-ugly out.

Now Olgivanna opened the door and came in. 'Don't, we must make the best of it, Frank.' And I saw that I was only making scene for copy. The usual circus.

'Please take it quietly,' she said.

I did.

Of course it was a newspaper frame-up with the 'lawyers'. A reward had been offered and the 'mother's son' found his information profitable. Cameras had already been set up around the house to illustrate the story as we came out of the door.

The horror of such impotence as mine! I pleaded with the valiant sheriff to take me and leave the mother and children where they were with a guard over them until morning. The trap had been sprung late on purpose—after ten o'clock—and after having pretended to call up his superior at Minneapolis (it would have spoiled the story to leave them behind that way) he came back to say that it was impossible to get him.

But he agreed now to leave my little family in custody where they were. And I went out in the face of puffing flashlights, got into his car and was driven down to the sheriff at the country jail in Minneapolis. His name was Brown.

Brown was a man of some parts in the Hennepin County community. A sheriff, but serving as a patriot without pay to clean up the Baptist belt and make it moral or something. A reporter volunteered the information that he had got himself into the newspapers a few days before, handcuffed to two thugs—to show 'the people' how serviceable a sheriff they had.

He knew of us only as he had read newspaper reports of the case and scented more publicity.

Well—I argued with the great Brown and I pleaded in vain. At length and with reason I pleaded with this sacrificial honour-man to leave the nursing mother and the two children at the cottage until morning . . . I would go to jail willingly if he would be considerate of them.

'I give you my word, Mr. Wright, I couldn't do that. No. Not even for my own brother. No. I am an officer sworn in to uphold the law.'

251

There was a cast-iron sense of duty for you. They had said of him that he would accept no salary either.

'Not for your own mother either, I suppose,' I said . . . again at wit's end. 'Well . . . then, will you let me call my little family and tell them what to expect, and what to do in the circumstances. I want to call them long distance,' I said.

'No need,' he said, 'they are here. And in any case you are not allowed outside communication. You are under arrest.' Ignoring the sheriff's promise, they had been brought along to jail in the car following the one that brought me.

And the crowd was busy now doing their daily stuff. In the next room they were word-painting the noble 'volunteer' sheriff as a hero. This was his reward for playing up to their game, I suppose. I hope.

Coming to me now was the sovereign insult a free country has to offer one of her own sons.

If only I were alone! Olgivanna!—The two children!

But my sin had been done two by two. And that can never be paid for one by one, even in a free country such as ours. Not while sheriffs volunteer anyway.

So I went up in the elevator with my distinguished republican jailer, the impeccable Brown. And Brown turned me in.

'They' searched me. Took away my money all but the small change: entered my family pedigree in the jail record of Hennepin County. And with businesslike hospitality, representing Minneapolis whose dishonoured guests now I was, Brown, getting a little dubious by now I thought, said 'Good night'.

A warden took me down a long corridor along brutal heavy animal cages built tier on tier within a great empty space arched over by a high trussed roof. The clang of the gates he opened and shut as he went echoed and reverberated behind us in space. He clanged our way to the far end where the 'better element' of jaildom, the high-swindlers and bootleggers were kept. All was quiet. They were asleep. He opened the little door of a cell a little longer than I am tall, a little narrower than I am long, a soiled mattress on one side and a dirty water closet at one end: the government allotment of squalor for manhood on such terms as had fallen to my lot.

I went in.

The warden said 'Good night'.

My country! To one of your own free sons this 'Good night'?

The ponderous door of the animal cage slammed shut and automatically shot its heavy bolt. My sensation was one of suffocation.

But I reached up and took hard hold of the cold iron bars to keep my mind clear and tried to hold on to my sense of humour. It was all that could save me now.

Then I turned and used up the three steps in one direction—there the filthy water closet. Nausea. Again dreadful suffocation.

252

Scarcely able to breathe, I sat down on the mattress. Saw it stained. Was it blood? Whose and how?

I looked above. The polished steel ceiling. I could reach up and touch it.

Where was Olgivanna? Where were the children? I had begged for information but prisoners are not allowed to communicate although convicted of nothing.

'Let me send a note to their mother?'

Said Brown, 'No, it's against the rules.'

This was the machine-made Brown. Brown the volunteer driver—by rote and routine or . . . wreck of this machine. A jail.

Intelligence? All on the outside.

Humanity? Outside.

Life, love, work, honour? Outside.

Cut down? Cut off!

Dung and dishonour!

Man's cruelty to man!

The blackest mark in human life is man's deep distrust of his fellow man! The deepest chasm dug by himself across the course of his own future.

I say every citizen, good or bad, as a feature of his education should be condemned to spend two nights in one of his own jails.

Let the good, the obedient, the wary-wise sense the endless repeat of the monotonous 'forever' they call a jail and keep to defend their own goodness, their obedience, and their wisdom.

Impotent, I cursed.

Again to my feet to measure my length against the bars; head far back and I could breathe.

Footsteps along the corridor.

The warden-watch was reaching the end of his beat—outside my cell.

He glanced in. He was just in time. I found myself. And I found 'they' had overlooked a piece of paper in my pocket. Strangely, a broken stump of pencil, overlooked, lay on the mattress. I said, 'Wait a second?' I scribbled a note.

'Take this to her. They brought her in here with me. Will you?' And wrapping a fifty-cent piece in the paper, poked it through the bars to him. He put his finger to his lips, nodded his head as he pushed back the fifty-cent piece and took the note. He went away.

Next time around.

'Did she get it?'

'Sure,' he said, 'She's all right. The Missus is looking after her and the kids.'

This fellow's sense of duty was remiss. He broke the devil's rules in hell.

And a little light came through. I could breathe now. It would be morning sometime. It always was. My sense of humour was on its way back. What remained of the night I sat up on the one clean corner of the mattress or pacing the few steps to and fro—to rest—paced in my stocking feet so as not to wake the good neighbours.

At daylight a distant clanging. It came toward me with an increasing roar until the tumult seemed to rock the very jail and it must fall of its own insane weight. The door to the cell suddenly flew open with a reverberating clang following all the others by electrical release. The tumult died in echoes.

The narrow paved passage connecting my cage with the other cages was there in front. I could now go out into that. A tin cup of Brown's chicory appeared at a little door set in the bars—a piece of Brown's bread beside it. I tasted his liquid and swallowed a bit of his bread. Without choking.

After a while my next door comrade came to say Hello. He had the morning paper. It gets to the cells too.

There were our pictures.

'Say,' he said, 'you got a swell girl. She sure stands by you.'

'Yes, she sure does.'

'Well,' he said, 'it's something not to be in here for nothing. You got something to tie to.'

'Trouble is she's tied up here too.'

'Aw, they won't do nothing to her though. They'll let 'em go all right.'

'Will they?' I said. 'I wonder why? The sheriff said he couldn't do anything for his own mother in the circumstances.'

'Yeah!'

'What are you in here for?' I asked.

'Me? Sellin' a little likker. Second time. Say, I got a swell girl myself,' he went on. 'Do you know what she done?'

'No, what?'

'You see that place out there where visitors come to see us fellows?'

I looked and saw a broad space with a shower on one side where an inmate might go, stand up and converse through a screen wire with someone standing in the outer space. You could have pushed a pencil through the screen but that is about as big as anything that would go through.

'You see, she hears that I'm in, from the papers. She comes up out there and they calls me. Then I goes out to see her. She watches the warden go away. "Stand up close, Jimmy," she says. I stands up close. Say! She unbuttons the bosom of her dress and what do you think she's got in there between 'em? Guess?'

'I couldn't.'

'A quart, by God! A quart!

'The warden goes by and she waits. Then she slips me three straws out of her pocket. "Go to it, Jimmy," she says, "go to it. It'll do you good, besides helpin' you." And I slips them straws into the stuff and I takes it all. Say! Can you beat that?'

'No,' I said, 'I don't believe anybody could beat that.'

254

I stepped out into the gangway to walk a little way but ran into another prisoner. There was room for only one in the width of the avenue.

'Hello,' said this one. 'You look funny in here.'

'Yes, I feel funny,' I said.

'I read the papers about you and her this morning. Say I had a bigger spread than that when they got me in here.' He pulled out a greasy old clipping and proudly showed it to me.

'I'm in for the bogus bail racket. Trial coming up soon, see. But, I've got a good lawyer. Nash! The best in the state. He'll see me through, all right.'

'Nash is his name?'

'Nash,' he said.

'How can I see him? They won't let me call anyone.'

'I'm going out to see him today and I'll tell him to come in and call you out to see him.'

That is how I got another lawyer to add to the collection.

Nash was a good lawyer, too.

He soon found out I was in jail for no reason that anybody knew except a telegram from some bailiff in Sauk County, Wisconsin; that a warrant had been sworn out for my arrest there. This telegram had reached Brown. Confirmation was lacking. Who sent it? We were all in jail on suspicion, so far as the beneficent Brown was concerned. Not so the newspapers. I was taken out by Brown to be interviewed by them that morning. And we were eventually formally released in another public court scene when the authorities at Baraboo, Wisconsin, appealed to to go ahead, refused to prosecute.

The case, such as it was and whatever it was, was dropped. The thing had been set for late enough at night so that no correction or relief was possible without going to jail, for copy. Such is the ingenuity of lawyers with reporters.

The law in the hands of any professional blackmailer is a mean instrument of revenge with many angles, all fertile 'points'. We were not yet free to go. No, not yet. The Federal authorities had meanwhile been seen. We were to be held there in jail pending appearance before an arm-chair Federal, famous in the Northern Baptist-Belt for 'moral' tendencies. He had grown to the chair with comparative affluence. I forget his name.

We now went before this august limb of the Federal law on the charge of having violated that malign instrument of revenge diverted from its original purpose to serve just such purposes as this for many years past: the Mann Act. Mr. Mann and his wife used to sit across the aisle from me at my uncle's church, All Souls. His law was dead letter so far as public sentiment went. But a law for ulterior purposes just the same. Instead of walking, we had ridden across the State-line.

So, accompanied by the press-gallery and cameras, we went through the streets to the Federal hearing together with the American public invited by the announcement in the enterprising press. I had successfully shielded my little family from both press and camera until this episode. For twelve months I had beaten the reporters at their own game at every

255

turn, although my little daughter had to go out of the Union Station three days old at her mother's breast to get away from them. I had saved Olgivanna from a single interview. Now it all ended in this triumph for them, hoi-polloi, rag, tag, and bobtail.

Bail was fixed in the sum of fifteen thousand dollars for us both. A separate count was lodged against each by Lafayette French, a resourceful, politically ambitious young prosecuting attorney with a flair for salacious detail, as appeared at the investigation.

Bigger and Better publicity the objective.

But our case now seemed serious. Far too serious for our friends, and they began to protest publicly. It seemed serious enough to us all by this time. Nothing could keep my sister Jane from rushing down from Philadelphia to Minneapolis to reassure herself concerning us. And Maginel called attorney Nash from New York for such reassurance as he could give her. We were released on bail after this second public appearance—the public again invited—after another night in jail for us all on account of this new ruse.

This second night in Hennepin County Jail was not so bad as the first. I had not been allowed to see Olgivanna except in court. The children not at all. But I now knew from her that they were well, and Olgivanna, though ready to drop, was facing it all like the thoroughbred she is. Tomorrow we would all be together again. Meantime after the new 'case' was lodged and before my new attorney, Nash, could get to Olgivanna, a Federal officer had insinuated himself to get her story. She had no more sense of wrongdoing than I had, and told him everything. Puerto Rico included. All of which he duly recorded—with the matron's kind assistance to supply missing details. No detail was omitted, questions asked in terms Olgivanna did not at all understand. The Federal game seems to be a game of points—or at simplest a game of hide and seek.

Thus the confession was complete. We were now involved with Immigration Acts.

Nash raged against the exploit of the Federal. But that was that. The Federals, too, are resourceful. I guess they have to be to get enough points to live on.

Our Puerto Rico sojourn for two months after the birth of Iovanna, to try and get peace and restore Olgivanna's health, it seems could be made into another violation of the complex immigration-law, because Puerto Rico was the United States but was so without grace of legal technicality as such. It was still a foreign country. So, by the moral virtue of technicality, 'they' said we had 'entered the country for immoral purposes'. And so the Federals could do with us as they pleased. We had made it all as simple for them as that. The law is an implement only. Technique is the lawyers.

Going back to jail I found Brown had sent in a clean mattress. The water closet was cleaned. I lay on the clean mattress that second night getting the sense of jail prisoners had told me they got—a sense of pro-

256

tection. At least nothing can happen to you in jail. And, after the evening feeding of the animals through the trap-doors in the bars, some of them in the upper animal cages begin to sing—one or two taking turns leading —fine manly baritone voices. Other caged animals picked up the familiar songs and joined in. It was tremendous. They sang familiar song after song. Some popular, some were religious. Were there hundreds of the sinners singing? Reverberations, I suppose. Twenty-five or thirty, maybe more at times. And they kept singing up to nine o'clock. Everyone then must be silent. A splendid sense of unity in their misery.

They made me feel ashamed of my shame because, after all, I was there for a passing moment while they were there for years, maybe for life.

The little chap, second cage over, in for bogus bailing, had gone out to his trial this day. Late I heard him come in. He was whistling a popular tune softly. I rapped a little on the bars to let him know I wasn't asleep.

'How now?' I whispered.

'Twenty years,' he hissed back and went on whistling. Soon he was asleep. I heard him snore. Callous? Or was this fortitude?

Next morning I saw him in the corridor.

'Nash will get it cut,' he said.

He gave me the details of his game. These illegal details were as complicated as the legal details to which we were subjected, and almost as ingenious. A crook has technique too. This fellow had professional pride in a scientific piece of work. Initial direction gone wrong, that's all, gone wrong for such curious, haphazard reasons. He had turned left instead of right.

After Court opening at ten o'clock, my turn came to go up and be dismissed. I asked Brown for permission to set up porkchops and mashed potatoes to the singers of the night before and all their listeners.

'Sorry,' said Brown, 'against the rules.'

The boys themselves bade me good luck. Their jailers all shook hands with me warmly, they had done their best for me. Even so had Brown. But a man no bigger than his job has no right to have a job where humanities are concerned even though he makes himself a gift to the job.

A few days afterward I was sitting in Cleaver Thayer's car near the railway station waiting for Cleaver. A Ford suddenly stopped by the curb opposite.

A man got out, grinning, rushed across the street holding out his hand to me: 'Hello, Mr. Wright, Hello! Say—my wife is in the car over there. And I want her to meet you. Can I bring her over?'

It took a second or two to recognize the warden. His uniform changed him—or was it the other way round?

'No,' I said. 'Let her stay where she is. I'll come over with you to meet her.'

She was pleased to meet me. He had a nice girl, too.

But after it all was over it took some time longer to get permission to leave the State. Some other kink in the endless coil of law in which we were now entangled. I forgot what kink or what coil of what law but the State was Minnesota.

The Thayers and Devines had been most kind. Cleaver put me up at his club. Both families were at the jail early to see Olgivanna and took the children for an airing. I don't know how they ever got them out. Brown must have been having his photograph taken. Cleaver was fine all the time. He coined a phrase that pleased him enormously. 'From Who's Who to the Hoosegow.'

His father signed our bail bond and another flood of publicity had gone over the dam.

While marking time in Minneapolis awaiting the swell young Prosecuting Attorney's permission to leave the State a demand came from the bank to 'pay up'.

A little surprised I wrote the bank reminding them of the circumstances of their mortgage. No reply to this. The circumstances were unfit for record or publication, so it seems. Only another technicality out of line with other technicalities, that's all. The classification is minute and the differentiation arbitrary but the consequences are often amazing. Maybe my situation, in view of this Federal action, looked bad to the bank. The bank soon threatened foreclosure and insisted upon the immediate sale of the print collection I had placed in New York in Mitchell Kennerly's hands to be, sometime, sold! It was a bad time to sell. But the bank insisted on sale. The block of rare prints was therefore disastrously sold for $42,000. And Kennerly took a 'commission' of nearly thirty-five per cent, which didn't help very much. I had understood it would be only fifteen at most. When you fall into the rut I was now in you went down the line while you lasted or there was anything on you to get.

During the months that followed the Minneapolis debacle in the northern 'Baptist Belt', we were in New York. My sister Maginel took us in. We had some respite because my little sister and her home are charming. She did everything in her power—and she is resourceful—to mitigate the desperation of our circumstances. And we were together—to fight it all. But the resources of the ultra-legal publicity persecution were by no means exhausted. A deportation story got into the papers. And 'they' were now after Olgivanna. She was formally arrested by immigration officials at the door to my sister's home and I gave a Liberty Bond—the last one— to be posted for bail.

This latest aggression added to our other woes was a cup too full. My sense of humour began to fade. The immigration service is notoriously cruel, almost never kind. It too is a merciless machine with minor officials for cogs.

So is a bank a machine. The bank, now stirred again to action by all this impending disaster, pressed harder and harder for money. I had nothing to give the bank because everything I had was in its hands. The bankers knew this. Under pressure of these desperate circumstances I conceived the idea of incorporating myself—selling myself to such friends and clients as would 'buy me' in order to raise the money to rid Taliesin and such collections as remained in the bank of the claims of the pressing bank itself. This would allow me to go to work again unmolested. The proceeds of the work would then be safe from suits that were sure to be brought by the 'persecution' were I able to earn anything at all.

With this scheme in mind, soon subscribed to by the bank itself, we returned to Taliesin. But owing to that blanket mortgage we were liable to eviction at the bank's pleasure unless we completely paid up.

Now began the incorporating of what looked like a lost cause.

Darwin D. Martin liked the idea. He subscribed and his lawyer drew up the first papers. I took them to others. My client, Mrs. Avery Coonley, subscribed. My best friend, Dr. Ferdinand Schevill, Joe Urban and my sister Jane, too, among a number of others who could ill afford to subscribe. Finally I had seventy-five thousand dollars subscribed. Alexander Woollcott helped at this crucial time in more ways than one. Charlie McArthur did what he could—to keep a smile on my face. Phil La Follette now stepped in, sympathetic.

'Frank, you have had bad legal advice.'

'I have, Phil. And I have taken it far worse than the advice itself. Suppose you help?'

'All right,' he said, 'but not to take the case directly. Leave Jim (Judge Hill) where he is. And I'll do what I can from the side lines.'

He went to see Ferdinand Schevill and Mr. Martin to see if they would stand by me. Their response was satisfactory. Things had quieted down. The figure-head of all the persecution, the outraged wife, was now in Hollywood without funds. Her lawyers were without funds, so the press was suffering time-lag. The story was dragging for them. Something had to be done.

The corporation if now executed as originally designed would keep them all outside funds entirely and no news either until prepared to treat fairly and reasonably in the circumstances. A drive along this line would have been effective. The various creditors pressing for settlement were proposing fair terms.

But Phil reversed the plan for procedure. He began negotiating for divorce. To get this we must go into court with 'clean hands' as the choice phrase runs in legal circles. To do this he advocated the voluntary deportation of Olgivanna. And eventually handed a thousand dollars of corporation money to me for the purpose.

Phil took Levi's ground: 'District Attorney Knudson (of our home county) could not stand against popular prejudice moved by the press.' Phil said he knew district attorneys. But attorneys do not seem to know each other very well. They too frequently surprise each other.

'But,' I said, 'he has stood up pretty straight for what he sees as right. I don't believe they can stampede him. Let me go to see him myself.'

'Keep away from him,' said Phil. 'You will only compromise him and tie his hands if you go near him.'

This looked reasonable to me.

'Frank, there is only one way. Send Olgivanna and the children away for a year, or with her defective passport the government is going to send her anyway. There is no way that feature of your case can be fixed up. Go to work and make some money meantime. Then you can go over like a man and get them back. A year after you get your divorce you can live a regular life.'

'How long to get the divorce on your revised plan?' I asked.

'Don't know. Say six months.'

'A year and six months for Olgivanna and the children with no home at all? And little if any money? No, Phil,' I said. 'Your plan is no good.'

But again Phil and his partner Rogers put me into the sweat box.

'You are unfair to Olgivanna because they'll arrest you both, sure. And then what? One of the provincial juries around here? What chance would you have?'

Said Phil, 'You're thinking more of yourself than of the woman, Frank. You might stand this but she can't. You are vain and selfish in all this. Take care of her now as you should have done so long ago. Send her away. Your courage is commendable but your cause is illegal!'

This high moral tone offended me.

Phil did not seem to me like his father's son.

I said, 'You may be "legal", Phil, but you're neither human nor radical. Your idea of "taking care" of Olgivanna would put an end to her and Iovanna. Yes, of course I am selfish. I started all this apparently in selfishness. I might as well end it that way. I'll take my chances standing together where we are, at my own home. We'll fight this thing out—and we will have to take what comes.'

More pressure. My legal advisers brought in friends who were contributing money to untangle our affairs and give us protection. The advice I was now getting was really their contribution, too. This was cited. Well, I gave in—took the money and the embarrassed parent went home to his little family to break the news.

'Get ready, Olgivanna,' I said. 'We're going straight to Washington.'

I thought I'd try my own hand as a last chance on the way to New York. And so I took Olgivanna to Washington headquarters. Laid the cards all on the table—told the unvarnished truth of the case as it stood, supported by the affidavits from Judge Hill and Svetlana's father which I already had.

Of course Olgivanna, by all moral standards, was my wife: the mother of a desired child born in our own country. Her daughter, Svetlana, was the child of a naturalized father. We had all been legally tangled up in a coil of legal rope—legally trapped for a 'story'. The truth was continually ignored in order that we might continually be exploited for more story. The law was also being used merely as a cat's paw to pull chestnuts out of the fire for an irresponsible woman urged to unseemliness and indiscretion by a free-for-all press—not an unfamiliar form of persecution to the department at Washington it seemed when I listened to them.

Well, Superior officialdom is not minor officialism. At last I had reached intelligent responsibility.

'Could we have a respite to straighten out?'

'How long?'

'Six months.'

We could.

I wired Phil no need to carry out the plan.

We were coming home.

Indignant letter came from him. I had broken an agreement made with him. 'On no account come back to Taliesin.'

But we came. There was nowhere else to go and no money to go there with if there was. 'Clean hands' or no 'clean hands'.

Without funds, her attorneys now pressing for settlement and already confiscating her many 'things', Miriam Noel came into court for separate maintenance and eventually sold the divorce she had already agreed to and signed two years and some months previously for exactly the same price she had agreed to then but plus the ruination she had planned and wrought by the false and sentimental appeal of 'outraged wife'.

But that Wisconsin divorce, desirable as it seemed, was a divorce with a curse on it. Wisconsin law forbade re-marriage within one year after divorce, though divorce was—in the language of the judge—'absolute'.

I had thought this divorce was to end our trials. I had heard the word 'absolute' from Judge Hoffman's own lips.

But it seems the curtain had only been rung up by divorce. Legality now wiped out personality, character, courage, common sense. We were playing a legal game of tag—of legal hide and legal seek. If I was caught in any 'immoral situation'—in other words with my own little family— during the year to follow, the 'absolute' divorce was null and void. Phil so informed me.

Lawyers know only the legal aspects of cases. It is for that they are lawyers.

Clarence Darrow had given me some good advice—long before. He said, 'Your case is not a legal case, Frank. What you need is the advice of some wise man of the world who will be your friend and who will see you through. Keep away from lawyers.'

No doubt Phil was all right and his advice was sound as life ran popularly or regularly. But as Clarence said, the case never was a legal one, except in certain superficial aspects of the whole matter.

Well . . . no sooner was the money divorce-settlement paid over to her than the 'outraged wife' and a group of reporters were besieging the truly upright and independent young District Attorney of our county. The 'case' so far as the press was concerned was still more game now. There was more cheap drama. Scene after scene. Staged by the resourceful as news.

The 'outraged wife' was still played to the absurd limit by them all. She snatched a revolver from the district attorney's desk and telling the reporters to 'come on' started for Taliesin.

Divorce 'absolute'!

We were at Taliesin standing our ground and at the same time trying to work. Several projects were at hand.

But the course of the corporation had changed. This was not what the subscribers had anticipated. The bank was not satisfied. My clients were not satisfied. If my friends could pay $75,000 to end a clear case of persecution with no better effect than was now visible, they could be made to pay up all down the line . . . legality was a success. It has many diverse legal forms.

If only they would go after me hard enough now why should anybody wait any longer for their money? And the bank itself refused to stand by its subscription to the corporation. Several other subscribers, none too warm, learning this, and that my sole property consisted in a divorce that left me more than ever at the mercy of unscrupulous exploitation—cancelled their subscriptions too.

What corporate money had been paid in had gone to Miriam Noel and her lawyers.

So the creditors stiffened up. I was powerless. The situation by now was out of hand so far as the man in it was concerned. He was written off and the case was no longer a matter of live and let live, but a mare's nest of legal quibbles that each and every one involved and demoralized life, and added costs to more costs.

One afternoon during our absence, the bank president came up to Taliesin and hired our help to remain there in the bank's employ. They were all told we were going away. I learned this from a faithful young apprentice in the studio, John Davis, who had heard it from some of the help and thought I ought to know it myself.

But next day, by way of the bank, we received a long legal notice from Judge Hoffman's court in Madison to the effect that the premises were being used for immoral purposes—the mortgage was outraged. And the mortgagee objecting, we were asked to leave.

I called Phil at once.

No surprise to him. 'Well?' he said, 'I don't see what *we* can do about it.'

'Do you mean to say I shall have to take this, too, lying down?'

'I don't see what we can do about it, Frank!'

So we got to Chicago to see what *I* could do.

Nothing.

We went adrift.

The day before I had received a telegram from Albert McArthur: 'Can you come out to Phoenix?' It seemed providential. You see, the corporation was an unfinished fragment—helpless now, in these or any other circumstances.

262

We had the coveted divorce but not clean hands. And so we were homeless and about penniless. We got to Arizona. I went to work with Albert
on the new Arizona Biltmore Hotel. The bank entered into legal possession of Taliesin as a whip to enforce collection of the sum due them, now
augmented by attorney's fees, court proceedings, foreclosure suits, interest
on interest. Interest on a $25,000.00 mortgage given them as general
security for current loans and held by them seven years was charged into
the sums due, when judgement was entered. Forty-three thousand dollars
had become fifty-seven or eight thousand.

Yes. Legality was supreme!

Strange how legally right any man may be and how utterly wrong and
outside all decency and equity! Legal might now makes right.

What went on thereafter was in my client Darwin D. Martin's hands.
Phil La Follette worked with the bank, at Mr. Martin's request, to effect
a fair settlement. Law and Money now at deadlock. Meantime to whip
my friends into line over my shoulders, the bank went through the business of auctioning Taliesin equipment, furnishings, and collections. The
bank had thrown Taliesin into the street. Whereupon many saw it who
otherwise would never have seen it. But the bank changed its mind when
a few bids came in.

Then Money tried to sell the whole place, whole.

No one wanted to buy it. For several reasons. Some of them humane as
I afterward learned.

Finally in September a compromise was effected and a telegram from
Mr. and Mrs. Martin reached us at La Jolla—'Taliesin open for your
return'. After all the harrowing circumstances of nearly four years past,
words that set us all madly rejoicing. The same real friend and client,
Darwin D. Martin for whom I had been building a summer home on
Lake Erie when we agreed to leave for parts unknown. I had sent John
to Mr. Martin to finish up the work. 'No,' said Mr. Martin, 'there can be
no substitute for Frank Lloyd Wright. We will wait till he is out of his
troubles.'

I could help him now, a little. The bank accepted substantially what had
been offered and due in settlement before I had been forced to leave
Taliesin and the legal machinery had begun to pile up waste costs in
ruinous legalities.

The bank vacated the premises which it had used during the summer as
a rendezvous as it pleased, to the detriment of the place. But we were now
free to return. That was the main thing. A settlement, too, had been
meantime made with the creditors. Darwin D. Martin and Ferdinand
Schevill were the substantial means by which this settlement was finally
effected.

Many stories of this incorporation of myself now appeared. An idea
gained credence that my financial troubles were over. That I could now
work with no financial harassments or restrictions. The reports had me

263

taken over and managed by Capital so that my usefulness might be indefinitely extended. Later the original corporation was somewhat extended by Harold McCormick and Mr. George Parker. And Charlie Morgan came forward as a volunteer, and interested a few others. But I wouldn't have liked the sound of this immunity on such terms if it were true.

As a matter of fact a few staunch friends, Mr. Martin at their head, had invested what money they could, and some of them at a sacrifice to themselves, to save me for any future usefulness at Taliesin, merely using 'incorporation' as a legitimate means to secure their loans by owning Taliesin and my earning-capacity. They owned all the corporation's preferred stock. I owned the common stock which could have no value until the preferred stock was paid up.

The corporation paid up, non-assessable, had no capital whatever, nor any means of getting any, except as my earning-capacity could produce it. And unless I could carry on from this point of incorporation there was no point whatever in incorporation. I and mine would starve, and the stockholders of course would lose their money.

Now appeared a singular reaction. I could get no life insurance anywhere. Sound and acceptable in every physical requirement, but—'too much publicity'.

But before the final return to Taliesin was effected, one more act in the cheap drama of 'legality'—divertissement. We were discovered by the persecution in our little cottage on the beach at La Jolla. In our absence the 'outraged wife' from whom I had had 'absolute' divorce for nearly a year, invaded the premises. Smashed up the interior. Appropriated what she liked.

She then went into court at San Diego in the practiced rôle of 'outraged wife', 'absolute' divorce notwithstanding, and swore out a warrant for 'immorality' on the part of 'her husband'.

Another story went broadcast. And by the present arrangement of 'absolute' divorce I was legally financing these various legal strangleholds, public entertainments and other insane private aggressions to entertain readers of the daily newspapers.

Instead of allowing me to use my reputation as an architect myself, in order to earn a living, publishers were capitalizing it in headlines for news to profit themselves.

The fact that I had made a wide reputation as an architect was all but ruining me in the circumstances. Were I obscure or a nonentity I should have been left in peace. So, after all, I was being shown up and plucked solely because of what I had myself built up by painstaking labour with some degree of success during a stormy twenty-two years.

Shortly after my marriage to Olgivanna, which took place quietly at Santa Fe following the year of probation which had followed the absolute divorce, this sort of crazy exploitation ended with a final move by the persecution—at Milwaukee.

Miriam Noel, now on her way to Paris, reached Milwaukee encouraged to start suit to keep the trust fund, established in her behalf, up to level. My earning capacity having been cut off by her, the trust fund established by me in her behalf had been drawn down by monthly payments to her as agreed upon, to a balance of some eleven thousand dollars. This suit started, she fell seriously ill. Her malady of long standing was aggravated by an operation in a Milwaukee hospital and she became unmanageable. A long distance call from a friend she had made in Milwaukee told me of this. And I confirmed it.

Several months later, having been removed in a state of coma from the asylum to a private sanitarium, she died without regaining consciousness.

Her several children, two married daughters and unmarried son, were near her at the time. But their mother was buried with no assistance from them.

What was left of a remarkably vital high-spirited woman, who for fifteen years psychopathic had been going up in flame, seldom knowing real rest unless by some artificial means, had found it. At last she was beyond reach of exploitation.

A mercy to herself and to all who had ever cared for her.

At no time did any newspaper dare print the truth concerning her mental state. For one thing, it would be actionable to use the word insane. In the next place it would have spoiled the entire setup for their stories.

As her own children refused to touch anything that was hers, the Milwaukee woman who claimed her as a friend and a Milwaukee lawyer became the unfortunate Miriam Noel's 'estate'.

RETROSPECT

This recitation of matter disgraceful to my country as to myself was written some twelve years ago. Resentment shows too plainly in the recital. None would show were I now to write the record of the persecution aroused by my own indiscretion. But the facts were so grossly misrepresented and so destructive then that I could not refrain from recording the truth as it should have been known at the time. The truth is bad enough, but I have never felt uneasy with truth. With true-speaking there can be no resentment.

I know that recounting facts does not constitute truth. Truth lies deeper. It is something we feel but can seldom touch with facts. So I am no better off to have got the facts on the record. At that time I thought I would be.

I have left it all in this book as it was and for what it may be worth. It is worth less than nothing to me—since I have it off my mind. And I don't see how it is going to help anyone else unless in danger of being in my case and in the fix I was in at that time.

I hope no one ever will be. Not even my worst friends nor my best enemies. No, not even the man who hadn't an enemy in the world but whose friends did not like him.

BOOK FOUR

FREEDOM

AUTUMN

Nature is now visible song.

Scarlet sumach runs like forest fire along The Valley hills.

The Future lies perfected in the seeds of bright fruits still hanging from naked boughs to tempt the present.

Acorns drop from the oaken bough to be eagerly sought in the mould beneath and carried far away. And bright berries, devoured by birds and beasts, are gone to new life in new ground. By appeasing Hunger and Desire—the Species makes sure of the Future?

Another life by way of infinite veins and arteries has added stature to the trees, given consequence to shrubs and flowers. The grass still green.

Flaming creeper wreathes the singing bough as leaves take on the hues of bloom, growth's greatest moment—until now.

Gentle touches of coming frost bring natural response to inner rhythm. Work done, the trees and shrubs, the flowers, return precious sap to the root.

To sleep.

In the little family chapel, 'truth against the world' there under the mass of dark green firs planted by Uncle Thomas—the old Welsh family stands up. To sing.

Again hear 'step by step since time began we see the steady gain of Man'.

The grey old heads; the not so young; the not so old. The young and the very young. All together the false, falsetto, and the flat lift that brave assurance to the boards of the chapel ceiling: an ancient challenge ever new, going out through open windows to fade away in the many-coloured hills beyond.

The boy, too, sings. Human exaltation. Fervour all about him floods the masses of gold and purple plundered from the roadsides to wreathe the pulpit with the gold and purple cloth and to match the purple berries of the woodbine pulled from trees twining the branches of scarlet sumach gathered from the hills.

White antimony from the pastures shines through them all like stars.

The family slowly sits down, and the grey heads, those not so grey, those not so young furtively wipe away their tears.

This boy wonders why they always weep? And they weep most when everything is best!

The book . . . lies open on the purple cloth, gilded edges flashing gold.

The white-haired preacher for today—the boy's Aunt Jane—now rises behind The Book.

Her text: 'The time of Grace has come.' Gratitude!

'Freely we have received.

Freely then, let us give.

Grace? The gift of freedom to the strong soul.

The time of grace has come: yes, the time of grace to others.

Living up to life—Man loves Beauty.

So it is that Beauty loves Man.'

'Beauty loves Man' sinks into this boy-mind.

Tenderness for all life suffuses this thought with happy feeling.

Freedom?

No.

Faith.

TO WORK AGAIN

1927. The load of debt has mounted, beyond any fair reckoning, but the familiar creative urge has gathered energy once more. Debt and urge still seem to go on together. Objectives once only dimly felt, gropingly sought, are coming pretty clear now. Confusion and the distress of disgraceful turmoil have ended? Sanity? The normal? Both are the true basis of human freedom. But Taliesin has been stripped to join the destitution of Hillside; Taliesin is there plundered by the bank and abused by curiosity as the Hillside Home School buildings were defaced by it and all but destroyed. The water comes in through the decayed and broken roofs at Hillside. The entire place is rapidly becoming a ruin. Taliesin itself is unkempt. Bank-rented fields are grown up with weeds. The buildings, in this climate so destructive to buildings, need repair. But the next move, even the next meal, is becoming a problem to be solved somehow without money. There is less than none.

But the sky is clearing a little. Familiar signs of the better thing in a better way are gradually bringing hope back to life again at Taliesin. There is more definite encouragement from Europe. I should be grateful for this at this time. I am.

But the last actual work on plans was done at Taliesin in 1923-24 nearly seven years ago. I am hungry for work, not honours. Some further work on the cantilever glass and metal skyscraper for Mr. Johnson of the National Insurance Company, and a study for the automobile objective for Gordon Strong, these seemed to have ended my active period of work.

The several young couples recently come from Zurich, Vienna and Tokio to work with me—Werner and Sylva Moser, Zurich; Richard and Dione Neutra, Vienna; Kameki and Nobu Tsuchiura, all talented. Faithful William Smith, a young major from Ottawa, in his ninth year at stormy Taliesin—all that life had gone on to other fields, there was no one working with me here now that I was, at last, free to work.

Denied work and what Freedom have you?

267

NOT WORK BUT ECHOES. MORE HONOURS

At this time, to join the earlier publications of my earlier work by Wasmuth in Berlin in 1910, Holland contributed by the way of the fine art publication *Wendingen*, a splendid volume. I had never expected anything like it, nor had I known anything about this one. I suspect no architect ever had a greater tribute than this one: *Wendingen*, a Dutch-English-German fine art publication, organ of a group of some nineteen architects, sculptors and painters of Holland and Belgium. It was edited by the distinguished architect, H. Th. Wijdeveld. In Holland they said that but for my work the modern architecture of Holland would not have existed. So Wijdeveld easily found support for this work. There are now many publications if that work is to end now. Four in German, two in Japanese, two in French, one in Czech. None yet in my own country, however. Honorary membership in Académie Royale d'Anvers, an ancient Flemish academic institution of the fine arts beginning as far back as Rembrandt and Franz Halls, came as another surprise. An honorary membership too in the German Royal Academie, first recognition of modern architecture by the Reich. These and other appreciations from European contemporaries reached me at this time when for several years I had walked the streets of many American cities, an exile with the now all too familiar worm's-eye view of society.

After four years of such exile from Taliesin—and from Architecture, it is much the same thing—I again began work on more definite plans for Mr. Johnson's cantilever office building, the standardized gas-station, San Marcos in the Desert, and especially upon St. Mark's Tower. Meantime the mutilated box had appeared in the offing. The box offering itself as new and naming itself the 'international' style.

Yes, now the ideal of an organic architecture, gone abroad, comes back deformed, turned up on the ground edgewise. So it names itself an international style? As though any universal 'style' were not more than ever offensive, now. Of course, undemocratic.

But a certain eclectic emulation by the perennial novice is seen along the much too obvious, extremely meagre lines of this new candidate offering itself for a 'style'. Emulation, too, begins to show itself. Architects, by nature born propagandists, begin to push this offshoot or left branch of modern architecture by characteristic propaganda, by advertisement *à la mode*. Little cliques keep forming within the original clique, all of them trading upon the narrow margins of an 'originality' meanwhile carefully concealing actual origins. All and each in turn, or out of it, pushing each other aside while all alike as two peas in a pod. All denying the pod though, and especially denying the vine on which the pod containing the peas grew. Small matter. But poor Usonia! Because of her ubiquitous publicity she is prone to this sort of thing it seems beyond all other lands. But why? Why have these United States of America never allowed themselves to learn something of architecture? As for my own place in my own work, at this peculiar moment of bogus-renaissance, along came

ARIZONA

While we were still in exile, anxiously waiting first at Phoenix and then at La Jolla for the legal *Yakamashii* to finally clear away from Taliesin, the unit-block system I had first used in Hollywood in 1920, with my help, had built another building: the Arizona Biltmore. A million-dollar fashionable resort hotel near Phoenix, Arizona.

This project was promoted by Charles and Warren McArthur and their brother Albert, who was one of my boys in the old Oak Park Workshop. Albert was accordingly commissioned to build this building. Albert—rich man's son—at this psychological moment of my exile and unemployment appealed to me to help him establish the block system as the construction of this project. Wanderer, now, myself, although no longer 'fugitive from justice', I gladly turned into quarters at Phoenix and worked some nine months during a characteristic Phoenix summer (118° in the shade) to help Albert establish the thing we wanted to do. I was to remain behind the scenes and glad to do so. The building was finally built, but meanwhile Albert encountered the inevitable opposition to the unusual in design and the new in construction; he was totally unable to stem the co-lateral tides of suggested changes engineers proposed in my building technique. Soon the system was robbed of any economic value whatever. When they had left off their services the unique block system was standing as a novel and beautiful outside only for a most expensive and unintelligent engineer's beam and wall construction; whereas great structural economy was first and foremost an integral feature of the system itself it was now a beautiful extravagance. Had it been naturally allowed to work with its own integrity, several hundred thousand dollars would have been saved in the cost of building. But the cost of the building seemed nothing in the circumstances.

Having then no authority myself beyond bullying Albert, making unofficial threats and suggestions behind the scenes, I was powerless to prevent this tragic waste or the addition of a fourth storey to the building although I conducted many tests to prove our case and all were more than merely successful. But such figures as the engineers could use could not be used in this case. In the building of the hotel cottages later, however, the details of the original scheme were better followed with somewhat better results of course. There should have been more of these and no fourth storey.

But the story of this building—the Arizona Biltmore—Albert should himself tell someday. It would be a valuable warning to young architects and a reward, maybe. I don't know. But he is too near to it yet, too personally involved in its various equivocal implications, meum and tuum, to tell it straight, even to himself probably, for another twenty years at least.

Meanwhile, during this debacle we had the salvage of reunion at Phoenix with the McArthurs—old friends of my family—the mother and her three sons all living in a group of charming homes near the Country-club, built by Albert. Mother McArthur's hospitality made our exile much

269

more bearable. If Phoenix had not had the McArthurs, it would certainly have had no Arizona Biltmore.

While working in behind the scenes thus with Albert in 1927, I met Dr. Alexander Chandler of Chandler, Arizona. He came over one day from the little town named for him, 'Chandler', to see me. His own town was on the mesa near the Mormon town of Mesa, about twenty-two miles east of Phoenix. Already in building that decent little town named for himself, and in other serviceable ways, he had built himself into the region. It had taken him forty years to do it, but it was done to good purpose, for he was widely known as a man of superior taste and judgement.

A dream of Dr. Chandler's it seems was an undefiled-by-irrigation desert resort for wintering certain jaded eastern millionaires who preferred dry desert to green, wet fields. He wanted to build this characteristic resort on a tract of several thousand acres in great stretches of pure mountain desert. The site was over there in the Salt Range ten miles from his still successful San Marcos, a successful hotel in his little town. So, learning I was in the neighbourhood, he came over to invite my little family to come with him and stay awhile to talk it all over at the pleasant, aristocratic Hotel San Marcos.

Dr. Chandler had certain definite ideas concerning this new desert resort. They were good ideas, or better, I thought. He said he had waited ten years before planning the building because he knew of no one who could give him what he wanted, unless I could. And as he said this he smiled his beautiful smile. There is only one smile more beautiful than his and that is his wife's.

So, together we went to see the spot, his inimitable black driver Harris at the wheel. Harris, too, is an artist . . . portraits. And there is only one Harris! But sometimes he takes a severe cold and says he finds it necessary to stay in bed next morning as late as ten o'clock to be rid of it.

Well, there could be nothing more inspiring to an architect on this earth than that spot of pure desert in Arizona he took me to see, so I believe. At last here was the time, the place and here was, in Dr. Chandler, the man. And he looked like the man of strength and independent judgement always necessary to characterize a thoroughbred undertaking in building, or in anything else. I immediately liked him and in spite of tragic failure still do. I went to work *for* him and *with* him, making the first sketches for the building while living by the seaside at La Jolla. We were there still in exile but anxiously awaiting at any moment the promised opportunity to return to Taliesin. I showed him these drawings on my way back there in October. The design pleased him. During the coming winter, 1929, he proposed to begin to build.

We had got back to Taliesin. I was at work on this project for some two months, when a telegram came from the Doctor suggesting we all come out and make the plans for the new resort right there.

Joyful news. A swift 'comeback' at last! A $40,000 fee in that direction. And we were, at the moment, housebound at Taliesin in a blizzard, twenty-two degrees below zero and blowing hard. Nevertheless, ignoring mentor La Follette—Phil—secretary now of F.L.W., incorporated, we broke away and went out into a blowing snowstorm on the way to Arizona. A real blizzard. The household and workshop at Taliesin were quickly closed and the trek by automobile to Arizona began, fifteen of us in all because I had gathered some boys together to work on this project and a few other prospects.

This desert resort I meant to embody all worthwhile I had learned about a natural architecture. First it was to be considerably better than any thoroughly practical layout I knew about. The building was to grow up out of the desert by way of desert materials. The block system naturally as the Sahuaro grew up. The Sahuaro should be the motif that inspired its style and the details. I had played with it a little in the plans for the Biltmore. Creation so long denied—after nearly seven years of waste and turmoil here a great opportunity came to me: an ideal site unspoiled, the man promoting it well up to the thing he wanted done. Something like this is the rarest good fortune in any architect's life. If the United States is ever to have creative architecture more such opportunities are needed by her creative architects.

Held off so long from active creation, I could scarcely wait to begin. I could not get the project off my mind. The sketches were successful. And important too. I had pretty well mastered block technique by this time—a good desert technique. With a man like Dr. Chandler to work for and this mastery I felt certain of results.

So we all finally arrived at Chandler after extraordinary risks in early January, 1927, only to find that suitable quarters to live and work would cost us several thousand dollars if we took them for the rest of the winter, spring and summer. And they said we couldn't live there in summer. Too hot. I knew the heat though I had always wanted to camp in that region. Why not camp now? Why not spend the inevitable 'several thousand' on a comfortable camp spacious enough to use not only in which to plan the building but from which it might be officered later during construction? I took this idea to Dr. Chandler and said that if he would give me a site somewhere we would build the camp ourselves. He reached for his hat, led the way to the little gray Ford coupé which he drives around the mesa at an average of fifty miles an hour and we went over toward the Salt Range.

Ten miles away we came upon a low, spreading, rocky mound rising from the great desert floor—well away from everywhere, but within view of the site of the new resort.

'How would this do?' said he.

'This—do you mean it—can we have this to build on?' I said.

(Ground where I came from was hard to come by.)

He nodded.

'What more could anyone ask?' I said.

'But,' he suggested, 'let us go a little further over toward the hotel site, you might like that better.'

271

'Oh, no—I'll take this as it is, right here.'

It was all too good, but it was true.

Lumber began to arrive that afternoon. Native $1 \times 10''$ boards and 2×4's (unluckily undersized and very green) and two-inch battens.

I sat down in a cold, vacant office upstairs in the little town to make the plans. The shivering boys stood around me watching, handing me the tools. We set up the drawing board on boxes. And it was cold. They said in Chandler 'unusual' weather, but wherever I have been it has been always 'unusual' weather: 'the coldest or warmest or wettest or dryest in thirty or fifty years.' The scheme was soon ready. Next morning we started in to build a camp. In fact we ate breakfast at the campsite as the frost came out of the air and a great red sun-disc rose over a sublime spectacle of desert mountain ranges and gorgeous sky.

We made such progress that day that one of my boys, Donald Walker, slept that night outside on a pile of lumber, rolled up in blankets. But by the next night we had set up the first 'box-bottom' of the tent tops and put cots in it for three more boys. Next day there was room for all to sleep except my little family of three and myself. Reluctantly we went back to Mesa to the hotel. But we came back for early breakfast in that wonderful dining-room sixty miles wide, as long and tall as the universe. We were shivering, oh, yes. But we were all singing happy in that clear cold sunrise. A great prospect!

We had a sweeping view all around us of this vast battleground of titanic natural forces, called Arizona. It will make *the* playground for these United States some day. But too soon yet. The 100 per cent American would spoil it now, *à la Hopi* or Mexicano-Hispano, or perhaps even 'the latest'—the international boxment *à la mode*.

Out here in the great spaces obvious symmetry claims too much, I find, wearies the eye too soon and stultifies the imagination. Obvious symmetry usually closes the episode before it begins. So for me I felt there could be no obvious symmetry in any building in this great desert, none especially in this new camp—we later named the place Ocatillo and partly for this reason. No, there would be nothing like obvious symmetry in the new 'San Marcos in the Desert'.

The sound constitution of any entity is pregnant with graceful reflexes. Seek those, young architect! Now by way of an architect's work-camp comes fresh adventure in the desert. We called the camp: 'OCATILLO'.

Victor Hugo wrote: 'The desert is where God is and Man is not.' Arizona desert is like that. But the Arizonian living in these desert towns has got himself a carpenter-built Mid-Western cottage, or sometimes, more fortunate so he thinks, a mid-Mediterranean or Mexicano palazzo. And believe it or not, he has already built a few skyscrapers in towns on the mesa. He would build more if he could.

The Yankee-Hopi house is the Phoenix favourite just now. In all this weird, colourful, wide-sweeping terrain nothing is quite so deciduous as

Arizona buildings, unless the crows lighting on the fences of the irrigated fields only to fly away.

Unspoiled native character insulted like this. Arizona character seems to cry out for a space-loving architecture of its own. The straight line and flat plane must come here—of all places—but they should become the dotted line, the broad, low, extended plane textured because in all this astounding desert there is not one hard undotted line to be seen. The great nature-masonry we see rising from the great mesa floors is all the noble architecture Arizona has to show at present and that is not architecture at all. But it is inspiration. A pattern of what appropriate Arizona architecture might well be lies there hidden in the Sahuaro. The Sahuaro, perfect example of reinforced building construction. Its interior vertical rods hold it rigidly upright maintaining its great fluted columnar mass for six centuries or more. A truer skyscraper than our functioneer has built.

And all these desert remarkable growths show scientific building economy in the patterns of their construction. The stalks especially teach any architect or engineer who is modest and intelligent enough to apply for lessons. In these desert constructions he may not only see the reinforcing-rod scientifically employed as in the flesh of the sahuaro but he may see the perfect lattice or the reed and welded tubular construction in the stalk of the cholla, or staghorn, and see it too in the cellular build-up of the water-barrel, Bignana. Even the flesh of the prickly pear is worth studying for scientific structure. In most cacti Nature employs cell to cell or continuous tubular or often plastic construction. By means of plasticity Nature makes continuity everywhere strongly effective without having to reduce the scheme to post and girder construction before she can figure it out. She has this great advantage in this architectural adventure over our very best engineers. Engineers are quite often as silly as architects. Plasticity is the new problem now ready to be met in building construction. I have seen that experts *can* be 'wrong for more than fifty years'.

Yes, Desert is rock-bound-earth prostrate to the sun. All life there above the crystal is tenacious sun-life. All life there dies a sun-death. Evidence is everywhere. Sometimes ghastly.

Here in this wonderland an architect and his helpers are actually working away to build a simple camp, a camp we shall call it. A human inhabitant of unmitigated wilderness of quotidian change—unchangeably changing Change. For our purpose we need fifteen cabins in all. Since all will be temporary we will call them ephemera. And you will soon see them like a group of gigantic butterflies with scarlet wing spots, conforming gracefully to the crown of the outcropping of black splintered rock gently uprising from the desert floor. This mound where Dr. Chandler first took me. A human gaiety in the Desert is under way.

The box-board cabins themselves are to be connected by a low staggered box-board wall with a horizontal zig-zag—(for the same reason Thomas Jefferson worm-walled his brick). It will be self-supporting and complete the enclosure just referred to as the 'compound'. Necessary openings in the canvas-topped box buildings we will close with canvas-covered wood frames. Flaps hinged with rubber belting. No glazed doors or windows. Glass is not for this type of desert camp if indeed glass belongs in the Desert at all.

Now, when all these white canvas wings, like sails, are spread, the buildings—butterfly simile aside—will look something like ships coming down the mesa, rigged like ships balanced in the breeze.

Yes, the group *will* look like some new kind of desert fleet. We painted the horizontal boards with cold-water paint, continuing around the varied board wall connecting all the cabins about the mound. I chose dry rose as the colour to match the light on the desert floor. The one-two triangle we used in planning the camp is made by the mountain ranges around about the site. And the one-two triangle is the cross section of the talus at their bases. This triangle is reflected in the general forms of all the cabins as well as the general plan. We will paint the canvas one-two triangles in the eccentric gables scarlet. The one-two triangles of the ocatillo bloom itself are scarlet. This red triangular form in the treatment is why we called the camp 'Ocatillo'. 'Candle flame.'

I presently found that the white luminous canvas overhead and canvas used instead of window glass afforded such agreeable diffusion of light within, was so enjoyable and sympathetic to the desert that I now felt more than ever oppressed by the thought of the opaque solid overhead of the much too heavy mid-western house.

The desert devils would come whirling like a dancing dervish and go in drifting spirals of dust rising high in the air. Occasionally a devil would cross the camp and it would shudder in its grasp like a ship—but hold fast. No damage.

I believe we pay too slight attention to making slight buildings beautiful or beautiful buildings slight. Lightness and strength may now be synonymous.

Usually we spend so much too much to make buildings 'last', as we say. Unqualified to build, we are still busy making caves for cave-dweller survivals.

So, 'Ocatillo'—our little desert camp—you are 'ephemera'. Nevertheless you will drop a seed or two yourself in course of time.

Meantime my draughtsmen—at this moment Heinrich Klumb, Donald, Vladimir and Cy and brave George Kastner, he was still ill, Frank Sullivan, Will Weston and I: we made most of the camp between ourselves. We put it together with nails, screws, rubber belting for hinges; rigged up the flaps with ship cord, all designed as carefully, probably more carefully than any permanent building. Not as carefully as a ship nor so well executed, of course, but done as well as we knew how with such technique and endurance as we had to give. Good enough. All to pass away in a year—or two?

274

As a matter of fact it did in less time than that. The Indians carted it all away during the winter after we had turned our backs upon it and characteristic disaster befell the U.S.A. No, not prohibition, I mean the fall of 1929 when Architecture and architects ceased to function throughout the U.S.A.

UBIQUITY

Yes, the Indians carried it all away. But, I have learned not to grieve long now that some work of mine has met its end; *has had short life*, as we say, even though it happens that a better one cannot take its place. I am consoled by the thought that today any building *design* may have far-reaching effect on the record, and because our machine—publicity—so easily gives it, as an idea of form, to the mind's eye of all the world. For an instance, 'Ocatillo' with no help or suggestion from me was published in German and Dutch magazines two months after it was nearly finished. It has appeared in magazines all over the world. Thank the machine for that: for this universal ubiquity. Or curse it as the case may be.

Dissemination and consequent prevalence of the Idea in some graphic thought-form—certainly that is one of the best—or maybe worst—things the machine has done for us in this age?

When *organic* architecture finds its way to us we shall have no such senseless destruction of life as we see going on around us now. Could striving for such establishment as we now have end, life would be more abundant for all. It would be much better in quality for everyone. These foolish little differences without any difference to which we so pridefully cling lead continually to the tedious repetition of infinitely insignificant resemblances. We seem so afraid of any seeming differences. How afraid we would be of any genuine 'difference'! I have reason to know.

And this is the evil of such philosophy as we have in our educated thinking today; that it never does nor ever can go to seed that can grow anything at all fresh *from our own soil*. Indigenous growth is the essential province of all true art and culture. It is so today as it was yesterday, or there will be no tomorrow for us! So rather than ponderous permanent blunders, until we learn more of good appropriate building, why not ephemera as preliminary study, say? Usonia proves it. America was given permanent building materials to work with—much too soon. Say a century.

RETROSPECT

The little camp is finished. We love it. The canvas windows and doors of Ocatillo *are* like ship-sails when open and may shut against dust or may open part way to deflect the desert breezes into the interiors. Screened openings for cross ventilation are everywhere at the floor levels, a discovery I made in seeking coolness, to be used during the heat of the day; closed at night. The long sides of the canvas slopes lie easily with the lines of the landscape, stretching themselves wide open toward the sun in order to aid a little in warming the interiors in winter. This long canvas roof-side is to have additional cover of canvas, air blowing between the two sheets, if the camp is ever occupied in summer. We can add this later we stay on in summer, and make it 'belong'.

It is gratifying to look and see as we look around us how well we fit into this strange, stern, well-armed, creeping cover of abstract land and its peculiar *growth* almost as abstract. This inexorable grasp of growing vegetation upon the earth itself is more terrifying to me as a principle at work than what we call death. Growth is everywhere more terrible and terrifying to me than all the other evidences of inexorable force put together.

There seems to be no mortal escape, especially not in death, from this inexorable earth principle—or is it sun-principle—of growth: this creative creature of the great sun?

And what of the subsidence we see now in the streamlines of these end-less ranges of mountains coming gently down to the mesa or going abruptly up into the sky from the plains. In this geologic era, catastrophic upheaval has found comparative repose by way of the sculptors wind and water. To these vast, quiet, ponderable masses made so by fire and laid by water—both are architects—now comes the sculptor—wind. Wind and water ceaselessly eroding, endlessly working to quiet and harmonize all traces of violence until a glorious unison is again bathed in the atmosphere of a light that is, it must be, eternal.

Finally to 'justify' our wild adventure, Ocatillo cost not so much more than the rent and keep asked for equivalent accommodations in Chandler or in Phoenix for the one season we were to stay, were the same number of persons provided for. The cost was about two hundred dollars per cabin. The labour was mostly our own. We are the better for that labour. We have met the Desert, loved it and lived with it, and the Desert is ours.

SAN MARCOS IN THE DESERT

Our camp was practically finished January 19th, 1928. Something of lively human significance had come alive. Under the suffused glow of the translucent canvas overhead we worked away on Dr. Chandler's resort for such jaded millionaires as might still be able to love beauty and seek solitude in beautiful, quiet surroundings. We were going to call it San Marcos in the Desert. We worked on it until the middle of the following June. Often we worked at night by gasoline light until we put in a Kohler plant and had all the electric light we wanted.

We worked out the 'resort' as a great block-system series of intercommunicating terraces facing to the sun of the south. There were three of these terraces, each room with its own pool and garden, one terrace rising above the other against the mountainside: a mono material building and the latest expression of the block-shell system started in La Miniatura and that miscarried partly at the Arizona Biltmore. The block system in this case is genuine reinforced masonry, the same within and without. The block shell here will be integral with structure. It is the structure itself.

The deep 'wash' or ravine rising as a gorge between the two great hills back of the terraces we used to conceal the road leading to the main entrance of the building. This entrance was placed well back under the building in the gorge itself. An organ tower of copper and block-shell design rose like a giant sahuaro from this gorge to emphasize this entrance. It is intended to give voice to the whole. Echo-organs are to be planted in the hills—Dr. Chandler's idea—for open air vesper concerts in the desert at sunset.

The dining room? It is simply a top-lit glass and copper arbour topping the living room central mass and is so connected to the hill slopes on either side by the terrace tops of the upper stories of the wings that adjacent dwellers in the mountain cottages—to be built later on as a part of the whole—may reach it along the top terrace comfortably on foot.

The plan of this far-flung, long-drawn-out building, owing to the placing of the levels of the sun-lit terraces, is such that each room, each bathroom, each closet, each corridor even, has direct sunlight. Every portion of the building to be lived in is free to the sun and also to magnificent views. The whole building has the warm southern exposure every winter resort so covets. And, the whole structure would approximate what we call permanent. Say three hundred years at least. Three hundred large rooms with bath, all appurtenance systems being more than adequate and virtually indestructible too.

Now, observe if you will that every horizontal line in San Marcos in the Desert is a dotted line. Every flat plane is grosgrained patterned like the Sahuaro itself. The entire building is in pattern an abstraction of mountain region and cactus life, set up in permanent masonry shells. The whole building is made more cactus than any cactus can be in itself, if you know what I mean. But none the less, rather more a human habitation to live in as long maybe as the mountain lasts.

Human habitation here comes decently in where God is. Man is come in as himself something of a God. And just that is what Architecture can do for him—not only show appreciation of Arizona's character but qualify him in a human habitation to become a godlike native part of Arizona for so long as any building ever endured. Arizona desert itself was architectural inspiration to me and because it was actually the architect's workshop in this endeavour, the feeling of the whole building in all its parts now designedly belongs to the terrain. This is what I mean by indigenous architecture. San Marcos in the Desert proves it is not only possible but that it is here.

So, of course, it was all too good to happen. Sometimes I think it was just a dream. But here are the completed plans, there you may see the carefully studied details. Responsible estimates were complete: the contract was signed by Paul Mueller the good builder, awaiting the Doctor's signature.

Then at that moment as Dr. Chandler took the train to complete the arrangements for coming to build came the crash of 1929. Where was

Dr. Chandler? There with the quick 'comeback'. Now instead of a $40,000.00 fee I found myself with a deficit of $19,000 to add to the mounting mountain of debt at Taliesin. $2500.00 was all there was to set against the whole.

Never mind. Something had started that was not stopping thus. Later you will see consequences.

By this time May heat was becoming the heat that made the desert the desert and keeps it one. The season now passed, dormant desert life was coming alive. Nine rattlesnakes were found in the compound. All must have a care. Nevertheless we planned, worked and drove about the region in a free sun-life of the wide spaces for several weeks more and watched our step.

For the homeward drive we acquired a used Packard sport Phaeton wide open to the sky. Camp broken, contents stored against return the following winter, the car stands by the gate to the compound to begin the drive overland to Taliesin . . . the full extent of the 1929 breakdown and its effect upon our enterprise not yet more than beginning to be known. There was still some hope.

Olgivanna and I sat in front to take turns driving; Svetlana and Iovanna were snug in the tonneau behind the rear windshield we had installed. We waved goodbye to the gay camp and drove off to pick up Dr. Chandler who was going with us as far as Holbrook. We wanted to investigate a new natural cement found in that region, as perhaps an ideal material for our block-building. This material—a magnesite, I believe, was found in drifts on the mesa floor. It was white, set quickly and hard. It was waterproof. We had left a plaster-model made of the actual block units proposed for use in building San Marcos in the Desert, standing white and brilliant in the centre of the camp compound on the crown of the hill. That was as far as the structure ever got on the ground itself.

Chicago was finally reached by way of long Midwestern commonplaces. The long overland drive further west so full of incident and interest monotonously continued on the way to New York City. I was to consult with Reverend William Norman Guthrie, brilliant Rector of St. Marks on the Bouwerie, and his vestry, concerning the tall apartment building to be built in the little park at Tenth Street and Second Avenue for revenue to help support the church. We found our Eastern cities and towns very like Western and Midwestern cities and towns. General lack of resourceful individuality, except that in the East there was less new construction. The village carpenter of New England had spread out and styled them all. I could not escape the feeling while there in the East that the young men had all left home and taken the East out West with them never to return. Eastern towns and villages all seemed waiting for their 'young' to come back again to help do something about the smug-ugliness of it all. They will never come. We drove through the new Holland tunnel into urban scenes of indescribable confusion. The erstwhile village streets of New York were in unusual uproar and turmoil of reconstruction—new subways, taller buildings all soon to be gripped and paralysed in the now rapidly spreading panic. The little Iovanna had heard of the Empire State Skyscraper as the ultimate. As we caught a glimpse of it her face fell. 'Daddy,' said she, 'they could have made it higher—couldn't they? . . . Then why didn't they?' You see that is really all 'height' can really 'mount to'.

SIGNIFICANT INSIGNIFICANCE

Seen here in New York is the same architectural insignificance found all along the wayside from coast to coast except bigger and better insignificance in every way. The insignificance we had seen all along the line had some rights. None here. There in the greatest metropolis of the U.S.A., in ambitious but fatal variety, is the same deadly monotony. Man-eating skyscrapers were all tall but seeking false feudal monumental mass for 1929 rivetted steel skeletons. This utter contradiction of structure and idea is what is most remarkable everywhere in New York. Chicago architects long before had discovered the possibility of using iron and steel to make a stone and brick building stand up so it could go on making masonry faces at admiring throngs all the way up, piling storey on storey. Of course, the tenuous open steel frame of these tall buildings is, in character, the reverse of feudal masonry mass. Lightness, openness and tenuous strength combined are its building characteristics. These ought to be associated never with heavy stone or concrete as the building code still insists it shall be, but with light insulated covering metals with glass insertion instead of heavy walls. The whole be so designed and the fabric so insulated as to emphasize the pattern of the structure itself and with a fresh beauty not belie the way it was actually built. An old, old story now, this pet American falsehood. Masonry materials do not only belie such steel structures but the practice is really a threat to the life of the structure itself by adding enormous useless weight to the frame of the whole. That very human equation, the factor of safety—really it is as Dankmar Adler used to say 'the factor of ignorance'—was seriously put to work behind all this crowded mass of pier buildings and crenelated tops of feudal masonry walls. The vaunted 'sky-line' was a haphazard anyhow. Its vaunted picturesque was a make-up of senseless feudal-masses standing there on steel stilts to mask and belie the real appearance of the purpose and character of the building itself and betray to all the real insignificance of this new man-unit in the old style city: a kind of bastardizing of great opportunity. The engineering was here functioneering, with architects merely putting the architecture on the outside. Looking in behind these false masonry masses . . . what, really, was it all? The urbanite lost in urbanism, that's all—helplessly drifting toward extinction by the domination of the machine and its unearned increment.

AN ANGRY PROPHECY AND A PREACHMENT:
THE CITY

Is the great city the natural triumph of the herd instinct over such sanity as humanity may know? Or is it only a temporal hangover from the infancy of the race, to be outgrown as the performance of humanity grows—modern? Civilization has seemed to need and feature the city meantime or I suppose it wouldn't be with us now? And, no doubt the city *has* expressed what the civilization that built it most cherished. So the city may truly be said to have served civilization.

But history records that the civilizations that built the greatest cities invariably died with them. Did the civilizations themselves die *of* them? I think they did.

Urban accelerations—history records this fact—always preceded such decay and we are seeing just such acceleration in our own cities, today.

So in the streets and avenues of this great city of New York, accelerations due to the skyscraper—itself one of the accelerations—may be singularly dangerous. Increasingly dangerous to any life the city may have even though its very own interests fail to see it as a danger until circumstances take hold of the situation by force. They are beginning to do so.

RENT

As I believe in Freedom as ideal, so I believe that the American city as we know it today is not only to die but is dying. In this intensified urban-activity seeming to the thoughtless like success, we are only seeing this characteristic acceleration that goes before ultimate urban dissolution. This ceaseless to and fro in the gainful occupation of this army of white collarites. Is it an activity of parasites upon the various forms of artificial 'rent'? Money itself now being a most lucrative form of rent. RENT is become the fetish of an artificial economic domination that now really owns and operates the great city. The city is itself now money-coming-alive as something in itself to go on ceaselessly working to make all work useless and wars a continuous commonplace to keep gold the 'standard' of all work.

Yet our American civilization may not only survive its great cities but eventually profit by them because the death of these cities—it is now conceivable—will be the greatest service the machine has to ultimately render to human beings, if by means of his machine man ever does conquer his own machine. What beneficent significance to him otherwise has his machine? The cities are already outgrown. Overgrown. And any great city must feed upon itself now until its present carcass is past redemption. But, should the machine conquer man, man will remain to repeat urban history. He will perish with his city as all other urban civilizations have so perished. The city, like all minions of the machine, is grown up only in man's image. But when it is minus the living impetus that is man, the city is only man becoming or already become—the machine. Even now the city is only the baleful shadow of the sentient man that once did need a city and who built it and maintained it because he did need it. That ancient city once a necessity and a proof of some greatness is now dying or dead of its own excess. Humanity must find a means to go beyond it to a Freedom undreamed of before. Humanity has already found it in the machine itself.

What built the cities that have invariably died? Necessity primarily. That necessity gone and now only a dogged tradition, no sentimental habit can keep any great city alive for a great length of time. Necessity built the city on the basis of 'leg-work or the horse and buggy; wood and coal consumption; food distribution. And when the necessity for communication was to be had only by personal contact.'

No effective mobilization of the individual making ten miles as one block nor any electrified means of human intercommunication then existed. Various physical contacts in that earlier day needed a certain congestion to facilitate and stimulate life. Life does not need them now in that way. The ancient city naturally grew and existed as the great aid and abettor of human intercourse. A city became the immediate source of wealth and power by way of such human intercourse as was essential to social, industrial and financial growth. Only by congregating thus in aggregations, the vaster the aggregation the better, could the fruits of human living then best be had. In that day the real life of the city lay in the stress of individual ties, the contacts of super-individuals encountering upon other individualities. The electric spark of curiosity and surprise was alive in the streets, in public meetings. In the home it was found only occasionally as people congregated there. All was excitingly gregarious and gregarious in order to be exciting.

Government, the city had as now. Fashions and fads it also had. But the salt and savour of individual wit, taste and character then made the city a festival of life; a true carnival as compared with any drab over-run city of our day. Even Paris. But this original human concentration is not to be so quickly changed as the conditions of its existence would warrant change, because human habit changes slowly as water wears away a stone. Perhaps less rapidly. It would seem so.

So our Architecture, fundamentally, were it a living architecture would reflect this livelier human condition were it here today. The modern common denominator, the machine, had not then arrived in the ancient city. Now? The common denominator has not only arrived but it has come down by and with and where the man is imprisoned and growing helpless just because of the machine. So at the moment new machine powers are rendering so many of the old powers impotent if not entirely obsolete. It is only natural that the sudden release of all these new scientific machine factors and forces should at first be fearfully and selfishly held back to the old habits. And to ulterior purposes bred by fear. What so timid as a million dollars? Several millions.

But machine-prophecy grows. And it shows, if nothing else shows, that

281

we are to deal with the fact and principle of machinery in its most dangerous form right here among us and now. The social results of machine use forcibly show that the cultural sentimentality in human affairs that tries to break these new forces down to old habits is impotent to deal with this new phase of our new 'daemon'—this mechanistic element. But, architecture will deal with it soon or the new devil will finally deal with our posterity not only as common denominator but as dominator extraordinary under some other name. Political significance no less.

To deny inherent power of growth and virtue to our new common-denominator the machine which, were man in his senses, might soon be the common-emancipator—would this be absurd? But the eventual city that this new common denominator will build with its common machine will be so greatly different from the ancient city or from any city of today that we will probably fail to recognize its coming as the city at all. At any rate it will not be, I think, a graveyard for individuality nor obliteration of the man. Any city of *futurism* to be valid will be only more individual than in ages ago. Not less so.

To put a new outside upon any existing city is simply impossible now. The carcass of the city is far too old, too far gone. It is too *fundamentally* wrong for the future we now foresee.

Hopelessly, helplessly, inorganic it lies there where the great new forces moulding modern life are most concerned. Those forces are making its concentrations not only useless but deadly or poisonous by force of circumstances being driven inward, meantime relentlessly preparing within, to explode. Reactions that should by reasonable natural organic change drive the city somewhere into somewhat other and else are everywhere at work. The new city will be nowhere, yet everywhere. Broadacre City.

The human-element in our modern equation is not yet recognizing an acknowledged equivalent. But it may already be seen drifting—or pushed—going it blindly. But *going* just the same and in several different directions.

No, the congestion of super concentrations was no great evil until electric power, electric intercommunication, individual mobilization, and ubiquitous 'publicity' became common denominators and the true decentralizing agents for human life. Add to these decentralizers the airship when it lays away its wings and becomes a self-contained mechanical unit. And add many other things kept under cover in our heavy and still hardy capitalist hands, all in safe keeping at this moment.

If we accept these modern, moulding agencies that science has ready to confer upon us at this moment, the form of everything changes, as time runs, for better or for worse. Everything but human nature changes—whether we will it or we will against it. Though 'Nature her custom holds', here and elsewhere we do change, none the less and notwithstanding. But how slowly!

Organic consequences of inevitable changes unperceived at first begin to appear all about us.

Freedom of human-reach and movement, therefore of the human hori-

282

zon as a sphere of action, is in a decade enormously widened by the new services rendered by the machinery. Horizontality has received immense impetus, an impulse that will soon make human activity immeasurable and therefore unendurable on any present terms or scale of city spacing.

The pain of additional human city-pressure is senselessly caused if we take a sensible view of our coming of age in this new era, this amazing Twentieth Century of ours.

But here we are helpless to face this issue, though really witnessing fatal internal collision between these mechanistic factors, we neglect their significance and thoughtlessly find release, new pride in piling high up into the air. Cowardly human tendency in any emergency is either to run or to stay right there where we are. We do both with animal fear and exaggerated human sentimentality. But mostly we pig-pile in consequence.

To meet this human weakness—eventually it is fear of freedom—under economic pressure, the skyscraper was born. Invention, for twenty years, looking for salvation to the engineer, the streamliner, and the elevator, has been trying to thus hold the profits of superconcentration. But the skyscraper is now seen as but a landlord's ruse to have and hold the profits of thoughtless super-imposition. In our thrilling skyscrapers we see only a commercial expedient, one that enabled landlords to exploit the herd and to the limit. By government ordinance and official order, as usual, it was done and is maintained.

Thus the greater human freedom, ability to spread out on the new space terms without personal inconvenience (and this is the most valuable gift brought by the undreamed-of powers of these new servants: electrical intercommunication, the automobile, the telephone, the airship, the radio and the press), which by twist of the capitalist wrist the skyscraper represented for the moment, every great city perverts from the man himself to be exploited in some form of profit to lucky realty. As the realtor's super-concentrations boomed, 1929 was inevitable.

Let us readily admit the thrill for the thoughtless in such acceleration and superconcentration directly due to this unwise exaggeration. But no one just now as socio-economic temperatures run high seems to want to know whether the acceleration is the healthy excitement of normal growth or really the fever of disease. Few seem to care much whether such acceleration means human progress or is only some form of the disease commercial exploitation, likely to be and make this machine-age the swiftest but the shortest-lived civilization in all history. The architect, however, does care. He must.

TIME

This iteration and reiteration of an idea is probably wearing upon my reader even now when the story of the idea has hardly begun. I feel the matter so important that at the risk of turning an autobiography into propaganda I will go on with it.

Forces themselves are blinded by it. Our lives are a sacrifice to it. Reading between the lines, history will show that human beings, unaccustomed to thought as organic and helplessly involved with organic forces, also remain time-blind. Over long stretches of time. But—there is a saving clause; today along with these new revolutionary factors, there come new means of communication amounting to the realization of a new human faculty that may wipe out Time. An ubiquitous publicity often succeeds in getting done in a month now what formerly might have drifted a decade. Yes, we are Time-bound in all forms of our life today and thought today. But to be conservative, what took a century in human affairs now takes but ten years. What emancipation is ahead?

Ten years, in our twentieth century, is an epoch. Thirty years, an 'age'!

So Time reactions to any human activity—notwithstanding machine ownership of this agency as of all other popular agencies—show to all men in less than one lifetime either the wisdom or the folly of such perversion of life-ownership. Humanity may yet call for correction before the affair has gone too far. Since we are prone to publicity. Publicizing needed organic influences may help nowadays to avert the organic disasters that overtook earlier civilizations. It may also precipitate disaster, be it said, if it is unnaturally used for precipitate purposes.

TRAFFIC

The traffic problem—a compulsion—already forces economic attention to tyrannical super-building in cities.

Although our economic attention seems to be our very best attention, yet the traffic problem—a time problem where time is said to be money—is yet wholly unsolved. But the call for solution is increasing. But there is, of course, no solution. The metropolis started all wrong on the ground for any organic development now. The gridiron originally laid out for the village horse and buggy, when that same village is now grown to the metropolis is a basic cause for this human cramp, economic waste and constant danger we call the traffic problem. High blood pressure in the veins and arteries of the village gridiron daily becomes more intolerable to the citizen.

The pretended means of relief eagerly specified by space-makers for rent—the expedient skyscraper—renders this human distress only more acute. The same means of relief carried only somewhat further down along the line and 'relief' by these experts will soon have killed the patient—the city. Witness the splitting up of Los Angeles and Chicago into several 'centres', each again already splitting up into several more. You may see the wise decentralization of the big department stores and the mail order houses. The migration of factories has already begun. The financial centre, alone, holds its place by the sheer main strength and awkwardness of civic authority. Nevertheless the population of the big cities decreases steadily.

And yet, in the face of all realistic evidence we view such prophecy as

284

the cubistic city of '*futurisme*'. 'La ville radieuse' for an instance. The tyranny of the skyscraper finds there a sophisticated philosophy fortifying itself as 'ideal' by proposing to get new cities built—*on the sites of the old ones!* Standardization way up on stilts again is seen as our Salvation. Enormous exaggerations of avenues of traffic is suggested but making all intercommunication utterly impractical because the actual nature of circumstances is surely making such exaggeration entirely unnecessary.

And made the plainer by this kind of 'drawing-board' architecture, we may see how the humanity involved in any machine-made city of this machine-made future of a machine-manipulated humanity is to be 'dealt' with by machine-made aesthetics in order to hold and render such human benefits as electricity, the automobile, the telephone, the airship and the radio into a systematic herd-exploitation of mankind instead of rendering mankind more free.

IN OUR NATION WHY BUILD POVERTY IN AS AN INSTITUTION?

Along with such skyscraper solution-by-picture of uptown confusion worse confounded as this modernistic myopia, there now goes the vexing problem of the tenement. This extensive would-be beneficent government 'housing of the poor'. Yes, the poor are not only to be with always, but the poor are to be recognized and multiplied *per se* as such. And so multiplied officially too, they are to be built in as official fixture of the cities of the great free United States of America. Yes . . . the 'poor' are to be so poor as to be accepted, confirmed and especially provided for as inevitable factors therein. As seen in any Federal plan, catastrophe is to be made organic. The poor are to be *built in!*

Yes, the slums of today are to be made into the slums of tomorrow.

That the poor will benefit by increased sanitation may be granted at a glance. But, not only are the living quarters of the poor to be more germ-proof, but life itself where individual choice is concerned is to be rendered antiseptic. If we trust our eyes.

The skyscraper is to be let down sidewise or the flat-plane tipped up edgewise as traps to crucify, not liberate, humanity.

And the poor man's life is to become just as the rich man's office— No. 36722, block 99, shelf 17, entrance K, with a few twists and turns thrown in to distract attention from the fact. The 'poor' man gets a bath-tub and a flower-box, a patch of lawn, but what Freedom to say and believe what he says, were he to say his soul is his own?

Surface and mass architecture thus *extinguishing* the poor man has already *distinguished* his landlord: therefore why should the poor man complain? Has the poor man not still his labour for his pains? And what has the rich man for his, I ask you? Ask him.

Yes, there he is, the poor man! No longer in a rubbish heap. No.

The poor man in the United States of America when Government is through with him is a comparatively decent mechanized unit in a

285

commercial system paying more rent with public help for his new blessings. But so far as he himself goes, there he is a form of 'rent'. Still a cog in rent—for rent and to rent, forever. Still the poor man's life is but two by twice. He has been toned down, but he has further been plucked of individuality and tucked in line. The unsightly 'slum' has thus been white-washed and fumigated. It will be recognized in future, as, still, the slum.

Nor can the poor—thus made surface-and-mass of the great institution of poverty individually (or collectively for that matter) choose anything aesthetically alive to live with. At least not if neighbours and landlords can see that he has it. But the 'social' objective is attained . . . the dirty rags of the poor have been temporarily covered from sight by a clean smock.

Yes, the poor man in this hard governmental picture, exhibit B, is cog 3,000,000,128 in the new model for the standardized city, is it 'La ville radieuse'—to come. The poor man it seems has no other choice. Because his choice is either sentimental or senseless? But observe now the simple aspect: housing the poor. How easy it all is!

This, indeed, by government or by order, is the 'Ne Plus Ultra' for the poor man of the 'E Pluribus Unum' of such social progress as the machine has forced upon us where authority by order takes architecture in charge.

These dreams of the new city where and when no real need exists for any city at all are delightfully impartial. These new 'ideals' distinguished no one, nor perceive anything except certain routine economies and the rent paying rituals sacred to a business man's civilization. These routine economics are to be shared with the ubiquitous-numericals (they are still the common-denominator), sharing them with the nominators of the system, the system being officially perfected as still, Ideal! Well, the economics are shared fifty-fifty? Half to the initial nominator—the Federal Banking System—and half distributed among the too numerous numericals? Fair enough—or—who can say what fairness is in so equivocal a system as ours at this time?

In any case, the division of these economic benefits within the range of this authorized official standardization of the man must be either left out or left entirely to the generosity of the initial nominators, the same as always before. We learned to speak of democracy, only.

And yet, what would you? Humanity is here orderly. Decent on the surface again—rank and file—in the great war behind all wars, the great to-have and to-hold. The common denominator in this scheme is here gratuitously officered, standardized like any army, marched not only to and fro, but up and down no little less. Six stories. The common denominator (the plain citizen) on such terms would be no more able to work without the initial nominator (the capitalist) than the machine would be able to work without the human brain. No, the growing ranks of the poor themselves, they are here become the government pawn. They have become the machine itself. In theory and in fact.

'The Noble Duke of York, he had ten thousand men,' they all go six floors up, and up six floors again. And none may know just why they go,

286

so narrowly up, up, up, to come narrowly down, down, down—instead of freely going in and out and comfortably round about among the beautiful things to which their lives are related in horizontal lines on top of this green earth. Why not spend the money on transporting them?

And is not this modern system of devising life on what we may call skyscraper terms (the skyscraper may be laid down flatwise and its occupants be not much better off) intended to reduce all but our mechanistic supervisors and the devisors who may live in pent houses or on the top floors—or those who may secure the privileges of the upper stories, to the ranks of the poor? Themselves the poor in spirit?

A free country and democratic in the sense that our forefathers intended ours to be free, means *individual* freedom for each man on his own ground. And it means that for all, rich or poor alike, as the true basis of opportunity. Or else Democracy is only another Yankee expedient to enslave man to the machine, and in a foolish way try to make him like it. Why not, now that the means comes to hand, let his line of action be *horizontally* extended: and give him the flat plane expanded parallel to the earth, gripping all social structure to the ground! A true capitalist system, apex in the air, broad base in the ground. This awakening sense of interior space in the man as in the building and ways of life to match it must break through to sunlight, sky, and air, or we will have a communist factory hand instead of a democratic citizen of free initiative in a land of opportunity for that worker. As for the cave? Our present idea of a building? It is ancient, vanishing with the walls now seen standing there as feudal-masonry. When that idea vanishes only, then will the machine be the natural conqueror of the drudgeries and demoralization of earth and fit to use for the extension of the spirit of man.

THE NEW FREEDOM

Freedom? Yes, when the margin of human leisure and the culture of every man who works may widen with his work. And every man works with joy and self-respect in his work. The machine thus comprehended and controlled would succeed for the man himself and the widening margin of leisure be increasingly spent in a field or on the stream or in the public or private gardens or the wood and the wild so easily reached now on great architectural roads.

There is spaciousness for all in Usonia. The great highway is becoming, and rapidly, the horizontal line of a new Freedom extending from ocean to ocean, tying woods, streams, mountains and plains and great and small together, tapping an outflow from the overcrowded urban fields for the better building of men in a better way. All human occupation thus expanded will add intrinsic beauty of feature to the truly noble nature-environment into which our nation has been born. Only then will we be justified in bringing children into the world. They will become the United States (our Usonia) of tomorrow: each pair of expectant little feet born to

287

its own acre. What right, else, has intelligent parenthood to exercise its function?

If our enormous machine power were humanely thus used it would enable all that was ever desirable in any city to go at any time now to a greater natural beauty and enjoy the freer life we could honestly call democratic. True culture must grow up with the ground. I believe that only when Machine increment, placed there where it belongs, enabling human life to be fruitful because Man is *with* his own ground and not merely a parasite upon it—only so and then will indigenous culture ever come to us as a truly Democratic Nation.

The better personal element are already withdrawing from what is now urban, leaving it to the dregs or to the bucket-shop or the business of the port of call or leave. The better elements are already so far withdrawn from the city that gang-rule is hard to break: The city infested by evil as a wharf is infested by rats.

When we become thus frankly utilitarian we can go with the new reality to the order that is beauty, and the simplicity of its expression to which our machine facilities, were they in proper as well as competent hands, entitle us.

I see such organic change soon defeating 'establishment'. Already it shows us that Centralization is giving way to decentralization and that we must take a hand in re-integration or be the shortest-lived civilization in all history.

THE ROAD IS ALWAYS BETTER THAN THE INN

Meantime these United States afford increasingly great road-systems. Splendid highways are becoming ours. Telephone and power poles that everywhere mar these highways and the countryside were long ago obsolete. The old pig-tight, horse high, bull strong fence is no longer needed as modern farming goes. Electrical fencing makes it unnecessary. And these great road-systems, hastening movement toward the city at first, are facilitating reaction now. The country-side is steadily rising in importance.

Railroads, once dominant metallic lines of communication strung in competing lines across the country, are growing gradually useless except for the long haul overland. These private roads will soon be turned into great natural concrete arteries for mobile uninterrupted traffic on several levels. Clumsy heavy coaches dragged roaring along on hard rails are already obsolete. The present heavy railway no matter how amended is too cumbersome and slow for the requirements of modern mobilization, and will pass with the passing of the city.

As new and greater road-systems are added year by year they are more splendidly built. I foresee that roads will soon be architecture too. As they well may be. Great architecture.

Leading toward the city, at first to gratify a hindered or frustrated socia and civil life, our great Usonian roads are working the normal way now, in

27. View in winter

TALIESIN III. 1927

28. The South

29. The Bell Tower in the rear middle wing
TALIESIN III. 1927
30. Glimpse of the living room

the right direction, leading away from senseless urban congestion and competition to a new life and greater integrity; the Freedom of the country when man with machine leverage in his own hand takes it over.

LAND

Thanks to provisions of Government, great natural and National Parks are becoming everywhere available for recreation.

There are millions of individual building sites, large and small, now easy of access and available owing to our great continually developing road-systems. These sites may be seen everywhere neglected—but they are good for little else. Why where there are so many billions of acres of idle land now easily reached by cheap transportation should land longer be parcelled out by realtors to needy families in strips 25 feet or even 100 feet wide, and the slum be transferred next door to itself? The rank and file survival of feudal thinking comes to its end. Routine establishment striving to preserve traditions of the ancient city to perpetuate the social and economic crimes practised by might upon the serf is less fashionable. Yes, an acre to the individual should be democratic minimum in our nation if this machine of ours is ever to be a social success.

What is standing in the way of coming liberation? Nothing but Habit, Greed and Fear.

It is only necessary to realign the standardized efficiency of the machine in this new direction, confine the concentration of its operation only wherever it may belong, and manage the distribution of benefits at large not as speculative profits but upon a basis of decentralization. We are learning that machine-benefits are human-benefits or they are bitter fruit. Much bitter fruit already hangs in the city tree, rotted, alongside the good —to eventually, and soon, rot the whole. Only a small part of our enormous machine increment is where it naturally belongs. Circumstances are inexorably taking it first to the regional field on the way to the country fields. By evolution certainly—by bloodshed maybe. -

THE GAS STATION

One more advance agent of reintegration, an already visible item in the coming decentralization of the City, may be seen in any and every roadside service station happening to be well located along the highways.

The roadside service station may be—in embryo—the future city-service-distribution. Each station may well grow into a well-designed convenient neighbourhood distribution centre naturally developing as meeting place, restaurant, restroom, or whatever else will be needed as decentralization processes and integration succeeds. Already, hundreds of thousands occupy the best places in the towns or, more significantly, pretty well outside the towns.

Eventually we will have a thousand new city-equivalents at work detracting from every small town or great city we now have. Proper integration of these would help overcome the super-centralization now trying to stand against human Freedom.

Added to many such minor stations destined to someday become beautiful countryside features there will be larger traffic stations at main intersections. There may be really neighbourhood centres where there will be more specialized commerce and such special entertainments as are not yet available by every man's own fireside. They are increasingly few because soon there will be little not reaching any man where he lives, coming by space-annihilating devices such as broadcasting, television. And incessant publication, of course. The cultural quality of these new means is steadily advancing in spite of the old commercial tides of advertising now swamping them. The neighbourhood garage is an 'eating' place—the auto camp or 'motel' are features of mostly all Western service stations. All these roadside units are increasing in numbers and in scope and scale as well as in range and desirability.

Perfect distribution, like the ubiquitous publicity that serves or destroys, is a common capacity of the machine probably never to be completely realized. Nor can it ever be even approximately realized in such 'centralization' as the back and forth haul of the big city. This affair of auto-mobilization for distribution to auto-mobilization, once it really begins to operate, will soon revolutionize present arbitrary, wasteful transportation arrangements.

The hated chain merchandizing linked to chain-servicing, decentralized but reintegrated in countryside markets, may give more direct and perfected machinery for all kinds of distribution of all kinds of stores in connection with traffic-stations than ever could be had by the out-dated back-and-forth haul.

THE MOTOR CAR MORE AND MORE

Complete mobilization of our American people is one natural asset of the machine, fast approaching. Opportunity will soon come for the homeward-bound individual to pick up by the wayside anything in the way of supplies he may require, just as the stranger may find there entertainment and satisfactory lodging. In these United States great highways are becoming arteries of the integrated but otherwise decentralized great metropolis of the future: Broadacre City.

Yes, these common wayside interests, plus entertainment because of the motor car, will soon be a highway as well as a byway commonplace. As the importance of Freedom appears to the human mind the need of it increases in the human heart. So no doubt a new sense of quality in all these expressions will appear. The luxurious motor-bus travelling over superb road systems is making travel and intercommunication not only universally available but highly interesting. And the aeroplane will be remodelled some day as a self-contained mechanical unit. Then it will pick up and continue this surface traffic as super-traffic in air, routed anywhere on earth. Then, and not until then, the airport will further develop as integral feature beside the highways, infinitely extending space-arteries and the possibilities of our modern life.

Even now, a day's motor journey is becoming something to be enjoyed in itself—enlivened, serviced, and perfectly accommodated *en route*. No need to get tangled up in spasmodic stop-and-go traffic in some wasteful stop-and-go trip to town nor to any 'great' city centre for anything whatever except to 'view the ruins'. These common highway journeys may soon become the delightful modern circumstance, an ever-varying adventure within reach of everyone. Already as Cervantes said, the Road is always better than the Inn.

DISTRIBUTION

Our cities today are voracious mouths. And New York is the greatest and greediest mouth in the world. A terrific drain on national transport. But with generally perfect and economic distribution of food completed within the immediate area of the countryside, a vital element that helped to build the city to its present extent has left it forever to spread out in direct relation to the soil from which the produce to feed it came. Local products should find a short haul to direct consumption. An expensive long haul to the city and then a haul back again is a wasteful feature of present urban centralization, and freshness has to be sacrificed.

Within easy distance of any man's dwelling anywhere soon there will be everything needed in the category of food-stuffs and factorialized or cultural products which the city itself can now supply. And so many the city never dreamed of. Yes, the centralized city of the future may become only a depot of some kind. One will be found at the ports or where vast supplies of natural material are located for manufacture. But wherever it is, it is certain that it will be only a degraded mechanistic servant of the machine, because man himself will have everywhere escaped to find all his city ever offered him, plus Freedom and privacy the city never had and is now busy trying to teach him that he does not want. He will have gone to seek and find the man-like freedom for himself that any free democracy ought really to mean to him today: Beauty of life—man's birthright where men are really free. This can be his on individual terms when the country he lives in is in fact a truly great Free country in this expanded extended sense of space.

APPEASEMENT

Then with this appropriate ideal of democratic freedom, how to alleviate, how to mitigate meantime the horror of life held helpless or caught unaware in the machinery we now call the city? How easiest and soonest assist the social unit to escape the gradual, growing paralysis of individual independence which characterizes the 'educated' machine-made university moron. Paralysis of the emotional nature is necessary to the ultimate triumph of the machine over man—serves only to quicken man's ultimate subjection to the entrenched machine of 'capital'. It is interesting to observe that we have no United States equivalent of the English Cockney to stand out against the universal standardizing practised upon us in our nation.

To stand up against that standardizing is the architect's real job as I see it. I wish I could have clearly seen it, instead of only feeling it many years ago when I walked out of the University of Wisconsin—to take the open road.

Measured over the great areas, the living human-interest today should be persistently uneducated, inspired to try along this fresh contact of free-individuality with growing faith in the freedom of work in and for sun-light and air in the breadth and beauty of the new spacing, the new scale, with and of the new ground. That I am sure is the greater *human* interest in our Democracy such as and where it is, and that should now characterize our free land even though it might be necessary to close the universities, museums and especially the art institutes now to get it into effect. Were I a Rockefeller—Ford—or Du Pont, I mean as rich, I would buy up our leading universities—close them and hang out the sign—closed by the beneficence of one, Frank Lloyd Wright.

'TASTE', THE TRAVESTY

Taste is still a matter of ignorance. But let us, for the purposes of this hour together, not regard this all too characteristic recession by way of 'educated' taste, our fashionable eclecticisms, too seriously. Let it be as it is, travesty, not tragedy. And proceed to pick up the latest architectural issue in sight. Miss Flat-top has, innocently, perhaps hopefully even, been calling it a bad name, 'modernistic'. Let us stop a moment to think . . . and reason a while together concerning her infatuation.

Such licentious waste of ourselves as we have called 'Taste' in getting ourselves built does become, at long last, more vitally important than Education. No eclectic affair, nor any eclecticism whatever can see our national life struggle coming along toward us so fast in this twentieth century. 'Out of the ground into the light' is the true way of growth. Not groping or fancifully two-stepping by way of more artificial background into complete outer darkness. We have had quite enough of background seen as foreground. Now let us clearly see background as background and we will advance.

Sheldon Cheney somewhere said, truly, in his book, *New World Architecture*, I think it was, 'we are, as a nation, standing at the beginning of a world slope in this obscured human interest called architecture.' Well . . . we as a people, can descend culturally no lower than we are, so however steep or slow that upward slope may be for us, it can only be upward toward the time when it will be just as natural for things to be genuine and grow beautiful as it is nowadays for things to be false and remain ugly. Great art has always been inseparably connected with the full bloom of a country's life? Wherever art has declined—that is to say, got itself as antique, anybody's antique, into the hands of the connoisseur or 'the dealer', either coming or going—the whole country never grows, or, having grown must soon degenerate. I do not believe we are a people—as has been said—'passing from barbarism to degeneracy never having known a civilization.' We are too ignorant and new for anything to happen to us on the high plane of degeneracy.

No, we are an ethically confused but still morally strong and simple-hearted people, a people that will yet instinctively bring forth a strong and healthy art when ethics and a true philosophy take hold. Let us, therefore, at the moment console ourselves with the thought that we cannot yet degenerate. We cannot degenerate because in art, generation itself is something American culture has not yet known. This affair we choose to call taste may pall and change—as it does continually. But thank whatever Gods may be it is not high enough as a quality to degenerate.

THE OLD ORDER

The United States of America while still very young in years is grown old at a tragic rate. But unfortunately for the new architectural opportunities trying to emerge as natural, or native, we are too old—because all that such pseudo-classic architects as we have had to copy from as architecture was never more in the original than a kind of antique sculpture. That is to say, all these ancient buildings we owe to pseudo-classic traditions were at one time some great block-mass of building material, 'sculped', that is to say fashioned from the outside into taste-conceived and desired or necessary 'features'. They were therefore exterior in Idea and relatively exterior in every sense. Always there was an 'outside' as an outside. And the 'inside' was there merely as an inside. Outside and inside were usually quite separate, wholly independent of each other. Holes were cut into the block-mass at intervals for a little light and some air; the deeper the hole looked to be, that is to say the thicker the sides of the hole were—the architects called these sides the 'reveal'—the better. Great attention was paid to a rather pretentious hole to get inside by, or to get out by . . . So, pseudo-classic buildings resembled more or less trimmed-up masonry fortifications. Often the originals were actual fortifications. Quite necessary to be fortified in those days.

Yes, the houses and public buildings had to be fortifications, for civilization itself was first and foremost fortified: that is to say, it was frankly founded upon force. So, usually, so-called classical and even feudal dwellings were little masonry caverns. If more pretentious, they were, at best, great caves.

Thus viewed in the perspective of this new ideal of lightness and strength conquering space, we must conceive this old architecture a sculptured block of building material as hollowed out within. Or we cannot imagine anyone living in it at all. All life then was living in the heart of a hollowed-out masonry block if the grammar of building in that time had any meaning.

Yes, that is the essential sense of the aesthetic whole in all that we call 'classic' architecture.

Now this ancient, honourable enough at the time, idea of a building, that is to say, masonry-mass as such, ornamented outside and ornamented inside, is now a serious set-back for any plastic architecture in our civilization that would look toward freedom to form a sound ethical basis in the proper use of entirely new materials by entirely new methods. Indeed, the survival of this 'classic' ideal, be it modified as 'Colonial' or what have you in the circumstances, is mostly what interferes with any hope we have for a fruitful pattern for living a free democratic life in our great country as of today.

THE SYMBOL OF AUTHORITY

The dome, this hang-over of the ancient and feudal (still pagan) ideal of building received its final illumination, therefore its ruination, in the 500-year-long decadence of the European Renaissance. Michelangelo, great sculptor that he was, crashed the crumbling ruin when in Rome he finally hurled the Pantheon on top of the Parthenon. The result of the great Italian's impulsive indiscretion was named St. Peter's. The world agreed that it was a day, celebrating the great act ever since in the sincerest form of flattery possible. Specialists in it ourselves, as we well know that supreme flattery is *imitation*.

Now, Buonarotti, being a sculptor, naturally set about making the grandest statue (call it a building) that he could conceive coming out of the Italian Renaissance of his day. This great new church dome of his, St. Peter's, was empty of meaning, had no significance at all except as the Pope's mitre has it, or had it. But although this upstart dome was violating all the principles of good construction, it nevertheless seemed to be just the sort of thing temporal *authority* had been looking for as a showy symbol. A label. And the unnatural dome up on stilts became the symbol of great authority, holy or unholy. A ponderous anachronism has become accepted officially to characterize and idealize authority in all civilized countries both great and small.

Before Michelangelo turned architect, domes had their haunches, that is to say the thrust of the dome (a dome is an arch), well down within the building itself. St. Sophia is a noble example of true doming, but it was built when the Roman empire was oriental. The Orientals first knew the beauty and value of a real dome.

But the great sculptor now divorced his dome from the mere matter of reality. So he got it up higher than all other domes. He got it way up above the building, up into the blue sky resting on high stilts. He called the stilts columns. Ah, that was better. So much more grand! But history records cracks seen opening in the base of the dome before it was finished. The massive masonry arch—a dome is an arch—was pushing out on all sides, with nothing but air to push against. Thus the dome itself and the stilts upon which the great arched mass stood became an awful threat to human

294

life there below. A desperate call was sent out to the blacksmiths of Rome. A grand chain demanded—links the thickness of your leg. And desperate was the hurry at the forge to keep the great sculptor's monumental grandeur way up there long enough to do its deadly work upon the imaginations of subsequent generations of by no means stupid men.

Well, the blacksmith's chain was finally secured, fastened round the haunches of the great dome that had been impulsively lifted so high above its natural bearings (but nevertheless lifted to immortality) by our hero, the great sculptor. As an architect, I can imagine the relief with which the sculptor crawled back to bed when the obliging and competent blacksmith had made all secure, and slept for thirty-six hours without once turning over.

This ponderous anachronism thereafter proceeded to project other continental domes, finally our own national Capitol. Then on it went downward to the domes of our various state capitols—some forty-eight of them? And then to the lesser domes of county courthouses. From them it went on down to the little domes of the minor city halls. There the accepted symbol, saved by the blacksmith, the accepted symbol grandly stands. Seen everywhere in this great new country dedicated to Freedom, it proclaims our debt to a great artist's indiscretion. And see it, too, as democracy's greatest heritage from the rebirth of architecture in Italy, called the Renaissance. Our native grando-mania took that form. That's all. It might have taken any other form, but it happened to take the dome.

Sir Christopher Wren on behalf of England had previously borrowed the sculptor's dome—and before we got hold of it—but wisely and beforehand this time, Sir Christopher borrowed the chain for St. Paul's from the Florentine blacksmith. Amusing record: canny Sir Christopher said his masonry dome would have stood without the chain! All the same he did not try it. His caution showed him more a man of sense than his remark showed him competent as an architect.

Worshipping at the false shrine of that dome, Usonia's architects were more shrewd, even, than Sir Christopher. Our grand masonry domes are all blacksmith now. They are cast iron shells imitating the sculptor's masonry, all nicely bolted together at the seams!

So well has the blacksmith arrived that the architect has all but gone out. Certainly so far as domes go. Whether the poor architect has gone for a recess or never to return, who can say? We may now honestly say that unless he comes back converted to the kinetic energy of this age and a true master of the blacksmith's iron work, seeing it clearly as no imitation whatsoever but seeing it as good and true iron work, there soon will be little use for him to come back. Here as anyone may see, out of a great sculptor's sense of grandeur in an art not quite his own arises a tyranny that might well make the tyrannical skyscraper—our own St. Peter's of the present hour—sway in its socket, sick with envy.

How dangerous imitation always is! How tragic it always is to allow authority ever to usurp the functions of validity. That once done, what Freedom then? Take warning, America.

Paying thus our equivocal respect to the dome—no longer a dome now but complicated iron work still imitating the unnatural masonry of St. Peter's—is only by way of emphasis of the fact that all ancient architecture of monumental character, the duomo, the temple, the palazzo, even the minster was mostly all sculp, sculpturesque, sculptorial or sculptoretto. And I must also insist that all artificiality as such, always was and will always be carried to excess. Hyper-artificiality invariably becomes commonplace grando-mania . . . either in the parlour, the class-room or the big building: really a form of senility or mere child's play. Depending on the circumstances.

How ridiculous, then, when not dangerous or positively vicious, this extravagant senility that would obliterate the living by sentimentalizing over the dead! Erecting monuments to the dead-and-gone instead of erecting memorials to the here-and-living.

THE ENEMY

Well, our country is now where choice has to be made between such spiritual senility made official and called academic, or true progress. President Hoover, lining up with much other official timber over the same dam, officially recommended this senility. Showing the folly of automatically constituting a pretty good executive, in some respects, an authority in the Fine Arts. Political or established Authority, I have observed in my lifetime is, and so soon, the enemy of all validity.

To sum up: Because it was then the only order, this ancient sculptorial sculptoretto order was at least moral. But subsequently the old order has become betrayal, immoral because of the hyper-artificiality called the Renaissance or 'rebirth' of the ancient order. Eventually this rebirth came to us in virulent form and is seen everywhere in our great cities as current eclecticisms. The ancient order always was economic crime and soon, I hope, a public nuisance. But worse than all beside it has become the cultural curse of these United States of America. The provincial grando-mania of the cultural lag.

YOUTH

Hope is not yet dead. The minority report is yet as it always will be the life of any true Democracy. And architecture has arrived as that vital minority report. As architecture today taking shape in the noble realm of ideas to make our machine power and our undemocratic millions really beneficent, there is one great new integrity—the sense of the within as reality—and behind this dawning sense of reality there are four more limitless new resources to make it ours.

The first resource is this sense of the within as Reality.

The second new resource is Glass, a super-material. Glass, air in air to keep air out or keep it in.

The third new resource is a new standard means of spanning spaces by way of strands of steel. Tenuity. The spider spinning.

The fourth new resource is an awakened sense of Materials. Their nature understood and revealed.

The fifth new resource is Pattern as Natural—Integral ornament. A spiritual element no less real than the first three resources.

All five together are modern in the best sense and may be used to create a new grasp on building we call organic. All are demanding new significance as architecture and making architecture again natural to our way of life in this twentieth century. But all five resources are not only the basis for Modern Architecture in this century; altogether they are no less a lesson to be learned by Modern Life itself, because what Life is, Architecture now is in this new sense.

Because of our infinite new riches in materials, because of our infinite new power in work, notwithstanding our present educational culture-lag and distraction, a deepening sense of life sees all these new resources at hand at this moment as *modern* and sees them as the stuff our culture will be made of.

This being the book on Work, you are in it now with me and you shall have another talk. I had to give a great many during these idle years to many thousands of people all over the United States. Should they seem too much like lectures, just skip them because I know they were intended for the young man in architecture. After all, you know, an architect is writing this autobiography and you have no right to forget the fact.

IN THE NATURE OF MATERIALS: A PHILOSOPHY

Our vast resources are yet new; new only because architecture as 'rebirth' (perennial Renaissance) has, after five centuries of decline, culminated in the imitation of imitations, seen in our Mrs. Plasterbuilt, Mrs. Gablemore, and Miss Flat-top American architecture. In general, and especially officially, our architecture is at long last completely significant of insignificance only. We do not longer have architecture. At least no buildings with integrity. We have only economic crimes in its name. No, our greatest buildings are not qualified as great art, my dear Mrs. Davies, although you do admire Washington.

If you will yet be patient for a little while—a scientist, Einstein, asked for three days to explain the far less pressing and practical matter of 'Relativity'—we will take each of the five new resources in order, as with the five fingers of the hand. All are new integrities to be used if we will to make living easier and better today.

The first great integrity is a deeper, more intimate sense of reality in building than was ever pagan—that is to say, than was ever 'Classic'. More human than was any building ever realized in the Christian Middle Ages. This is true although the thought that may ennoble it now has been living in civilization for more than twenty centuries back. Later it was innate in the simplicities of Jesus as it was organic 500 years earlier in the natural philosophy, Tao (The Way) of the Chinese philosopher, Laotze. But not only is the new architecture sound philosophy. It is poetry.

Said Ong Giao Ki, Chinese sage, 'Poetry is the sound of the heart.'

Well, like poetry, this sense of architecture is the sound of the 'within'. We might call that 'within', the heart.

Architecture now becomes integral, the expression of a new-old reality: the liveable interior space of the room itself. In integral architecture the *room-space itself must come through*. The *room* must be seen as architecture, or we have no architecture. We have no longer an outside as outside. We have no longer an outside and an inside as two separate things. Now the outside may come inside, and the inside may and does go outside. They are *of* each other. Form and function thus become one in design and execution if the nature of materials and method and purpose are all in unison.

This interior-space concept, the first broad integrity is the first great resource. It is also true basis for general significance of form. Add to this for the sake of clarity that (although the general integration is implied in the first integrity) it is in the nature of any organic building to grow from its site, come out of the ground into the light—the ground itself held always as a component basic part of the building itself. And then we have primarily the new ideal of building as organic. A building dignified as a tree in the midst of nature.

This new ideal for architecture is, as well, an adequate ideal for our general culture. In any final result there can be no separation between our architecture and our culture. Nor any separation of either from our happiness. Nor any separation from our work.

Thus in this rise of organic-integration you see the means to end the petty agglomerations miscalled civilization. By way of this old yet new and deeper sense of reality we may have a civilization. In this sense we now recognize and may declare by way of plan and building—the *natural*. Faith in the *natural* is the faith we now need to grow up on in this coming age of our culturally confused, backward twentieth century. But instead of 'organic' we might well say 'natural' building. Or we might say integral building.

So let us now consider the second of the five new resources: glass. This second resource is new and a 'super-material' only because it holds such amazing means in modern life for awakened sensibilities. It amounts to a new qualification of life in itself. If known in ancient times glass would then and there have abolished the ancient architecture we know, and completely. This super-material GLASS as we now use it is a miracle. Air in air to keep air out or keep it in. Light itself in light, to diffuse or reflect, or refract light itself.

By means of glass, then, the first great integrity may find prime means of realization. Open reaches of the ground may enter as the building and the building interior may reach out and associate with these vistas of the ground. Ground and building will thus become more and more obvious as directly related to each other in openness and intimacy; not only as environment but also as a good pattern for the good life lived in the building. Realizing the benefits to human life of the far-reaching implications and effects of the first great integrity: let us call it the interior-space concept. This space interior realization is possible and it is desirable in all the vast variety of characteristic buildings needed by civilized life in our complex age.

By means of glass something of the freedom of our arboreal ancestors living in their trees becomes a more likely precedent for freedom in twentieth-century life, than the cave.

Savage animals 'holing in' for protection were more characteristic of life based upon the might of feudal times or based upon the so-called 'classical' in architecture which were in turn based upon the labour of the chattel slave. In a free country, were we ourselves free by way of organic thought, buildings might come out into the light without more animal fear; come entirely away from the pagan ideals of form we dote upon as 'Classic'. Or what Freedom have we?

Perhaps more important than all beside, it is by way of glass that the sunlit space as a reality becomes the most useful servant of a higher order of the human spirit. It is first aid to the sense of cleanliness of form and idea when directly related to free living in air and sunlight. It is this that is coming in the new architecture. And with the integral character of extended vistas gained by marrying buildings with ground levels, or blending them with slopes and gardens; yes, it is in this new sense of earth as a great human *good* that we will move forward in the building of our new homes and great public buildings.

I am certain we will desire the sun, spaciousness and integrity of means-to-ends more year by year as we become aware of the possibilities I have outlined. The more we desire the sun, the more we will desire the freedom of the good ground and the sooner we will learn to understand it. The more we value integrity, the more securely we will find and keep a worthwhile civilization to set against prevalent abuse and ruin.

Congestion will no longer encourage the 'space-makers for rent'. The 'space-maker for rent' will himself be 'for rent' or let us hope 'vacant'. Give him ten years.

These new space values are entering into our ideas of life. All are appropriate to the ideal that is our own, the ideal we call Democracy.

A NEW REALITY: GLASS

A resource to liberate this new sense of interior space as reality is this new qualification called glass: a super-material qualified to qualify us; qualify us not only to escape from the prettified cavern of our present domestic life as also from the cave of our past, but competent actually to awaken in us the desire for such far-reaching simplicities of life as we may see in the clear countenance of nature. Good building must ever be seen as in the nature of good construction, but a higher development of this 'seeing' will be construction seen as nature-pattern. *That* seeing, only, is inspired architecture.

This dawning sense of the *Within* as *reality* when it is clearly seen as *Nature* will by way of glass make the garden be the building as much as the building will be the garden: the sky as treasured a feature of daily indoor life as the ground itself.

You may see that walls are vanishing. The cave for human dwelling purposes is at last disappearing.

Walls themselves because of glass will become windows and windows as we used to know them as holes in walls will be seen no more. Ceilings will often become as window-walls, too. The textile may soon be used as a beautiful overhead for space, the textile an attribute of genuine architecture instead of decoration by way of hangings and upholstery. The usual camouflage of the old order. Modern integral floor heating will follow integral lighting and standardized unitary sanitation. All this makes it reasonable and good economy to abolish building as either a hyper-boxment or a super-borough.

Haven't senseless elaboration and false mass become sufficiently insulting and oppressive to our intelligence as a people? And yet, senseless elaboration and false mass were tyrannical as 'conspicuous waste' in all of our nineteenth-century architecture either public or private! Wherever the American architect, as scholar, went he 'succeeded' to that extent.

ANOTHER REALITY: CONTINUITY

But now, as third resource, the resource essential to modern architecture destined to cut down this outrageous mass-waste and mass-lying, is the principle of continuity. I have called it tenuity. Steel is its prophet and master. You must come with me for a moment into 'engineering' so called. This is to be an unavoidable strain upon your kind attention. Because, unfortunately, gentle reader, you cannot understand architecture as *modern* unless you do come, and—paradox—you can't come if you are too well educated as an engineer or as an architect either. So your common sense is needed more than your erudition.

However, to begin this argument for steel: classic architecture knew only the post as an *upright*. Call it a column. The classics knew only the beam as a *horizontal*. Call it a beam. The beam resting upon the upright, or column, was structure throughout, to them. Two things, you see, one thing set on top of another thing in various materials and put there in various ways. Ancient, and nineteenth-century building science too, even building *à la mode*, consisted simply in reducing the various stresses of all materials and their uses to these two things: post and beam. Really, construction used to be just sticking up something in wood or stone and putting something else in wood or stone (maybe iron) on top of it: simple superimposition, you see? You should know that all 'Classic' architecture was and still is some such form of direct super-imposition. The arch is a little less so, but even that must be so 'figured' by the structural engineer if you ask him to 'figure' it.

Now the Greeks developed this simple act of super-imposition pretty far by way of innate tasteful refinement. The Greeks were true aestheticians. Roman builders too, when they forgot the Greeks and brought the beam over as a curve by way of the arch, did something somewhat new but with consequences still of the same sort. But observe, all architectural features made by such 'Classic' agglomeration were killed for us by cold steel. And though millions of classic corpses yet encumber American ground unburied, they are ready now for burial.

Of course this primitive post-and-beam construction will always be valid, but both support and supported may now by means of inserted and welded steel strands or especially woven filaments of steel and modern concrete casting be plaited and united as one physical body: ceilings and walls made one with floors and reinforcing each other by making them continue into one another. This Continuity is made possible by the ten-uity of steel.

So the new order wherever steel or plastics enter construction says: weld these two things, post and beam (wall and ceiling) together by means of steel strands buried and stressed within the mass material itself, the steel strands electric-welded where steel meets steel within the mass. In other words the upright and horizontal may now be made to work together as one. A new world of form opens inevitably.

Where the beam leaves off and the post begins is no longer important nor need it be seen at all because it no longer actually *is*. Steel in tension enables the support to slide into the supported, or the supported to grow into the support somewhat as a tree-branch glides out of its tree trunk. Therefrom arises the new series of interior physical reactions I am calling 'Continuity'. As natural consequence the new aesthetic or appearance we call *Plasticity* (and plasticity is peculiarly 'modern') is no longer a mere appearance. Plasticity actually becomes the normal *countenance*, the *true aesthetic* of genuine structural reality. These interwoven steel strands may so lie in so many directions in any extended member that the extensions may all be economical of material and though much lighter, be safer construction than ever before. There as in the branch of the tree you may see the cantilever. The cantilever is the simplest one of the important phases of this third new structural resource now demanding new significance. It has yet had little attention in architecture. It can do remarkable things to liberate space.

But plasticity was modest new countenance in our American architecture at least thirty-five years ago in my own work, but then denied such simple means as welding and the mesh. It had already eliminated all the separate identities of post and beam in architecture. Steel in tension enters now by way of mesh and welding to arrive at actual, total plasticity if and when desired by the architect. And to prove the philosophy of organic architecture, form and function are one, it now enters architecture as the *aesthetic* countenance of *physical reality*.

301

To further illustrate this magic simplifier we call 'plasticity': see it as *flexibility* similar to that of your own hand. What makes your hand expressive? Flowing continuous line and continuous surfaces seen continually mobile of the articulate articulated structure of the hand as a whole. The line is seen as 'hand' line. The varying planes seen as 'hand' surface. Strip the hand to the separate structural identities of joined bones (post and beam) and plasticity as an expression of the hand would disappear. We would be then getting back to the joinings, breaks, jolts, and joints of ancient, or 'Classic', architecture: thing to thing; feature to feature. But plasticity is the reverse of that ancient agglomeration and is the ideal means behind these simplified free new effects of straight line and flat plane.

I have just said that plasticity in this sense for thirty-five years or more has been the recognized aesthetic ideal for such simplification as was required by the machine to do organic work. And it is true of my own work.

As significant outline and expressive surface, this new aesthetic of plasticity (physical continuity) is now a useful means to form the supreme physical-body of an organic, or integral, American Architecture.

Of course, it is just as easy to cheat by simplicity as it is to cheat with 'classical' structure. So, unluckily, here again is the 'modernistic' architectural picture-maker's deadly facility for imitation at ease and again too happy with fresh opportunity to 'fake effects'. Probably another Renaissance is here imminent.

Architecture is now integral architecture only when Plasticity is a genuine expression of actual construction just as the articulate line and surface of the hand is articulate of the structure of the hand. Arriving at steel, I first used Continuity as actual stabilizing principle in concrete slabs, and in the concrete ferro-block system I devised in Los Angeles.

In the form of the cantilever or as horizontal continuity this new economy by means of tenuity is what saved the Imperial Hotel from destruction during the great earthquake of 1922. It did not appear in the grammar of the building for various reasons, chiefly because the building was to look somewhat as though it belonged to Tokio.

Later, in the new design for St. Mark's Tower, New York City, this new working principle economized material, labour, and liberated or liberalized space in a more developed sense. It gave to the structure the significant outlines of remarkable stability and instead of false masonry-mass significant outlines came out. The abstract pattern of the structure as a complete structural-integrity of Form and Idea may be seen fused as in any tree but with nothing imitating a tree.

Continuity invariably realized remarkable economy of labour and building materials as well as space. Unfortunately there is yet little or no data to use as tabulation. Tests will have to be made continually for many years to make the record available to slide-rule engineers.

In the ancient order there was little thought of economy of materials. The more massive the whole structure looked, the better it looked to the ancients. But seen in the light of these new economic interior forces conserved by the tensile strength of a sheet of plastic or any interweaving of strands of steel in this machine age, the old order was as sick with weight as the Bounarotti dome. Weak . . . because there could be no cointerrelation between the two elements of support and supported to reinforce each other as a whole under stress or elemental disturbance.

So this tremendous new resource of *tenuity*—a quality of steel—this quality of *pull* in a building (you may see it ushering in a new era in John Roebling's Brooklyn Bridge) was definitely lacking in all ancient architecture because steel had not been born into building.

The tenuous strand or slab as a common means of strength had yet to come. Here today this element of continuity may cut structural substance nearly in two. It may cut the one half in two again by elimination of needless features, such elimination being entirely due to the simplification I have been calling 'plasticity'.

It is by utilizing mass production in the factory in this connection that some idea of the remarkable new economics possible to modern architecture may be seen approaching those realized in any well-built machine. If standardization can be humanized and made flexible in design and the economics brought to the home owner, the greatest service will be rendered to our modern way of life. It may be really born—this democracy I mean.

Involved as a matter of design in this mass production, however, are the involute, all but involuntary reactions to which I have just referred: the *ipso facto* building code and the fact that the building engineer as now trained knows so little about them. However, the engineer is learning to calculate by model-making in some instances—notably Professor Beggs at Princeton University.

The codes so far as I can see will have to die on the vine with the men who made them.

MATERIALS FOR THEIR OWN SAKE

As the first integrity and the two first new resources appeared out of the interior nature of the kind of building, called Architecture—so now, naturally interior to the true nature of any good building comes the fourth resource. This is found by recognizing the nature of the materials used in construction.

Just as many fascinating different properties as there are different materials that may be used to build a building will continually and naturally qualify, modify and utterly change all architectural form whatsoever.

A stone building will no more *be* nor will it *look* like a steel building. A pottery, or terra cotta building, will not be nor should it look like a stone building. A wood building will look like none other, for it will glorify the stick. A steel and glass building could not possibly look like anything but itself. It will glorify steel and glass. And so on all the way down the long list of available riches in materials: Stone, Wood, Concrete, Metals, Glass, Textiles, Pulp and Plastics; riches so great to our hand today that no comparison with Ancient Architecture is at all sensible or anything but obstruction to our Modern Architecture.

In this particular, as you may see, architecture is going back to learn from the natural source of all natural things.

In order to get Organic Architecture born, intelligent architects will be forced to turn their backs on antique rubbish heaps with which Classic eclecticism has encumbered our new ground. So far as architecture has gone in my own thought it is first of all a character and quality of *mind* that may enter also into human conduct with social implications that might, at first, confound or astound you. But the only basis for any fear of them lies in the fact that they are all sanely and thoroughly *constructive*.

Instinctively all forms of pretence fear and hate reality.
THE HYPOCRITE MUST ALWAYS HATE THE RADICAL.

This potent fourth new resource—the Nature of Materials—gets at the common centre of every material in relation to the work it is required to do. This means that the architect must again begin at the very beginning. Proceeding according to Nature now he must sensibly go through with whatever material may be in hand for his purpose according to the methods and sensibilities of a man in this age. And when I say Nature, I mean inherent *structure* seen always by the architect as a matter of complete design. It is in itself, always, *nature-pattern*. It is this profound internal sense of materials that enters in as Architecture now. It is this the fifth new resource that must captivate and hold the mind of the modern architect to creative work. The fifth will give new life to his imagination if it has not been already killed at school.

And, inevitable implication! New machine age resources require that all buildings do *not* resemble each other. The new ideal does *not* require that all buildings be of steel, concrete or glass. Often that might be idiotic waste.

Nor do the resources even *imply* that mass is no longer a beautiful attribute of masonry materials when they are genuinely used. We are entitled to a vast variety of form in our complex age so long as the form be genuine—serves Architecture and Architecture serves life.

But in this land of ours, richest on earth of all in old and new materials, architects must exercise well-trained imagination to see in each material either natural or compounded plastics, their own *inherent style*. All materials may be beautiful, their beauty much or entirely depending upon how well they are used by the Architect.

In our modern building we have the Stick. Stone. Steel. Pottery. Concrete. Glass. Yes, Pulp, too, as well as plastics. And since this dawning sense of the 'within' is the new reality, these will all give the main '*motif*' for any real building made from them. The materials of which the building is built will go far to determine its appropriate mass, its outline and, especially, proportion. *Character* is criterion in the form of any and every building or industrial product we can call Architecture in the light of this new ideal of the new order.

304

31. HOUSE ON THE MESA: project, 1931. Model exhibited at the Museum of Modern Art, New York, 1932. Machine-age luxury

32. WALTER DAVIDSON SHEET STEEL FARM UNITS: project, 1932. The fire-proof farm concentration of Broadacres City. Model exhibited at the Museum of Modern Art. 1934-5

33. MALCOLM WILLEY HOUSE: project, 1932. A typical Broadacre City dwelling, or Little Farm unit. Model exhibited at the Museum of Modern Art, 1940

34. View from below waterfall

EDGAR J. KAUFMANN HOUSE. 1936

35. Ramp connecting Falling Water and Guest House

THE NEW INTEGRITY

Strange! At this late date, it is modern architecture that wants life to learn to see life as life, because architecture must learn to see brick as brick, learn to see steel as steel, see glass as glass. So modern thought urges all of life to demand that a bank look like a bank (bad thought though a bank might become) and not depend upon false columns for credit. The new architecture urges all of life to demand that an office building look like an office building, even if it should resemble the cross section of a bee-hive. Life itself should sensibly insist in self-defence that a hotel look and conduct itself like a hotel and not like some office building. Life should declare, too, that the railroad station look like a railroad station and not try so hard to look like an ancient temple or some monarchic palazzo. And while we are on this subject, why not a place for opera that would look something like a place for opera—if we must have opera, and not look so much like a gilded, crimsoned bagnio. Life declares that a filling station should stick to its work as a filling station: look the part becomingly. Why try to look like some Colonial diminutive or remain just a pump on the street. Although 'just a pump' on the street is better than the Colonial imitation. The good Life itself demands that the school be as generously spaced and a thought-built good-time place for happy children: a building no more than one storey high—with some light over-head, the school building should regard the children as a garden in sun. Life itself demands of Modern Architecture that the house of a man who knows what home is should have his own home his own way if we have any man left in that connection after F.H.A. is done trying to put them, all of them it can, into the case of a man who builds a home only to sell it. Our Government forces the home-maker into the real-estate business if he wants a home at all.

Well, after all, this line of thought was all new-type common sense in architecture in Chicago only thirty years ago. It began to grow up in my own work as it is continuing to grow up more and more widely in the work of all the world. But, insulting as it may seem to say so, nor is it merely arrogant to say that the actual thinking in that connection is still a novelty, only a little less strange today than it was then, although the appearances do rapidly increase.

INTEGRAL ORNAMENT AT LAST!

At last, in this fifth resource, so old yet now demanding fresh significance. We have arrived at integral ornament—the nature-pattern of actual construction. Here, confessed as the spiritual demand for true significance, comes this subjective element in modern architecture. An element so hard to understand that modern architects themselves seem to understand it least well of all and most of them have turned against it with such fury as is born only of impotence.

And it *is* true that this vast, intensely human significance is really no matter at all for any but the most imaginative mind not without some development in artistry and the *gift* of a sense of proportion. Certainly we must go higher in the realm of imagination when we presume to enter ere, because we go into Poetry.

Now, very many write good prose who cannot write poetry at all. And although staccato specification is the present fashion, just as 'functionalist' happens to be the present style in writing—poetic prose will never be undesirable. But who condones prosaic poetry? None. Not even those fatuously condemned to write it.

So, I say this fourth new resource and the fifth demand for new significance and integrity is ornament *integral to building as itself poetry*. Rash use of a dangerous word. The word 'Poetry' *is* a dangerous word.

Heretofore, I have used the word 'pattern' instead of the word ornament to avoid confusion or to escape the passing prejudice. But here now ornament is in its place. Ornament meaning not only *surface qualified by human imagination* but imagination giving *natural pattern* to structure. Perhaps this phrase says it all without further explanation. This resource —integral ornament—is new in the architecture of the world, at least insofar not only as imagination qualifying a surface—a valuable resource —but as a greater means than that: *imagination giving natural pattern to structure itself*. Here we have new significance, indeed! Long ago this significance was lost to the scholarly architect. A man of taste. He, too soon, became content with symbols.

Evidently then, this expression of structure as a pattern true to the nature of the materials out of which it was made, may be taken much further along than physical need alone would dictate? 'If you have a loaf of bread break the loaf in two and give the half of it for some flowers of the Narcissus for the bread feeds the body indeed but the flowers feed the soul.'

Into these higher realms of imagination associated in the popular mind as sculpture and painting, buildings may be as fully taken by modern means today as they ever were by craftsmen of the antique order.

It is by this last and poetic resource that we may give greater structural entity and greater human significance to the whole building than could ever be done otherwise. This statement is heresy at this left-wing moment, so—we ask, 'taken how and when taken?' I confess you may well ask by whom? The answer is, taken by the true *poet*. And where is this Poet today? Time will answer.

Yet again in this connection let us remember Ong's Chinese observation, 'Poverty is the sound of the heart.' So, in the same uncommon sense integral ornament is the developed sense of the building as a whole, or the manifest *abstract pattern of structure itself*. Interpreted. Integral ornament is simply *structure-pattern made visibly articulate* and seen in the building as it is seen articulate in the structure of the trees or a lily of the fields. It is the expression of inner rhythm of Form. Are we talking

306

about Style? Pretty nearly. At any rate, we are talking about the qualities that make *essential architecture* as distinguished from any mere act of building whatsoever.

What I am here calling integral-ornament is founded upon the same organic simplicities as Beethoven's Fifth Symphony, that amazing revolution in tumult and splendour of sound built on four tones based upon a rhythm a child could play on the piano with one finger. Supreme imagination reared the four repeated tones, simple rhythms, into a great symphonic poem that is probably the noblest thought-built edifice in our world. And Architecture is like Music in this capacity for the symphony.

But concerning higher development of building to more completely express its life principle as significant and beautiful, let us say at once by way of warning: it is better to die by the wayside of left-wing Ornaphobia than it is to build any more merely ornamented buildings, as such; or to see right-wing architects die any more ignoble deaths of *Ornamentia*. All period and pseudo-classic buildings whatever, and (although their authors do not seem to know it) most protestant buildings, they call themselves internationalist, are really ornamental in definitely objectionable sense. A plain flat surface cut to shape for its own sake, however large or plain the shape, is, the moment it is sophisticatedly so cut, no less ornamental than egg-and-dart. All such buildings are objectionably 'ornamental', because like any buildings of the old classical order both wholly ignore the *nature* of the *first* integrity. Both also ignore the four resources and both neglect the nature of machines at work on materials. Incidentally and as a matter of course both misjudge the nature of time, place and the modern life of man.

Here in this new leftish emulation as we now have it, is only the 'istic', ignoring principle merely to get the 'look' of the machine or something that looks 'new'. The province of the 'ite'.

In most so-called 'internationalist' or 'modernistic' building therefore we have no true approach to organic architecture: we have again merely a new, superficial aesthetic trading upon that architecture because such education as most of our architects possess qualifies them for only some kind of eclecticism past, passing, or to pass.

Nevertheless I say, if we can't have buildings with integrity we would better have more imitation machines for buildings until we can have truly sentient architecture. 'The machine for living in' is sterile, but therefore it is safer, I believe, than the festering mass of ancient styles.

GREAT POWER

A far greater power than slavery, even the intellectual slavery as in the school of the Greeks, is back of these five demands for machine-age significance and integrity. Stupendous and stupefying power. That power is the leverage of the machine itself. As now set up in all its powers the machine will confirm these new implicities and complicities in architecture at every point, but will destroy them soon if not checked by a new simplicity.

The proper use of these new resources demands that we use them all together with integrity for mankind if we are to realize the finer significances of life. The finer significance, prophesied if not realized by organic architecture. It *is* reasonable to believe that life in our country will be lived in full enjoyment of this new freedom of the extended horizontal line because the horizontal line now becomes the great architectural highway. The flat plane now becomes the regional field. And integral-pattern becomes 'the sound of the Usonian heart'.

USONIAN ARCHITECTURE

This new sense of Architecture as integral-pattern of that type and kind may awaken these United States to fresh beauty, and the Usonian horizon of the individual will be immeasurably extended by enlightened use of this great lever, the machine. But only if it gets into creative hands loyal to humanity.

By way of these five new means—all 'Architecture'—this monster power, reawakened now and quickened by the creative artist, must gradually come into completely new uses. Instead of crucifying all integrity by stupid eclecticisms, monotony in variety, and utterly wasting life by way of the academic sham capitalized and sold under by our own academic 'captains of industry', our American life may again know the salt and savour of good work in true creation. The culture-lag we inherited with our various nationalities, especially that one washed up on our Eastern shores, will be overcome in time.

The 'captains' both of the cap and gown and the shop and counting house can only see machines as engines of wealth founded upon convenient economic business systems of exploitation. They are the only one means they know. But the captains themselves, I observe, when sufficiently enriched, become culture curious, turn traitor to their own machine-increment and waste it all in bigger and better imitations of the already sufficiently devastating antique. Ask Sir Joseph Duveen! He was not Knighted by the English for nothing. Do the people need further proof of the system's sterility than that Knight? Then look for what it is in these recurring wars settling nothing except the necessity for more and greater wars. Empire, the apotheosis of War.

HE WHO LOOKS AND SEES

I must believe that notwithstanding shallow newspaper hokum our people are weary of this shallow commercialized life of 'taste'. I believe they see more clearly through academic lies. The American in the street looks and sees the aeroplane fly overhead, emancipated from make-believe, free to be itself and be true to itself. He looks and sees the steam-ship ride the seas, triumphant as the superb thing it is, for what it is; sees the motor car becoming more the machine it should be, daily less like a horse and buggy, gradually acquiring freedom to be itself for what it is. In all modern mobilizations or utensils whatsoever in architecture, awakening, he may see this age of the machine more freely declaring for Freedom to express the simple facts of structure. Malformations of material and the misuse of tools and utensils grow less.

I believe that in the new uses of these new and valid economic stan-dards in architecture here enumerated, you may see and measure the cure for the causes of oncoming urban decay. And urban decay may be a real service rendered twentieth-century mankind by what we are here calling the 'Machine'.

Well, up to and including the nineteenth century, mechanical forces *did* place a premium upon centralization. None the less, twentieth-century mobilizations—electrifications in multiple forms—*are* advance agents of decentralization and fresh integration.

It is not so difficult to see now that man has only to get this monster, the Machine, into the service of his trained imagination and get machine-increment where it belongs—into the hands of his better self—and the big city is a survival fit only for burial: dead. The natural consequence of that grand mechanical success which today is only a form of human excess. A finer ideal of machine-age luxury as primarily human is coming out of, or coming along with, our modern architecture today. And this will live to bury the corpse of every great city in America. Some day.

Meantime journeyman, beggarman, merchant, chief—beware! This group of ideas is set forth here as one great demand for a finer integ-rity of human life, and we must repudiate any symbol it may itself create as likely to relapse into imitations as minds are now educated in our popular colleges. Institutions are the enemies of creative thought and work.

Nor can this new sense of reality look to any ready-made abstraction—Greek, Hindu, Chinese, whatever is authority. This thought must look all full in the eye for the impostor it may finally become by way of current standardized philosophy. Whatsoever.

Yes, I must and I do believe that this new demand for life as organic—therefore life as itself a noble kind of architecture—architecture is life—must read first lessons afresh in the great book of creation itself, despising with the fervour of youth all that lives either ashamed or afraid to live an honest life *as itself*: proud to live for what it is or may become because of *its own nature*.

A common integrity of life will then carry these five significances as one great integrity to full expression as the great Usonian architecture of Life, the great universal life of our own true democracy.

309

America, there is no need to be afraid! 'We may disregard the laws, but if we are for NATURE . . . we are never lawless.'

The circumstances at Taliesin made it necessary to go on more talking tours North, South, East—West. I became a sort of

JOURNEYMAN PREACHER

Young men and young women in many communities of our country were themselves the great fact in the various lectures I gave at this time pretty much upon this same subject upon which you have just been lectured. And these young men and women were the circumstance that encouraged me to openly assume the hateful unpopular guise of the preacher. They paid me thousands of dollars to talk to them, and were eager to help me send exhibitions of my work to various places here at home and as it had already gone abroad. I have recounted some of the experiences of the congenital preacher somewhere in me, here, to show how the on-coming generation in our country is keen and coming clean, a fresh strong voice, where the present generation has been so stultified by the stupid sentimentalities of our Victorian past. I believe and you will soon believe that at least the coming generation is trying to learn to differentiate between sentiment and sentimentality. Not so easy, either, in these times of double-barrelled reaction, high-powered commercial radio, cinema salesmanship and graphic propaganda for all other and else.

So from what I have myself seen, I say to you with confidence that the next generation but one will overturn the falsity in which it was reared—and themselves with their feet on the road to Freedom, give a fairer break to fine-sentiment, so it be honest, than the generation before them of which they will become expositors. That future generation will have its meed of action. I feel that it cannot be denied.

ANOTHER MODERN INSTANCE

One evening came the New York Town Hall meeting. A meeting called to protest against the non-employment of myself by the Chicago Fair authorities.

What an embarrassing anti-climax!

I had given plenty of good reasons already for such non-employment. I was only too ready to give more. Surely it was better to have one architect out of employment in such parlous times than the eight or ten or fifteen already employed at the Fair? Were I to come in they would go out.

Another group entirely would have come in with me if ever I came in at all. They all knew that.

But this Town meeting was prefaced with a dinner at the Crillon to which a congenial exponent of the Fair, good old Ray Hood, had invited me. He came over to shake hands before whatever it was that was coming at the Town Hall later. I didn't know what was coming. Nor did Ray.

No, I didn't know what was coming. And I guess, by the way Ray looked, he didn't care what came.

The hall was packed. Alexander Woollcott in the chair. I have seen Aleck bubble with wit in his lair by the river and scintillate in his seat with the mutual admiration society at the Algonquin. But that night Aleck was effervescence itself. At least living in New York City does keen the rapier and polish the thrust, if he is a fair example.

At once the meeting took on an air of laughing gaiety. But that changed when Lewis Mumford got up to speak. With the essential manliness and nobility seen in the man as seen in his work he made no attempt to be apologetic or conciliatory. He was earnest and seriously wrote down the matter of the Fair where modern architecture was concerned more clearly and effectively than I had done the evening before.

As for me, still embarrassed, caught off guard in all this, and up on my feet now for something or other, I hastily decided to pay my respects to the Fair by building, building while the crowd listened, a fair or two of my own quite for myself and by myself—three in fact—and of diverse character.

In a flash it seemed to me this would be constructive criticism worth something to architecture, entertaining to me at least, and fun for them —maybe—meantime. As for the rest, it was dead issue so far as I was concerned.

Because the only real interest I had in the Fair since first hearing of it, or any hope of it whatever, was to prevent any such catastrophe to our culture as occurred in 1893. Pro or con.

I did hate to see the careful, devoted sacrifice of so many faithful years in building up a great cause again played up, and probably played out, down and out, by the clever pictorializing and the current salesmanship that I knew would be snatching the great cause to feather the architectural offices of a few New York and Chicago plan-factories. However much I might like or be flattered by the factors of those factories, I could see no more than that coming out of the circumstances.

So I *was* placed in an embarrassing, awkward position by this meeting because it would seem that I was present and spoke because I myself resented being left out of the Fair. Whereas the truth was I resented only their quick turnover to my work and the pretentious scene-painting I knew coming of it as unworthy the modern architecture I had myself given them. Only for this exploit?

Standing there to speak, having given no previous thought to the matter, several contrasting ideas of a fair that would be worthy modern architecture because square with our new structural resources came into my mind. These ideas not unnaturally, as I was simply talking and thinking out of my everyday self, developed as I talked.

I had given the schemes no study. They were spontaneous.

311

THREE PROGRESS FAIRS IN ONE

Scheme One:

As skyscraperism characterizes the thought of the group characterizing the fair—and they had themselves idealized the fair in so many words, as 'like New York seen from one of its own high buildings . . .'

Why not, then, the Fair itself the apotheosis of the skyscraper?

Build a great skyscraper in which the Empire State Building might stand free in a central interior court-space which would be devoted to all the resources of the modern elevator.

Instead of the old stage-props of the previous fairs, the same old miles of picture-buildings faked in cheap materials, wrapped around a lagoon, a fountain or theatrical waterfall in the middle—to be all eventually butchered to make a Roman holiday—let there be, for once, a genuine modern *construction*.

If elevators could handle the population of New York, they could handle the crowds at the Fair. Why not handle the crowds directly from several expansive tiers of mechanized parking space as great terraces from which the true skyscraper itself would directly rise? The construction should be merely the steel itself designed as integral pattern in the structural framing. Then concrete slabs for floors projecting as cantilever balconies from floor to floor—garden floors intervening as restaurants.

Instead of glass for enclosure—some of our many light, transparent glass substitutes might be used. The multitudinous areas thus created could be let to the various exhibitors. The entire feature of the top stories could be garden observatories, pleasure places. A vast auditorium might join at the base to the skyscraper and handle such great aggregations of people on the ground. This tower construction of steel might rise from the triple-decked parking terraces, one corner of the terraces projecting and extending into the lake two ways at right angles to make piers and harbours for all water craft. Beneath the lake nearby where the reflections of the tower would fall, powerful jets of the lake itself rising by way of inserted power pumps to great height. All to be illuminated by modern light-projecting apparatus, projecting toward the tower and projecting from it. The lake thus at contingent points becoming a series of great fountains irradiated by light.

The Lake Front Park itself would thus become merely landscape adjunct to the great modern structure which might easily, and modestly, rise two hundred and forty-five stories. The total construction say two thousand five hundred feet above the lake level—or about a half mile high.

The clouds might naturally or artificially drift across its summit. Or effects be created by aeroplanes laying down coloured ribbons of smoke to drift across it.

Such construction—the fake architecture of the New York functioneer obsolete—today would be no impossible feat, financially or structurally. In fact, entirely within reach as safe and reasonable. Practical.

And it could stay thus, a feature of the Chicago Lake Front beautiful

312

as the Eiffel Tower never was. And the Eiffel Tower would reach only well below its middle.

Every floor would be a practical resource for future affairs of every sort. The business of the city itself might move into it with all its multifold minor branches. Still there would be room enough left for a mighty, continuous, never-ending industrial fair that would embrace the products of the entire civilized world in Chicago.

Something accomplished worthy of a century of progress? The beacons from the top would reach adjoining states: the radio from the antennae lifting from the tower crown would be in touch with all the world.

But if not skyscraper-minded and preferring to roam instead of to be lifted up on high . . . then . . .

Scheme Two:

A weaving characteristic of this age of steel in tension. Accept from John Roebling his pioneer work—the message of the Brooklyn Bridge.

Build noble pylons—since the Fair commissioners seemed to like the word 'pylon'—on the Lake Front 500 feet apart each way until enough park, including threading waterways, have been covered to accommodate all exhibitors on the park level and in one balcony lever surrounding the enclosed area. This canopy to be anchored by steel cables to the outer series of appropriate pylons. Weave, in the main and minor and intermediate cables, a network that would support transparent fabrications such as we have as modern glass substitutes in our day. And thus make an architectural canopy more beautiful and more vast than any ever seen. The canopy could rise five hundred feet at the pylons to fall to one hundred and fifty feet above the park between them. The fabric should fall as a screen at the sides to close the space against wind. The rain water, falling, would wash the roof spaces clean or they could be flushed from the pylon tops as fountains, the water dropping through openings at the low points of the canopy into fountain basins, features of the system of lagoons that would wind and thread their way through the greenery of the park beneath the canopy.

All trees, foliage and waterways could be combined for the beholder by moving walkways to reach the individual plots allotted to the individual exhibitors. Little footwork. Each individual exhibitor would thus be free to set up his own show and ballyhoo it how he pleased.

The old fair-spirit, exciting as of old—but thus made free to excite the sophisticated modern ego once more by great spans and wondrous spinning.

Well, this type of construction with appropriate illumination and hydro-electric effects should cost less in standardization thus extended and made beautiful than the pettifogging, picture-making, privatistic individual buildings of so many architects all only interfering with exhibits and exhibitions in order to say exactly nothing. Yes, and say it in the same old way. Tagged—only publicity tagged—as 'new'. And, at least, the great 'pylons' might remain always as lighting features of the Lake Front Park.

313

Whereas the privatistic buildings faked in synthetic cardboard and painted would all have to be thrown away some day.

Or . . . more romantically inclined? Then why not—

Scheme Three:

There on the Lake Front is the Chicago harbour already enclosed against the turbulence of Lake Michigan.

Why not use that for a genuine holiday? A gay festival for the eye. Why not a pontoon fair?

Make sealed lightly reinforced metal cylinders, air exhausted from these like those of the catamaran; use them for floating foundations. Fabricate light thin tubes, some large and others not so large. Some slender and each in any desired length. Fabricate them in pulp in order to be very light, soaked and stiffened in waterproofing or in transparent synthetics. Use these 'reeds' in rhythmic verticality, grouping them to get support for light roof-webbing. Again use the steel strand anchored to the metal drums to get and hold the webbing for roof cover. Large pontoons for tall buildings, long buildings. Square for square buildings. All to be connected by interesting floating bridges. Floating gardens too could be connected to the buildings—the whole ground plan of assembled floating units to be connected together by characteristic linking units, themselves attractive features, so that while all were joined, yet all might gently undulate with no harm to any unit.

Then introduce transparent coloured glass tubing among the coloured pulp tubing. Why not illuminate the glass and have, for once, the airy verticality as a sheer legitimate modern fabrication, only aimed at as 'a charm of New York' and seen there only at night in the rain?

The parti-coloured opaque and transparent verticality would be doubled by direct reflections trembling in the water.

The water itself could again be thrown up by inserted force-pumps to great heights and in enormous quantity, effects costing nothing but power. The fair a whole world of illuminated illumination, irradiating and irradiated light—an iridescent fair or a fair of iridescent, opalescent 'reeds'.

The great whole would be a picturesque pleasurable 'float'.

Modern pageantry, this?

And genuine in itself. Appropriate space could be easily created for specific purposes and adapted to suit each commercial purpose: all these varied units linked together as a continuous, varied, brilliant modern circumstance.

Then, after the Fair was over, certain appropriate units could be detached and floated to an anchorage in the lagoons of the varied parks and waterways of the Lake Front Park to serve as restaurants or good time places, as concessions rented from the city.

And I said that if there are these three ideas genuine and practical as Modern Architecture, they could be sure there were, as easily, three hundred to choose from.

Well, I had done my best to get out of a trying situation. Of course I

314

can hear the eclectic group saying they had thought of all these schemes themselves and rejected them as impractical. To reject them so would be their judgement, and no doubt their necessity, too, as things were with them. But not as things were with me.

MILWAUKEE: STILL ANOTHER INSTANCE

The several exhibitions of my work were now over and the material safely back again at Taliesin, always a great relief. It is perishable stuff. Charlotte Partridge, curator of the Layton Art Gallery, Milwaukee's centre of culture in Art, had asked me to send over an exhibition. Give a lecture. She volunteered to raise necessary money if I would come.

The last place I could imagine interested in anything modern (or ethical) would be Wisconsin's own Milwaukee.

I agreed therefore. Miss Partridge seems to have had her private troubles getting the necessary funds. But the exhibition went forward. I was busy directing the boys who were busy setting it up when Miss Partridge introduced a tall, fair young person 'doing the show' for the *Milwaukee Journal*. I thought she was much too good-looking to know much about architecture. And I went on working. She was persistent and followed me about as I worked at this and that, asking questions meantime. I answered between moments here and there. Finally: 'Mr. Wright, would you mind telling me what you think of our new nine million dollar courthouse?'

Now this new courthouse was a steel structure surrounded by three stories of vertical solid walls punctured occasionally by small windows all according to architect's Hoyle. Above that, a tall stone classic order ran all around. Surmounting the whole 'Classic' mass was a heavy stone cornice. A steel building inside. A stone building outside. I did not know at the time who the architect was.

'Well, the new courthouse will set Milwaukee back fifty years from any cultural standpoint,' I said and went on working, not thinking I was talking for 'publication'.

'Oh, I'm so glad to hear you say that!' dancing up and down with glee.

Then from her, conscientiously: 'Would you mind if I put that in print?' This request was so considerate that, touched, I stopped. Thought a minute. What did it matter? It was at least true. 'No, go ahead.' The interview continued and I thought no more about it.

Got home late that evening. Next morning, early, a long distance call from Milwaukee. The *News*. The *Journal* was out with a statement (it is always 'statement') headline quoting you: ' "New courthouse sets Milwaukee back fifty years from any standpoint of culture." How about it?'

'All right,' I said, 'make it a hundred. I've been thinking it over.'

The fight was on. The pottage began to boil. Other newspapers called wanting confirmation. They got it. Then came the usual follow-up interviews with Milwaukee's 'leading' architects by these journals. Reporter comment upon this, 'All afraid to express an opinion, not caring to incur shafts of radical architect's wit.' This pleased me. One of their number, Tullgreen, said, 'Wright always was twenty years ahead of the time.' The inference being, 'and so why worry'. Albert Randolph Ross, I soon found out, was winner of the competition for the new courthouse. He was himself interviewed now by the *Journal* and he explained why his design was 'Classical' instead of Modern.

Here is Randolph Ross:

'Mr. Hoover, talking in Washington recently on the occasion of appropriations for public works, said it was a good thing to carry on the traditions as established in Washington.

'When I went into the competition I considered whether to design a building in the modern and experimental trend for a great public courthouse. I made modern sketches, but in my opinion they fell flat for this purpose. They were not typical and expressive of public work, so I turned to that type established by our forefathers.'

Turning to a defence of the courthouse design, Mr. Ross said, 'It was chosen unanimously by three of the country's most brilliant architects as the plan that completely met the requirements of beauty, plan, and utility.

'I have no quarrel with trends in modern architecture. I take a fling at it myself. I even considered it for the courthouse. But it simply won't do for public buildings. It violates the dictates of a definite style built up through one hundred and fifty years of our history.

'A departure into modernism would not be suitable for a courthouse. We must be trained slowly to things violently new. The public's money cannot rightly be used to force experiments down its throat.

'The aesthetic side of the new courthouse counts only ten per cent. All that is needed in a building is a design that will arrest light in such a way as to give it a pleasing effect. That has been accomplished. The plan of the courts, offices and corridors and the building's utility are most vitally to be considered.'

The point of view of America's casual eclectic is here completely expressed. But if the aesthetic design of the courthouse is an affair separate from the courthouse and estimated by Ross at 'ten per cent', why spend fifty per cent on an extravagant showy useless stone envelope?

Reply to Ross:

Milwaukee should look at Chicago's county building, twenty years ago the last word in pseudo-classic, it was chosen in the same way. Today that building is manifest to all as a ponderous anachronism and cultural crime. A lie.

And I say that the Milwaukee county building is today just the same crime, modified only by Ross's superior taste. Within a few years this crime will be manifest to all the citizens. The thought of the world is gradually growing more sensible.

Architect Ross says 'he is unwilling to spend the heard-earned millions of Milwaukee's money on any experiment'. This may sound good to Milwaukee. If so, it is one of the things that is the matter with Milwaukee and that eventually will leave her a permanent backwater in civilization.

316

Architect Ross says he is not willing to 'experiment'. No. But as an architect he *is* willing to 'bet' nine millions of the people's money on a narrow margin, the unsure taste of a transitory period. 'Taste' as he sees it is no risk.

But why should the future have any more respect for the Milwaukee-lie than for the Chicago-lie? And there was some excuse for the Chicago-lie. The age had not awakened to engineering architecture. For the Milwaukee-lie there is no such excuse. The world has waked up.

Were Architect Ross utterly blind to the progress of the last decade in his own profession in architectural circles the world over, then he might still consider honest engineering architecture an 'experiment'.

Notwithstanding all conservative opinion the Milwaukee county will stand as a late 'experiment', an experiment in sentimental falsehood, foredoomed to failure.

Since *experiment* the courthouse must thus be, Mr. Ross, why not *experiment* with sanity and truth?

'Our forefathers' notwithstanding, monumental stone mass disappeared as a truth when steel in tension, clear glass and ferro-concrete became the actual body of the machine age. To combine stone and steel, even in the name of the 'forefathers', is dangerous, Architect Ross. And young men in architecture all over these United States see this fact today. That means, every man who thinks will see it soon.

Then why bet on or 'experiment' with pure sentimentality to your own taste, Architect Ross?

Why not *know*?

So much public talk infuriated the official city fathers. They got together, argued the question as to whether or not I should be called before them to explain the disparaging remarks. A vote was taken. The vote stood ten to ten. The opposition claiming I was a notoriety-seeker and to call me down publicly would only add fuel to my flames. So I was not called after all.

The press had a good time adding editorials to the headlines.

ANOTHER LITTLE STORY

Children and students were pouring into the exhibition. Miss Partridge said nothing the gallery had given attracted so much interest among the young people of Milwaukee.

The Milwaukee architects, a few exceptions, kept away. To be seen going into that show was too much for most of them. Merely to gratify their curiosity? And not much curiosity.

But there was a lecture yet to come. For some reason I forget I had to postpone it for several days. Friday of the week following the Wednesday the exhibit opened I got to Milwaukee about four o'clock. I was to speak that evening.

Charlie Morgan and I were at the Pfister Hotel . . . a bath and getting

317

dressed for a little dinner Miss Partridge was giving . . . A knock at the door. Loud.

Charlie opened it. A life-sized Milwaukee sheriff stepped in with a warrant for my arrest.

What charge?

A judgement entered against me to pay seven thousand dollars to the deceased Miriam Noel. Brought by her estate!

The payments due her by contract were all made to her during her lifetime from a trust fund deposited in a Madison bank at the time of the divorce. There were eleven thousand dollars still left in the fund when she died. The balance of this fund reverted to me at her death, so the charge was only my failure to pay myself this seven thousand dollars, to bring the trust fund up again to its original standard.

Ridiculous? Of course. But it worked. It served their 'legal' purpose. The attorney of the 'estate', whoever and whatever the 'estate' unless myself, had sworn to the document, so I was taken into custody, entered in the record at the county jail (not finger-printed this time) and motored over to the justice before whom I was to be tried, of course photographed all along the way as I went. Prearranged. Camera men stood around all posted where they could do the worst good.

Angry enough I understood the foolish situation, but I put the best possible face on the whole affair. Keeping my head up.

'Justice' asked questions. Got answers. Lawyers having gratified the curiosity of the assembled press, then urged the 'court' that I be kept in custody over night. (The lecture in mind, I suppose.)

But the 'court' thought this might be carrying things rather too far, I imagine, for he denied the motion. Cold feet at the last moment, he set me free. So the 'plan' only partially succeeded. The evening papers were on the street with fresh headlines opening old sores as Charlie and I went back to the hotel.

Miss Partridge had been reproached by Milwaukee architects for bringing a disgrace upon the city. Having me there. She didn't seem to care. She is something of a captain herself.

It was now six-thirty. Time for the little dinner. We got there. Charlie more raging and furious than I. We dined pleasantly and nevertheless, reaching the lecture hall only a little late. I think none of us knew just what might happen next. And I remembered Olgivanna's reluctance to have me go to Milwaukee at all: her plea to cancel the lecture and stay away.

The place was overflowing, one of the courthouse commissioners in the audience. And there was a general feeling, they said, that when I talked I would modify the remark concerning the nine million dollar courthouse.

Instead of the 'arrest' putting a damper on my spirits that evening, the dinner and kindness of all concerned, even the complimentary sheriff himself, more decent than his superiors, restored them for as enthusiastic and appreciative an audience as I've ever had anywhere. They heard me through.

Then I stepped down to give them all the half hour I knew they expected.

Many questions came and were answered.

The commissioner got to his feet: 'Mr. Wright, we had hoped you would modify your remarks concerning our new courthouse, or at least explain them. Will you do this?'

'I will,' I said and proceeded to say:

'Milwaukee's new nine million dollar courthouse belongs to the nineteenth not the twentieth century. A great stone mass over steel such as the building is can be memorial to Milwaukee only as a backwater in civilization. Their courthouse can only advertise to posterity that Milwaukee was neither scholar nor gentleman. No scholar because Milwaukee was ignorant of the current of advanced thought abroad in the world at the time. No gentleman because regardless of her duty to herself.

'A steel building inside and a stone building outside is an anachronism inviting destruction,' I said, and turned to leave the hall.

The commissioner, strangely enough, seemed pleased. The audience was no less so.

The commissioner, on his feet again, said, 'Well then, why not tell us just what kind of a courthouse we should have had, were we "scholars and gentlemen".'

So turning back again, I gave them a modern building as I saw it, as it came to me.

'The solid preparation of solid masses of terraced stone or concrete. Rising upon this "stylobate" an iridescent light-enmeshing fabric of steel and glass. All, within, luminous and brilliant. The whole structure light, free of space and economical of materials. Free in thought, an expression of our own new opportunity in our own time.' I carried it on into some detail and delivered the whole to them where they sat for about five million dollars. More than enough to build it.

I had made it so obvious that the audience broke into applause, including the commissioner and his party. And Milwaukee was a closed episode so far as anybody but Ross was concerned.

So I wrote a note to Ross saying I hoped and believed no harm had been done to him. I had really meant none. I felt called upon to at last openly champion the cause to which I had already given everything.

Unfortunately I soon began to find that behind every pseudo-classic plate-glass window, however small the window, there is some fine, well-meaning individual to be hit by any brick thrown by anyone. It was the cause with me however, in this case as ever. Not the man. And Ross, I think, was intelligent enough to know this. Never before had I thrown a brick directly at any classic performance. But now it seemed high time to make that performance a public issue. The modern hat was in the pseudo-classic ring.

My note to Ross received a gracious reply, 'no harm'.

And saying guardedly that he envied the future its coming freedom.

319

The lawyer for the 'estate' dismissed his fake suit with profuse and servile apologies, offering to pay all costs. And he volunteered this interesting information in the presence of Jim Hill, my own lawyer: he hadn't wanted to go through with the thing but no less than five leading Milwaukee citizens had insisted upon his 'going through'. So he did.

Interesting to follow this up? I had the means. But like all persecution by publicity, of what use? More publicity? Yes.

That is always the final weapon where publicity is not wanted. Where it is wanted, well, it is for them to sell it or not.

And this is fair enough?

HONOURABLE INTERVAL

A letter comes from Holland saying the exhibition was opened at Amsterdam in the State Museum by our American Ambassador, name Swenson. He tried to say something about the show but could talk only of America and the flag. The president of the Architects' Society then got up and made the speech for him that he might have made if he had known at all what the exhibition was about, or why it was over there at all. A cablegram: my Dutch colleagues congratulating me in many kind words upon my 'consistency in a great cause'.

That word consistency! It is seldom the word for the imaginative man in action, is it?

I was inclined to deny the allegation for conscience' sake.

And I sincerely don't believe I have been 'consistent'. Off on holidays too often. But direction has never changed nor development been hindered. I've always returned refreshed for the work in hand—having learned much more from every 'aside' than from the 'line' itself.

Is that consistency? Well, then I should plead guilty to the soft impeachment and I will.

Next the exhibition goes over to the German *Academie der Kunste* at Berlin; the erstwhile Royal Academy. The first time I believe the 'Reich' has honoured modern architecture? From there it went to Frankfort, then to Stuttgart and finally to Belgium. It came home to Taliesin again in October so that it might go to work in our own country where I believe it is most needed, even if not so much wanted. A country once so hectic an eclectic as ours is forever eclectified? The years go by.

Solicited again and again by the New School of Social Research and many others, I went as journeyman preacher to a week of preaching in New York City to earn the only fees anywhere in sight at that bad time in my life. This began to look like recognition at home. Or was I only losing my grip on the future—by gaining on the present?

MORE INSTANCES

From the excellent state university at Eugene, Oregon, came a hand-lettered appeal for an exhibition of my work signed by all the architectural students and their shepherd, Walter Wilcox. Walter Wilcox is one of the best shepherds. That it came at all touched me at this time. And though so far away I managed with their help to get there with the exhibition. Then I went on to Seattle. A success. Two lectures, failures I thought, had been given in Denver following the six at Princeton. The Princeton six were built by the Princeton Press into the published book, *Modern Architecture*. Five lectures were given in New York City, a pleasant one in Philadelphia at the Contemporary Club—charming dinner given a small group by courteous Paul Cret. Two more lectures and exhibition again at Madison, Wisconsin. Two at Minneapolis—I hope Sheriff Brown came. He would have felt at home in the enormous fashionable throng overflowing the Art Museum and barricading the museum grounds with motor cars until I got in myself with great difficulty. Two lectures and an exhibit at Chicago Art Institute, since published by the Institute. Many of these meetings, so crowded by the young sons and daughters of my fellow men and women, affected me strangely. Those 'at home' in Chicago and Wisconsin especially, where warm welcome in places of long association aroused the sleeping sentimentalist in me, though not to the point of modifying my ideals of sentiment to accept sentimentality as such. But dangerously near their demoralization of these ideals often, just the same. What did this awakening appreciation mean, I wondered, a little uneasy.

Sometimes overheard: 'the man is still an iconoclast!' Often whispered indignation. Gossip: he must be lonely, etc., etc.: perhaps any or all the surmises usual in the circumstances. But I used to wish they would dub me 'radical', and let me go home to stay. A good honest word, that word 'radical'? It means of the *root*. And how know life unless through knowledge of the 'root'? But 'radical' on the academic tongue usually spells 'red!' because as I have said, the hypocrite instinctively hates the radical in the United States. But if so, was I no longer radical, or were they overtaking me?

Well, everywhere I found the halls overflowing. And everywhere I went I found youth eager, questioning and enthusiastic. Natural modernity seems to have captured the imaginations of Usonian youth. I hope the new integrity will possess the heart, making indigenous culture on more liberal terms than the substitute the schools have accepted and offered so far. More fundamental concepts of natural law as organic are necessary at first. Under the fire of intent and intelligent questionings by youth, I began to feel a 'youth' myself, to take free and deeper breaths. I began to feel less alone in my work.

What effect this would have upon me and upon my work I did not know.

CATHERINE

At Chicago, I remember an echo of my earlier youth. One afternoon in the gallery at the Art Institute where the exhibition stood, a tall graying but still handsome woman came toward me smiling. A moment's hesitation. And then I recognized Catherine. I had not seen her in fifteen years. These years seemed to have dealt with her gently and she looked—frankly—young and happy—as she said she was. She was married again —now Mrs. Ben E. Page. We went about the exhibition together noticing many a work that had grown up out of the 'other half' of the Oak Park establishment where her children had run about with my thumb-tacks in the bottom of their shoes. However ill-advised Catherine's attitude had been toward me, she had never been other than loyal to anyone she ever loved.

THIS AUTOBIOGRAPHY

Writing these pages trying to be honestly autobiographical, telling only what is true, I see why all autobiography is written between the lines. It must be so written.

No matter how skilled the writer or how spontaneous he may be, the implication outdoes his ability or undoes his intention. The law of change is at work as he writes and the circumstance flows from beneath the fixation at the point of his pen into endless other forms and significances— except as a single facet may catch the gleam of the reader's intelligence and he writes truth in between the lines for himself.

Autobiography is impossible except as implication. And for the life of me, I cannot see why I recounted so many episodes that were far inferior to those I delight to remember and tell now. I do not know why I have not written of many features and incidents of my life so much more deeply intimate, so much more suggestive even in architectural thought. More picturesque certainly. They come crowding into mind at odd moments. Press upon my heart for utterance too late, and go away again.

Even those I have tried to utter here go away mocking, unsatisfied if not dissatisfied.

Does this fluid nature of life, I wonder, really allow nothing to be wholly held? Is nothing to be arrested and directed in human experience —so far as the essential quality, the *life* in it, goes except by the greatest of art? Is the writer helpless, as the surgeon is helpless with his anatomical study of the corpse on his dissecting table, to put his hand even for a moment upon what was the life of that corpse?

To me, it seems so.

The sufferings of growth itself, as growth, the agonies of the sentimentality that vainly tries to hold life by 'institution' and 'establishment', trying to extend the fleeting hour until the simple inevitable becomes high tragedy to the soul: are not these sufferings our own punishment for violation of the first simple law of Freedom? What is that law except the law of organic change natural to whatever changes. Does not all live to change?

As I remember, the best of life is a becoming. And so I record the barren lines and leave the rest to go the way of life.

322

BELATED MEMORIES

I remember the third week after I left my first home in Oak Park, the misery that came over me in a little café somewhere in Paris on the Boulevard St. Michel. Caring neither to eat nor drink I was listening to the orchestra. It was the end of a rainy day in a long depressing rainy season. The Seine most of the time over its banks. Late at night.

The cellist picked up his bow and began to play Simonetti's madrigale. Lloyd had played on his cello the simple old Italian sentimentality often. I would play with him, on the piano. But the familiar strains now gave me one of those moments of interior anguish when I would have given all I had lived to be able to begin to live again. The remembered strains drove me out of the café into the dim streets of Paris with such longing and sorrow as a man seldom knows, I hope. It was not repentance. It was despair that I could not achieve what I had undertaken as ideal. I wandered about not knowing where I was going or how long I went, at daylight finding myself facing a glaring signboard—still, somehow, somewhere near where I had started out on the Boulevard St. Michel.

I remember:
When all was well with the new life at Taliesin, during my first two years of life there, whenever I would go to Chicago to keep track of my work I would take time somehow to go out to Oak Park. I would go there after dark, not wishing to be seen. Go to reassure myself that all was going well there too—with the children.

I would see the light streaming from half-open windows and hear their voices.

Or perhaps they were playing the piano or cello. The violin.

Perhaps singing.

Perhaps calling to each other. Oh, yes, I might have known it. All cosy enough.

And I would turn away to town again. Relieved.

I remember:
Llewellyn coming down to stay with me occasionally as he did at the Congress Hotel, bringing his mandolin to play for me. It gave me pleasure to see him fold each garment neatly and put it carefully by on a chair when he went to bed. And I would tuck him in. The 'deserted' child.

He is a lawyer now . . . well, fate would . . . etc.

I remember:
The little suppers with Catherine and Frances at Hironymous' Tip-Top Inn atop the old Pullman Building. These young ladies . . . my 'deserted' daughters. So much 'young ladies' they were now that I was suspected by acquaintances of mine of dereliction from the straight and narrow path of the devoted though unconventional lover by conventional attentions to gay young things.

323

I remember too . . . but this volume must reach timely if unseemly end, or if not timely, then some kind of seemly end.

So, 'I remember' to forget most of what I should have written to make writing at all the full, expressive record I wanted it to be.

As with the stories of adventure in building I left out those I should have liked best to write, so these pages lack the faces and names and places, the times and circumstances that would be most revealing, really more significant than any I have recalled. But that mutability, is it not the charm of life, alive?

Live up to life bravely, sensitively, conscientiously or even philosophically, how we may, this fleeting and becoming defies fixation the more we do so live it.

Therefore who can put his own life into his own hands? Or put it into words of his own mouth? Then how to put it into the pen on this paper?

Unlucky he who could, however lucky we might be if he did.

TALIESIN III

Again Taliesin! Three times built, twice destroyed, yet a place of great repose. When I am away from it, like some rubber band stretched out but ready to snap back immediately the pull is relaxed or released, I get back to it happy to be there again.

At sunrise last late September I stood again with bare feet on the virgin sod of the Taliesin hill-crown. Looking off to the South I saw the now big dark-green clump of fir-trees Uncle Thomas had planted there fifty years ago to keep the little family chapel company and shade the Lloyd-Jones picnics on a Sunday.

A little farther to the left—East—above the farm that used to be Uncle James', rises the range of hills I sometimes walked along at night as a barefoot boy in search of Peace, Beauty, Satisfaction, Rest. Over to the right a little, West, there beyond are the far away hills where I went to look for the cows: and where I believed the surplus of the fervent hymns sung there used to go. Below and between are the many-coloured rolling fields where Uncle James used to call to the young dreamer, 'Come back, Frank, come back!'

Over the nearby ridge, wasting away, lies a reproach and a sorrow to me—what is yet left of Aunt Nell and Aunt Jane's Hillside Home School.

'Romeo and Juliet', the windmill tower, stands still bravely at work on the hill crown to the right there, West, just above the old home-school. Again a new wheel needed now: the third to be wrenched from its moorings by the severe northwest storms. But the tower still stands. Uncles, aunts, nephews and nieces—they have all gone elsewhere—or forever gone beyond. Occasionally, as in that boyhood time, come moments of the other where . . . inner abstraction of the spirit. But now I hear no one calling, Frank! come back! 'Come back, Frank!' Of that past there is only the free, long retrospect of Time, Place and Otherwhere to come drifting back through the present moment: a retrospect now many times strung around the earth—probably to go stringing around it again. Who knows?

Many but not so many dreams of the future? Moments of anguish? Oh, yes—of course—there are many; but no moment of regret. Day by day I enjoy more the eternity that is now. At last I am realizing that eternity *is* now. And that eternity only divides yesterday from tomorrow.

It is now as though the mind itself at times were some kind of recording film in endless reel, to go on perfecting and projecting pictures endlessly, seldom if ever the same as the moment changes. But the same scene and scheme may show itself from infinitely varying angles as the point of view changes if informing principle, the *impulse* living in it all, stays in place. Else the impotence of confusion, the chaos of madness: vain imprisonment in the Past.

No—the several years since Taliesin first steeled itself and settled down to its work and its deal have been free, but of course they have not been carefree. Sad memories not excluded—they have been happy years. Short. And Hope never really dies. Because of those troubled years, my life is richer than ever before, though with 'hard times' as we like to say—and we must say it—lying all around us. Coming nearer every day to Taliesin. The menace of its mounting load of debt.

AGAIN HOME

Olgivanna, Svetlana, Iovanna and I were up at sunrise this late September morning walking in the thick blue-grass, bare feet in the thick white rime of frosty dew. The rime so cold that every few steps we would have to stop to warm our feet in the hollows back of our knees.

The tall red-top, the grass on the hill beyond the garden, gleamed in the slanting rays of morning sun, the tall grass everywhere, hung with a gossamer covering of spider webs of amazing size: a sunlit brilliance. All their delicate patterns were sparkling with the clinging dewdrops, myriads that turned each separate strand of each marvellous web into a miracle of dotted light: a kind of construction that might well inspire this age, because it is a beauty we might realize in steel and glass buildings. If we would we could.

The German Shepherd, Kave, always leaping, nosing, nipping and biting at our bare heels, we reached the melon-patch on the hillside below the reservoir. Once there, we gathered ripe melons, cool with the frosted morning dew, broke them across our knees and ate our fill of the rosy, watery sweetness, crushing in our mouths handfuls of the pink flesh decorated with black seeds. So many melons were lying all about that we ate only the hearts and threw the rest aside for the birds.

Fruit seeds were invented for birds and animals, and for us too this morning.

The faithful Kave shepherds us, sleeping by my bedside at night. Or sometimes by his mistress. If he is shut out, his howls and protests are not to be borne. He gets in and lies down there to waken us in the morning by brushing a cold nose to our faces or giving a warm tongue to the cheek at precisely a few moments before the breakfast bell regularly rings in the tower on the hill. Then we get up and go into the big living room with its expanse of cypress, waxed wide-board floor, turn on some favourite dance music and have the morning frolic we call setting-up exercises, but really they are more like dancing. Olgivanna learned some of them at the Institute at Fontainebleau and taught them to us.

Winter nights—all in the frosty white outside—we love to build a great blazing wood-fire in the big stone bedroom fireplace, closing the inside shutters of the whole house, and lie there story-telling, arguing or reading until we fall asleep. Sometimes we take turns reading aloud, Iovanna's fairy-tales always coming first. Carl Sandburg's 'White Horse Girl and Blue Wind-Boy' is her favourite at the moment and ours too. I read it to Olgivanna on our first trip to New York—in a lower berth together.

So, you see, Taliesin scenes are homely scenes. These latter years—Iovanna is nearly six years old now—have been a succession of possessions, changing hours made up of changing moments each with its own lovely picture to be treasured among pictures. Curly heads and loving dark eyes, lithe supple bodies, eager minds living life make beautiful pictures. And all make constant demands.

But though life is homely at Taliesin, life is never monotonous. Taliesin days are one continuous series of changing play and changing work, hard to say usually which is which, but emergency always. Always an emergency. The landscape itself changes outside the windows as the sea changes, only these valley changes are more immutable than the sea, I think.

There are no fixed habits yet. Not even good ones. Unless it is that breakfast bell. We avoid them still as I did when as a young man I made up my mind that they killed imagination. I have always avoided them, feeling them the enemy of imaginative well-being in creative work.

Good company rarely comes our way, but will sometimes find its way to as far away as we are. But we are still pretty far away. We do not often regret it.

Here we are, free now for the time being. This winter living in quiet seclusion at work and play all over the house and workshop. We do not see much difference between our work and play. Usually if the weather is severe seven or eight of the great stone fireplaces at Taliesin are burning holes in the forest. Some of them burn oak most of the time at evening. Our fireplaces have established a pretty good market for cordwood in the neighbourhood and 'stabilize' it now, although the fireplaces are really for good measure since the whole place is heated by steam and lighted by our own hydro-electric plant. A pull on a switch-cord by the bed-side lights the grounds about the house. I am a little ashamed of this precaution, because that is what it is.

We love the snow at Taliesin. And icicles. Yards long, hanging fringe from the eaves.

In summer our range of activity widens somewhat, takes in the farm and gardens, our wooded hills, the rolling fields and country roads. We still plunder, as I did when a boy, the roadsides, choice branches of bloom or berries to 'arrange' in the house or studio. And there is the broad, sand-barred Wisconsin River's changing flow in the broad bottom land below the house—for walking and swimming. Our entire resources are constantly taxed. 'Something is always happening in the country,' as Wilhelm Bernhard—a draughtsman—used to remark.

We dream and are planning great things. Good music is essential to our life at Taliesin. A grand piano stands by the living room fireplace, a cello resting against its hollow side, a violin on the ledge beside it. There are several recorders there also. A harp is coming. Olgivanna plays Bach, Beethoven, old Russian music. I let the piano play itself a few moments sometimes while the feeling lasts, knowing nothing. Something comes out. And I can never play any of the things, such as they are, a second time. Olgivanna says she likes to hear me play. Hers is a gentle encouraging soul and she would not hurt even such outrageous pride as mine.

Svetlana too plays now, and the young Iovanna plays with perfect style all the while. Finger movements perfect. But the notes she selects are not always or even often well-suited to each other. No matter, Iovanna plays too. We all play.

My little five-year-old daughter Iovanna and I among constant inventions have invented a game. An architect's daughter, she has many kinds and sizes of building blocks, among them all a set of well-made cubes about an inch square painted pure bright colours, red, yellow, blue, green, black and white. Some of the cubes are divided on the diagonal into contrasting colours. Well, whoever deals, deals seven blocks to each and two diagonals. Iovanna's turn to play. She chooses a colour-block—not fair to start with a diagonal—and places it square on the waxed board floor. Then I select a colour-block and put it, say, touching hers at the corner. Her turn. She studies a little, head one side, finally putting down a block in whatever way she chooses, but however put down it will now make a decided geometric figure. So imagination begins to stress the judgement to decide the next play.

Instead of extending the figure on the floor, she may now put a block on top of the one already 'played' by me. She does so. The figure on the floor begins to look more and more interesting as the 'third dimension' enters and the blocks creep up into the air. The block group begins to be a construction. I may follow up and down, or I go crosswise with whatever colour I may have. But whatever I do, I will change the whole effect just as she will when her turn comes to play.

Sometimes she sees she has spoiled the figure with her 'turn' and asks to change it.

Always she may.

The fourteen blocks in place we take in the result, critical or enthusiastic.

Sometimes these little form-and-colour exercises in block-pattern make a good thesis in 'Modern Art'. The fact is, I intend them to be so.

Yes, Taliesin life at this time, not too late, is one continuous round of movement, usually in happy rhythms ending in sound sleep for all . . . only to begin again with play and laughter at sunrise, settling down after breakfast into serious work that is play too—for we love the work we do, even when we are all adding tired to tired and adding it again.

Usually we are together all the time and everywhere, too, whether in work or in play. Iovanna does nearly everything we do as well as she can. Her half-bushel of gold-brown curls pile up on her head. They lie in ringlets there and look at you like eyes. Her name was made from her maternal Grandfather's—Ivan, or John, and her paternal Grandmother's Anna. Literally John Anna, Johanna or Iovanna, to go with Olgivanna, properly Olga Ivanovna. And the name of the charmingly disposed little daughter before we met, Svetlana. In Russian the name means 'light'.

Iovanna's own stories often astonish us.

Buddha, whom she sees all about in various forms, intrigues her imagination. She romances with Buddha. But recently she has become interested in another great personality. Here is something concerning that new interest Olgivanna wrote down, word for word, changing nothing.

I am calling it Ave Maria. But as I have already assured you, I am not in the least sentimental.

AVE MARIA

'Go to bed now, you have run around enough. Come now, it is time to go to sleep,' I said to my little daughter Iovanna.

'Wait, Mother. I must go and tell God "goodnight".'

I was surprised, as I heard this for the first time. I followed her into the living room and she stood there in the middle and said clearly, right into space, 'Goodnight, God.'

We went back to the bedroom, I tucked her in bed.

'Stay with me, Mother, sit down. Mother, I would like to see God. Will you buy me some flying wings at Marshall Field's, so I can fly up into the sky to see him?'

'But God is not in the sky only. Remember what your Father told you in the church in New York, that God was in your heart?'

'Yes, Mother, I know, only I think my heart is too little for God. You see it is too little. When it gets cold, he gets cold in my heart and he goes up in the sky to build a big fire there to keep warm.'

'But your heart is a fire. Your heart is love, it is like a flame, it keeps God warm.'

328

'Oh, no, Mother, I told you it is too little for God. He is big and my heart is just little, just like—well, you see just like a little grain of seed.'

'But think of all the hearts there are in the world: children's hearts and grown-up people's hearts, all together they make a great big fire for God to keep him warm.'

'Oh, but he needs food, or he will get very hungry. We must give him something to eat. He is very kind you know. We must take care of him.'

'He does not eat. He lives on love. He is never hungry if he has enough love.'

'But, Mother, we should send him something just the same. We should make a big bouquet of flowers for him. You know he loves flowers. And he loves shells, too. You see, all the shells of the sea come to him. They bring him food and flowers and everything he needs. I want to send him something.'

'Send him your love by being good, minding your Mother and Father. You should also work if you want to please God.'

'Oh, I am working. I swept the sitting room. I brushed Svetlana's dress for her, I rubbed Auntie Maginel's poor neck. I work very hard. Do you have to mind God too?'

'Certainly.'

'And Father too?'

'Of course.'

'Would God punish you if you and Father were not good?'

'God never punishes, we punish ourselves.'

'Would God punish me if I were not good?'

'No, but I would have to punish you if I could not make you good by being nice to you. I don't like to do it, but I have to do it so God can be warm in your heart. He is very cold and sad when you are not good.'

'Is he warm right now?'

'Very.'

'Mother, I wish I could see him.'

It became very quiet in the room. In another moment she was asleep.

And so these three books within a book. A fourth to come.
All of them to the Anna who is my mother.
To the Ivan (John) whose daughter
Olga Ivanovna, called Olgivanna, is
Mother to Iovanna—little 'John Anna' . . .
the last of the generation calling me father. Svetlana included . . .
And to Olgivanna herself.
Because, but for her this book were never written.

POSTLUDE

Here on this low hill in THE VALLEY there is Freedom to make life and work really synonymous terms. In the retrospect is a vast panorama of life. Human experience a colourful tapestry shot through with threads of gold as light gleams whenever truth is touched and love rose worthy of noble selfhood or life rose higher because of death.

Or where living faith justified defeat.

Sincerely sought, well-loved, may be seen that principle—is it the very quality of life itself vaguely felt by the boy as left out in that early lesson preached by familiar feet in the snow up the slope of the valley field?

The order of Change is limitless and profound.

As a natural order I have sought the Nature of this order. I have been trying to see it as Principle. I have long seen it as Reality. Perhaps as Heraclitus said—the only reality we may see.

In so far as changes come by law of natural growth, we need not fear change. Though we may fail to see it, change is beneficent. So no menace.

Inevitable and good friend, organic change is not mere chance. To any natural order or a true culture founded upon reality change would be friendly. Age then becomes a desirable qualification. Where age is not so, then what civilization have we?

Our life here on earth should be blessed not antagonized by this true attribute of all natural growth . . . death—but a change—in itself only a crisis of growth.

I have encountered many violent breaks in my field of work, studying as normal this element not in the reckoning. I am reconciled now to respect. Armed also, but not to establish. Armed to foresee and forefend the flow that is human life wherever I can see it or feel it to flow true.

Romance to me is become Reality in this fateful, flowing sense.

And I have been seeking ideal life as I have been seeking ideal building, just as at the beginning of *An Autobiography* I sought naked weed rising above blue arabesque, sunshot on spotless white.

Thus my life has been, as it must be, a changing test of Principle. Eternal.

Now leading Life-adventure is this keen new romance of Time, Place and Man I have called modern, flowing on together, going out from my hand into the making of a changing world: a world so instituted— if institution still must be—as to be capable of change without the constitutional disorder we so dread now, or any fear of fatal disaster.

Freedom is the title of this book, four, but there is this to acknowledge: there is no such thing in itself. Freedom has not been attained on earth by mortals, least of all by the one who professed to have discovered it, the Buddha himself.

Escape is not freedom.

The only freedom we have a right to ask is the freedom to seek—to be —to believe—and to love the beautiful as our souls conceive it, perceive it or as we can feel it.

That Freedom is the only freedom for men.

And, it is freedom enough. It is Our Country.

BOOK FIVE

FORM

WORK-SONG

We have battle hymns. We have war songs, anthems, and we do have some few Negro labour-chanties. But we have no work-song of our own that is a thing of the militant work-spirit.

These T-square and triangle verses, a kind of disturbing fife-and-drum corps coming down the street—in a straight-line pattern—were spontaneously written early in my work life and should have preceded the previous book *WORK*. They were omitted there because the song then seemed, and still does, to be shouting 'damn'. Why not? It takes an ego shouting 'damn' to withstand emasculation by such imitative erudition as ours and the 'cultivation' any true ego, upright, is sure to receive at our very best hands. So, here, to you is the militant work-song. Not as literature whatsoever, but for better or for worse.

Olgivanna set the lines to music and the song is now sung upon occasion by the Taliesin Fellowship.

The only time these curious verses came out of hiding was long ago, when, urged by well-meaning friends, I sent them on under the title of *THE DRUM* to Richard Watson Gilder, then editor of *The Century*. The Work-Song came back with a polite 'The rhythm of the drum, Mr. Wright, can hardly be translated into poetry.'

Life seems to disdain our very best literary measurements: especially our scholastic appraisals. Even so our approved popular standards.

All such become a frozen asset, or upset where cultural growth is earnestly sought or deeply desired.

Outside our current of conventional ideas of what constitutes literature, who knows Poetry?

The quest begun by the child in this beloved Valley, young feet woollen-warm in fresh-fallen snow; both aching arms full of 'useless' dried weeds: the structure-pattern of a multitude of lives already given, the search for FORM here continues. It *is* a self-seeking—yes, of course, with what freedom I could win—or take.

Well . . . after the first four books *FAMILY—FELLOWSHIP—WORK—FREEDOM* are done, like the 'Freshman at the Party' I look back. Ten years later, wistful now, I imagine what I might have truly said to go deeper and come off with more credit. Perhaps make a better book for you to read. With some chagrin I realize I have not written an autobiography at all. What I have set down is more an anti-Broadway creed. I do not regret the 'anti' nor the 'creed' because the 'anti' is needed badly and *An Autobiography* has been with me an act of faith in what lies deeper. Every word I have written is fact, at least. But facts no more make Truth than boards, bricks and mortar make Architecture. Only Imagination using facts honestly as mere structural material can so imbue fact with Spirit as to make another life, the life of Man, take fresh inspiring Form. The work of art.

This fifth book is the continued search for FORM.

THE CHARACTER OF FORM

Meantime among so many disheartening discoveries stands the all-heartening important truth (something at least to 'tie to') that true FORM is always organic in character. It is really nature-pattern. In nature-abstraction, therefore, lies the difficulty as well as the simple centreline of the honest ego's search for integral FORM. And since all Form is a matter of structure, it must be a matter of government as well as a matter of architecture; a matter of the framework of a society:—the constitution of a civilization.

Proved by my own experience, I too can say that 'every problem carries within itself its own solution', a solution to be reached only by the intense inner concentration of a sincere devotion to Truth. I can say this out of a lively personal adventure in realizations that gives true scheme, line and colour to all life and, so far as Architecture goes, life to what otherwise would remain mere unrelated fact. Dust, even if stardust.

Any good architect is by nature a physicist as a matter of fact, but as a matter of reality, as things are, he must be a philosopher and a physician. So the new spiritual physiognomy of old world-wide philosophy is still at work on the pages of this belated haunted fifth book of *An Autobiography*. Here you will find the outlines of a true social pattern hidden by the realisms which may enrich but which can also obscure Reality.

What we are seeking together must be found between the lines.

An Oklahoma editor claiming to be a cousin of mine (great printer but no editor) once blazed at me in disgust and anger, 'Hell, Frank, if you don't like the system on which this country's run, why don't you get out of it? Go somewhere else! Goddammit.'

'Not to please you, Richard, nor any of my relatives,' I said. 'If I see something wrong with my country I am going to stay right here doing my damndest to set upside-down right-side up.'

Now, as a matter of course, to get my own conscience or yours on straight, or for you to get yours or mine on straight, we may trouble each other's cousins and annoy a good many good people. Such as they are, and we are. But if to you and to me Democracy really means anything at all it must mean just that kind of trouble with our cousins and our sisters. Our uncles and our aunts. Not to mention our parents and especially our dearest friends and trouble thrown in, maybe, with the Police. As things are. But, millions of consciences like yours and mine, likewise uneasy, struggling against what seems so unnecessarily stupid, so utterly inferior, are essential to the life of any honest country wherein Democracy may be, after all, only that 'state of unhappy consciousness', which Hegel said it was.

But no! I have a better right to stay here dissatisfied out loud than you have to stay down there in Oklahoma satisfied out louder just because you happen to own a newspaper or something, Richard.

If this country of ours (it *is* one of God's many good countries, either won—self-baptized in our name by our own blood—or inherited, stolen, or bought, isn't it?) were incurably lame, halt or blind, the Cousin Richards of these States might be all right. To criticize would then be only cruel. But I don't think this country is *incurably* lame, halt or blind. At least, the people in it are not while I belong here and love the belonging as well as I do: loving the country not so much for what it is—no, but more for what it meant to be and for what a good many of us still hope it is going to be. I know, with good enough reason now, there are many loving it just the way I love it: a love that means eventually, if not soon, a true democratic FORM not only for our buildings, but for the appropriate lives we will live in them, and even the cultivation of the ground on which they shall stand.

Meantime, in any sound—that is to say *honest*—Democracy, Peace or War, true discretion from now forward consists in the resolve to speak and act the living Truth where it concerns us as we honestly understand it and squarely face the consequences of so acting and speaking, gentle reader or reader ungentle. If we do make a general practice of such wise honesty freely, then I am sure there are enough among us with sufficiently developed intelligences to find the true social, economic (and therefore *truly architectural*) FORM normal to the culture of such Freedom as we profess. That Freedom is now the new Integrity not alone in this Nation but in all the world. We will call it, hereinafter, the new Reality.

But we are in great danger of entirely running out of ideas concerning the very simple but startling idea of human freedom we once professed, because we who ran away from the 'old country' and came over here for safety, scared out of our native wits, now run back to the mother country for safety, waving not our own flag but an ism.

The Lloyd-Joneses were all handsome folk. But my mother and my maiden aunts, Aunt Nell and Aunt Jane, were, I think, the handsomest of the ten. Their five brothers, shaggy-maned, bearded, patriarchal, handsome. Four of the five: James, Enos, John and Jenkin, happening into Madison one fine day were driving along in an open rig on University Avenue (two of them were University regents) when someone shouted from the sidewalk—'Where are the other eight?'

The neighbouring uncles all called the Lloyd-Jones sisters 'the girls' and the boys and girls all called them Aunt Nell and Aunt Jenny. The two sisters were disciples of John Dewey by way of Francis Parker under whom they once taught school. They were nearing seventy and their school was becoming harder than ever for them to manage. Added to the naturally unprofitable nature of their enterprise, the unfortunate, tragic death of their brother James (my favourite uncle) had thrown them into acute financial distress. Bankruptcy threatened the Hillside Home School where for twenty-seven years 'the Aunts' had mothered some forty to sixty boys and girls, aged seven to seventeen—preparing their forty to sixty boys and girls for college by keeping a staff of thirteen teachers in residence besides themselves. They had done a pioneer work in home-school co-education. The Hillside Home School was perhaps the first—certainly one of the first—co-educational home schools in our country: probably in the world. Mary Ellen Chase has drawn their portraits with a sympathetic hand in her book, *The Good Fellowship*.

Meantime 'the Aunts' tried manager after manager. Some of the managers were their own nephews or nieces. Some they brought in from educational enterprises in the cities. But none was ever able to do very much. And there were good reasons. My beloved Aunts themselves were those good reasons. Their plant had grown old with them and they were deeply in debt without realizing it. But, in fact, they were themselves as mentally alert and potent as ever. They simply could not reconcile themselves to be directed by others or see any of their prerogatives go into other untried hands. I myself never thought of them as old. They really had no age, these maiden sisters of five brothers and three sisters, aunts of some forty nephews and nieces, foster mothers of hundreds of other women's children. But their very strength became their weakness now. Their famous brother Jenkin had been a strength to them and he tried to help them now. It was the same with them even where he was concerned. They would take neither domination nor advice, and while he could have found money for them if control went with the money, he could not get control himself nor deliver control. So they got no financial aid at this crucial time. And some blamed me for this.

As it was with Jenkin Lloyd-Jones, so it was with their own alumni who might have been expected to come to their assistance. And I don't know why some of them didn't come to the rescue of their faithful old teacher-mothers. But none came. I believe a few hundred dollars did come in from several sources. But they needed thousands—some forty-six of them. Finally thing at the school came to such a pass that Aunt Nell quite lost her mind with worry. She would wander up and down the room wherever she might happen to be, talking to herself, wringing her hands —moaning. Aunt Jane, still a quick and sympathetic soul, would try to comfort her when these fits of despair darkened the mind. Sister Anna (my mother)—a great help to them always—was especially helpful now. There seemed no way out; no one to help. So I did. To 'pay up' and give them a little rest—rest they so much needed but which no one, least of all myself, believed they knew how to take. They wanted to turn everything over to me, asking me to promise that their work would continue. I promised.

That promise comforted them.

They had put their best into the advanced ideas of co-education on liberal principles which they now represented. I had found money for them before when the 1902 buildings were built. One of my clients, Mrs. Susan Lawrence Dana, gave them the little Art and Science building next the School building and equipment, complete. She loaned the Aunts twenty-seven thousand dollars more to help complete the main school building. Another client, Charles E. Roberts, gave nine thousand dollars to help in a subsequent pinch. I think there were other helping hands at that time but I don't know whose.

This, partly, was why they had turned to me now when all else had failed.

About the time the new buildings were built—1902—there was some family feeling (and saying) that they would ruin the Aunts. But all the Aunts ever put into them from first to last was about half their cost plus the considerable work volunteered by the family. The new buildings were their pride and joy.

I did think of finding some schoolmaster to carry on but could not imagine anyone in their place. There could be no one.

Neither Aunt long survived after giving up active participation in the life of the school.

Aunt Jane, a gallant fiery disposition in contrast to the cool, more managerial disposition of Aunt Nell, about this time had not been so very well. I think she suffered the loss of the School most, for 'loss' they both regarded it when only a promise took the place of the reality they had both so loved. Occasionally, when weather permitted, she liked to go back to sleep in her own room at the School. She was found there, dead, one morning when we all least expected it.

Aunt Nell had contracted smallpox while young. Her hair turned snow-white when she was twenty-six, but her health, subsequently, had always been good—her outdoor activity kept it so. She now lingered along for another year or two, finally losing control of the fine clear mind she always had—becoming, because of her indomitable will which had always had its way, not at all easy to manage. But finally, she too found release—in the boys' cottage of the school where the Aunts had mothered seven boys aged seven to twelve. There was where she preferred to be.

And now a strange thing concerning the 'property' that was quite generally believed to be the plant of the Hillside Home School. It appeared that the individualities expressed by the glowing personalities of Aunt Nell and Aunt Jane had been all there was of the Hillside Home School except the idealistic buildings I had built for them, 1902-3, into which went some of the enthusiasm and faith they had put into their own work.

335

The physical side of their work was otherwise slight. The several other buildings were so ugly and worthless they were only waiting to be torn down. Out of an old metal bedstead and clean fresh bedclothes, a print on the wall, a piece of rag carpet, an improvised stand, a wash bowl and a nicked pitcher skilfully combined with a vase of flowers and a bowl of fruit, the lovely view through the windows, the living presence of the Lloyd-Jones Sisters had evoked a miracle to go with the shining waxed-boards of the floor.

With Aunt Nell and Aunt Jane gone, their 'property' vanished into the surrounding air—all except their ancestral ground and the buildings standing upon it to which their spirit had given concrete form. But even these buildings were suited only to their own school work and, placed where they were, of no value unless they could be used as farm buildings, which they could not be. The old octagonal barn in bad repair had been badly placed, as had the dormitory and servants' building—all were carpenter-built buildings (no design) and were in such a state of disrepair that, all things considered, it seemed best to tear them down as they spoiled the buildings that did express their spirit. All of the active Hillside Home School plant other than the 140 acres of farm land (worth about eighty dollars an acre without buildings) had little or no value. There were almost no Lloyd-Jones Sisters' 'assets' so called. Were all such gathered into a heap they would hardly bring one thousand dollars.

What a lesson in the enlivening, characterizing, saving power of human individuality the old Hillside Home School was! The only thing in which faith should ever be placed, the only faithful 'asset'. Things grow old and vanish like that. But individuality once achieved, perhaps by way of the use of 'things', is immortal—beyond reach of age, or better to say is developed and strengthened by age—until age itself should bring the most desirable of qualifications.

These great women possessed such individuality and to such a degree that where they were, there was consequential order out of insignificance —the usefulness of even the inferior object, atmosphere, warmth and light out of nothing.

The Hillside Home School, high-hearted in the service of a great ideal— such service is too seldom seen in this world—became toward the end of its life a kind of eleemosynary institution which the Aunts were supporting. Parents who were bereaved or had separated would send their children to the Aunts. The Aunts would become attached to the children, the dues would be paid for at a little while and then as various disasters would befall the parents payments would cease, but the Aunts would keep the children on and on. And this in so many various forms was the story until at the end the too many teachers were unpaid; faithful old employees had not asked for pay in years; uncollectable bills mounted to the impossible. A ledger of accounts which came along with other assets after their death shows bills due and receivable of some forty thousand dollars. Not one cent collectable.

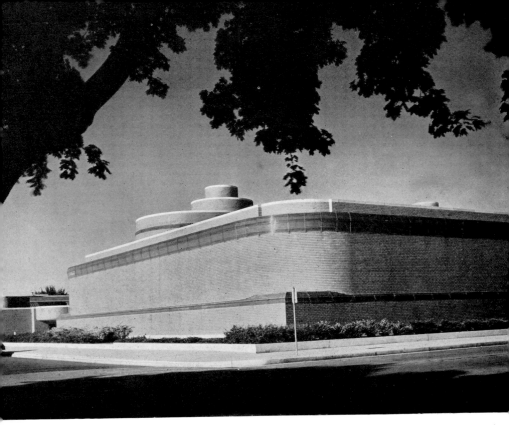

36. General view. Walls of glass tubing, brick, and Kasota stone

S. C. JOHNSON & SON INC., ADMINISTRATION BUILDING. 1936-7

37. Side wall of offices. Glass tube lighting

38. Detail

39. Dendriform columns of the hall. Shaft nine inches diameter at floor; ceiling spread twenty feet

S. C. JOHNSON & SON INC., ADMINISTRATION BUILDING. 1936-7

40. View through interior wall of glass tubes

41. Detail: entrance to car park

POST-MORTEM

For years (and even now) after the Aunts passed on (typical experience) —some old farmer would step out into the road ahead of me and say, 'Frank, I never ast no pay for the forty cords o' wood I hauled "the girls" back there February nineteen-fifteen.'

'Well,' I would say, 'why didn't you ask them for the money, and why have you said nothing about it to them nor to me until now?'

'Oh,' he would say. 'I knowed they was hard up then and I didn't need the money bad. But it's differ'nt now. Yes, *sir*, it's differ'nt.'

Trying to read the man, I said, 'But your bill is outlawed now.'

'Oh, sure,' he'd say. 'Outlawed sure, but you're their nephew, Frank. You're willin' to pay me *somethin'* on the old account, ain't ye?'

'Of course,' I'd say, 'how much do you say?'

'Oh, pay me half—sixty dollars and I'll call her square.'

'But I haven't got sixty dollars right now.'

'Oh . . . ain't ye?' he would say. 'All right then. I'll jest as soon come 'round sometime I'm down thet a way and pick it up. I knowed you wouldn't let your old Aunts down, Frank,' said he.

And he would get the money when I got it. Such bills were outlawed, of course, but, worse, some were undoubtedly false. I used my own judgment. Grew to be less and less easy. Paid some, and told others to go. What else?

PERSPECTIVE

To anyone looking back over the life and work of these two dear grand maiden-aunts of mine, work of great consequence to us all is still living. I see it so cruelly set and hard beset by the circumstances of their provincial environment which is of course still our own environment at Taliesin. Age was a disqualification when the life work of these great women was endangered. They were wasted as though they were animals in a market. Their wisdom and rich experience went for nought. Just as in the provinces the age of a horse determines his useful value, or a cow her desirability, the chickens their egg-laying and edibility; so the deadly provincial American mind carries this over into human life. Instead of growing old gracefully, with the distinction and genuine honour we see it attaining in wiser ancient civilizations (the oriental, for instance), if we look about us we will see all that finer quality of living thrown away, cancelled by this characteristic animalistic view of age. Age driven to conceal its venerability under devices of the cosmetician—the plastic surgeon— devices of dress. Age tries so pitiably hard to 'look' young because it *is* young and in most precious ways stronger than ever. But when the traces of use are regarded as mere wear and tear, they do become ugly indeed. A 'lived in' face should be no disqualification in our provinces and even less so on the hard pavements of our urban centres. But the young have their fling and then they are flung, flung upon the scrap-heap of the Old, while youth persists and the best time of life is ahead: instead of the fruiting of the tree, a dreary waste. Our people are doing this thing to themselves, a damning count against all Western Civilization.

If age brings no great reward to others and itself in a society, something is radically wrong with the individual or the society. Perhaps with both. I remember well a great woman, friend of my mother's—Mrs. Lydia Avery Coonley-Ward, herself an example of what she was saying—'If a woman is not attractive at twenty it isn't her fault, but if she isn't at fifty, it certainly is.'

A PROMISE

I have made many promises in my life, always intending to keep them. I think I never made one that I didn't intend to keep. But my corner of hell will be paved with those that turned out to be only intentions. Time and circumstances destroy promises as distance dims one's view. But one promise would not let me go. My love for my mother and my aunts, my admiration for their grand gray heads and the dignity of their beautiful persons which age had brought were bound up in that promise as though they lived on in the promise: a promise I had made to see their educational work go on at beloved Hillside on the site of the pioneer homestead. That filial promise would go along with me wherever I went. If I settled down, it settled down with me. In course of time it became a subjective urge as well as an objective. If I lived I was sure to keep the promise whether I wanted to or not. I became an Instrument of Fate.

No matter what reason might dictate I would keep that promise in good time. And, since I was what I was, I would keep it in my own way. As yet I had no idea in what way; procrastinating as always, this time for many years, I had faith in myself or whatever it is that keeps the promises we make.

And I believed now, *from within*, that whatever I deeply enough desired I should have, because it first had me.

No, it was no longer necessary to bend my mind in that direction. Something had taken place that would simply turn circumstances and events in that direction. In good time what was desired would be there.

ANNO DOMINI 1929

This economic, now historic nationalistic failure of the attempt by Production to control Consumption, so ignorantly termed a 'depression', is here. Economic breakdown is so complete at this time that no workman's hammer is ringing in our great state of Wisconsin. Native workmen of my own countryside, labourers, carpenters and masons of Iowa County as in the next Dane County and the next Sauk County are all but starving while I watch the shingle roofs of the 1902–1903 Hillside School buildings falling in for lack of some such labour as theirs. All of them (yes, labourers included) are rotting away. Roof water is coming in on most of the fine interiors. Waxed sand-finish walls of the rooms are completely scribbled

338

over with proper names like some provincial privy, desecrated by this ever
devastating passerby whose better name is Curiosity. Should what is still
left of these buildings I so proudly built in 1902 for those gallant pioneers,
my Aunts Nell and Jane, go through one more winter in this agonizing
condition, then no use ever attempting to repair them. The matchless
flesh-coloured sand-stone walls built under my direction by twinkling-
eyed, bewhiskered Timothy, the old Welsh stone mason ('and what-
ever-r-r') would be left standing. Not only was there no money to pay
long outstanding money-debts but there was now hardly carfare to get to
the big city in order to find work there, should there be any work to do.
Where might work come from? None could say. Except as we could raise it
ourselves there was no food. My friends were losing what money they had
or had already lost it. How did I know? They knew how they knew I
knew!

If he has no ground of his own and if he cannot go to work on some
farm, no architect in these United States of America has anything to do
unless he is 'related' to someone who happens to be sitting pretty, and
(because the more cautious were hit hardest) sitting pretty meant, merely,
lucky. Barely subsisting from day to day the architects in our great
country trying so hard to control Consumption by Production were still
in 'pursuit of happiness' but, while living upon 'savings' or money-means
bought by insurance, got by marriage, or some inheritance. Or more than
likely, got by borrowing something somehow from someone while Production was impatiently waiting to be consumed or trying to force Consumption. Not only my own 'earnings' (merely what 'they' call them) are
gone, but any credit I may ever have had whatsoever is gone because of
them. But we were only sharing now in all this the fate of the far more
provident: mortgages, judgments, private chagrin, humiliation private
and public, disgrace—nation-wide. Blackmail and slander still accumulate
in the foreground of this glum national picture.
A motley horde of outstretched hands comes frequently to Taliesin's
door in the valley! They come knocking in all too familiar guises: legal
'repossessions', press interviews, duns, more repossessions, more threats.
Private blackmail, private and public 'adverse examinations' by shyster
lawyers, long-distance telephone duns, duns by friends, duns by relatives,
duns by employers. All desperate. No money—and at last, sabotage.
Threats: some more threats. And assassination. These all stand outside the
door, lit by the sinister flares of interior treachery. And the usual self-
righteous 'saviours' heap the sordid measure of tragic defeat to running
over with well-meant (and too well-known) advice.
Worse than all, like Festus Jones, I myself, not having much conscience
anyway, find that what little I have is pretty solidly guilty!
My trouble too is, I know, that I still yearn to be on good terms with
myself and have never yet succeeded in getting rid of this deep-seated,
inherited, tragic ancestral plague—the desire to stand well with my kind
—to win the esteem and affection of my fellows. And to heap the cup, I

have always been ready and willing—I still am—to do without the Necessaries of Life if only I may have the Luxuries. This has seemed the only way to do 'the things that are more excellent' while the Criterion—Money—secretly calls the turn.

A STATION FOR THE FLIGHT OF THE SOUL

Many times before, in desperate circumstances (perhaps because of them) came AN IDEA. I, too, can get a bad idea—but not this time. The now subjective promise came to its object as the idea? No buildings to build at the harrowing moment but, capitalizing thirty-five years of past experience, why not build the builders of buildings against the time when buildings might again be built?

Congenital Education, dormant family influence, up and out—at last! To make a promise good?

Numbers of young men were always coming from around the world to work with me at Taliesin. Several were at Taliesin now. After talking the 'idea' over, pro and con, we, a son of Wisconsin Welsh pioneers and a daughter of Montenegrin dignitaries aiming to be educators, composed and sent out during the summer of 1932 the following circular letter to a small list of friends. Here is that circular letter:

AN EXTENSION OF THE WORK IN ARCHITECTURE AT TALIESIN TO INCLUDE APPRENTICES IN RESIDENCE

Frank Lloyd Wright together with a number of competent assistants will be in residence at Taliesin and will there lead the work of a new Fellowship of Apprentices to be now established.

Three resident associates: a sculptor, a painter, and a musician, eventually chosen for the work to be done, are contemplated. An inner-group of seven honour-apprentices having the status of senior apprentices and three technical advisers trained in industry will also be chosen to assist.

Leaders in thought from many countries may also come to occasionally share for a time in our activities, perhaps temporarily reside there.

We believe that a rational attempt to integrate Art and Industry should coordinate both with the everyday life we live here in America. Any such rational attempt must be *essential architecture* growing up by way of social, industrial, and economic processes natural to our way of life.

Not only must this framework and background of future Democracy be developed in itself as a kind of organic architecture, but the very qualities most basic and worthwhile in Philosophy, Sculpture, Painting, Music and the Industrial Crafts are also fundamentally Architecture. Principles underlying life and the arts are the same. So it is the Architecture of Life itself that must be the fundamental and therefore first concern of any true culture anywhere if the world is to be made safe for Science.

340

No alliance between 'Art' and Commercial Industry is ever enough because no mere 'alliance', however useful, can be Creative. Appropriate forms must be developed from within and they must be forms having worthwhile relation to our actual industry. The necessary original work will be best done where the workers will have not only spontaneous recourse to modern shop and working conditions but have at the same time, as workers, benefit of the inspirational fellowship of some genuinely creative architect. Constant working contacts with the nature of structure and materials, the ground, and of nature-growth itself are the only reliable texts to be used in this connection. Only as these are actual forms of daily experience directly related to daily life and work are they the texts we must now use to begin again at the beginning.

What little creative impulse survives among us in the confusion of this machine age might thus have some chance to live uncontaminated by the old human expressions already dead or dying around us. The Big City is no longer a place for more than the exterior applications of some cliché or sterile formula, where life is concerned. Therefore the TALIESIN FELLOWSHIP chooses to live and work in the country. The FELLOWSHIP establishment is located on a fine farm forty miles west of Madison, four miles from the nearest village on State Highway 23 in beautiful Southern Wisconsin. Near the Wisconsin River.

THE WORK IN ARCHITECTURE first done at Oak Park and Chicago, and later at Taliesin, has proved itself during the past thirty years. It has gone far enough in the world-current of contemporary change so that good work may be done in full cooperation with our more advanced producers and manufacturers: those who sincerely desire to improve the nature of their product. American industry need no longer depend for artistic excellence upon the copying of imitations nor need ever do so again if our country will learn to utilize resources such as our resources at Taliesin.

As the TALIESIN FELLOWSHIP therefore, we now propose to extend apprenticeship from the several draughtsmen to whom it has been limited to include seventy* apprentices working under leadership as described.

Each apprentice will work under the inspiration of direct architectural leadership, toward machine-craft art in this machine age. All will work together in a common daily effort to create new forms needed by machine work and modern processes if we are to have any culture of our own worth having. A number (a hundred or more) of such young workers in Architecture have already come to Taliesin from various parts of the world. Others may now be immersed in the many-sided activities of a growing Fellowship of apprentices. Our activities, we hope, will be gradually extended to include collateral arts by way of such modern machine crafts as we can establish. Living in direct personal contact with modern concepts and the currents of thought in the world now demanding new form we believe young architects, artists, and craftsmen may here find means to build up spiritual forces and a technique that will guarantee a life work in *the essential architecture of all the arts* and be enabled to practise them as

* Changed to twenty-three.

341

the natural fulfilment of an experience and training belonging peculiarly to our own time and country.

SO WE BEGIN this working Fellowship as a kind of daily work-life. Apprentices at work on buildings or in crafts which have a free individual basis: a direct work-experience made healthy and fruitful by seeing Idea as work and work as Idea take effect, actually, in the hand of the young apprentice.

OUR HOME LIFE MUST BE SIMPLE. Meals in common. Fixed hours for work, recreation, and sleep. Each worker will have his or her room for study and rest. Suitable toilet accommodations will be made convenient to all rooms. Entertainment too will be a feature of our life at home. Plays, music in the evenings; the cinema and conferences to which musicians, literary men, artists, and scientists will sometimes be invited and (occasionally) the public. The beautiful region itself is never failing source of inspiration and recreation for all concerned. Daily life will be planned to benefit by its beauty.

Fellowship work in its manifold branches will come directly under the influence of an organic philosophy: organic architecture for organic life. At Taliesin this life will be lived with such sense of the Future as may belong to the present.

The actual study of Architecture *as a kind of practice* will in this broad sense be taken into detailed studies of building designs and principles of construction. Eventually biology, typography, ceramics, woodcraft, and textiles will be further taken into consideration. These practical studies will go hand in hand with characteristic model-making and soon will go on to practical experiments in the crafts made by such apprentices as go into the workshops which we hope to build.

Apprenticeship not *Scholarship* is to be the actual condition and should be the attitude of mind of the Fellowship. A fair division of labour in maintaining all branches of work will fall to the share of each member. Especial predilections or idiosyncrasies, although respected, will not be separately encouraged. There will be no age limit for apprentices but the qualifications of each will be decided finally by Mr. Wright after a month's trial in the Fellowship work. The right to reject any applicant at any time is reserved—either before or after being formally received into the Fellowship. The Fellowship, however, is not on trial. The apprentice is.

TALIESIN AIMS to develop a well-correlated human being: the correlation between hand and the mind's eye most lacking in modern education.

As a primary requirement therefore each member of the Fellowship will be asked to engage in all the daily work of necessary Fellowship maintenance. Wage slavery will be eliminated so far as possible.

THE LABORATORIES AND MACHINE SHOPS are not yet built but, eventually, they will be planned next to the draughting room as shown in the accompanying illustrations.

Studios and galleries are already built or being built. The first experimental units ready are those of architectural construction and design, the philosophy of architecture, typographical design, the printing of a publication *TALIESIN*—organ of the Fellowship; also moulding and casting adapted to modern systems of construction in glass, concrete and metal. Woodworking by modern machinery. A collateral study of philosophy and the practice of sculpture, painting, drama and rhythm. These units are to be followed by actual glass-making, pottery, weaving, modern reproduction processes in any form we may be able to establish. We believe that business men in industry will find it worthwhile to cooperate with us in setting up these crafts.

A personal testimonial, only, will be given to each worker at the end of his or her apprenticeship. Each year will have a holiday of six weeks for each worker but arranged only as the work permits.

THE FELLOWSHIP IS NOT YET THE 'FOUNDATION' IT HOPES TO BE but is an independent cultural enterprise and the sustaining revenue of the Fellowship for the next several years must come mainly from apprenticeship fees and maintenance work, four hours each day, of the apprentices. Added to this may be Architects' fees, compensation from industries for services rendered or to be rendered; the sale of complete art objects; a publication to be printed by the Fellowship. And the possible but not probable contribution of money or equipment from 'Friends of the Fellowship', a group to be organized among those who believe in our work and who are able and willing to add scope to our usefulness.*

Undoubtedly, prosperity of the Fellowship must depend upon the quality of its membership but more upon the spirit of cooperation felt and practised by the members and myself in the work we do. Only the apprentices themselves can make apprenticeship useful to a master or to themselves. Therefore no apprentice will be accepted without trial: the right to terminate any Fellowship without notice, reserved.

EACH WILL BE REQUIRED TO PAY THE FIXED FEE for tuition as stated on the application blank herewith. And as a necessary feature of their training, each will be required to contribute his or her share of work each day on the grounds or new buildings or on the farm, for the privilege of participation in the experimental work going on in the studios and workshops and such production of art objects as practical exemplars for industry and building as may be for exhibition and sale. An account will also be kept of the money had from such sales. At the end of each year a fair dividend will be paid to each member which may eventually reduce or abolish the tuition fee.†

A BUSINESS-LIKE ORGANIZATION will manage the affairs of the FELLOWSHIP.‡

THE FARM AND GARDEN will be so managed to employ the help of the apprenticeship that a substantial portion of the living of members may come from their own labour on the ground, thus enabling apprentice fees to remain low as possible.

* The group has not yet been organized.
† The original fee was six hundred and fifty dollars for a full year, but, next year, for cause, changed to eleven hundred dollars.
‡ This was never established because not needed.

343

No sooner was this ambitious scheme proposed than we abandoned it. After sending out the circular we decided we would do better to stick to what we already had than to go too far institutional or 'educational'. I had certain qualifications; Olgivanna had others to add to mine. So we put our heads, as well as our hearts, together, simplified it all to come within our immediate capacities, so we thought, and wisely cut down possible membership to twenty-three. But the foregoing text—text by no means simple enough—was nevertheless sent out. It had the effect we hoped for and intended. Twenty-three young men and women brought twenty-three times six hundred and fifty dollars—one year each—to work it out at Taliesin. And a fair cross-section of Young America assembled there October 1, 1932, eager to go to work at something—ill-prepared for anything except academic study of some sort. Least of all for the Freedom Taliesin had to offer.

TO THE ENEMY

Since we had now started something, supplementing the foregoing statement, the following letter replying to a *Manifesto* issued at that time by the Beaux Arts of the United States was directed to the heads of the 'Beaux Arts' schools. The letter was mailed with a request to post the letter where students might see it, should the institution be so inclined. In some cases it was so posted.

The reader understands quite well by now that the servile Beaux Arts societies in these United States would be anathema to any ideal of indigenous USONIAN culture.

If this dull lack of indigenous culture ('pattern') in the fabric of our weaving is not wrong then should we be content with no pattern at all? Better off sterile? None will say so. As the matter stands we cannot afford to lose one single strand native or natural to our growth as a free nation or allow one fresh attempt to build it that may be destroyed by the old patterns and prejudices we jealously drag along. In this cultural lag we have completely stultified instead of inspired the to-and-fro of mere artifice that we are fond of calling Standardization. If we do allow this cultural back-drag to be 'Art' much longer, there can be no life of the Spirit left in our weaving. We can never have the inspiring culture of our own that can lift these inevitable routine standardizations above the belt, because Civilization is truly this matter of inspired and inspiring pattern (culture) in the social fabric (our society).

Civilization is this affair of Pattern.

A witty Frenchman has said of us: 'The United States of America is the only nation to plunge from barbarism to degeneracy with no culture in between.'

Here is the reply to the innuendo 'by circular' of the *Manifesto* of the Beaux Arts in the U.S.A.:

TO THE STUDENTS OF THE BEAUX ARTS
INSTITUTE OF DESIGN: ALL DEPARTMENTS

A notice to you, taking my name in vain (together with the names of two other modern architects whom I respect, Gropius and Le Corbusier), has been sent to me.*

If this circular is proper evidence of the quality of inspiration to which our young architects are now subject this may be the time for them to help themselves. Reading between the lines of this lively circular which contains a threat, I see that the Beaux Arts establishment in America realizes that neither its old practices nor the old doctrines can be made to apply longer, except by force.

But as this circular bears witness, the Beaux Arts is now ready to speak-the-language of the new thought in architecture. Must then the Beaux Arts leadership deny or betray modern architects before it can 'come over' to modern architecture as gracefully as it thinks becoming to its dignity? Or else, say (it does so in this circular) it won't come over to modern architecture at all and 'all the students will be pushed back to classicism'?

And, are you, as students, reliably informed concerning what constitutes modern architecture? You are officially told that 'it is not going to become a style based upon Wright, Gropius and Le Corbusier.'

Now . . . it *is* true that much that passes for modern architecture is not organic because it is already contaminated by American Beaux Arts standards of imitation. To unfortunate young architects so contaminated I am a friendly enemy. But architecture as 'modern' has a future only because these modern architects, whatever their faults (from whom I am sorry to say the circular in question derives only language), are what they are, and because they have done what they have done.

Yet it is because of their work that the Beaux Arts is now ready to modify its programme or 'push you all back into classicism'!

I admit that the principles and practice of *organic* architecture are yet insufficiently familiar to some of these modern architects against whom you are officially warned. But they will be the principles you will be moved by and that you will master if you do not betray your country to the 'Beaux Arts' as it will betray you now and everywhere if it can do so by assuming a virtue it cannot have. Unfortunately the Beaux Arts training in architecture has been all the academic training Young America has had a chance to get.

But today no man able to think for himself believes in such pseudo 'training'. No training like it can aid any young man to grow into a creative architect. These very principles of an organic architecture (modern architecture) which the Beaux Arts 'views with alarm' and from which it derives the unfamiliar language it tries to use in this circular—'the meaning of materials', etc., etc., would blow their method and practice away were they or their students able to grasp the real meaning of that language.

* See Notice to Students and Correspondents—Architectural Department— School Year 1931–32, April 20, 1932.

When 'in all history', for instance, has 'the meaning of materials' or anything deeper than fine composition been found in these academic circles until the men whose work you are now officially told—'modern architecture is not going to resemble' came along? The simplest knowledge of simples, 'the meaning of materials', my thesis in particular, would utterly destroy these native 'Beaux Arts' establishments. It has already gone far toward doing so because of utter ignorance in the practice of the very nature of materials and the uses of modern methods and that misunderstanding of modern architecture which is a sublime American Beaux Arts characteristic! 'Composition?' *That* only is the shrine of all Beaux Arts training.

Well, 'Composition' is dead.

The silhouette of masonry mass over steel only lives as a festering feudal hangover, a false gesture. But in organic architecture, Creation still lives as the Magna Charta of your Liberty. Yet you are told your work must not resemble it!

So it is natural and inevitable that hypocrisy should flower as the result of this system of eclectic imitation not only fostered, but now *featured* by the institution calling itself the 'American Beaux Arts'! The result must be—no fruit.

But, should fault be found with an ostrich because it persists in sticking its head in the sand, because no ostrich is a lion? Where, I ask you, young man—are you going to learn the truth that 'intelligent mass', 'consideration of the three dimensional block of the building' are not *fundamentals*, and learn that merely as such, all are properties of good design no longer applying, fundamentally, to youth in architecture? These items are not principles but qualities—mere *by-products* of good design. No longer 'fundamental', I assure you.

So if you *are* to be 'pushed back to classicism' (the threat is contained in the circular) and therefore confined to these old reactions referred to as 'the fundamentals of good design' which the ancient Beaux Arts once learned and the modern institution now refuses or is unable to forget, then this moment seems the proper time to hold out to such of you as are really in love with architecture, opportunity to learn something of the principles that make 'modern architecture' so objectionable to the Beaux Arts; and make it so chiefly because it has become a threat to their own self-preservation. The accompanying plan must explain to you what I mean by opportunity. Taliesin has already established a living, worldwide Tradition. Now it has good reason to know that Youth everywhere is hungry for this new reality. Everywhere Youth is rocking in an old academic boat no longer seaworthy. Even in the dock for repairs, that old 'classic', the 'American Beaux Arts' can no longer be made safe for youth. Nothing modern architecture has to give any student can reach him by way of such eclectic imitation as now captains and sails that old caravel.

However reformed, the Beaux Arts cannot forget that it must never learn.

Taliesin, January, 1932.

Training for Democracy will thus always be beginning at the beginning with the young or else breaking through all training with its naturals.

The Taliesin hat was thus, without equivocation, 'in the ring'. Some twenty-three young men and women had already responded. Although Taliesin rambles over a good many acres of hillside, we had to make-shift to house the twenty-three—even temporarily. We could manage to feed them with outside hired help. But we had to go to work with them and forty outside workmen to get them all becomingly sheltered, bedded down and provided with adequate places to be planned, in which to work together as promised. I felt in duty bound to use what money they paid me (in the usual instalments, of course) for that purpose only. And this use, notwithstanding the circumstances of importunate debt—debt well armed, as always, with lawyers, advance agents of bolted doors and barred windows, or even worse, the still small voice of Conscience that is my misfortune—steadily carried on. I suspect numbers of our young people borrowed the money to come to Taliesin.

Dankmar Adler once said to me that he got his start in life by owing money to the right people. He borrowed money to pay for his education as an architect and being unable at the time to pay it back, the people who loaned it to him (he said) felt that the only way they could ever get it back again was to give him a job—a building to build. So he got his first job. I pass this along (in confidence) to posterity for what it may be worth.

As the plan for the Taliesin Fellowship unfolded itself, I had hoped that apprentices—like the fingers on my hands—would increase not only my own interest and enthusiasm for my work as an architect, but would also widen my capacity to apply it in the field.

The first came true. But the second, as yet, is a temporarily frustrated hope. We somewhat overshot the mark. But I have not yet given up hope. We are steadily improving.

We had designed a heading (one, Hillside roofs in snow; one, Taliesin roofs in snow) and started a weekly column beneath it, one in Editor Evjue's Madison paper *The Capital Times*, one in the *State Journal*. The articles, beginning in 1932 and signed by the apprentices, ran for several years. Although apprentices themselves usually wrote the articles (architects, I thought, had need to be especially articulate), occasionally Olgivanna and I would take a hand. Here follows one of mine. The articles, hundreds of them, are hard to come by now.

WHAT IS THE MATTER WITH HUMAN NATURE?

A young apprentice for a year—now an architect, young friend of mine[*] writes concerning the Taliesin Fellowship: 'Your idea is good and your work should succeed, but you are asking too much of Human Nature.

[*] Alden Dow.

I wish you had attempted something in which you had a greater chance of success.'

To my solicitous young friend:

Taliesin *is* preaching an unpopular gospel, I admit: preaching by practice, the gospel of Work, and Work has been pretty well knocked out of American youth by way of inflated 'Education'. It is going to be no easy matter, I can see, to put the joy back into work that alone can make work creative and lift it above drudgery.

There have already been many youths here at Taliesin who had applied themselves to a college curriculum four to six years and had come out with the usual 'degree'. Some of them honour men. They could sufficiently concentrate to arrive at that. But they know, as I do, that this is less, much less, than half the right thing.

'Less than half' means that most college-grown men today are rather less than half-men. They are sometimes interesting, often informed, controversially conversational, pettily egotistic, but usually impotent. Any skilled labour involving their physical resources is beyond them. They imagine it is beneath them but, really, it is beyond them. To use tools well, especially a shovel, a hoe, or an axe requires at least as much Science and more Manhood than swinging a golf club on a golf ball correctly or rooting at a football game.

To stay with a good piece of work in the field or a building requires more stamina than football because football is showing off and field work or building is a kind of skilled sacrifice to nothing immediate but something stored up in the Future. The man who plants a tree knows something of this non-showing but deeply satisfying aspect of work. And if the Taliesin experiment in apprenticeship does fail, it will fail because our modern youths have been left high and dry above the capacity to surrender to work in its rich, full, manifold forms. And because the individual educated youth, where his physical nature is concerned with his head, is unable to be and continue as a good workman—per se, as such. That is to say, where his head and hands should be.

So I look with increasing disgust (alarm too) at the coddled addled product parents turn adrift upon society by way of the colleges. Yes, by hundreds of thousands, half-baked novitiates congregate in universities all looking for dignity, worth and wealth outside the only source from which either can spring for them: the creative energy of their whole manhood, projected with enjoyment into useful creative employment: work wherein physical force must be so related to mind that none can say where the one begins and the other ends.

I have the same feeling of repulsion for the one-sided development of, say, a sedentary musician, that I would have for some man with an enormous muscular right arm hanging from an undernourished, undeveloped body. I should consider that arm a spiritual deformity as well as a physical monstrosity. 'Specialities' are usually developed at such expense to the health and soundness of the whole man. They offend me even more now since I have been leading youth into action by way of the axe, the saw, the plane, the hammer, and the scythe, the shovel and the hoe. The stone chisel, the paint brush, as well as just cooking and washing up. And then comes the use of the T-square and triangle on the drawing board.

No more drawing-board architects at Taliesin! Not if I can help it. Nor, if I can help it, any more one-sided specialists who can't and won't take work as though their daily bread did not depend upon a modicum of sweat on the brow and some joy in their own decent skill. The sedentary specialist has had his not sufficiently brief hour in capitalism. For fifty years, at least, the academic pigeon hole has had its fill of peripatetic young human lives conditioned to capitalism and here we are as we now are, a nation of employees of some employee of an employee. We do not know who our Employer is. Increasingly few have the heart or the brains to inquire. Of what use to know?

And what 'Educated' youth is worth employing as a workman on his own stark merit? Lack of correlation and stamina is what is the matter with him. Here in this work at Taliesin we are seeking to find and build up in the young lad that joy and stamina in work which will enable him to take hold of life afresh and *anywhere*! Were the world of men and things destroyed as it stands, he could take hold and make a better one in every way. If the weakness and indolent habits of sedentary American college life are incurable—well then, Taliesin hasn't much chance to succeed. But there are young men here already *enjoying* work, enough to prove that essential manhood is still potential in the *insurgent* college-man at least. But we have our Ups and Downs. Our Ins and Outs.

These several background sets—stage props?—must serve to give you some idea of what the Taliesin Fellowship meant to meet as best it could. They will also give you the attitude of the Fellowship at the time.

For weeks I had driven up and down the ramifying valleys of our matchless countryside looking for lumber and other materials to work with. We needed, and desperately, lumber, stone, lime and labourers of all sorts. As you see in the lines (and between them), we had very little or no money at all to pay for these coveted desirables at first. The search lasted for months. Finally, materials still lacking—having failed to secure most of the essential materials, I got forty workmen together from the neighbouring small towns—laid my scheme before them and made them the following proposition—anxious and still wondering where I could get the materials for them to work with if I succeeded and they did come to work. I proposed to dissipate what money the apprentices brought in by putting most of it each week into the pockets of the all but starving workmen, sheltering them in comfort, feeding them well, and paying for the food they consumed. They willingly signed the following agreement. I suppose in the circumstances they would have signed anything. Most of them were a hungry-looking lot.

GENERAL NOTICE*

All workmen, as party of the first part, and Frank Lloyd Wright, as party of the second part, representing the Taliesin Fellowship, agree to work in partnership as follows: suitable board and lodgings are to be provided by the Fellowship and one-third of the wages as agreed upon in each individual contract as signed by each workman will be paid in cash weekly. The balances are all to be paid when the buildings now under construction are completed and ready for occupancy and increased apprenticeship fees can be obtained.

(Signed)

—————————————
FRANK LLOYD WRIGHT

Each workman was asked to sign the following contract:

INDIVIDUAL CONTRACT†

Charles Curtis, as party of the first part, and Frank Lloyd Wright, as party of the second part, representing the Taliesin Fellowship, hereby agree to work in partnership as follows:

Charles Curtis is to go to work as mason on the buildings as planned for the Fellowship by Frank Lloyd Wright, and work as directed by him from the date hereof until October 15th, 1932, for the sum of four dollars ($4.00) per working day—to be paid as follows: twenty-five dollars ($25.00) a month as work progresses, the balance due to be paid to Charles Curtis October 15, 1932, by Frank Lloyd Wright out of the funds of the Fellowship.

While Charles Curtis is with the Fellowship it is agreed that satisfactory board and room shall be provided by the Fellowship.

(Signed)   (Signed)

—————————————   —————————————
FRANK LLOYD WRIGHT   CHARLES CURTIS

In some cases, Karl Jensen, secretary at the time, neglected to get some of the men on the dotted line, but when they were taken in on the work they were all told and knew well enough what the terms were upon which they were working. The general notice, lettered in black and red on a white placard, was posted in the Dining Room and in the buildings where they worked.

The men were appreciative and grateful. So I believed. Be that as it may, I soon had forty of them for partners and put all to work saving the Hillside Home School buildings. Other workmen (they were continually tramping by), learning of our set-up, asked us to take them on. Some

* Posted on the walls of Dining Room, Oct. 1, 1932.
   Specimen.

350

came from as far away as San Francisco and New York City. That man-power of ours was a motley of urban, rural, married, unmarried, young and old, good, bad and indifferent America: the dregs of the system at the bottom, fairly good country workmen at the top.

We fixed up the old laundry building at Hillside with a wood range and managed running water, hot and cold. We made long board tables and covered them with white oil cloth, and put hard benches beside them. We fixed up the old place until it seemed inviting and homey, and began to feed our men comfortably. Workmen are captious where food is concerned. But we fed them so well that, believe it or not, they really admitted it. There was very little drinking on the premises. Some few of the men went to town for that and would come back and fight. We could always start a backfire. A little room near their dining room, we—the young Fellowship—set aside as a dining room for ourselves. We had our noonday meal there together every day (pretty well cooked farm produce) to consider things in general, and argue in detail when exciting problems were pressing, using the white plastered walls for illustrating details. Problems were plenty and always pressing. Activity was soon gratifying and exciting. The men were glad to get to work after long enforced idleness.

And to keep them all going on in the right order and direction was a problem mostly solved afresh each night about four in the morning and worked out on the drawing boards next day. During that wakeful early morning hour, which I have known ever since, I can remember creative work, an hour devoted to prospect, retrospect and perspective when all is still and I am rested, and I know I can turn over and rest several hours more: then things come clearest. At that time the unsolved problems seemed to work themselves out with comparatively little assistance from me.

We had man-power. About forty men.

MATERIALS VERSUS CASH

LUMBER

We were now where we had to have more lumber or stop work altogether. Standing around in the woods of our country, were many piles of sawed oak. I coveted them all as I coveted gravel, sand, and cement. The surrounding farmers had cut the timber on their own wooded hillsides and were keeping the lumber for barn building. I tried to buy some of these lumber piles, pay part down, part on credit. But nothing could be done. The hard financial going all around had made everyone, especially the farmers, doubly suspicious, especially so of me, the spender of so much money with no visible means of support. So far as they could see. For many weary patient weeks I met the same answer to all my propositions and petitions. 'No—we must have cash.' 'Cash is what we need most of anything. Pay right now, or else!' They really did need 'cash' desperately.

351

Of course they did. Cash was more than ever, absolutely now, King. But I finally learned that Herb Schoenmann (ten children), a decent neighbouring farmer, had 400 acres of virgin oak timber standing just over the ridge from Taliesin. I drove over to see Herb, offered him a fair price and terms for his four hundred acres of timber, on the stump. And Herb accepted. (Yes—he was paid.) Then I found a good sawer on the other side of the river who agreed to saw the logs at the regular price if we cut them and brought them in. I found another farmer (a good fellow out on parole for stealing his neighbour's chickens) who would cut the trees for a price and his old father and two young sons (really nice boys) would haul them in, he said, if we would help in the logging with our caterpillar tractor and some of our Fellowship boys.

So back to first principles for us.

Forthwith, we went headlong into logging. The place became a logging camp. Soon, after overcoming innumerable difficulties of a time-consuming, painful but picturesque character, green-oak timber was going up into the walls and trusses of our coveted buildings. Sap was still running from the boards. Green twigs were still on the logs when we sawed them into boards, scantling, and beams according to Henry's lumber lists. None too evenly sawed timber either. But never mind.

We had lumber. Seventy thousand board-feet.

It was our own.

The boys—yes, the girls—enjoyed the hard work as well as the painful picturesque experiences. Those experiences were consequential too, in unexpected but perfectly natural ways.

We had incurred a debt of several thousand dollars besides our own labour and what money we had. But we now had something to build our superstructure with. Rather hard to manage but we would have taken anything that could not positively crawl off the building lot. You should have seen those inexperienced boys tackle that heavy logging job! No worldly-wise, pavement-sore urban parents could ever believe their boys capable of such hard continuous physical punishment as their boys took. They liked it. I mean the boys.

Lumber-yard lumber was still way beyond us. Prices were far too high. About double what we paid for the green oak. Lumber, like telephone and telegraph service and other 'System' items, had not dropped one cent during the 'depression' nor were any concessions made if headquarters knew what was going on. They were all holding the fort: which means prices. Meantime work on the buildings continued. And the workmen, no longer hungry, were not grumbling. They were satisfied with what money we paid them. The framework was now there in the rough.

A LEGAL EPISODE

After a few months, however, we again ran out of lumber and into a characteristic snag.

352

42. Model

HERBERT J. JOHNSON HOUSE. 1937

43. Interior of wigwam living room of Johnson House. Four-sided fireplace; tiara lighting

44 (**below**). Detailed view of living room, fireplace, and top lighting

45 (**below**). Balcony from playroom

46. Erected on the Mesa at foot of McDonnell Range, Maricopa County. Desert stone and Redwood. Canvas-covered frames overhead, movable for air and light

ARIZONA DESERT CAMP. 1934-6

47. Office studio of the Desert Camp

Again I went about the country, covetous—seeking another piece of timber.

Finally, I located some logs just out. Young Richardson, another farmer some miles away, had dropped about twenty thousand feet of red oak to the ground and the logs were lying there on the slippery hillside to be hauled. We bought and paid for them! I borrowed that money from an apprentice, Alden Dow.

But unfortunately we were soon on our way to Arizona. The Fellowship is an outdoor affair. We need to be outdoors on buildings as much of the time as possible. Inasmuch as it costs thirty-five hundred dollars to heat all of Taliesin and Hillside, we go out to Phoenix, Arizona, in winter, and on into the desert to build a camp of our own to work with and work in. We called it Taliesin West.

Meantime Tom King, local attorney-banker, had accepted a collection item against me of several hundred dollars for a disputed account with an eastern publishing house. This house was receiver-holder of Payson (*Disappearing City*) from whom I had bought back the copyright and 'remainder' of that book. I disputed the account because I had returned the 'remainder' when I found the books unbound. Nevertheless the long arm of the law, learning of the logs (the 'long arm' owned the local lumber-yard too) the neighbouring banker-lawyer 'attached' them. We, who merely bought and paid for them, first learned of the act upon our return from Arizona the following spring when we went to haul our logs. The Law and taxes never sleep where money is at stake, and often make very little noise on the way to execution. Tom, the lawyer's banker (and the bank's lawyer), had posted a sign on the fence near the family chapel yard conforming to legal requirements (so he said), but a notice which none of us ever saw, nor could see because we were two thousand miles away.

This was a blow, hard as it was unexpected—another kind of boot with a hard heel, a hustling sort. But recovering and visiting the scene we found a few thousand feet the Law had left behind. (Overlooked.) The Law should never play that way.

We ruefully hauled these remaining logs. But no use.

CATASTROPHE

Before we could get them into boards came the national CATASTROPHE! Labour in the U.S.A. went on 'RELIEF'.

On account of 'relief' we, the Taliesin Fellowship (in partnership with labour), had no more use for building materials for several years to come. Our labour had been 'bid in' to rest—relieved.

I mention this entirely legal interference with our plans and specifications as the final blow, but characteristic of the very many ultra-legal, but entirely unjust interferences from first to last, partly because, though all were desperate for 'money', none could be had by labour, none at all unless by gift. It would be too tedious to remember most of the circumstances to say nothing of narration. But just the same, though dashed, our work on the buildings did partly keep on for a time.

The buildings kept on growing up a little. The Taliesin boys themselves were begging to be able to carry on.

The workmen were no longer satisfied.

All had gained weight except Will Schwanke.

Will was foreman of carpenter construction, a faithful Spring Green carpenter. He was lean because he was faithful, perhaps. Will was not half dominant enough though, for that tough gang. I had to step in continually. His wife, who told Will all about himself frequently, strongly objected to us also. She kept telling him so. It jarred him frequently, but Will stayed faithfully by us on the carpentry just as Charlie Curtis, the seventy-nine-year-old Cornish mason from Mineral Point (whose wife took it from *him*), stayed with us on the masonry.

Both stayed for the duration.

Both were fine characters. A good influence on the boys and good instruction too. Stone walls as fine (almost as fine) as Timothy's, which are the finest in the world, were nobly standing there now ready for the framing.

'I don't want you to pay me much, Mr. Wright,' said Charlie. 'I am a contributor to the Fellowship because I think it's a grand idea.'

The boys made a lot of the old mason, while he made a good mason out of a lot of them. I liked Charlie.

John Commons, grand old man of the University of Wisconsin, came to see us discouraged and about beaten down. He declared he was all in—an old man at seventy-two. He did look as though he hadn't long to live. But we went to work on him, gathered round him and made much of him. I took him out to see Charlie working on a new stone fireplace in my bedroom. 'John,' I said, 'this is Charlie Curtis. He is eighty-one years old and a grander mason than ever.'

John Commons looked as though he had seen a ghost.

His jaw dropped. But the lesson went home.

He began to 'come back' as the saying is. After a week or two with us he went home.

His friends wanted to know what we had done to John.

'Oh, nothing,' I said, 'we just put him on good terms with himself, that's all.' That was six years ago and John is still going strong.

Charlie Curtis was kind and tolerant to all the amateurs except one rather elaborate travelling philosopher who came hitch-hiking in, enthusiastic, from the Colonial belt. All the screws needed for correlation were loose in him. But he had a polished mind and brilliant ideas to expound. He *would* keep on expounding them. I put him on as helper for Charlie, chipping stone and carrying mortar. One day, after a week of surplus theory and excess lack of correlation, Charlie put his hand up to my ear and said, 'For God's sake, Mr. Wright, take 'im away. Take 'im away before I kill 'im. I can't stand 'im no more.' I took him away and kept him in general circulation for the duration.

354

Charlie Curtis often used to say to the lads, 'You've got to get the feel of the rock in your 'ands, m'boys. It hain't no use 'til y'do! No use 't all'.

We had tripped the ledges and again opened the old quarry from which the beautiful stone for the Hillside buildings was taken. This quarrying was a mighty experience for the inexpert—we were all amateurs but, Charlie Curtis helping, we did it. We had plenty of stone which we had quarried, hauled ourselves, and piled about the buildings. Our fellows were getting splendid in action. Blocks of flesh coloured sandstone, cords upon cords of it out of the ground, two miles away.

The buildings kept on growing up by way of more and more long fine stone walls. We now had four local masons working under Charlie.

LIME

But we had to have lime or stop. The prideful Cord, getting tired, started travelling again. Finally I found some lime freshly burned but it was way up north in the state. However, they agreed to deliver it to us at a low price partly on credit. But weird stories were beginning to travel. They travel fast (and fixed) in 'The System'. So, on the way to deliver the lime, stopping at the local lumber yard in Spring Green, the up-state dealer was told by the local Spring Green dealer that if he sold us any lime at all he (the local man) would have him declared unfair by the 'Association' (the Association, like the T & T and the lumber companies, hadn't relaxed a bit during the breakdown) and if he did so, he said, no lumber yard in the state would buy any more from him. The lime-burner came to us with the story instead of the lime—apologetic, of course, very. He really believed in us. He was willing to help us but was actually up against it.

He said, 'You buy lime but once. The lumber dealers keep on buying lime.' So he said he could not afford to go against them and sell lime to us.

What to do? Conspiracy in restraint of trade? Undoubtedly. But what of it? We were out on a limb.

The men were soon entirely out of lime. We couldn't afford to buy cement. The lumber yards were full of cement—but for us to keep our workmen going, deliveries were only for cash-down. The cement dealers, like the lumber dealers, all knew their way out of the scraps they were in: stick together. Keep prices up. We came up against this fine fellow-feeling of theirs for their fellow-creatures on more than this one typical occasion.

Things were pretty tightly interlocked, I can tell you. There was little or nothing lying around loose in our county or those next to it. And rarely was there an 'independent' to be found anywhere. Independents were soon 'brought around'. It cost too much—this independence.

The principal materials were all under 'production-control'.

Strictly up against it again, under pressure, I remembered that lime for the original Hillside Home school buildings that old Timothy had used back in 1902 had all been burned in the hills not more than several miles away. The old kiln might be there yet! August Cupps owned the place now. So we went up over the hills to see August. 'Sure,' said he. 'Sure,' said tall awkward August, the sorghum-maker. 'Sure, go ahead, fix up the old kiln. I'll sell you wood to fire it at three-fifty a cord. Cut it myself.' There were yet lots of wood on the hillslopes nearby, and still plenty of limestone near the old kiln. So up went the boys to bring the old wrecked lime-kiln back to life again and themselves learn how to burn lime: a bunch of greensters. I got an old-time lime-burner from Black Earth to instruct them. We fixed up the broken grates with old ones we took from the old buildings at Hillside—patched up the tumbled walls, stripped a section of the old stone quarry and filled the patched-up restoration with good raw lime rock; piled cords and cords of wood alongside in long ranks to feed the roaring fires. Our boys took their food up to eat beside the kiln and would also take turns sleeping there by the kilnside on the ground under blankets, getting up every two hours all night long to keep the old kiln burning.

We got good lime . . . hundreds of bushels of it. We could have gone into the lime business, and thought seriously of doing so. We were A-1 producers of an essential building material.

We burned many full kilns of lime from first to last and we all loved it.

Somehow we grew strong by it. All of us. And that old kiln there on the hillside in the woods was a sight at night—lighting up the countryside for miles around.

We watched that light in the sky from Taliesin itself. When the iron door would open to engulf more cordwood, the boys, stripped to a loin-cloth, looked like stokers in the hold of a battleship. That old kiln *was* a battleship. Back to the primitive again to beat the tieup—the 'bottleneck'.

We had good lime.

It was our own.

SHOPPING FOR THE FELLOWSHIP

The old Auburn Cord (four thousand two hundred pounds in itself) became a beast of burden. But a handsome thing it was when not put out of sight by provender and put nearly out of commission by our weekly trips to the wholesale grocers in the neighbouring towns of this Iowa County and the next, Dane County, and the next, Sauk County. The car had taken several foreign prizes for body design and it was the nearest thing to a well-designed car I had ever seen outside Europe. And right here the feeling comes to me that the Cord should be heroic in this autobiography somewhere.

On the edge of entering the Money breakdown when several large commissions loomed in the foreground, I gave up the Packard for the Cord, taking it on an instalment-plan contract that ran us ragged for years. But it (the Cord) seemed to have the right principle—front-wheel drive pulling instead of pushing along, and certainly it looked becoming to my houses—the best design from my 'streamline' standpoint ever put on the market. I had myself driven myself (my own hands on the wheel) some five different top makes of car (beginning with the Stoddard-Dayton roadster in 1910) the equivalent in miles of some seven times around the earth—and, believe it or not, with never an accident—not even a smashed fender. But let me say I did not drive in Japan. I had four or five different drivers during that sojourn—they are a special class and how, over there —high silk stockings (ladies'), patent-leather shoes, knickers, and a military cap. And they high-saluted each other as they passed. Owing to narrow tortuous high-on-a-bank roads of Tokio countryside, their proficiency was similar to that of a slack-wire performer in a circus.

Due to a compound fracture of the wrist got while cranking the heavy Knox roadster I owned (after the Stoddard-Dayton), I kept a driver at Oak Park for a time. He was very careful of my broken member—but eventually stole the car. He turned out to be one of a gang of auto thieves. The police finally got the car in a St. Louis barn as they were putting a coat of green paint over its beautiful gunmetal finish.

I never cared for the Knox anyway. At high speed it would settle down and shake itself almost to pieces in a perfect frenzy (the garage-doctors call it a shimmy). And they couldn't show it how not to.

I think I got almost as much enjoyment (1922, '23, '24) out of the long, low, black, specially built Cadillac as out of the Cord. Patent-leather Victoria hood over the rear seat, windshield between first and back seat, no footboards, sides built down. I drove it in L.A. when I returned from Japan. That Cadillac thus had mostly the look of the later Cord—stream-lined—very compact. Wherever we parked the crowd would gather to see the 'foreign' car—trying to guess the make.

But the Cord was a prideful car—an innovation along right lines that changed the whole field of body design for the better—for one thing.

I was headed for Chicago one fine morning, very early. Between Madison and Evansville a florist's truck turned up ahead. I drew aside, about to pass, honking hard, when suddenly the truck with no warning at all turned and drove directly in front of me, turned sharply left—I jammed on the brakes, but the Cord caught the already careening flower-wagon full on the side—nosed it over and over again and again and again as a hog might nose a truffle. Over and over went the Madison florist, three times, and he was well on the way to the fourth turnover before the truck finally collapsed in a heap—the head of the Madison florist coming up through the debris—cursing loud and cursing plenty.

Never were swear-words sweeter to my ear. The man was not even hurt.

He recognized me with a 'G— d—— it, Mr. Wright!!!! G— d——!! Jesus Christ, why don't you look where you're going!!!' He got disentangled from the collapsed top, got up just a little wobbly, and galloped off to the nearby roadside station to call up—whom do you suppose? The press! He was asking them to send a photographer out to get the wreck. A left turn into traffic rarely gets damages, especially as we were three to testify to the fact that the florist had given no warning whatever; and had

357

he perjured himself to the contrary, why, he was only one. Our journey was interrupted, but the Cord was not badly hurt.

They picked up what had been the florist's truck and threw it away.

Where were we? . . . going shopping . . . going in the Cord to German's Wholesale Warehouse at Richland Centre, thirty miles away. (I was born in Richland Centre.) We did all the shopping in person because long sojourn in Japan had cultivated my bargaining instincts, and my technique. We usually got good measure and good prices wherever it was possible. After selection we would start loading—sacks of flour on the fenders—crates of fruit on the bumper. Rump and back seats piled high with everything a grocer keeps, and a green-grocer as well. And when we would finally lash the load to the Cord the springs were on the bumpers. If we hit anything with that load we never could have been distinguished from the groceries, unless by colour.

Reaching home, unloading began. The Taliesin storeroom filled up a little for a week maybe, and then again we went, sometimes West or East or North or South. We traded with the neighbouring wholesalers for years —until added to my practice in Japan buying prints was so vast an experience in the lore of provender-buying that I would have made a bet with you that I could buy anything you had to sell for one-quarter less than any sum you had secretly made up your mind was the very least you would take for it.

Sometimes there was remaindering going on. That was where we would shine and the Fellowship would be fed that particular bargain—say, dried apricots or pink salmon or melons or whatever you can think of—until that particular 'success' was out—which really means in.

Our rapid-fire gatling-gun buying pleased the storekeepers. Pointing with my stick I would indicate what we wanted with little or no hesitation, and we would be off on our way loaded down (and almost out) while another customer was buying a crate or two of something or other. They used to say of me in the old family days at Oak Park that I was a 'good provider'. But I was a grand 'good provider' now.

I have always liked to 'provide'—especially luxuries, and spread them about in a decorative fashion on the tables. The apple-barrel-with-the-head-knocked-out of my boyhood, I suppose. The bushels of roasted peanuts set around in big bowls; grapes lavished in big bunches in glass semi-globes; all kinds of nuts—rare fruits like persimmons—figs—grape-fruits —strawberries—from the South. Pomegranates—avocados, etc. And we were especially fond of small fruits.

I always judge a hotel by two things—do they have fresh fruit, and are the toilet accommodations clean? Many a time we have walked away both in Europe and America after the invariable preliminary inspection proved unsatisfactory.

Herb (Jacobs of Usonian House number one) told me of the Elam Mills, an old brick building down on Halsted Street, Chicago, where the best cereals are ground in good old ways. Corn, wheat and oats. That delicious taste of corn, wheat and oats! And that mill ground it with all the life-

358

giving features (vitamins, I suppose) left in. Good stuff to maintain bodily vigour, good complexion, active brain. Add, from our Guernsey herd good milk, our own fresh eggs, fresh fruit in and out of season, and a glass of good wine on occasion, and our own inimitable Wisconsin cheese—and what have you? Well, that is about what we have.

Only now we raise most of it ourselves.

The Cord is gone.

The boys haul the provender into the root cellar at Taliesin and pile it up. We 'put down' this year (1942) one thousand quarts of tomatoes, besides many hundreds each of green beans, peas, and vegetables. But that isn't much.

That underground reservoir of food can take several carloads and ask for more.

A tunnel leads to it, and at the arched door in the masonry wall you switch on the light—the sight that meets the eye is a treasure-filled cave, not unlike Aladdin's. To the left are Olgivanna's wine casks: wild grape wine, elderberry wine, chokecherry, rhubarb, dandelion, potato wines, beet, tomato, tame grape, wild grape, plum brandy, cider, chokecherry mead. Apples, cider, vinegar. Rows on rows of jams, fruits, marmalades, jellies, sauces, pickles, vegetables. Sauerkraut. To the right, on sand, are piles of potatoes, squash, beets, carrots, cabbage, onions, parsnips, and rutabagas. Melons in season. Hanging from the ceiling are dried herbs from the herb garden.

If a barbed-wire entanglement were put around Taliesin for the winter we would all come out next spring with double chins.

This fifth book of *An Autobiography* is destined to be no work of art, but actually the sorry tale of a congenital urge which found itself anew in this rash determination to make architects while making architecture: the consequent 'sweat, blood and tears', and laughter, connected with that structural phase of our national revolution: a rebellious banditry itself which, instead of being merely punishable by death, is cruelly subject only to the severest social penalties and economic sacrifices our fearsome body-politic staggering under its overload of government can devise or inflict by Ignorance, by Neglect, or by Law.

Thomas Jefferson. Where are you now? Is the muddy wave of an ism closing over your gracious head?

But I am reconciled to punishment. Why should this adventure not be punishable?

Any established order must yield to growth iota by iota. And then it will yield only when well undermined or it falls by its own excess or by duress. Lucky if after yielding, it is not frightened back and forth again and again. But at Taliesin we have managed somehow to live on and keep on working appreciatively in the direction and actual service of a great Ideal, no less in these ten years past than single-mindedly for a lifetime.

359

We have, however, been compelled to work for the construction of an indigenous Architecture as revolutionaries in a far too uncommon War (I say, the right kind of war if war must be): earning another half million to go with the million dollars already 'earned' in my lifetime. Yet, never really having any money. No . . . throughout these forty-five years an out-and-out culture-bootlegger, forced by the nature of our national tumbled house to work and live under the banner of a bandit: that is only to say, the banner of the Radical!

Never solvent as banking goes. No, but all the time and overtime, the honest counter-revolutionist where the social system under which we live is concerned for its way of life . . . concerned for what it calls its own safety! Its 'safety', does it say? It too is 'out on a limb'. But, God! I should say that what it deems and calls its 'safety' may be seen as ultimate destruction unless in common with our enemies we lose what we try so foolishly hard to win . . . not yet understanding that no world-revolution can be won as any nation's war unless it is a people's war. And then? We wouldn't like it.

Walt Whitman! Dear old Walt, we need you more than ever: your salt and savour in this dish of humble-pie we are called to eat in shame and defeat, win or lose! Your robust soul might save us even now.

We have taken the wrong way. We must wait for you on a closed road.

If you are sympathetic you may see, between these lines at least, how the Taliesin Fellowship could only come into being and get into open service of its Ideal as a threat to such smug 'safety' as the current agents (broadcasters of our current 'morale') advocate. I say the Taliesin Fellowship could have come into actual social service only as a special kind of social bootleggery. Yes, unhappily, not being 'regular', our Fellowship has had to be thievery in some kind. At any rate, an Indigenous Architect, a Native Architecture, and the Taliesin Fellowship could have come to be in no legitimate way under the despotic Money criterion of present-day Usonian life.

STARS AND BARS

And thus it comes to be in a new free country which has become a kind of hard-up 'tour-de-force' speaking English far too fluently but none too plainly, that any Ideal above the belt or below the Bank is illegitimate! As things go, only Money can justify Work or pay for it or should ever talk above a whisper . . . if at all. Like the Administration-extraordinary of all this blood-letting money-getting, I have had, so far as the Ideal is concerned, somehow to get into unrepayable money-debt myself for everything related to me or directly related to this Cultural Ideal which we call the Taliesin Fellowship. Even the warm pioneer family-life so enjoyed by us as children in this beloved Valley by the broad sand-barred Wisconsin River—life so warm that it warms me still, eventually had to go away; go by way of the bad choice of its own numerous offspring, some forty of my cousins, to scatter in faraway towns to seek the cash-and-carry yeshood of the white collarite. So the hired man of the humanly glowing, noble family life of that pioneer day now owns most of the original family farm-steads: 'own' (and so exploit regardless) the ground which my people broke and loved so greatly in the wise breaking, conserving the wooded hills and the tilth of the soil. Yes . . . my people, the Welsh pioneers lived and died for this, their Valley.

And now even the architectural forms I myself may discover honestly and try to practise around the world are themselves revolutionary.

So they, too, are a kind of banditry? They must be so because if we find a better way to build a better building and actually build it that way, we change and probably destroy existing values everywhere. Even overnight. Therefore in modern times let us say the Taliesin Fellowship *is* on the modern social level of ancient Robin Hood with his medieval band of freebooters.

We don't cut the throats of our neighbours or rape the women of the neighbourhood. Nor do we ever disturb the overflowing hen roosts much as the boys—loving eggs—would like to. But if we are true to ourselves we must do violence to their most 'sacred feelings'. Continually we insult hallowed 'tastes' and do outrage upon the established property rights and 'beliefs' of our most worthy creatures of social habit. We do this, whenever we build a new building, furnish it and plant the grounds. An outrage! And the educational system of our country (the greatest mass-production, by the way, next to motor cars, gadgetry, engines of war and munitions) is not that establishment, endangered, too, by this inevitably ruffian attitude when we go seriously—that is to say, naturally—to work in search of our radical Ideal? So this search of ours for democratic FORM is revolutionary. Necessarily. But a Revolution utterly essential to the life of this our country.

If the Republic is ever going to grow up to be *itself*, a true self-support-ing Democracy, independent of foreign exchange, safe from Money in the rôle of arch-commodity we as revolutionary are essential.

Since the Taliesin Fellowship is here (we celebrated our 520th Sunday evening—October, 1942—together in the living room at Taliesin Sun-day) and has actually come to be a cultural entity (it has lasted ten years to this moment), it follows that unless what we have done is a miracle, it is illegitimate. Inasmuch as I am but a half-hearted believer in miracles except as they are the uttermost commonplaces of nature, I must declare us illegitimate: myself Usonia's illegal but natural, therefore, inevitable, son. Prodigal? Yes. But not contrite. Not yet. No. No revolutionary Evolu-tionist is ever penitent.

And yet: to look back is almost more than can be borne. An overwhelm-ing pity rises for the defeated ones, those who aspired and are dead, those who expired in isolation, desolation, and despair.

Our boys were getting a new view of things and I was back to boyhood. They were no longer strangers to the Reality I wanted the young architects to meet and that was omitted from their college education. Taliesin was by now itself a kind of kiln—burning not cord wood but labour, materials, and food. Year in and year out. The buildings kept on growing. The roofs were going on. Tile roofs: a story in itself. . . .

ETTA

Standing there in the half-light of this, to you, confusing picture is a graying, gay, gray-eyed little woman—daughter of old Mr. Parsons—a fine old citizen of Dodgeville, up over there on the ridge seventeen miles away.

Olgivanna and I and the young Iovanna, tired of tough breaks and tough steaks, used to drive up to the Parsons' meat market. Father Parsons would go back into his box, take down his best, and cut off a rib roast for us. It would be the best we ever ate.

Etta was helping her father. She would wrap it up, hand it to us with a salty remark and the friendly smile that only Etta knew the secret of. The neighbours were all fascinated by or fearsome of Etta's native wit. She was kind but she was shrewd. She knew them all right and they knew she knew. She was a staunch 'La Follette man'. Her ideas were her own and she missed nothing of what went on. 'I see Phil is getting around again speaking to the farmers. He was over at the "Point" yesterday,' she said. 'It was a hot day so when he warmed up too, he threw his coat away, tore his collar off. Then he rumpled up his hair, and went after them.'

Her gay, light-hearted laughter would let you know what she thought of the act that Phil had put on. Mother Parsons (the family lived back of and on a level with the shop) would look in through the door between the shop and the living room—a gentle soul with the same captivating sweet smile as Etta's and ask us how we were. Somehow we were always all right. And sometimes we would go back and sit down by her windowsill full of plants and have a slice of bologna sausage and a cracker and tea, or a cup of coffee and a cookie.

Well—Mr. Parsons died. Etta and her husband, Hocking, carried on the shop—selling meats, groceries, a few plants in season. And seeds. They were pretty well off. But soon Etta lost Hocking. We went to his church funeral. They were greatly respected so the whole town attended —all feeling deeply sorry for Etta, now a widow in black; her mother now in black too.

The shop went on just the same. Etta now in a white butcher's apron behind the block, sometimes cleaver in her small hand with the plain gold wedding ring on her finger, mother still sitting by the door looking in occasionally. They didn't butcher any more now. Their meat came in by truck from 'the System'.

Our need of groceries and meats grew and we thought it might do Etta some good to have it, but things turned out the other way around. For years we drove seventeen miles to Dodgeville to trade with Etta,

362

leaving everything pretty much to her. We gave her a few hundred dollars now and then, and she never sent us a bill—except, as she would say—'You are in about three hundred now.' And we would pay up. She gave us pretty near wholesale prices—'Good idea you've got down there. Want to see it go through—think I'll come down and strike you for a job just as soon as you've eaten us out of house and home here.' And she would gaily laugh that one off.

'Any time, Etta. Come on and run us. The place is yours that way, and anytime you want it.'

Things were going fair and well enough until Relief came. Some of our Dodgeville workmen spent the money we paid them with Etta. From first to last a good deal of Fellowship money went into her till—and still no bills. We didn't ask for them.

'How many boys and girls have you got down there now?' she would say, as the groceries heaped up on the Cord and hid it from sight (I carried out the provender and stacked it).

'Oh, about twenty-five—say.'

'My,' said Etta, 'they must eat an awful lot, don't they?'

'Guess they do—why? Are we buying an awful lot for twenty-five?'

'How many workmen now?' she would ask.

'Oh, about thirty now, I guess.'

'Which eat the most?'

'Why . . . I don't know. I guess the young apprentices do,' I said.

'I'll bet you're right,' she said. 'I'm going to bring Mother down and see 'em at it myself.' She did come several times, watching everything with an amused half-smile as though she had indulged them in food—herself. We got good advice from Etta. She would say, 'Good work you're doing down there—but your bill's running high.'

'How much?'

'Oh, about fifteen hundred,' said Etta. And then panic. We would get after some money right away and turn in all we could. A stern chase is always a long chase, but we were getting even when Relief befell. Then we went behind. We were beginning to see that 'the good idea down there' was a good deal of a money affair, after all. Etta didn't seem to care much. The men who got money to spend at her shop didn't get it from us now but they got it just the same from the government and gave it to her. She had a fair share of the town trade. We were in a fix though, and Etta knew it. We expected the worst—that Etta would have to cut us off. Etta was warned by friends. 'Nope,' she'd say, 'I know they haven't got it now, but they'll get it some day—some way, I'll bet. Good work they're doing —smart people. But not too smart.' And she would gaily laugh that one off.

She would never tell us any more what our balance was but our best thought on the painful subject would have been about three thousand at one time. That was the stock Etta took in the Taliesin Fellowship—the good idea she liked.

Etta is a good business woman and has plenty of good ideas herself. She is there, business as usual, to prove it.

She went into partnership with the good idea. Will Etta ever be paid in full, do you think? I'll bet she will. What do you bet?

THE LIGHTER SIDE

Our Fellowship gatherings on Saturday and Sunday evenings began—October, 1932—in the living room at Taliesin, continuing at Taliesin West in Arizona. These Fellowship gatherings for supper and a concert, or a reading and perhaps pertinent discussion (probably a little of these together), as I have said, have been going on for ten years. As for me, I have never failed to enjoy one of them. They were always happy and always fresh—not only composed of perfectly good material, good music, good food, enthusiastic young people, good company, but something rare and fine was in the air of these homely events by way of environment—atmosphere. No one felt, or looked, commonplace. The Taliesins (Middle West or West) are made by music for music and enter into the spirit of the occasion as if the one were made for the other. Eye music and ear music do go together to make a happy meeting for the mind—and the happy union charms the soul. This happy meeting is rather rare as independent intelligence is rare. We lived in it.

Olgivanna felt that the Fellowship—looking like the wrath of God during the week—should wash itself behind the ears, put on raiment for Sunday evenings and try to find its measure and its manners. Most of it had both. In the right place too. The girls all put on becoming evening clothes, did look, and were, charming. That clothes make a difference is one of the justifications for our work as designers. On Sunday I scarcely recognized some of my own Fellows of the workday week. There was something vital and happy radiating from them all on these happy occasions when everybody served everybody else as though he were somebody, and willingly took the part in the entertainment he had been rehearsing. Part of it, of course, was because they were where they all wanted most to be—volunteers—doing what they most loved to do. Very much at home. I am sure none will ever forget his share in Fellowship life on these eventful but simple occasions, and while the fellowships change with time and circumstances—these events keep their character and charm nevertheless.

Many of the Taliesin young people would come because they had read something I had written or seen my work, probably both, and dreamed of someday working with me. They had come somehow with money begged, borrowed, or received as a gift, from all over the United States and many foreign countries, gratefully giving their best to Taliesin. And most of our boys and girls were individuals by nature with an aesthetic sense rejecting commonplace elegance. That rejection by Taliesin itself would be the natural attraction Taliesin would have for them: the artificiality that passed current for Art and had no place in Taliesin's instincts nor in theirs. To a man, the boys were naturally averse to the dull convention, either social or aesthetic. The girls were likewise. Alexander Meiklejohn—himself the experiment at my old University (Wisconsin) and on several

364

occasions a guest at Taliesin, said to me one evening, 'Yours is the most alive group of young men and women I've seen together since I became an educator.'

ESPECIALLY DESIGNED

Taliesin Sunday Evening Occasions take place in the Taliesin living room number three, the third living room to stand in the same space. The most desirable work of art in modern times is a beautiful living room, or let's say a beautiful room to live in. And if perpetually designing were perpetual motion the world would have in Taliesin that much-sought-for illusion for the millennium. The Spirit of Design was pervasive, presided really, at these Taliesin events. The Saturday evening rehearsals and these Sunday night occasions were natural Fellowship festivity. But discipline at Taliesin in doing anything at all anywhere, lies in the fact that throughout, all must be especially designed. In none of anything can anything go that is not as especially designed to be perfectly natural to itself and Taliesin as sheep, crows, and butterflies are out of doors. And I want to insist that no discipline from the exterior is so severe a strain as this discipline from within.

This discipline applies to our boys and girls when they take turns providing the customary house decorations in appropriate scale or getting 'especially designed' effects with native wild things or familiar trees and garden flowers, effects that were invariably as original and charming in seasonal arrangement as they were fresh in touch and idea with each individual who took charge. The seeds of good design fell about the place as naturally as apples fall from trees or thistledown drifts from the thistle crown. 'Design' even in festivity—why not especially—was like air, the thistledown, because of what was around about, like the thistle crown, to fill and excite the mind. Every move in any direction is an opportunity. To be a developed designer or a designer in embryo was simply to be a natural member of the Taliesin Fellowship. Every member from the first to the last one was in active service to Organic Design.

From the very first we have had these pleasant distinguished company weekends—although guests are seldom invited because we were not really ready, we felt, but they were always welcome just the same and plenty came. Soon after the first years of professionals playing high quarters, we got our own Taliesin trio and quartet going into rehearsals. Soloists were plentiful among us from the first. Professionals from the various orchestras had come to join us for the summer but we soon got tired of playing second, ourselves merely entertained. We found, also and soon, that the musical activity of the Fellowship languished when the professionals did come. There were many reasons for this. So now, as I had desired from the first day of the Fellowship, we have our own male choir singing Palestrina, Bach, Negro spirituals, folksongs, and other good music: a repertoire of some seventy-five songs. We have a quartet, a trio, and as usual, many

365

soloists. Svetlana has cultivated the old-fashioned recorder too. Recorders now form a choir, and we mingle harp, piano, strings, recorders and voices. A really good Bechstein concert piano takes the corner in the Living Room, and one is in the Playhouse. A harpsichord in the blue loggia has joined the group. Iovanna's harp stands alongside. A César Franck cantata last Sunday evening brought out our present resources. The young people have lately gone all-out for folk dancing Friday evenings.

You should see our grand-piano collection. We have seven appropriately and usefully placed about the buildings, not to mention the harpsichord.

About twenty-five years ago I sat playing the piano in my own way (no notes, so no pattern) letting the piano play itself for its own amazement. Carl (Sandburg) was listening. I suddenly stopped and wheeled around toward him with one of those mischievous impulses that I like to practise upon my friends and that so often ruin me. I said, 'Carl, if my mother hadn't decided for me that I was to be an architect, I should have been a very great musician. It would have been my next choice. And since the mind required for greatness in either art is the same, I should have ranked with Beethoven, I am sure.' I turned back to go on playing. But Carl didn't forget the episode and tells the story to this day to illustrate my colossal ego. I suspect he uses the word egotism when he relates the episode as I have heard from others. Ego, yes. Egotism, no.

BEETHOVEN

In Beethoven's music I sense the master mind, fully conscious of the qualities of heartful soaring imagination that are god-like in a man. The striving for entity, oneness in diversity, depth in design, repose in the final expression of the whole—all these are there in common pattern between architect and musician. So I am going to a delightful, inspiring school when I listen to Beethoven's music—music not 'classic'—soul language never to be classified. Because of soul-depth and breadth of emotional range, Beethoven's music is in itself the greatest proof I know of divine harmony alive in the human spirit. As trees and flowering things under the changing lights of a beclouded sun pervade the all out of doors, so Beethoven pervades the universe of the soul.

When I was a small child I used to lie awake listening to the strains of the Sonata Pathétique—Father playing it on the Steinway square downstairs in the Baptist minister's house at Weymouth. It takes me back to boyhood again when I hear it now. And the other sonatas were as familiar then as the symphonies and later quartets are now. When I build I often hear his music and, yes, when Beethoven made music I am sure he sometimes saw buildings like mine in character, whatever form they may have taken then.

I am sure there is a kinship there. But my medium is even more abstract—so kindred spirits who understand the building are even more rare than in music. There is a similarity of vision in creation between

366

Music and Architecture nevertheless. Only the nature and uses of the materials differ. The musician's facility is so much greater than the architect's can ever be. The idiosyncrasy of the client does not exist for the great composer. Utilitarian needs play a small part in his effort. The rules and regulations imposed by the laws of physics upon the performances of the architect are not present to any great extent in the scheme of things submitted to the musician. But both must meet and overcome the same prejudice—the same cultural lag. The limitations human stupidity puts upon insight and appreciation—these are the same for both.

I keep on saying that an artist's limitations are his best friends.

So perhaps the more severely limited art when success does crown creative effort is the greater and more abiding achievement—if for no other reason than that the one is the Abode while the other is the Song. Both are best when the song dwells and the abode sings: both may when creative power and the passion of love makes them glow from within.

Mastery is no mystery. Simple principles of Nature apply with peculiar emphasis and force to all the master does: a scheme in keeping always with the nature of materials (instruments), materials used in such a way as to reveal the beauty in tone and texture they possess. The strings were his, par excellence, but percussion, brass and woodwind—he knew them all so well that he never gives one away nor asks of the one what belongs to the other; continually enriching each with all and all with the character of each. But what gives *consequence* to mastery *is* a mystery. It is Inspiration.

And the planned progressions, thematic evolutions, the never-ending variety in differentiation of pattern, integral ornament always belonging naturally enough to the simplest statement of the prime idea upon which the superstructure is based: Beethoven's rhythms are integral like those of Nature!

Once organic character is achieved in the work of Art, that work is forever. Like sun, moon, and stars, great trees, flowers and grass it *is* and stays on while and wherever man is.

Other musicians have this mastery also, and greatly, but none I understand so well, none so rich in the abstract idiom of Nature as he—whose portrait Meredith drew in the sentence: 'The hand of the wind was in his hair; he seemed to hear with his eyes.'

I am humble and grateful in his presence. 'Who understands my music is safe from the world's hurt.'

AN 'I REMEMBER'

I remember John Fiske (the great historian) coming to the little brown house by the lake, coming there to dine with Father, Mother afterward remarking upon the great man's voracious appetite (as famous as his histories). I see his thick lips nesting in the great brown beard, eyes hidden from sight by the light glancing of his enormous spectacles. After dinner the great historian sang and even I could see how he loved that. In fact, Father (who played his accompaniments, of course) said that he was utterly proof against any compliment or blandishment where his powers as an historian were concerned but let anyone be so indiscreet as to compliment his singing, even a little, and he was singing on their hands thereafter. So it is with me, I love to sit in on chamber music rehearsals of the Fellowship talent and criticize—knowing as much of the particular composition probably as John Fiske knew of the art of singing—but dreadfully pleased to have my criticism—regardless of the composer's notations (and perhaps sometimes his intentions too) heeded.

Such are the joys of the amateur, and far from innocent they are. I am sure Franklin Roosevelt gets much the same reaction where his command of the Army and Navy is concerned.

THE UPKEEP OF THE CARCASS

Food under Olgivanna's guidance was excellent and very well served to the Fellowship and our guests by the Fellowship itself. Olgivanna started this. She said, one summer day, early in the second year of the Fellowship, 'Frank, let's have no paid help. They don't belong here, you know. They vulgarize everything. There is no reason why these young men and women themselves can't learn to cook and serve their own meals gracefully without hiring help. Our boys and girls do their own rooms anyway and many of them do their own laundry. Do let me try! I want to see what I can do. You will see they will feel all the more at home, more a part of all this activity they are in here with us, if they take their share of the household routine upon themselves and serve each other.'

Sceptical at first, I was afraid of the time consumed and the interruption it would be to our other labours. And I didn't believe in trusting our own good health and well-being to that extent to amateurs. But I soon found she was right. We fared very well indeed. Better than ever before. But it took a lot out of her from first to last. Nevertheless she made the plan work. And while there were plenty of individual breakdowns and many failures, she did succeed in making the Fellowship see the light in it and soon learn to discount the hardships. And the garbage, and the perpetual dishwashing.

There were many unexpected reactions. It appeared, for instance, that the nearer to the habitual wage-earner class a boy or girl was, the more rebellious he or she felt when doing what seemed to him 'menial' labour. Just as those Fellows we would sometimes take into the Fellowship without fee, allowing them to work their way along with us, would be the least co-operative, most of them instinctively 'keeping shop' with us. Being there only to 'get' what they could, they gave the least and left the soonest.

But Taliesin kept on growing. The buildings were under roof. The boys had not only 'the feel o' the rock in their 'ands' but the science of a board among boards, and what the stick was good for in a building, as they went

48. Interior of Garden Room. Redwood and canvas overhead

ARIZONA DESERT CAMP. 1934-6

49. Another view—opposite side of the Garden Room

50. The alley behind the draughting room at the camp

ARIZONA
DESERT CAMP.
1934-6

51. Bridge connecting the lit·
theatre with the main camp, lo·
ing out towards entrance to t
camp

52. View of camp at entrance,
looking from office studio out
over the desert

53. Fireplace at end of Gard·
Room

from drawing board to the actual sticks and boards and learned what tools can do with them.

We put a scheme of rotation into operation in our work out in the fields and on the buildings. I named a head man for the fortnight just ahead who was free to choose his first aid or right bower. The first aid became next leader. He named the leader to follow him who chose his own aid. After consultation with me the leader each day laid out work for the others. The work of the following day was thus planned the evening before. Something resembling this way of directing was now applied to the housework.

MUTUAL SERVICE

Olgivanna tells of this: It takes years for the young people who join this work to throw off the old concept of academic schooling. At first they are unhappy because they are not all the time at the draughting board, they miss the class lecturing, they want formal discussions. They are suddenly dropped into a world of interior discipline, yet without a rule written down. A discipline which turns them to their own resources and makes them act with the sense of their own conscience. The concept that all work is important is new. There is no menial labour. There is no backyard. Taliesin is all front yard. The field work is as important a responsibility as the work in the draughting room, or in the garden, the kitchen or the dining rooms. This seems very difficult for young America to accept. One of our young men could not see the work in the kitchen as anything but menial work to be done by a servant. When he was told he didn't have to do it his conscience troubled him because all the others were doing that work. They began to tease him about it—'til he felt foolish in making an exception of work which was part of the whole. Later he became one of the best in making beautiful decorations in the dining room when in turn it came into his charge and the tables were arranged in new original ways, and he became a good cook. After the work in the kitchen he would sit and make drawings for the new arrangements he felt we needed. He would suggest new systems in serving, which would eliminate waste motion. He was just as interested in that work as in any other. His knowledge of the working of a kitchen and dining room on whatever scale is instilled into his very being—a knowledge earned and gained by him by way of actual experience—not by way of a superficial inadequate theory of designing.

This participation in our maintenance has a strengthening and unifying effect on the group. Taliesin has become their real home. One part of the group is headed by one with experience in planting the garden in the spring. Every morning all of the young people work in the garden for an hour or two. Afterwards the seniors go directly to the draughting room, some go planting trees (there have been hundreds of them planted about Taliesin), some go checking and fixing the electric fence, hauling gravel, grading roads. They learn how to handle stone by building the walls, laying the floors, putting up piers. They learn to work with wood, metals, and textiles. They arrange their own rooms, rebuilding the interiors according to the plan made by them which they submit to their master for approval. The large draughting room is like an abstract forest with light pouring from the ceiling in between the interwoven oak trusses. The atmosphere in it is always one of intense quiet concentration—which sometimes under pressure keeps the young people voluntarily working on drawings until the late hours of the night. Yet the draughting room responds to lively relaxation when tea is brought in at four o'clock and everyone gathers about the large fireplace, or in the stone-circle on the hill talking, discussing Fellowship problems, or getting engaged in dynamic political social discussions. The tea is prepared in weekly rotation by the young women of the Fellowship. Most intriguing recipes are tried. Those the group particularly enjoys are put into the Taliesin Cook Book, which is already a rich collection of Taliesin favourites.

It is fun to plan meals with our young people. For instance, as to what meat we shall use this week—shall we butcher the calf or the pig, or the goat-kid, geese, or chickens? We would wander together through our old cook books, some of them fifty years old: American, Russian, Yugoslav, Polish, of all nations really, and find new delicacies, always learning new exciting ways and always succeeding in getting interesting meals prepared. And when the wine-making season comes, we all go in automobiles, station wagons, trucks—taking picnic lunches with us—to gather wild grapes, chokecherries, blackberries, elderberries. Permeated with warm autumn sun we return home. The following weeks we crush and prepare our grapes and berries for wine. We gather our apples and the golden season of apple cider sets in. Large crocks are filled with cider and tin cups hung by them stand in the court for the boys to drink while the cider press keeps on working, making more for the hard cider we will drink next spring and the vinegar we need.

About that time the rapid plans for the annual Hallowe'en masked ball are being made. The committee of entertainment is appointed. Small secret group meetings are held and all of Taliesin is sensitive to a mysterious mood that pervades everything. The party will be full of surprises—original and exciting—since each one of the young people is talented and designs with spontaneous quick imagination.

Many of our young people, as I have said, are musicians and keep up their work in music. They have programmes to prepare for every Saturday and Sunday evening. The chamber orchestra has been in existence for five years, playing Bach and Beethoven, Brahms and Haydn trios, quartets, sometimes quintets. The choir of eighteen young voices sings Palestrina and beautiful old English and American songs. On Saturday night we go to the Playhouse, where buffet supper is served, and listen to chamber

370

music and solos. Sometimes a short play is put on the stage. Then we see moving pictures which come to us from all countries of the world. Every Sunday noon we go picnicking, exploring new places, going back to our favourite ones.

The social life of Saturday and Sunday ends the week and begins the next by an evening at Taliesin when all dress in their best clothes, and where we entertain our weekend guests, many famous artists among them. They frequently entertain us, and taking their turn, sing or play for us, or speak or read to us. The gathering usually breaks up in small groups engaged in quiet discussions gradually dispersing one by one 'til quiet descends upon Taliesin and the graceful figure of Buddha stands unperturbed in this warm human movement projected into Space.

REHEARSALS

Meantime Fellowship life went on in the original Taliesin studio: designing, drawing. Always details of details for the buildings steadily growing up at Hillside in spite of RELIEF and all other obstruction. Our own boys were learning to *build* our own buildings. Designs were perpetually made by the apprentices for the fittings and furnishings of their own rooms to be executed by themselves (if a boy's room were changed he threw out what his predecessor did and started 'fresh'); perspective renderings; abstractions of plant life; studies from nature, and the nature of materials especially. And all the while our hands were in the mud of which bricks are made. We saw the designs we made take shape in the actual work of our hands and stand there before us in actual materials. But what was more important, the boys had to live with their errors or successes in building themselves into their own rooms and see the mistakes corrected. We do not learn much by our successes: we learn most by failures—our own and others', especially if we see the failures properly corrected.

To see a failure changed to a success—there is what I call Education.

Photography too we tried to include. Without much success, although several of the boys showed remarkable ability in that resource. We didn't have the money. As for music: at the beginning we tried several professional musicians, composers, to get that side of our work going, but it was too soon for that—we were much too engrossed in construction. Just for that perhaps, we didn't go very far or very fast. However, the intimate little Saturday evening rehearsal dinners in the Playhouse, and the Sunday evening event, music and supper in the Taliesin Living Room, went on to give relaxation its place in our lives.

Formal introductions in the Fellowship were dropped where guests were concerned. The guest would be introduced by Olgivanna or myself or one of the apprentices to the Fellowship as a body. Then the boys and girls would step up and say, if addressing a junior—I am John; or an adult,

371

I am Lautner. The girls likewise. A little too much to expect guests or callers to carry in mind both given and surnames of thirty or more young men and women at one time. Casual guests were so frequent.

CAPITAL INSTANCES OF THE CASUAL

Sophie Breslau, for instance (She said with a laugh, 'A thousand-dollar package where singing was concerned.'), coming out from Madison, bringing Ima Roubleff, her accompanist, standing up in the Living Room singing gloriously and happily there until three o'clock in the morning. There were many others from time to time.

We were all music lovers, or else mad about music, which is not quite the same thing. Many such informal occasions were thus stolen from the system—another kind of bootlegging, you see?

The most extraordinary instance of casual evaporation by translation I ever knew occurred when Mies Van der Rohe was to be inducted as Pilot into the chair of Architecture at Chicago's Armour Institute. Mies and I have been fond of each other. He has known of me all his architectural life. I believe him a sincere man as well as an architect. He had asked me to come as speaker to a big dinner given in honour of that occasion. The dinner took place in the ballroom of the Palmer House. I sat near the centre of the platform table at which were ranged various architects and dignitaries. My turn to speak, after listening to Emerson and other professional speakers reading from notes, and another lot of other bores intending eulogy of 'the talented German' now their guest, taking over the helm of Armour . . . but saying nothing.

It was all most superficial blah or laboured lip service, so when I rose I put my arm across Mies' shoulders (he was next to the speaker's place), and simply said, 'Ladies and gentlemen, I give you Mies Van der Rohe. But for me there would have been no Mies—certainly none here tonight. I admire him as an architect and respect and love him as a man. Armour Institute, *I* give you my Mies Van der Rohe. You treat him well and love him as I do.' I abruptly stepped down and walked out.

When Mies' turn came to speak he spoke in German, as he knows little or no English. For some five minutes he went into the origin of his discipleship and reverence for me. He told how much he was indebted to me, frankly and to the point. He was proud to stand there and say it. The German architect paid a well-considered tribute to an American architect, an affectionate tribute such as is rare in the history of the world, the architect's world at least.

The interpreter said (he was Walterdorf of the A.I.A.), after Mies had paused before going on with the rest of his speech, 'Mr. Van der Rohe says he is sorry Mr. Wright left so soon.' And unless you understood German, that is what you got from Mies Van der Rohe so far as he went up to that point at the crowded dinner in his honour.

The many boys and girls of Taliesin, hundreds from first to last, all behaved themselves with self-respect. And so far as Olgivanna and I could see (none too far, of course)—with circumspection. The first several years, however, there were some exceptions to the latter. But during all ten years of Fellowship-in-residence we have yet to look back and complain of an insolent act, or any unwillingness to carry on as required—or very much shirking. While free occupation was a hard lesson to be learned, we had only a few slackers, some with native disabilities, some dazed—not knowing what it was all about, but few real incompetents. Perhaps a dozen that I can remember. Naturally such would not last very long in our atmosphere and activity anyway. This loyal Spirit of the Fellowship in face of such handicaps of accommodation and equipment as ours was truly remarkable. I look back upon the circumstance with astonishment and no little gratification.

In the first years we had much altered and reconditioned the old buildings. We were trying to complete a large new one—our Draughting Room, flanked by sixteen small apprentice rooms, eight on either side. The old buildings had a new lease on life now—all protected under good tile roofs. The tile roofs that are a separate story. I don't want to forget it.

These first years of Fellowship went rapidly by for young and old. Young fellows would hitch-hike across the continent—and from as far away as the country was wide—to join us if they could. We were compelled, for lack of means and room, to refuse more than four hundred. Had I enough money to keep and feed them we could have filled the valley with hopeful young workers and might have started Broadacre City right then and there, ourselves. They have kept on coming in from all sides though we have never proselytized for apprentices as we never have for clients. But the sad fact is, those we were compelled to refuse were often the most desirable ones. Skilled workers they were, often.

THE OFFICIOUS SAMARITAN

And then one day when we were looking forward to getting into our buildings the blow fell—not prohibition this time, but 'Relief'. The Administration of our government suddenly placed some forty or more of our workmen in a position where they could figure out that by doing nothing at all they could have a few dollars more in pocket from the government than they were getting from us. We had been keeping about seven families in Iowa County out of the poorhouse and about as many more in neighbouring Dane County. All our men had good quarters in which to sleep. They had good food, the best, and plenty of it. They were pleased and satisfied. But now the men—several or more at a time—would decide to quit; more and more would come in to me and say, 'We are going to take advantage of Relief.' I had no argument to advance because the only inducement I could make would be to outbid the Administration

373

and I couldn't. Many men probably would prefer to get their money without working anyway. Thus this matter of Money still stood with us.

Just to make this affair of money worse, of now being able to eat without working, an I.W.W. or two from New York City (I had a couple of them in on the work) got a dozen or more of the worst ones among the local men to join up in repudiating the partnership agreement, demanding that I pay up all the balances *right now*. Someone in Madison had told Mike Lazar, the lather, about an old dead-letter law on the Wisconsin statute books to the effect that no wage labourer had a legal right to make any contract whatsoever for his labour. The worker was thus so classified that legally he was nobody but a slave to be paid in full at least every two weeks, or he and his employer, too, would go to jail. He had no right to himself. The workmen got together on this, shamefacedly at first, but the get-together soon gained headway. The men formed in queues outside my study door and then several at a time would come in to my corner of the studio and ask for 'pay', reckoning the sum due them on the overall contingent wage agreement, but those sums were stipulated as wages only if they stayed on until the time came when I could get the buildings into use. *Now* this unexpected demand struck in addition to the board, room, and weekly cash payments we had agreed upon and that I had managed to pay them so far when they could do a little better by living on the U.S.A. and doing no work at all.

Of course, I had already given these men all the money I had. There was no source from which I could then get more. There was no relief for me or mine. The agreement I made with them stated that I could get the sums stipulated only when I got use of the buildings. And unless I could get those buildings we started to build together for the apprentices, I could get no money to pay the balance of their stipulated wages. The buildings were only about half-done. But all the money I had already paid for labour and materials (some forty-five thousand dollars) was tied up in unfinished buildings as useless to me as to them.

The buildings now stopped growing altogether. Instead of getting suitable places in which to work in three years, it was to take seven, until we learned to build them ourselves for ourselves.

RELIEF

Karl Jensen was secretary at the time, and Henry Klumb was right bower. They would be with me at these trying times as I sat over there in my little corner of the old Studio by the big stone fireplace. The gang (gangsterism was what they were in now) had formed this habit of lining up outside, and kept on day after day, for months, coming in to me for this money they were really only entitled to when they had kept their word as men and performed their part of the partnership agreement.

Well, I thought of making a test case of the foolish slave-law—one of those 'three laws passed to cure one flaw'. But it so appeared, after appealing to the State Industrial Commission (which, I suspected, suspected me of exploiting labour), that under this law the labourer was made a slave, and that any attempt to make an agreement with him only laid us both liable to jail, just as they had been told. And although most of the men had gone on government relief at the time, that did not stop them from tearing the agreement down and pressing me for money which they proceeded to do. This feature of relief where wages were due was not 'legal' and I might have informed the authorities of the money coming to them in the circumstances, but I felt ashamed to knock the men out of anything they could get when they had so damned little. And I have always rather shied at any appeal to 'authority' anyway. No good ever came of the policeman where I am concerned. So foolishly I made promises. We kept the promises just as well as we could, all the while looking and hoping for miracles.

The miracle would be 'work'—buildings to build.

There was no building. Little money was coming in to go into so many hands, and without any, some of the men began to get ugly. But they would go away with a little. During many ensuing weeks there were outrageous scenes. One, Jones, a troublesome ringleader, attacked me in the studio one late afternoon—got his hands well on towards my throat when Henry jumped at him, yelling so loud with anger that Jones was scared into 'taking his hands off Mr. Wright'. Human nature in the bunch and in the raw was not unfamiliar to me. But I had not yet learned *to make no promises to anyone*.

Karl was now like a secret-service man, prolific in subterfuges and stallings—untiring and resourceful. But Karl was scared—really. In Karl's mind probably was an incident that took place in an obscure street in Madison where Jimmie had driven me in the Cord to get some tools for Fellowship work. Blackhand letters had kept coming from 'a nice character' every now and then—after he saw us, as he soon did, carrying on our buildings under the Fellowship banner while he—a pre-Fellowship creditor—was not yet fully paid. Evidently he felt himself entitled to desperate measures. So one hangover from pre-Fellowship days, but now a situation, was an attack upon me in the street by an angry farmer—Indian blood in him.

A COARSE INCIDENT

Business transacted, I was about to get back in the Cord when someone came up behind me, struck me violently several times on the back of the head. Partly stunned, I turned toward the Indian farmer, saw Jimmie some distance away on the sidewalk struggling violently, his arms pinned behind by the farmer's son brought along for the purpose. A planned, well-timed assault. I took this in at a glance; as I caught other blows in the face I turned toward the assassin. Instinct warned me not to strike the man. So I clinched with him and he went down into the gutter on his back. I held him down there until he said he had enough. But, in the split second when getting off him I stepped back to let him up, he kicked backward and up at me with his heavy boot, caught me on the bridge of the

375

nose with his boot heel. I pinned him down again. Blood spurted all over him. This time I had both knees on his chest, his head still in the mud in the gutter. While holding him down there I deliberately aimed the torrent of blood with a broken nose full in his face. His own nose, his mouth too, clotted with blood, he gagged and gasped for breath. Jimmie, meantime frantic, was unable to break away and come to the rescue. The nice character was cursing and appealing to the several astonished bystanders. . . . 'God damn it, men, take him off,' he shrieked. 'Take the man off me, for Christ's sake! He's killing me!' But I had not struck him. I was careful not to. I was only holding him down there in his own gutter in his own mud, painting him a gorgeous red until his features were clotted with my own blood. I let him up and he disappeared in the astonished crowd, which must have thought a murder was being committed.

I didn't know but that I was disfigured for life. Jimmie now free to drive, I got in the car. 'Jimmie,' I said, 'my nose is broken. Drive me to the Clinic.'

Everything I had on was saturated in front with what the doctor assured me was remarkably young blood, and it must have been so, for the break mended with astonishing rapidity, the perfectly good nose showing no trace. That boot was a symbol.

So was the nose.

Never mind, dearest . . . I know what the moral is.

This adventure with 'ideas plus work' as against 'money plus authority' was thus ushered in. When I got home, bandaged, unknown to me, my boys (four of them) went out after their man, got into his house to find him there on the other side of the dining table, holding his wife in front of him for protection. Later he got a kitchen knife in his hand and the ugly fellow threatened them from behind his wife, she and the daughter meanwhile screaming imprecations and calling for the police. Of course, the police came and arrested the boys and the assassin. All were in the county jail when I heard of their well-meant sympathetic 'strike' and got there to take a look at them behind bars. There they were, a nice-looking lot of boys, but a nice case for the District Attorney. Before I could get the young lads released, they spent a couple of nights in the county jail. But the nice character himself stayed in for quite some time to await trial. The case was finally settled in court, the nice character leaving the state. The boys were paying a fine of several hundred dollars. On the 'instalment plan', of course.

The Taliesin Fellowship had got off to a very bad start. Indeed.

DEFENCE

There were subsequent approaches now, to a similar thing until it was suggested that I employ a bodyguard or, at least, carry a weapon. Both suggestions were ignored because I believe any man is safer unguarded and unarmed in almost any emergency.

376

The time that perfidious gang spent standing around trying to get money out of me in such equivocal circumstances would have paid them much more in work—ten times over—than the money they now declared I owed them. But there was no work for them to do if they would work, except that which I offered them. Were they enjoying this act, sitting pretty and being paid for it while they shook me down? A situation? Yes . . . and no.

I kept on faithfully handing out to them whatever I could get—collected dues, or fees if any, sums I might still borrow somewhere, somehow (it is amazing how gullible my friends have been)—something I might sell—but still on and in came the gang. I was frequently without a cent in my pocket. But I was used to that. And I grew to believe that if I parted with my last cent more would come. And more—a little—always did come. I got rid of that gang finally, one by one, though not until black-hand letters had been in my mail for a year or two. Anonymous always. And for many years afterward, some of the men would turn up still asking for forgotten unpaid balances. But I must say that a few were really decent, a half-dozen or more, and one of the tragedies of the situation thus created by my effort to put ideas-plus-work against money-plus-authority was that the more decent the men were, the longer they had to wait for money in the circumstances. Of course, ethically the men were not entitled to be paid. Morally I suppose they were. I don't know. I knew there could be no more building until we could do it ourselves.

We had boys now who could handle carpenter's tools, do good masonry, plastering. Painting was easy. They learned to weld and use woodworking, as well as road-building and farm machinery.

Just at this high moment in our mundane affairs the Employer's Mutual Insurance moved in on us: stepped up for money for past-due protection for these men which they hadn't needed. Well, enough is enough. Let's not labour the details but say that from the advent of 'RELIEF' and its innumerable consequences we hung fire on construction, except for what the boys themselves could do, for nearly five years. Then my work in Architecture began to come back, and I could add my fees as an architect to apprenticeship tuitions, pay for the materials we needed, keep some expert workmen, and go ahead to salvage what we had already done. Even this was now in a state of decay. But altogether thirty-five thousand dollars a year would not keep us going for materials—and Fellowship upkeep. I had found that I had got into something that only a multimillionaire should have attempted. But, of course, none such would have attempted anything of the kind. That I kept up in the circumstances and was not murdered, as well as still further 'disgraced' as they say (ungraced would be nearer), was a surprise even to myself.

'I don't know whether you are a saint or a fool,' said my lawyer. I said, 'Is there a difference?' As I've looked around me I never could see that there was. Much.

377

But I had made a promise worth keeping. A promise to myself. When I remember my promise to my grand old Aunts—Nell and Jane, and my mother, I often wish they, and the Lloyd-Joneses, might look in now upon what we have accomplished these ten years past, and say—fool or saint! But who cares to be either one or the other even in the fond eyes of one's own family?

I know something better, but who wants to know?

FELLOWSHIP MARRIAGES

The current of Fellowship life flowed on.

Davy and Kay decided to be married. There was nothing we could do about it, except help celebrate. Theirs would make the sixth marriage in the cause, or is it the course, of nature since the Fellowship began. First there were Rudolph and Betty, then Vernon and Margaret. Quite an interim, then the tragedy—Wes and our own Svetlana—that turned out so well. Then came Hulda and Blaine, followed by Cornelia and Peter. Now it was Davy and Kay. We conceded to all appropriate wedding parties and probably there were six happy honeymoons.

There would be other weddings—the one certainty in co-education? Another couple already in sight: My God, is propinquity necessarily fatal? Or are Olgivanna and I too good an example to set before young bachelor girls and boys?

Now came the question of the weather—we who live in the country become weatherized if we are not weatherwise. We have learned that to run from it, hoping to escape from 'bad' weather (of course, we mean bad for us) is to run into worse. I have learned that everywhere in the world the weather is unusual and unless one learns to 'land on one foot', so to speak, concerning it, nothing ever happens as planned. So we planned the wedding with the weather. The weather turned out to be fine. And so did the wedding part of the wedding.

Davy and Kay were both favourites. Davy, a talented manly chap; Kay, a natural-born charmer. (Let that be sufficient introduction.) Olgivanna laid things out. Inspired, she planned another Taliesin fair-weather wedding in the little old family chapel. (Truth Against the World.) It was Spring, and we threw open the windows and doors. The birds flew clear through the chapel without stopping, and the boys went out in the big truck, as they liked to go, after wayside decorations. The old chapel walls under the high wooden ceiling of the interior which I had put there when a boy, became a festive bower of sun-splashed branching green with masses of spring flowers arranged around the pulpit where the bridal couple would stand for the simple ceremony. The auctioning of the virgin in the Roman slave mart still looked down on it all from the wall behind the pulpit. A family heirloom, our old Steinway square piano (Father rapping my fingers into proper position every time I see it) stood beside the pulpit under the golden Bible laid there as centrepiece: Olgivanna set slender stacks and groups of tall white candles (Greek Orthodox childhood

378

—she loves candles) here and there in the foliage to burn in the shadows; they seemed somewhat religious, nevertheless they were a good decoration too (even in religion isn't that always the primary motif?); Iovanna's golden harp brought in from home was placed to the rear for pervasive incidental music. She played Debussy softly while the ceremony was taking place.

The cooks for the week were standing back there in the rear room, ready in tall white caps and white jackets and eager to carve the feast. They had baked the traditional ring into the wedding cake. Olgivanna's best wine was bottled from her big cellar casks for this especial occasion. The milieu and the menu were quite festive enough and too beautiful, I should say, even for the wedding of some Russian Lady-of-the-Bed-chamber.

Then, as had Kay and Davy (Davy's little sister alongside to carry the bride's bouquet), we all got dressed up. The wedding party climbed into the old Hillside carryall to be driven in state by the old farm-team over the hills to the place where the wedding bells had been ringing for at least half an hour. The bride's headdress got pretty well jolted on the way over because the tallered canopy of that old rig had been wreathed with wild grapevines, as a substitute for split covering, and they kept coming down and mixing in. Thus embowered, beflowered and bedizened, too, we, the happy Taliesin wedding party, reached the chapel gates (Truth Against the World) without further incident. Very like the other gay weddings, although, to me, each seemed nicer than the last.

The ceremony went off with a few tears from the next of kin, but mostly there were smiles all around. The feast so attractively spread, itself a superlative decoration, we soon reduced to a mere remnant of its former self as healths were drunk in our homely wine. And then (indiscretion) the boys—Edgar in the lead as usual—in the rôle of the local-devil, rushed the old chapel organ out into the chapel yard, set it down in the grassy space between the graves and the road. Shaded by the gigantic cotton-wood that grew by the gate, the youngsters danced old-fashioned square dances with the bride and groom. Our Fellowship talent took turns playing the dance tunes on the chapel organ. Some friendly village folk attended standing there against the dark evergreens to watch the gaiety, and also some of the old family group were there by another group of evergreens not seeming too happy, and I soon had reason to know they publicly disapproved of this gay use of the sacred chapel and family churchyard shrine. I noticed their expressions and they were not good. A gathering storm.

Davy and Kay disappeared after a little of this—but soon a small airplane zoomed overhead and there they were above and off on wings, for a wedding journey the modern way. The bride's bouquet had been thrown to Gene. Upstretched hands waved happiness to the bride and groom as they sailed away.

Another Taliesin man and wife.

Thereupon followed a family scene in the chapel yard. The storm broke. Bitter reproaches were lavished upon Olgivanna and myself, the guilty

379

promoters of this violation of sacred family traditions (which I had thought I fairly well understood—and represented too). But no, such callous disregard of family dignity! Besides (and this was true) the chapel wasn't mine anyway. It belonged to the Lloyd-Jones family.

Something well worth keeping had thus, in a self-righteous moment, been ruthlessly spoiled. Well . . . the organ was hurried back as it had been hurried out, and put into its accustomed place none the worse for the dance tunes. The music and the harp were gathered in with the remnants of the guilty feast. The tall candles (a little shorter now) were blown out and all came away from the beautifully decorated Lloyd-Jones chapel depressed.

Where happy Fellowship had been in high spirits a few moments before, chagrin was in our hearts.

Hatred had struck at Joy. The Fellowship hurried away.

Evening shadows, no longer blue but long and lengthening, had about crossed the valley to the opposite hills. The slender marble obelisk in the chapel yard gleamed tall and white against the chapel evergreens: Ein Mam, the simple legend on one side; Ein Tad on another. This simple monument marked the graves of my old Welsh Lloyd-Jones grandparents. Around this central obelisk were the surrounding headstones marking the graves of five pioneer sons and five daughters. Further away but surrounding them were the graves of the grandchildren. About all the pioneer life of the beloved Hillside valley. They—the Lloyd-Jones family—were all there safely, according to clan tradition, gathered in around the family shrine: the white ancestral marble obelisk.

I sometimes sat there under the trees and wondered and remembered, partly because Taliesin's tragedy had sent its share of graves among those of this charmed old pioneer family circle. I went there now.

The sun had set. The afterglow was dimming in the sky as again I sat there on the grass to wonder and remember. And I remembered my dear aged mother dropping to her knees, reverently pressing her lips to the cold white marble monument, to Ein Mam and Ein Tad, as I was taking her by on my arm to stand beside the open grave then waiting for her brother Jenkin: another faithful daughter soon to join the ancestral group. And I remembered standing alone, just over there by the abounding evergreen trees, beside another open grave, at this same fading time of day; a new grave I filled to the brink with flowers and then, joined by two nephews waiting at the chapel gate, filled in with solid earth—covering the earth-mound with evergreen branches. Both were grass-covered mounds now, still waiting for their headstones.

THE ALLEGORY THAT FAILED TO CONVINCE EVEN THE AUTHOR

Read aloud in the family sitting room: Olgivanna and Iovanna listening. The title of this Allegory is 'Truth Against the World', and I began to read:

As I sat disconsolate on a low grass-covered mound in the chapel yard, I wondered, and pondered and remembered as twilight deepened to dusk and darkened under the evergreens—the sacred chapel evergreens. They were sighing, stirring to and fro in the gentle breeze. As I carelessly listened I thought I heard . . . Was it possible? A human sigh, then the whisper of my name. Listening now intently, I heard nothing more. Wondering, I still listened . . . still remembering. Silence for a time. Then the gentle human whispering of intelligible words began, extending all around me. Intent as I peered into the dusk, pale blue wraiths were wreathing upward out of the family graves like pale blue mist rising all around me, but wreathing slowly; wraiths taking on familiar human shapes. A moment more of the gentle sighing and then the whispering of the pallid shapes began again, the wraiths now quite blue, flames swaying with the breezes to and fro, to and fro as the breezes rose and fell. The ghostly company all seeming to sit there on their own headstones.

Olgivanna: Oh, Frank dear, oh, this is too much! This Thornton Wilder graveyard thing. He got away with it but you simply can't.

Listen . . .

Nearby a shade arose in shimmering silver, head bent forward, hands folded in her lap. A whispered name—again—my own! The ghostly family conclave rising now, one and all and standing there together in one group, swayed gently to and fro, and as gently nodded and whispered together in the dusk. I leaned, looked and listened for the secrets of the dead.

Olgivanna: Frank, you simply can't put this sentimentality into print. They'll say of you as they did of Turgenev's later and so sentimental work, 'Age is breaking in on him.'

Listen . . .

Again my name. The wraiths grew luminous as the dark deepened and their whispered words grew more distinct there on the edge of the dark. In wonder—I whispered, Mother . . . why are you here like this . . . my mother . . . surely *you* are a spirit in heaven!

Olgivanna: Terrible! Terrible! Oh, Frank, how can you be so foolish! Trite—you convince no one, not even yourself as I can see.

Listen . . .

A pause . . . 'A spirit in heaven, yes, my son: but spirits in heaven cast blue shadows here on the green earth as the golden sun casts the blue shadows of the green trees. Our shades may rise and go whenever the breezes blow if they but blow gently.' The family shades gently swaying with the breeze nodded assent. Again soft whispering as before.

Olgivanna: Pah! Frank, you are gone, gone, gone. This must never get into print, that's all.

Listen . . .

The breezes for a moment grew stronger, and I listened to all the family in chorus. They were whispering, 'If they still love us, we may rise. When breezes gently blow our earthly shades may rise. Arise and go to those who love us.' In bewilderment I looked around more curious than amazed, still listening, still wondering, as the family shades, these flickering

381

ghostly flames in lambent blue resting on their graves were again gently swaying and nodding assent. Silence for a time, but gently as ever, timed with the breeze in the trees, the gentle swaying to and fro, to and fro, went on.

The nearest shade, the one in shimmering silver, now whispered, 'When gentle breezes fan your cheek or stir your hair, my son, it may be the gentle touch, the caress of those whom you love but have lost on earth, those who still love you in heaven . . . their caress may be upon your head.'

Olgivanna: Oh! Oh! Oh! this spiritualistic thing! Frank, how can you?

The dusk deepening to dark the breezes now dying down. Again silence. . . .

(Now sweet-sixteen) Iovanna: Why, Daddy, that is something I might have written, but not you. It's not like you at all. Please don't.

But an author is desperately determined.

Listen, World . . .

The evergreens were now hard to see, gently stirring still, faintly sighing as before—but the sighing and whispering grew more indistinct . . . 'When you live most, then we come. . . .' The shades still slowly bent their heads and still were swaying assent.

Oh, Daddy—Daddy! That swaying business—it's just awful. AWFUL! *can't you see?*

Listen . . .

The silver shade gently lifted the semblance of a beloved venerable head, eyes hidden deep in shadow as, more faintly than ever, now that the breeze was dying, scarcely audible whispered . . . 'You will know what your beloved want you to know, my son, if you turn to look at the symbol on the chapel gate.'

For heaven's sake, Frank! Do wake up! This is the end. I won't listen to another word. How awful!

Nearly done.

Listen . . .

The breeze now barely stirring the sombre evergreens, the shades are wreathing downwards into their own graves, each swaying gently and as they grew to resemble the family ones so long beloved, so now as slowly surely sinking, wreathing away . . . vanishing as dew vanishes from the grass into nightly mist. As, utterly, all was still.

A lurid howl from Baby Brandoch, hitherto peacefully playing on the floor. Svetlana rushes to pick him up: Gosh, Daddy Frank, what are you up to?

If it's all like the little I overheard—well, I just don't see how Mother and Iovanna stand it.

Listen, all of you! The idea at least is good. . . .

It is now dark, the wind so dreaded by ghostly shades was rising as the moon arose. I got up and went out by the way I came in. Wondering still and remembering I looked back at the gate. There it was in stone . . . Truth Against the World, the revered, ancient Druid symbol old Timothy had carved there on the gatepost for the Lloyd-Joneses, those whose 'shades' had just wreathed upward for a ghostly gathering of the whispering clan and gone away. Had they come to give their verdict?

Strange . . . a new meaning . . . Why had I not seen it so before? . . . The downward rays of the sun were Joy! Joy set against and dispelling the mean hatreds that were all the sorrows of this world.

That then was what the old Druids knew? Was that what the family ghosts flickering in lambent blue there above the graves in the graveyard had been trying to whisper to me?

'The truth to set against the woes of this world is Joy!'

Joy it is that elevates and transfigures Life.

Olgivanna in despair:Pah! And you think you have discovered something? Why, the old Greeks all knew that. Everybody knows it. And here you are just picking it up! Oh, Frank, my dear, throw it away and forget it. Just stick to Architecture. You are safe there.

Of course, my girls were right. They always are! So we all laughed and I threw the thing away. My innocent little excursion into 'writing' was one more blasted hope.

THE MORAL

And I here admit that like all truth, this one—the ancient Druid symbol **\/** which the Lloyd-Jones family adopted as its own is dangerous because so few of us ever learn here on earth to know the difference between Joy and Pleasure. The dead know. When will the Living learn?

Sentimentality is not sentiment, although if I had the skill to make the Allegory stand, sentimentality might have persuaded the more foolish among you otherwise. And Selfhood is not selfishness, though it is often hard for any but a Lloyd-Jones to know when the one is eating up the other. No, Joy is not pleasure. And the abuse of the good is so often taken for the good itself, that symbols are no longer good themselves.

That is truth.

And what can American wagery know of Joy when it is working so desperately hard and overtime in order to live for pleasure?

THE FOUR SEASONS IN FOUR VERSES

Somewhat akin to the unconvincing Allegory, here is an early study in aspirates: sibilant verses to be whispered. My mother came over when she read 'the study' and said gravely, 'My boy, when a young man starts versifying it is a sign.' She didn't say a sign of deterioration, but I knew.

This early abstraction and design in the fashioning of a verse to render the movement of the subject—the Breeze—into its own rhythm, starting slowly, enlivening and dying down, belongs to the same period as the Work Song. Both, as you see, are experiments in straight-line or streamlined design that really belong on the drawing board because both are abstract-pattern in line and colour. Unfamiliar at least, and unlikely in words, although Edgar Allan Poe seemed often to come pretty close.

383

Emphasize the aspirates a little.

Slender grows the tender mesh of silken threads and films of green,
Sunbeams glimmer through between the leaves in nestling sheen,
Gently wavering and fluttering like butterflies awing,
As in melody the raiment of the Spring . . .

Stirs and is still.

Languid vapours veil in torpid heat the deep of azure,
Lazy insects drone in drowsy bloom and glow of verdure,
Faintly uttering the gutturals of Summer's lush o'errun,
As in sultry ease the ripe of Summer's sun . . .

Stirs and is still.

Gleaming crystal overarches seas of gilded leaves,
Flaming vine entwines the flowing oak, and deftly weaves
Rustling radiance in fashioning of iridescence fair,
As with transient heat the rhythmic Autumn air . . .

Stirs and is still.

The frozen earth in starry night lies waiting tense and proud,
Glistening moonbeams shadow askance her glittering shroud,
Frail with frost the breath of life wreathes and rises to a shrine,
As the dying breeze, adream in Wintry pine . . .

Stirs and is still.

Meantime the buildings grew. They were worthy of what they cost us all from first to last. And there were many compensations down the line. Tough as the going mostly was, there was continual accomplishment. Both inside and outside, this thing we wanted most, a suitable, characteristic place to work and play in, grew in integrity, beauty and usefulness, kept on growing up on the hillside at 'Hillside' as though it belonged there. It did belong there. We saw now ideas familiar on paper becoming useful and beautiful features of life and important effects that stood on the ground and would live long.

We worked, we sang, we played with the enthusiasm of youth undiminished. Love's creative labour well spent.

OUR GOODTIME PLAYHOUSE

For one thing, we got our little recreation room—a happy thing—(call it The Playhouse for lack of a better name) with the Bechstein concert grand below, and above in the balcony a fine cinema (35-mm. equipment). Operation began shortly after 'Relief' had thus laid *us* in the gutter and on *our* back. That playroom was fun (on the instalment plan, too—three years to pay for the piano, seven to pay for the equipment, etc. etc. etc.).

Originally we cut up the old Hillside Home School gymnasium and rearranged it into a bright nightspot in Fellowship life. Then we changed it and cut it open more. Then we changed it some more by deepening it.

54. RALPH JESTER (MARTIN J. PENCE) HOUSE: project for a house of plywood.
1938-(1940)

55. SUNTOP HOMES. 1939. Model exhibited at the Museum of Modern Art, 1940.
Quadruple apartment building for the Tod Company, Philadelphia. Four apartments
shoulder to shoulder. Sundecks for children's playgrounds

56. Concrete and stone over stream

KAUFMANN GUEST HOUSE. 1939

57. Living room terrace and steps to water

Ever since we have continued changing it here and there and lavishing upon it all our scheming skill to make the great oak-roofed and oak-walled room a lovely, likely place to be expectant in: sympathetic to sound as a viol.

For our events we combed the available supply of the best foreign films in the world as well as our native products.

The education I myself have received from that source alone would justify the Playhouse.

And I may as well confess right here that it appears to me that, after all has been done and said, it is my own education that the Taliesin Fellowship has undertaken—much more so than I have undertaken that of incidental Fellowships. . . .

An amazing additional wealth of experience and broad range of travel is stored up in me, already the much-travelled traveller, as the result of those films. It would be impossible to travel about the world and see for one's self as deeply or richly the life of the strange parts of the world as the cinema in the hands of great writers and good directors working with the historic resources of the various great nations that have gathered it can now present it.

We have had from Austria and Germany thirty-three splendid features; from China, three; from Czechoslovakia, one; England, forty-four; France, fifty-nine; Ireland, two; Japan, three; Mexico, three; Norway, one; Russia, seventy-two; Sweden, two; Spain, two; and the United States, forty-four. To date a total of two hundred and sixty-nine top films of the world.

The stage curtains were the first craft-work of the Fellowship—rectilinear, brilliant, coloured-felt abstractions (I made the design) applied to a neutral coarse cotton fabric. We bled the silver screen (the screen is about eight by ten feet). The screen is luminous white instead of beaded silver.

We let the sound track play through on a red felt band about one foot wide, up and down on the left side of the picture. Straight-line sound patterns were there in light to harmonize the moving picture with our characteristic type of design.

We indulged in some interesting experiments in sound—reflexes ending up with the loud-speakers beneath the stage pointing toward the rear wall of the recess in which the screen stood. Sound to permeate the house instead of hitting hard on the ear. From this back board wall, the sound—now a reflex—spread to the audience. Integral sound. Many guests having seen the films elsewhere which they now happened to see in our playhouse, would say they enjoyed them as though they were seeing them for the first time, discovering more in them than they had ever thought was there.

Incorporated in the Playhouse:

1. Reflex seating arrangement instead of seating on centreline with eyes directly in front.

2. The stage, part of the audience room.

3. Bled screen for cinema.

4. The sound track playing through beside the picture on a red band. A straight-line decoration in light, harmonizing the picture with the house.

5. Electric lighting without glass.

6. Sound magnifiers beneath stage floor—directed against rear wood wall of stage—sound thus becoming part of the room instead of directed at the ear.

7. A dais for quartet, one for the piano, and seating for choir, arranged and related sympathetically to the stage at one side—instead of pit in front of the stage.

8. A real 'Foyer'—a fireplace in the Playhouse itself. The use of architectural screens to reproportion the room and provide service for feasts and cloakroom space.

9. The top of the seat-ranks a broad ledge on which colourful table service is arranged for ear-and-eye feasts. Good interior decoration.

The whole construction in native oak aside from the supporting walls is stained dark, with a brilliant play of polychrome against the dark throughout.

SNATCHING VICTORY FROM THE JAWS OF DEFEAT

Our special act: this 'snatching victory from the jaws of defeat'.

We had quite a time getting seated in this Playhouse of ours. After looking about a good deal and being refused often, we had finally decided on some movable metal chairs manufactured in Elgin, Illinois. About eight hundred dollars for about the one hundred chairs we needed. We accepted the terms offered. But nothing happened. The Company, after agreeing to deliver, refused to deliver, demanding the never-to-be-forgotten 'cash'. We had waited some weeks in blissful ignorance of this—setting our opening date to correspond with promised delivery. But the characteristic blow fell. So, what to do? Eight hundred wasn't much, but we couldn't spare eighty dollars at the time. We might have expected it by now; it had blocked us *ad libitum—ad nauseam*. But strangely hope does spring eternal in the Taliesin breast—we still believed in Santa Claus. Though in the toils of the System, we have never yet learned how to lose hope.

Thus driven to pay for the trifle which was not trifling, in order to open on time we again sat down at the drawing boards to see what we could do with green oak boards, 1″ × 9″, a keg of nails and a few screws. We evolved a system of bench seating, more appropriate than the coveted Elgin metal product. Far more interesting in character. Rough green lumber was all we had to put into it, but we fitted it all together into a new idea—the comfortable reflex seating arrangement you may see there now —where seating an audience was concerned. The girls cut up cotton bed-pads and tripled them to pad the seats and backs of the benches which had a broad top rail to hold the supper service. We found some cheap red enim (ten cents) to cover the cushions, sewed coloured cords to the covers, and tied them on to the seats. And we had seating.

Pretty hard, but not impossible if the play was really good. Most always it was.

But the Playhouse was becoming charming entertainment in itself— entertainment that could never fail. The magic of something new and interesting appeared among us again 'to snatch victory from the jaws of defeat'.

I had wanted a theatre of my own ever since when, as a boy, I read of Wilhelm Meister's puppet-theatre in the attic of the house Goethe designed for him. Here it was—far beyond Wilhelm Meister's or any Goethe himself could have designed. This surely counted us *one*?

Every time we were cut off from an unexpected source of 'cash-and-carry' supply, we came up smiling, really better off for the rebuff because of the demand upon our own resourceful inspiration. Of course the middle-men were all hanging by their eyebrows from sky-hooks. Their bosses were taking no chances.

Nevertheless we found generous co-operation enough so that we are not yet convinced that no one wants to go into partnership with us. We thought we were a good thing at a time when all was dead or dying. We are surer than ever now, now that dead and dying are actually here all around us and it is war in place of economic distress.

REST FOR THE WICKED

We kept on trying to get and give co-operation whenever need for accommodation appeared, as it did, constantly. But always the risks seemed too great to those who could help us on our way if they would. So far as they went, our cause was beside their mark. It never could 'pay'. And (seriously) why should the System want to compromise itself by helping us anyway? What interest to the 'make' of the middleman were we, or was anything whatever, if there was no cash profit in 'the deal'? They had to live. So they said. So their discounts were naturally not only very few but very suspicious.

Help was spaced far apart on centres in those equivocal trying days. We might say that in the early days help was invisible. Or in reverse.

I may as well confess, at this point, however, that I was certain financial help from some source *would* appear when we really got something going to show the nature of the cultural effort to which we were committed. But we never got to the point where I was ready to show what we had done and ask anybody for financial help. We are not there yet. So all the friendly help we've had has been small and haphazard; you might say, accidental, but none the less appreciated on that account. The more welcome for that, I should say. I should like to tell the stories of several such. And some day I will write them.

I am no longer so sanguine where substantial help is concerned. This effort of ours is far too individual to attract it. No nameplates of donors nor much glory in substantial giving to us. And I guess that we must make ourselves or break. Only the Institution can get help. And we don't want to be an Institution. Neither are we 'all dressed up and no place to go'.

We are not much dressed up at all.

In many desirable ways we would like to be. And yet, in many respects our self-respecting poverty stands as itself for the thing it *is*—the open countenance of principle: something out of our own soil belonging to our own time and place, naturally.

It is crude as the bark on a tree.

But the tree itself is there—under the bark the branches are springing, the green leaves spreading to the light—as the whole endeavour grows slowly, painfully but happily according to the true principles within it.

We believe that we have planted a fruit tree and that our cultivation will bring the tree into bearing.

There is no source of inspiration the West won't copy. In this substitution of experienced example and exemplar experience that we call master and apprentice, we have met certain characteristic traits of character, certain liabilities as well as assets. And while we believe we are fundamentally democratic, we are as anti-'cash-and-carry' as we are anti-war.

Here are some of our principal liabilities and, in general, they would be those of a true democracy:

When we were building Edgar Kaufman's house at Bear Run, I had one of my enthusiastic, faithful boys, Bob, 'Little Sunshine', on it on the usual apprentice arrangement made with every client. 'Take him away,' said E. J. in despair at an early stage of the proceedings. 'His blunders will cost me money. Take him away!'

'No, E. J.,' I said, 'not yet. Be patient. He may be, and he is, costing us both a little money, but not much. You gave me a thousand dollars to help make the models of Broadacre City. Well, it's only fair for you to pay your small share of the education of these young fellows—America's future architects. It is fair, if for no other reason than just because they are giving you and me, where your opus is concerned, something no money can buy: an alive and enthusiastic interest in our work and the eager co-operation that goes with it too, as well as they can. None of them are fools. I know it is an intangible I am talking about. I know. But your building will come out right-side up in the end, and you'll have something in the way of a building experience as well as a building that money could never pay for. And I assure you that the building won't have cost you as much either as it would have cost you were the whole thing "regular".'

'All right,' said E. J., but unconvinced (he is a good business man as well as a good fellow too). 'We'll see.' And now, to tell the truth to E. J. (and the same goes to all my clients in this struggle for superior character and integrity in building), the experienced professional would be just as much or more at sea in the way of doing things where I am concerned. And the experienced professional would be much harder to inform and convince of his error in trying the new way than my amateurs would be. He would make mistakes and he would stick to them to save his face, where one of my boys would say, 'Sure, how stupid of me—I see it all now.' The boys did add a lively human interest element all down the line, on every house we built. For better and some for worse. Sometimes prospective clients coming to see the work on a new building and being shown about by the boy, would like him so much they would give their work to the boy!

A system was then in force allowing a Fellow to do work with his name on the plans but all designs and details to be submitted to me for approval. The same fee, ten per cent, to be charged; divided one-third to apprentice, one-third to cover the cost of plans made by the Fellowship, and one-third left in the Fellowship for it to grow up on. This was a mistake from every standpoint as I will explain in a later chapter. While authentic originals are available, why devote the resources of the Fellowship to warmed-up or warmed-over amateur productions, especially as they seemed to destroy the Fellowship rather than build it up? More on this subject later.

And it is only fair to say that on all the buildings I have built with the Fellowship alongside (there are some thirty-five or -six or -seven such buildings now), from the very first I have found quicker comprehension and more intelligent faithful co-operation, counting in all the aggravating dropping of stitches from first to last, than I ever got out of 'experienced' professionals at any time. This would not apply were we doing the standard thing done by the regular architects for which the channels are all cut. I well know that. But once we do go afield from the beaten track, not for novelty—no—but for the necessarily different because it *is the better thing*, we (my clients and myself) are better off (the time limit aside) with the honest amateur than we could ever be with the conventional 'expert' in the rut. The expert is usually a man who has stopped thinking and so is perfectly able to be utterly wrong for at least the rest of his lifetime. He has made up his mind, not upon principle, but upon expedient practice. So he is quite likely to be, himself, a rule of thumb already out of date where we are concerned.

As a matter of fact, during the rational pioneering of these past forty-five years, I have developed a technique of my own—still flexible—therefore still growing with each new experience, which means each new building we build. Not only is it not probable that 'the practical man of experience' would be likely to grasp and apply it: he *wouldn't* do it if he could. But in all frankness, let me say he couldn't do it without more study than he can afford to give it, and on the way that study means more failures. Failures which would be more numerous, more difficult to remedy and as much more costly to apply as he was certain of his experience. Saving his face would be more costly to my clients, therefore, than the quickly corrected blunders of my amateurs. But I realize that my proximity to the work done is more than ever essential. That is not likely soon to change except as I have in time trained good builders myself. The Fellowship should now have several such, and will soon have more like

389

Harold Turner and Ben Wiltscheck. We have a score of boys though who could already build one of our houses and build it well if backed by capital.

But the time when we can thus build our own buildings, milling our own materials, is not yet.

We are looking forward to it, however.

No more drawing-board architects if I can help it, contractors trying to build buildings they know nothing about.

To bear me out, about all my clients have testified to the joy and satisfaction they get from their own particular building, believing theirs to be the best house I have built, as indeed it is for them. Their experience with the sincere try for the organic in character—the honest experiment made in their behalf—has often opened a new world to and for them. Were it not likely to be misleading—looking like boasting, or a plug—I should like to introduce here letters from many, even from most all of the clients, testifying to that as a fact. And my clients are a cross-section of the distinctly better type of American—I should say Usonian, to be specific— most of them with an aesthetic sense of their own, many of them artistic, accomplished, and most of them travelled. They have sometimes learned about us from abroad.

We seldom get the real provincials. The provincial doesn't dare trust his own judgment as to cultural causes and effects. If he has been abroad, his education such as it is, usually confirms his instinctive eclecticism. He is the country's characteristic cultural coward.

The houses we build are usually enjoyed by people who are rich in other things than money. It seems as though the appreciation of our work is inversely proportioned to the financial standing of the person involved.

But sometimes when Usonian houses are very far away and proximity to the work therefore is not possible, after work is 'practically complete', we have had to go back to the opus as a body of workmen ourselves to straighten out mistakes, meantime perhaps bettering the original, correcting faulty workmanship and materials in order to save the owner harmless trouble and generally establish or re-establish what was originally intended but perhaps in this or that particular instance, by the owner's interference, unhappily lost in execution. We do this. And we ought to have and will soon have a Fellowship follow-up group organized to help furnish and use the house after it is done, in the style intended, with the ease, grace and distinction which the new forms make possible. We are already doing this, often.

Our Fellowship method grows steadily more effective as we go along, until I am assured by my clients, comparing their own costs with the known costs of neighbouring buildings, that one of our operations will result in more actual space accommodation and greater material advantages in every way than the more 'regular' houses much more easily had, that abound around them. What style and distinction our buildings possess is therefore 'thrown in'. 'No charge.' But it is also only fair to say that it *is* more difficult to find ways and means to get our houses built.

The distinction of our buildings (the countenance of principle will stand out in any crowd) is inevitable. It marks them and makes them, should they fail at any point—temporarily leak or show defects and especially should they exceed expected costs—immediately become a common mark for the envious sceptic. Most of the sceptics are architects. Or friends and neighbours who live in fashionable homes.

We are yet, thanks to our lucky star, unfashionable.

Our faults are those, not of a common system but of an independently growing thing: a challenge to Fashion. But our faults are corrected much more easily than the faults stock-and-shop would be sure to perpetrate. Because every problem carries within itself its own solution, and, because we make the buildings what they are, thoroughbred, we are perfectly competent to cure evils and rectify errors as they arise. We have the secrets conferred by our experience with the type we originate.

Any experiment we make is not on our part a seeking for novelty—but is sincerely and intelligently an experiment made in the client's own interest. Cure and correction are a matter of pride with us because, in a peculiarly intimate sense, every building we build is not only the client's own, but also *our* own. We must and will see that that building becomes what we intended it to be or we would soon be ashamed to look ourselves in the face. And since the building is always a public mark, the building must be maintained as intended even if we have to help. It is sometimes a matter of enough money of our own to be able to do this. But we get the money eventually. And no client who has stood by us has yet been let down. It is also only fair to say that most all of them have not let us down either. Many of them have taken a lot that seemed at the time beside the mark in order to get what they were certain was coming, glad to stand by the principles we practise, principles in which they as firmly and faithfully believe as we do.

Their investment in the building is dated some years ahead (say, ten years) and increases in value with time because our buildings cannot go out of fashion. They are not and never will be dated.

THE CONQUEST OF THE DESERT

Taliesin West is a look over the rim of the world. As a name for our far-western desert camp we arrived at it after many more romantic names were set up and knocked down. The circumstances were so picturesque that names ran wild—so we settled sensibly to the one we already had.

To live indoors with the Fellowship during a Northern winter would be hard on the Fellowship and hard on us. We are an outdoor outfit; besides it costs thirty-five hundred dollars to heat all our buildings at Taliesin, so it is cheaper to move Southwest. The trek across continent began November, 1933. Each trek was an event of the first magnitude. The Fellowship's annual hegira with sleeping bags and camping-outfit, big canvas-covered truck, cars and trailers for thirty-five, *was* an event even in Fellowship life. To conquer the desert we had first to conquer the intervening two thousand miles in cold weather. The first years we stayed at Dr. Chandler's hacienda at Chandler, Arizona. Very happy there, too, but crazy to build for ourselves.

We were growing in proficiency.

A major rule in the Fellowship has always been 'do something while resting'. So we preferred to build something while on vacation. I was earning something again, now, as an architect, and we could get materials. But first we had to settle on a site. By this time that vast desert region, Silence and Beauty, was as familiar to us as our part of Wisconsin. There was plenty of room and plenty of superb sites, high or low—open or sequestered. Every Sunday, for a season, we swept here and there on picnics. With sleeping bags we went to and fro like the possessed from one famous place to another. Finally I learned of a site twenty-six miles from Phoenix, across the desert of the vast Paradise Valley. On up to a great mesa in the mountains. On the mesa just below McDowell Peak we stopped, turned, and looked around. The top of the world!

Magnificent—beyond words to describe! Splendid mystic desert vegetation, but what a bad road. The only trial crossing the great wash of Paradise Valley, the broad wash to the Verde River was this miserable G—— d—— Hell of a road that that trail across the desert was in wet weather, so we found. And there was a rainy season until later it got to raining all the time.

But roads can be improved. The site could not be. The land could be bought from Stephen Pool at the Government Land Office. Pool said he was keeping it for some fellow (he said 'fool') who would fall in love with it and 'do something with it'. We got about eight hundred acres together finally, part purchase, part lease. Next year we began to 'do something with it'. We made the plans and were all ready.

We knew about what thirty apprentices, our little family alongside, needed—one of the things was 'room'.

There was lots of room so we took it and didn't have to ask anything or anybody to move over. The plans were inspired by the character and beauty of that wonderful site. Just imagine what it would be like on top of the world looking over the universe at sunrise or at sunset with clear sky in between. Light and air bathing all the worlds of creation in all the colour there ever was—all the shapes and outlines ever devised—neither let nor hindrance to imagination—nothing to imagine—all beyond the reach of the finite mind. Well, that was our place on the mesa and our buildings had to fit in. It was a new world to us and cleared the slate of the pastoral loveliness of our place in Southern Wisconsin. Instead came an aesthetic, even ascetic, idealization of space, of breadth and height and of strange firm forms, a sweep that was a spiritual cathartic for Time if indeed Time continued to exist.

The imagination of the mind of man is an awesome thing to contemplate. Sight comes and goes in it as from an original source, illuminating life with involuntary light as flashes of lightning light up the landscape.

The Desert seems vast but the seeming is nothing compared to the reality.

But for the designing of our buildings certain forms abounded. There were simple characteristic silhouettes to go by, tremendous drifts and heaps of sunburned desert rocks were nearby to be used. We got it all together with the landscape—where God is all and man is nought—as a more permanent extension of 'Ocatilla', the first canvas-topped desert camp out of Architecture by youthful enthusiasm for posterity to ponder.

Superlatives are exhausting and usually a bore—but we lived, moved, and had our being in superlatives for years. And we were never bored.

From first to last, hundreds of cords of stone, carloads of cement, carloads of redwood, acres of stout white canvas doubled over wood frames four feet by eight feet. For overhead balconies, terraces, and extended decks we devised a light canvas-covered redwood framework resting upon massive stone masonry that belonged to the mountain slopes all around. On a fair day when the white tops and side flaps were flung open the desert air and the birds flew clear through. There was a belfry and there was a big bell. There were gardens. One great prow running out onto the Mesa overlooking the world, a triangular pool nesting in it—another garden sequestered for quiet with another plunge-pool with water raining down from the wall in one corner of it.

There were play-courts for the boys, spacious rooms for them, and there were pleasant guest-quarters on a wide upper deck overlooking the garden and the Mesa.

Said the local wise-man, 'No water on that side the valley—waste of money to try.'

But we tried and got wonderful water at 486 feet—85 degrees when it emerged at the pool. All went forward pretty much as usual, etc., etc., only on a less inhibited scale and upon the most marvellous site on earth.

Our Arizona camp is something one can't describe and just doesn't care to talk much about.—Something like God in that respect?

And how our boys worked! Talk about hardening up for a soldier. Why, that bunch of lads could make any soldier look like a stick! They weren't killing anything either, except a rattlesnake, a tarantula, or a scorpion now and then as the season grew warmer.

No, they weren't killing anything: stripped to a pair of shorts they were just getting something born, that's all, but as excited about the birth as the soldier is in his V's when they come through. More so if my observation counts.

The reward came.

Olgivanna said the whole opus looked like something we had been excavating, not building.

That desert camp belonged to the desert as though it had stood there for centuries. And also built into Taliesin West is the best in the strong young lives of about thirty young men and women for their winter seasons of about seven years. Some local labour went in too, but not much. And the constant supervision of an architect—myself, Olgivanna inspiring and working with us all, working as hard as I—living a full life, too full, meanwhile.

The difficulty was for us, that the place had to be lived in while it was being built.

We were sometimes marooned for five days at a time. The desert devils would swirl sand all over us when it was dry. We could see whole thunderstorms hanging below us over the valley, see the winds rushing the clouds toward us, and we would get the camp ready as though we were at its mercy out on a ship at sea. At times on the way to and from Phoenix for supplies I would sit in the car, Olgivanna by my side, when my feet were on the brakes under water up to my knees.

The Masselinks coming to visit their son were lost in the desert waterwaste overnight, and water was up to everybody's knees until the afternoon of the next day. The son in an attempted rescue was almost carried away.

Frequently visitors trying to see us were nearly drowned in the desert.

Hardships toward the latter end of the experiment were almost more than flesh and blood could bear. Olgivanna and I, living in the midst of a rushing building operation for seven years, began to wear down.

Otherwise our Fellowship life went on much the same, Taliesin or Taliesin West—except that the conspiracy of Time and Money was a little less against us.

Once you get the desert in your blood—look on the map of Arizona Highways for Taliesin West.

N.B. I've forgotten to speak of our desert playhouse: a 'kiva' solid masonry inside and outside, with a sunken fireplace and an outside hangar for our cinema to peep in through the thick stone wall, arrangements for feasting and music. A triumph of imagination by way of simple form and limited space in the heart of a great cubical masonry block.

FELLOWSHIP LIABILITIES OR DEMOCRATIC BACK DRAG

I have said they would not be peculiar to us but would be those common to Democracy.

I. The Servant Mind

The servant mind is a menace to us as it is a menace to Democracy. And it is a natural inheritance of the melting pot. It comes from the lower ranks of society and permeates the upper ranks to destroy them—the drag of innate servility on the struggle for independence: the congenital curse put upon the true or innate aristocracy we call Democracy, placed there by feudal servility. The servant mind is inbred and not likely to be cast off except as it is unbred.

For instance: a well-to-do country gentleman was visited by a friend. The gentleman's valet met the guest, showed him to his room, meantime complaining of his master. In small invidious ways he deprecated him until the exasperated friend, who was a true friend, said:

'Well, Michel, if you don't like the way your master treats you, why don't you leave him? Go somewhere else . . .'

'Oh,' said the valet, 'no, it's all right. I gets even. I spits in his coffee every morning.'

Now there are as many variations and modifications of that cup of coffee as there are people and circumstances. A general example of what I mean by 'the servant mind'.

And, of course, since the freedom of Fellowship is impossible except on terms of self-respect and equality—some form of kick-back or treachery is the inevitable consequence of the servant mind, should it get into our midst, which is more and more unlikely.

II. The Inferiority Complex

Not far removed from the servant mind, probably descended from it in some way, is this troublesome inferiority complex. But it is even more dangerous to Fellowship than the servant mind because it is harder to diagnose and deal with. It is something that will make a young fellow ashamed to pick up a walking stick dropped by an elderly man, or a companion, for fear of seeming servile; something in the boy that makes him bad-mannered and awkward in fear of his own inherent servility. And the fear makes him look as he is—cheap. That same thing prevents him from ever earning the title gentleman, and stands in the way of his ever becoming a truly manly man. We have observed it sometimes in the Fellowship in the more feminine types of young men. But the girls are not entirely exempt. In them it may stem from their attempt to throw off the domination by the male.

Of course, it is only a man who believes in himself that can ever give loyalty to an idea or be faithful to the master of one, or to one who is master of the idea.

In true apprenticeship there must be an interchange between the two which puts them into a trust with one another.

So the inferiority complex is dangerous to us.

It cannot safely be put upon a footing of equality in comradeship nor, because it cannot trust itself, is its loyalty to masterhood or to mastership to be trusted.

Always a questionable type.

Judas was probably the better sort of the type in question who sought to save his Master from himself, seeing his Master as he (Judas) saw himself.

The consequences of discipleship where the complex is concerned are always dangerous.

The inferiority complex shows itself most in unnecessary unbecoming self-assertion—trying hard to make itself believe what it wants others to believe: that it is not inferior. It is the opposite of modesty and protests too much always because it wants too much so much, and fears it has too little. Nothing is more damaging to Fellowship or harder to root out, because, for one thing, it is a hangover of the umbilical cord. For another, it is the same inevitable subjective association of ideas that goes back to aristocracy not natural but false, false because hereditary.

Dr. Spivey (the hero of Florida Southern College) once said to me that the boys who came in to work their way through college were usually the malcontents, and eventually the troublemakers. Instead of gratitude for the privilege extended to them, they themselves were suspicious that they were not in the same category as the paying students, and fancied slights, soon or late, developed resentment.

The Fellowship has found that the less a boy or girl actually has had in life before coming in to the Fellowship, the more supersensitive to fancied slights or resemblances to servitude he is.

But there is something deeper than that, undermining good fellowship, that tries to set up artificial barriers in order to 'even up' the score, something not openly acknowledged even to itself. Perhaps the same thing happens that happens when an article is 'marked down' for sale. What we get cheap we seldom value except as something cheap.

III. The Umbilical Cord

The grown-up child seldom casts it entirely off—especially the unregenerate. Usually it is the sentimental tie-back to prejudices of the former generation: the 'hold-back' of the parent who wants to see the child grow up, but suspects and dreads the consequences of enlightenment. The Father who was a conservative fears for the son who is becoming a radical. Mother instinctively hovers over her young, perhaps in the position of a hen who has hatched out a duck. Or Father is the cock who has fathered a feather. The cord drags after the offspring or coils about its neck, preventing, so far as it can, the free action of the free spirit of the child. Because, if affectionate and dutiful, the child is sentimental where Mother (sometimes Father too) is concerned; the cord hurts them, and drags the boy or girl back if going too far or too fast ahead. So the 'cord' is no asset to Fellowship. And the cure for it is always tragic. When the Spirit-parent encounters the flesh-and-blood or carnal parent, there is usually an uneasy feeling on the part of the carnal parent that parental authority is getting a bad break or being betrayed, his offspring being led astray. Usually the parents feel that the child's individuality is being sacrificed. He is being misled. Certainly the only place a young mind can or should be led when the umbilical cord remains around the neck is 'astray'.

396

IV. The Pin-Feather Ego

Worthless cargo. But the Fellowship falls heir to it not so much in the refugees from Education as those who come to Taliesin after four, five, or six years of fairly successful college life. These 'degree' men, even more than those who break with college, come to us with a habituated mind and a tightly strung nervous system to boot. Characteristic always is premature (which is immature) criticism. On a moment's notice, categorical wisdom! The premise and the thesis. Always the stock-and-shop point of view. Disjecta membra on every subject ever catalogued. The damage thus done to Youth by the classroom authority is incalculable. This type is the Expert in embryo.

It is living what life it has on information but never really able to learn.

Young men living the vicarious life of the devotee vicar, they are the individuals who try to escape the herd by herding.

By way of the mere association of ideas we call wishful thinking, it is easy for most of us to make ourselves believe what we want to believe. For the young man educated far beyond his capacity, it is possible to erect a complete synthetic 'ivory tower' and live there in it if his experience stands still long enough to allow him to get into it. But in certain circumstances in Urbania such intellectualism does stand up. I have seen it so stand, as potato sprouts do on potatoes in a dark cellar. This vicarious character is a prematurity and eventually an utter emasculation of soul where the manly ego should be. It is the result of Education that is destined and designed to die on the vine. 'Designed mis-education.' But meantime it has occasionally been a Fellowship stumbling block. Time, often months, sometimes years, must be given the victim in which to relax before he becomes sufficiently receptive either to perceive or acknowledge the mastery he would meantime subconsciously emulate. Nothing can be put into hands self-conscious nervous tension has shut so tight. When the hands are open, palms upward, voluntarily held out together in the dignity of true humility, then is the time to give without fear of wasting the giver and what is given.

V. The Ever Womanly

The woman always wins.

This, the Eternal Feminine, is a Fellowship problem of no mean dimensions: the one we have not yet solved and may never solve so long as we hold to our co-educational ideal. The woman always wins. This is her civilization, her day, and her hour. When left to her choice in our country she dresses her figure to emulate the broadshouldered style of the male, and her sons grow more and more to resemble the silhouettes of her own figure. The figures of the sons of their mothers and the daughters of their fathers are thus growing more and more to resemble each other, and they trade characteristics with disconcerting, increasing frequency.

Woman is steadily winning away the Fellowship.

She can turn a Fellowship into a nursery without half trying.

To what extent co-education, under ideals like ours, can be trusted as desirable, we have no mind, as yet, except that we are not for the average woman. Certainly married companionship should be no bar to Fellowship were the average woman less possessive. But the average woman is the natural cup to be filled—to which her man is to bring not only himself, but the makings of a future for her children. She is seldom cultured to be honestly idealistic in herself. She is pragmatic because of her biological character. She is concerned, subjectively if not objectively, for the little shovelful of coals that will enable her to start a little hell of her own at the very earliest possible moment. She is co-operative only until she gets her man. Thereafter she is only waiting to establish herself wherever man can be the bringer to her, for hers.

Now the average woman is a wise provision of nature for the survival of the species. We, the Fellowship, cannot and should not quarrel with her, but we must, for the time being, go around her. The average man may still be a true servant of an Ideal, but his inspiration comes frequently from his love for a woman and so long as she sees him turning toward her, all is well. But she has to have a place for this and the place is not in Fellowship. He must make a place especially for her, so either we must include in our plans separate households, independent but associated for the purpose of raising children—which we are considering—or accept only such womanhood as has evolved the satisfactions of the artist, the philosopher, in short the Idealist who does not sacrifice but rather intensifies womanliness. Such women are rare. We hope to have them, but how are we to recognize them before it is too late?

VI. The Cashandcarry

Democracy badly needs a new Success Ideal. The present one is a form of damnation. Not only does Democracy need a new one but must have it soon or democracy perishes. Cashandcarry 'Success' knows no qualities nor can admit or permit of any mastership but Money. Money must be in the very nature of things as things are, the proof of Success in such as our System. So most American universities inculcate and prepare for that venal sort of Success. Inevitably our American colleges and universities are similar to enlarged Trade Schools—all qualifying the youth of the nation to cog in somewhere in the commercialized social machine, and so —earn money. We who are not so constituted find that many youths must go back into the wagery of Cashandcarry to pay back the money they borrowed to be thus educated. So the wires get crossed. It is unfortunate for us that the trader-instinct, shopkeeping, lies in ambush everywhere: the price tags already fixed on humanity as they are fixed upon any other commodity. But so it is. We of the Fellowship can scarcely hope entirely to escape the mark-up and the mark-down continually being made by American educational institutions. The result of this institutional idiocy is what I am calling the Cashandcarry mentality we live in. That mentality is a routine, commercialized, middle-of-the-road substitute for a mind. You can move anybody in it around for a little more money than he has been getting.

But it is more than merely difficult to set up, and almost impossible to maintain, a way of life for young men and women otherwise.

Such life as ours in the Fellowship *is* otherwise and it is not only in sharp contrast, but in unfair competition with that surrounding mentality. We (the one) must come and go in the other (the many) to a certain extent. That is inevitable.

It is due to the opposing philosophy of our surroundings that we suffer most.

Just as Democracy always suffers most in War.

A Cashandcarry nation needs every man a wage-slave just as the nation in war needs every man a conscript. Because, in its false economy, production controls consumption, it would have to be so. The Commander-in-Chief of the Cashandcarry would have to be the banker as it stands now. Professional commercial propaganda, using the proper names, could make either defeat out of victory or victory out of defeat in any commercial circumstances if the prop could be kept up long enough. That faith in production and continuous unrelenting advertising propaganda is the touching faith of the average-man of our day in Peace. And so it is the same in War.

The most dangerous characteristic of the System however, from any cultural standpoint, is the short-cut to burial for the inherited inferiority complex which the System affords.

Money can do it.

Fellowship is looked upon by the Cashandcarry, and naturally, with suspicion. 'You are a kind of Art Colony, ah!' Or: 'You are a kind of country club for art students'; or, well, there are dozens of their own ideas ᴜof what we are. 'Fellowship' sounds to them like some sect or other. Anyhow, no good can come of 'getting off the beaten track'. 'The machine can't go there.' 'Stick to the boulevard, my boy, if you can.' 'Main travelled roads are best, you know.' 'No patience with this assumption of the try for something different.' 'It is insulting to *our* intelligence.' 'Who the hell are the people anyway?' 'And what *is* the assumption?' 'We aren't good enough for them? All right, who cares a damn about them?' Etc. etc.

If the Cashandcarry mentality (it is wage-slave) gets into Fellowship, it would probably soon be found mixed up in some kind of secret exploitation inside or outside of the Fellowship. The Cashandcarry mind is constantly worried: 'What am I getting out of this?' 'Will it pay?'

'Never mind what I am giving to it: let them get what they can out of me.'

The natural fundamental of the profit system is here. It gets us when we get it. We don't get it if we can see it first. Often we can't. It is only under pressure that it appears.

Suggested motto for the Cashandcarry: 'Let us then be up and doing'— for *me*.

Running along with this mundane membrane Money, there is another parallel invention: Time as a kind of policeman. Time, the policeman. But a policeman subsidized by money gangsterism.

VII. The Broadway Creed

Belittlement is its business.

Confusion of the best with the worst is its avocation.

Concerning the wisecracker. We have always a supply of him in the Fellowship. We laugh at his cracks and in good turn take a crack at him. He comes most frequently from the large urban centres of the East, but he comes also from Kansas, Dakota, California, or Minnesota.

The Broadway Creed has covered the country pretty much until it has Hollywood for its other end, and is pretty much commonplace all the way between. Especially where the upper region of the pantaloons is concerned . . . Box Office. The particular cynicism of our era is a kind of smart smut which the breed of the creed instinctively uses to besmirch the common faith of the common man.

Faith of any kind is a mark for the creed's experts, especially any surviving faith in human nature. Selfishly bred, children of pleasure herding on hard, crowded pavements in congested urban areas, the breed naturally gets the worm's-eye or low-down view suited to the Cashandcarry mentality.

But, more important, the Broadwayman's Creed is the solace and the front line of defence for the inferiority complex. Its performances are the instinctively inferior smart-boys' flag and release.

In spite of the Immigration laws, it has grown up among us as the natural product of the melting pot.

As Carlyle said of Democracy, so we say of the Broadway Creed, 'It is a disease. Let us have it so we may have done with it and get on to rule by the bravest and the best.' Nevertheless, human conduct may eventually grow to be a little wiser for the Broadwaymen's worm's-eye view. But a sense of the ridiculous assuming the airs and graces of humour which is really what it is not, has robbed us of too much of our native salt and savour. A Winchell is a Broadway substitute for a wholesome manly Will Rogers.

Among us there is enough punctilio to puncture. There are enough stuffed shirts to thump and enough hypocrisy to play up, infested as the country is with the flood of commercial exploits idiotically extolling their own cheap merits, hoping to knock off a good piece of business by so doing.

The rat-like perspicacity of the breed raised on the Creed is worth much where that work is to be done. How much?

Well, there's Mickey Mouse. He's amusing.

Amusement is the indispensable as things get to be in Urbania. And while the laugh provoked by ridicule and the funnies is not the same as the laugh provoked by the salt and savour of true humour, even that cheap laugh is worth something to our plight. The Creed thus serves a turn.

And the breed does serve the Box Office. Its Box Office is social poison. Its laugh is a cheap laugh. But a laugh is our best medicine—that and a good physic.

Well . . . perhaps both save the day for some purpose for which neither was really intended.

But the search for FORM must reject the Broadway Creed entire, because the laugh it produces is not only a cheap laugh, but the breed itself is antiseptic, in itself sterile. It is inorganic and therefore it cannot reproduce. The future dies with it, or of it.

THE CREATIVE CONSCIENCE

The ALTER EGO is the distorted mirror (concave or convex as the case may be) in which mastership sees its own reflection. The alter ego may be a form of flattery but it is more often a distressing caricature which must be borne for the good of some cause. If any.

The young, if innocent, are hardly conscious of being guilty of alter-egoism, but the more sophisticated ones who do know they are guilty soon grow a hatred of the original of their image, the pictures they make. And in time the alter ego thus becomes the instinctive detractor of the coveted original. His trouble is that the original is there behind his cupboard door as a threat to his own sense of himself, when he himself performs. He would like to escape and to destroy his original in the short cut.

The disciple is a legitimate form of the Alter Ego. Jesus had twelve disciples, such as they were, and they were such as they always are. But, occasionally, even Jesus got up into the high mountains to be relieved of his disciples for a time. Nevertheless, I think the Alter Ego is a justified necessity. But he is an asset to Fellowship only just so long as his alter-egoship is an open door or window through which he may look out upon a natural world otherwise dark to him, a world wherein his alter-egoship will gradually grow independent by way of the sincerity of his devotion to his master; his devotion becoming the door or window through which he sees what his master sees—gaining direction at least for going, as time goes, further on: perhaps being saved years of wasted effort by the light that shines from his master, who under certain conditions can himself be the door and the window. Then the alter ego is justified. Then only is he an honest asset to Fellowship. His apprenticeship is a stepping stone to his own independence; even if his aim continues sympathetic, it continues as collateral. It is always unfair to accuse an alter ego of that type of plagiarism. He steals nothing. He gives himself to his master simple-mindedly with no reservation, while his own sense of himself in whatever is to be done by him is forming within him. I have found that those in the Fellowship who had least Individuality worried most about it. Those who had it most were seldom concerned about it. It would take care of itself naturally without offence or defence. The Cashandcarry seldom lets it come through alive.

The ALTER EGO never consciously 'copies' his original source of inspiration although he is usually no more than promoting a natural implication which was inherent in the masterpiece in the expression of which he participated. If he is a good disciple he is himself an implication of his master. Maybe for life. But most disciples are a weariness to the future and to the mastership which sees before very long that he has not inspired them but is only being used by them as a shield for inconstancy, or vain exploitation.

To enter sincerely into the spirit of a master, standing loyally by his side in his work is, so it has always seemed to me who have myself been such a one, the greatest privilege any novice may ever have.

Education has nothing so precious to offer to youth.

Usonia needs thousands of Taliesins, not one only.

But to go too far with the letter of any master in any implications of his own work is to insult both the master and the apprentice himself. Both become a source of grim amusement.

Men of achievement in the Arts and Sciences should continue their activities by placing themselves where their experience may serve the oncoming tide of life. But how far should the Alter Ego go with his apprenticeship? The answer is that all depends upon circumstances and the Creative Conscience. With that Conscience developed both the novice and the master are safe and happy in each other. Time is of no essence in the matter. Apprenticeship may go on five—ten years profitably to both, perhaps for life. It all depends. The sincere search for FORM can use the honest alter ego. He can go along. He will be there when FORM becomes a matter of fact.

The Creative Conscience then lies in the artist, as in manhood, in himself. As the fashioner of FORM it demands the whole truth or suffers. It gives the whole truth—or suffers.

It is marvellous to stew, like fruit, in one's own juice and then be set back to simmer for a while.

FELLOWSHIP ASSETS

    I. AN HONEST EGO IN A HEALTHY BODY—GOOD CORRELATION
    II. LOVE OF TRUTH AND NATURE
    III. SINCERITY AND COURAGE
    IV. ABILITY FOR ACTION
    V. THE AESTHETIC SENSE
    VI. APPRECIATION OF WORK AS IDEA AND IDEA AS WORK
    VII. FERTILITY OF IMAGINATION
    VIII. CAPACITY FOR FAITH AND REBELLION
    IX. DISREGARD FOR COMMONPLACE (INORGANIC) ELEGANCE
    X. INSTINCTIVE CO-OPERATION

These human attributes of Fellowship when inspired by love will eventually evoke THE CREATIVE CONSCIENCE.

THE FIRST-PERSON SINGULAR

The only thing a man has that can't be taken away from him is himself. He cannot afford to be selfish. In Selfhood the more of himself he gives the more he has to give. The less he gives the less he has to give.

As I have already said: I find that those young men who had most individuality were troubled least about it. To be too much concerned with it is a pretty sure sign that there is little there to be concerned with. A sound man does not think or speak much of his health nor willingly speak of what he thinks most deeply. So until a man knows the difference between individuality and personality he may confound them in any issue where either is concerned. What he is worrying about is really his personality. Individuality is the essential innate character of the man. His personality is merely the way he looks, walks, speaks, his form, features and habits. Idiosyncrasies are matters of mere personality. None of these personal things is the man's Individuality. And because Individuality lies deeper and is the soul, it is probably looking out at you from the eyes of him you are looking at, looking from under the roof of his mind quite all unconscious of itself.

We don't labour the first-person singular much in the Fellowship. We let it pretty much alone, as it likes to be if it is genuine. And we have found none getting in here without enough of it to be respected. We are bored, however, with the intellectual disguise which is the abuse of the thing—mistaking mere egotistic curiosity for a thirst for knowledge but seldom able to draw the line between the curious and the beautiful. The first-person singular is always born. It grows best and becomes strongest and most fruitful when it is most unaware of itself and is not encouraged to pull itself by the roots every now and then to see how it is growing.

Walt Whitman said he loved the companionship of animals—they were not worried, or worrying others, on account of their souls.

And I like Emerson, walking out under the elms: 'The great trees looked down on him and said, "Why so hot, my little man, why so hot?" '

Why indeed!

ALDEBARAN

Among the very first to come in to Fellowship, a tall dark-eyed young man turned up at Taliesin. He was the son of an Evansville editor. *Who's Who* says the editor was the man who drove the Ku Klux Klan out of Indiana. He did and practically single-handed. The lad came from a course in engineering at Massachusetts Tech, was a fountain of energetic loyalty to the ideas for which Taliesin stood. He soon took a leading hand in whatever went on. His mind was alert, his character independent and generous. He was young—about nineteen.

Svetlana, my charming adopted daughter (she came to Taliesin with Olgivanna), was sixteen. Soon it appeared that Svetlana liked to ride in the truck Wes drove. A general sympathy amounting to a conspiracy grew up behind these young people, and everybody but Olgivanna and myself was aware of a budding romance. Not we. When we did wake up—there were some accusations and unkind words. Too soon! Both too young! The budding romance which looked like a kind of treachery went underground, but partisans for the young couple formed to fight their battle for them. No use. We wouldn't have any of it. So after a while the principals and their partisans struck out for parts unknown. We had been so fond of both of them that we couldn't see the thing as other than the treachery of ungrateful irresponsible children.

We didn't hear from them for a year or two. But we greatly missed them and the inevitable reconciliation took place after they had been married—Svetlana studying music in Chicago, Wes building buildings in Evansville. Were we happy to have them back—giving good accounts of themselves? We were. Perhaps the break was a good thing all around. Certainly both were much improved by the break on their own. And we were a good deal the wiser. I guess we had improved too.

Wes's father died soon, and Wes had a small income and a widowed mother. Taliesin had a son-in-law as well as a devoted follower.

There is a picturesque group of hills to the West—nearby. A farm on the river next to Taliesin, a farm of about three hundred and fifty acres. Wes coveted it and I egged him on to buy it. He seemed the kind of lad who could use ground. And I wanted to see Taliesin expand—expecting someday to see its collaterals owning as much of the countryside as together we could well use.

Wes bought the ground—named it Aldebaran (the follower), and Taliesin soon after that jumped to the control of about one thousand acres with about three miles of water-front. The naming of the place shows the spirit of the lad. He was a genuine apprentice. His ambitions were not cheap. His individuality was strong. He didn't need to worry about that. He was glad and proud to stand by and contribute his strength to Taliesin and Taliesin appreciated him, believed in him now as much as he believed in Taliesin. Here was apprenticeship in flower. Wes planned a good house on a near-by hill—a well-conceived house for his young wife, who gave him a young son they have named Brandoch, a name which puts it up to the boy to be a hero.

Taliesin had a son, a daughter, and a grandson. Taliesin has other faithful competent sons—many of them an asset to Fellowship, but none so close in as Wes—none with more strength or more energy and loyalty than the young man Olgivanna and I drove away years ago with the unkind assumption that he was stealing away a daughter. Well, Svetlana is now somebody in her own right. Here in the Wisconsin Hills is Aldebaran, Taliesin's first real extension—collateral human growth. But inside Taliesin Wes is a leader and the charming lively Svetlana has a large share

404

in cultivating the music life of the Fellowship. She has an innate sense of music. Wes is so interested in farming that I can scarcely get Architecture out of him or into him any more. But it is there. They make, I guess, a Taliesin showpiece.

Wes (now ten years at Taliesin) is a right bower, the best example of What-Taliesin-Can-do-for-a-Young-Apprentice (his wife thrown in) and what a young apprentice can do for Taliesin.

THE STORY OF HIBBARD THE JOHNSON WHO DID MUCH FOR THE OLD HOME TOWN—WAX OFFICIATING

Hibbard (the Hib) was an attractive young waxmaker, son of a wax-maker, who was also the son of a waxmaker. Hib's father, so they say around Racine (the old home town), was famous for his 'hunches'. Not only did Hib inherit the ancestral factories but the ancestral hunches. And this now world-famous modern office building to house the administration of the ancestral wax-manufacturing company was one of Hib's hunches. Hib's remarkable house, now standing broad, wide and handsome, out in the prairie countryside near by, was . . . but of that, later. Hib's hunches made him, for one thing, the only Racine boy to do anything really worth while to culture that industrial ace: the big graceless Wisconsin factory centre by Lake Michigan where millionaires originate and from which they always go somewhere else for fun. And cultivation too. If any. Along with Hib's family inheritances was a valuable lieutenant-general, John Ramsey by name, manager by nature. And no manufacturer, I believe, ever had a better manager or a better man than Jack. Jack, like Hibbard, had seen the education manufactured at Wisconsin U. but both refused to bite off more standard erudition than either could well digest. Hib's brother-in-law, Jack Louis by name, was head of a prosperous advertising firm in Chicago near by, guiding the publicity side of S. C. Johnson Wax by radio. 'Johnson's Wax' gave Fibber McGee and Molly a long ride, eventually greatly to the benefit of the wax-polish industry, and no doubt —Fibber and Molly McGee.

Well, this hunch of Hib's so had it that the prosperity of his now over-crowded and solidly prosperous wax concern should enable the company to do something worth while for the daily lives of its numerous office employees, young and old. So the limit in convenience and beauty in a building for this purpose that intelligence could find and the best in quality that the Johnson money could ever pay for, was none too good for Hib.

When the sky at Taliesin was dark and the days there gloomy, as I have described, Hib and Jack were the ones who came out to Taliesin to see about that new building. They came, you might say, like messengers riding on white steeds trumpeting glad tidings. Jack Louis had been willing, but sceptical; architecture was not radio. But, some time before, a group of art directors from Chicago had visited Taliesin—egged on by good Bill Kitt-redge, I believe. And Willis Jones came along. Willis, a discerning and

405

greatly appreciative young art director, was working for Jack Louis at the time, making designs for his Chicago advertising company. After his visit, of his own volition, Willis got after the Johnson folk. And also a talented young architect, Howard Raftery, put up a sacrificial fight for Taliesin. As a result, the official visit (gratifying annunciation) occurred simetime in July 1936. The occasion was pleasant all around. Next day came a note from Hib enclosing a retainer (one thousand dollars) testifying to his appreciation of what he saw on that occasion. And, the pie thus opened, the birds began to sing again below the house at Taliesin; dry grass on the hillside turned green, and the hollyhocks went gaily into a second blooming. The orchard decided to come in with a heavy crop of big red harvest apples and the whole landscape seemed to have more colour; Iovanna rode more fiercely through the Valley; and both Olgivanna's responsibilities and mine were doubled—with smiles. Work was incessant. Taliesin galvanized into fresh activity.

Well . . . pretty fine sketches for the administration building, the best I could do and just about as the building stands there in its utterly unworthy environment today, went forward. Returning home after that momentous visit, the abandonment of plans resembling a fancy crematorium which some local architect had already contributed was enacted and Hib gave over the coveted commission to the architect Jones and Raftery had persistently recommended—an architect held back outside the current of building for seven years. Here and thus his feet were put back on the road to an activity almost 'struck out' by the very long chain of untoward circumstances hereinbefore related. So I now look back upon that visit—July 20, 1936—with a deep and pleasant satisfaction, never ceasing to be glad that I have for friends the two men who came to see me that day.

What a release of pent-up creative energy—the making of those plans! Ideas came tumbling up and out onto paper to be thrown back in heaps— for careful scrutiny and selection. But, at once, I knew the scheme I wanted to try. I had it in mind when I drew the newspaper plant at Salem, Oregon, for Editor George Putnam, which he had been unable to build. A great simplicity.

Owing to a high ideal of simplicity, this building was bound to be an exacting piece of work. And for quite some time I conducted myself like a pregnant mother.

There were enough headaches to go all around on all sides: the 'union' universally strong in Racine, the building codes strong in Wisconsin. Also, in addition to the law of gravitation, there was the terrific time-lag of Innovation to be overcome: they are similar. But no cultural lag! None. Both Hib and Jack were at the head of the procession from start to finish. 'They' say I am 'hard to get along with' (meaning, really, hard to go along with), but I was never too much for these boys, even if they did finally begin to chafe a little as the inevitable began to happen and the original building kept on growing up. The opus added unto itself a vast

406

domiculated carport, a small hemicycle for the entertainment and instruction of employees got up over the entrance and then came squash courts,
garages, etc., etc. All these, and more, came knocking for admission. We
started with a paltry $250,000 in the 'rock pile'. Before we started, it
jumped to $350,000—and as time went on landed in a pile nearer
$850,000. But we had more to show for that pile than anybody who ever
built a similar industrial administration building of the first rank. The
entire thing thoroughly fireproof, air-conditioned, floor-heated (gravity
heat), and, including appropriate furnishings designed by the architect,
was built for about seventy-eight cents per cubic foot. And observe—
although a building is not radio, it was the psychological world-moment
for the more serious sort of thing we now did. Hib knew it (his 'hunch')
and he took the gaff with only a stab or two at his architect now and then
just for luck.

But no stabs in the back.

Jack kicked around a little—managerially. But why not? Some kicking
was a necessary feature owing to the great simplicity of that building.

Also, to preserve the great simplicity, I made some 132 trips by motor
car from Taliesin to Racine (a distance of 165 miles) to superintend the
structure, and over a period of two years in all weathers, just to get it
built the way I thought it should be built—carrying on until, towards the
end, pneumonia had me down to interrupt proceedings. More patience
had to be added to infinite patiences that great simplicity had required up
to that time. Perhaps only Ben, the Wiltscheck, our builder, can quite
realize how much was required. Ben was no contractor's contractor. He
was educated at Penn for an architect. Failing to satisfy himself with his
own designs he went out to build buildings for others. Ben was 'au fait'.
He went about everywhere in Racine society on equal terms with his
employers. But more to the point, he was a careful builder—well aware
of the great importance of keeping the architect right there on the job.
Not one move would Ben make until the detailed drawings of the original
drawings were detailed some more. And so far as I know, for once in a way
the Builder did not try to destroy the Architect. There was real co-operation, confidence in each other's ability all around, and all the time. Without that circumstance no such building as that modern thoroughbred
could ever have been built at all. It was, and altogether, such a Simplicity
as is never found in stock. It was in no sense and nowhere—shop.

When the building was opened the world seemed to have been waiting
for the event because it was there outside trying to get in to see it. When
finally it did get in, reams of newspaper copy began to pour from the
press, and such talk!

Everyone who saw the building tried to describe it. 'It is like a woman
swimming naked in a stream. Cool, gliding, musical in movement and in
manner. The inside of an office building like a woman swimming naked
in a stream? Yes, that's right.' (Leading feature article: *Life Magazine*,
May 1938.)

Bill Connolley, competent 'man on the job' for the advertising of the S. C. Johnson Co., calculated that (with no help from him at all) two or more millions of dollars could not have bought the front pages in newspapers and top-notch magazines which the building had attracted to itself.

And, the movie 'shorts' took it up and carried on.

The radio came chiming in. Meanwhile the stream of visitors from all over the world went on and continues to go on to this hour.

Why? Because of something in the universal air, that's why. It was high time to give our hungry American public something truly 'streamlined', so swift, sure of itself and clean for its purpose, clean as a hound's tooth —that *anybody* could see the virtue of this thing called Modern. Many liked it because it was not 'modernistic', but seemed to them like the original from which all the 'streamlining' they had ever seen might have come in the first place. As a matter of fact, the word streamlined had been first applied to buildings by the architect of this one.

It is a trifle hard to hit the bull's-eye *every* time *all* the while, and we expected certain minor troubles to develop. They did, but mostly as expected—annoying of course, even so. But they were remedied eventually, and also as designed. Nothing developed sufficiently important to mar the integrity of the building as a whole which was lengthwise, crosswise, and in cross section an Experiment in design and construction. An experiment though, and mind you, in behalf of the S. C. Johnson and Son's Company. All the time. There is an important difference between the merely 'experimental' and a genuine experiment. The one may be a feeling for novelty. The other is rationally based upon experience seeking a better way.

The Wisconsin Industrial Commission vexed us for some time, wouldn't say yes and didn't say no to the plans. But I've learned since from contacts with other building commissions in other states (let's say Missouri for one) how sensible and considerate that Wisconsin Commission under Mr. Wrabetz et al. was. This was partly, I believe, because Hib himself stood up at the board meeting beside me and squarely told that commission that he wanted that building that way and he was damn well prepared to stand back of it to the limit. Finally, if we would agree to make tests as the building proceeded, should the commission require them, we were told to go ahead. We did make several important tests. We made them with such startling and gratifying success that new precedents for reinforced concrete construction were established. The Industrial Commission raised no further objection.

When I went to the Tokio Building Commission (1914) for a permit to build the international Imperial Hotel earthquake-proof, the Japanese authorities enacted a scene somewhat similar. They couldn't say yes and didn't say no because they had never seen anything like the scheme proposed, but said—'Go ahead: we will watch you with the hope that you, world-famous architect [deferential bows both sides] may have something.

408

So we will follow carefully. Please proceed.' We did. And they followed. Very carefully, let me say.

There was never a permit to build the Imperial Hotel earthquake-proof. It was all a gigantic experiment in behalf of Japan by the *Kenchiku ho* of the Imperial Household—myself. An experiment not yet understood nor fully granted success by my own people, except with a grudge. The Japanese, however, were pleased with the results.

After all, it was their affair?

And there never was more than a conditional permit to build the unique Administration Building of Johnson's Wax; nor ever a permit to build the original textile block houses in California, nor the later board-and-brick Usonian Houses in seventeen different states. No. Nor—but we are talking about the building that Hib's 'hunch' set up life-size in his native Racine partly for the edification and amazement of the home town. But not so, too much.

Organic architecture designed this great building to be as inspiring a place to work in as any cathedral ever was in which to worship. It was meant to be a socio-architectural interpretation of modern business at its top and best.

The building was laid out upon a horizontal unit system twenty feet on centres both ways, rising into the air on a vertical unit system of three and a half inches: one especially large brick course. Glass was not used as bricks in this structure. Bricks were bricks. The building itself became—by way of long glass tubing—crystal where crystal either transparent or translucent was felt to be most appropriate. In order to make the structure monolithic the exterior enclosing wall material appeared inside wherever it was sensible for it to do so.

The main feature of construction was the simple repetition of slender hollow monolithic dedriform shafts or stems—the stems standing tip-toe in small brass shoes bedded at the floor level.

The great structure throughout is light and plastic—an open glass-filled rift is up there where the cornice might have been. Reinforcing used was mostly cold-drawn steel mesh—welded.

The entire steel-reinforced structure stands there earthquake-proof, fireproof, soundproof, and vermin-proof. Almost fool-proof but alas, no. Simplicity is never foolproof nor is it ever for fools.

Weight herein this building by way of a natural use of steel in tension, appears to lift and float in light and air; 'miraculous' light dendriforms standing up against the sky take on integral character as plastic units of a plastic building construction entire, *emphasizing* space instead of standing up in the way as mere inserts for support.

The main clerical work force was all correlated in one vast room, 228 by 228 feet. This great room, air-conditioned, besides the top lighting and rift for light at the cornice level, is daylit also by rifts in the brick walls. And the heating system of the main floor of the building is entirely beneath the floor slab. The structure is hermetically sealed and air-conditioned with this gravity heat.

The building complete, being destined to stand in unimpressive surroundings bounded by three ordinary village streets, we settled upon the main entrance as interior to the building lot; thus the motor car was provided for as a modern indispensable and with new hospitality. Ample parking facilities are under cover of this great domiculated spread of carport.

The main building itself in which the dendriform shafts are floated is set back from the street on three sides; a colourful band of planting dividing the main brick walls from the sidewalks, enlivening the dreary environment. Above, the carport, tile-paved, was to have become a playground for the workers.

The hemicycle—a cinema seating 250 for daytime lectures or entertainment, wired complete for sound, is placed at mezzanine level at the middle of the floor arrangment. An enclosed glass-roofed bridge spans and connects the officers' quarters in the penthouse to a tall wood-lined squash court rising high above the garage. President Herbert Johnson's private office, an office for his stenographer, and a private chemical laboratory ride at the apex of this penthouse; the officers, Jack Ramsey at their head, are built in on the same level (roof level) in each of the wings extending from it.

Below this penthouse arrangement of officers who, by way of the open court under the glass ceiling, have a view of the big workroom on the ground level, are the several hundred office workers sitting at especially devised desks on chairs that belong to the desks. Sub-heads of various departments function just above them in a low gallery, mezzanine to the big room where direct vision and prompt connection with the workers in the big room itself is had directly at convenient points by spiral iron stairways.

The few enclosures within the big workroom are low glass walls, screened by Aeroshades. Thus the plastic sense of the whole, most stimulating, is well preserved in various parts even to the uttermost detail.

The main toilet accommodations are located, conveniently, directly beneath the working staff and are directly reached by means of small circular iron stairs located at appropriate intervals.

The entire building operation, generally by way of cost-plus arrangements, was in the architect's hands, ably managed by Ben Wiltscheck, supervised by myself and superintended by the Taliesin Fellowship, mainly by Wesley Peters and Edgar Tafel.

To enumerate in detail or even catalogue the innovations to be found in this one building would require more time and patient attention on your part, and mine too, than either of us cares to give it. So let's say here that it is technically, and in the entire realm of the scientific art of Architecture, one of the world's remarkably successful structures. I like it. They like it. Let it go at that.

For once in a way, again an up-to-the-minute thoroughbred, daughter of the Larkin Building—1906—was born—1938—on provincial American soil. A great modern building completely furnished, planted complete in perfect keeping with the original idea of a more feminine building as a whole, was its sire, the masculine Larkin Building of Buffalo.

The legitimate offspring is now there to be seen. But, you can only see as much of the harmonious whole as your inner vision permits you to see.

And that will be however much your prescience of innate rhythm in building construction enables you to perceive. It takes a developed 'some one' to see the Johnson Administration Building altogether. That is, to see it *all*. But most folks see enough to delight them or make them envious. Or make them mad.

There is no escape from the building otherwise.

Hib's hunch not only worked out in advertising returns—it began to work out in terms of increased work and morale. Work and morale increased one-tenth to a third the first year the building was in use. The officials loved the place as much as the help did, and some of both of them said they hated to leave it to go home. Jack Ramsey (who had a fine new happy home) was one of these. But there were many others. And Hib must have felt something that way himself . . . because just as I had got out of bed with pneumonia, the idea of building a house of his own, to match it, grew up in his mind. One day he had taken me out to see the tract of prairie (a small lake running it length) that he owned by the big lake (Michigan), and had for years been keeping as a kind of wild-fowl preserve. Some days after we had walked about and talked about a house on that site and I had explained a zoned house to him, Hib brought me a little sketch plan he had himself pencilled of the general outlines of a house pretty much as his stands out there on the prairie now.

Just before I had come down with a devastating fever, Hib had been dining with us and, after dinner, I was demonstrating with a Victrola the essential lack of modern music as compared with Music—jumping up and down meantime to change the records. 'Man', he said, 'don't you know you waste a lot of energy that way when you might be resting?'

Shortly after this, an agent of the Capehart, Cushing, came out with instructions from Hib to measure the house for a complete three-station installation of that remarkable record changing and playing instrument. A superfine record player with a radio attachment just as the Scott is a superfine radio with a record-playing attachment. Hib put in the most complete installation I have ever seen. More complete than his own. He was like that sometimes—a 'hunch', you see?

I respect 'hunches' in others if they correspond with mine. This one—the little sketch made with T square and triangle—did. And soon the new house for the young bride Hib was to bring in to it was designed, laid out, and under way. He had mumbled something to me in a vague sort of way about 'cost', but I knew he didn't mean *me* to be too much interested in

411

that. That was *his* affair—after all. So I laid the house out on a scale befitting a young industrial prince of the Johnson line, who all his life long had had about everything he wanted. Now I intended he should want something finer than he had ever seen to want. What else than a house such as that one would be, could he buy with money or time that would yield him such large returns? This house I would build for him should be, definitely, 'capital' not only safe during this lifetime, but go on as true capital into the lives of his children and their children—a joy meantime and a distinction. A proof of quality. What more capital use to make of 'capital'? There were some arguments about that point later on. And some feeling about it. Not much though, because Hib is, after all, pretty much right.

Two youngsters—a charming girl and a nice boy were his own as a result of a former marriage and now his newly promised bride already had two boys of her own—hence the children's wing for four. Here was the high Wigwam (living room) under the mass of wild grape vinery at the centre shooting out four independent wings—one wing (a luxurious mezzanine), with a continuous balcony toward the great lake, for Hib and wife, and one on the ground floor for the four children—another wing on the ground for workscape and help, and another on the ground also for guests and motor cars.

We called the house 'Wingspread' because spread its wings it did. We set a cast bronze door plate into the wide stone slab of the doorsill with abstract wings upon it in low relief to signify the name.

This structure is of the common 'prairie-type' of the earlier years. A type proving itself to be a good one for a home in the climate around the Great Lakes. It is popularly known as brick veneer. Outside upper members are wide cypress plank, roofs tiled, floors of concrete, four-foot-square concrete-slab tiles over floor heating, here as in the Administration Building itself.

Thus 'Wingspread', unique Herbert Johnson prairie house near-by Racine became another zoning experiment which began in the articulation of the Coonley House at Riverside, built 1909, wherein Living Room, Dining Room, Kitchen, Family Sleeping Rooms, Guest Rooms, were separate units grouped together and connected by corridor.

The building is orientated so that sunlight falls in all rooms and the ground plan shows a completely logical expression of the Zoned House. (The first design for such a house was printed in the Taliesin Monograph, December 1934.)

At the centre of four zones forming a cross, a spacious wigwam of a Living Room stands. A tall central brick chimney stack with five fireplaces on four sides divides this roomy vertical central living space into four spaces for the various domestic functions: Entrance, Family Living, Library, and Dining Room. Extending from this greatly dignified, lofty central wigwam are the four wings. This extended zoned-wing-plan lies,

412

very much at home, quiet and integral with the prairie landscape which is, through it, made more significant and beautiful. In this case, especially, green growth will eventually claim its own; wild grapevines swinging pendent from the generously spreading trellises; extensive collateral gardens in bloom, extending beneath them, great adjoining masses of evergreens on two sides and one taller dense dark green mass set on a low mound in the middle of the entrance court—the single tall associate of this spreading dwelling on the prairie. Lake Michigan lies well off ahead but within the middle distance, and is seen over the wild-fowl pool which stretches away in the direction from just below the main terrace of the house. A charming foreground.

But this house, while resembling the Coonley House at Riverside, Illinois, is more bold, masculine, and direct in form and treatment. It is better executed in more permanent materials. The building has a heavy footing course of Kasota sandstone resting on rock ballast laid deep in broad trenches, has the best brickwork I have seen in my life, and the materials of construction and the workmanship throughout are everywhere substantial. Especially the woodwork and furniture by Gillen show fine craftsmanship. The house is architecturally furnished throughout in fairly good keeping with the quiet character established by the building.

Here, because Hib rubbed his lamp and parted from a little 'capital', another prairie house in 1938 came out of the blue to join the earlier ones of 1901-1910.

The young bride never lived to enter the furnished house. Out of the blue (the house three-fourths finished) one day an old workman on the house told me that a white dove we had seen frequenting the belvedere of the building—and in which both he and I were interested—had flown away and disappeared. The workman shook his head. A bad omen. 'The young mistress will never live in this house,' he said. And she too, as we soon learned, had passed away.

Hib's interest in our building went way down. It took good persuasion to get him interested in ever going on with the house again, although it was three-fourths done at the time this blow befell him. I, friend now as well as architect, did my best to represent to him what I thought his young wife would wish were she living. I felt sure she would want to see him finish what he had so happily begun with her; he needed, and now more than ever, a refuge such as that house would be for his children (they were fast growing up); he owed it, if not to himself, if not to her, then to Racine not to leave an empty shell of a house desecrating in desperation instead of nobly memorializing the memory of the wife he had lost. After a while I guess he began to see it something like that. Because we began the work on it again. We completed the house in every particular as planned for a wife and four children. Hib seemed to sigh with relief upon seeing actually realized the building—the house they had both worked on with me and of which he had fondly dreamed. The house, not yet a home, began

413

to justify the hopes we had from the first invested in it. It turned out a veritable thing of the Spirit: a true consort of the prairie. The 'last of the prairie houses' it shall be, so I thought—though I don't know why.

Should you ever see it, observe this fact . . . . the house did something remarkable to that site. The site was not stimulating before the house went up—but like developer poured over a negative, when you view the environment framed by the Architecture of the house from within, somehow, like magic—charm appears in the landscape and will be there wherever you look. The site seems to come alive.

Hib saw this. He felt it did express, in a finer sense, human feeling for the young wife lost than anything else he could have done. And soon he began to wake up really and actually live in the house. That house, more than anything else, I believe, brought Hib back again. But he might be unwilling to say so.

HERESY

A test is usually heresy. Ever since I can remember trying to build, tests have been going on under my supervision. A test of some kind was always either in sight or just around the corner, or was just evaporating results and another necessary. The supreme test, I suppose, was the earthquake's grasp of the Imperial Hotel. Leading up to that final test were foundation tests with borings and pig-iron leadings; slab tests; cantilever tests; tests of the value of continuity in heavy concrete beams; tests of stair-flights extending from floor slabs like extended arms. Not to mention plumbing tests, wiring tests. Test by test we arrived at the ultimate: the Imperial's flexible stability.

Nearly every structure I have built, large or small, required some test. Or many. Floor-heating tests; novel wall-construction tests; tests of new details of fenestration. Fireplace construction to be tested; roof construction in new materials to be tried out. Experiment following experiment. Frequently one test would require others. One experiment would lead to the next until the building process extending back over a period of forty-five years resembles the continuous test to which life itself subjects the architect himself.

It is true that nature never puts an idea of Form into practice, plants a new type or species, that she doesn't plant its natural enemy beside it. Nature has her equilibrium to maintain. She is continually maintaining her sense of proportion in all things. So when we make tests we are really trying to discover her *status quo* (for so it is), or, shall we say, the laws of proportion inherent in her own designs. Her equilibrium is an unknown quantity. It is probably God and we cannot reach God on a stepladder, which is what a Code is. And probably a very short and rickety one. But lightness and strength in erection, volume and weight at the ground levels, certain obvious limited patterns, we may see make sense before our eyes. There are many variations of this. Hence the test.

414

An architect comes closer to certain secrets of nature in his practice if he is master of organic FORM than most artists and scientists. Although in any final analysis we are all in the same category—making tests according to calculation or better than calculation—inspiration. Testing an inspiration? An expert in building construction would declare it an absurdity.

But that 'absurdity' has characterized my life.

An architect is either on the winning side grasping the laws of nature or on the losing side, the side of dead data, the *idée fixe*, the rules of the Code.

Most book data are the result of some testing process limited at the time by this and that circumstance. The most important of such data as we know serves only for a time, the length of time determined by how flexible the mind of the man and the formula were when the datum was fixed.

Flexibility is the only chance a mind or a datum has for survival.

Heraclitus was right.

So Codes are the mental limitations of short men, short of experience, short of imagination, short of courage, short of common sense.

A federal law should be enacted compelling the bureaucrats (those 'blessed by a little brief authority') to throw the codes out of the window every five years and enact new ones. Meanwhile (as it has already been done in England) a referendum should be set up as a Court of Appeals with better mental equipment than can be expected of the administration of codes. The referendum qualified to listen to ideas and give sanction to a likely experiment in structure—proper safeguards provided—in order that the data for the next five years may be a matter of record.

Inevitably a bureaucrat is a short man, however long his legs may be. His is a mind only fit for a bureau. He is undersize in most respects. Being a limb, or out on one as some member of an Authority, he worships Authority and since the Authority is all the strength he has he cherishes what little he has with all his strength.

Justice, truth, advancement—these are not his concern.

These are his enemies. He does not feel safe with any one, not to mention several, of these vital concerns of humanity.

Tradition—the formula—this it is that invests the bureaucrat with whatever power he has. Anything irregular inverts him. So he is one of the grains of sand in the sandbags that ballast the flying ship. And that is good enough for him. It's all he asks—'but little here below'. So never submit tests to a bureau or a crat. Both are in the position of the black crow who declared, after the other crow had tried hard to convince him that he could sing, 'No, it's no good. No, I don't like it. No. Youse is wastin' your time—'cause I wouldn't like it, even if it was good!'

Here is the fatal weakness of Democracy: the bureaucrat. The fatal weakness of Democracy does not lie in gangsterism or political chicanery or civil disobedience or anything like them. It lies in this dumb sheep-like submission to Authority, 'the drinking of the vanity of office'. And

415

especially this taking sanctuary in Authority by the bureaucrat. That is why Democracy sets Authority under Authority which is set under another Authority that can go to court and have the lower Authority reversed. But how long? O Lord, how long?

The Wisconsin Building Commission, Wrabetz et al., is a superior building commission as commissions go, but enforcing an antique code which they revise from time to time, calling in for the purpose those architects who abide by the Code and do not make trouble for the commission by experiments. Thus the body of the politic is safeguarded.

In the story of the Johnson Administration Building, I referred to a board meeting wherein Hib and I appeared to ask the commission to give us permission to proceed on a test basis. . . . One of those tests, not because it is more important than a dozen others but because it is recent, should be recounted here.

The Code allowed a maximum height of six feet for a concrete column nine inches in diameter no matter how constructed. Concrete is concrete, n'est-ce pas?

To go to the height of the dendriform shaft twenty-four feet high, spreading into a ceiling as was now contemplated, three feet in diameter would thus have to be the senseless size at the base—for a spacing of the shafts 24' 0" on centres—because two thousand five hundred pounds was code-limit on concrete. There would still be space to sit around in the building but little visibility. Hence the scene in the board room described in that story of the building.

My dendriform shaft was predicated on cold-drawn steel-mesh reinforcements, a steel integument embedded in the outer concrete flesh of the shaft—the circular membrane of steel thus becoming one with the flesh of concrete. The resultant strength was far and away beyond anything the usual rod-reinforcing, on which the code had been framed, could do. Also by agitating the concrete while pouring, it was quite easy to raise the code-limit from twenty-five hundred pounds to an actual twelve thousand at least.

A field test was decided upon and declared open: no objection to publicity. Having the expensive steel forms already made (we were that sure of success), we set up an exact duplicate dendriform out on the site in plain view, steadied it by slight diagonal wood braces and with a steam shovel we started dumping weighed gravel and cement bags on the extended flat floor of the top of the shaft. By the time the load appeared in sight not only the commission but the town and neighbouring press were observers. I sat with several apprentices looking on—woollen shawl on my shoulders (it was cold) but was soon walking around with Hib watching for the first telltales of failure. The crane kept swinging and dumping, swinging and dumping, until the sun went down. We were still there waiting for collapse. Long ago any requirement by the commission had been passed and doubled. Still the heap up there on top kept growing.

416

58. Entrance

KAUFMANN GUEST HOUSE. 1939

59. Rear view in summer

60. Front view

61. Side view

KATHERINE WINCKLER AND ALMA GOETSCH
HOUSE. 1939. USONIAN TYPE

62. Living room with
Usonian fireplace

The sight was incredible. The police had taken charge and roped the populace from the vicinity of that heroic slender stem, standing up there a graceful thing on tiptoe, standing straight and true, until sixty tons instead of the twelve tons required were on top of a shaft nine inches in diameter at the tip on the ground, and the concrete was only eight days of age. Slight cracks were now discernible in the upper part of the shaft where it splayed into the top. No more load could be put on without sliding off, so I gave the word to break it, wanting to see where failure would come first, although it was pretty evident where. A lateral push against the shaft brought the enormous overload tumbling to the ground causing a tremor felt to the surrounding streets. The shaft, still unbroken, lay on the ground. The spreading head had broken off. The commission, saying nothing, disappeared.

Their silence gave consent.

We went on with the building scheme that had been trembling in the balance but in the balance only up to twelve thousand pounds. The code was satisfied at that figure of twelve thousand. Yes, silence gave consent. We proceeded.

There were other tests. An amusing one wherein the circular metal elevator and its enclosure was challenged. Could anyone get the car released from the outside? None of us could. But a clever operator appeared from the bureau, who, having had much practice in picking elevator locks by a means no layman could have thought of, did finally succeed in starting it. So we lined the car with a transparent substitute for glass.

Such is the expert and his Bible—his good old Code.

No doubt the Code as a check for the jerry-builder has saved some lives where jerry-builders are the quarry. But it didn't save the new capitol wing at Madison where code sizes were as prescribed but superintendence was so faulty that I had my first lesson in building collapse while, in a former chapter, you have seen me hanging on to the iron fence looking in on Catastrophe.

THE CHURCH OF THE FUTURE

Here's to the good old Reverend Dr. Burris Jenkins of Kansas City, Missouri, and his young right bower in the parish, Joe Cleveland, both wholeheartedly trying to do the right thing by the future . . . but hampered by two good Kansas City lawyers working with a zealous (not to say jealous) building commission composed of one good 'old foundation man' and one ex-architect (his clerk) both strictly of Yesterday.

So far as these building-committee lawyers were concerned, they never cared much for that sort of thing anyway. But this church-of-the-future business was all right enough, if Dr. Burris wanted it, though everything must be strictly legal . . . as it is in heaven.

The church plans were hurriedly made because all were anxious to get a start. Money was insufficient for needs but everybody, even the lawyers, thought it likely to be easier after we got going. So we tried to get going in a hurry in order to get the necessary money. The building scheme had to be simple—a thousand seats at least, Sunday School rooms, a separate chapel, offices for the church officers, kitchens, and a clubroom or two. Such a programme as would have cost about five hundred thousand dollars under ordinary conditions. We had to get the congregation inside and fairly comfortable, if possible, for one hundred and fifty thousand. The scheme was therefore the simplest thing that we could imagine. Incredibly simple and economical. And, if I do say so myself, a damn good scheme. The plans called for a light *tenuous* steel frame, flexible in shape —a hex—*resting for the sake of flexibility on rock ballast foundations*. The same foundations as used in the Johnson building at Racine and all the other buildings I have built. The light steel skeleton was to be covered on each side by heavy paper strung with steel wires (Steeltex) securely wired to the skeleton and then the cement-gun process, so successful on the West Coast and used in K.C. itself to waterproof old brick buildings, was to be used to put a thin but sufficient shell over the insulating paper: the shells were $2\frac{1}{4}''$ apart, held by the wires to the paper like plastering on a lathed wall. This was to go on both inside and outside. Probably, I thought (and still think), the most advanced and desirable cheap building construction yet devised for any climate. Provided the Gunite is good. There was little or no detail involved except the open framework of two shallow sloping roofs over the two channels. All surfaces were plain. All corners were slightly rounded to aid the Gunite process. The structure depended upon its shape, graceful simplicity, and lightness of treatment for aesthetic effect. The cost figures came in finally, but only after no one in K.C. had confidence enough in the church and its architect, or faith in the novel technique, to bid.

I turned to Ben Wiltscheck in the circumstances (emergency), and in the midst of a turmoil such as conflicting interests and ideas can set up on a building built by lawyers and a building commission enforcing an antique code, Ben took on the main structure at about one hundred thirty-five thousand dollars, but leaving the chapel and the parking terraces and the block of Sunday School rooms to be built at a cost of about twenty-five thousand more. We all then felt sure that the twenty-five thousand would come in on top of the other forty thousand we needed, when the character of our effort was recognized.

We went after a building permit. Snag one. The newly elected commissioner himself said he was an old foundation man and I couldn't put anything like that foundation over on him.

'Never heard of pounded rock for foundations,' he said.

Said I, 'Look at the railroads of the country. Their heavy loads (moving too) have been on rock ballast for a hundred years.'

Said he, 'Nothing to do with Kansas City foundations; peculiar conditions in K.C. ground; cracks open in dry weather and walls settle.'

'But the thick rock ballast would be just the equalizer for a thing like that, wouldn't crack nor could it harmfully settle.'

'Oh, no! No! Not here in Kansas City. Nothing but concrete here. Only

418

concrete. Nothing but concrete footings can go underground in Kansas City.' This, unalterable, was a serious knockdown blow because there is a certain lateral come-and-go possible to the light superstructure in a hexagonal form when the light steel fabricated structure rests on coarse broken stone; in this case, particularly, a necessary flexibility that would be lost if the frame were fixed to solid concrete at the bottom. There is a contraction and expansion going on in solid footings that is not present in rock ballast. I protested and tried again and again with all I had, but the legal committee of disbelievers itself insisted that 'all should be perfectly legal'.

Well . . . the time to assert the rights of an owner to his own building had arrived. The essential scheme should have been rejected or accepted by all and sundry, right then and there, the building committee fired, and a new start made.

But Dr. Jenkins, Joe, and I wanted to save the thing and trusted to our ability to subsequently 'snatch victory from the jaws of defeat'. So I proposed, 'Allow us to go ahead and we will make any tests you require.' The lawyers hesitated, hemmed and hawed, deliberated and visited the commissioner, looked wise, and looked for compromise. They found the compromise by employing a local engineer (recommended by the commissioner himself) to design solid concrete foundations. I don't live in Kansas City and heard it only from some reporter who dug up the story.

Some eleven thousand dollars up on building costs.

Again—right then and there—I should have stopped the building where it was and have withdrawn from any connection with it whatever. The building was, henceforth, in the hands of the enemy. The fundamental condition of success of a rational experiment in behalf of the church was gone. The flexible hex-frame could not contract and expand in its own way, so cracks were sure to appear in the envelope. But I too am an optimist. I hated to 'abandon the child', hoping to find something if they did appear as expected, that would serve—perhaps another coat of Gunite after the first winter was over. It is always possible to build up the thickness of the shell indefinitely.

But no—the worst was far from over. Snag now after snag was set up. The building was soon no longer mine except in shape—the shape which had already lost some of its meaning. And 'the good foundation man', egged on by the inside K.C. engineer, began stiffening up the frame. Making the frame rigid where I wanted it to be and remain flexible.

Some fifteen thousand dollars more up on the building costs.

Ben Wiltscheck had a contract and had to build the building. Ben also thought that by making these concessions he could get by and save the thing somehow at the end in spite of all legal interference. But the lawyers intended to win the case.

We made tests but were warned there must be no publicity. The commissioner suspected and the engineer challenged the strength of the balcony. On the condition he made, that there should be 'no publicity', we made the tests with loads prescribed. There was no visible deflection anywhere.

The new floor construction next came under suspicion. Still specifying 'no publicity', the commissioner observed that test: twice the required load and no deflection whatever.

These proofs seemed to make 'Authority' thoroughly mad.

Of course, there was no way of testing the footings the building needed, except the hundred or so buildings that had been standing for generations.

But behind Ben now was no church and no architect. There was only the good old foundation man, his clerk, their stand-in, the local engineer (the blind leading the blind), and a pair of lawyers. The lawyers knew their law; masters of the profession, they were sure they could take care of anything when the time came, especially any contract they themselves made. They knew how to make them.

Now Kansas City is just about as near Taliesin as New York City, so far as accessibility goes. Had I been able to go down and live on the job, the wrecking crew might have been checked even then, if there had been a building committee less legal and more rational—faithful to the idea we started with. I offered to go down if that could be set up. Dr. Burris Jenkins had himself fallen very ill. He was a sick man. Joe, succeeding to the chief ministry, did all he could and did (eventually) do so much that he resigned, which is probably the same thing as being fired.

Dr. Burris himself, now somewhat better, was told to 'keep out' and leave the affair to the lawyers. He did. Worn out, I guess. The usual game was being played. It looked as bad for Ben as it had for me.

The Church of the Future was now a row between lawyers and the K.C. building commission, their local experts, the various others that the lawyers had called in over Wiltscheck's head, and Ben Wiltscheck himself. There had been no reference by them to me in the matter since the essential foundation scheme was wrecked and the frame 'strengthened', 'made safe', as the K.C. engineer said. I don't know what superiority over Wisconsin-licensed engineers (we had two of the very best beside myself) the Missouri engineer (unlicensed) could have except that he was down there in Kansas City working.

I have always known that lawyers make the poorest builders in the world. They are narrow-minded dealers in and for and with the strictures of the law. And they are poor sports because they are men of opinion.

If only we could have had several forthright practical American business men as we did in Racine to back up the novel experiment in housing a deserving congregation for much less than half the usual cost of the ordinary thing, housing it with comfort, beauty, and distinction, success would have been ours. It will be yet.

Meantime . . . well . . . Joe Cleveland, elevated to the ministry by Dr. Burris Jenkins himself, wants a job. I'll never get another building to build in Kansas City, which is less than no matter at all. But Ben is out about twenty thousand he could ill afford to lose, and just because he stuck his head out. And I am now 'ex-architect'. Kansas City, Missouri, just missed something that might have been a jewel in the town; it will now resemble a busted pearl in a swine's snout, until finally after all the

420

messing around is over, we do go down there ourselves to take what will be left of the whited sepulchre and make it what it was intended to be before it went all-out 'legal'.

The lawyers meantime are busy. They have their hands full of the sort of thing that makes them what lawyers are. But some lawyers I know are pretty decent fellows at that. Out of court.

There must be something, too, about 'this here Missouri' that makes Kansas City what it is today—Yesterday . . . no place for the Church of the Future.

BREAKFAST AT TALIESIN

There may be other breaks for a fast, but none so far as I know, like a Taliesin breakfast on any one of Taliesin's seven terraces, the one where the view is best or the sun is right, or the one where the wind is most agreeable, or where all are right together. Light early supper, early to bed the night before, are the conditions on which digestion is willing and happy to break-fast. Push the button of the Capehart as you pass? Haydn pouring from the built-in speaker over the hill garden this morning. But, fresh as dew themselves, the breezes are blowing the scent of sloping clover fields over our way, birds in the tree-tops below are singing as though delirious with joy, perhaps nothing at all is best. Yes, it is. Let's sit down (ourselves fresh) in comfort to a wide well-spread tastefully set low table, ample cloth of Chinese linen fancifully coloured and great big napkins to match, big enough to tuck into the neckband and spread all over whatever it is you wear for breakfast. This morning Alec (Woollcott) wears dark-blue silk pyjamas, belted coat to match, large white polka dots the size of a dime sprinkled all over his person.

The table decorations this morning? By Herbert. Unusually good. A big shallow glass platter brimming with clear water: anemones nestling in a big branch of fern brake held up by a curious yellow moss-covered stone set in the water.

Ribbons of the white mist into which the morning sun has already resolved the dew are lifting, going up to ride as clouds in the blue while the shadows are still wide and long.

Alec is just looking, not talking.

Cowbells are tinkling, gently dinning away on the meadow running up the valley by the stream. White peacocks gather nearby on the roofs and Yoo-hoo-oo!

Olgivanna, picturesque in a big hat tied on her head with strings under her chin, to shut out the sun which was shining in everybody else's eyes, presides over all. Iovanna fluffs out, coming on the breeze already dressed for school and sits down opposite. Because both of them like Alec, Svetlana, wearing bright slacks, bright ribbons perched in splendid dark blowing hair, and Wes come in for this occasion.

Me? Oh, I have no raw linen. Loose wide-sleeved jacket buttoned at the wrist, wide baggy trousers tied close around the ankles. Carl (Sandburg)

421

once visited me when he was working on his 'Lincoln'. I dressed him up in similar style. Lloyd Lewis was there and got a good 'shot' of us in the artistic semi-elegant négligé. For years Carl has been trying to buy that picture from Lloyd for fear someone will see it! Well, anyway, that is what I have on.

Everybody wishes everybody an affectionate 'good morning' as we finally draw up to the table.

First, we all look around and listen, then look again.

A few fresh strawberry leaves laid over them, here comes a heap of noble Taliesin strawberries in a big old Chinese Celadon bowl. The stains of the strawberries are lovely on its cool pale-green surface. Just picked the berries in the garden there below, dew on them, still. With Devonshire cream perhaps?

Then some real Scotch oatmeal (Elam's)—four hours in a double boiler —with Guernsey cream? Fresh eggs with *baked* bacon—ours, too: the eggs still warm from the nest. Will you have yours, white or dark, in the original package?

And here comes Billy with a wide old Celadon platter of fine asparagus freshly cut—he has just this moment gathered the asparagus. You cannot fail to observe how the colour of asparagus agrees with Celadon. Beside each place is a tall glass of our fresh Guernsey milk—from the herd tinkling there on the green meadow. Cold? No? All right then, hot. Comb honey? Our own: Hans is a good bee man. As the honey is passed somebody tells the story of Wilde's important urban lady who asked for some more of 'that extremely delicious honey' to be passed, with the remark,
 Do you know! Were I too, to live in the country, I assure you that I too, should keep a bee!'

Alec looks at me more in sorrow than in anger and I feel suitably ashamed.

Novel jams and preserves of many novel sorts Olgivanna now presses upon us. She made them all herself. What colour! And what flavour! We are served by ourselves, ourselves this morning meaning Kenn, Billy, and Kay of the Fellowship.

Naturally, steaming coffee is right there on the service table. And crisp original-Graham toast (one side only, please) comes from the toaster tended by Olgivanna.

After that awful break concerning the bee has somewhat evaporated, we sit back and just enjoy being there forgiving each other everything. Eating meanwhile with appetite . . . everybody all right.

Our fast is completely broken.

There is no 'Let us then be up and doing' for us this morning.

As he begins to do the talking, Alec continues to sit with his hand on the handle of a special coffee pot we have set beside him (no, the pot is not Celadon nor is it distinguished) pouring out a fresh cup, now and then. (I could hardly get a word in edgewise for three or four days even if I had wanted to.) But I always prefer to listen to him. He is charming us one and all by the play of his wit—waving a fly away now and then as though he were waving a flag.

Alec is not like 'the man who came to dinner' when he comes to breakfast. I can tell you that. I look at his fine square face, firm shapely chin—a distinguished mature man of a becoming age, whatever it is or ever will be . . . something very fine in Alec's face due to innate kindness of heart. His is a really warm heart-beat generosity possessed by few men I've met. I watch him now seeing that steaming coffee-bowl carrying cargo to his liver between sallies. We are enjoying the real conversation of a friend among friends, Alec making brilliant marvellous things out of commonplaces as other less gifted people make marvellous things commonplace. And we sit there oblivious of Time until it is time for lunch.

I have misgivings about such 'goings on' with coffee. No physical weakling myself, perhaps because I had my first cup when I was fifty-five, I can't drink one without some slight dizziness, liver spots or something or other an hour or so afterward. So I remonstrate with Alec a little. No effect.

Lieber Meister used to come down to breakfast, pound the table for coffee, his hand shaking, and be morose until he got it. Then with it, soon pleasant, expansive as a blooming rose. Different, certainly, but good too, when in his coffee.

I've never seen a match for Alec. He makes me feel as though I had just come down from way-back yonder on a load of poles when I listen to him . . . damn him! You know.

'The Man Who Came to Dinner' can't compare with The Man Who Came to Breakfast. He too is wit, a colourful cynic, a man of the world but a bitter smart Alec. The man who came to breakfast is a true friend, an aesthetic enthusiast, lover of fine things, one who well knows why he loves them—a man of rare discrimination as well as master of a wit seldom at its end. The kindest, most generous man I know is Alec. And I know many kind and gentle men. Put that beside 'The Man Who Came to Dinner' which you've probably seen. Try to figure it out.

If you get Alec straight he will be both and probably as many more in between as there are occasions. No Chameleon either. He just takes circumstances as a diamond takes light—that's all. And flashes.

I like the distinguished kindly man who came to breakfast. So do we one and all. I speak for the Fellowship too.

Olgivanna put into his hands as he departed a simple little matt-glass Madonna because he admired it so much: a *chef d'œuvre* a little taller than an overcoat pocket is deep. And because I don't know why Alec should have a Madonna or what he might do with one I tried to be a little jealous and failed. Somehow you can't do that to Alec.

THE USONIAN HOUSE I

The house of moderate cost is not only America's major architectural problem but the problem most difficult for her major achitects. As for me,

423

I would rather solve it with satisfaction to myself and Usonia, than build anything I can think of at the moment except the modern theatre now needed by the legitimate drama unless the stage is to be done to death by 'the movies'. In our country the chief obstacle to any real solution of the moderate-cost house problem is the fact that our people do not really know how to live. They imagine their idiosyncrasies to be their 'tastes', their prejudices to be their predilections, and their ignorance to be virtue— where any beauty of living is concerned.

To be more specific, a small house on the side street might have charm if it didn't ape the big house on the Avenue, just as the Usonian village itself might have a great charm if it didn't ape the big town. Likewise, Marybud on the old farm, a jewel hanging from the tip of her pretty nose on a cold, cold day, might be charming in clothes befitting her state and her work, but is only silly in the Sears-Roebuck finery that imitates the clothes of her city sisters who imitate Hollywood stars: lipstick, rouge, high heels, silk stockings, bell skirt, cock-eyed hat, and all. Exactly that kind of 'monkey-fied' business is the obstacle to architectural achievement in our U.S.A. This provincial 'culture-lag' in favour of the leg which does not allow the person, thing, or thought to be simple and naturally itself. It is the real obstacle to a genuine Usonian culture.

I am certain that any approach to the new house needed by indigenous culture—why worry about the house wanted by provincial 'tasteful' ignorance!—is fundamentally different. That house must be a pattern for more simplified and, at the same time, more gracious living: necessarily new, but suitable to living conditions as they might so well be in this country we live in today.

This need of a house of moderate cost must sometime face not only expedients but Reality. Why not face it now? The expedient houses built by the million, which journals propagate, and government builds, do no such thing.

To me such houses are stupid makeshifts, putting on some style or other, really having no integrity. Style *is* important. *A* style is not. There is all the difference when we work *with* style and not for *a* style.

I have insisted on that point for forty-five years.

Notwithstanding all efforts to improve the product, the American 'small house' problem is still a pressing, needy, hungry, confused issue. But where is a better thing to come from while Authority has pitched into perpetuating the old stupidities? I do not believe the needed house can come from current education, or from big business. It isn't coming by way of smart advertising experts either. Or professional streamliners. It is only super-common-sense that can take us along the road to the better thing in building.

What would be really sensible in this matter of the modest dwelling for our time and place? Let's see how far the Herbert Jacobs house at Madison, Wisconsin, is a sensible house. This house for a young journalist, his wife, and small daughter, is now under roof. Cost: Fifty-five hundred

424

dollars, including architect's fee of four hundred and fifty. Contract let to P. B. Grove.

To give the small Jacobs family the benefit of the advantages of the era in which they live, many simplifications must take place. Mr. and Mrs. Jacobs must themselves see life in somewhat simplified terms. What are essentials in their case, a typical case? It is not only necessary to get rid of all unnecessary complications in construction, necessary to use work in the mill to good advantage, necessary to eliminate so far as possible, field labour which is always expensive: it is necessary to consolidate and simplify the three appurtenance systems—heating, lighting, and sanitation. At least this must be our economy if we are to achieve the sense of spaciousness and vista we desire in order to liberate the people living in the house. And it would be ideal to complete the building in one operation as it goes along. Inside and outside should be complete in one operation. The house finished inside as it is completed outside. There should be no complicated roofs.

Every time a hip or a valley or a dormer window is allowed to ruffle a roof the life of the building is threatened.

The way the windows are used is naturally a most useful resource to achieve the new characteristic sense of space. All this fenestration can be made ready at the factory and set up as the walls. But there is no longer sense of speaking of doors and windows. These walls are largely a system of fenestration having its own part in the building scheme—the system being as much a part of the design as eyes are part of the face.

Now what can be eliminated? These:

1. Visible roofs are expensive and unnecessary.
2. A garage is no longer necessary as cars are made. A carport will do, with liberal overhead shelter and walls on two sides. Detroit still has the livery-stable mind. It believes that the car is a horse and must be stabled.
3. The old-fashioned basement, except for a fuel and heater space, was always a plague spot. A steam-warmed concrete mat four inches thick laid directly on the ground over gravel filling, the walls set upon that, is better.
4. Interior 'trim' is no longer necessary.
5. We need no radiators, no light fixtures. We will heat the house the 'hypocaust' way—in or between the floors. We can make the wiring itself be the light fixture, throwing light upon and down the ceiling. Light will thus be indirect, except for a few outlets for floor lamps.
6. Furniture, pictures and bric-à-brac are unnecessary because the walls can be made to include them or *be* them.
7. No painting at all. Wood best preserves itself. A coating of clear resinous oil would be enough. Only the floor mat of concrete squares needs waxing.
8. No plastering in the building.
9. No gutters, no downspouts.

To assist in general planning, what must or may we use in our new construction? In this case five materials: wood, brick, cement, paper, glass. To simplify fabrication we must use our horizontal-unit system in construction. We must also use a vertical-unit system which will be the widths of the boards and batten-bands themselves, interlocking with the brick courses. Although it is getting to be a luxury material, the walls will be wood board-walls the same inside as outside—three thicknesses of boards with paper placed between them, the boards fastened together with screws. These slab-walls of boards—a kind of plywood construction on a large scale can be high in insulating value, vermin-proof, and practically fireproof. These walls like the fenestration may be prefabricated on the floor, with any degree of insulation we can afford, and raised into place, or they may be made at the mill and shipped to the site in sections. The roof can be built first on props and these walls shoved into place under them.

The appurtenance systems, to avoid cutting and complications, must be an organic part of construction but independent of the walls. Yes, we must have polished plate glass. It is one of the things we have at hand to gratify the designer of the truly modern house and bless its occupants.

The roof framing in this instance is laminated of three 2 × 4's in depth easily making the three offsets seen outside in the eaves of the roof, and enabling the roof span of 2 × 12″ to be sufficiently pitched without the expense of 'building up' the pitches. The middle offset may be left open at the eaves and fitted with flaps used to ventilate the roof spaces in summer. These 2 × 4's sheathed and insulated, then covered with a good asphalt roof, are the top of the house, shelter gratifying to the sense of shelter because of the generous eaves.

All this is in hand—no, it is in mind, as we plan the disposition of the rooms.

What must we consider essential now? We have a corner lot—say, an acre or two—with a south and west exposure? We will have a good garden. The house is planned to wrap around two sides of this garden.

1. We must have as big a living room with as much vista and garden coming in as we can afford, with a fireplace in it, and open bookshelves, a dining table in the alcove, benches, and living-room tables built in; a quiet rug on the floor.

2. Convenient cooking and dining space adjacent to if not a part of the living room. This space may be set away from the outside walls within the living area to make work easy. This is the new thought concerning a kitchen—to take it away from outside walls and let it turn up into overhead space within the chimney, thus connection to dining space is made immediate without unpleasant features and no outside wall space lost to the principal rooms. A natural current of air is thus set up toward the kitchen as toward a chimney, no cooking odours escaping back into the house. There are steps leading down from this space to a small cellar below for heater, fuel, and laundry, although no basement at all is necessary

if the plan should be so made. The bathroom is usually next so that plumbing features of heating kitchen and bath may be economically combined.

3. In this case (two bedrooms and a workshop which may become a future bedroom) the single bathroom for the sake of privacy is not immediately connected to any single bedroom. Bathrooms opening directly into a bedroom occupied by more than one person or two bedrooms opening into a single bathroom have been badly overdone. We will have as much garden and space in all these space appropriations as our money allows after we have simplified construction by way of the technique we have tried out.

A modest house, this Usonian house, a dwelling place that has no feeling at all for the 'grand' except as the house extends itself in the flat parallel to the ground. It will be a companion to the horizon. With floor-heating that kind of extension on the ground can hardly go too far for comfort or beauty of proportion, provided it does not cost too much in upkeep. As a matter of course a home like this is an architect's creation. It is not a builder's nor an amateur's effort. There is considerable risk in exposing the scheme to imitation or emulation.

This is true because a house of this type could not be well built and achieve its design except as an architect oversees the building.

And the building would fail of proper effect unless the furnishing and planting were all done by advice of the architect.

Thus briefly these few descriptive paragraphs instead of a floor plan may help to indicate how stuffy and stifling the little colonial hot-boxes, hallowed by government or not, really are where Usonian family life is concerned. You might easily put two of them, each costing more, into the living space of this one and not go much outside the walls. Here is a moderate-cost brick-and-wood house that by our own new technology has been greatly extended both in scale and comfort: a single house suited to prefabrication because the factory can go to the house.

Imagine how the costs would come down were the technique a familiar matter or if many houses were to be executed at one time—probably down to forty-five hundred dollars, according to number built and location.

There is a freedom of movement, and a privacy too, afforded by the general arrangement here that is unknown to the current 'boxment'. Let us say nothing about beauty. Beauty is an ambiguous term concerning an affair of taste in the provinces of which our big cities are the largest.

But I think a cultured American, we say Usonian, housewife will look well in it. The now inevitable car will seem a part of it.

Where does the garden leave off and the house begin? Where the garden begins and the house leaves off.

Withal, this Usonian dwelling seems a thing loving the ground with the new sense of space, light, and freedom—to which our U.S.A. is entitled.

427

THE USONIAN HOUSE II

We have built some twenty-seven of them now in seventeen different states. Building costs in general in the U.S.A. were rising and are rising still. We find that seventy-five hundred dollars is about the sum needed to do what the Jacobs bought for fifty-five hundred. The Usonian house would have cost from seventy-five hundred up to ten, twelve, and in some certain extensive programmes, fifteen, sixteen, and on up to twenty thousand dollars. We have built several extended in every way that cost more.

The houses cost, I should say, one-third more to build than when we started to build them in 1938. But this holds true—any comparison with the 'regular' houses around them shows that they are more for the money physically for the sums they cost than the 'regulars'. Their freedom, distinction, and individuality are not a feature of that cost except as it does by elimination put the expenditure where it liberates the occupant in a new spaciousness. A new freedom.

It is true, however, that no man can have the liberation one of these houses affords with liberal outside views on three sides becoming a part of the interior, without incurring extra fuel—say twenty per cent. more. Double windows cut this down—but also cost money.

GRAVITY HEAT

Concerning floor heating. Heated air naturally rises. We call it gravity heat because the pipes filled with steam or hot water are all in a rock ballast bed beneath the concrete floor—we call the ballast with concrete top, the floor mat. If the floor is above the ground it is made of two-inch-square wood strips spaced 3′ 8″ apart. The heating pipes are in that case set between the floor joists.

It came to me in this way: in Japan to commence building the new Imperial Hotel, winter of 1914, we were invited to dine with Baron Okura, one of my patrons. It is desperately cold in Tokio in winter—a damp clammy cold that almost never amounts to freezing or frost—but it is harder to keep warm there than anywhere else I have been, unless in Italy. The universal heater is the *hibachi*—a round vessel sitting on the floor filled with white ashes, several sticks of charcoal thrust down into the ashes all but a few inches. This projecting charcoal is lighted and glows—incandescent. Everyone sits around the *hibachi*, every now and then stretching out the hand over it for a moment—closing the hand as though grasping at something. The result is very unsatisfactory. To us. I marvelled at Japanese fortitude until I caught sight of the typical underwear—heavy woollens, long sleeves, long legs, which they wear beneath the series of padded flowing kimono. But as they are acclimated and toughened to this native condition they suffer far less than we do.

Well, although we knew we should shiver, we accepted the invitation to dine at Baron Okuro's Tokio house—he had a number of houses scattered around the Empire. As expected, the dining room was so cold that I couldn't eat—pretending to eat only and for some nineteen courses. After dinner the Baron led the way below to the 'Korean room', as it was called. This room was about eleven by fifteen, ceiling seven feet, I should say. A red-felt drugget covered the floor mats. The walls were severely plain, a soft pale yellow in colour. We knelt there for conversation and Turkish coffee.

The climate seemed to have changed. No, it wasn't the coffee; it was Spring. We were soon warm and happy again—kneeling there on the floor, an indescribable warmth. No heating was visible nor was it felt directly as such. It was really a matter *not of heating at all* but an affair of *climate*.

The Harvard graduate who interpreted for the Baron explained: the Korean room meant a room heated under the floor. The heat of a fire outside at one corner of the floor drawn back and forth underneath the floor in and between tile ducts, the floor forming the top of the flues (or ducts) made by the partitions, the smoke and heat going up and out of a tall chimney at the corner opposite the corner where the fire was burning.

The indescribable comfort of being warmed from below was a discovery.

I immediately arranged for electric heating elements beneath the bathrooms in the Imperial Hotel—dropping the ceiling of the bathrooms to create a space beneath each in which to generate the heat. The tile floor and built-in tile baths were thus always warm. It was pleasant to go in one's bare feet into the bath. This experiment was a success. All ugly electric heat fixtures (dangerous too in a bathroom) were eliminated. I've always hated fixtures—radiators especially. Here was the complete opportunity to digest all that paraphernalia in the building—creating not a heated interior but creating climate—healthful, dustless, serene. And also, the presence of heat thus integral and beneath makes lower temperatures desirable. Sixty-five degrees seems for normal human beings sufficient. But neighbours coming in from super-heated houses would feel the cold at first. It is true that a natural climate is generated instead of an artificial forced condition—the natural condition much more healthful, as a matter of course.

I determined to try it out at home at the first opportunity. That opportunity seemed to be the Nakoma Country Club but that Indianesque affair stayed in the form of a beautiful plan.

Then came the Johnson Administration Building. Just the thing for that and we proceeded with the installation, but all the professional heating contractors except one (Westerlin and Campbell) scoffed, refusing to have anything to do with the idea. But as chance had it, the little Jacobs House turned up meantime and was completed before that greater venture got into operation.

So the Jacobs House was the first installation to go into effect. There was great excitement and curiosity on the part of 'the profession'. Crane Company officials came in, dove beneath the rugs, put their hands on the concrete in places remote from the heater, got up and looked at one another as though they had seen a ghost. My God! It works. Where were radiators now?

As usual.

Articles on 'radiant heat' began to appear in testimonial journals. But it was in no sense 'radiant heat' or panel heating or any of the things they called it that I was now interested in. It was simply *gravity heat*—heat coming up from beneath as naturally as heat rises.

Some thirty or more Usonian buildings now have floor heating. We have had to learn to proportion the heat correctly for varying climates and conditions. We have accumulated some data that is useful.

There is no other 'ideal' heat. Not even the heat of the sun.

THE UNKIND FIREPLACE

Lloyd (Lewis) is not only my own client after my own heart but he is one of my warmest and most faithfully insulting and insulted of friends. Long ago when I was down getting a worm's-eye view of society and Lloyd was a rising young 'publicity man' I engaged him to keep me out of the newspapers. He lasted a little less than three months. Then I paid him off and fired him for cause. The thing couldn't be done. He blamed me. But why blame me for my own fault?

Now his turn. He employed me to build him a house. He was a hard client. But not hard enough.

Having been there myself, often, I knew it was so damp and hot out on the prairie by the Des Plaines River that I set Lloyd well up off the ground to keep him high and dry in Spring, Fall, and Summer, his domicile winnowed by the wind . . . beneath! Thereby I exposed him in Winter not unnecessarily, but somewhat expensively. For the good of his health? Yes. But more for the good of his soul.

That type of house I believe ideal for a prairie site on low, damp land of that type. But no such proceeding could be called cheap.

So, up there off the ground, the beautiful river landscape coming in through three sides of the beautiful house and the woods showing beneath, it was hard to keep Lloyd warm in Winter. Kathryn, his wife, didn't cool off so readily as Lloyd did, but the sixty-five degrees we set for normal in a floor-heated Usonian house just didn't jibe by about twenty degrees with the Daily News office where Lloyd worked. And there was something the matter with the boiler pump there which we went down to fix or else the house would have risen to seventy-five. I am glad of an excuse to go to Lloyd's home anyway.

With usual bravado, pretending to make light of the thing, I thought of various ways of keeping the writer warm. I thought of wiring him to an electric pad inside his vest, allowing lots of lead wire so he could get around. But he waved the idea aside with contempt as a passing of the 'buck'. No patience at all, so we dropped that. Then I suggested we appeal to Secretary Knox to turn down the heat at the Daily News from eighty-five gradually to sixty-five so he could become acclimated. But Lloyd said the cold-blooded Daily-News-men couldn't get their stuff out at that temperature. Anyway he didn't want to be educated; he said he *was* educated. So we dropped that one too.

There was nothing left for me to do, since I had made the house part of the landscape and the landscape all around it came in on three sides (and underneath as well) but put on some double windows at Lloyd's expense just like the other folks do, in hiding around there in those fashionable woods. It was humiliating to get down thus into that clandestine society but we just had to go through with it.

Still in the same spirit of bravado, knowing that it is not at all in my own interest I now refer to the unkindest ordeal of all. The innocent very simple little fireplace I built for Lloyd to sit by when he writes just refuses to draw . . . too simple, I guess, to know how. We have built some three thousand fireplaces that do draw and a few that didn't know how at first but that do know how now. This particular one, though, Lloyd's own, doesn't know how yet. It will. We haven't given up.

Meantime, the curious neighbours are coming and parking their cars in the vicinity to watch and see if there is any smoke coming out of that part of the chimney top yet.

But was the house doing it to Lloyd or was Lloyd doing it to the house?

There it is . . . my beloved most intimate friend, the Historian, Drama Critic, Sports Editor, sitting there by that damn little fireplace, an especially unobtrusive little one I designed especially for him (brick) now so obtrusive you can hear the midget miles off by way of a sort of clinical or morbid interest on the part of the neighbours. Those who had undergone operations of their own?

Well, there it is, one out of three thousand, to speak truth, that did draw.

But I know what: should we fail to teach that fireplace the law and it still refuses, we can put a little fan, a kind of policeman, up there in the chimney with a switch down nearby where Lloyd sits so when he has enough fire he can turn it off and when he doesn't want smoke he can turn it on. In the whole galaxy (or is it phalanx) of three thousand fireplaces that little one (it is a sidekick of the successful big one) will thus be unique.

We'll let you know how everything turns out.

If we don't, the neighbours will.

Although if it turns out well they will have lost interest and dropped the whole matter.

The house made a gardener of Kathryn and a farmer-without-a-barn

431

out of Lloyd. You should see the boy around the place in those coveralls! He raises pigs.

There is a lot of the best in both of them built into their house because I knew and loved them so well, well enough to put it there. And they earned it and deserved the best I could do. They were up to it too. They loved the house.

Nevertheless the tragedy that befell so many of my clients happened to the Lloyd Lewises. They just liked to stay in their house and didn't care to go out anywhere unless they had to go.

Many of their friends, like the Alfred MacArthur's, for instance, just pretended to like the house because they like Lloyd. But I know some of the neighbour's didn't. But those who didn't were living in period houses dated way back when and furnished 'way back' to match.

In fact, the new dwelling made quite a stir in the society of that squeamish, highly stylish neck of the flat woods where Old Mexico, Norway, Ancient Sweden, and Camden village were in hiding behind the trees and to no good purpose, believe me.

Lloyd and Kathryn also furnished their exciting but very quiet Usonian House 'to match' and in such good Usonian style that even I like to go back to enjoy it myself. So does Marc (Connelly). So does Alec (Woollcott). Alec wrote a nice little letter to me about the house which was fine. And generous again.

Hoping Alec won't object, if Lloyd doesn't, here is the little letter which I cherish. I'll share it with you.

DEAR FRANK:

I hear you will be returning to Spring Green tomorrow so I am leaving promptly for Rochester, New York, but not before making a second visit to Libertyville to see that exhilarating house you have built for Lloyd Lewis. I was there last Sunday and went to confirm, by a second visit, the impression it made upon me. On the strength of that house alone I think I could go forth and preach afresh the gospel of Frank Lloyd Wright.

I see now more fully than ever before what effect the right house can have upon the person inside it. I told Lloyd that this one makes even a group of *his* friends look distinguished.

Lloyd, whom I admire and enjoy, never did anything so wise in his life. Just to be in that house uplifts the heart and refreshes the spirit. Most houses confine their occupants. Now I understand, where before I only dimly apprehended, that such a house as this can liberate the person who lives in it.

God bless you.

A. WOOLLCOTT.

April 15, 1941.

THE STAMPEDE

I refused to be stampeded by the wave of urbanism which swept the U.S.A., affecting such of our architects as Harvey Corbett, Lamb, Van

3. Outside sleeping porches for bedrooms connected to spacious halls and dining [rooms]

SYDNEY BAZETT HOUSE.
1940

64. Living room

Fireplace and dining table in
ng room

LLOYD LEWIS HOUSE. 1940

66. On the Illinois prairie, in deep woods. Living quarters entirely above ground. Cypress and common brick

67. Living room. No plastering in Usonian houses

Allen, Ray Hood, Bel Geddes, to name but a few, and so very many others: in fact, *all* of our commercial architects, both great and small. I could see little more in La Ville Radieuse, a greater New York by Hugh Ferris, or the soulless dreams of Bel Geddes et al. than exploitation of what was already an excess. The taller Chicago, the more-up-in-the-air San Francisco, etc., etc., were stupidities that bored me. Higher and higher up and up went the visionless race for skyscraper distinction. Skyscraperism by way of the urban man-eaters became, by way of false civic pride, popular and science monthlies, T-square and triangle clubs, a startling dream of a stunning future in which man himself as a feature of that future became a speck of no significance whatever. Except as he had brought to an apex his own abnegation in this splendiferous, hard-as-nails design for his own tomb.

The skyscraperist craze was due to our commercial vanity played upon by the false pride of Science itself in our day and hour. Or I should say the pride of false science.

The skyscraper itself, however, was the needed hallmark for modern commercial *Success*! And certain civic ambition *was* served by it. But really it was, at bottom, a mere unethical exploitation by the landlord of the profits of superconcentration. Socially a menace; architecturally, false. An exploit of the blind perverted mechanization of the period. The realtorific faith and fatalistic promotion that are the danger and the curse of this mechanistic age came to a death's head in the American skyscraper.

My faith went the other way.

I could see the very tall building only in the country. And Broadacre City, as agrarian as it was urban, was eventually the answer I found to this spectacular folly of prevalent commercial vanity. But the 'man-eater' had captured the imagination of American business men to such an extent that nearly every city of the country had its skyscraper in the worst possible spot in order to keep up and be anybody at all, at least be 'up to date', a 'going institution'. It was *on* the street but not *for* the street. Why the skyscraper so readily found so many false prophets among our American architects until their work could be seen standing up and out even on the Western prairies, under circumstances that made them similar to headstones in the cemeteries of those same places, is a question I could answer if it were really worth while.

Nevertheless and notwithstanding all consideration, ethical, aesthetic, economic, the skyscraper was serving as the banner of American commercial success: the success that was running the nation ragged. And down and out, Anno Domini 1929. America's cow, so to speak, was, by this ruse, taken indoors, spoonfed in a stanchion behind glass for advertising purposes only. The cow was steadily declining in health and productivity in consequence. All this when the national cow from any standpoint of health or real wealth should have been turned out to grass.

TO THE AMERICAN EAGLE

If you must have a skyscraper—he is a flyer. You will see his symbol on the back of most of our coins. And he is a square American. I sent him the following telegram: 'We knew you could fly straight, but now when everywhere is equivocation and cowardice you not only think straight but you dare speak straight.' You know whom I mean. And this goes for his brave little wife.

Honour, too, to the true American who put him into the service of his country for better or for worse. A staunch man, Henry Ford.

And the Usonian hat is off to John Haynes Holmes, a courageous hero fit for a sky pilot for the American Eagle.

ON TAKING EFFECTS FOR CAUSES

For forty-five years I have seen, intimately, the origin and growth of the movement in Architecture in which the work I have done myself has been a major factor. And now that I am principal witness to its inception and subsequent development (the inception and development of that movement which is now called Modern architecture for lack of a better name), I am still seeing History made, able to compare the making as seen by our very best critics with facts with which I am myself familiar. What I have seen makes me more than ever suspicious of the critical Historian. And this applies to any Historian of himself. Yes, I am suspicious of myself sometimes. Three Scotch highballs would call for suspicion.

I have seen the original work spread world-wide as an original impulse, take general form on the surface of the globe, and increase both here at home and abroad, but take superficial general form only—a superficial resemblance.

I have contributed to it new forms, again and again—hundreds—only to see them exploited, put forward wrong end to, and if not exactly upside down—then certainly inside out. I have seen since 1910 (I then for the first time visited Europe) the European reaction to this work I have myself done and I know full well its contemporary effects on other architects at home and especially abroad. I have seen the direct and creditable obvious implications of my work often credited to others as their own original idea or impulse, although I have never seen the obvious implications of the work of others credited to me—that were creditable to me.

I have seen the critical view of what were mere effects persistently, often wilfully, mistaken for causes. And vice versa. So equivocal and confusing, so far astern were they in their necessarily posterior view of the situation so far as origins are concerned that I usually read critical reviews of my own work in relation to the work of my contemporaries with grim amusement and appropriate profanity. Since I cannot read them backward. Reviews are so far out of focus and (designedly or not) so badly out of drawing as to put effects forward as causes and set causes back into the category of mere effects.

Such, I say, is the History of the so-called Modern Movement in Architecture, 'a designed miseducation' in general. Instead of growing more simple with time, the mere Effects multiply and further obscure actual Causes.

The gift of seeing a source rise, take its natural course and begin to flow—become a rivulet, then spread to a steady, broad flowing river in contemporaneous life—maintaining a just proportion in the seeing and the writing: well, it is simply not done.

Perhaps origins are entitled to the seclusion ensured by such confusion?

A nice provision of Nature?

But artificial subsequences are soon universally looked back upon as of primary consequences and there is no remedy.

Higher education is too much a cheap conceit hoping to thrive on mere Information but never really able to learn the net result, inferiority mistaking patriotism for Honour—sacrifice for Duty—money-punctilio for Character and a hectic noisy self-assertion for a good time.

No wonder this great provincial nation has such faith in propaganda.

Perhaps there is something in the English tongue that makes it an efficient prevaricator, a natural equivocal perverter of truth. Yet how could things have been very different in other and earlier times? How can we be sure that all History is not made in the same way: effects mistaken for causes, causes mistaken for effects?

I have seen the long arm of mere coincidence thus play strange tricks on the Critic. I have seen appearances too often be the only basis for his rationalizations after the fact, and all entirely beside the mark; no more than a pleasant fiction or an interesting speculation. Amusing as well as exasperating.

I could name a long list but would only open profitless controversy because the critic, *per se* as such, is no respecter of an original source of information. And certainly, even were he a competent judge, no respecter of an original source of inspiration. The thing is too simple for him on any such basis. There is not room enough for his own expansion. History 'à la mode' is, I suspect, mostly the personal view of reflections, a sort of mirage in a distorted mirror: the mind of the Historian. In our day true proportion in true perspective does not go with our temper or our pace *or* the effects we aim to produce. 'Speed', as Meredith says, 'is a kind of voracity.' And voracity is by nature none too particular. That for one thing. But, for another, out of our academic pigeon-holes we are swamped by the departmental mind. A mind which has its uses but a mind that sees in parts only and patches the parts together to make a case for its own sake, or for himself and, unfortunately, for the future.

Thus any sincere search for FORM is meantime betrayed to the inimical, and worse, perhaps confused from Generation to Generation.

We need something safe to build on. Of course, that something is the Truth. But the real seeker for Truth always gets back to simples—and

435

with rectitude, amplitude, and impartiality lets the shallow surf of erudite self-assertion break upon itself and roll back where it came from.

Bred to greatness and splendour by Art and Science, Architecture has cosmic destinies yet undreamed of . . . by the critics.

DR. FERDINAND THE FRIEND

Did you understand me to say that the Taliesin Fellowship had received very little help from anyone? I should take that back. It was in pre-Fellowship days, to be sure, but there probably would have been no Fellowship at all, but for the occupant of the Chair of History at Chicago University—by name, Ferdinand W. Schevill. In book four you have been told of the incorporation of Frank Lloyd Wright: how seven of my friends and clients contributed between them some fifty-seven thousand dollars to defend and get me back to work again and keep me working at Taliesin. They were Dr. Ferdinand Schevill, Harold McCormick, Mrs. Avery Coonley, Darwin D. Martin, the principal subscribers. Ben E. Page, Mrs. Jane Porter, and George Parker of Parker-pen contributed also.

Well—Dr. Ferdinand was president of that corporation (much against his will, I suspect), an enterprise wherein all of the fifty-seven thousand was lost in the national collapse of 1929–1930 except the objective for which the money was originally intended and subscribed. And that had a narrow escape.

The purpose was getting me back to work again where, protected, I could keep at it.

Ferdinand won't like this—but most of the corporation subscribers were 'rich', while he had only a good revenue from his historical textbooks and his salary as Historian at the University. Only recently I learned that he had not only subscribed his original quota, seventy-five hundred dollars, but had secretly put up five thousand more in the name of a friend who afterward became secretary of the corporation. And, moreover, to show you what use the man has for money, Ferdinand was a heavy subscriber to Sherwood Anderson's publishing venture—no more profitable, I venture to say, than my venture as an architect. Poor, great Sherwood! Ferdinand loved him more than he loved me, because Sherwood was so much more lovable.

It all goes to show, I think, that money is no stricture in the hands of a man like Ferdinand, the recluse. For he now lives and writes—retired—in a nice little home Woltersdorf built for him in the woods near Michigan City, Indiana, not far from the Carl (Sandburg), he who took a national hero to pieces, put him together again, and got rich. The true Carl was born to be a poet, a glorious failure, not a Success. 'Success' is very unbecoming to Carl.

That I didn't build that house for Ferdinand hurts me more, I guess, than Ferdinald helped me—because I would gladly have given the price of his subscription to have built it for him. But at that time I was far away, the going still uncertain, and Dr. Ferdinand was in a hurry and . . . well . . . you will probably have your own idea as to why he didn't want to take the trouble to go through the building operation with me. The circumstances I admit were not propitious. But do you know what? I believe Ferdinand didn't try to overcome the obstacles so that I might pay back to him at least that much because he is so essentially modest and retiring. He wanted a commonplace house. If I had built his house he might have been rooted out at all hours of the day by tourists and young students of architecture; he would have been exemplar, a showpiece. And having no mind to charge fifty cents for the privilege of viewing his abode, he chose the obscurity that went with Woltersdorf.

I am therefore jealous of Woltersdorf—and obscurity.

Obscurity is so much easier to live up to.

Had I followed in my own youthful, shy bent, I might have been allowed to build a house for my best friend.

They say the woman always pays. . . . Nonsense!

It is the fool who has allowed himself to be famous who pays—and pays.

THE MERRY WIVES OF TALIESIN

While I was alone at Taliesin after coming back from Japan, I had three wives, Sylva, Dione, and Nobu, looking in on me and keeping my spirits up. But they were not mine. They were the wives respectively of Werner (Moser), Richard (Neutra), and Kameki (Tsuchiura)—apprentices from Zurich, Vienna, and Tokio. But I can't imagine what I would have done without them at the time. On the rocks mentally, morally, emotionally.

We had music in the Living Room of Taliesin II evenings as we do now in the Living Room of Taliesin III. We occasionally drove about in the countryside. Werner (Werner played the violin) and Sylva had a fine little boy, Lorenz. I liked to hold Lorenz sometimes. I loved to have him around. He was a beautiful boy. Richard and Dione had a small son, too (named for me before leaving Vienna); Kameki and Nobu were only just married. Together with Major Will (Smith) they were all my immediate family. A happy one because they were all good to what was left of me at that bad time. The boys kept my mind on my work; the girls kept kind attentions and flowers all through the house. While they did make me feel less lonely, they only made me feel all the more need of 'the woman in my life' in these several pre-Olgivanna years. That Sylva-Werner baby especially made me long for a little soft one of my own at Taliesin. After all, what was Taliesin without young children? I guess the happiness of these young couples pushed me gently over the precipice of divorce and marriage to really live again.

The young women were three entirely differing individualities. Their young husbands were talented fellows, but not to be compared to their wives. Sylva was a true-hearted beauty; Dione was a genius, good to look

437

at, played her 'cello and sang while playing, doing both with real style: her own. And like most Europeans she played the best of music. Nobu was like a petite Japanese doll—when exquisitely dressed in her native costumes. Kameki was extremely competent, blinking intelligently behind his glasses. I look back upon that period of life at Taliesin as a quiet prelude before the storm. The outside storm broke when Olgivanna appeared upon the scene, which she did some time before they had all left, two of them going home (their terms were up), and one to the West Coast to 'get jobs'.

Werner had come to me with a letter from his distinguished father, Herr Professor Moser of Zurich, probably then the leading architect of Europe (Herr Professor Otto Wagner gone), asking me to take his son Werner as a pupil. I was happy to have the great architect's son. Kameki came by way of the Imperial Hotel to study with me. Richard had been knocking on my door from Vienna for admittance to Taliesin for several years, until at last, coming over anyway and finding me gone, he camped down with Holabird and Root a few months to wait until I came back. All are building reputations for themselves in, respectively, Switzerland, Japan, and California.

Autobiographers publish a good many letters, I believe. So here is one I have recently received from Herr Professor Moser's now distinguished son, Werner, himself author of many important interesting buildings in Switzerland.

DEAR MR. WRIGHT:

Since we have this terrible totalitarian war in Europe there is much uncertainty, much dissatisfaction and opportunism in our European architecture. There is a great need for a constructive, clear, direct mind. You can demonstrate in your life-long work one continuous line of architectural development, of course expressed in a big variety of applications of the one principle. Your work is a consolation today for every sensible architect, and an encouragement not to resign, because it shows to us the deeply rooted belief in everything which is positive today and the possibility to express it beautifully with the characteristic elements of this time.

(It is bad English but I hope you know what I mean.) I had a great pleasure to follow your new ideas from the recent publications in preparing a lecture about your work. There were many young students and a really spontaneous interest in all your achievements. It was a good thing, in comparing it to your designs, to show up the weaknesses in Swiss architecture. The lack of thoroughness, of coordination and imagination, and so on!

Of course, you never can replace an ingenious mind, you can only try to follow his basic idea! Sylva and I had many thoughts for you since we saw Olgivanna and you three years ago in Paris. I remember well your critical call referring to my designs: 'Werner, you need a good spanking!'

We would enjoy strongly to hear how you and your inner-Wright family are going through these times!

In your work we feel the never-tiring youth, which is over-shadowing everything done by the younger generation, in respect to inspiration and courage.

You certainly know how precarious the situation in Switzerland is. We are trying very hard to keep independence.

I would like to forward pictures of my works to get a severe critic from you! I hear of your big exhibition in New York and regret very much not to be able to see it. It is about time to have an exhibition like that in Switzerland!

Sylva and the three children are very well, we are for a few days in the winter sports to do ski-ing. Lorenz is almost my size and wants to be an architect. He will be through school in a few years and I should like him to be some day apprentice to you.

Very many thanks and sincere wishes for 1941 to Mrs. Wright and you from all the Mosers, especially from your Werner.

LULU BETT

Zona (Gale) once told me, 'I think the wisest thing you have ever done is to stay in the country.'

I pondered this. She might have meant so many things.

While Sylva, Dione, and Nobu were all the wives I had at Taliesin, I occasionally drove up the river to Portage with one or another of them to see Zona—in spite of the columnar village-palazzo she lived in. The old-colonial box (of course, she didn't build it) stood baldly and emptily forward on the street leaving a great lawn to the rear—a few nice trees on it —running to the Wisconsin River bank—the same sand-barred river that flows below the windows of Taliesin. My people all knew Zona. My Mother and my Aunts much admired her. While in Japan I read *Lulu Bett*. Straightway I made up my mind to know Zona Gale better when I got home; if not, to know the reason why. I had met her at Taliesin with Charlotte Perkins Gilman.

We used to come in to the house with our arms full of wild flowers gathered on the way up the river. Once or twice we were compelled to throw them all out on account of the violent reactions, none too kindly, of old Father Gale. Hay fever.

Sometimes I used to take Nobu and Kameki along in costume (Japanese umbrella too, you know) and pose them on the lawn by the river—making pictures for Zona. Zona and her friend (it might be the Lulu who wrote the play *Sun-up* or some other literary celebrity—they were always around) would get a little supper together for us.

Of course, I hated her environment as utterly unworthy of her (she was an exquisite thing, Wisconsin's Zona Gale). I hadn't met Olgivanna and I thought Taliesin would be a much more appropriate place for the author of *Lulu Bett*. But I had been spoiled, or something. Perhaps I had always expected the women to make love to me. I just didn't know how to make love to Zona Gale.

439

But she was always glad to see us, asking me to come, although she said she valued her Regency at the University of Wisconsin too much ever to be seen with me in public. (There were other reasons I guess, because it wasn't so very long before she married.) For any woman to be seen with me in public *was* pretty dangerous for the woman (not to mention dangerous to me). So I loved the Zona who wrote *Lulu Bett*. And after I knew her a little better I told Zona that I didn't believe she ever wrote the book, she was so unlike Lulu Bett, herself. But you couldn't quarrel with Zona. She was too complete and lovely in herself. She was like something exquisitely carved out of ivory.

I wonder, though, what she meant when she said 'the *wisest* thing you have ever done,' because it was no *wisdom* of mine that kept *me* in the country. No, it was something constitutional. My mother so deeply loved life in the Valley that I am sure I nursed at the Valley's breast when I nursed at hers.

Terrestrial beauty so grows on me as I grow up that the longer I live the more beautiful it becomes. A walk in our countryside when the shadows are lengthening is to look and drink a poignant draught—and look and drink again. I wonder if anything there can be in 'Heaven' is so lovely. If not, how tragic Death must be! Death or no death, I see our countryside as a promise never to be broken.

THE AMERICAN CITIZEN

And here in the midst of this small trilogy of reminiscences, where and when and how she appeared in my life, between The Merry Wives of Taliesin and Lulu Bett, is Olgivanna. Fate the dealer dealt her to me at this particular moment. And since Fate so decided and this is, in a way, an autobiography, I do not have either the hardihood to fly in the face of Fate and change the place of her appearance or leave her out. These eighteen years she has been a vivid living presence, next to my heart and in the hollow of my arm, a joy and inspiration.

She is here under the casual title 'The American Citizen', which, though a triumph of understatement, is a true and becoming title for Olgivanna.

Were I to keep on 'growing up' I had reached a jumping-off place. At least a critical stage in the growth of this thing which is me. Things had been going pretty low so far as I was concerned. Something was past due. What was it? Was it me?

When I met her at the parting of the ways, a mad genius-of-the-pig-bristles, Jerry (Blum) was alongside. A better than good, much-travelled, diamond-in-the-rough painter but rather terrifying. His parents had spoiled him with too much easy money. There was a fury in him now damned by trouble with his wife Lucile. I myself, lower down in my own estimation than I had ever been in my life, was staying at the Congress for a night or so. Jerry of auld-lang-syne (the Midway Gardens) happened in and all unsuspecting we, 'Les Misérables', strolled over a block or two to the Sunday matinee of the Russian ballet. Our tickets landed us near the stage in two balcony box-seats, by the rail. A third seat in the box was empty: apparently the only unoccupied one in the big overcrowded house. Karsavina was to dance and her performance had just begun when an usher quietly showed a dark, slender gentlewoman to the one empty seat in the house. Unobtrusive but lovely, I secretly observed her aristocratic bearing, no hat, her dark hair parted in the middle and smoothed down over her ears, a light small shawl over her shoulders, little or no makeup, very simply dressed. French, I thought—very French . . . and yet perhaps Russian? Whatever her nationality I instantly liked her looks and wondered who she was and where from. And why. Losing all interest in the stage. Although I can perfectly see Karsavina poised on one toe as she stood when the gentle stranger entered the box and my life.

Jerry, more intent on the dark, slender lady with the graceful movements who sat beside him than on Karsavina, moved a little closer—but evidently frightened the gentle stranger for she moved a little further away. I looked over the rail to see where he would land if I dropped him bodily out of the box, but he would hurt too many people down there below. He addressed a remark to me intended for her, foolishly complimenting Karsavina, so I gave him one also intended for the gentle stranger.

'No,' I said. 'No, Karsavina won't do. She's dead.' And waving toward the audience below, 'They are all dead: the dead is dancing to the dead.'

A quick comprehending glance from the young Frenchwoman with the sensitive feminine brow and dark eyes . . . or was she a Russian princess?

The glance went home: a strange elation stole over me. Suddenly in my unhappy state something cleared up—what had been the matter with me came to look me in the face—it was, simply, too much passion without poetry. Starved . . . for poetry . . . that was it . . . the best in me for years and years wasted—starved! This strange chance meeting, was it . . . poetry? I was a hungry man.

I didn't notice Jerry after that until the intermission. Something long since out of drawing had come to life in me. The intermission came soon. Evidently Jerry intended to find out who the lady was. 'Pardon me, Madam, we have met somewhere before?' She seemed unconvinced and unimpressed. 'In New York, at Waldo Frank's perhaps?' She gave me a startled look. A long shot. Yes, it so happened that the gentle stranger did know Waldo Frank's wife, Margaret Naumburg. That clever knight picked out a few more names she recognized and Jerry had opened the way to introduce me: 'My friend; he is Frank Lloyd Wright, the famous architect. You may have heard of him?' She hadn't, but she looked at me as though she had seen me before. So much so that I thought she had for a moment. I thought I must have met her—somewhere? But no, no one like her—that I could remember—and yet—where? There was something . . . coming clear.

441

She spoke in a low musical voice. In a sentence or two she criticized Karsavina from our point of view, showing unusual familiarity with dancing and dancers. No longer quite so strange, the emissary of Fate, mercy on my soul, from the other side of the known world, bowed her head to my invitation to tea at the near-by Congress. She accepted with perfect ease without artificial hesitation.

I was in love with her.

It was all as simple as that. When nature by the hand of Fate has arranged her drama all else is beside the mark. It is as it should be.

Over tea cups the obvious conversation ranged the gamut of Philosophy and Art. The implications were colourful overtones, deep undertones. She held her own in either: and 'her own' was a famous architect. Manifestly well educated she was unusually well trained in self-possession in a more profound school than anyone I had ever met. And, incidentally, not so important, I learned what you already know, that Olgivanna—that was her name—was born to an official family in Cettinje, Montenegro, was educated by her sister in Batum, Russia, had just arrived from Paris with her seven-year-old little daughter, Svetlana. She had come to Chicago to confer on business matters with her husband from whom she had separated. She was intending to return to Paris as soon as possible. You already know, too, the attractive name Olgivanna was made by her friends out of Olga Ivanovna as it had been in Batum—Russian for Olga, daughter of John. The nickname Olgivanna was a respectful form of address not unlike our Mrs. or Miss.

The *Institute Gurdjieff* for the harmonious development of man, I had already heard about. The Asiatic savant had brought his group to New York the summer before and performed remarkable studies in human correlation at Carnegie Hall. She herself had been in the group and I now learned from her more of that remarkable training. The Institute took unrhythmical neurotic human beings in all the social strata, took them apart, and put them together again better correlated, happier, more alive and useful to themselves and others. I am putting here what Olgivanna said with her own inimitable accent into my own words. It seems that Ouspensky, Orage, Lady Rothermere, Katherine Mansfield, and many others were Gurdjieff beneficiaries and disciples. Olgivanna, Jean Zartsman, Lili Galounian, the Hartmans, and Schoenvalls were all star leaders in the teachings Gurdjieff had promulgated and was preaching—nearer Dalcroze it seemed to me than any other well-known system. But more profound. It was fascinating revelation as she described it. She seemed to approve and like what I had to say about it. Between us across that tea table went more from each to each than I can ever describe. It was not in words, although the words were good. I am no novelist. Meredith might do it. But I should be dissatisfied with what he did and so would Olgivanna.

Jerry kept on gushing. Even more than her acquaintance with philosophy I admired the more than lady-like art, art is the word, with which

442

Olgivanna let Jerry slide off without hurting his feelings too much. Jerry was a good talker though, and discussion at the table had been stimulating, so let's forgive him his trespass. After a half hour Olgivanna arose to go (arose is the word), to go to her child, she said. But I couldn't bear the thought of letting her go—I was afraid I should lose her. She hesitated, but only for a moment when I said, 'Olgivanna, please leave your address so we may call on you? I want to learn more. I can't think we should let our remarkable meeting end here.' But I was eager to teach as well as to learn as anyone could see. Jerry took the address because he, being a painter, had a pencil. I, being an architect, never have one.

Olgivanna (what a winning name) was gone. The light went off when she went. But I knew well enough that nothing could stop us from seeing each other again, nothing either for her or for me. I went East for a week, but sent a little note from the train. I dropped back into the aching void.

As soon as I got back I called Jerry to come over and stay with me, knowing that he would have been to see her. Poor Jerry was all broken up over the affair Lucile. I had to listen to that first.

'Jerry, have you seen Olgivanna?'

The unhappy painter-wretch had been to the address Olgivanna had given. 'But,' he said, 'Olgivanna only wanted to talk about you and that bored me.'

I felt grateful to Jerry for being bored that way, and much that pleased me more he imparted with a few characteristic curses.

I wrote another note asking when I might come. The time fixed, I went to take Olgivanna to the theatre. Neither of us can remember, nor care to, what the play was. She has several faithful North Side friends, music-makers some of them, and some on whom we began to impose.

Some days later I invited Olgivanna to Taliesin to have her meet Sylva, Dione, and Nobu, and their clever husbands. Olgivanna and 'the merry wives of Taliesin' had much in common all being European. Next afternoon she left. My 1924 household, knowing full well what had happened to me, was sure that Taliesin was the place for *her*. None so sure as I. Her divorce was in court—granted. So was mine, waiting for signature—so why wait? Two fountains of arrested energy didn't wait. Waiting was not in our natures—never was. Never has been. Isn't now.

Although we didn't know then how much would have been saved to both if we had 'waited', it probably would have made no difference.

We had each other for better or for worse.

Olgivanna was mine. The night we were off to New York together I read her to sleep with Carl's fairy tale of *The White Horse Girl and The Blue Wind Boy*. I guess he so intended it. I had just discovered the 'Rootabaga Stories' and they delighted me so much I wrote him a little letter, appended hereafter in gratitude.

The story of the plight that followed this brave flight into a new life—passion with poetry now—you have read in the fourth book of *An Autobiography*. What you have not read is how well the chance meeting dealt by the hand of Fate—kind for once, at least—turned out for us and for everyone else who had any right to be at all interested in how it turned out. For more than eighteen years, the perfect mistress, Olgivanna, and I have lived and worked in luck and out of luck at Taliesin, constantly together in any case. And this in sickness and in health. Mostly health. No fair-weather friend was Olgivanna. There was great work to be done there as well as a full life to be lived. But one that would have destroyed any human being less well trained for the struggle for the better thing, and less inspired by natural gifts, mutual love and understanding for that high struggle.

Just to be with her uplifts my heart and strengthens my spirit when the going gets hard or when the going is good.

We were married, certainly, but we wouldn't know it unless you insisted on the point, because we don't need to be. I found that the girl who was qualified by years of hard, patient trying to understand, inspired by ideas similar to my own, was qualified to be an imaginative vivid inspiration and a real mate.

Whatever we undertook, she never shirked.

And strangely enough—or is it so strange—she, whose parents were Montenegrin dignitaries, had pictures of her Montenegrin forebears that looked just like my Welsh forebears. They might have been of one family although we ourselves resembled each other only in spirit.

John Commons (of Wisconsin U.) told us there was nothing to wonder about in that because the Montenegrins, the Basques, and the Welsh were all a related mountain people. Her severe bringing-up was so similar to mine that we liked not only the same fundamentals, but what went with them in much the same way. There was just enough difference in the non-essentials to make whatever she did the more interesting to me. She would take a case of any kind in the Fellowship, straighten it with a grasp and effectiveness that could not be matched. She could paint, or sculp, or cook, or dance, or play and sing. Svetlana is like her in that respect. It isn't mere versatility. There is a driving fire in it all.

Svetlana is Olgivanna's little daughter's name. After some legal difficulties which you have read about already, she came to live at Taliesin with her mother where she is now married to the stalwart Wes.

As for the little 'soft one' that I wanted to complete beloved Taliesin in the valley—Iovanna? Why, she is already a lovely plus-seventeen, as tall and with as gracious a manner as her mother, a young lady with beautiful masses of brown hair, hair such as mine was at her age. She looks at you something like me, but enough like her mother to make the resemblance of not too much consequence.

This isn't much of a story. It is all too close to home to write much about it. But too long a time elapsed before Olgivanna and I finally found each other. It was pretty late. Olgivanna often says, 'Oh, why didn't we meet before all the Past ever had a chance to be the Present?' Well . . . after all, that is probably a little ungrateful because Olgivanna wouldn't have liked me until I had been battered into shape by the many untoward circumstances of outraged previous experience, passion properly starved for poetry, and the harm done by too much damage and too much flattery, somewhat undone. I don't like myself much back there. And if she hadn't been properly starved too, probably I wouldn't have such faith in Olgivanna as I have now—with that serious noble look in her face of which I am proud, the greying hair drifting back from her sensitive temples that proves my point.

She is brave and has the heart of a lioness.

No, I think we mated as planned behind the stars—just right. I don't even wish I were younger because we both seem to add up to just about the right age for us, and I admire maturity much more than youth. I would prefer to die to going through my own 'youth' again.

When she was 'inducted' to citizenship, standing up straight in court to answer the question asked by the old judge, she answered all the questions correctly in a firm clear voice, except one. She made one ridiculous mistake. 'Mrs. Wright,' said the judge, 'what form of government do we live under?'

Unhesitatingly she said, 'A democracy, sir.'

The judge bent his head, smiled a little, while poking at the blotter on his desk. 'No,' said the judge. 'No, Mrs. Wright, but we *are* a Republic.'

The American Citizen . . . Olga Ivanovna.

TO CARL SANDBURG, POET

DEAR CARL:

I read your fairy tales nearly every night before I go to bed. They fill a long-felt want—Poetry.

I'll soon know them all by heart.

Have you sent the book to Lord Dunsany? It would make him feel sorry he was born a Lord and so had to fool around with Gods and Goddesses.

I've tried so long to play the guitar with my mittens on that Henry Hagglyhoagly is mine—and O Man! the beauty of the White Horse Girl and the Blue Wind Boy! And the fairies dancing on the wind-swept corn! The Wedding Procession of the Brown Stick and the Rag Doll! The Skyscraper that Decided to have a Child!

All the children that will be born into the Middle West during the next hundred years are peeping at you now, Carl—between little pink fingers —smiling, knowing in their hearts they have found a friend.

And Lucky Spink and Skabootch—to have a daddy—'fire-born' who understands blue. Blue is happy imagination. Something that wakes and sings no matter how much it hurts—or is it always singing?

Yes, Carl, only the Fire-born understand blue. You are the kind of artist for me. Stick this little posy in your hatband for a day. I fling it to you from where, as always, the tracks leave the ground for the sky and I'll be waiting for you at this station in the Rootabaga Country to bring Spink and Skabootch to play with their Uncle:

FRANK

Taliesin.

445

And then Carl, the genius, had to ride to riches by way of counting the hairs on the head and fingering the buttons on the clothes of our most beloved national hero: that great leader who truly believed the Union could only live if half of it was destroyed in the name of Freedom by the other half: the agriculturists on the wrong track, slavery, wiped out by the industrialists on the wrong track, machine production controlling consumption.

The great fanatic who invented conscription-in-a-Democracy and by way of white-slavery drove black-slavery into the body-politic, instead of banishing it—enthroning the money-power and the machine to wave the stars and stripes over a wrecked and devastated South, where a culture might have taken root that would have cured its own evils from within if any real help had come from the North.

Napoleon said: 'Do you know what amazes me more than anything else? The importance of force to organize anything.'

War itself is a denial of Civilization.

THE INVITED GUEST

BRAZIL—RIO DE JANEIRO

October, 1930

An invitation came from the Pan American Union to go to Rio de Janeiro, as member of the jury representing North America, to judge the accumulation of drawings in the world-wide competition for a memorial to Columbus. Herbert Kelsey (Kelsey built the Pan American building in Washington) was engineering the affair. The programme included wives and we thought the excursion might be beneficial—although Olgivanna and I were both bad sailors. Perhaps this time in quiet southern seas we might do better.

All right, we packed up, caught the boat as she was casting off the pier the Grace Line—United States built boat.

Kelsey was already in Rio.

Diplomats were on board, and Saarinen, the Finnish architect, who for some reason was representing Europe from America. The two great continents, Europe and North America, would see something of each other by way of Wisconsin and Finland. I had always resented Saarinen a little, regarding him as our most accomplished foreign eclectic—a little jealous too of his easy berth, bestowed by the hand of American riches, while I had to wait and work and scrape for mine, the hard way. Yes—I know, this seems pretty small. But our provincials feel that culture comes from abroad if at all, and the importation is looked upon in the provinces, especially at Detroit, with great favour. I suppose they think we can't have much at home that should be looked up to.

But it is only, of course, because they wouldn't know how to look.

446

Saarinen, the Finnish cosmopolite with the Norse accent, spoiled all that mild ill feeling. We became fast friends and had no basis for disagreement on anything whatsoever. I wouldn't disagree with Saarinen and he couldn't disagree with me if he would.

Which reminds me: some time ago we met at a railway restaurant in Chicago—he was on the way to a church he was building in Columbus and I on my way to a church I was building in Kansas City. He had a million dollars to do his (his usual luck). I had one hundred and fifty thousand dollars (maybe) to encompass about the same thing (my usual luck). He asked me if I had seen his design. I had, in a newspaper. 'What do you think of it?' he asked.

'Well, Eliel,' I said, 'when I saw it I thought what a great architect— I am!'

We laughed and he slapped me on the wrist. Well, that's Eliel Saarinen and that, I am afraid, is me. Saarinen was born and will die—a Finn.

By way of the British, I was born native . . . and I refuse to die.

Speaking of Saarinen always brings to mind the power behind the throne at Cranbrook, Carl Milles.

Carl is a sculptor—probably the greatest.

In the hall of his house he has the whole wonderful Barberini collection of Greek sculpture which he bought outright and brought home from Rome.

He will give it all to Taliesin.

Cranbrook cannot have it.

I wish this simple disposition of the wonderful Barberini collection were true.

We were on the way to South America. . . . The old half-freighter pushed up to the great pier at Rio in early morning—that wonderful harbour at sunrise! There were a lot of boys (students, I thought) climbing on board. They surrounded us. Only one (and a half, say) spoke English.

They were a delegation from some seven hundred or more students of the Brazil Belles Artes, out on what they called (borrowing from us) a 'strike'. The institution was modelled by and on the French, of course. Latins for the Latins. The Beaux Arts professors of the Belles Artes had ruled me out altogether by banning my books and forbidding magazines on modern architecture in their library, together with all of my kind.

The youths were a delegation sent by the student body to ask me for help.

Would I help?

I would.

'Look out,' said Saarinen. 'This is a revolutionary country—first thing you know SSSKKK [he drew his finger across his throat]—and it will be all over with you.'

'Never mind,' I said. 'Come on. Get in and help.' He stood on the side-lines, however.

But I was soon in over my head.

My head still on my shoulders I met Herbert Moses, editor of *El Globo*, one of Rio's leading newspapers, and I soon learned how to make a speech in a foreign tongue. Moses was not only remarkably intelligent, but also (an experienced editor) remarkably articulate. I filled him up with the point of view. He was enthusiastic.

The first meeting with the enemy was in the old hall of the Belles Artes. The Beaux Arts dignitaries, myself, and the handsome president of the University of Brazil presiding. I sat next to him. 'How do,' he said. I did a little better, but it was in my own language. I knew less Portuguese than he knew English. He knew no more English than that. And only one and a half boys out of the seven hundred at Belles Artes spoke English! Many read it, though.

El Globo spoke English like a Yankee.

Our ambassador, Morgan, a genial competent one, was there and spoke.

We, the dignitaries, were all ranged at a long elevated bench such as judges use in our court rooms. The boys were massed down there below.

The meeting began with Latinesque formalities. The President offered a welcome, a professor or two chimed in. My turn—but without waiting for me to speak, bedlam broke.

When they let go a little I got *El Globo* by the arm and, standing that way, would tell him in a sentence or two what I wanted to say. He would put it over to the young rebels with such effect that they would go wild.

The Latins love to go wild.

I gave them all I could—pleaded their cause as the future of Brazil. If Brazil was to have a future, how could she deny her youth the advanced thought of the world whether or not her elders disagreed with that thought and—well, my reader knows by this time what I would say. I stopped; Moses (*El Globo*) stopped.

And then the masses of youngsters charged the judges' bench, pushed their dignitaries aside, *El Globo* and the Ambassador too, picked me up and carried me down to the street, called a taxi, and sent me off to the Copacabana with all on board who could stick.

There was now meeting after meeting.

The affair Columbus took a back seat although we finally did judge the show. And there were great dinners and celebrations galore. I wrote the opinion and the other judges politely concurred—not looking for argument. What was the use anyway? A young Englishman got the prize and deserved it. The whole mass of entries, with a half-dozen exceptions, was a bad form of grandomania and wonderful draftsmanship. Like most competitions it was all in vain. What can a competition be except an averaging upon averages by the average? The first thing the jury (a picked average usually) does is to go through and throw out all the worst ones and all the best ones, and then the jury, itself an average, averages upon some average design as it could only do. But I wouldn't have it that way.

Well, the Belles Artes 'strike' began to turn on the heat. I don't remember where or how many times I spoke, or how many newspaper

448

Model exhibited at the
seum of Modern Art, 1940.
nian type on slope. Natural
ress and red brick

EGOR AFFLECK
OUSE. 1940

Fireplace

Living room

71. ANN PFEIFFER CHAPEL, FLORIDA SOUTHERN COLLEGE. 1940. Open
tower trellis for flowering vines planted in concrete holes in place of steeple

72. KANSAS CITY COMMUNITY CHURCH (in construction). Perspective drawings. Searchlight beams arranged under perforated roof instead of steeples. Cement
over metal laths

articles I wrote for *El Globo* and *El Manha*, the leading newspapers of Brazil.

The boys would come after me and I would go, and Herbert Moses would 'interpret'—if that is what he did. He became fiery eloquent—I suspect he frequently put more into me than I had put into him. I met the 'modern' professors the boys wanted. They were good architects and excellent men. The authorities were very negligent or else indulgent because they didn't arrest me, but finally they did arrest one of the coveted professors who spoke alongside me—Araujo.

Saarinen said my turn was next.

He enjoyed the whole affair in a very refined sort of way, peculiar to the Finns.

They have a National Academy in Brazil, a medal dispensary something like the National Académie Française. The Academy tendered me an honorary meeting and subsequently an honorary membership. I accepted on condition that the society help the boys in their struggle for Freedom.

They agreed.

The Architects Society of Brazil gave us a dinner, with wives. I was in the very thick of the struggle then, and I pleaded the cause of the boys until I brought tears to their eyes to go with the seven different kinds of wine—and my own eyes came to tears without wine. They tendered me honorary membership in their National Society. I accepted conditionally: on condition that they help the boys at Belles Artes.

They agreed.

Ah—the Rio de Janeirians are a fiery, gallant folk. I never thought I would ever like the Latins so much. Olgivanna and I hardly touched the ground during our stay. We went from place to place with a grand set of fellows and their handsome wives. We week-ended at Petropolis, bathed on the beach before the Copacabana, rode in the suburbs and along the marvellous Rio waterfront dominated by curious mountain silhouettes.

Kelsey must have hated me for it all—because what had it to do with the competition for the Columbus Memorial? He attended to that and made a good job of his knitting.

A famous French landscaper was there at the time with plans for the replanting of the Versailles-like gardens of the waterfront. The Rio de Janeirians brought the architect and the plans to exhibit both to me . . . for criticism.

I didn't feel competent.

The *Atlantique* came to harbour one day during our six weeks' stay and the great city turned out to meet her at the pier. Our Ambassador had a stalwart bodyguard who fought a clear-way in the crowd so we might follow the Ambassador up the gang-plank, get on board, and see what I thought was France's greatest contribution to modern architecture.

Truly, the elegance and beautiful craftsmanship of the interior of that ship were stunning. I sat and marvelled.

The Rio de Janeirians have but one social fault. They are committed, heart and soul and therefore so are you, to photography. Everywhere we went in public or in private at unexpected moments there was the puff, puff—or startling flash—of flashlights. Ambassador Morgan was usually around somewhere. Our Ambassador was popular in Rio. They couldn't have a function public or private without 'El Ambassador'.

After the dinner-in-honour at which everybody photographed everybody else, the architects took me over to be especially photographed again by their famous star portrait-photoist. The photographs were good and I had to sign them all for all the architects of Brazil.

Time came to come away. Things had been tremendous. The students came to say they wanted to do something for us. They said they had been 'out' so long that (like me) they had no money left. Some of them wanted to bring flowers to Olgivanna but they could not afford to buy them.

Might they not then come to the Copacabana and serenade us that evening? They could. And they did—hundreds of them.

They rushed the piano out to the middle of the ballroom floor. Some of the boys improvised instruments and native costumes, sang and danced till three in the morning while we looked on from a balcony. I wish an American movie magnate could have filmed that show for our country. But down there I couldn't say *American* movie magnate without giving them offence or to think that I meant one of *their* own magnates. The Rio de Janeirians always resented any reference to ourselves as the Americans. So I said Usonia when I talked about our country to them. They liked the term. They had never heard it before but thought it appropriate.

We got home after a long journey in perfect weather on an old United States steamer (why do we build them half-freight, half-passenger, I wonder?). Probably the subs have sunk it. Anyway, we were happy to get home.

Taliesin was a beautiful dream again realized. There is nothing like homecomings for that realization.

A cablegram from Ambassador Morgan, a fortnight after we were settled again, said that the boys had the professors they wanted.

The students of the Belles Artes were free to grow up to serve the future of Brazil!

We brought along such a mass of photographs, newspaper pictures, and clippings that Henry sat down and compiled an album, thirteen inches square and two inches thick, which you may see at Taliesin to this day.

SNIFF TALIESIN

Independently of wide-open windows seldom shut, letting in the varying smells of the four seasons, Taliesin is pervaded by its own very especial smell. The visitor on coming in for the first time will sniff and remark upon it, ask what the fragrance is.

In Spring and Summer the windows at Taliesin are thrown wide-open. The odour of the long white drifts of wild-plum bloom on the nearby hill-

450

sides drifts in—the crabapple and hawthorn in the meadows send their scent on, over the treetops. Later the sweet breath of the clover fields rides in to the rooms on the morning and evening breezes. Soon the scent of new-mown hay pervades the place. So our windows, like the doors, are seldom closed in Spring and Summer. In Autumn, when they are closed, mingling with the odour of freshly burned oak, is the smell of bowls of apples and unshelled shag-bark hickory nuts—the prince of all perfumes. And the sumach. But for the Winter, there inside the rooms is newly gathered, everlasting, cream-white antimony. This gentle pervading odour of antimony is to the sense of smell what the flavour of slippery elm is to the young boy's sense of taste. Oak fires then start in the seventeen ever-present stone fireplaces to go out but seldom until the following Spring, unless fuel gives out.

A few of the many fireplaces smoke just little enough to contribute the fumes of the burning oak when the evenings are chill in Autumn or Winter, and Taliesin is covered with its thick protecting blanket of snow, thin white wood-smoke going straight up toward the evening star.

So it is in Winter especially that Taliesin is most itself and smells best.

The Taliesin smell, then, is compounded of the acrid odour of oak-wood fires, overlaid and softened by the odour of great bundles of antimony gathered from the fields in Autumn. Great masses of the decorative creamy white herb-blossoms stand about on tables and ledges in big old Chinese jars. The tang of burned oak and the strange odour of antimony together in fresh air—this is the authentic recipe for 'the Taliesin Smell'.

AGGRESSIVE FOREIGN POLICY—A FABLE

There was once a nice Johnnie on his way to school with a lot of other little Johnnies and Tommies and Jennies all around him. Johnnie saw a curious thing he hadn't noticed before—a hornet's nest hanging in the bushes. Not knowing much about hornets, he got a stick and poked the nest—whereupon the hornets swarmed out, stung all the little children except Johnnie, who went bravely on to school. At school, in the midst of the boo-hooing and wailing, Johnnie told his tale. The teacher said, 'Why, Johnnie, you are a *hero*! I didn't know hornets were so dreadful.' So Johnnie, the hero, sat up front. And all the children went out instructed to destroy all the hornets everywhere to make the woods safe for such as Johnnie.

JAPAN—TOKIO

Invited to Japan to build the new Imperial Hotel, the Teikoku at Tokio—during that four years' residence, and a preliminary visit in 1906, I learned some little something of a culture that I had studied and worshipped from afar. Owing so much to Old Japan, it would be absurd for me to leave her culture to the mercy of the 'patriotic' destructive 'white eyed' ignoramus who will write and rate her now. Typical trash is this dedication of a new book just published: 'Dedicated to the gentle, self-effacing and long-suffering mothers of the cruellest, most arrogant and treacherous sons who walk the earth—to the women of Japan, who will as always, reap the richest harvest of suffering as their reward.'

Well—there you have it—about the general, generous size of the average Western comprehension of the Orient.

Extraordinary that for so many centuries 'the arrogant sons' should have sired this paragon of virtue and she should in turn have mothered 'the most treacherous sons on earth'? But no common sense nor any sense of decency stays with our travelling provincials when they undertake either to underwrite or destroy Japan. The basis for any sense of proportion whatever is lacking.

Kipling said, among other things he said with a grain of truth in the saying, 'East is East and West is West and never the twain shall meet.'

I am sure they should not meet, at least not yet because, except for a few culture-hunters (and exploiters?) like myself, the West has no tolerant comprehension whatever to give to the East—from the first to the last. And the East has conceived a thorough, grossly exaggerated contempt for the culture, honour, and character of the West. Both China and Japan have preserved a great deal of their sense of beauty and artistry. And it is true that the Japanese have from their first knowledge of us regarded us as vulgar barbarians. From their standpoint we are.

The Commodore who in 1854 fired the shot that compelled Japan to 'open up' was no violet.

That rude awakening of Nippon—the Land of the Rising Sun—from the peaceful pursuit of culture for four hundred years, during which time her Art and Craft rose to high-water mark in all the culture of the world, was a terrible shock to the Sons of Heaven.

'What is the secret of this strange power? These vulgarians have neither character, manners, nor brains,' said the Nipponese wisemen. And they sent their elder statesman, Count Ito, journeying around the world to find out. He was absent some two years, staying longest in Germany. Japan's Number One statesman came back with the secret: 'Explosives. In Machines.'

Japan (and this is hard for the West to understand) went into hysterical self-abnegation and began to destroy her beautiful works of art, casting them upon sacrificial bonfires in the public places surrounding the palace moat in the capital, Tokio: virtually throwing her civilization upon these fires as on a funeral pyre, a national form of that *hara-kari* which is also incomprehensible to the West. A young American at that time helped save many of the proofs of their great culture from this wanton destruction. His name was Ernest Fenollosa.

Japan whose religion was Shinto—the severe 'be clean' religion, overlaid with a colourful Buddhism, had reached the parting of the ways. She had 'lost face', an Oriental spiritual tragedy which again we fail to understand. Her centuries of severe interior discipline, more severe in poverty than any the world has ever seen, had gone for nought. The culture of Dai Nippon—the Land of the Rising Sun—must have been wrong if a crude barbaric people with cold white skins, cruel noses, and white eyes that frightened their children and made them cry, had the power to destroy them; these coarse men who had no power of thought, or true spirit of courage, so they said. But they could destroy them only because they were masters of explosives in engines of destruction!

Soon after Count Ito's return, the Japanese schools were being modelled on the German. A military system was set up Germanizing the Japanese. Official Japanese delegations were for years and years continually travelling the West and picking up the details of the new power all over the world, almost invariably finding the best applications in Germany. It was such a delegation that picked me to build the second or new Imperial Hotel, a social clearing house for official Japan, after first having heard of me in Germany. So German architects built Japan's new Parliament buildings, built the first Imperial Hotel. The Imperial University became, virtually, a German university. Japanese music went 'Ich liebe dich' on the stages of modernized Japanese theatres. The conviction had settled deep in the Oriental breast and in official Japan's national conscience that the Asiatic yellow peoples must some day meet the Western white-eyed peoples on a footing that would save Asia from barbarous double-dealing England and her stooge America. They saw nothing to admire in Western culture except that as a means to an end, it would serve them better than their own in the undertaking now ahead.

Many years later, one day when an American architect, myself (almost by accident), was building the new Imperial Hotel for them at Tokio, came the news that American statesmanship had declared them an inferior race. The United States of America had denied them the privileges of civilized nations.

I remember the fury of the indignation meetings that took place at that time in Tokio.

I was not allowed abroad without protection for more than two weeks until the ancient capital quieted down again. The infuriated Sons of Heaven were now completely confirmed in their belief that Asia must prepare to save herself from the international shopkeepers and peddlers of the white variety with their gods and their goods: and *everywhere* on the Asiatic continent or on any sea that washed Asia's shores.

They did prepare with thoroughness and efficiency: preparations that seemed entirely to escape the military eye of the purblind dominant race except for one intelligent mind: the mind of the hunchback Homer Lea. His books, *The Valour of Ignorance* and *The Day of the Saxons*, when issued thirty years or more ago, should have had attention which they failed to receive. He is one of the few minds—like Napoleon's—to realize that the military mind is a dead mind.

The largest populations of the world—about three to one—and the most ancient, were no longer innocent of a leader-nation who had mastered the great secret of cruel western barbaric power—explosives. The West was riding a new horse. Not only had Japan made that discovery but she learned how to ride. She felt she was therefore the saviour of the sleeping, unaware Yellow races of All Asia. That leadership, even if in their ignorance of danger it had to be fought for among themselves, was her Destiny.

It is a common saying under the flag of the Rising Sun that the East is the morning land, the West the evening land. All the dirty seven hundred commercial tricks in streamlined Western commercial duplicity practised by the worst of Westerners found apt pupils on Asiatic shores. Soon the slant-eyed yellow-men everywhere, but especially in Japan, learned another secret of Western power—the monkey moneyism of commercial empire, wherein the sophisticated whites were pitted against the un-awakened, as yet untaught, yellow-men. The yellow-man was no match for the streamlined commercial experts of the West now in action. No, not yet, but coming: tricks against tricks. Being a more ancient people, the Asiatics were more easily degenerate and demoralized even than the relatively cold whites.

Two episodes seem to drop into place here of their own accord, since my persistent absorbing pursuit of the Print is so involved with Oriental experience. The first was one for me. The second was one for them.

From time to time I had collected superb Actor prints: Hosoye—about eleven hundred Hosoye of the first rank—Shunsho, Shunko, Shunyei. Single sheets, diptychs, triptychs, pentaptychs, and several septyptich—iridian sheets of soft paper stained with soft colours portraying ancient famous actors in classical roles on the ancient Japanese stage. Any collector will know what that collection means. 'Wrieto San' was already on the map of Tokio as the most extensive buyer of the fine antique print. Already de-scribed to you is what an avocation the pursuit of the rare print made in ancient Yedo, had become to me in Tokio. The prints, extremely rare and expensive, were still going up in price at this time. It was often said—'It is finished' and 'Japan had been raked with a fine-tooth comb for a quarter of a century, so give it up.'

Frederick Gookin of Chicago was the foremost reliable connoisseur in our country. A fine person in himself. When I was about to return for the fifth time to the building of the Imperial Hotel, he introduced William Spaulding to me. The Spauldings were cultured Boston (Beacon Street) people who had got into this most absorbing, exciting, and expensive game known to aesthetics very late. As bride and groom, William and his bride, Virginia Fairlie of the Chicago Art Institute, had tried to start a collection while on their honeymoon in Japan but they could find almost nothing. I myself had been able to find very little. Learning from Fred-erick Gookin of my extraordinary collection of actor prints, Mr. Spaulding came to my rooms in Orchestra Hall to see a group I had brought in for my own pleasure. Delighted with the portfolio of one hundred prints he offered me ten thousand dollars for them. It was at the time a fair price.

For a number of reasons I accepted although, except as collections were abandoned, it was quite impossible to find first-rate prints.

A few days later about ready to return to Japan I received a telegram from the Spauldings inviting me to come to Beacon Street for a conference. I gladly went and at dinner that evening the subject was broached by the Spauldings. I imagined the interest was Mr. and Mrs. William's but John also sat in with us. 'Would you consent to try to find prints for us in Japan, Mr. Wright? We are both impressed by your experience and your knowledge of the subject and your opportunities in Japan and feel we can trust you completely. We know it is no longer possible for us to find prints unless you will help us.' I had expected something like this and had been trying to arrive at something but had nothing definite in mind.

Suddenly I decided. I said, 'I will take whatever you want to spend, spend it and divide. I'll keep what I think in the circumstances I should have and you shall have the others.' 'Well,' said John as he laughed, 'that's hardly a business proposition, is it, Mr. Wright?' I said, 'No, I am not a business man, Mr. Spaulding.'

They wanted to know why I would not do it on commission. I said, 'Too much book-keeping.' We left it at that and went to bed.

Next morning John and William said they had all thought it all over. 'We will be glad to acept your offer. You will find twenty thousand dollars to your credit in the Yokohama Specie Bank when you arrive in Tokio.'

There was no scratch of a pen to record the agreement.

Neither the Spauldings nor I thought I could find enough prints worth buying to spend the money.

When I arrived after the usual tedious Pacific crossing, the fifth, I went directly to Shugio. He who was Mutsushito's 'connoisseur' and my intimate friend. Hiromische Shugio had charge of all Japanese fine art exhibits, in the foreign expositions—a friend of nearly all the great artists of Europe, Whistler especially. He was a lover of London, which he liked to compare with Tokio. Shugio was a Japanese aristocrat (there must have been some Chinese blood in him with that name) and highly respected by everyone. He had access to court circles and enjoyed a universal reputation for integrity. I laid the case before him.

It was my feeling that, hidden away Japanese-fashion in the go-downs of the court beyond the approach of the merchant class, were many as yet untouched collections of the somewhat 'risqué' prints.

Shugio wasn't very sanguine but agreed to talk with a few friends. He wasn't very energetic either. But finally by tactful pursuit he was moved and soon we did hear of a private collection that might, with proper circumspection, be bought. Shugio had the tact. I had the Spaulding money.

Well, it was simply amazing. I bought the first collection that turned up on that trail for much less than I ever thought possible. The news (a secret) got around just how and where we hoped it would. Money was very scarce then (1915–1916) in Japan. The interest rate at the banks was nine per cent.

I was getting excited. Already I had established a considerable buying power and anything available in the ordinary channels came first to me. I picked up some fine things in this way. But aristocratic Japanese people lose face if they sell their belongings, even such taboo things as the prints. But evidently Shugio had found a way. Well, it had begun. The twenty thousand was soon gone and already I had priceless things. Anything unique or superior went to the Spauldings. I kept the prints together in Shugio's own *go-down* and mounted and grouped them as I got hold of them. I would cable for money from time to time during the five-month campaign. The money always came, no questions asked. And nothing from me except excited demands for more money until I had spent about one hundred and twenty-five thousand Spaulding dollars for about a million dollars' worth of prints.

Many were unique on the record.

A superb collection almost beyond price—most of it is now in the Boston Museum of Fine Arts, a gift from the Spauldings.

Finally a cable: 'When are you coming home?' I cabled back: 'Taking next boat,' boxed the prints, and caught the next boat but one. I was to bring the prints to the Spaulding country home at Pride's Crossing. By this time both the Spauldings, William and John, and Mrs. Spaulding were proficient judges, but they had Gookin (as consultant connoisseur) present. For three days we laid out prints and prints and more prints and some more prints until neither the Spauldings nor Gookin (he was now leading expert in America) could believe their eyes. Even to me it seemed like some fantastic dream. Sated with riches in the most exquisite graphic art on earth, after three days at a marvellous feast we sat back and rested.

Gratified was hardly the word. William Spaulding especially delighted, said, 'Mr. Wright, this goes far beyond any expectations we had. You can't have much of your own after turning this over to us?'

'I have enough,' I said. 'I have done pretty well by myself, I assure you.'

'No, I don't believe it.'

He walked over to his desk and wrote a cheque for twenty-five thousand dollars and handed it to me. I genuinely hesitated to accept it but of course I did. And he came downstairs with an exquisite slightly toned copy of Utamaro's Ryogoku Fireworks—black sky—and said, 'My brother and I want you to keep this treasure and never part with it. You have brought us a better copy—probably the finest in the world—but this is the next best, we believe. We bought it from Baron Sumitomo.'

After lunch we went out for a drive in the Spaulding Stearns-Knight— top down. I was sitting on the rear seat between John and William. Not going very fast, enjoying the relaxation, we were passing the school grounds, boys playing ball, when I heard the crack of a bat on the ball: a square hit. I glanced up just in time to see the ball sailing over us. Instinctively I reached up for the ball, caught it and threw it back into the game.

'Well!' said William Spaulding in astonishment. 'So that is it! Well, Mr. Wright, I know now how you got those prints! It's all clear at last!'

Hiromische Shugio got some of the twenty-five thousand, but I wish now I had given him all of it.

You have here before you a perfect picture of the West looting the Orient. I make no apologies. You may judge for yourself.

A fascinating game had now developed as an avocation: this pursuit of the print—but on a scale never originally intended.

My own buying—buying for the Spauldings—for the Metropolitan, for the Buckinghams, Chicago Art Institute, had automatically, no such intention on my part, given me command of the print market in all Japan. Nothing much now got away. I had spent nearly a half million dollars in Japan at a time when money there was scarce indeed.

You may well say, the East got the money, didn't it? But what did the West get? Priceless art treasures running into millions. And it was always the same story, in either Japan or China.

Wrieto San's 'avocation' was great pastime, but profitable to him and to the West. I grew ashamed of it finally.

All right. The Japanese merchants didn't like it, of course. But it went deeper.

Howard Mansfield was treasurer of the Metropolitan Museum at the time. He had asked me to pick up some treasures for him next time I got back to Tokio if anything extraordinary should turn up. Emissaries used to come to me from various country places, frequently, to offer their 'finds' first to me.

Wrieto San is getting to be too much of a merchant, I thought.

I believe I lost caste a little in Japan by way of it. But one more chance came from Nikko—very secret. I went up by train with the well-known Tokio dealer, Hayashi, a name as common in Japan as Smith is common in America. Then we went by rickshaw to a little Japanese house hidden in the woods in the outskirts in the country.

There we found the 'collection'. My God! I thought I had seen every subject extant by now. I hadn't. There were things in that collection still unique—things like a large-size Harunobu (printed in gold leaf in heavy goffered paper) that later brought twenty-five hundred dollars at auction in New York. Kyonagas—stunning subjects I had never seen. Noble primitives: Sharaku by the dozen, Shunsho, charming Kiyonaga, Shunko, Yeishi triptychs, Toyokuni I five-piece, the Shunman black-and-white septyptich, Hokusai almost complete, the Hiroshigo Saruhashi, the gorge, the snow-triptych, ah well . . . why go on? Suffice it to say that this clandestine collection beggared imagination and so description. I who had so eagerly read of Aladdin and his wonderful lamp when a boy . . . well, again this was Aladdin's cave. All the prints were of the first quality. *Ichiban,* as the Japanese say.

I, still the hungry orphan turned loose in the bakeshop, spent about two hours there and bought it all for fifty thousand dollars. They needed

457

money badly. And I who had crowded out other buyers by now—practically had things my own way. I was accustomed to getting about three for one anyway, which was not greedy as things were going. Ten for one is about what the West expects from the East, and takes.

Again the tedious return voyage across the vast Pacific. The eleventh.

But I had my treasures on board to study and gloat over. Glutton? Absolutely.

When I returned I had them all classified and properly mounted and took them to New York and Howard Mansfield. Howard, really by this time our most fastidious American collector, was the centre of a group of more or less wealthy but, nevertheless, very discriminating collectors. He himself was by now a veteran. The group called in experts (several of them) and excluded me from their conference, which hurt me. Why should they exclude me? I couldn't understand.

Finally Howard, pencil and paper and lists in hand, offered me forty-five thousand dollars for about half of the collection. Make it fifty thousand, I said. Agreed.

Some months after returning to Tokio and back to work on the Imperial already sick of the rôle I had been playing, I received a cablegram from Howard Mansfield:

WRIGHT. IMPEHO. TOKIO. KYOTO MATSUKI, NEW YORK DEALER, TURNS INFORMER ON TOKIO RING REVAMPING PRINTS. SOME FROM YOU HAVE PIN-PRICKS SHOWING REVAMPING. BETTER INVESTIGATE. MANSFIELD.

I investigated at once and knew where to go to do it. I found that Matsuki told the truth. Several leading dealers, the smartest in Tokio, had for years been keeping a famous craftsman with helpers working in the country on genuine old prints, as rarities in poor condition turned up, putting months of work on a single rare specimen that would bring several thousand dollars, probably.

They would first discharge the colour—restoring the paper to normal, soak old worthless prints to obtain the proper colours, and then, by an ingenious system of pin pricks at certain angles of the drawing, guide the reprinting of the original print from blocks cut solely for the purpose of reprinting that one print. The result was not an imitation. It was a genuine restoration and valuable. But who wanted it? No collector, certainly.

The jig was up. Staying away from me until this last trip, they had previously loaded up many collectors like Sir Edwin Walker of Canada, and a half-dozen less well-known collectors in our country, but they had fought shy of me—either not daring to try me out before or emboldened by their success with others thinking it time to retaliate.

Wrieto San had fallen. I went after the ring, wiped it out, got the ringleader (he was Hayashi) in jail. After he had been there a year his case came up. The court sent for me. The police brought Hayashi to me where I was sitting in court at a small table to judge him. The court wanted to know what I wanted done with him. He knocked his forehead to the floor and begged for mercy as tears streamed from his eyes. I said, 'Take everything of the sort he has away from him. Forbid him to ever deal in colour prints again and let him go.' This was done. He had very little of anything. They would have hanged him if I had said so, for the Japanese authorities were furious.

The trickery greatly humiliated them. So I had 'cleaned up the market' in quite another way than I originally intended.

The Japanese authorities openly apologized. The dealer was banished. He was last heard of in London. The print business, but not Japanese prints.

He was a product of the West and belonged there.

I dare say he is successful in London.

Was I satisfied? I was. Satisfied that the East was one up on the West. And somehow, not sorry. It was a sop to my own conscience.

But now I had to square myself with Howard Mansfield and friends. When I got home again, much later, we held at Taliesin what was known as 'The Print Party'. I threw open the vault at Taliesin with its collections to Howard and his friends. They were free to choose what they would in exchange for the restored prints. About one-third of the 'treasures' I had brought them had been 'restored'.

That party cost me about thirty thousand dollars.

'Wright,' said Howard Mansfield, 'I knew we could count on you!'

'Yes, Howard,' I said. 'But you are as culpable as I am. You excluded me, you called on your own experts and picked out your own prints. And I had no responsibility really. But "Wrieto San" couldn't afford to "lose face", as the Japanese themselves say.'

'Yes, Wright, I know,' said the treasurer of the Metropolitan, 'I know.'

The game was all played according to a pattern set by the West. And it all served me right for getting into something I had no good right to be in. I woke up. There was no one now to say to me—No, you are no American! I was a pretty good 'American'.

And I have always maintained, without pride, that had I ever desired to become one of the successful commercial gamblers of the West they would now be taking my money away in freight cars.

Came the Japanese war with Russia. Japan, the novice, put her schooling to the test and to the amazement of the dominant race she won that dubious prize. From that time on she began acquiring the stance in the Pacific that would some day stand her in good stead: valuable coast lines and some ten thousand islands. One of those, near by, became a vast secret training ground for trying out Western ideas with German schooling and Japanese improvements.

At one time—it was just previous to the Exclusion Act—Japan evidently looked upon the United States as an exception. Many of her people and many of her statesmen looked upon us as a possible trustworthy friend. I do not know why, unless because of our extensive (and expensive)

459

interest in her culture. But she soon lost that hope and with it went what little respect she ever had for us when she saw us selling coveted iron to her for war purposes at the same time that we were encouraging China to resist her. That act tallied with her firm faith in Western depravity and duplicity.

Japan has always adored the motherland, China, as we adore the motherland, England.

When I went to Peking, 1918, to let contracts for the rugs for the Imperial Hotel, I learned facts regarding China and Japan from Dr. Ku Hung Ming of Peking. He had once been secretary to the Empress Dowager of China. Dr. Ku was an Oxford graduate, but wore his cue (a Manchu inheritance) curled up under his red mandarin cap as a protest against what he called the motor-car Chinaman. While in Peking (Peiping) he wrote several famous books—one, *The Spirit of the Chinese People*, I had read which so impressed me that I determined to look him up when I arrived in Peking. I had a chance to sit and learn from him.

The sage and I went about off the beaten track exploring Peking. Since he hated the motor-car Chinaman, we took a strapping young Mongolian (six feet seven for me and another smaller for Dr. Ku—he was not very tall) and we would usually take along a guide who had attached himself to me—not very welcome he, but useful often.

We saw the old palaces, the blue-tiled Temple of Heaven, the Imperial Palaces, the great Gates, dusty caravans of camels going through from the Gobi Desert—loaded with furs. And then branched off into the unknown. One day he took me to an ancient temple little known to tourists. He was continually showing me the obscure but significant, interpreting it all to me in the spirit of the Chinese people. This particular temple-roof was down, water coming in on the sculptured walls—one entire wall was covered with pottery figures in complete relief set into niches in the wall. There were several hundred in several ranks, each some two and half feet high—brilliant in colour.

Dr. Ku walked away to take in the view.

I was again like the 'hungry orphan turned loose in a bakeshop' for the moment coveting the sacred images. Satan in the bulky form of the guide stole up alongside me and now that Dr. Ku's attention was on the landscape that came through the fallen walls, he said in a low voice, 'You like statues very much? Yes? All right—you pick out one, two, t'ree. I bring you hotel tonight, you see in mornin.'

I was tempted for a moment and then came a reaction—a revulsion of feeling would be it. I couldn't bribe this fellow to plunder the place—sacred to such as Ku Hung Ming—a plundering process across the years that was stripping China of her finest things. I said, 'No, no, I don't buy that way. Some day this temple might be restored.'

'Never,' said the guide. 'Soon all gone. Somebody else will get.'

'Not me.'

The little sage's ears must have been sharp. The dialogue had all been

460

sotto voce, but I heard steps behind me and felt an arm laid over my shoulders as the old philosopher's voice almost down to a whisper in my ear said, 'No, it is not so. *You* are no American.' The token of affection and respect, for so he meant it to be, touched me and I have never regretted abandoning those marvellous figures to the 'somebody who would if I didn't'.

We stood looking at the figures. Dr. Ku talked, told me about them. He too said there was not much chance of saving them. But it was better to leave them to their fate than go to perdition (or at least purgatory) with them.

The little old scholar, grey cue still curled up under his little red mandarin cap, said many wise things. He truly was a wise man—one of the few I've met. He was neither old school nor new school. He was the timeless sort so far as his mind went. I remember he said, as we walked about the ruins, there were almost no original Chinese left in China—all were now Mongolized. They had, during many, many centuries, been gradually Mongolized from the North. The only remaining original Chinese, due to an early migration by way of Korea, were the Japanese. The Japanese were Chinese who had met there on their islands the native Ainu and absorbed most of the small Ainu population. The secret of their excessive fertility was phosphorescent food, their diet of fish. And he said the rapid rate of their increase would soon raise a serious problem. A Japanese family of thirteen is a small family. A Japanese sire having sixty children to his credit was nothing unusual; of course, this would be a rich man with several wives. But the Oriental birth rate, including Russia (more largely Asiatic than is generally realized), was such as to be quite capable, were a gun put into its hand, of forming a deluge of manpower which under capable direction might easily swamp any further attempts by the West to subjugate Asia. They would multiply faster than they could possibly be killed, even by modern mechanized warfare. They could ride the wild horses of destruction three to one!

Now, he said, Japan looks upon herself as that 'gun in the hand' of Asia. Both Japan and China worship at the shrine of India. Should India gain her independence, she is their natural spiritual leader. The Hindus—Buddha—conquered China and Japan. Dr. Ku said the Asiatics regard Russia as the connecting link between the East and the West. Japan, no doubt, would some day, probably by way of China as a natural bridge, join with Russia. And it was not unlikely, in the opinion of Dr. Ku, that India freed from Western domination, would join with the yellow races led by Japan and China, and that all Asia would make a defensive treaty with Germany which would give a good four-fifths of the population and area of the world over to the power and uses of the yellow man. He said the Africans were sure to go with the Asiatics whenever the time came.

And in Dr. Ku's philosophic view was perhaps whatever biologic basis there was in the Emperor Wilhelm's 'Yellow Peril': an overwhelming opposite, an entirely separate race genius—one which we do not and cannot, even if we cared to, understand. Dr. Ku told me that we of the West

461

not only could not understand but could only ascribe to that genius the motives which we would ourselves have in whatever the circumstances might be, and be completely deceived every time as to whatever they might be actually. Russia and China were already, and soon Japan would be, glacial in the human mass due to the fecundity of population and limitless natural resources when modern sanitation and arms came to them.

No Asiatic nation could ever be thoroughly conquered for long by any outsider.

Never would Japanese conquest of China be the end of China or German conquest be the end of Russia.

But Japan's conquest of China *would* be the end of Japan. As the Mongolian was the end of the original Chinese, so the Mongolian-Chinese womb would be the end of Japan. Every Japanese man covets a Chinese woman. Even a well-to-do merchant will gladly take a Chinese coolie-woman for a wife. She would add at least nineteen half-castes the first generation, who would in the second generation add at least three hundred and forty-four three-quarterites, etc., etc., *ad infinitum*. In seven generations there would be no Japanese left in China nor probably very many left in Japan itself. 'Henceforth', said the tiger to the lady, 'henceforth you ride inside.' The fanaticism and cruelty of Orientals is something we can stay away from but that we can't change by fear of us or our power any more than we can level their eyelids to a perpendicular with their noses. Because they are not afraid and they fight not for revenge but for their own.

Now in 1942, remembering the words that Dr. Ku had spoken a quarter of a century ago and judging from my own experience, I find it utterly wrong to classify Hirohito with Mussolini and Hitler. Japan is an entirely different racial quantity and spiritual quality. She is pro-axis. That is all. She is really Asia for the Asiatics, dead or alive, and for whatever that may mean she will fight to the death. Anything that will serve that end she will embrace with indescribable Oriental faith and fatalistic fervour.

She feels the liberator's sword is in her hand and she feels free to use it in ways that seem treacherous to us of the Western world but which to her seem only good strategy.

She feels that but for the white bedevilment of China, the Indies, and India, she would even now be secure in her position as qualified leader of what she calls and feels to be the great Emancipation.

What the Western world calls and would like to believe to be the Chinese Republic was ridiculous to Dr. Ku. The Chinese Republic in his view was only a coastal strip which the great uncounted—even, to modern times, undiscovered—masses of Chinese know little and care less about. To refer to China as a Democracy was to refer to Dr. Sun Yat-sen, his remarkable family and friends, and a few million Chinese all looking to the U.S.A. for a hopeless confirmation and support, which could in any final issue only *betray* and *not* liberate the Chinese people. There was no realistic basis, not even a commercial one, for calling our support of China our fight on the side of 'Freedom'. No. Freedom of the Asiatics will, he said, never come by such external means. It would gradually grow from within, Japan or no Japan. And it was to be a matter of many centuries.

The West, Dr. Ku thought, failed utterly to take into account that China and Japan are of one blood. Their own natures within the range of their own fanaticism and cruelty can do best for and with each other in due course of time. He saw nothing the West could do for either nation or their collaterals except further bedevil and destroy them, postponing their inevitable future—the yellow races solidly linked by way of Russia with the West and Germany—if Germany should survive—retained as a paid schoolmaster. But the schoolmaster would probably be no longer needed.

ENGLAND—LONDON

April, 1939, an invitation came from the Sulgrave Manor Board by way of the British Ambassador to the United States to take the Sir George Watson Chair for that year and deliver the lectures that a bequest from Sir George had made possible. The lectures were to alternate, one year by an Englishman, the next by an American. The lectures were intended to serve the better acquaintance of British and American culture. Lord Bryce, Woodrow Wilson, Hadley of Yale, Theodore Roosevelt, the Governor of Canada, and many others, had delivered them.

The Sulgrave Manor Board, as you may know, took over the old home of George Washington in England and was taking good care of it—common ground in American and English history. The lecturer was free to deliver the famous lectures in any one of the English universities he might choose, and as many or as few lectures as he chose. The honorarium of twenty-five hundred dollars might be for but one lecture if the recipient of the honour so decided. The rights of publication went with acceptance by the lecturer. I accepted the honour, for so it was. I decided to give four evenings at London University. But the Royal Institute of British Architects, upon learning that I was chosen to give the lectures, proposed to join in sponsoring them, asking that they be given in the new hall of the new building of the Royal Insitute in Portland Place. As a preliminary attention, the Institute made me honorary member of their body so that I might not set foot on England's soil a stranger. At least I like to think that might have been one characteristic English reason.

The most coveted honour among architects in our country is this one from the Royal Institute of Great Britain. Unlike many of our own similar societies, its honours are honourably bestowed. They do not go by fashion or by favour or prestige and are so recognized throughout the United Kingdom. The Royal Gold Medal of the Royal Institute therefore goes a long way with any Britisher anywhere on earth and so as a matter of course it should go with any American anywhere. It rounded out the honours previously received from seven other countries. This last should have been

463

first—but that the first shall be last and the last shall be first is standard old prophecy.

We decided to take Iovanna with us. She would soon be thirteen and needed the educational experience. So we went by the *Queen Mary* again to London, this time staying at the old Garland Hotel which, standing not far from Trafalgar Square, put an end to Suffolk Street. On the boat we met a *Manchester Guardian* man who told us enough about the hotel to decide us to visit it. Henry James had stayed there to write. Whistler and his cronies had often turned up there. I remember that Ashbee said he stayed at the Garland when he came up from the country—Camden Town—to London. Lady Sandwich said people from the English country estates coming up to London often stayed there. We found the old place delightful. English homeliness and quaint ugliness. As English as anything in *Pickwick*.

In giving lectures, if that is what they are, I've found that I do my best if I do not make preparation for them whatsoever. When *I* get enjoyment out of delivering them, I am sure others get some. Trying to remember spoils the delivery of what I want to say when on my feet. Since I am only talking out of myself anyway, I need no rehearsal as I would if I had collected material for the occasion. The audience is an inspiration, too, not to be forestalled. So when I wish to do my best as I always do, I am careful not to think of what I intend to say. And this was the only careful preparation I made for the lectures—four evenings at the Royal Institute—lately published by Lund Humphries under the title *Frank Lloyd Wright*. A well-illustrated and tastefully printed book issued while the bombs were dropping on London. The first copies reached us in Arizona, February, 1941.

While listening to the New Year's Eve broadcast at Taliesin West, 1941, that same winter I learned that among the King's birthday honours of that year, His Majesty's Royal Gold Medal for Architecture had been bestowed upon me. If my friends were astonished, you may imagine my astonishment. I think they were all startled except Russell Hitchcock, who seemed to know something about it as being in the air.

I accepted with the cablegram: YOU PROPOSE A GREAT HONOUR. I ACCEPT GRATIFIED THAT DURING THIS TERRIFIC WAR ENGLAND CAN THINK OF HONOURING AN ARCHITECT. FRANK LLOYD WRIGHT.

Former American recipients had been Richard M. Hunt, Charles McKim, and Thomas Hastings. I took it as remarkable evidence of the great change taking place in the currents of thought in the modern world. It pleased me that the young lads who had been working with me would have less opposition to overcome in the years ahead than I had met. I regarded the award as a distinct break for them although perhaps there are worse enemies than open opposition. Popular success, for example.

The British lectures in the Sir George Watson Chair I regard as a great experience: one of the most gratifying of my life. Young men came from

73. Entrance. Redwood and desert stone

OBOLER GATE LODGE. 1938-9

74. Interior

CARLTON DAVID WALL HOUSE. 1940
Usonian type

75. View of dining room window scheme. Three arboretums enclosed in plate glass

76. Exterior view in winter. Cypress and brick

Edinburgh, Cambridge, and in between, until there was seldom even standing room in the splendid hall. Notably, the audiences were young. The audiences increased until they were turning many away.

Said the Earl of Crawford, leaning over toward me on the platform—'What is this, Mr. Wright? The board has never seen anything like this before.'

I said, 'Your lordship, I can't imagine.'

That same Lord, the evening on which I had taken perhaps too gloomy a view of the cultural state of things in general, got up and remarked that the proceedings had rather puzzled him. He said he felt somewhat in the position of Sandy at the funeral being held in the old Scotch churchyard. Sandy, curious to see what was going on, got too close to the edge of the grave, slipped and fell in, barking both shins on the coffin. Next day the local paper, commenting on the funeral, said, 'The unfortunate incident cast a gloom over the entire proceedings.'

And the good-natured laugh was on the 'lecturer'.

There was an affable Lord in the chair always. There is no better nor more competent company on earth than the English gentleman, but one or two of the M.P. Lords who came over to preside were, unlike the Earl, 'rather a bore, don't you know'. Olgivanna was present at all the lectures and many would ask her if it was true that my speaking was entirely spontaneous—not because it didn't seem so, but because it *did* seem so spontaneous. She assured them it was so: perfectly spontaneous. During post-mortem discussions of the lectures many interesting things were heard. One ponderous Duchess next seat to a friend of mine raised her lorgnette and asked, 'Who *is* this charlatan from Texas who comes way over here to talk *us* down?'

Iovanna was castle-crazy but was disappointed so much by the adding and patching that didn't 'belong'. She found a companion in John Gloag's little daughter who took her about. She was particularly offended by S Christopher Wren's additions because they so invariably ignored the original work as to be really not additions but subtractions. Nor could she reconcile the plumbing hanging over or on or showing under the ancient dignity of the outside walls. No amount of explaining squared the facts with budding Romance. She loved the Tower—but was eager to be on the trail of François Villon in Paris.

On the whole I who have the most intelligent of audiences have never had such a high level of intelligence and fine character in the audience as in London—nor such awareness and purposeful heckling. I always enjoy a heckling, and so does a British audience. I won't quote any of the many evidences of this because an old court reporter was present and got the whole thing down, so accurately that for once in my life there was little to correct in the copy he presented. The tasteful book, heckling and all, edited by Secretary of the Royal Institute, Carter, came out as I have said, when London was raided, bombs exploding, and the walls of London falling or in ruins.

There is something indomitable in British pluck and splendid in British character that makes you wonder what England might have been like in the culture of this world were it not for the 'white man's burden'—her Empire. Surely such qualities as hers are good for far more than war and conquest and the conduct of subjugated peoples. If England had a chance to be a free England on her own—developing slowly the characteristics and strength of Englishmen from within, the nation might have been small, but the world would have had one mighty, genuine democracy by now. A shining light, the great examplar needed. Her great were among the world's greatest, irrespective of conquest. Empire has ruined England. Her successes for three hundred years did her, as England, no real good. A disease took root and spread by way of her success. Dismal reflection it has now spread to us.

About a year later a telegram came from the *News-Chronicle* to the Arizona desert, asking for 1,500 words of cabled suggestions for the rebuilding of London, January 21, 1942. I sent the following:

The greatest creature of habit on earth is London. Slums and ugliness that would have taken centuries to overcome have been blasted out of the way in a few days. While sentiment is entitled to its tears, the art and science of human habitation may get a break. If English-speaking culture by way of grit and the will of Englishmen takes the break, goes ahead, and builds in line with this age of mechanical power the Empire may die, but English dominion will survive to triumph.

Power so capable to destroy is just as capable to create, we shall soon see. And we shall soon see whether England is humanitarian or only English, and whether Germany is humanitarian or only Germanic. If England is humanitarian London will decentralize. Even the bomb overhead points to that as a necessity. London reintegrated should be twenty-five times the area of old London. The new space-scale of our mechanical era is just about that—twenty-five feet now to one foot then.

Human congestion is murder; murder if not of the carcass, then murder of the most desirable human sensibilities. There is room and crying need for the greater London. The plan for it should be laid down now keeping in mind that Tradition with a capital T is greater than the manifold traditions to which it gives rise. Traditions must die in order that great Tradition may live.

Great buildings always begin at the beginning, so the necessary items are:

1. No very rich nor very poor to build for—no gold.
2. No idle land except for common landscape—no real estate exploiters.
3. No holding against society the ideas by way of which society lives—no patents.

In short, no speculation in money, land, or ideas; not one of them must be a speculative commodity but *must be used* as actual necessities of human life like air and water. This is the true basis for what we could honestly call Democracy. It is a necessary basis upon which to build a city of the mechanical age that will take the place of the feudal monster now being destroyed.

This liberation of human individuality is not so terrible a leveller of human fortunes as it may seem to be. It is the only basis for true capital, the life of human initiative. Base capital broad upon the ground, not as now with apex on the ground, base in the air. Except for the disabled, unemployment of any kind would be unthinkable in a State so founded. England could be that State and would be forever impregnable.

The physical body of the democratic city of today would have no one centre but would have many centres all well correlated, the height of the buildings increasing as the perimeter of activity was approached.

Were Old London to fairly accommodate the partial motorization it already had B.B. (Before Bombs), there could be no building at all in London. And London motorization had only just begun. London should be a motor-car, aeroplane London, the new spacing all laid out upon the new scale of human movement now set by car and plane.

But the sentimentality of our elders blocks the path of true progress and continually begs for compromise. Make none. Make none whatever, because all the vision we have is not enough to prevent such sentimentality from catching up and holding us back again. Keep this static out, and keep the traffic centres all wide open. Historic London could be featured in a great central London park-system. Conduct power from the mines. Do not cramp industrial areas around piles of raw material or fuel with the usual deadly-dull collateral 'housing'-by-Government. Abolish the back-and-forth haul of people, fuel and supplies. Do not be afraid to build factories and farms as fit associates for country homes, schools, churches, theatres and parks.

Railway arterials should be elevated with continuous storage space beneath the tracks: lorry traffic should be set low on each side so that lorries may be free to take on or take off anywhere. All traffic should be fluid and undated. Yes, it can be done. Such grandomania as survives the bombs should expend itself by extensions parallel with the ground—going up into the air only as activity thins out. Old building codes should be thrown away. New ones simplified and broadened in keeping with the opportunities of the new age should be written.

There must be no traffic problem. That has been solved in Broadacre City. Make broad streets concave instead of convex, with underpasses for foot passengers. Provide top-turn left inter-sections for traffic, and over- and under-passes for the criss-cross: no traffic lights because the roads themselves would be low-lighted ribbons. For all this the likelihood of accidents is reduced to about one tenth of one per cent. And away with poles and wires forever.

Along with speech honestly free goes free life for the individual on his own ground in his own house, all his own way, yet in no man's way.

No, not Utopia, just a way of building from a good modern plan for a Democratic people. That's all. What luxury and pagan beauty the Greeks knew or medieval Christianity knew is, by comparison, an exterior thing,

467

like some stage setting. There need be no difference in quality of thought between the house of a man with more and the house of a man with less: only difference in extent.

The home is the real citadel of the human race in any democracy. And where and while the private home has the integrity I here bespeak for it there will be no war.

All may harmonize. Individuality could inform and enliven all private homes now without mutual detriment if architecture could live again, even if it must live again because of bombs in irresponsible hands. Maybe it could yet only live because of bombs. Who knows?

It is easy to do this with fluid power and integral architecture. The necessity for the old pigeonholing aggregations of the horse and buggy past belong back there now with the horse and buggy mind and the manure pile. A new kind of beauty comes back to life—integrity. That is beauty. Plan for an integral economy. Integral building and economy is cemented to democratic culture. It is not a mere phrase. We are building it a little here and there, in spite of ancient codes, ignorant interference and wanton waste. Though international now, it spoke English first and can save England from bombs forever because the pressures that made war inevitable cannot exist in a Democracy so planned. Dictators would be out of luck.

No use blinking the fact that mechanics have outrun the social and aesthetic forms, the philosophy and ideas of your Yesterday. Why use Yesterday's rules for laws today? 'If we are on the side of nature we are never lawless.' We are safe. Were such organic planning executed, the Empire might disappear, but British Dominion would be safe. Were Germany to win this war it would be to lose it on any basis of a plane-and-gun future.

Don't grieve too much, Britain. Empire is no essential.

F. LL. W.—*Taliesin West.*

'The Empire of Imagination is more enduring than any Empire of mere fact.'

A note from Sir Ian McAllister said the cablegram had been published throughout the United Kingdom. In due course a *News-Chronicle* cheque for twenty guineas made 'the crossing'. In the circumstances a touching affair—that cheque.

RUSSIA—MOSCOW

May, 1937

An invitation came to travel as Honoured Guest of the Soviet Union to attend, in Moscow, the great world conference of Architects to which a number of the great architects of the world were being invited. So again we set out. We debarked from the *Queen Mary* at Cherbourg, went by way of Paris to Berlin, and after a short stay in both capitals, finally landed at the Russian border for customs' examinations. The examination (something like looking the gift horse in the teeth) was getting acrimonious and

468

more and more complex, when a telegram from Moscow called it all off and we took the old European leftover parlour-and-dining-car to Moscow.

There was a wide blank space at the frontier, trees all cut down, a kind of no-man's land, a barbed-wire entanglement both sides. Towers with sentries were overlooking this cleared space. Russian sentries were marching up and down the station platforms on the one side, Polish sentries on the other. I ran into one and was waved back into the Russian station.

The famous trials were just over. The Army had been purged of an army. It was said in Paris that both the frontiers were closed and we could not get into Russia. In Paris they tried to scare us out of going there at all. We wouldn't be scared.

I should like to write at length of Moscow, but this chapter of *An Autobiography* for a hundred reasons, all good, must come to an end.

The enthusiastic Russian people were wonderfully kind to us. Warm hospitality. Their works were even more wonderful. Old churches were going up in the air, dynamited to make way for wide avenues for the new Moscow. Moscow was being made ready for five million citizens. The great road-making programme going on toward Leningrad, young girls with white kerchiefs over their fair hair driving great steam-rollers. Tractors and trucks were everywhere. The old buildings, some good, contrasting sharply with the new ones, mostly bad. Of their kind, many of the old Russian Greek Orthodox churches were fine. Of course, the beautiful Kremlin.

But the modern buildings were hard and coarse, unsympathetic and badly proportioned. This would apply to all but a score of them with perfect justice. I don't wonder the Russian people reacted to them as they did, rejecting them in favour of the old classic order. The so-called modern buildings must have been hateful to the mystic emotion, the passion of the people of Russia. I met many of the Russian architects and writing for *Soviet Russia Today* when I came home, have described them and their work.

We went over to meet our Ambassador and had luncheon with Mr. and Mrs. Joe Davies. Joe was a Madison U. boy and we enjoyed a private talk, with a glance now and then at the walls, because there was reason to believe that outsiders were under espionage. But that wore off and not a single basis for suspicion could we see from first to last during our visit.

We were allowed to buy nothing for ourselves. Even our telegrams, personal laundry, went in with the hotel bills to the Soviet. The architects carried this so far that when we wanted to bring back some antique Russian instruments to Taliesin they wouldn't hear of anything but buying them and presenting them to us.

So warmly attached did we become to the Russian Spirit that I came nearer to tears in leaving them than I remember in my life.

What a land of opportunity was Russia! In the street or in private homes, in all places public or private, it was *we, ours*: our theatre, our subway, our schools, etc. Too much going into building up the defence which

would inevitably have to be used, and perhaps just because it was buil
up to such proportions! It was a subject of which no one spoke. I don'
know. The world was in a jam. Great changes coming. And there wa
something in the air then—May, 1937—that made everyone afraid o
something he couldn't define.

The American newspapers were nasty because I said publicly that the
had not been telling us the truth over there at home about Russia, an
were I in Stalin's place I would kick them out, all correspondents, and fo
the good of everyone concerned. There were a few exceptions. I name
them. Walter Duranty was one.

There were at the Congress architects from Spain who told us of the
restoration of old Spanish buildings undertaken as soon as the bombing
had ceased—long before either side had won the war. There were architects from Turkey, Ankara, Jerusalem. From Finland, Rumania, Sweden
Norway, and, of course, England and France. But most interesting were
the native architects from the fifty-eight Russian States stretching of
toward Tibet and toward Batum on the Black Sea. In all there was a
ideality, an eagerness to learn, I had never seen before. A solidarity difficult to believe in. Comradeship was everywhere as they filled the great
circular foyer of the Hall of the Nobles and gathered in groups for discussion of what had already or was just about to take place.

When we got further in to the country I was surprised to find the same
flowers and trees we have here at Taliesin, and see them fighting the very
same weeds at the Kolkhoz until I learned that the latitude is the same.

The belts of similar foliage, bird and animal life seem to encircle the
globe in strata according to latitude. Longitude doesn't matter much.

We stopped at the Metropole—historic old Europeanized caravansary—
until we went to Sukhanov. Sukhanov is the Russian Taliesin. The same
rural loveliness—oaks, pines, white birches, and wild flowers. The same
herds and the same birds and similar architects.

But the buildings were of the ancient order—an old palace, a big circular room with a big circular table at which the architects sat with their
families and guests, to be fed from provender which they raised themselves.
Their herd was twice the size of ours on four hundred acres where we have
about a thousand.

We liked the Russians and they liked us. I had liked them back in 1915
to 1919 when I had invited Russian refugees from the Revolution (there
were so many in Tokio) to my apartment at the old Imperial. Then it was
the Russian of the old Regime I liked; now in 1937 it was the Russians
of the Soviet proletariat. The women I thought much the same in both
regimes. In them the Russian spirit, regardless of circumstances, shone
through. With the men it was quite different—in favour of the proletariat.

In my Tokio apartment was that rarity in Tokio, a grand piano. (I had
found a fairly good one on the Ginza and bought it.) The food at the
Imperial was probably as good as anywhere in the world, so I used to in-

vite them frequently and we got to know each other pretty well. So well, in fact, that they would sometimes put an arm around me and say, 'But no, it cannot be that you are an American! Surely you are a Russian!'

'No,' I would answer, 'I am very much an American. And so are you! It isn't that we are one or the other but alike, that's all.'

But they would say, 'We don't like Americans.'

'Well, the reason for that is that you really know Americans. The ones you would like don't come here often. Come to America and see them where and as they really live and you will like Americans. The travelled ones aren't the natural or even the more cultivated ones. I can think of a dozen American men with whom the princess (Cheremissinof) would fall in love and the Countess C, Countess Metaxa, and Countess Lubienski, too. Perhaps you would like our American men better than our women. I don't know. The women can be awfully nice. Your men would like them. They aren't too much like the movie stars you see. The little shop girls take the stars for patterns, but our American women, those not Frenchified too much nor Anglicized out of their natural lives, would resemble Russian ladies more than any other nationality. I assure you— you would like us at home.

'Nobody likes us abroad because the best of us don't go much abroad.'

And this little speech to the Russian refugees in Tokio twenty-five years ago goes for the proletariat in Moscow today. There is something native to present-day Russians which is also native to Americans. It is the simplicity of freedom. Or should I say the freedom of simplicity? Strange that I could see but little difference between the women of the old regime and the women of the new. The men? Yes, there was a difference there.

I love the Russian spirit. I am glad my wife speaks Russian. She was a wonderful interpreter for me and frequently cleared up points for them. She was educated in Russia even though it was under the old regime, so she speaks the soft beautiful language like a native. Soviet Russia and Usonia are capable of perfect understanding and sympathy. It is inevitable. But the Russians are richer in human content and in colourful spirit owing to their Oriental heritage. I, too, think they combine the East and the West. The best of us not only have sympathy to give them, but an experience that might show them much to avoid. I guess we ought to have a revolution over here.

TO RUSSIA

As the Honoured Guest of the Russian People I had come to deliver the following speech from the speaker's box in the great Hall of the Soviets where the famous purge trials were held. Inasmuch as I couldn't speak the language, I wrote the speech and had the text translated by *Pravda*. The translation was carefully checked by Olgivanna before giving it to Colle, the President of the Institute of Architects, to read. I spoke the introduction and conclusion, leaving him to read the body of the text. The place was filled to overflowing with six hundred architects from all the

471

states of the Soviet Union, and many from abroad. I have never had so great an ovation in my life. Many young architects crowded around Olgivanna, she who could speak to them, saying, 'We know your husband's work so well, and we even knew his face before he got here.' The place resembled a convention hall electing a president. Again and again I had to go back, the applause continuing until I reappeared to take my seat beside Olgivanna in the box at one side when the entire audience rose to its feet, turned our way with a new burst of applause. The Soviet fliers had just won the plaudits of the whole world by reaching Seattle across the North Pole. There was great excitement in Moscow—flares, music and triumphal marching day and night.

ADDRESS TO THE CONGRESS OF ARCHITECTS
SOVIET RUSSIA

MY DEAR COMRADES: I have travelled across the frontiers of five nations, from one great hope of the world, the U.S.A., to greet another great hope of the world, the U.S.S.R. I find that I, your guest, could now go home crossing but one, and that one the frontier of my own nation. And I can return by travelling only one-third of the distance I travelled to get here. The U.S.S.R. and the U.S.A. are both moved into a central position among the nations of the Northern Hemisphere by the supreme aviation of the Soviet Union. Thanks to Science we are next-door neighbours. But the Soviets are now to build fine buildings: a very different matter. A great art. I am glad to be here because I am already familiar with your struggle to find suitable architecture for your new Soviet life. I am sympathetic because we of the new life of my own country, the U.S.A., were ourselves where you stand now. We once had the great opportunity—'a clean slate', as we say. We had to choose between crawling back into the shell of an old culture or going bravely forward to the new one we needed in order to become a strong new culture ourselves. In our new-found freedom we made the wrong choice. We chose the inferior path of the slave.

The rapid growth of Science, apparent success of mechanical appliances and industrial technique, these achievements exploiting vast natural resources gave us great wealth, suddenly. All these advances had so far outrun our knowledge of the principles underlying the right practice of Art that, needing Architecture as much as you do now, we freely plundered such tombs of preceding civilizations as we liked, and foolishly built upon forms we took from the bargain counter of dying or decayed cultures. So today our official architecture is a disgrace to the name of freedom owing to that ignorant licence.

Our official buildings only serve to betray by way of our commercial vanity our significant triumphs in the realms of Industry and Science. As it is elsewhere in the world, only now are genuine architectural forms suited to our new life breaking through. We see them, if we look for them, among these stage settings with which we ignorantly sought to camouflage our lack of growth from within: the growth that alone is worthy to

472

be called Culture; the integrity which gave ancient nations whatever greatness they had in their day. That we have done pretty well at this prostitution is poor enough consolation. What we have done is not good enough because meantime the U.S.A. has allowed herself to learn nothing of architecture. All of the arts in our country have suffered atrophy in consequence.

Our skyscraper? What was it? A triumph of engineering but the defeat of architecture. Steel frames standing hidden by facings of thin stone tied on to the steel frame—fascinating pictures—imitating feudal towers; but Architecture as false as the civic economy that allowed them to be built in congested urban areas. I have seen a dismal reflection of that falsity in your own work palace. This work palace—only proposed, I hope—is good if we take it for a modern version of St. George slaying the Dragon: that is to say—Lenin stamping the life out of a capitalistic skyscraper.

And elsewhere among you, I see our old enemy—Grandomania. I see it even in your subways. I see you repeating underground what the nobles did for themselves (and to themselves) in this hall in which we stand now. Suitable enough, no doubt, for their parasitic life, but too far beneath the level of the new integrity we are learning to call organic architecture, naturally becoming to those ideals of freedom for which you fought.

The 'palatial' will not be easily destroyed in Russia as I see. Cut grandomania down here and it lifts up its head somehow over there (which means among you over here) when and where we least expect it. But I believe it is popular here only because the finer expressions of modern architecture have been allowed scant standing room among you.

A new thought comes to us fresh from the new freedom of humanity: a more exacting and exciting ideal has come with these new freedoms than the Old Cultures ever knew. The old cultures could only flourish by externals, but the new must and may now flourish by growth from within. Slow growth, I know. But it is the only growth that is safe for Russia now.

I dread to see the Soviet Union making the same mistakes our American Union made. When buildings must be built before culture has had time to come abreast in order to make them true architecture, it is better for the Soviets to make buildings scientifically sound with as much good sense and intelligent use of good materials as possible. Then stop there!

The left wing of our new movement toward an organic architecture professes to do this but they did not do more than make flat-topped plain-wall surfaces ornamental. They will pass.

The right wing was not content to do less than make ornament of the building itself. They are therefore in senile, bad company. But the true centre of the movement, organic architecture, has gone on developing the scientific, sound material conditions of building into a higher manifestation of the human spirit suited to modern life.

At this moment were the Soviets to concentrate on good proportion, good planning and construction, building great highways and bridges, great planting schemes, retaining walls and terraces, refraining from much ornamentation of her structure and refraining from any attempt to make them elaborate in form until her young architects by way of experiment gradually evolve new Russian types as true to the New Russia as the Kremlin was true to the Old Russia—then the U.S.S.R. would justify our new world hope. A genuine culture at last! I am hoping the U.S.A. will some day undo what it has so badly done, and itself not do less than this.

Comrades, in building, do not waste yourselves upon these mere affairs of 'taste'. Architecture, in the advanced thought of the time, is fast becoming a matter of scientific knowledge applying philosophical ideas wherein Art is again free and supreme.

Take no less than this.

Another great matter coming to light in our modern world is the inevitable decay of great cities. Urban life has served its turn even for you, and cities great or cities small are definitely dated. The factory worker's view and version of life, and his vision now especially, needs the co-operation and healthy inspiration of Russian ground. The agrarian needs the industrialist, yes, but the industrialist needs the agrarian far more. The ground is the natural and national birthright of every man and is more important to him than anything he makes out of it or puts upon it. Of that fundamental basic ingredient of the good life—Russia has plenty for all and forever to come. So it would seem to me.

Russians, make good use of your ground for the new Russia! Can the Soviets not see that electricity, machines, automobiles, radio, television—the architecture of splendid highways and spacious, farflung Agriculture—can make the old form of city (centralization) not only useless, but harmful to the future? Vertical is vertigo, in human life. The horizontal line is the life-line of humankind. An entire nation will some day be one great free extended city. Its citizens will be living broadly spaced on ground of their own in a free pattern where workers in field and factory, in art and craft, science and education, commerce and transportation, will harmoniously intermingle. Each human endeavour will be related to every other on organic lines natural to all. And human life without waste motion, distraction, dissipation, interference, or imposition will take on new forms—better ways of doing everything. If that is what Russia means to do, then I am a Russian. Everybody in Russia, whatever his nation, will be a free man. Organic architecture has already so far evolved the pattern of such a higher life on earth as to be able to know and show the City of the Future. I would much like the young architects of the U.S.S.R. to see, and some day they may see, Broadacre City—the city that is everywhere and nowhere.

The United States is still far from such a plan. Her economic waste and the attempt of production to control consumption prevent it. Private Ownership and the Profit System supreme and raised to the nth degree in all branches of life prevent it. These economic follies make the greater city impossible for another half-century at least. But Russia could have that freedom of democratic form now, if she wanted it enough. Her architects have the vision and the ability.

This new freedom is the great integrity modern life lacks and needs. This integrity is the service organic architecture could render the U.S.S.R. at this critical stage in the national life of the Soviets. And later it will extend from Russia to the continental world at large—if by that time there should be any of it left.

To you architects of the Soviet Union: I, who admire and love your spirit, I say, Go slowly into the higher realm of building that we call Architecture. No matter what the pressure, prepare to begin at the true beginning! Learn structure, yes, but first study thoroughly the *principles* beneath the technique and forms of organic architecture, and by way of your own high Russian spirit, grow an architecture as true to yourselves living the new Soviet life as the forever beautiful Kremlin was true to the old life of the soil, so that the great work grew out of itself where it stands.

The Kremlin—divested of its parasitic Renaissance improvements— stands as one of the great human treasures of all time.

The Soviet must not imitate the Kremlin. But the Kremlin honours the Soviet. And it is my great hope that the Soviet will honour itself by growing up to be a true cultural entity in terms of today's tomorrow. When Architecture is really Architecture it is timeless. Out of the young Freedom that is now the U.S.S.R., other great treasures for the Future should come. But, patience. They cannot be forced. They also must humbly begin at the beginning and slowly grow.

Returning from Russia the American papers were openly hostile because of what I said about them in Moscow. But I wrote the article below: 'Architecture and Life in the U.S.S.R.' in August, 1937. It was published in *Soviet Russia Today*. Russia was then 'red', and therefore to the entire United States, news and radio, disreputable.

No one wanted to hear anything good about the U.S.S.R.

To commend anything Russian got you in wrong with the powers-that-be—socially, financially, and especially morally.

My God, of what hypocrisy we are capable!

ARCHITECTURE AND LIFE IN THE U.S.S.R.

Now that I am back at Taliesin again, my Moscow colleagues are far enough away for perspective to assert itself. I enjoyed them so much, was personally so much in sympathy with them while there, that appraisals made on the spot might easily have been overdrawn. They were not.

As I look back now across the Pole—my friends in Moscow and their work appear the more extraordinary. I went to them intending to do what little I could to end the confusion in the reactionary practices in Architecture I saw among them. I particularly disliked the Work Palace of the Soviets. I had hoped to alter the minds entangled with its erection. But the foundations were in.

And I found that in Russia, as in the United States long ago, the masses who had nothing and to whom the landed aristocracy appeared to have everything, now had their turn to be pleased. Nothing pleases them so much as the gleam of marble columns under high ceilings, glittering chandeliers, the unmistakable signs of luxury as they looked up to it when it decided their fate, and they ate out of luxury's hand if they ate at all.

But reassurance for me lay in the attitude of the Soviet architects themselves. I may mention Alabyan, Collé, Yofan, the Vesnins, Nikolsky, Chusev, and the editor, Arkin, as personal acquaintances in this connection. All of them took the present situation with a humour and a touch of fatalism characteristically Russian.

Just now is no time to offer the liberated ones the high simplicity which repudiates the falsity of that sort of luxury. This is not the time to insist upon something they could not understand—the higher simplicity that has turned upon that flagrant artifice as the people themselves turned upon its possessors. So in the Soviet Union I saw the cultural lag again as I have seen it and fought against it for a lifetime in these United States. With the Russians, as with the Americans, several more generations must pass before a more natural way of life and building takes the place of the old order. The Russian people see viciousness in that old order where human rights are concerned. But the masses of the Russian people are yet unable to see that viciousness in the higher realm of created things of which architecture is the highest, and that what they fought to destroy still lives on among them in the parasitic forms of the life they destroyed, to destroy them in a more subtle and far-reaching destruction.

The architects, however—at least those I have named—are men who realise this. But they are men who say, 'Never mind—we will tear it down in ten years.'

'It will take nearly that long to finish the Palace of the Soviets.' I said.

'Never mind, we may tear that down too—even before we complete it.'

'But this popular rush to get into Moscow? Are you right when you prepare Moscow to take five million country people, instead of sending Moscow out to the five million?'

'But Russia needs a cultural centre for her uneducated millions for years to come. Let the city be that cultural centre for a time,' said they.

Such resignation would not be possible for me. I can understand it, perhaps envy it, but cannot approve it. Notwithstanding the tragedy of the first essays in the direction of the new simplicity, I would see the Russian opportunity as a mighty incentive in no way diminished by a false start.

But the attitude of the Russian architect is sincere and far in advance of the social consciousness of our own American architects. I do not know one architect among us who looks so far into the future, able to smile indulgently at his own present effort—perspective given by a fine sense of humour mingled with idealism.

Said Alabyan: 'I thought I would put all the columns I would have to use for the rest of my life into this building [the new Theatre] and have done with it.' Said Vesnin, concerning his Palace of Culture and Rest (a very desirable improvement on Le Corbusier et al.), 'It lacks colour. It is only a preliminary study. It is not yet Russian.' Said young Yofan, not yet

476

disillusioned concerning his highly decorated eclecticism, the Palace of Soviets: 'Never mind, Mr. Wright, it will improve as we go along. We are studying it continually.' And I saw proofs of that statement in Yofan's studio (Napoleon's old residence in Moscow by the Kremlin wall).

Who could help loving such liberal, great-hearted, imaginative fellows? What colleague would not do anything he could do under heaven to help them? The result might be help *from* them. Said they to me: 'Have faith in our people. We Russians are by nature artists. We love the beautiful. Our sense of life is deep and rhythmic. We will create a new Russia. You will see.'

I believe I do see in their efforts a new organic Russia slowly entering into their buildings 'through closed doors'. And I see no necessity for Russia to die that the Soviet Union may live.

If Comrade Stalin, as disconcerted outsiders are saying, is betraying the revolution, then, in the light of what I have seen in Moscow, I say he is betraying it into the hands of the Russian people.

In Moscow the architects enjoy a large old palace complete, as their Academy. There you find a gallery and supper rooms on the top floor. Libraries, studios, and collections below. Just before leaving Moscow we joined some of the architects I have named for retreat and recreation at their Sukhanov, a four-hundred-acre park, thirty miles from Moscow, where another old palace stands. There, their own herds and flocks around them, they are putting up new buildings. All stand in a beautiful forest with fine vistas of beautiful countryside. To this wooded retreat whenever they will, they may and do go with their families and friends for recreation. The architects are about to build small studios for preliminary study and shops for technical experiments.

There seems to be none but friendly rivalry among them. Why should there be other than willing cooperation? Worldly rewards cannot benefit them. They are economically independent for life and so are their loved ones. One man's success hurts no one else but is a stepping stone for his fellows. The sting has been taken out of competition. There is no humiliation in today's defeat because failure today may be retrieved by tomorrow's triumph. The road is open. And their 'tomorrow' is today in the sense that Eternity is Now. You will feel it so when you talk to them.

Good fellowship at Sukhanov, as Olgivanna, my good interpreter, and I found, is an unforgettable human experience. Have you ever known Russian hospitality? No? Well, then, be an architect and go to visit Russian architects. They will take you to Sukhanov.

Being a farmer myself as well as an architect, I visited a collective dairy farm. The farmers were at their work in the fields and barns, all sharing according to their contributions. They milk three times a day—at sunrise, at ten o'clock, and at sunset. All live together in a village like the farm village of the old order except that now there is the crèche filled with babies cared for while their mothers are at work. The babies are nursed by their own mothers. Nearby is a kindergarten, along modern lines. Both crèche and kindergarten are maintained by the Soviet itself. The *kolkhoz* is a nucleus characteristic of Soviet effort, but his agrarian effort is far less developed than industrial effort, as it still is with us in the U.S.A.

The factory is better built and run than the farm. For one thing, the farm requires so much more. This is partly because the Revolution first came from organized labour in the factories and the farms at first resisted the subsequent movement to collectivize their work. At one time the farmers destroyed their pigs and crops rather than turn them over to the collectives. We well know how difficult it is to bring any cooperation to bear upon American farm life, or within it, even now. The Grange came the nearest of anything we had but it does not flourish.

The agrarian hurdle seems to have been taken by the Soviets. Co-opera-tive farming is likely to prove the same blessing that socialization proved to be in factory industry. The houses of the farm village range about a central square that might be a beautiful park, with loud-speakers there connecting each farm group with the voice of their leader and the cultural efforts of the urban centres. In time, these farm units are sure to become the most desirable of all places in which to work and live.

Plans for the new Moscow are still wrong from my standpoint but far ahead of any city planning I have seen. There is splendid opportunity to make the city over because no private property nor sentimentality can say 'no' when the great plan requires the blowing up of whole sections of old buildings. Even sacred old landmarks are blown into the air to make spacious streets where dirty obscure lanes existed. The scope and liberal character of the proposed changes and extensions are astonishing.

When completed, Moscow will inevitably be the first city in the world. But to me, that can only mean something already dated and outlived by the advanced thought of our today, Broadacres.

All of the new city will be much too high—the same premium put upon congestion that landlordism places there. And I suppose this is partly be-cause the industrialist, still clinging to his habits, is ahead of the agrarian in the U.S.S.R. He is still ahead in our own U.S.A. For some reason, there will be regimented areas too in the 'classic' manner, where inevitable freedom should be. There will be four-storey school-houses—knowledge factories—where two stories would be too high. And while the entire outer-belt is a park area, it should be the other way round. The best of the traditional and official buildings should stand in a big central park, buildings growing higher as they extend outward into the country.

But much that is splendid is already done—wide avenues and park spaces. The ancient Moscow River is being walled with cut granite blocks sweeping in a fine curve from the water to the upper levels. The ancient Kremlin walls and domes stand nobly above these great new granite-slopes.

The Moscow subway is a succession of well-planned palatial stations. I like the more simple ones, built at first, with columns containing lights, the shafts rising and spreading into the overhead. Later ones are richer and more spacious. The Moscow subway makes the New York subway look like a sewer.

But cutting across the road to culture there is a barrier—the same barrier that is here with us: the popular demand for spiritually unearned, luxurious grandeur. But in their case, no wonder or reproach. The Russians outside the aristocracy and bourgeoisie had less than nothing. Now it is their turn. Millions looking toward Moscow as a Mecca can go there at last! Of course, they go and want to stay, because the lash of unrequited toil on the land has left its scars.

Concerning new construction: their buildings are no better or worse than the best work of other countries. Misfortune befell Moscow when her modern architects took after the left wing. That mistake in direction left some very negative and foreign results—indeed, drab, lonesome, technically childish. The popular reaction from that fiasco could only be luxurious picture-making in the antique, the picture-making which the older people learned as children to admire and covet.

Chusev and I stood together in his great Soviet hotel, a huge constructed thing, done in what I told him should be called 'the Metropolitan style' because you could see it with such virtues as it has and all its faults in Philadelphia or any big city of the world. A comfortable hotel though, and I exaggerated a little because in many respects it was better done, and more comfort provided for the occupant, but still the building was the type of hotel we Americans are learning to hate.

Mere size seems to captivate the Soviets as it seduced our provinces earlier. Of course, all this is the reaction in action which I was afraid I would see.

The Palace of the Soviets, to be the crowning glory of the new construction, suffers likewise from grandomania of the American type in imitating skyscraper effects way up to the soles of the enormous shoes of Lenin, where the realistic figure of that human giant begins to be three hundred feet tall. Something peculiar to the present cultural state of the Soviet is to be seen in the sharp contrast between thick shoes and workman's clothes and skyscraper elegance. These perpendiculat skyscraping motives are surmounted at the characteristic New York setbacks by sculpture, pygmy by comparison.

Lenin, enormous, treads upon the whole, regardless. Nothing more incongruous could be conceived and I believe nothing more distasteful to the great man Lenin if he could see. And yet Yofan, the young architect whose design was accepted for this work seven years ago, has this year built the most dramatic and successful exhibition building at the Paris Fair. The general motive of that building is not dissimilar to that of the Palace of the Soviets. It too is a building surmounted by gigantic sculpture.

But the Paris Fair building is a low, extended, and suitable base for the dramatically realistic sculpture it carries, whereas the Palace of the Soviets itself is a case of a thoroughly unsuitable, badly over-dramatized base underneath realistic undramatic sculpture.

I went with Yofan to see a sanatorium he had done near Moscow and that too was a very well-designed, very well-built structure. Any Soviet citizen needing attention and care may go there to luxury seen only on our trans-Atlantic liners. An ingenious arrangement of balconies and rooms gives outdoor enjoyment to indoor comfort. On the whole, here is a performance that could not be, has not been, excelled anywhere. The building occupied by *Pravda* I saw as the more creditable of the 'modernistic' attempts by the Russians. But, because of its negative and unconstructive precedents, such building is not for the Russians—it is too laborious a stylization of too little spirit and small content. I see the Russians discontented with less than something profound, when culture catches up—say, in ten years.

The extensive Palace of Culture, a recreational centre for the studious or artistically minded citizen, was better in many respects. It contains as good a design for an auditorium as I, a specialist in auditoriums, have ever seen. The scope and extent of the whole is good in conception, not bad in execution. I liked its architects. I will like their work better when it is more like them, and that means more Russian in spirit and character. Both architects are capable, invaluable to the Soviet as are many others besides the friends I have mentioned. The Soviet sent more than four hundred Russian architects to the Congress at Moscow. And invited many from other countries.

Leningrad is to be, I take it, the Soviet showpiece in cities. Nikolsky showed me his design for the new stadium at Leningrad: stadium spaciously monumental, a broad treatment employing masses of trees in an architectural way I liked much. A sensible relief from ponderous masonry, it will be a fine work on a grand scale.

The Russian cinema has made its buildings the finest good-time places for the people to be seen anywhere in the world. The Vesnins have designed some of them. Collé, my interpreter at the Congress, President of the Architect's Society—the A.I.A. of the U.S.S.R.—has a fine sense of proportion and style, at present leaning classic-ward, however. Alabyan, President of the Congress, shows himself a competent designer in the new theatre, giving some life to the old mode. And so it goes on, this tremendous social construction that is calling upon Architecture for help and direction. Competent architects able to build great buildings are there. And alongside are sympathetic employers, critics, editors like Arkin, the editor of *Pravda*, and many others, among whom the heads of their fine arts academies may be included although now, as here, on the side of reaction. I hope temporarily.

What a pity that architecture in Soviet Russia is not as free as the man —so that the millennium might be born at once, where the road is still more open than anywhere else, without all this wasteful wearisome temporizing with the old time-lag and back-drag of the human predilection for ignorance where culture is concerned. It is hard for me to be reconciled to the delays Russia is experiencing, no matter how cheerfully, in getting architecture characteristic of her new freedom.

I saw the admirable models for Soviet Russia's new towns and cities in various places—all better than good but too many concessions to the cultural time-lag. I suppose the marvel of it all is that a country so backward as Russia should have these fine things at all—at least, have them so soon. Perhaps too soon!

I grant all that and still regret.

But I saw something in the glimpses I had of the Russian people themselves which makes me smile in anticipation: the Russian Spirit!

There is nothing like that spirit anywhere in the world today.

I felt it in the air, saw it as a kind of aura about the wholesome maleness of her men and femaleness of her women; in this new gospel of work; in the glad open expressions of the faces of workmen and workwomen. Freedom already affects them unconsciously; proud they carry themselves. Especially the women. I could not help feeling, 'What a mother this new Russia is going to have!'

A kind of new heroism, one more integral with humankind, is surely growing up in the world in the Soviet Union where men are men and women are women; where God has ceased to be an expensive abstraction to the people; where abortion is abolished; where there is no illegitimate child and the resources of the state stand behind the mother to reinforce her in the care of her sons and daughters. In Russia, there is a place in the sun ready for the little newcomer when conceived. Wherever and whenever the child is born, there is really another citizen with rights guaranteed by the state—education ready and waiting and opportunity to work. There is no discrimination between the sexes.

All this is surely wise.

And how wise are the premiums placed upon *quality* in work—integral industrial rewards which build up the man in his effort—the 'Stakhanov Principle', they call it. Rewards of a social and substantial character devised by a wise leader to develop an entirely new Success ideal. It is hard for us *here* in our society, our Success ideal as it is, to conceive this new freedom for the individual without grasping several fundamental things totally changed there in the human objective. I find myself continually needing a more simple viewpoint than our complex order of 'meum and tuum' allows. Until we get that viewpoint, however, we cannot understand Russia. We of the grasping West will marvel at her vitality and strength, her heroic growth and richness of expression, and admire expecially her colourful individuality, never knowing the secret of such happiness.

That secret is too simple for us because it does not longer consist in our way of to-have or to-hold but in acceptance of a life consisting in neither except insofar as having or holding may have human benefits each to each and each to all. The relief of such release from ignoble fear, economic anxiety and false shames, you may already see in Soviet faces, Soviet acts. Heroes and heroism will glisten naturally in the fabric of this new Soviet life.

Having seen and sensed the Russian spirit, I should say that enemies interfering with the Soviet Union would not only have to reckon with the whole male population bearing arms, but with the women too, and every child above nine years of age.

Nothing less than total extermination could conquer Soviet Russia.

A true poet and philosopher, Dr. Ku [I have quoted him when talking about Japan], had the faculty of thinking and speaking 'in simples'. One day, while sitting on the edge of an old stone terrace overlooking a lotus pool, he summed up and characterized the various races of the world with what seemed to me great insight and justice—especially with regard to America. 'Soul' seemed to him to be the element most lacking in all the nations—the French having a substitute. The substitute was delicacy.

But, he said, it was Russia who would give soul to the world.

At that time I knew Tolstoy, Turgenev, Dostoevsky, Pushkin, and Gogol; I knew Russian music and theatre too, somewhat. And I thought I saw what he meant.

Today I believe what he said. It is true. Russia may yet give to this money-minded, war-minded, quarrelling pack of senile races that make up the Western world the soul they fail to find within themselves—and, I hope, in time to prevent the suicide the nations are so elaborately preparing to commit.

Taliesin, August 10, 1937.

One of the many repercussions to the foregoing article, which was copied by the *Capital Times* of Madison, was this letter:

AN OPEN LETTER TO FRANK LLOYD WRIGHT

In the many years that your name has been associated with excellence in Architecture, you have won a reputation for honesty and fearlessness, and your opinions are listened to by many Americans. It is therefore regrettable that you should have seen fit to couple a favourable account of the Soviet Union with a serious slur on the Communist Party of the United States.

We, who have visited your Taliesin and have seen your buildings with uncompleted floors, without light, and without heating facilities, have witnessed a melancholy illustration of how art is forsaken by an economic system whose one God is profit. We have admired the integrity which has kept you from accommodating your talents to the erection of the kind of structures Capitalism is willing to buy.

We wondered what you would say of the land of socialism where art as well as industry belongs to the *whole* people, and a great architect's creations do not need to stand about without electricity, gloomy symbols of the enchainment of art under capitalism. And we were not mistaken in your integrity. You came back with frank praise, you gave the lie to the distortions of the press, you said: 'If Stalin is "betraying the Revolution" as people are constantly shouting, he's betraying it into the hands of the Russian people.' We are therefore completely at a loss to fathom your assertion that the Communists in America are racketeers. Can it be that you have momentarily forgotten your distaste for 'Grandomania' and disdain us, merely because as yet there are only fifty thousand of us and we are not quite in a position to do the things the Communist Party in Russia can do?

Or can it be that even after learning that a first-hand knowledge of Soviet Russia is quite different from what the capitalist press supplies us with, you are still content to get your information about the *American* Communist Party at second hand from that same press? If the statement in the *Capital Times* was not an error, we hope that you will find time to make an accusation more explicit and that the fairness you have shown in your description of Russia will prompt you to give us a chance to answer. We feel convinced that only a lack of direct acquaintance with American communists—coupled perhaps with the all too common mistake of confusing some campus bohemians with Communists—can be responsible for your statement.

The Faculty Branch of the Communist Party, University of Wisconsin.

REPLY TO THE FACULTY COMMUNISTS OF THE UNIVERSITY OF WISCONSIN:

TO OUR UNIVERSITY COMMUNISTS: I have read your open letter. First, let me assure you that I have not said Communists in America were Racketeers. That was a slip between the Press and the lip—over the telephone. To say that would be as untrue as foolish. I did say, Trotskyites and campus intelligentsia in mind, that the Communists in our country seemed to me, now that Racketeers were in among them as they are among the labour unions, the worst enemies of Russia.

I confess that I do not know what your 'communism' is. I do not believe it is like that, but I am inclined now to see any ist or ism as alien and shun the ites.

I have lived to see the organic architecture I put my life into exploited in the name of an ism—made istic by the 'ites'. I refer to 'internationalism', now the 'modernistic'. So perhaps I am too ready to believe that whatever communism may once have been, it too has been exploited by 'campus sharp-wits', the lazy irreverent sharp-wits who flourish on ists and isms. Inevitable ites that curse truth by living *on* it instead of living *for* it. Theirs is the kiss of Caiaphas. For that reason, what does the term Republican mean now, or Socialist, or Democrat? Yes, or Communist? Any ideal or movement is more vulnerable from beneath and from within than it is from the outside or from above. Communism in the United States is a conspicuous example. Or that term Progressive? Already just about as ambiguous. Let's drop the corrupted and corrupting labels and be specific!

'Social Justice' sounds better to me than any ism, but that too is only label. I could march under a banner that stood squarely upon that idea if made definite.

The United States might unite under the banner of some unequivocal idea, and win any honest social objective.

483

Democracy itself, like Social Credit, is no more or less than Social Justice. But even the grand term, Democracy, has been bought and oversold by party politics and fakirs until it is now merely 'Americanistic'.

TO YOU, AMERICAN COMMUNISTS

FROM RUSSIA TO THE UNITED STATES AND BACK AGAIN TO RUSSIA . . . AS TO 'FORM':

1. Every man guaranteed the right to work.
2. No able man to eat unless he works.
3. Free ground and a free medium of exchange.
4. General decentralization: less crowding everywhere, and less government except as government consists in transacting the impersonal business of the whole people.
5. No speculation in natural resources or in the utilities common to all by way of which our people live. No exploitation of earth, water, air, or sky; of natural resources like oil, gas, coal, common carriers, or radio; no speculation in telephone and telegraph, press, or post; education and medical help to be free.

A short cut to all this, to becoming a country owning itself; in debt to itself only government *from within itself*. A far greater simplicity than Russia. A new Success ideal would soon supplant the one that went with the old profit motive, one more organic, and therefore more *humane*.

How could this be brought about? Gradually. By taxation and some form of purchase by capitalizing the country itself over and above a fair living for every man, woman, and child in it—selling the margin back to the people as stock in their own country.

A genuine system of private ownership, a system of capital with its broad base on the ground in the lives of the whole people, instead of standing precariously on its apex for the few. Is it communism I am describing? Is it socialism? No? Well, gentlemen, if you must have an 'ism' I see it as true capitalism—the organic capital of an organic Democracy: the only basis of an organic architecture or for indigenous Usonian culture.

N.B. And, comrades, please don't put my plight at Taliesin up against Russia as a reproach to my country. I've been pretty 'trying', you know. I am still trying.

Taliesin, August, 1937.

THE SAFETY OF THE SOUL DEPENDS ON ITS COURAGE

The long view is the cool view.
'Tolerance, experiment, and change gives a culture strength.'

Life always rides in strength to victory, not through internationalism or through any other 'isms', but only through the direct responsibility of the individual. It bears a royal characteristic called Initiative. Where Individual initiative is active, strong and operative, there you may see the mainspring of life in abundance, operating.

Nature herself places this premium upon Individuality. And it applies to Nations. Nations are only the Individual raised to a common-power which should act as a check upon idiosyncrasy. The fact that a Nation does not so act is the weakness of the Nation.

Organic Democratic FORM: TRUTH ever fresh has not yet come to our Civilization.

So we have the sorry spectacle of a venal world substituting blows for ideas: a whirlpool of destruction and hate into which our leaders draw us with too great ease.

When I returned from Russia many friends, reading what I had written and hearing me talk of our experiences there, were all curious to know how the visit had affected my 'point of view'. Said Lloyd (Lewis), for one, I remember, 'Frank, come now, what do you really make of Communism in Moscow?' 'Oh,' I said, 'the Russians have done remarkable things considering their start with such tremendous illiteracy. But the Revolution has been only partial; they've kept our idea of Money—the System that is destroying us and will destroy Communism too; they still believe in great concentrations of human beings on hard pavement for educational purposes (it will probably prove to be for military purposes). She has fallen for machine worship—it will turn and rend her as it will rend us.' 'Then,' said Lloyd, 'you don't come home a convert to Communism?'

'No,' I answered. 'No isms, private or international, for me. I believe in a capitalist system. I only wish I could see it tried some time.'

The Fifth Book of *An Autobiography* ends here.

'KEEP THE YOUNG GENERATIONS IN HEALTH AND BEQUEATH TO THEM NO TUMBLED HOUSE.'

Like Sinan, the famous Ottoman architect of Agra who, centuries ago, built a city for Babar, I wish to build a city for Democracy: the Usonian city that is nowhere yet everywhere.

Since this search for FORM ends there, the Usonian City, Broadacres, will be the sixth book of *An Autobiography*. The natural Conclusion.

INDEX

For the writing of this work I have long ago consulted and occasionally remembered Pythagoras, Aristophanes, Socrates, Heraclitus, Laotze, Buddha, Jesus, Tolstoy, Kropotkin, Bacon, William Blake, Samuel Butler, Mazzini, Walt Whitman, Henry George, Grundtvig, George Meredith, Henry Thoreau, Herman Melville, George Borrow, Goethe, Carlyle, Nietzsche, Voltaire, Cervantes, Giacosa, Shelley, Shakespeare, Milton, Thorstein Veblen, Nehru, Major Douglas, and Silvio Gesell.

Louis Sullivan's writings I have not read: he whose thought was, in his own person and presence, an open book to me for many years.

And innumerable are the various collaterals, diagonals, and opposites that went into the place where this book might have come from but did not. I said at the beginning that the real book was between the lines. It is true of any serious book concerned with culture.

Gene (Masselink) of the Fellowship and his helpers have untangled day by day, month by month, the mass of inter-lined and defaced scripts that would tease anyone, especially myself. Gene is the only one who could read them.